NATIONAL GEOGRAPHIC

# TRAVELER
# Great Britain

Christopher Somerville

# Contents

How to use this guide 6–7  About the author 8
The regions 47–334  Travelwise 335–90
Index 391–97  Credits 398–99

## History & culture 9

Great Britain today 10–15
Food & drink 16–17
History of the land 18–21
History of Great Britain 22–37
The arts 38–46

## London 47

Map 48–49
Introduction 50
The City 51–55
A walking tour of the City 54–55
Westminster & the West End 56–67
A walking tour of Westminster 62–63
Soho & Covent Garden walk 66–67
Bloomsbury 68–72
Knightsbridge & Kensington 73–82
Feature: London's parks 78–79
Knightsbridge & Kensington walk 80–81
Following the Thames 83–92

## Home Counties 95

Introduction & map 96–97

## The South Country 115

Introduction & map 116–17
Feature: Hardy's Dorset 136–37

Page 1: Horseguard in London
Pages 2–3: Cows grazing at dawn near Barrow Mump, Somerset
Left: Market day in Barnstaple, Devon

## The West Country 139

Introduction & map 140–41
Feature: West Country moorland 148–49
A walk around Bath 154–55

## Wales 159

Introduction & map 160–61
A drive from Dolgellau to Conwy 168–69

## South Midlands 175

Introduction & map 176–77
Two Cotswolds drives 181–83
Feature: William Shakespeare 188–89
A walking tour of Oxford 192–94

## East Anglia & Lincolnshire 199

Introduction & map 200–201
A walk around Cambridge 204–206
Feature: Constable Country 214–15

## North Midlands 223

Introduction & map 224–25
A drive around the Peak District 229–31
Feature: Wedgwood & the potteries 236–37

## Northwest England 243

Introduction & map 244–45
Feature: Wordsworth & the Romantics 254–55
A drive around the Central Lakes 256–57

## Northeast England 261

Introduction & map 262–63
A walk around the city walls 268–69
A drive in the West Riding 272–73
North York Moors drive 276–77

## Scottish Lowlands 287

Introduction & map 288–89
Two Edinburgh walks 300–303
Feature: The game of golf 304–305
A drive from Glasgow to St. Andrews 306–307

## Highlands & Islands 309

Introduction & map 310–11
A drive through Royal Deeside 316–17
Feature: Outdoor Scotland 320–21
Scottish Islands 325–34
Feature: Islanders 328–29

## Travelwise 335

Planning your trip 336
How to get to Britain 336
Getting around 336–38
Practical advice 338–41
Emergencies 341
Hotels and restaurants 342–87
Shopping in Great Britain 388–89
Entertainment 390

Index 391–97
Credits 398–99

# How to use this guide

See back flap for keys to text and map symbols

The *National Geographic Traveler* brings you the best of Great Britain in text, pictures, and maps. Divided into three main sections, the guide begins with an overview of history and culture. Following are 12 regional chapters with featured sites selected by the author for their particular interest and treated in depth. Each chapter opens with its own contents list for easy reference.

The regions, and sites within them, are arranged geographically. London is further divided into five smaller areas. A map introduces each region, highlighting the featured sites. Walks and drives, all plotted

on their own maps, suggest routes for discovering an area. Features and sidebars offer detail on history, culture, or contemporary life. A More Places to Visit page generally rounds off the regional chapters.

The final section, Travelwise, lists essential information for the traveler—pre-trip planning, getting around, communications, money matters, and emergencies—plus a selection of hotels, restaurants, shops, and entertainment.

To the best of our knowledge, site information is accurate as of the press date. However, it's always advisable to call ahead.

---

**Floors** We have used the British convention for naming the floors of a building. Hence, in this book ground floor refers to the first floor, the first floor refers to the second, and so on.
**National Trust properties** These are identified in the text by the abbreviations NT and NTS (National Trust for Scotland).

### Color coding
Each region is color coded for easy reference. Find the region you want on the map on the front flap, and look for the color flash at the top of the pages of the relevant chapter. Information in **Travelwise** is also color coded to each region.

**Kensington Palace**
<br>🄰 48 B3
<br>✉ Kensington Gardens
<br>☎ 020-7937 9561
<br>💲 $$$
<br>🚇 Tube: High St. Kensington, Queensway

### Visitor information
for major sites is listed in the side columns (see key to symbols on back flap). The map reference gives the page where the site is mapped, plus the grid reference. Other details are the address, telephone number, days closed, entrance fee ranging from $ (under $4) to $$$$$ (over $25), and the nearest tube stop for London sites. Visitor information for smaller sites is provided within the text.

## TRAVELWISE

| | |
|---|---|
| **THE SOUTH COUNTRY** | Color-coded region name |
| **BOURNEMOUTH** ———— | Town name |
| 🏨 **ROYAL BATH** <br> **$$$$ ★★★★** | Hotel name, price range, & star rating |
| BATH ROAD, BH21 2EW <br> TEL 01202-555555 <br> FAX 01202-554158 | Address, telephone & fax numbers |
| Large Victorian hotel with fine views out to sea. Health club in a pavilion in the grounds. Choice of restaurants—either the Garden Restaurant or the celebrated Oscars. | Brief description of hotel |
| ① 140 🅿 70 ⊟ ☎ 🔻 <br> 🅰 All major cards | Hotel facilities & credit card details |
| **BRIDPORT** ———— | Town name |
| 🍴 **RIVERSIDE** <br> **$$$** | Restaurant name & price range |
| WEST BAY, DT6 4EZ <br> TEL 01308-422011 | Address & telephone number |
| Lively restaurant specializing in fresh local seafood. The kitchen relies on the day's catch for its repertoire. | Brief description of restaurant |
| 🍴 80 🕐 Closed Sun. D, Mon., Dec.–Feb. 🅰 Major cards | Restaurant closures & credit card details |

### Hotel and restaurant prices
An explanation of the price bands used in entries is given in the Hotels & restaurants section beginning on p. 342.

## REGIONAL MAPS

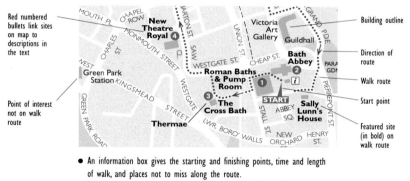

Point of interest

Adjoining chapter

Grid reference

Drive start point

County name

Important point of interest

Important featured town

- A locator map accompanies each regional map and shows the location of that region in the country.
- Adjacent regions are shown, with page references.

## WALKING TOURS

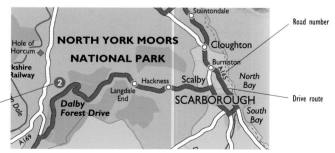

Red numbered bullets link sites on map to descriptions in the text

Point of interest not on walk route

Building outline

Direction of route

Walk route

Start point

Featured site (in bold) on walk route

- An information box gives the starting and finishing points, time and length of walk, and places not to miss along the route.
- Where two walks are marked on the map, the second route is shown in orange.

## DRIVING TOURS

Road number

Drive route

Red numbered bullets link sites on map to descriptions in the text

- An information box provides details including starting and finishing points, places not to miss along the route, time and length of drive, and tips on the terrain.

NATIONAL GEOGRAPHIC
# TRAVELER
# Great Britain

## About the author

Christopher Somerville spent his childhood in a remote village in rural Gloucestershire, where he reveled in the freedom to roam the woods, fields, and riverbanks. This upbringing gave him a lifelong love of walking in the open air and a taste for the quieter corners of the British countryside.

During the 15 years he spent as a schoolteacher, he wrote several books about walking and landscape. A lucky break gave him the chance to swap the rigors of the classroom for the pleasures and uncertainties of travel journalism. He has written some 20 books, including guidebooks, walking guides, and personal travel accounts. He writes regularly for *The Daily Telegraph* (he is their Walking Correspondent) and *The Sunday Times* about his travels, on foot and otherwise, in the hidden corners of Britain and Europe. He also presents his own walking series on regional television.

Island communities and their way of life fascinate him, particularly in the Celtic fringe of Scotland and Ireland. He enjoys walking, talking, listening, laughing, singing, and playing music.

# History
# & culture

Great Britain today 10–15
Food & drink 16–17
History of the land 18–21
History of Great Britain 22–37
The arts 38–46

**Stonehenge, Wiltshire**

# Great Britain today

YOU COULD DRIVE THE 900-ODD MILES FROM LAND'S END IN SOUTHWEST
Cornwall to John O'Groats in northeast Scotland in a day and a night. That is how small
Great Britain actually is—the distance, say, between New York City and St. Louis. Yet this
little group of islands off Europe's northwest coast has influenced world culture as pro-
foundly as any nation in history.

Visitors are coming in growing numbers to
Britain—not just to enjoy the celebrated
beauty of its green hills and meadows and its
historic towns and villages, nor simply to see
where William Shakespeare was born, or
where the Queen lives, or where the Beatles
started out. Many come because they feel an
empathy with these islands and their people,
perhaps because of a shared language, perhaps
because strands of so many cultures all over
the world are closely interwoven with Britain's.

The British themselves—this motley
mingling of Saxons, West Indians, Celts,
Normans, Indians, Chinese, Africans, Danes,
and others—stand at a cultural crossroads
these days. They are justifiably proud of their
history, of the great poets and writers, statesmen and thinkers, scientists and social
reformers who have been nurtured in these
small islands. They cherish the rich theater of
pageantry bequeathed to them by history.
They look with deep satisfaction on their
ancient patchwork of farming landscapes,
their half-timbered medieval houses, their
remote mountain ranges. They take pride
in their regional chauvinism, their strongly

differentiated local accents, the subtle changes
of flavor in beer, or nuance of humor from
one county to the next.

Yet they see themselves at the same time as
only one smallish society in a modern,
competitive world. They accept that their
country's God-given right to a seat at the top
table of world politics is no longer automatic.
Their former certainties and sense of superiority
are largely gone.

The political union among Scotland,
England, and Wales—perhaps between these
three and Northern Ireland, too—seems to be
easing apart, not necessarily for the worse.
The nation's hesitant, equivocal attitude
toward closer links with Europe—a legal
reality since 1973, but certainly not yet a
political, social, economic, or emotional one—
reflects this fairly general desire to preserve the
historic status of the British as independent
islanders, while engaging positively with the
wider world.

**Known for its display of fashion, in partic-
ular huge hats, Royal Ascot is the social
highlight of Britain's racing year.**

## Off the beaten track

Almost every visitor to Britain wants to
see Big Ben, Shakespeare's birthplace,
Edinburgh Castle, and the other main tourist
attractions. But there is another Britain, one
that most visitors never see or even guess at.
If you want a taste of that, you will need to
slow down, take time for conversations, and
penetrate odd corners of the country. Here
are a few suggestions for quirky, stimulating
sidesteps that will introduce you to the
other Britain:

**The South Country** Romney Marsh and
Dungeness in southeast Kent.

**The West Country** The Lizard Peninsula
and Bodmin Moor in Cornwall.
**Wales** The Valleys north of Cardiff; the Wye
Valley; the wild tip of the Lleyn Peninsula.
**East Anglia** The beautiful Deben estuary and
bleakly haunting Orford Ness in Suffolk.
**Northwest England** Bowland Forest moors
and former mill towns; the little-visited coast-
line west of the Lake District.
**Northeast England** Out-of-this-world Spurn
Head on the Yorkshire coast.
**Scotland** Unvisited southwest Galloway; the
Moray Firth coast; any of the islands. ■

Meanwhile, that wider world continues to value the British for qualities which, with characteristic self-deprecation, they themselves would hardly admit to possessing: a sense of fun and fairness, a politeness and consideration for others developed of necessity by this multicultural society that lives cheek by jowl on an overcrowded island, dry humor laced copiously with irony, and a balanced way of dealing with each other and with strangers.

## LOCAL FESTIVITIES

An aspect of British life that has resisted all attempts to stifle or dilute it is the nation's remarkable penchant for local customs, festivals, ceremonies, and other forms of more or less eccentric ritual. Some have deep traditional or religious roots and mysterious significance; others are bogus bits of invented hokum. All are good fun, and worth a look if you are in the area.

**Hunting on horseback, a British tradition still pursued in several counties**

### January

*1*—New Year's Day.
*25*—Burns Night: Scotland's celebration of national poet Robert Burns.
*Last Tuesday*—Up Helly Aa': The Shetland islanders' vigorous celebration of midwinter, featuring the burning of a full-size Viking longship.

### February

*Late January/early February*—Chinese New Year: Firecrackers and dragons, celebrated in London, Glasgow, Manchester, and other cities.
*Mid-month*—Viking Festival: Ceremonial boat-burning and reenactments of Viking battles in York commemorate the founding of the Viking city, Jorvik.

## March

*17*—St. Patrick's Day: Celebrations by Irish communities of their patron saint.
*Shrove Tuesday*—Pancake Day races; street soccer game at Corfe in Dorset.

## April

*Maundy Thursday* (Thursday before Easter)—The Queen distributes ceremonial Maundy money to senior citizens at a selected venue.
*Easter Monday*—Hare Pie Scramble and Bottle Kicking at Hallaton, Leicestershire.

## May

*1*—Obby Oss at Padstow, Cornwall: Crazy capers, mesmerizing music.
*8*—Furry Dance, Helston, Cornwall: In and out of the houses in a floral dance.
*Ascension Day* (40 days after Easter)—Well-dressing in Tissington and other Derbyshire villages: Decking the wells with floral pictures.
*Last Monday in May*—Spring Bank Holiday: Cheese-rolling and breakneck running down a precipitous slope at Cooper's Hill, near Brockworth, Gloucestershire.

## June

*Mid-month*—Appleby Horse Fair, Cumbria: Gypsies and horse dealers assemble for the great annual travelers' get-together.
*24*—Druids welcome Midsummer Day dawn at Stonehenge.

## July

*Second Saturday*—Durham Miners' Gala: Banners, speeches, and pit-related nostalgia.
*Third week*—Swan-Upping (see p. 98) on the Thames, Berkshire: Counting the Queen's and others' swans on the Thames.

## August

*First Week*—Royal National Eisteddfod: Welsh arts and music; changing venues.
*Third Wednesday*—Priddy Fair, Somerset: Sheep auctions and fairground hucksters on top of the Mendip Hills in a unique country fair, over 650 years old.

## September

*First Saturday*—Braemar Gathering: Caber-tossing and traditional sports in the presence of the Royal Family.

## October

*First Thursday, Friday, and Saturday*—Nottingham Goose Fair: One of Britain's most spectacular fairs. In medieval times this was the largest hiring fair in the Midlands. Thousands of laborers and servants came to find work. As for the geese—upward of 20,000 were sold in one weekend.
*31*—Hallowe'en: Children hollow out pumpkins to make faces and dress up as witches.

**Cavendish Village Fete, Suffolk, one of the local summer events across the country**

**November**

*Early in month*—Bridgwater Guy Fawkes Carnival, Somerset: Britain's largest nighttime carnival starting in Bridgwater and visiting small Somerset towns over ten days.

*5*—Bonfire Night/Guy Fawkes Night: Fires and fireworks commemorate the failed Gunpowder Plot of 1605. One of the largest events is at Lewes in East Sussex, with politically incorrect-effigy burning.

**December**

*26*—Boxing Day: Traditionally, a day when the gentry gave presents to servants.

*31*—Allendale Tar Barrelers, Northumberland: Men parade with blazing headpieces.

*31*—Hogmanay: Traditional Scottish celebration of New Year. ■

# Food & drink

BREAKFAST, AS YOU EXPERIENCE IT IN HOTELS AND BED-AND-BREAKFAST places, will probably be a variation on what is known as the Great British Breakfast—a mixed grill or fry of some combination of eggs, bacon, sausages, tomatoes, mushrooms, black and/or white pudding, and fried bread, followed by toast and marmalade, and washed down with tea.

**Smoked herrings, known as Orford Butleys, are a local delicacy in the village of Orford, Suffolk. The traditional method of woodsmoking fish is becoming a thing of the past.**

## BRITISH PUBS

These days pubs, formerly purely drinking establishments, almost all put on some kind of lunchtime menu. Many also offer evening meals, eaten either in the bar or in a separate restaurant area.

British food has greatly improved over the last 20 years and dishes have become more varied and innovative. But traditional dishes are making a comeback. Combinations are the name of the game: roast pheasant and bread sauce, roast beef and Yorkshire pudding with horseradish sauce, sausages and mashed potatoes with hot English mustard, steak and onions, steak and kidney pie, shepherd's pie with Worcestershire sauce, bread and cheese with pickled onions (known as a Ploughman's Lunch), fish and chips with salt and vinegar.

Desserts tend to be simple but effective: spotted dick (steamed pudding with raisins) or treacle tart with custard, strawberries and cream, steamed ginger pudding with ginger sauce, apple pie with custard, plum or rhubarb or gooseberry crumble with cream.

Rural pubs are places to sample the locally brewed beer, served without gas pressure from a hand pump or straight from the barrel, drunk a little cooler than room temperature, and savored for that elusive combination of the sweet richness of malt and the bitterness of hops that always tastes of beer and yet shifts and modulates in emphasis and balance almost from one town to the next. Once you have weaned yourself off the thin, cold, corporate blandness of lager and cottoned on to the many-layered, ever changing, subtly developing flavors to be found in a pint glass of beer—you'll be hooked for life.

## SCOTTISH & WELSH SPECIALTIES

In Scotland, try game (venison, grouse, wild salmon), kippers, Arbroath smokies (smoked haddock), and Scotch broth; also the epic and iconic haggis, a savory concoction cooked traditionally in the lining of a sheep's stomach.

In Wales, cawl (mutton broth), lamb, freshly caught fish, crumbly white Caerphilly cheese, and the long and luscious leek—the national vegetable—can all be excellent.

These two countries come into their own at afternoon tea time. In Wales, try laverbread, made of seaweed and oatmeal, and a fruit bread called *bara brith;* in Scotland opt for shortbread, scones, and oatcakes. ∎

**The atmospheric British pub—a place to gossip, relax, and socialize**

# History of the land

MAINLAND BRITAIN HAS AN ASTONISHING VARIETY OF LANDSCAPE, FROM rocky northern mountains nearly three billion years old to flat fields in East Anglia that were only reclaimed from the sea within the last century.

Reading the landscape from the oldest to the newest means starting in the west: the volcanic rocks of the Scottish highlands and islands, the highest peaks of the Lake District in Cumbria and Snowdonia in Wales, and the granite heart of Dartmoor and Cornwall down in south-western England. Some of these hard materials were formed of solidified molten rock—granite, basalt, gabbro, and dolerite. Some were transformed by immense heat and pressure—quartzite, gneiss, schist.

Around 400 million years ago, upheavals exposed rocks around central and southern Scotland and the mountains of Wales. They formed gigantic mountain ranges, which were gradually worn away by wind and weather into the confused jumble of shales, slates, gritstones, and schists that now underlie some of Britain's most beautiful mountains, and moorlands.

Looking at a geological map of Britain, you can see great snaking bands of limestone, gritstone, and old red sandstone. This sandstone underpins the cliff and coastal country of southwest Scotland and northwest England, parts of the Welsh Borders, and north Devon and Exmoor; it was formed of compressed sand from a vast red desert that filled the center of Britain 400 million years ago.

The gritstone that underlies the moors of southern Yorkshire and Lancashire is an amalgam of particles of sand and stone deposited by ancient rivers in prehistoric estuaries.

The carboniferous limestone of the Pennines, where flower-rich pastures grow, was formed from the shells of countless marine creatures. In parts of Lancashire, Yorkshire, Nottinghamshire, County Durham, and South Wales it contains layers of vegetation, compressed and hardened into coal.

Oolitic limestone forms a thick 300-mile belt that crosses the country from the North Yorkshire coast by way of the Lincolnshire Wolds, the eastern Midland uplands, and the Cotswold Hills, running down through Bath and Somerset into Dorset and on to the Devon coast. Formed some 200 million years ago from grains of sand surrounded by calcium carbonate, it is sometimes called "roestone," or "eggstone," because of its surface, which looks like a mass of close-packed fish eggs. Oolitic limestone varies in color from pale silver to deep honey-orange and enriches buildings in towns such as Stamford, Cirencester, and Bath.

Chalk, the foundation of much of southern England, is also formed from the shells of marine creatures—in this case minute organisms called foraminifera, which lived and died in the shallow waters of the Great Chalk Sea that drowned most of northern Europe about 100 million years ago. Unimaginable numbers of these minuscule shells accumulated on the bed of this sea—enough to have formed a layer which today, at Walbury Hill in Hampshire, extends down from the 1,000-foot hilltop to sea level, and on down beneath the water for a further 650 feet. The chalk blanket covered most of Britain after the sea receded; but subsequent weathering, along with a breaking up and sloughing off during subterranean upheavals, saw the erosion and disappearance of much of the layer. What remains is especially impressive in the curves of the chalk downs, and in the rampart of cliffs along the south coast.

Until the coming of the four great ice ages, rivers continued to drag clay, sand, and pebbles southeast toward the North Sea coasts of southern Britain. The ice ages themselves (about 600,000 B.C. to 12,000 B.C.) finished the shaping of Britain, as their glaciers gouged valleys through the hard rock of the mountains and smoothed out the softer rocks farther south. Meltwaters during the thaws brought down more silt and gravel, spreading a thick blanket of tilth and clay across East Anglia and the southeastern corner of the island that today—along with land reclaimed by man from the sea—provides Britain's most fertile arable soil.

**Cows find sustenance in a grassy hedgerow containing cow parsley (wild chervil).**

## FLORA & FAUNA

The wildlife of Britain has taken a tremendous hammering in recent decades, due to postwar farming policies that set great store by production through intensive agricultural methods. More than 80 percent of all hedgerows, wildflower meadows, and wetlands has been lost. Pesticides, herbicides, and fertilizers have been sprayed wholesale. Meanwhile, development of roads and housing has destroyed farmland, meadows, and woods. Songbird, butterfly, insect, hawk, owl, and mammal numbers have all dropped, and wildflower diversity has diminished drastically, too.

But legislative protection by European Union designation, by conservation groups, and by individual action is now, at last, on the increase. Recent changes in EU agricultural policy, too, mean that intensive agribusiness monoculture is less attractive than it was.

There are still plenty of primrose banks and bluebell woods in spring, lane verges full of campion, wild garlic, cranesbill, and sweet cicely in summer, hedgerows sheltering the nests of yellowhammers, dunnocks, and chaffinches. Up on the northern moors you can hear the haunting, bubbling call of curlew. In the Scottish mountains golden eagles, mountain hare, and pockets of relict post-ice age flowers are still there. Red kites in Wales

**The Farne Islands, Northumberland, have sheltered birds since the seventh century.**

and elsewhere have flourished, bringing the species back from the brink of extinction. And blue-legged, high-stepping avocets now breed on the marshy islets of the Suffolk coast, having returned after the war to a Britain in which they had been shot to extinction during the previous century. ■

# History of Great Britain

THE FIRST HUNTERS WERE ACTIVE IN BRITAIN FROM THE END OF THE FIRST
great ice age, around 250,000 B.C. Some probably ventured across the Channel and North
Sea land bridges during the warmer periods between the following ice ages, but it wasn't
until after the last big freeze, around 10,000 B.C., that Paleolithic or early Stone Age
hunter-gatherers arrived in any numbers. They shot and trapped the aurochs, mam-
moths, elks, and other animals that were following the northward creep of the tundra as
the climate warmed up.

Gradually it became possible to cut down the
developing forests with the aid of crude but
effective stone tools. By the time the Neolithic
or late Stone Age farmers arrived from the
Mediterranean region around 3700 B.C., a trib-
ally owned, patchwork landscape was appearing. Britain was now an island cluster, thanks
to rising sea levels. The newcomers brought
skills of animal husbandry; they planted wheat
and barley, and slashed and burned more forest, especially across the downs of southern
England with their easily worked chalk soils.

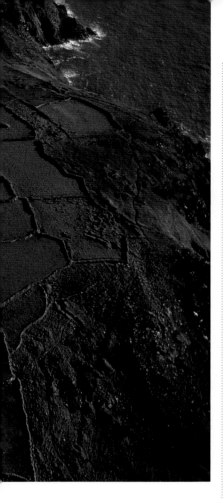

**Stone walls mark ancient Iron Age field patterns around Rosemergy farm in Cornwall, creating a patchwork landscape characteristic of Britain.**

The clever immigrants known as "Beaker Folk"—from the fine pottery vessels they buried with their dead—arrived in about 2000 B.C. With them they brought the secret of bronze from the Iberian Peninsula and the Low Countries of Europe.

The dark-haired Celts who came across from France in about 600 B.C. imported iron-making and efficient plows. They were skilled warriors, too, builders of hill forts, druidical worshipers, jewelers and swordsmiths, singers and poets. On the outer and western fringes of Britain, such strains live on.

## Relics of early Britain

Much of Britain's ancient history still lies imprinted on the landscape, preserved for millennia through chance, superstition, or cultural awareness. Notable Neolithic examples are Belas Knap long barrow in Gloucestershire, the Callanish stone circle on the Isle of Lewis, Grimes Graves flint mines in Norfolk, the village at Skara Brae in Orkney, and Uffington White Horse in Oxfordshire. There is a very well preserved Iron Age village at Chysauster in western Cornwall, and an enormous hill fort at Maiden Castle in Dorset, scene of a fierce battle between Britons and invading Romans. Wiltshire is particularly rich in ancient monuments: Silbury Hill, West Kennet long barrow, Avebury stone circle and avenue, and mighty, enigmatic Stonehenge (see pp. 134–35). ∎

### ROMAN OCCUPATION

The Romans' first attempt to invade Britain was tentative—Julius Caesar arrived in 54 B.C., met some resistance from the Britons, and departed. In A.D. 43, four tough legions landed, with orders from Emperor Claudius to stay put. By A.D. 50 they had captured Caractacus, chief of the Catuvellauni; by A.D. 61 they had weathered and survived the hurricane rebellion by the Iceni under Queen Boudicca. By A.D. 84 Julius Agricola, working with small units of well-trained, efficient soldiers, had subdued all of England and as much as was thought necessary of Scotland and Wales. Between A.D. 122 and A.D. 128, Hadrian's Wall was built across the 73-mile neck of land between the Tyne and the Solway Firth—a solid northern boundary to the whole mighty Roman Empire.

For 250 years, the Romans dominated life in Britain with their effective, practical methods. They laid down well-engineered highways such as Ermine Street from London to York and Hadrian's Wall, and Watling Street from London to Chester. They built a network of byways to open up the forested hinterland. They cultivated an extensive acreage of corn, and cleared pastureland. They drained fens and marshlands. They mined coal, silver, tin, lead, and gold. They built towns such as Verulamium (St. Albans), Glevum (Gloucester), Camulodunum (Colchester), and Eboracum (York). They laid out estates with beautiful villas and created wonderful mosaic floors, intricate gold ornaments, marble statues, delicate glassware.

**The Great Gold Buckle, found at Sutton Hoo in Suffolk, contains 14 ounces of solid gold, and dates from the seventh century.**

Yet they could not keep the barbarians away from Rome, nor maintain their over-stretched empire indefinitely. Shortly after A.D. 400, the last of the legions packed up and marched away.

## PASTORALISTS & NORTH SEA WOLVES

There was a hiatus of perhaps 40 years, during which the works of the Romans began to crumble back into encroaching fen and forest. Then the blue-eyed, fair-haired Saxons came from the Low Countries in waves of immigration that lasted 200 years. King Arthur, often taken to be a mythical figure, may in fact have been a Romano–British chief whose battles against the new invaders passed into legend.

### Taming the land

These Anglo-Saxons established villages, usually near rivers which offered them drink, transportation, and irrigation. Their laws were democratic, the rules being hammered out in council rather than imposed from on high. They made huge inroads on Britain's remaining wildwood and cleared big swaths for agriculture, plowing with cooperatively owned ox teams. We read their settlement names in suffixes today: "-ton," a settlement by a river; "-ley," a clearing; "-ham," a flat pasture; "-wick," an animal farm. And we find their memorials all over Britain, from King Offa's great dike (see p. 174) along the Welsh Borders to the gold and garnet treasures of the Sutton Hoo ship burial in Suffolk, now on display in the British Museum (see p. 71).

With a certain amount of fighting and feuding, the Saxons parceled part of Britain into a number of adjoining kingdoms—the

## Lasting legacy

The Romans built to last and left their treasures scattered in the earth when their 400-year occupation came to an end. What they built can be seen most dramatically along the 73 miles of Hadrian's Wall (see pp. 284–85) in Northumberland, and in the foundations of the Roman baths (see p. 154) at Bath, the town of Verulamium (see p. 111) at St. Albans, the palace at Fishbourne (see p. 127) in

Sussex, the villa at Chedworth (see p. 183) in Gloucestershire, and the foundations of Colchester Castle (see p. 213) in Essex. Their jewelry, statuary, and glass is shown in county museums up and down the country—most stunningly in the intact and beautiful silverware of the Mildenhall Treasure, found in Suffolk and now displayed in Room 49 of the British Museum (see p. 72). ■

chief ones were Wessex (southwest) and Kent (southeast), Mercia (Midlands), East Anglia (east), and Northumbria (northeast). But the seafaring, warlike Vikings, chiefly from Denmark, had other ideas when they began their three centuries of raiding and forcible settlement across the North Sea around the end of the eighth century.

The monastic communities that had established themselves on the east-facing coasts were the first to suffer from the Vikings' hunger for new land. The raids became a long-drawn-out immigration surge, violent and unstoppable. Some compromise and alliance-building became possible after Alfred the Great, King of Wessex (R.871–899), defeated the Danes in 878. Some of the Norsemen settled the north of the country, as place-names on the map tell us—"beck," a stream; "-by," a farm; "thwaite," a meadow clearing. They themselves endured attacks from their former compatriots. It was not until after the next—and last—successful invasion of Britain that the North Sea Wolves ceased to bite.

## NORTHMEN FROM FRANCE

It was their great castles that symbolized the power of the Normans, and their determination to stay and to dominate after they had defeated the Anglo-Saxon army under King Harold II (R.1066) at Hastings on October 14, 1066. These Frenchified Norsemen were—like the Romans 1,000 years before—efficient, ruthless, and highly effective. Under their dynamic king, William I (R.1066–1087), they crushed resistance in the north. The epic Domesday Book survey (1085–86) showed the king exactly what he and everyone else owned, and what it was worth—a typically Norman achievement.

## Their influence

The Normans changed the flavor of Britain. The Anglo-Saxon landlords were replaced by barons and bishops, whose power soon grew to challenge that of the king, and French and ecclesiastical Latin became the official languages for the next 150 years. With their close blood and trade links to the Continent, the Anglo-Normans invited French monastic orders to establish branches in Britain, bringing with them an increase in learning and culture.

Once the Norman succession had been resolved after the Civil War of 1135–1154, Henry II established the Plantagenet dynasty. It lasted through the 12th-century Crusades to the Holy Land, the murder of Thomas à Becket (see p. 122), the Barons' Wars of 1215–17 and 1263–67, that saw the power of the barons reduced, and on to the end of the 14th century, by which time the Normans' successors were venturing back across the water to fight for the throne of France.

## MIDDLE AGES

During the Middle Ages, wool-rich East Anglia became Britain's most populous and prosperous region. The feudal system, in which peasants worked their own strips of farmland and their lord's under allegiance and obligation to him, was in full swing. Monks drained many marshland areas and built sea banks, behind which the land was reclaimed for agriculture. Houses began to be built unfortified as the barons' feuds subsided; roads improved; towns grew apace, usually around castles, and their craftsmen organized themselves into powerful, self-protective guilds. The signing of Magna Carta in 1215

## Norman castles

The first castles, built shortly after the Norman Conquest, were of wood—a keep (stronghold) on a motte (mound), with a bailey (walled garrison enclosure) on an adjacent motte. None of these now remain.

Henry II (R.1154–89) ordered his turbulent barons to seek his permission before building a castle, and from then on building was in stone, with elaborate defenses—moat, portcullis, murder holes, offset entrances. Curtain walls were introduced early in the 13th century to divide the bailey into three wards (walled areas), and gatehouses and projecting barbicans (fortified courtyards) were added.

Castles were the focal point of warfare until the introduction of gunpowder and cannon, and a sharp reduction in the power of the barons, tipped them toward obsolescence. ■

underpinned the establishment of an independent legal system based on trial by jury, in which everyone had the right to be judged by his or her peers in a court uninfluenced by church, state, or monarch.

King Edward I (*R*.1272–1307) was known as the Hammer of the Scots; in fact he failed to subdue Scotland, but conquered Wales in 1284. He introduced a Model Parliament in 1295, in which representatives of rich townsmen and well-to-do country dwellers served as members.

### End of an era

Society was devastated by the outbreak of the Black Death in 1348–49, spread by fleas that had arrived on ships in the coats of black rats. About one in every three of Britain's four million population died, and after the plague many villages were left abandoned. In the depopulated countryside labor was scarce, and the peasants became aware of the power they possessed to offer or refuse their labor. In this sellers' market a new relationship between landowner and worker began to emerge, one based on money rather than social obligation. It was the beginning of the end of the feudal system. The peasants had not escaped repression, however. When they raised a revolution in 1381 under their leaders, Wat Tyler and John Ball, and marched on London in protest against a poll tax levied to raise money for the Hundred Years' War, they were put down with measured savagery. More than 1,500 were hanged.

Ten years before the outbreak of the Black Death, the Hundred Years' War with France (1337–1453) had been initiated by King Edward III (*R*.1327–1377) when he claimed the French throne. The conflict staggered on for well over a century, with cross-Channel expeditions culminating in battles such as Crécy (1346), Poitiers (1356), and Agincourt (1415) that were proving grounds for the British bowmen.

Hostilities lurched to a halt in 1453, by which date the French had recaptured all their national soil except the port of Calais, which was finally regained in 1558.

### Deeply divided

There had been trouble enough at home, meanwhile. In 1399 the direct Plantagenet line was broken when ambitious Henry Bolingbroke seized the throne from King Richard II (*R*.1377–1399) and initiated the rule of the House of Lancaster. This is the stuff of William Shakespeare's plays *Henry IV Parts 1* and *2*, and *Henry V*, sagas of plotting ending with bloody defeat at the Battle of Shrewsbury in 1403 for the rebel Earl of Northumberland, his tempestuous son, Henry "Hotspur" Percy, and the Welsh leader Owain Glyndwr.

In 1455, only two years after the end of the very expensive and draining war with France, civil strife broke out across England in what became known as the Wars of the Roses. Shakespeare chronicled this protracted struggle between the Houses of Lancaster (red rose) and York (white rose). For 30 bloody years the war went on, until Henry Tudor decisively won it for the Lancastrians in 1485 at the Battle of Bosworth. The victor himself married a Yorkist princess, thus drawing a line under the whole business and ushering in, peacefully, the Tudor era.

## Everyday building

Medieval builders used materials that were available locally. Skeleton frames of timber were filled in with brick in the Midlands, flint in East Anglia. Wattle hurdlework could be pegged into gaps in the frame and daubed with cob—a mixture of cow dung, horsehair, straw, lime, clay, or whatever lay on hand.

Cotswold yellow oolitic limestone needed no timber support; given good foundations, it built churches, houses, and barns of enduring beauty. Roofs were thatched with straw or reed; later, as tilemaking spread, they were laid with baked red pantiles. House floors were of earth with rushes laid on top, or flagstones in better-off households.

In the **Clergy House** at Alfriston near Eastbourne (*NT, The Tye, tel 01323 870001, open Sun. all year & Tues. April–Oct.*) the floors were of rammed chalk, sealed with 30 gallons of sour milk. ■

The big cruciform church of St. Mary's in the village of Hambleden, near Henley-on-Thames

## MEDIEVAL CHURCH BUILDING

Britain contains, mile for mile, one of the greatest collections of medieval ecclesiastical architecture in the world. There are many reasons for this extraordinary density of superb churches and monasteries, most of them to do with the trading prosperity of an island country where top-quality wool grew naturally on the hoof. Church-building was not just an act of piety; it was a very visible benchmark of how well donors were doing, economically and socially.

Most sensitive of all about juggling their worldly and spiritual standing were the bishops, several of whom were as powerful as any baron. Where the latter built castles, the former built cathedrals, and continued to build them and add to them long after the castles had become all but redundant. Bishops and aristocrats keen to be floated to heaven on prayers and psalms would endow the building of chantry chapels within or at the side of cathedrals, where Masses could be said or sung for their souls. Many of these little chapels survive, delicate stone cells of exceptional beauty.

The presence of a saint's relics, particularly those with miraculous powers of healing, would guarantee a flow of pilgrims through the shrine, each adding a contribution to the construction funds. The monastic communities, too—smooth-mannered sophisticates such as the Benedictines, farmers in remote sites like the Cistercians, or the more austere

Augustinians—had far-flung estates and wide-spread commercial interests, and many could afford to build their abbeys and outbuildings in almost as much style as the grandest cathedrals.

## Evolving styles

Many of the great cathedral buildings took centuries to complete, and the often jerky

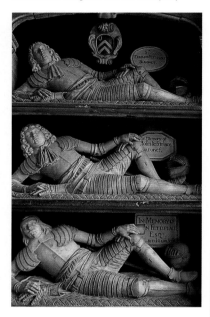

**Neatly stacked in tiers, generations of the Fettiplace family are commemorated in St. Mary's Church, Swinbrook, Oxfordshire.**

march of architectural fashion can be traced in their fabric. The Norman or Romanesque style (circa 1050–1150) shows round-topped arches, often embellished with firmly incised dogtooth or chevron carving, square towers, and heavy, massive pillars—a solid, confident, "here-to-stay" style, as at Norwich (see p. 216) and Durham (see pp. 278–79).

Early English (circa 1150–1280) brought in pointed arches and tall, narrow lancet windows. Flying buttresses and rib vaulting, taking some of the roof weight off the walls, slimmed down the pillars and helped to make this a lighter style, demonstrated at Salisbury (see pp. 131–32). Decorated (circa

1280–1380), exemplified in the chapter house of York Minster (see pp. 266–67) and Exeter Cathedral (see pp. 142–43), offered an ornamented, flowery appearance, with elaborate tracery in the enlarged windows and plenty of highly detailed carving in roof bosses, and on corbels and pillar capitals. Perpendicular, from 1350 to the 1530s, retreated from elaboration, flattening window and doorway arches and re-introducing uncluttered lines—though fan vaulting, as in Gloucester Cathedral (see p. 178) and King's College Chapel, Cambridge (see pp. 205–206), became ever more intricate and lacy.

At the Reformation (circa 1540), a violent revulsion against church privilege and decadence meant a virtual halt to development for the next hundred years.

## Parish churches

Humbler glories, but no less enjoyable to seek out and admire, are found throughout Britain in thousands of beautiful medieval parish churches. Between the 13th and 16th centuries, many areas of the country—the Yorkshire Wolds, for example, the broad East Anglian sheepwalks, the Cotswold Hills, and the close-turfed chalk downs of the South Country—became very prosperous through the quality of their wool and the (often imported) skill of their weavers.

When the medieval wool and cloth merchants became rich, many thought it fitting—or prudent—to thank God by paying for the creation of a new church, or the beautifying of an existing building. Most of these parish churches were built of materials available locally. Unfortunately, many are now kept locked, but inquiry at the nearest house may produce the key.

Inside, among the memorial tablets, the meticulously worked hassocks, and stained-glass windows with their tributes and dedications, you can read the story of any small community's continuing history.

Parish churches often contain signs from bygone masons and carvers—a wooden benchend of a fox stealing a goose, or a corbel head of a nun with toothache, or high on a roof boss the Green Man sprouting leaves from nostrils and mouth, a pagan guest invited by the mason to the Christian feast.

## AGES OF DISCOVERY & ELEGANCE

The House of Tudor was a very compact family affair, consisting of Henry VII (R.1485–1509), his son, Henry VIII (R.1509–1547), and three grandchildren, Edward VI (R.1547–1553), Mary I (R.1553–1558), and Elizabeth I (R.1558–1603). The two who began and ended this short-lived dynasty, the old man and his younger granddaughter, were chips off the same block—coolly competent people, bold yet crafty, not afraid to take a risk but prudently keeping one eye over their shoulder at the same time. Altogether the Tudors held power for just over a century. But what a century!

During its course, peace came to the troubled land and a whole new religious movement was founded in Britain. Adventurers sailed around the globe, established New World colonies, broke the power of Spain, and founded the British Empire in India. Britain's greatest dramatist was born and rose to literary glory. This, for Britain, was a time of renaissance, a golden age.

### Catholics & Protestants

Henry VIII is famous forevermore for his six wives—Catherine of Aragon (divorced), Anne Boleyn (beheaded), Jane Seymour (died), Anne of Cleves (divorced), Catherine Howard (beheaded), and Catherine Parr (survived). Henry's virulent quarrels with the pope, and his abolition of Britain's monastic communities, stemmed from his inability to father a male heir with his first wife, Catherine of Aragon. Between 1533 and 1540 he divorced Catherine, split with the pope, announced the formation of the Church of England and declared himself head of it, and oversaw the Dissolution, destruction, and selling off of the

monasteries. Henry batted aside opposition like the blunt instrument he was. His son Edward—by his third wife, Jane Seymour—succeeded to the throne in 1547 at the age of nine, and was dead by 1553. Five years of mayhem followed, as Protestant churchmen and thinkers were hounded and burned by Roman Catholic Queen Mary.

**German artist Hans Holbein the Younger (1497–1543) captures the menacing spirit of Henry VIII.**

Elizabeth succeeded in 1558, with civil and religious life in turmoil. But "Gloriana," a tough cookie when she needed to be, could

## Tudor building

You see it everywhere, in timber church roofs and stained-glass windows, on pargeted plaster walls, clipped into hedges, inset into brick terraces—the Tudor rose, symbol of the pride of the country's best-known ruling dynasty. Tudor building was solid and self-confident, exemplified by the heavily carved timber frames of merchants' houses, by

fine oak paneling, by superb guildhalls such as that at Lavenham in Suffolk (see p. 212), and by the building of the great Elizabethan country mansions (Hampton Court Palace, see pp. 84–85; Burghley House, see p. 221; Hardwick Hall, see pp. 234–35), with their tall chimneys, acres of brickwork, and miles of glass that have so gracefully mellowed over 500 years. ■

also listen to advice. A self-confident national mood grew up. The English sea captains Sir Francis Drake (1540–1596), Sir Walter Raleigh (1552–1618), Sir John Hawkins (1532–1595), and Sir Martin Frobisher (1535–1594) diminished Spanish power on the sea. Raleigh founded Virginia. The East India Company opened for business in India. When Elizabeth died in 1603, things were looking good for Britain.

The throne passed to the Stuart dynasty, already well established in Scotland. James VI of Scotland now also became James I of England (*R.*1603–25). This twitchy but clever man survived the Catholic Gunpowder Plot of 1605 and tensions with his government; it was during his reign that the persecution of religious nonconformists persuaded the Pilgrim Fathers to follow their consciences to the New World.

James's son, Charles I (*R.*1625–1649), believer in the divine right of kings, abolished Parliament in 1629 and attempted autocratic rule until 1640 when he recalled it. A confrontation was inevitable, and it blew up in 1642 when royalist "Cavaliers" and parliamentarian "Roundheads" faced each other in another civil war. Seven years later, defeated and discredited, Charles went to the execution block in Whitehall. The Roundhead leader, the stern Puritan Oliver Cromwell (1599–1658), initiated 11 years of nonmonarchical government by Parliament (1649–1660), a dour time in the "Republic of England" during which merrymaking around maypoles and in theaters was banned, and war with the Dutch severely restricted trade and prosperity. This unsatisfactory hiatus ended when Cromwell died and the not entirely reliable

An eyewitness representation (Weesop 1649) of the execution of King Charles I of England. His reign was marked by political and ideological conflict, but his republican successors fared no better and were in turn replaced by Charles II in 1660.

Merry Monarch, Charles II, returned from exile in 1660 to restore the monarchy.

The Restoration period may have given Britons some excellent stage comedies; but there were bad times, too, under the later Stuarts. A disastrous return of the plague in 1665, followed by the Great Fire of London in 1666, rocked the confidence of many. King Charles II (*R.*1660–1685) approved legislation that barred Roman Catholics from all official positions. His successor, James II of England (*R.*1685–88), made life difficult for himself by

swinging the religious pendulum overenthusiastically toward Catholicism. In 1688, James was deposed in the so-called Glorious Revolution and, apart from a brief and unsuccessful comeback in Ireland in 1690, the Stuarts faded off the scene. Their return in 1715 (the uprising of the "Old Pretender," son of James II) and 1745 (his son, Bonnie Prince Charlie) only confirmed their impotence.

The incoming monarchs, joint sovereigns William of Orange, who came over from Holland, and his English wife, Mary (the daughter of James II), were unimpeachably Protestant. There were still troubles on the Celtic fringes, notably the massacre of the Macdonalds at Glencoe in 1692 (see p. 313), and further bloody repressions in Ireland. Under William and Mary (*R.*1689–1702; William reigned alone after Mary's death in

1694), and then under Mary's younger sister, Queen Anne (R.1702–1714), however, the troubled kingdom settled down, coalesced further by the 1707 Act of Union between the English and Scottish parliaments.

## Georgian era

After the death of Queen Anne, none of whose children had survived into maturity, the Elector of Hanover was invited across the North Sea to take the throne. So began the succession of the four Georges, a time of relative peace and prosperity for the country. During the 18th century, the industrial revolution commenced along the fast-rushing rivers of the Midlands and the North, and soon made Britain the world's chief manufacturer. James Watt (1736–1819), the Scottish engineer and inventor, discovered steam power in 1781, and Sir Richard Arkwright (1732–1792), English industrialist, harnessed it for the weaving industry. A great canal system came into being, forerunner of the world-telescoping railways.

During the 60-year reign of George III (R.1760–1820), the arts boomed and manufacturing prospered. Rich men built and landscaped dream environments for themselves, while the northern manufacturing towns sprouted slums and open sewers.

America fought the old country and gained independence; the Scottish Highland clans disintegrated and all but disappeared. Napoleon Bonaparte (1769–1821) was faced and beaten; desperate agricultural and industrial workers rioted near to revolution.

It was a period of paradox. Indigenous rural ways of life collapsed as a new, powerful bourgeoisie emerged. Rich landowners parceled up the landscape for pleasure and for profit in the form of the enclosures, whose demarcating hedges shaped what we now think of as the "traditional" landscape. The dispossessed rural working class flocked into the little hells of the factories.

## GEORGIAN ARCHITECTURE

The distinctive architecture of the Stuart and Georgian Age of Elegance still seems stylish today. It was the early 17th-century "Grand Tour" of the Continent, undertaken by well-off youngsters, that opened British eyes to the ideals of the Italian designer Andrea Palladio

(1508–1580)—a symmetrical and harmonious use of colonnades, pediments, porticoes, balustrades, and other classical features.

### Palladian

This Palladian style, epitomizing perfection in simplicity and making the most of stone as opposed to the Tudor-era brick, inspired the great Inigo Jones (1573–1652) to produce masterpieces such as the Banqueting House in London (see p. 63) and his rebuilding of Wilton House near Salisbury (see p. 133). Eighteenth-century architects who developed this pure Palladian style included John Wood the Elder (1705–1754) and the Younger (1728–1781), who modeled most of Georgian Bath (see pp. 153–56), and Robert Adam (1728–1792), one of whose achievements was the building of Edinburgh's New Town (see p. 303).

### Baroque

Running simultaneously with the flowering of Palladianism was the far more exuberant and extravagant baroque style, which flourished from the mid-17th to the mid-18th century. Balance and symmetry were central to this style, too, but decoration was added with whimsical touches such as swags of drapery, luxuriant foliage, cherubim, and seraphim. At its best, as in the many London churches of the British architect Sir Christopher Wren (1632–1723), or in the solo works and collaborations of those such as Wren's pupil Nicholas Hawksmoor and Sir John Vanbrugh—for example, in Blenheim Palace (see pp. 196–97)—the style took fantasy and wild imagination to splendid heights.

### Regency

The Regency style, which was developing during the future George IV's long tenure as Regent for his periodically insane father, George III, is best shown at spa towns such as Brighton (see p. 126) and Cheltenham (see p. 181), and in elegant suburbs like Clifton (see p. 152).

The design of gardens and grounds at such fine places had been developing, meanwhile, from the 17th century's very formal geometric style to something much looser, epitomized in the landscapes of Capability Brown (1716–1783) and Humphrey Repton (1752–1818).

**"Industry of the Tyne: Iron and Coal" by William Bell Scott (1811–1890)**

## INDUSTRIAL ARCHITECTURE

Scattered all across the country are examples of specialized forms of architecture that followed one another out of the womb of the industrial revolution. The succession can be clearly seen in Calderdale and Rossendale, where West Yorkshire meets east Lancashire. On the hill slopes are the weavers' cottages with their out-size upper story windows to let in as much light as possible; beside the streams and rivers stand the water-powered mills that succeeded them; then, down in the valley floors, where roads and railroads ran, loom the great steam-driven textile mills with their multiple stories, long ranks of windows, and towering chimneys.

Ironbridge Gorge, just south of Telford in east Shropshire, was the cradle of the industrial revolution. Abraham Darby (1678–1717) pioneered the cheap smelting of iron with coke here in 1709; 70 years later his grandson, Abraham Darby (1750–1791), spanned the River Severn's gorge with the world's first cast-iron bridge (1779), which still forms a perfect circle with its own reflection in the water. Several excellent museums at Ironbridge tell the story.

### Monuments to wealth

Look to the great industrial cities of northern England such as Leeds, Manchester, Sheffield, and Bradford to see huge mills, factories, and cavernous warehouses—cathedrals of commerce, some of them lavishly decorated with glazed tiles, terra-cotta moldings, and elaborate door and window frames, to reflect the power and consequence of their owners. Around them, drawn up in regulated ranks, are the redbrick walls and slated roofs of the workers' terraced houses.

Transport left its own architectural stamp on the landscape: lock gates, quays, warehouses, and highly ornate Victorian stations

**Queen Victoria at age 78. Despite her dour expression and secluded lifestyle, her later years were marked by an upturn in the prestige and popularity of the monarchy.**

and multiarched viaducts along the railroads. In the valleys of South Wales and in the coal-mining northeast, a postindustrial landscape is emerging. Old pit heaps have been given new life as grassy hills, reservoirs as fishing lakes, and tramways as green countryside paths.

### VICTORIAN HEYDAY

The Victorian era has sunk deeply into the national psyche as a kind of Eden before the 20th-century fall. This image is a tribute to the Victorians' own mythmaking, based around the ideal of the Royal Family as a secular Holy Family, epitomizing goodness, stability,

and the progress of enlightenment. The Great Exhibition of 1851 (see box), drawing together threads of civilization from across the world, sums up what we think of the Victorians and what they thought of themselves.

### Massive changes

Yet the 19th century, most of it spanned by the reign of Queen Victoria (R.1837–1901), encompassed such social, economic, and spiritual deprivation in rural and industrial areas of Britain as had never been known before.

Illumination of ordinary people's pleasures, hopes, and sufferings in the Victorian era is provided now—as it was then—by the novels of Charles Dickens (1812–1870). The jolly, red-nosed heartiness of *The Pickwick Papers* (1836–37) was followed by the hollow-cheeked misery and brutality of *Oliver Twist* (1837–39) and *Nicholas Nickleby* (1838–39). *A Christmas Carol* (1843) set the standard for cheery, "traditional" Christmases; *Hard Times* (1854) exposed the wretchedness of lives in a northern industrial city.

Many writers were appalled and fascinated by the effects of the industrial revolution—already a century in existence by the time of the Great Exhibition—as, given an infinitely greater boost by steam power, its factories and mines, railroads and workers' slums spread out to cover much of the land. The resultant social change was on an epic scale. In 1800, about 70 percent of the population worked in agriculture; by 1900, it was about 10 percent.

### The Great Exhibition

It was the idea of Prince Albert (1819–1861) to celebrate Britain's mid-19th-century preeminence as a world imperial power and industrial giant. The Great Exhibition, held in Hyde Park inside the Crystal Palace—a colossal glasshouse designed by the Chatsworth House gardener, Joseph Paxton—ran from May 1 to October 15, 1851. Six million people admired 100,000 exhibits, from the mightiest steam engine to the most delicate filigree jewelry from India. ∎

**The Crystal Palace was so huge that it even enclosed trees within its structure.**

**During the Blitz, many children were evacuated from London to temporary rural homes.**

### Rebellion

The Factory Act limiting children's working hours to no more than 48 per week was not passed until 1833. Chimney sweeps still employed climbing boys, as portrayed in Charles Kingsley's *The Water Babies* (1863). Corruption in Parliament and the working man's lack of a vote led to the Chartist Riots of 1838–39, with mass marches and demonstrations by tens of thousands of people.

Two dozen were killed by troops in Newport, South Wales, in August 1839. Agricultural and industrial workers laid off due to mechanization went on machine-smashing sorties. There was a desperate undercurrent to the triumphant surface that 19th-century Britain showed to the world.

### New frontiers

And they were triumphant times. The world's first passenger railroad (1830) introduced geographical and social mobility. Slavery was abolished throughout the empire in 1833, the same year that the Oxford Movement revived evangelical missionary Christianity. Anesthetics arrived in 1846, ending millennia of surgical horror. Charles Darwin's 1859 *The Origin of Species* set minds off on hitherto unthinkable tracks. Compulsory education for all, up to age 11, was initiated in 1870. Electricity began to light and heat houses in the 1880s. There was even help for the countryside and its heritage with the Ancient Monuments Protection Act of 1882 and the formation of the National Trust in 1895.

## 20TH CENTURY

The 20th century brought enormous change to Britain. There was a brief golden Edwardian glow to open the century; then came World War I (1914–18) with its million dead, its traumatized survivors, and its terrible, unanswerable questions. War memorials can be found in almost every village, carrying long lists of the dead.

No society—especially such a rigidly stratified one as Britain's had become—could escape fundamental change after such an ordeal. In 1918 the vote was granted to all men over 21, all women over 30 (women's votes at 21 came in 1929). Primary education became free. The trade unions gained membership and power, leading to the General Strike of 1926 in support of miners' pay and conditions claims. The great depression of the 1930s put millions out of work and on the unemployment lines; some, from the hard-hit northeast, walked 300 miles in the 1936 Jarrow March to protest in London. That year Edward VIII (R.1936) succeeded his father George V (R.1910–1936), fell in love with American divorcée Wallis Simpson, and abdicated his throne to marry her.

### New Elizabethans

Six million Britons served during World War II (1939–1945), and 275,000 of them lost their lives. A further 58,000 died on home territory in bombing raids. Enormous pride in "winning the war" turned quickly into disillusion at "losing the peace," as rationing of commodities and austerity standards in clothing, cars, and buildings persisted well into the 1950s. At the time, locked into the uncertainties of the Cold War at the side of the United States, it seemed a tense yet gray period. Looking back now, many Britons see it as a golden age when they were cradled by the welfare state and their children could explore the streets and countryside in safety.

Queen Elizabeth II succeeded her father, George VI (R.1936–1952), in 1952. During her reign the pace of change in Britain has accelerated. In the 1950s and '60s, the British Empire was swept away by tides of independence, to be replaced by a surprisingly healthy and resilient Commonwealth of voluntary members. A multicultural society was initiated by immigrant workers from former colonies. "Swinging London" rose and fell as British pop music reached all corners of the world.

### Striking a balance

The 1970s were characterized by appalling labor relations, by an upsurge of trouble in Northern Ireland, by strikes and pickets, and "winters of discontent." In 1973 Britain joined the European Community (now the European Union)—a commitment she is still dithering over. During the last two decades of the millennium, consumerism, selfishness, and greed often seemed to be staking a claim on the soul of the country. Britons hated seeing their landscape under threat from development, their towns and villages swollen and homogenized, their much-maligned, but now belatedly appreciated, welfare state dismantled. Yet overseas visitors continued to arrive in Britain, in search of deep roots of history and culture, and to enjoy seeing a country where change and tradition still exist side by side. ■

## Postwar architecture

The widespread destruction caused by World War II bombing left great opportunities for postwar architects. Sadly, and with a few honorable exceptions such as Sir Basil Spence's 1955–1962 Coventry Cathedral (see p. 190), these were squandered. Brutalism in concrete was the order of the day in bombed and cleared town centers.

The 1980s and '90s saw ancient towns and villages surrounded by business parks and characterless supermarket complexes. Absence of local materials in their construction and a lack of harmony in color, scale, and appearance with their surroundings has made almost all this recent building unsympathetic—though some developments in London's Docklands, along with Richard Rogers' "inside-out" Lloyd's Building (1986; see p. 54) in the City, and the clean lines of his airport buildings at Stansted, are examples to the contrary. ■

# The arts

BRITAIN'S CONTRIBUTION TO WORLD LITERATURE, FROM GEOFFREY Chaucer's day up to the present, has been of the first importance. And Giraldus Cambrensis, the Norman-Welsh chronicler and ecclesiastic, twice elected but never consecrated Bishop of St. David's, predated Chaucer (circa 1345–1400) by 200 years when he wrote down his *Itinerarium,* a witty and gossipy account of his tour through Wales in 1188. Welsh, English, and Scottish bards and poets were creating an oral tradition of verse, song, and story for hundreds of years before the Dark Ages, when monks, traveling through Europe, brought back the notion of reading and writing. Education transferred the skills to the laity, and the great British literary tradition was founded.

Chaucer's *Canterbury Tales,* composed around 1387 to 1400, was a hugely ambitious project that death prevented him from finishing. A century would pass before William Caxton brought the craft of printing to the point where he could produce, in 1485, an edition of Sir Thomas Malory's *Le Morte d'Arthur,* an account of the life and death of the mythical "once and future king," that Malory had written 15 years before. And it would be another century before William Shakespeare (see pp. 186–89) began to create the plays and sonnets that would establish him as the greatest writer in history.

## 17TH CENTURY

The 17th-century preoccupation with the tensions between orthodox and nonconformist religion brought forth John Milton's (1608–1674) epic poem *Paradise Lost* (1667), and John Bunyan's (1628–1688) "spiritual travelogue," *The Pilgrim's Progress* (1678), written in Bedford Gaol where Bunyan was imprisoned for unlicensed preaching. Another classic is the witty *Diary,* begun by Samuel Pepys (1633–1703) in January 1660, an invaluable insight into 17th-century life and thought.

## 18TH CENTURY

During the 18th century, the English novel began to take shape and find readers. Daniel Defoe (1660–1731) led the way in 1719 with *Robinson Crusoe,* based on yarns he heard in a Bristol tavern from rescued shipwreck victim Alexander Selkirk. In 1749, Henry Fielding (1707–1754) produced his full-blooded *Tom Jones,* and the novel was off and running.

Defoe had also published his great, sharp-eyed travelog *A Tour Thro the Whole Island of Great Britain* (1724–26).

Dr. Samuel Johnson (1709–1786) and James Boswell (1740–1795) took up the literary baton after their 1773 travels through Scotland, with Johnson's *A Journey to the Western Islands of Scotland* appearing in 1775 and Boswell's *Journal of a Tour to the Hebrides* in 1785. These are splendidly characterful travel books, easy to read for enjoyment and instruction even today, and they set a standard few other travel writers could reach.

Two 18th-century poets who made an indelible mark were the Scottish national poet Robert Burns (1759–1796; see pp. 292–93), whose short life blazed so brightly; and the visionary William Blake (1757–1827), with his *Songs of Innocence* (1789) and *The Marriage of Heaven and Hell* (1790–93).

## 19TH CENTURY

A tremendous literary flowering took place in Britain during the 19th century. The prolific talent of Charles Dickens (see pp. 40, 124) laid bare some of the worst aspects of the industrial revolution while creating some of the most memorable characters in fiction: Mr. Pickwick, Oliver Twist, Nicholas Nickleby, Little Dorrit, Ebenezer Scrooge, David Copperfield, Pip and Abel Magwitch, Uriah Heep, and all the others.

During the second decade of the century, the country parson's daughter Jane Austen (see p. 129) wrote *Sense and Sensibility* (1811),

**Shakespeare's Globe Theatre has been reconstructed in London's Bankside just 200 yards from the site of the original building.**

*Pride and Prejudice* (1813), *Mansfield Park* (1814), *Emma* (1816), *Northanger Abbey*, and *Persuasion* (both 1817). Sir Walter Scott was turning out his "Waverley novels" among a great stream of historical romances—*Waverley* itself (1814), *The Antiquary* (1816), *Rob Roy* (1817), *The Heart of Midlothian* (1818), *Ivanhoe* (1819), *Kenilworth* (1821), and

**Charles Dickens worked relentlessly, producing several successful novels and campaigning against the social evils of his time.**

others—many of them written under frantic pressure to pay off creditors.

William Wordsworth (see pp. 254–55) was most poetically active during this period in Grasmere, too, and his fellow poet and admirer John Keats (1795–1821) showed brilliant promise in his early twenties before his premature death. Quite another kind of writing was being produced around this time with the publication in 1830 of William Cobbett's *Rural Rides*, a stinging commentary and exposé of southern England's depressed agricultural scene and corrupt local politics.

The literary talents of the Brontë sisters (see p. 272) shone during the 1840s. After a childhood spent writing about the imaginary realms of Gondal and Angria, in 1847 the three young women each produced a brilliant novel: Anne's *Agnes Grey*, Charlotte's masterpiece *Jane Eyre*, and Emily's demonic *Wuthering Heights*. Anne went on to write *The Tenant of Wildfell Hall* (1848) while Charlotte produced *Shirley* (1849) and *Villette* (1853). Within two years of their first work, Anne and Emily were dead, and Charlotte followed them in 1855.

Another writer to make her mark on the mid-19th century was Elizabeth Gaskell (1810–1865) with *Cranford* (1853) and *North and South* (1855); she also wrote the definitive *Life of Charlotte Brontë* (1857). Marian Evans, under the name of George Eliot (1819–1880), produced such classics as *Adam Bede* (1859), *The Mill on the Floss* (1860), *Silas Marner* (1861), and *Middlemarch* (1871–72). Later on came the romantic novels, short stories, and poems of Robert Louis Stevenson (1850–1894), the frail Scotsman with a wild gothic imagination—*Treasure Island* (1883), *A Child's Garden of Verses* (1885), *The Strange Case of Dr. Jekyll and Mr. Hyde*, and *Kidnapped* (both 1886) among a vast output. Sir Arthur Conan Doyle (1859–1930), another Edinburgh-born writer, introduced his detective hero Sherlock Holmes in *A Study in Scarlet* (1887), killed him off in *The Final Problem* (1893), and resurrected him ten years later through sheer pressure of public demand in *The Adventure of the Empty House* (1903). The Dorset-based writer Thomas Hardy (see pp. 136–37) produced all his epic Wessex novels—*Far From the Madding Crowd*, *The Mayor of Casterbridge*, *Tess of the d'Urbervilles*, and the others—between 1874 and the turn of the century. Literary treasures piled high. But of all the works of 19th-century British writers, the one that has had the most profound effect was published in 1859 by a middle-age geologist and biologist, and had the catchy title: *On the Origin of Species by Means of Natural Selection*, or *The Preservation of Favoured Races in the Struggle for Life* by Charles Darwin (1809–1882).

## 20TH CENTURY

The impact of 20th-century British literature is harder to assess; time will tell what is good enough to last. Some Americans—Henry James and T.S. Eliot, for example—honed their talents while living in Britain. The Irish playwright and polemicist George Bernard Shaw (1856–1950) wrote all his great plays—*Arms and the Man, Man and Superman, Pygmalion, Saint Joan*—while living here. In the 1920s, Virginia Woolf (1882–1941) and D.H. Lawrence (1885–1930) made their names. The interwar years saw Eric Arthur Blair (1903–1950), writing as George Orwell, produce *The Road to Wigan Pier, Down and Out in Paris and London, Animal Farm*, and *1984* just after World War II.

Another key literary figure is the novelist Graham Greene (1904–1991), with his piercing eye for downbeat atmosphere and characters caught between good and evil in such understated masterpieces as *Stamboul Train* (1932), *Brighton Rock* (1938), *The Power and the Glory* (1940), *The Heart of the Matter* (1948), *The End of the Affair* (1951), and *The Comedians* (1966).

Postwar writers included Kingsley Amis (*Lucky Jim*), Alan Sillitoe (*Saturday Night and Sunday Morning*), John Osborne (*Look Back in Anger*), and John Braine (*Room at the Top*). Iris Murdoch (*The Sea, The Sea*), Anita Brookner (*Hotel du Lac*), and John Fowles (*The French Lieutenant's Woman*) have made big names for themselves. William Golding was awarded the Nobel Prize for Literature in 1983; his *Lord of the Flies* (1954) opened a dark door into human behavior when all the rules of civilization are swept away. Salman Rushdie wrote the acclaimed *Midnight's Children*, about the birth of independence in his native India, and then went under sentence of death for offending orthodox Muslims with *The Satanic Verses*. Irvine Welsh carries the shock banner with his seamy dialect novels of drugs and crime in Edinburgh, notably *Trainspotting*.

Poetry has continued to flourish despite its customary shortage of funding, promotion, and public regard. The frontline trenches of Flanders forged the romantic Wilfred Owen (1893–1918) into the Great War's finest and steeliest poet. Since then England has produced W.H. Auden (1907–1973), Ted Hughes (1930–1998), and Sir John Betjeman (1906–1984). Scotland has discovered in Hugh MacDiarmid a native poet fit to share the plinth with Robert Burns, and out of Wales have come the two great Thomases: Dylan (1914–1953), and R.S. Thomas (born 1913).

## ART

Britain's global influence in art, compared with its contribution to world literature, has been fairly modest. Each age has thrown up its singular genius, though, and there have been some British leaders in the varied fields of landscape painting and watercolor, satirical drawing, and innovative design.

The native art of Britain can be enjoyed in county and municipal museums around the country, in private collections such as the Burrell Collection (see p. 296) in Glasgow, and Sir John Soane's Museum (see p. 93) and the Wallace Collection (see p. 94) in London, and on the walls of dozens of country houses.

Outstanding examples of early jewelry and pottery have survived dating back through the Iron and Bronze Ages to the Stone Age. The rich hoard retrieved from the seventh-century Saxon ship burial at Sutton Hoo can be seen in the British Museum (see p. 71), and the interlaced patterns and glowing colors of the Lindisfarne Gospels' illuminations are in the British Library (see p. 71).

Churches and cathedrals are good places to look for Dark Ages and medieval art, from stained-glass windows and carved rood screens to statuary, frescoes, and treasures such as the Mappa Mundi in the New Library Building adjoining Hereford Cathedral (see p.178) and St. Cuthbert's painted coffin at Durham (see p. 279).

Post-Renaissance Britain gave rise to a broad range of artistic expression that covered the Elizabethan portrait painting of Nicholas Hilliard (1537–1619), the baroque woodcarving of Dutchman Grinling Gibbons (1648–1721) in late 17th-century churches and country houses, and the biting social and moral commentary of the engraver and painter William Hogarth (1697–1764) in his serial conversation pieces "A Rake's Progress" and "The Election," (see p. 93) and admonitory prints such as "Gin Lane."

The Georgian era was a golden age for British art and crafts. Thomas Gainsborough (1727–1788) and Richard Wilson (1714–1782) were turning out their light-filled landscapes, and Joshua Reynolds (1723–1792), George Romney (1732–1804), Sir Henry Raeburn (1756–1823), and Gainsborough himself were raising the art of portrait painting to

new heights. Poet William Blake, meanwhile, was translating his apocalyptic visions into illustrations.

Thomas Sheraton (1751–1806), George Hepplewhite (died 1786), and Thomas Chippendale (1718–1779) produced delicately carved and upholstered furniture for the landed gentry who had their grounds land-scaped by Capability Brown (1716–1783). Josiah Wedgwood (1730–1795), Thomas Minton (1765–1836), and Josiah Spode (1754–1827) created beautiful ceramics in the potteries of Staffordshire. And satirical, witty commentary was made on the life of the country by the celebrated caricaturists Thomas Rowlandson (1756–1827) and James Gillray (1757–1815).

**"Mr & Mrs Clark & Percy" (1970–71) by David Hockney**

John Constable (1776–1837) and J.M.W. Turner (1775–1851) were learning their craft as painters around this time. During the first half of the 19th century they would reach triumphant fruition—Constable with his meticulous depictions of East Anglian rural scenes, and Turner—also in landscapes—with a style increasingly impressionistic. Later in the Victorian era the Pre-Raphaelite brotherhood of painters tried to turn the clock back to the more lyrical and pastoral approach of the early Middle Ages. Their leading lights were Sir John Everett Millais, Ford Madox Brown, Dante Gabriel Rossetti, William Holman Hunt, and Sir Edward Burne-Jones, who also designed church stained glass still to be found all over

Britain. William Morris (1834–1896) became the most influential designer of the later 19th century with his back-to-traditional-basics Arts and Crafts movement, a vision that influenced the stylish art nouveau design work of Glaswegian Charles Rennie Mackintosh (1868–1928) around the turn of the 20th century.

The boundaries between art and craft—and art and almost anything else for that matter—have become blurred during the past century. The crowded religious paintings of Sir Stanley Spencer (1891–1959) and monu-mental, threatening landscapes of Paul Nash (1889–1946) have given way to far more expressive painting styles, from light and airy interiors by David Hockney to the dark and obsessive portraits of Francis Bacon and Lucian Freud.

**Unfinished but beautiful, "Christ Preaching at Cookham Regatta" is typical of Sir Stanley Spencer's individualistic work.**

Sculpture moved into abstraction from Sir Jacob Epstein (1880–1959) through Barbara Hepworth (1903–1975) and Henry Moore (see p. 114). Caricature continued to be a British strongpoint, with stars of distortion such as Gerald Scarfe and Ralph Steadman.

## MUSIC

Traditional British music and dance has roots that go far back in time. Such traditions have preserved a more vigorous life in the Celtic nations of Wales, Scotland, and Ireland. Here wild dance music is still played, and unaccompanied singing is enjoyed in pubs, village halls, barns, and back kitchens. The folk music of England—songs of rural life and labor, vigorous and (some might say) galumphing tunes to accompany country dancing—still keeps a toehold in folk clubs and a specialist record market, but has nothing like the social or musical cachet of its Celtic counterpart.

British religious and classical music ran a fairly straight course from the great choral works of Tudor composers such as William Byrd (1542–1623) and Thomas Tallis (1505–1585), through Henry Purcell (1659–1695) and George Frederick Handel (1685–1759), into 19th- and 20th-century names such as Sir Edward Elgar (1857–1934), Frederick Delius (1862–1934), Ralph Vaughan Williams (1872–1958), and Gustav Holst (1874–1934). Perhaps it is characteristic of British musical tastes that none of these

serious composers finds quite such a niche in national affection as those Victorian spinners of sublime light opera, Sir William Schwenck Gilbert (1836–1911) and Sir Arthur Sullivan (1842–1900). This century has witnessed the flowering of Sir Michael Tippett, Sir William Walton (1902–1983), and Benjamin Britten (1913–1976), among others. Celebratory festivals of classical music such as those at Aldeburgh in Suffolk (Britten),

Glyndebourne in Sussex (opera), and the Promenade Concerts performed in the Royal Albert Hall in London are always packed.

Pop and rock composers and musicians have been influential since the early 1960s. The Beatles, of course, took off like an express train in 1963 with their magical mix of R&B, rock 'n' roll, balladry, country and western, music-hall, schmaltz, and soul. Since then, new music styles—some taken from

across the Atlantic, some genuinely home-grown—have continuously cropped up, keeping things fresh.

Pop, rock, glam, progressive, punk, pomp, New Romantic, acid house, rave, hip-hop, indie, happy, heavy, hairy…and crossovers and fusions, sometimes unsuccessful but always interesting, between the musical heritages of Asia, the Caribbean, and Africa have all slotted into this multiethnic society.

**Whatever kind of music you're into, you will find a club somewhere in Britain that plays it.**

## THEATER
In the world of British theater, William Shakespeare (see pp. 186–89) is as unassailable a benchmark as are the Beatles in pop music. More than 400 years after they were first written, his plays still pack theaters wherever they are produced.

The English theater was shut down during Puritan times, from 1640 to 1660, but apart from those dour decades it has flourished. Shakespeare's well-known contemporaries were Christopher Marlowe (1564–1593) and Ben Jonson (1572–1637).

After Charles II returned to the throne in 1660, audiences split their sides with laughter over Restoration comedies such as William Congreve's *The Way of the World* and George Farquhar's *The Beaux' Stratagem*. Irishman Richard Sheridan's *School for Scandal* delighted Georgian audiences, while Victorians were amused by Irish writer Oscar Wilde's bitingly witty plays *Lady Windermere's Fan* (1892), *An Ideal Husband*, and *The Importance of Being Earnest* (both 1895).

Today's crop of British playwrights includes names such as Tom Stoppard and Alan Ayckbourn, while Sir Andrew Lloyd Webber (*Cats*, *Evita*, *Jesus Christ Superstar*, *Phantom of the Opera*) continues to dominate the field of musical shows.

Twentieth-century stars of the stage form a roll call that features Dame Peggy Ashcroft, Paul Scofield, Sir Laurence Olivier, Sir John Gielgud, Richard Burton, Vanessa Redgrave, Sir Anthony Hopkins, Kenneth Branagh. The Royal National Theatre in London mounts innovative and challenging plays, while for Shakespeare the faithful flock to the Royal Shakespeare Company's theater at Stratford-upon-Avon (see pp. 186–87), or—for an authentic Elizabethan playhouse atmosphere—to London's reconstructed Globe Theatre (see p. 87), in Southwark on the south bank of the Thames.

## FILM

Many stage players and writers have crossed over into film, both cinema and television. British filmmaking has traditionally tended to survive in the shadow of Hollywood; directors who do make it very big, such as Sir Alfred Hitchcock (1899–1980), have done so via the Hollywood machine. Two fields have always proved fruitful—costume dramas (the Merchant Ivory films of the 1980s and '90s, some starring Emma Thompson, for example) and comedy. Wry, quirky hits such as *Four Weddings and a Funeral*, *The Full Monty*, and *Notting Hill* grabbed audiences in the 1990s.

Television's costume dramas (Jane Austen's *Sense and Sensibility* and *Pride and Prejudice*, Charlotte Brontë's *Jane Eyre*, George Eliot's *Middlemarch*) and comedy shows like *Monty Python's Flying Circus* and John Cleese's *Fawlty Towers* have shone the lamp for Britain, too. And while cable TV channels and commercial radio stations proliferate all around, "Auntie" —the BBC, or "Beeb"—continues to represent excellence and impartiality.

### Good locations

Dotted around the British towns and countryside, you will come across houses and landscapes that have been featured in classic cinema and television films. In the southwest keep an eye out for Saltram House near Plymouth in Devon, and Montacute House (see p. 157) in south Somerset, locations for *Sense and Sensibility*. Robert Bolt's *A Man For All Seasons* was filmed in and around Hampton Court Palace (see p. 84) on the Thames, just west of London. In Lincolnshire, East Anglia, the golden limestone town of Stamford (see p. 221) was a central feature of *Middlemarch*, while Belton House near Grantham was "Rosings" in the smoldering Colin Firth and Jennifer Ehle television version of *Pride and Prejudice*.

Farther west, in the north Midlands, Sudbury Hall, west of Derby, was used for the *Pride and Prejudice* interior scenes, while exteriors were shot at Lyme Park, south of Stockport in Cheshire. Two popular TV series were filmed in Yorkshire—*Last of the Summer Wine* around Holmfirth, northwest of Sheffield, and the James Herriot country vet series, *All Creatures Great and Small*, farther north in the West Yorkshire dales of Swaledale and Wensleydale. The monumental Castle Howard (see pp. 270–71) in North Yorkshire featured heavily in the television adaptation of Evelyn Waugh's novel *Brideshead Revisited* (1982).

Scotland's spectacular castles, lochs, and glens have provided backdrops for many films. Castle Tioram on Loch Moidart in the west featured in *Highlander* (1986), Glen Nevis, south of Fort William in *Kidnapped* (1986) and *Braveheart* (1995), while Blackness Castle on the Firth of Forth, west of Edinburgh, and Dunnottar Castle, just south of Stonehaven on the northeast coast, were filmed for Franco Zeffirelli's *Hamlet* (1990). ■

Everyone knows the famous London land-marks—St. Paul's Cathedral, Big Ben, Buckingham Palace, Westminster Abbey. But there are many intriguing byways and undiscovered corners, too, in this fascinating city.

# London

Map & introduction **48–50**
**The City 51–55**
St. Paul's Cathedral **52–53**
A walking tour of the City **54–55**
**Westminster & the West End 56–67**
Westminster Abbey **57–58**
Buckingham Palace **59**
National Gallery **60–61**
A walking tour of Westminster **62–63**
National Portrait Gallery **64**
Tate Britain/Tate Modern **65**
Soho & Covent Garden walk **66–67**
**Bloomsbury 68–72**
British Museum **69–72**
**Knightsbridge & Kensington 73–82**
Victoria & Albert Museum **74–75**
Science Museum **76**
Natural History Museum **77**
Knightsbridge & Kensington walk **80–81**
Kensington Palace **82**
**Following the Thames 83–92**
Tower of London **89–92**
More places to visit in London **93–94**
Hotels & restaurants in London **343–46**

**Big Ben, Westminster**

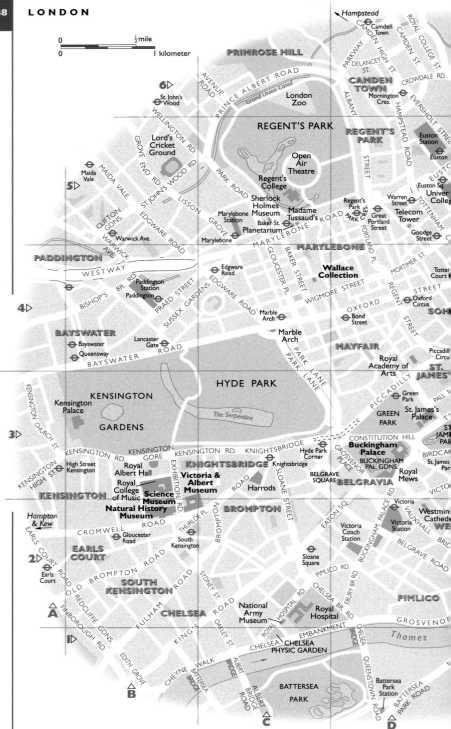

0 ½ mile
0 1 kilometer

PRIMROSE HILL

Hampstead

Camden
Town

CAMDEN
TOWN

6▷
St. John's
Wood

AVENUE ROAD

PRINCE ALBERT ROAD

Grand Union Canal

London
Zoo

ROYAL COLLEGE ST
CAMDEN HIGH ST.
CAMDEN ST.
CROWDALE RD.
DELANCEY ST.
ALBANY
PARKWAY
Mornington
Cres.
EVERSHOLT STREET
HAMPSTEAD ROAD

Lord's
Cricket
Ground

REGENT'S PARK

REGENT'S
PARK

Euston
Station

Euston

WELLINGTON RD.
GROVE END RD.
ST. JOHN'S WOOD RD.
MAIDA VALE

5▷
Maida
Vale

Open
Air
Theatre

STREET
Regent's
Park

EUSTON

Euston Sq.

Univer
Colle

Warren
Street

Telecom
Tower

TOTTENHAM

Regent's
College

Sherlock
Holmes
Museum

Madame
Tussaud's

PARK
Great
Portland
Street

CLIFTON
GDNS.

Warwick Ave.

WARWICK AVE.

LISSON GROVE
PARK ROAD
EDGWARE ROAD

Marylebone
Station

Baker St.
Planetarium

Marylebone

MARYLEBONE

MARYLEBONE

MARYLEBONE ROAD

BAKER STREET

GLOUCESTER PL.

Wallace
Collection

PORTLAND PL.

MORTIMER ST.

Goodge
Street

SOH

Totter
Court

PADDINGTON

WESTWAY

Edgware
Road

WIGMORE STREET

REGENT STREET

Oxford
Circus

STREET

4▷

BISHOP'S BR. RD.
Paddington
Station
Paddington

PRAED STREET

SUSSEX GARDENS

EDGWARE ROAD

Marble
Arch

OXFORD ST.

Bond
Street

Piccadill
Circu

ST.
JAMES

BAYSWATER

Bayswater

Queensway

Lancaster
Gate

Marble
Arch

MAYFAIR

Royal
Academy of
Arts

KENSINGTON
CHURCH ST.

BAYSWATER ROAD

HYDE PARK

PARK LANE

PARK LANE

PICCADILLY

Green
Park

GREEN
PARK

PALL M

St. James's
Palace

ST
JAM
PA

KENSINGTON
GARDENS

Kensington
Palace

The Serpentine

CONSTITUTION HILL

Buckingham
Palace

BUCKINGHAM
PAL. GDNS.

BIRDCA

St. James
Par

3▷

KENSINGTON RD.
KENSINGTON
GORE

KENSINGTON RD.

KNIGHTSBRIDGE

Hyde Park
Corner

GROSVENOR PLACE

Royal
Mews

KENSINGTON
HIGH ST.

High Street
Kensington

Royal
Albert Hall

KNIGHTSBRIDGE

Knightsbridge

BELGRAVE
SQUARE

BELGRAVIA

St. James
Par

VICTO

KENSINGTON

Royal
College
of Music

Science
Museum

Victoria &
Albert
Museum

SLOANE STREET

BUCKINGHAM PALACE ROAD

Victoria

Victoria
Station

Westmin
Cathed

WE

Natural History
Museum

Harrods

BROMPTON ROAD

EXHIBITION RD.

EATON SQ.

Hampton
& Kew

CROMWELL ROAD

Gloucester
Road

THURLOE PL.

South
Kensington

BROMPTON

BROMPTON ROAD

EBURY BR. RD.

Victoria
Coach
Station

BELGRAVE ROAD

PIMLICO

2▷

Earls
Court

EARLS COURT ROAD
OLD BROMPTON ROAD

EARLS
COURT

SOUTH
KENSINGTON

SYDNEY ST.

Sloane
Square

PIMLICO RD.

CHELSEA RD.

GROSVENOR

A

FINBOROUGH RD.
EDITH GROVE
OLD REDCLIFFE GDNS.

FULHAM ROAD

CHELSEA

KING'S ROAD

OAKLEY ST.

National
Army
Museum

ROYAL HOSPITAL RD.

Royal
Hospital

Thames

B

CHEYNE WALK

BATTERSEA BRIDGE

ALBERT BRIDGE

CHELSEA
EMBANKMENT

CHELSEA
PHYSIC GARDEN

CHELSEA BRIDGE

Battersea
Park
Station

QUEENSTOWN ROAD

BATTERSEA PARK ROAD

C

ALBERT BRIDGE ROAD

BATTERSEA
PARK

D

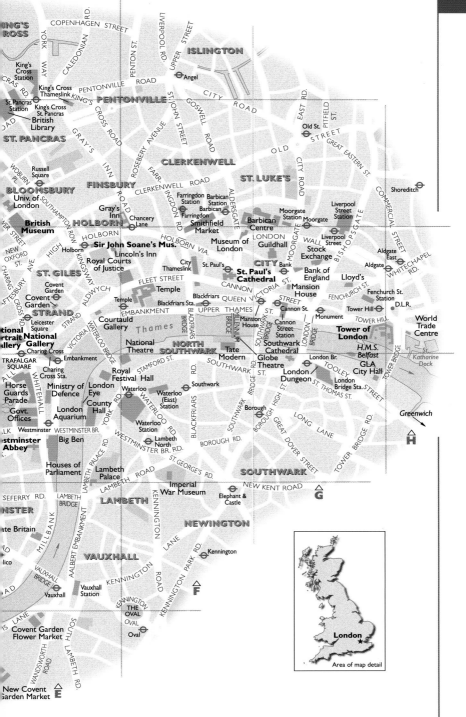

KING'S CROSS

COPENHAGEN STREET
YORK WAY
CALEDONIAN RD.
LIVERPOOL RD.
UPPER STREET

ISLINGTON

King's Cross Station
King's Cross Thameslink
PENTONVILLE ROAD
PENTON ST.
Angel

St. Pancras Station
King's Cross
St. Pancras
British Library

ST. PANCRAS

Russell Square
WOBURN PL.
SOUTHAMPTON ROW

BLOOMSBURY
Univ. of London

GRAY'S INN ROAD
ROSEBERY AVENUE
ST. JOHN STREET
GOSWELL ROAD

CITY ROAD

EAST RD.
PITFIELD ST.
Old St.
GREAT EASTERN ST.

CLERKENWELL
CLERKENWELL ROAD
FARRINGDON RD.

FINSBURY

ST. LUKE'S

Shoreditch

COMMERCIAL STREET

Gray's Inn
British Museum
HOLBORN

Chancery Lane
HOLBORN
Holborn
HIGH HOLBORN

NEW OXFORD ST.
CHARING CROSS RD.
SHAFTESBURY AVE.

ST. GILES

Covent Garden

STRAND

KINGSWAY
ALDWYCH

Sir John Soane's Mus.
Lincoln's Inn
Royal Courts of Justice

Temple
FLEET STREET
Temple
Blackfriars Sta.

EMBANKMENT
Courtauld Gallery

Farringdon Station
Barbican Station
Farringdon
Barbican
Smithfield Market

ALDERSGATE

Museum of London
LONDON WALL

Barbican Centre

Moorgate Station
Moorgate

Liverpool Street Station

Aldgate

Guildhall

Liverpool Street
LONDON
Stock Exchange
CITY
St. Paul's
St. Paul's Cathedral
Bank
Bank of England
Lloyd's

BISHOPSGATE

Aldgate East

WHITECHAPEL RD.

CANNON ST.
QUEEN VICTORIA ST.
Blackfriars

UPPER THAMES
Mansion House
Cannon St.
Cannon Street Station

FENCHURCH ST.
Monument
TOWER HILL
Tower Hill

Fenchurch St. Station

D.L.R.

World Trade Centre

National Portrait Gallery
National Gallery
Leicester Square
Charing Cross
TRAFALGAR SQUARE

Charing Cross Sta.
Embankment

VICTORIA EMBANKMENT
WATERLOO BRIDGE

National Theatre

Thames

NORTH SOUTHWARK

STAMFORD ST.

Tate Modern

BLACKFRIARS BRIDGE
MILLENNIUM BRIDGE

SOUTHWARK BRIDGE
LONDON BRIDGE

Southwark Cathedral

London Br.
London Bridge Sta.

TOOLEY ST.
ST. THOMAS ST.

H.M.S. Belfast
GLA City Hall

St. Katharine Dock

TOWER BRIDGE RD.

Greenwich

H

Horse Guards Parade
WHITEHALL

Govt. Offices

Ministry of Defence

London Eye
County Hall

London Aquarium

Westminster
WESTMINSTER BR.

Big Ben

Westminster Abbey

Houses of Parliament

Royal Festival Hall

YORK RD.
WATERLOO RD.

Waterloo
Waterloo (East) Station

Waterloo Station

Lambeth North
WESTMINSTER BR. RD.

Southwark

BLACKFRIARS RD.

SOUTHWARK ST.
Globe Theatre

London Dungeon

London Bridge Sta.

GLA City Hall

Borough
BOROUGH HIGH ST.
BOROUGH RD.
ST. GEORGE'S RD.

LONG LANE

GREAT DOVER STREET

SOUTHWARK

Tate Britain
MILLBANK

Pimlico

LAMBETH PALACE RD.
LAMBETH BRIDGE
Lambeth Palace
LAMBETH ROAD

Imperial War Museum

NEW KENT ROAD
Elephant & Castle

G

FERRY RD.

LAMBETH BRIDGE

LAMBETH

ALBERT EMBANKMENT

KENNINGTON

NEWINGTON

VAUXHALL BRIDGE
VAUXHALL

Vauxhall
Vauxhall Station

VAUXHALL

KENNINGTON ROAD
KENNINGTON PARK RD.
KENNINGTON LANE

Kennington

F

Covent Garden Flower Market

THE OVAL
OVAL
Oval

WANDSWORTH ROAD
LAMBETH RD.

New Covent Garden Market
E

London
★
Area of map detail

# London

WHAT CAN ONE SAY BY WAY OF AN INTRODUCTION TO LONDON? THIS IS ONE of the world's great historic and contemporary cities. Here are the seat of government at Westminster, the monarch's great royal residence of Buckingham Palace, and the nation's premier art galleries, museums, theaters, and arts venues. This is the home of one Briton in seven. London is endlessly adaptable, having converted itself from a walled Roman fort and Dark Ages stronghold to a great medieval city, to a baroque phoenix literally risen from the ashes of the Great Fire of 1666, to a Georgian dream of elegance, to a Victorian powerhouse of empire incorporating extremes of wealth and poverty, to a faded and jaded interwar imperial shadow, to Swinging London of the 1960s, and to today's sprawling, cosmopolitan, money-centered ants' nest of a place.

You will find elements of each and all of these in Britain's capital city. There are the truly great tourist attractions that demand attention: Westminster Abbey, St. Paul's Cathedral, the Tower of London, Buckingham Palace, the British Museum, the National Gallery, and Trafalgar Square, among many. And there are hidden, tucked-away delights and pleasures: Sir John Soane's Museum in Lincoln's Inn Fields, for example, or the waterfront walk among the architectural extravaganzas of Docklands, or Chelsea Physic Garden, or the crispy-duck sellers beneath the dragon arch in Soho's Chinatown.

**ON FOOT**
London is a safe and pleasant place to walk around by day. Four walks are suggested in the following pages: Around the City of London and St. Paul's Cathedral; from Westminster and St. James's Park to Buckingham Palace and back by Trafalgar Square; through seedy but latterly "hip" Soho and lively Covent Garden; and from the smart shops of Knightsbridge to the famous museums of Kensington and into Hyde Park. Do use the excellent Underground railway, better known as "the Tube," to discover for yourself more of this great and exciting city. ■

**St. Martin-in-the-Fields (1721–26), glimpsed through the fountains of Trafalgar Square**

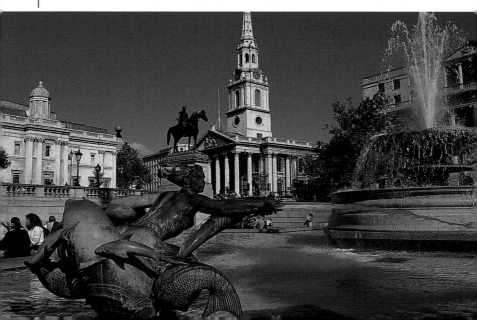

At the heart of the City is the Old Lady of Threadneedle Street—the Bank of England.

# The City

The City of London, or the "Square Mile," as the financial heart of the capital is known, is almost entirely given over to commerce, an exciting and sometimes jarring mishmash of solid Georgian and Victorian architecture alongside plate-glass modernism. It is a stimulating place to walk around—not the most restful part of London, though the many very fine 17th-century churches provide havens of peace.

The Square Mile covers approximately the same area as the walled city of Londinium founded by the Romans on the Thames shortly after they arrived in Britain in A.D. 43. It was the highest point that ships could reach at high tide, and the first feasible place upriver from the estuary mouth where a bridge could be built.

Londinium recovered quickly after being sacked in A.D. 60 by the rebel Iceni tribe under their warrior-queen Boudicca, and soon became the chief port and road junction of Roman Britain. The boundaries of the city did not expand outside the Roman walls until well after the Norman Conquest; then they commenced a gradual creep westward.

Following the restoration of King Charles II, two disasters struck London in quick succes-

sion. The Great Plague of 1665 killed a quarter of the capital's inhabitants, and the following year's Great Fire destroyed four out of every five houses. This was not an unmitigated tragedy, however, since it cleared away several disease-ridden warrens of badly maintained, insanitary housing. It also provided an opportunity—grasped by Sir Christopher Wren in particular—to build a more modern city, mostly of stone, much of it heavily influenced by the baroque style.

St. Paul's Cathedral is the showpiece of the 17th-century rebirth of the City of London, but the City walk (see pp. 54–55) shows you many more post-Great Fire architectural treasures, as well as a number of medieval gems that have survived fire, wartime bombing, and modern developers. ■

# St. Paul's Cathedral

**St. Paul's Cathedral**
- 49 F4
- St. Paul's Church-
  yard, EC4
- 020-7236 4128
- Closed Sun. except
  for services
- $$
- Tube: St. Paul's

ONE WARTIME PHOTOGRAPH ABOVE ALL CAME TO symbolize the resisting spirit of London during the 1940 Blitz—that famous shot of the dome of St. Paul's Cathedral silhouetted against a wall of flame and smoke, standing firm under fiery attack. There was an irony to the image, too, for it was the Great Fire of London in 1666 that destroyed the city's medieval cathedral and enabled Sir Christopher Wren (1632–1723) to build the magnificent new church that made his name and fortune. Wren dominated London's rebuilding after the fire, designing 52 churches, of which the great baroque cathedral of St. Paul (1675–1710) was his masterpiece.

Huge, domed, swagged, and magnificent, bulky St. Paul's sits marooned in a green churchyard. Twin towers guard the west front, built in 1707—the northern tower houses the largest bell in England, the 17-ton "Great Paul." Inside the cathedral, the saucer domes on the nave ceiling carry the eye forward to the crossing under the great dome.

Wren wanted to build a basilica cathedral with four arms of near equal length, but this was considered too Italianate and too modern and the church authorities insisted on the conventional long nave and shorter transepts. However, Wren's innovative genius was allowed full play in the construction of the dome, 364 feet high and second only to St. Peter's in Vatican City. It measures 157 feet from side to side of its famous Whispering Gallery, and bears down with the weight of thousands of tons of stone and lead—the lantern on the top alone weighs 850 tons.

Before climbing the 530 steps to the topmost viewing gallery, take plenty of time to enjoy a stroll around the body of the cathedral. Here, the beautiful wrought-iron choir screen was made by Jean Tijou, one of the Huguenot refugees who so greatly enhanced the cultural and artistic life of Britain. Another foreign settler, the Rotterdam mastercarver Grinling Gibbons (1648–1721) carved the choir stalls and organ casing to Wren's original decorative design.

## MEMORIALS

It had been Wren's wish that his masterpiece be left uncluttered with memorials, but the cathedral's symbolic importance made this impossible. Indeed, much of the interest of St. Paul's lies in its many monuments. Immediately on entry, you pass on your left the Chapel of All Souls with its deathly white effigy of Lord Kitchener of Khartoum. There is a touching and seldom inspected pietà located above the chapel's altar.

In the north aisle and north transept are notable memorials to famous men such as Dr. Samuel Johnson (see p. 55) and Field Marshal Lord Slim, as well as to forgotten heroes like Maj. Gen. Andrew Hay who died aged 52, "closing a military life marked by zeal, prompt decision, and signal intrepidity." Painter and sculptor Frederick, Lord Leighton (1830–1896) and the Duke of Wellington (1769–1852) both have remarkably hook-nosed effigies.

Wellington himself lies buried in the crypt in a giant marble tomb surrounded by lions, while nearby are images of Florence Nightingale (1820–1910) tending a soldier, and the hero of Trafalgar, Lord Nelson (1758–1805), lying in a huge, black sarcophagus under a rather flashy coronet and cushion. His coffin was originally commissioned for Cardinal Wolsey in the 16th century, then seized by Henry VIII. It remained unused until 1805 when Nelson was buried within it.

## DOME

Shallow wooden steps lead up to a short flight of stone stairs and the entrance to the Whispering Gallery with its wall paintings and good view down into the nave—one of the angles from which in 1981 TV viewers around the world saw the solemnization of the marriage between Charles, Prince of Wales, and the 19-year-old Lady Diana Spencer.

From here, more spiral steps climb to the windy Stone Gallery, and there is a final flight of iron stairs to the little railed Golden Gallery, dizzyingly high, where you stand in the open 350 feet above the churchyard and look out over London and the Thames. ■

# A walking tour of the City

From the Monument pillar, the walk leads into the financial heart of the capital, with the Bank of England and the Stock Exchange, and on past three City churches and the great St. Paul's Cathedral to Fleet Street and the Inns of Court.

The walk starts outside Monument tube station at the 202-foot Portland stone **Monument 1** *(Monument St., EC3, tel 020-7626 2717, tube: Monument)*, topped with a burst of brilliant gold flame. It stands 202 feet from the site of the baker's shop in Pudding Lane where the Great Fire of London broke out on September 2, 1666. The fire burned out of control for four days, consuming 13,200 close-packed medieval houses and 89 churches, including the classical-style St. Paul's Cathedral.

Walk along Fish Street and turn right onto Eastcheap. Turn left on Philpot Lane, cross Fenchurch Street, and go along Lime Street; turn left onto Beehive Passage.

**Leadenhall Market** on the left is a maze of curved, cobbled streets full of expensive food and gift shops, pubs, and chic restaurants. From Leadenhall Place view the boldly bizarre

**Lloyd's Building 2** (built in 1986 to the designs of Richard Rogers, architect of the Pompidou Centre in Paris), with elevators scuttling up and down its gleaming metallic walls like robotic insects. Some love it, some hate it.

Turn left along Leadenhall Place to Gracechurch Street; turn right, cross Cornhill, then go west on Threadneedle Street.

Here is London's financial heart. On the right are the new buildings of the Stock Exchange, then the impressive pillars of the grand Old Lady of Threadneedle Street, the **Bank of England 3**, founded in 1694, with its **Bank of England Museum** *(Bartholomew Lane, EC2, tel 020-7601 5545, closed Sat.–Sun., tube: Bank)*. Beyond on the left is narrow little Lombard Street, hung with elaborate signs—a banking center since Norman times when moneylenders from Lombardy set up shop.

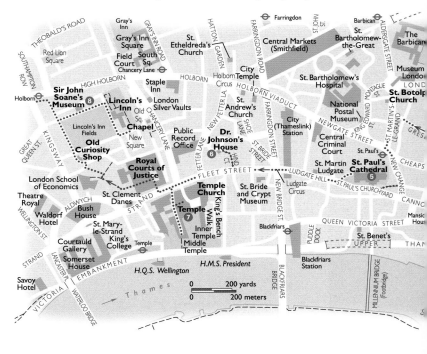

Cross the top of Lombard Street and take the second left on Walbrook to **St. Stephen Walbrook** (1672–79). Built by Wren, the church is peaceful haven of creamy-colored stone under an ornate dome, with a massive altar sculpted by Henry Moore (1898–1986).

Go along Bucklersbury, then turn left along Poultry; turn right and proceed north on King Street to Gresham Street. Here are the **Church of St. Lawrence Jewry,** containing a stained-glass portrait of Wren, and the turreted and crocketed **Guildhall** ❹ (*Gresham St., EC2, tel 020-7606 3030, closed Sun. Oct.–April, tube: Bank, St. Paul's),* whose Great Hall holds monuments to William Pitt, Lord Nelson, the Duke of Wellington, and Sir Winston Churchill.

From the Guildhall, go west on Gresham Street to the junction with Aldersgate Street. On the right is the Georgian **St. Botolph Church,** with a fine plaster ceiling and stained glass showing John Wesley preaching.

From the church, walk south along St. Martin's-Le-Grand and New Change to **St. Paul's Cathedral** ❺ (see pp. 52–53).

From the cathedral's west end, walk along Ludgate Hill, then Fleet Street (once home of

the British newspaper industry); turn right along Hind Court to Gough Square. **Dr. Johnson's House** ❻ *(17 Gough Sq., EC2, tel 020-7353 3745, closed Sun., tube: Temple, Black-friars),* is where the lexicographer Samuel Johnson (1709–1784) compiled his seminal *Dictionary of the English Language* (1755); cartoons and paintings by Johnson and his biographer, James Boswell (1740–1795) are shown.

Back on Fleet Street, cross and go right; past Cock Tavern, go left through Temple Bar gateway. In the early Middle Ages, the **Temple** ❼ *(Middle Temple Hall, Middle Temple Lane, EC4, tel 020-7427 4800, closed Sat.–Sun. & Aug., tube: Temple)* was headquarters of the Knights Templar. Here in a maze of lanes and courtyards are the Societies of the Middle and Inner Temples, where students train for the Bar (law).

Back on Fleet Street again, cross and go left past the **Royal Courts of Justice,** then right to cut through to St. Clement's Lane. Cross Portugal Street and continue on St. Clement's; turn left into Portsmouth Street opposite the tiny **Old Curiosity Shop** (claiming to be Dickens's inspiration).

At the top of the street is Lincoln's Inn Fields, where felons were beheaded and quartered. On the opposite (north) side is **Sir John Soane's Museum** ❽, one of London's great hidden treasures (see p. 93).

Enter **Lincoln's Inn** *(Chancery Lane, tel 020-7405 1393, closed Sat.–Sun., tube: Chancery Lane)* from the east side of the square. Here are more 17th-century houses and courtyards in the oldest of the four Inns of Court. The Great Hall has a huge hammer-beam roof and stained glass. Return to the northwest corner of Lincoln's Inn Fields; turn right to reach Holborn tube station. ∎

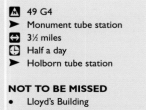

- 49 G4
- ► Monument tube station
- ↻ 3½ miles
- ⊕ Half a day
- ► Holborn tube station

**NOT TO BE MISSED**
- Lloyd's Building
- St. Paul's Cathedral
- Sir John Soane's Museum

**Unmistakable landmarks of London—the Houses of Parliament and Big Ben**

# Westminster & the West End

**Westminster is undoubtedly the heart of visitors' London. This area of the capital lying west of the Thames contains the Houses of Parliament and Big Ben, Westminster Abbey and Buckingham Palace, Trafalgar Square and the National Gallery—all guaranteed, perennial attractions. Yet Westminster is no tourist gimmick. The district is also the constitutional, political, and royal heart of the nation. All the great ceremonial occasions, from the State Opening of Parliament to Trooping the Colour, take place here.**

Westminster is the London residence of the monarch, and kings and queens have been crowned, married, and buried here for 1,000 years. The prime minister lives in Westminster; Parliament lays down the law here; and Big Ben strikes the national time signal.

The view across the Thames is of the pinnacled Houses of Parliament and Big Ben's rocketlike tower. This is not only the most photographed scene in the country, but an image most often associated with London.

The walk (see pp. 62–63) around the heart of the capital will show you the great sights of Westminster. It also introduces you to some less familiar delights, such as the beautiful but often overlooked Church of St. Margaret in the shadow of Westminster Abbey (see pp. 57–58), the secret subterranean hideout (the Cabinet War Rooms, see pp. 63) where Winston Churchill and colleagues planned the conduct of World War II, and the touchingly overblown ceiling paintings of the Banqueting House (see pp. 63) that Charles I commissioned to celebrate the divinity of the Stuart dynasty, never dreaming that his own head would soon be struck off by a common executioner. Leave plenty of time to look around the churches, galleries, and exhibitions en route. ■

# Westminster Abbey

FILLING THE SOUTH SIDE OF PARLIAMENT SQUARE, Westminster Abbey is not only the largest and loveliest Gothic church in London, but very evidently the point where the religious, political, and monarchical lives of the nation come together. This site has been the scene of 38 coronations since that of William the Conqueror on Christmas Day 1066—all the monarchs save Edward V, murdered in 1483, and Edward VIII, who abdicated in 1936.

The present church was refounded in 1065 by Edward the Confessor just before the Norman Conquest, replacing the former church of circa 960. Most of the abbey as it is today was begun in 1245 during the reign of Henry III. It was completed in leisurely medieval fashion; the nave, though in the same Gothic style, dates from later on in the 14th century. The Lady Chapel at the east end brings us into the Tudor era, while the towers at the west end are the 18th-century work of Nicholas Hawksmoor (1661–1736) to a design by his mentor, Sir Christopher Wren.

Westminster Abbey is enormous, and a good impression of its bulk is gained from outside the mighty Victorian Great North Door, whose porch is decorated with rank upon rank of offertory and musical angels, potentates, prelates, and saints. Inside, the immediate impression is of great height (the nave is 102 feet from floor to roof) and of narrowness, dramatically lit by the huge chandeliers.

## INTERIOR

One of the chief attractions of the church is its unrivaled collection of monuments to the great and good (and to the not so great or good).

After payment at the Great North Door, you can advance to see Statesmen's Aisle in the north transept. Here are some of the abbey's finest statues, including Benjamin Disraeli (1804–1881),

William Gladstone (1809–1898), and Sir Robert Peel (1788–1850). William Pitt (1759–1806) has a 25-foot monument. On your right, the north choir aisle close to the organ is dedicated to musicians, with monuments to Henry Purcell, Sir Edward Elgar, and Benjamin Britten.

### Royal chapels

At the east end of the church are the chapels where the monarchs rest. Walking around the ambulatory you get glimpses of the carved stone shrine of Edward the Confessor (R.1042–1066) and of

**Westminster Abbey**

49 E3

Parliament Sq., SW1

Abbey: 020-7222 5152. Chapter house: 020-7222 5897

Abbey: $$. Chapter house: $/$$

Tube: Westminster, St. James's Park

**Westminster Abbey contains not only priceless treasures of medieval artwork, but also examples of 19th-century design at its most elaborate.**

the later medieval royal tombs erected close to it. Standing at the foot of the stairs to Henry VIII's Chapel is the oak Coronation Chair, made in 1301 and used at every coronation since then. The richly fan-vaulted Chapel of Henry VII conceals some splendidly heroic and humorous misericords under the choir stall seats. Here lies Henry himself (*R*.1485–1509) in gilt bronze effigy. Below, in a vault, is the tomb of James I, far more modest than the overblown grandiosity of his adviser, the Duke of Buckingham (1592–1628), who lies surrounded by grieving bronze warriors. In the north aisle, Queen Elizabeth I looks coldly regal in marble; poor Mary, Queen of Scots, stares palely and piously up at a fine display of gilt flowers in the canopy above her tomb in the south aisle.

### Poets' Corner

Poets' Corner, in the south aisle, holds monuments to William Shakespeare, John Dryden, Henry Wadsworth Longfellow, Lewis Carroll, W.H. Auden, Henry James, Alfred Lord Tennyson, D.H. Lawrence, Lord George Byron, Robert Southey, Charles Dickens, and Sir Walter Scott. The 13th-century chapter house (reached from the east cloister) has superb stone carvings above a floor tiled in rich ocher and cream colors. The walls display mind-boggling 14th-century frescoes: St. John blissfully smiling in a vat of boiling oil, venerable saints casting down their golden crowns in a well-orchestrated shower, a snub-nosed dromedary, a one-hump "Kameyl," and a fiery red depiction of a "reynder" hunt.

### Nave

Toward the west end are floor slabs to politicians Stanley Baldwin (1867–1947), Clement Attlee (1883–1967), and David Lloyd George (1863–1945), among others, as well as to Sir Winston Churchill (1874–1965) and the symbolic Unknown Warrior of World War I. These contrast with monuments such as Captain Richard le Neve of the Edgar, killed in 1673 in a "sharp engagement with the Hollanders." ■

**The towers at the west end, designed by Nicholas Hawksmoor in 1734, were added in 1745.**

# Buckingham Palace

THE ROYAL FAMILY DO NOT PARTICULARLY CARE FOR Buckingham Palace, it is said: They always appear happier at Windsor, Sandringham, or Balmoral. The original Buckingham House was built in 1703 for the Duke of Buckingham in what were then rural surroundings, but it has been greatly altered since.

The palace you see now was built in the early 1920s. It is the official London residence of the monarch, whose presence is signified by the flying of the Royal Standard.

King George III bought Buckingham House in 1762. John Nash carried out an enlargement in the early 1820s for George IV, but was "let go" when his plans proved too expensive. In 1837, at the threshold of Queen Victoria's reign, it became the sovereign's residence in preference to St. James's Palace.

Nineteen of the 661 rooms are open to the public each summer, originally to help pay for repairs to Windsor Castle (see pp. 100–104) after the 1992 fire there (restoration was completed in November 1997). This arrangement will be reviewed in time but is likely to continue. You can view the red-and-gold Grand Hall, with Nash's curved staircase and glazed dome; the vaulted Picture Gallery, lined with a no-nonsense selection of Old Masters; the gold-ceilinged Throne Room; the sumptuous State Dining Room, and other ceremonial chambers.

Other, separate attractions are the **Royal Mews** *(tel 020-7799 2331, closed Fri.–Sun.)* with its collection of extravagant state carriages and cars; and the Queen's art collection, presented as a series of changing exhibitions in the **Queen's Gallery** *(tel 020-7766 7300)*. One attraction that has never lost its appeal is the **Changing of the Guard** *(11:30 a.m. daily April–early July, alternate days early July–March)*, when red-jacketed guardsmen under tall black bearskin hats march in front of the palace. ■

**Buckingham Palace**

- 48 D3
- Buckingham Palace Rd., SW1
- 020-7766 7300
- Closed Oct.–early Aug.
- $$$$
- Tube: St. James's Park, Green Park

**Late in the morning crowds gather in front of the Buckingham Palace gates to watch the Changing of the Guard just inside.**

# National Gallery

WITH ITS GREAT PORTICO FRONTING ONTO TRAFALGAR Square, the National Gallery is London's premier art gallery displaying one of the greatest collections of Western European paintings (from around 1260 to 1900) in the world. The four-wing layout is user friendly: 1260–1510 in the Sainsbury Wing; 1510–1600 in the West Wing; 1600–1700 in the North Wing; and 1700–1900 in the East Wing.

**National Gallery**

- 49 E4
- Trafalgar Sq., WC2
- 020-7747 2885
- Late opening Wed.
- Charge for special exhibitions
- Tube: Charing Cross, Leicester Square

To make the most of your time here, spend the first half hour of your visit browsing the gallery plan and catalog, selecting about 30 paintings or artists you would really like to see (a few star attractions from the collection are suggested below). But along the way you are bound to stumble across so much more, either familiar or new to you.

The internal layout of the National Gallery's Sainsbury Wing entices you on, though its small-ish rooms can become crowded around such star exhibits as the Leonardo cartoon and the "Wilton Diptych."

### SAINSBURY WING

**Room 51** contains Leonardo da Vinci's famous cartoon of "The Virgin and Child with St. John the Baptist and St. Anne." **Room 53** has the "Wilton Diptych," in which a flock of blue-robed angels with gull-like wings surrounds the Virgin and Child. **Room 56** holds Van Eyck's "Arnolfini Marriage."

In **Room 58** is Botticelli's "Venus and Mars." Raphael's tiny, exquisite "Madonna of the Pinks" is in **Room 60,** Hieronymus Bosch is represented in **Room 62** by "Christ Mocked," full of brutal faces and cruelly spiky armor, and in **Room 66** is an unfinished "Nativity" by Piero della Francesca (circa 1420–1492), in which a glorious, sleepy-eyed angelic choir sings hymns to Mary with her beautiful, almond-shaped face.

### WEST WING

**Room 7** holds a darkly passionate "Agony in the Garden of Gethsemane" by El Greco. Michelangelo's unfinished "Entombment," showing a pale Christ held in a sling of grave wrappings, is in **Room 8. Room 9** has several Titians, including the "Death of Actaeon," a savage composition in Titian's later, blurry style engendered by failing eyesight; a Veronese "Adoration"; and a superb Tintoretto of the seen-it-all face of Senator Vincenzo Morosini in old age. In **Room 12** are a Pieter Bruegel the Elder "Adoration," with the Three Kings unkempt and exhausted after their journey, and two ugly "Tax-Gatherers" by Marinus Van Reymerswaele.

### NORTH WING

Jan Vermeer is in **Room 16** and Franz Hals in **Room 23.** Room 23 also contains several Rembrandts. One shows the artist's wife, Saskia, in 1635, age 24 and bursting with life and warmth; another is a beautifully affectionate portrait

of Hendrickje Stoffels, the girl who was nursemaid to Rembrandt's child after Saskia died, and who later became the painter's mistress.

In **Room 29** is "Samson and Delilah" by Rubens, with Samson collapsed in a stupor on Delilah's richly sumptuous red dress. **Room 30** displays "The Toilet of Venus" (also known as "The Rokeby Venus"), painted by Diego Velázquez (1599–1660), celebrating the warm tints and curves of this narcissistic goddess.

### EAST WING

**Room 34** is crammed with treasures: Works by J.M.W. Turner (1775–1851) include his early, storm-tossed "Dutch Boats in a Gale," his later, poignant "The Fighting Temeraire" and tempestuous "Rain, Steam and Speed." Also here are superb landscapes by John Constable (1776–1837), including "Salisbury Cathedral from the Meadows" and "Stratford Mill." The famous "Hay-wain" is

also here, with many details revealed on close inspection— haymakers in the distance, piling a wagon; three red admiral butterflies in the foreground; a vase of red flowers in a window of Willy Lott's Cottage.

**Room 38** contains pictures of Venice by Canaletto; **Room 39** some nice dark Goya portraits, including a coldly efficient "Duke of Wellington."

**Room 43** is packed with Impressionists—Degas, Manet, Pissarro; Monet's "Bathers at La Grenouillère" and his foggy "Thames below Westminster." **Room 44** has studies for "Bathers at Asnières" by Georges Seurat (1859–1891), along with the painting itself of boys dipping in a calm Seine. In **Room 45** are sunny Cézanne landscapes, and his blue "Bathers"; and several wild van Goghs, including the spiky "Wheatfield with Cypresses," painted in the St. Rémy asylum, and one of his four "Sunflowers." ∎

J.M.W. Turner's vivid "The Fighting Temeraire" (circa 1838)

# A walking tour of Westminster

**From the Houses of Parliament, this walk leads to Westminster Abbey, then continues through St. James's Park to Buckingham Palace. From here it follows the Mall to Trafalgar Square before reaching Banqueting House.**

From Westminster tube station cross the street to **Big Ben,** the great clock tower named after its 14-ton bell, which has tolled time for Britain since 1859. Turn right and continue around to the left into **Parliament Square,** with its statues of national heroes.

On your left rise the **Houses of Parliament,** more properly called the **Palace of Westminster** ① *(Parliament Sq., line up at St. Stephen's entrance, tel 020-7219 4272, closed late Aug.–mid-Oct.; a.m. Mon.–Wed., some Fri. mid-Oct.–Sept., tube: Westminster),* a grand Gothic fantasy built between 1837 and 1860 by Sir Charles Barry (1812–1852) and Augustus Pugin (1795–1860) to accommodate the House of Lords and the House of Commons. The original palace was built here by Edward the Confessor. After the Reformation, the Commons were housed in what had been the palace's chapel. When that was burned in 1834, Pugin and Barry were

called in. As a bow to the history of the site, the Speaker's Chair stands where the chapel's altar used to be. Beyond the House of Commons is the 11th-century **Westminster Hall,** built for William II, where Guy Fawkes was tried for treason in 1605, as was Charles I at the end of the Civil War. Charles II had Oliver Cromwell's head spiked on the roof in 1661, in revenge for his own father's execution.

Cross to **St. Margaret's Church,** used by the House of Commons since 1614, a late medieval gem with notable stained glass—at the west end, the blind poet John Milton dictating *Paradise Lost,* with scenes from the fall all around him; at the east end, pain-wracked faces and bodies in a 16th-century Flemish Crucifixion; in the south aisle, daring modern spikes and slashes in gray, green, and yellow by John Piper. John Milton, Winston Churchill, and Samuel Pepys were all married here.

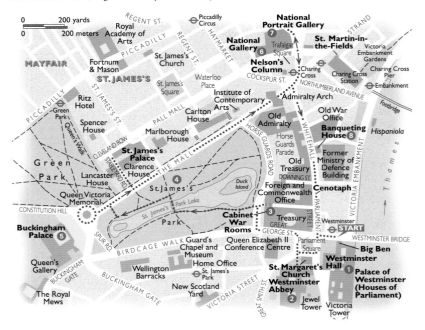

Continue into **Westminster Abbey** ❷ (see pp. 57–58). From the abbey, cross to the north side of Parliament Square. Go left along Great George Street to the edge of St. James's Park, then turn right to the **Cabinet War Rooms** ❸ *(Clive Steps, King Charles St., SW1, tel 020-7930 6961, tube: Westminster, St. James's Park).* Beyond the sandbagged entrance, stairs lead down to the complex of subterranean rooms from which Churchill and his staff planned the Allied conduct of World War II. The original maps, full of pin holes, are still stuck on the walls.

When this bunker was being prepared in August 1939, the outbreak of war was expected to be followed by the wholesale destruction of London by bombing. Although the scale of the bombardment proved to be smaller than feared, the Cabinet War Rooms continued to be used. By 1945 they had branched into 70 rooms, covering more than three acres underground. Some of Churchill's best known wartime speeches were broadcast from here.

Audio guides lead you around the rather spooky chambers. There are giant radio sets and scramblers, telephone exchanges, typing pools, and bedrooms with functional iron bedsteads—a complete secret citadel under London's streets. Churchill's own work room is on display, with two telephones and a green-shaded lamp; also his bedroom (seldom slept in) containing an ash tin for the prime ministerial cigar, and a plain white chamber pot.

Back at street level, cross into **St. James's Park** ❹ (see p. 79), London's oldest park, and walk through in a westerly direction to reach **Buckingham Palace** ❺ (see p. 59), your destination at the end of the park.

| | |
|---|---|
| ▨ | 49 E3 |
| ► | Westminster tube station |
| ⬌ | 2 miles |
| ⏱ | Half a day |
| ► | Westminster tube station |

**NOT TO BE MISSED**
- Palace of Westminster
- Westminster Abbey
- Cabinet War Rooms
- National Gallery

From the palace, it is a little under a mile to Trafalgar Square along the ruler-straight, tree-lined Mall. En route you could detour to Stable Yard to view the great Tudor brick gatehouse of **St. James's Palace,** the monarch's residence until Buckingham Palace superseded it.

**Trafalgar Square** is a never-failing tourist magnet, with its central **Nelson's Column.** Admiral Horatio Nelson towers 185 feet above the fountains designed by Sir Edwin Lutyens (1869–1944) and the four famous lions, the work of Sir Edwin Landseer (1802–1873). A pedestrianized pavement leads from the square to the **National Gallery** ❻ (see pp. 60–61) and the **National Portrait Gallery** ❼ (see p. 64). Alongside stands the early Georgian church of **St. Martin-in-the-Fields,** famous for sheltering the homeless and for its free Monday, Tuesday, and Friday lunchtime concerts.

Turn south on Whitehall to find on your left the **Banqueting House** ❽ *(Whitehall, SW1, tel 020-7930 4179, closed Sun. & for government functions, tube: Westminster, Charing Cross),* sole remnant of the great Royal Palace of Whitehall (burned down in 1698). Upstairs in the Great Hall, a Rubens ceiling celebrates the reign of Scottish King James VI, who in 1603 became James I of England. The scenes depicted are the Union of England and Scotland (overweight cherubs dropping roses on royal personages), the peaceful reign of the king (love, kisses, and plenty of rosy-cheeked health), and a curious kingly ascension in which a red-faced James is borne aloft into heaven by a bevy of brawny women. Charles I, who commissioned the paintings in 1629 to honor his father and to enshrine the divine status of the monarchy, was beheaded on January 30, 1649, on a scaffold built for the occasion against the wall of the Banqueting House. Wearing two shirts to prevent him from shivering (so that no one should think him afraid), the defeated king stepped out of the window onto the platform and went bravely to his execution.

Continue past the entrance to **Downing Street,** opposite, now gated to protect No. 10, the prime minister's residence. Pass the **Cenotaph**, Britain's national war memorial (by Sir Edwin Lutyens), to return to Westminster tube station. ∎

# National Portrait Gallery

THE NATIONAL PORTRAIT GALLERY, AROUND THE CORNER from the National Gallery in St. Martin's Place, contains some 9,000 portraits, drawings, photographs, and sculptures spanning more than 500 years. Many themes emerge. In old age Wordsworth broods poetically, Charles II like a cynical satyr, former Home Secretary Lord Whitelaw in gentle puzzlement; the poet Coventry Patmore stands dandyish and alert; the blind composer Frederick Delius raises a face pared by thought, as if hearing a long-forgotten melody.

**National Portrait Gallery**

49 E4

✉ St. Martin's Place, WC2

☎ 020-7306 0055. Recorded information: 020-7312 2463

🕐 Late opening Thurs.–Fri. until 10 p.m.

💲 Charge for special exhibitions

🚇 Tube: Charing Cross, Leicester Square

**"Emma, Lady Hamilton" by George Romney is in the National Portrait Gallery's collection.**

In all the flush of youthful beauty are actress Ellen Terry at 17; Emma Hamilton, Nelson's mistress, at 20; Christine Keeler, a call-girl at the center of a 1960s government scandal, shown naked astride a trendy Arne Jacobsen chair; and poet Rupert Brooke.

## SUCCESSFUL FIGURES

There are women accustomed to exerting power of one sort or another: a steely-haired Baroness Thatcher, photographed in 1991 just after her ousting from Downing Street; a cold, implacable Queen Elizabeth I with hooded, unfathomable eyes, and a 1918

portrait by Augustus John of Lady Ottoline Morrell, socialite lover of several of the artists and sitters in this gallery (including John himself), looking rapacious and rather mad under a huge black hat.

Then there is the self-confident power exuded by some of the most successful middle-age men, exemplified in the portraits of architect Sir John Vanbrugh (1705) and royal painter Sir Peter Lely (1660).

## HUMAN FRAILTY

As for the eyes being the windows of the soul, they certainly open up the inner being in Sir Thomas Lawrence's 1828 presentation of reformer William Wilberforce in late middle age, in George Romney's self-portrait of 1784 (both unfinished), and in Romney's 1792 depiction of the poet William Cowper.

Hollow-faced poet Alexander Pope, AIDS-ravaged film director Derek Jarman, and piercing-eyed scientist Stephen Hawking show the spirit's triumph over the weakness of the flesh.

By contrast, we see the cigar-chomping Victorian engineering genius Isambard Kingdom Brunel (see box p. 152), casually yet masterfully posed against giant chain links, and the glossy, air-brushed 1980s media couple Harold Evans and Tina Brown, icons of material success in their respective ages. ■

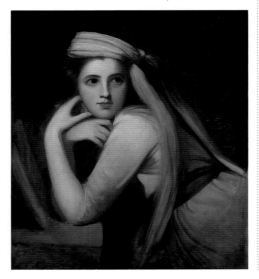

# Tate Britain/Tate Modern

**Tate Britain**

🅰 49 E2

✉ Millbank, SW1

☎ 020-7887 8000.
Recorded information: 020-7887 8008

💲 Charge for special exhibitions

🚇 Tube: Pimlico

**Tate Modern**

🅰 Map p. 85

✉ Bankside, SE1

☎ 020-7887 8000.
Recorded information: 020-7887 8008

💲 Charge for special exhibitions

🚇 Tube: Southwark, Blackfriars, London Bridge

**The annual rehang at Tate Britain is a winter highlight.**

TATE BRITAIN (FORMERLY THE TATE GALLERY) FACING THE Thames on Millbank, was a gift to the nation from Victorian sugar manufacturer Sir Henry Tate (1819–1899). It contains the best of British painting from Tudor times up to the 20th century. On the opposite side of the river is Tate Modern housing an eclectic, often unconventional collection of modern painting and sculpture from around the world.

Tate Britain holds the definitive collection of the works of J.M.W. Turner. He left his paintings to the nation, but it was not until the Clore Gallery was opened in 1987 nearly 150 years after the artist's death, that the Turner Bequest could be hung as one piece in all its glory. As well as the famous oil paintings, letters, sketches, and a fascinating display of the artist's working notebooks can be seen. The works are exhibited mostly around the ground floor in chronological order from the 16th century round to the present day. Like many great art galleries, the Tate does not have enough space to show all its works of art and displays are rotated on a yearly basis, enabling the gallery to show as much as possible of its extensive collection.

Exhibits range from the richly tinted fashion of 17th-century portraiture through 18th- and 19th-century landscapes and society portraits to a wide-ranging collection of Pre-Raphaelites, Impressionists, and 20th-century works by Pablo Picasso, Auguste Rodin, David Hockney, and others.

Housed in a stunning transformation of the Victorian Bankside Power Station at Southwark, Tate Modern is one of the world's leading modern art galleries. It contains international art from the 20th century, including works by Matisse, Picasso, Pollock, and Warhol. ■

# Soho & Covent Garden walk

This half-day walk introduces you to two of the most colorful areas of central London, Soho and Covent Garden, both of which have seen great changes in the past couple of decades.

Emerging from Piccadilly Circus tube station, you are confronted with one of London's best known landmarks—the statue of **Eros** at the center of Piccadilly Circus. In fact, the delicately balanced winged figure represents the Angel of Christian Charity, and was put up in 1893 as a memorial to the 7th Earl of Shaftesbury, a philanthropist who worked to abolish child labor in Victorian factories.

Head first for the **Rock Circus** ❶ *(tel 020-7734 7203, tube: Piccadilly Circus),* upstairs in the London Pavilion. This is a supremely kitsch piece of fun. You start by having your picture taken alongside a waxwork rock star, then inspect more or less successful tableaus (hopelessly thin Fat Elvis, excellent George Michael, laughable Beatles, first-class Freddie Mercury), while a crackly headphone sound-track jumps neurotically between songs. Final port of call is a risible "live show" of jerky wax-works and flashing lights in a revolving theater. No observer could fail to be moved.

From here turn into Shaftesbury Avenue, then left to Great Windmill Street into **Soho.**

This region of narrow streets to the north of Piccadilly Circus was built as a pleasant residential area during the westward expansion of London after the 1666 Great Fire. But the fashionable were swept farther west into Mayfair, and Soho became an immigrants' area where first Huguenot refugees and then Poles and Russians, Greeks and Italians set up house and small businesses. In Victorian times, Soho drifted into a darker era as a raffish night haunt for theatergoers and music hall devotees. By the 1950s it had declined into a seedy district of peepshows, strip joints, and sex parlors or—according to its many artistic and literary aficionados—a freewheeling refuge from bourgeois constraint. Both elements are still strong in today's Soho, but some of the sordidness has disappeared in the face of a new wave of decent small restaurants and food-centered businesses, many owned by the area's Chinese.

## EAST OF SOHO

Working your way north, there is an excellent fish restaurant, Zilli, on Brewer Street, with a window full of jars of exotic pickles and preserves. At **Berwick Street Market** (*Mon.–Sat.*) there are stalls piled with fruit, olives, and cheeses.

To the southeast, around Gerrard and Lisle Streets, is **Chinatown** ❷ (*Tube: Piccadilly Circus, Leicester Sq.*), marked by bilingual street names and a colorful ceremonial arch-way across Gerrard Street. During the Chinese New Year in late January or early February, this district is alive with firecrackers and papier-mâché lions and dragons. If you are hungry, try take-out crispy, aromatic duck and rice from any of two dozen restaurants—but watch your duck being cooked, so that you don't end up with all the fat!

North of Chinatown on Dean Street, above Leoni's Quo Vadis restaurant at No. 26, is a plaque recording the residence here of Karl Marx from 1851 to 1856, while he worked on *Das Kapital.* Across on the corner of Greek and Romilly Streets is the famous **Coach and Horses** pub, lined with cartoons and prints.

On Charing Cross Road make for Cambridge Circus, then go east along Earlham Street to Seven Dials, with its weird reconstruction of a 17th-century Doric pillar topped by sundials. Cross onto Shorts Gardens and turn left into **Neal's Yard** ❸, a little triangular oasis of New Age shops, "therapy rooms," alternative remedy emporia, and inexpensive eateries, all reeking of spices and patchouli oil.

## AROUND COVENT GARDEN

From Shorts Gardens bear right on Neal Street, past crafts shops, kite sellers, cobblers, and vegetarian cafés. Cross Long Acre by the nice art deco tube station of Covent Garden to reach the former fruit and vegetable market itself in its big open square.

On your left is the **Royal Opera House** (see p. 390), one of the world's great opera venues, a splendid building which recently

underwent a major and expensive overhaul. This is the home of both the Royal Ballet and Royal Opera companies. On the square's east side is the **London Transport Museum** ④ *(39 Wellington St., tel 020-7379 6344, tube: Covent Garden)*, whose collection of venerable old horse-drawn buses and trams, trolley buses, ancient underground steam locomotives, and vintage tube trains is housed in the old Victorian flower-market shed.

Just along Russell Street is the **Theatre Museum** ⑤ *(7 Russell St., tel 020-7943 4700, closed Mon., tube: Covent Garden)*, full of costumes from famous productions (*Alice in Wonderland* to Shakespeare), the handprints of showbiz and theaterland celebrities (Geraldine McEwan to Sir Cliff Richard), displays on the development of British theater and its great actors (Sir Henry Irving to Sir Laurence Olivier), and an enjoyable makeup exhibition in which visitors are the guinea pigs.

## OLD MARKET PLACE

Centerpiece of the square is **Covent Garden Market** ⑥ *(tube: Covent Garden)*, a beautiful 1833 hall of iron and glass. Covent Garden was the Soho of the 17th and 18th centuries, an unsavory mass of brothels and gambling dens that grew up around the market. The Victorians cleaned it up, and it remained London's chief fruit-and-vegetable market until 1974, when business moved

| | |
|---|---|
| 🗺 | 48 D4 |
| ► | Piccadilly Circus tube station |
| ⟷ | 1½ miles |
| ⏱ | 4 hours |
| ► | Leicester Square tube station |

**NOT TO BE MISSED**

- Rock Circus
- Chinatown
- Neal's Yard
- Covent Garden Market

across the river and the transformation began. Today the old hall shelters very chic restaurants, cafés, craft stalls, and stores, with entertainment from street musicians and jugglers guaranteed.

On the west side of the square is **St. Paul's Church** ⑦ *(Bedford St., tel 020-7836 5221, tube: Covent Garden)*, well worth a visit for its ornate gilt ceiling, baroque pulpit, and dozens of memorials to well-known stage stars—they include Boris Karloff, Vivien Leigh, Charlie Chaplin, Noël Coward, and Gracie Fields. Left of the door is a glorious wreath carved in limewood by Grinling Gibbons—his own memorial.

Back on Long Acre, turn left for Leicester Square tube station (one stop from Piccadilly Circus via the Piccadilly line). ■

# Bloomsbury

Bloomsbury lies northeast of Soho, north of New Oxford Street. The heart of the area is the British Museum, and around it lie the handsome garden squares laid out during London's 17th- and 18th-century shift west from the medieval city. A plaque in Bloomsbury Square pays tribute to the Bloomsbury Group, which was influential on early 20th-century thinking in the arts.

Sites particularly associated with literary figures (see box) are 46 Gordon Square, home to the Stephen family who founded the Bloomsbury Group; Russell Square, where the poet T.S. Eliot (1888–1965) worked for many years as an editor for the publisher Faber & Faber at No. 24; and Brunswick Square, north of Guildford Street, where Virginia Stephen (1882–1941) lived in 1911 at No. 28 with Leonard Woolf, whom she later married. The novelist E.M. Forster lived at 26 Brunswick Square from 1929 to 1939. Fitzroy Square was where Virginia and Adrian Stephen lived (No. 29) from 1907 to 1911; here they started Friday evening readings with Cambridge friends. Irish-born dramatist George Bernard Shaw wrote *Arms and The Man* and *Candida* (both 1894) at No. 39, during a stay of 11 years.

Charles Dickens, too, is strongly associated with Bloomsbury. On the eastern borders at 48 Doughty Street, now the excellent **Dickens House Museum** *(tel 020-7405 2127, tube: Russell Sq.)*, he lived from 1837 to 1839 and wrote *Oliver Twist*, and *Nicholas Nickleby*; from 1851 to 1860 his home was Tavistock House in Tavistock Square, where he wrote *Bleak House, Hard Times, Little Dorrit*, and *A Tale of Two Cities*, and made a start on *Great Expectations*. ∎

**Hundreds of blue plaques identifying the houses where distinguished people once lived can be found all over London. You can see this one outside the Dickens House Museum.**

## Bloomsbury Group

The Bloomsbury area is forever associated with the eponymous Group, a coterie of avant-garde writers, designers, and artists who shared a bohemian lifestyle here and in the country before World War I and for a few years after. Centered around the Stephen brothers and sisters—Thoby, Adrian, Vanessa (later Bell), and Virginia (later Woolf, pictured)—and their home at 46 Gordon Square, the Bloomsbury Group included the pacifist socialist painter and critic Roger Fry, poet and novelist Vita Sackville-West, Virginia's publisher husband, Leonard Woolf, eminent writer on economics John Maynard Keynes, and biographer Lytton Strachey: a powerhouse of independent and willful intellect. ∎

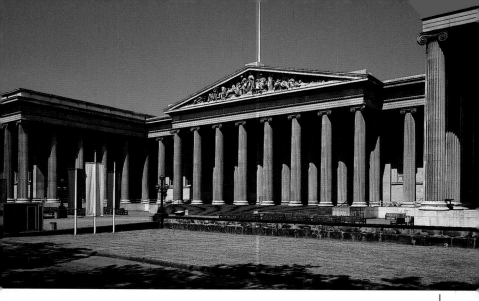

# British Museum

**British Museum**

📍 49 E4

✉ Great Russell St., WCI

☎ 020-7323 8299

💲 Donation. Charge for special exhibitions

🚇 Tube: Holborn, Tottenham Court Road, Russell Square

THE BRITISH MUSEUM IS ONE OF THE WORLD'S GREAT museums. It was founded in 1753, when the government paid £20,000 ($33,000) on the death of Sir Hans Sloane (1660–1753), the royal physician, to secure his private collection of 79,000 objets d'art for the nation. The museum has grown ever since; current holdings are seven million items, from every corner of the world. The British Library has recently moved from its home in the museum to a new building at St. Pancras, and the historic round Reading Room is now the Walter and Leonore Annenberg Centre and the Paul Hamlyn Library. The courtyard outside the Reading Room has been transformed into the Great Court, a two-acre square spanned by a spectacular glass roof.

**The British Museum was opened in 1759 in a 17th-century mansion, making it Britain's first public museum. It is now the largest, covering some 13½ acres.**

The museum is laid out on three floors—Rooms 1–34 on the main or ground floor, Rooms 35–73 and 90–94 on the upper floors, and Rooms 77–89 in the basement. Of course, it is impossible to see everything in the collection in one visit, so the best idea is to get a floor plan at the information desk and pick a few plum attractions.

### HIGHLIGHTS

**Room 8** contains the superb Elgin Marbles. This fifth-century B.C. relief frieze from the Parthenon temple in Athens was brought to London in 1801 by Lord Elgin, then British ambassador in Constantinople. In 1816 the British government paid him £35,000 ($58,000) for the marbles, and since then the Greek authorities have persistently asked to have them back—so far with no success. They are magical: an animated procession of horses and humans, among which agitated sacrificial heifers raise their muzzles to the sky. The Hellenistic theme continues in **Room 14** where artifacts include a fine gold oak-leaf wreath decorated with tiny gold cicadas and a bee (circa 350–300 B.C.).

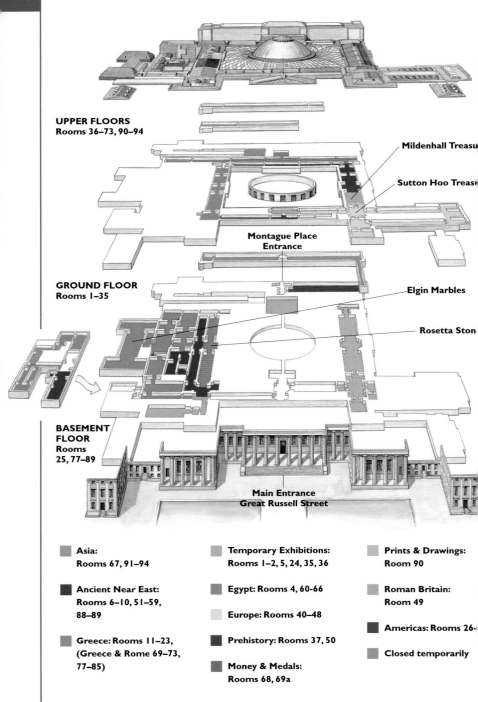

**UPPER FLOORS**
Rooms 36–73, 90–94

Mildenhall Treasu

Sutton Hoo Treas

Montague Place
Entrance

**GROUND FLOOR**
Rooms 1–35

Elgin Marbles

Rosetta Ston

**BASEMENT
FLOOR**
Rooms
25, 77–89

Main Entrance
Great Russell Street

Asia:
Rooms 67, 91–94

Ancient Near East:
Rooms 6–10, 51–59,
88–89

Greece: Rooms 11–23,
(Greece & Rome 69–73,
77–85)

Temporary Exhibitions:
Rooms 1–2, 5, 24, 35, 36

Egypt: Rooms 4, 60-66

Europe: Rooms 40–48

Prehistory: Rooms 37, 50

Money & Medals:
Rooms 68, 69a

Prints & Drawings:
Room 90

Roman Britain:
Room 49

Americas: Rooms 26-

Closed temporarily

**The Portland Vase was bought by the Duke of Portland and loaned to the museum in 1810. The museum purchased it in 1945.**

Enormous Assyrian friezes from the seventh century B.C. in **Rooms 17–21** include the "Attack on Lachish," showing massed bowmen, spearmen, and slingers, as well as two unfortunate prisoners being flayed alive. The "Royal Lion Hunt of King Ashurbanipal" is even more striking, with snarling lions being stuck with arrows and speared as they try to board the royal chariot.

**Room 25** has the celebrated Rosetta Stone, a big dark chunk of stone carved with three scripts—

**The Rosetta Stone is named after the town near the mouth of the Nile where it was found in 1799.**

hieroglyphic, demotic, and Greek—each recording the same decree of a council of priests in 196 B.C. The stone's discovery enabled scholars to decipher Egyptian hieroglyphics for the first time.

**Room 33** is laden with Oriental art including Tibetan inlaid jewelry, 16th-century Vietnamese altar vases, eighth-century Indian carvings of gods and demons, Chinese jades and Tang tomb figures of horses and warriors, and fragile Ming bowls.

**The detail on this ceremonial helmet from Sutton Hoo includes a gilt-bronze moustache and eyebrows of inlaid garnet.**

The Mexican Gallery in **Room 33c** contains wonderfully colored, stylized, and vigorous Aztec and Maya mosaics and sculptures.

**Rooms 37** and **68** hold the pre-Roman gold treasures of coins, armlets, and jewelry unearthed around the British Isles. In **Room 41** is the stunning Sutton Hoo Treasure, excavated in 1939 from a Saxon chief's ship burial in Suffolk—a chased iron sword blade, gold and garnet scabbard bosses, a whole-face helmet, worked gold-bronze shield fittings, a lyre, a huge bronze cauldron, a scepter crowned with a bronze stag, a gold and cloisonné purse.

## BRITISH LIBRARY

(*96 Euston Rd., St. Pancras, tel 020-7412 7332; tube: King's Cross, St. Pancras, Euston*)

The highlights of the Library's collection at St. Pancras are the Lindisfarne Gospels. These late seventh-century gospels were exquisitely colored and illustrated with birds and foliage by monkish contemporaries of St. Cuthbert on the island of Lindisfarne (see p. 283). Other precious exhibits include two of the four remaining copies of Magna Carta, the charter of liberty and political rights signed by King John at Runnymede in 1215 (see p. 99). ■

**Room 7 features a reconstruction of the Nereid Monument—a fourth-century B.C. tomb found at Xanthos in western Turkey.**

Head for **Room 42** to see the Lewis Chessmen: 12th-century carved walrus-ivory chess pieces—broad-faced, bulgy-eyed warriors, bishops, kings, and queens—from the Isle of Lewis (see p. 331). Next move on to **Room 49** to see the fourth-century Mildenhall Treasure, dug up in wartime Suffolk—beautiful, gleaming, masterfully worked Roman silver bowls and platters, and a great dish with relief scenes of the worship of Bacchus.

**Room 61** is filled with ancient Egyptian mummies with elaborately painted cases, including cat, snake, ibis, crocodile, and falcon—as well as human. Adjacent rooms contain examples of Egyptian jewelry and Coptic art.

**Room 70** holds the Portland Vase. Dating from the first century, this is a superb Roman work of art in cobalt blue, with a white glass relief depicting, it is thought, the marriage of Peleus and Thetis, and their offspring, Achilles. The vase was painstakingly rebuilt after being shattered into over 200 pieces by a drunken visitor. ■

# Knightsbridge & Kensington

Knightsbridge and Kensington, the heavenly twins lying south of Hyde Park, are two of the smartest shopping centers of London, where limousines pause on the Brompton Road or Sloane Street to decant expensive persons into elegant stores such as Harrods and Harvey Nichols, or into any one of several hundred top-flight boutiques. This glossy image grew from the 1820s when the Buxton-born builder Thomas Cubitt (1788–1855) built the beautiful houses of Belgravia, and picked up more cachet after the 1851 Great Exhibition in Hyde Park, when South Kensington, to the west of Knightsbridge, suddenly became immensely fashionable.

Other areas of London may come in and out of fashion, but the district of Knightsbridge takes the cake when it comes to top shopping. From Knightsbridge tube station, Sloane Street stretches south, lined with classic designer stores including Cartier, Armani, Chanel, Katharine Hamnett, and Christian Lacroix. Near the junction of Sloane Street and the Brompton Road, the Scotch House is tartan heaven for anyone with a dash of Celtic blood. Beauchamp Place (pronounced BEECH-am), off the Brompton Road, is another road full of fashionable and stylish little shops.

## HARRODS

All stores pale into insignificance beside the mighty Harrods *(87–135 Brompton Rd., SW1, tel 020-7730 1234, closed Sun., tube: Knightsbridge)*, indisputably the reigning world monarch of style, elegance, opulence, and mercantile savoir faire. Charles Henry Harrod opened his small family-run grocery store here in 1849, and the place has never looked back.

In the basement are the splendid marble halls of Harrods' own bank—Harrods Bank Ltd. On the ground floor, if you wish, you can scour the Room of Luxury for a $5,000 Christian Dior crocodile handbag, a $17,000 set of Louis Vuitton luggage, or a perpetual motion wristwatch, as designed for the Pasha of Marrakesh, retailing at just $22,000. Most people don't. They drift through to the irresistible Food Halls with their lavish, highly colored, sculptured ceilings and displays: Arts and Crafts tiles on walls and pillars; pigs and peacocks in flight above the *charcuterie* counter; a cupola full of hunters and shepherds; the lovely little mermaids above the iced fish display; and the aquarium at the oysters-and-champagne bar.

The rest rooms are stylish beyond belief: the Gents with their marble automated basins and hushed attendants, the Ladies in Georgian splendor with original tiles, woodwork, and marble, all with free scents and creams.

You could spend all day riding the Egyptian escalator with its sphinxes and acanthus capitals—up to the furniture department on the third floor to snap up a marble-topped cabinet at $42,000, or down to the basement barber shop with its padded red leather chairs and gleaming black-and-white walls.

## HARVEY NICHOLS

At the top of Sloane Street, where it meets Knightsbridge, is the famous department store of Harvey Nichols *(tel 020-7235 5000, tube: Knightsbridge)*, London's best known retailer of high fashion clothes. On the ground floor is every kind of celebrated perfume and accessory seller, from established favorites such as Yves Saint Laurent, Chanel, Versace, and Lancôme, through Jean-Paul Gaultier to up-and-coming companies like Trish McEvoy who are putting down roots. The first floor is given over to international women's fashion from Vivienne Westwood, Cerruti, Dolce & Gabbana, with bright knitwear from Rebecca Moses and Jasper Conran, to Jean Muir's plain lines, and little black dresses from Donna Karan.

Favorites in the designer collections on the second floor are Nicole Farhi and Tse, plain classic jumpers from John Smedley, and shoes from Joan & David. More shoes appear on the third floor—the hugely popular children's footwear range in primary colors at Buckle-My-Shoe. Up on the fifth floor you can relax in the bright, clean restaurant where the chefs prepare everything out in the open. Alongside is Harvey Nichols's very upscale Food Hall. ■

# Victoria & Albert Museum

**Victoria
& Albert Museum**

🏛 48 B3

✉ Cromwell Rd., South
   Kensington, SW7

☎ 020-7942 2000

💲 $$ (free 4:30–
   5:45 p.m.)

🚇 Tube: South
   Kensington

"WELCOME TO THE WORLD'S GREATEST MUSEUM OF decorative arts," says the map leaflet of the Victoria & Albert Museum, and that just about sums up the British institution known universally as the V&A. Somewhere along the 7 miles of galleries in this labyrinthine holdall of a museum, a representative sample probably exists of every form of fine and applied art known to man. It was Prince Albert's vision for the 1851 Great Exhibition— that of inspiring the ordinary British working man and woman with access to examples of excellence from all over the world—that generated the foundation of the V&A, one of the richest and most eclectic collections in the world.

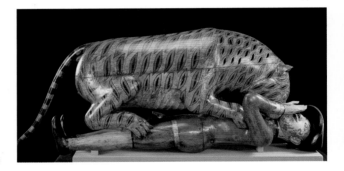

**Typical of the varied, empire-minded, often tongue-in-cheek collection in the V&A is "Tippoo's Tiger," carved in about 1790 for Tipu Sultan, the Tiger of Mysore —he was killed in 1799 fighting the British at the Battle of Seringapatam.**

There is a kind of logic to the layout, which divides the collection into Art and Design, and Materials and Techniques. The former is mostly on levels A, Lower A, B, and C; the latter on C and D. There is also the Henry Cole Wing, with six floors of paintings, drawings, photographs, and prints; and the small Frank Lloyd Wright Gallery.

As part of a major transformation project, the V&A aims to represent its entire British Galleries by 2002. As a result, these galleries are currently closed, though some of the objects are displayed in other galleries around the museum.

### LEVEL A

On the walls of a huge barrel-roofed gallery in **Room 48a** hang the enormous Raphael cartoons, templates for tapestries. These great colored pictures more than 20 feet long of scenes from the New Testament were commissioned by Pope Leo X for the Sistine Chapel in 1515. Especially striking is the "Miraculous Draught of Fishes," in which a flock of hungry cranes watches muscular men straining at a bulging net, while a wild-haired Peter kneels before Christ in the bows of a small boat brimming with fish. In the same room is a Spanish retable of 1410, carved with scenes of torture from the martyrdom of St. George.

**Room 41** contains the Nehru Gallery of Indian Art, with dazzling jewelry, amazingly detailed 16th-century gouache paintings of battle, the gold throne of Maharaja Ranjit Singh, and the celebrated "Tippoo's Tiger," a three-quarter life-size wooden tiger (with a pipe organ in its side) devouring a scarlet-jacketed official of the East India Company, while **Room 42** has beautiful Islamic tiles on themes of water and vegetation.

In **Room 43** is the Medieval Treasury, including the copper and enamel Becket Casket of circa 1180, which probably contained relics of the saint. Also here is the extraordinary English Romanesque 12th-century "Gloucester Candlestick," writhing with entangled men, monkeys, evangelists, and dragons; and the late 12th-century Eltenberg Reliquary, shaped like a cruciform domed temple in enameled copper, ivory, and bronze gilt.

The Japanese Gallery in **Room 45** displays exquisite miniature workmanship in ornamentation of dishes and cabinets, Samurai swords 700 years old, and tiny netsuke figures—a lion; Futen, the god of Wind; Hotei, the squat, obese god of Prosperity.

**Rooms 46A** and **B** contain the Cast Courts, filled with plaster casts of medieval sculpture— Michelangelo's heroic "David" from Florence and his sensual "Dying Slave and his Rebellious Comrade," the shaft of Trajan's Column from Rome, and the entire Pórtico de la Gloria of 1188 from the Cathedral of Santiago de Compostela.

The Gamble, Morris, and Poynter Rooms, near the back of the building, were originally the museum tearooms and are decorated in Arts and Crafts style. They retain their Minton tilework, Pre-Raphaelite panels, and stained glass.

### LEVEL LOWER B
**Rooms 52–58** form an L-shaped series of rooms with displays on Britain from 1500 to 1750—a Georgian music room; late 17th-century English silverware; a Grinling Gibbons limewood carving of the "Stoning of St. Stephen";

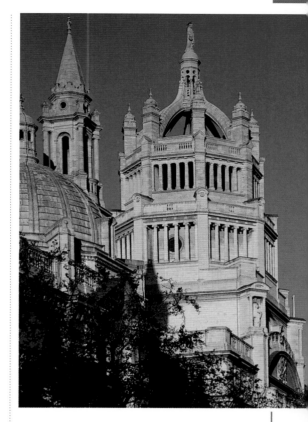

superb inlaid furniture; and the grotesque ten-foot Great Bed of Ware, made in 1590 by Jonas Fosbrook (who is said to haunt it).

### HENRY COLE WING
The Frank Lloyd Wright Gallery on **Floor 2** celebrates the work of the great American architect (1867–1959), and contains a 1937 office stylishly designed in wood.

On **Floor 6** paintings include J.M.W. Turner's "East Cowes Castle" (1828) and a pale, ghostly "St. Michael's Mount" (1836). Landscapes by John Constable include a rather slapdash study for "Dedham Lock and Mill" (1820), one of six painted "on spec." in hopes of a buyer. ■

**A splendid stone lantern and dome adorns the ornate facade that the Victoria & Albert Museum displays to Cromwell Road. Prince Albert's idea was to give the British working man a museum he could be proud of.**

# Science Museum

**Science Museum**

🅰 48 B3

✉ Exhibition Rd., South Kensington, SW7

☎ 0870-870 4868

💲 $$$ (free 4:30– 6 p.m.)

🚇 Tube: South Kensington

THERE ARE MORE THAN ONE THOUSAND INTERACTIVE displays among the hundreds of thousands in the National Museum of Science and Industry, better known as the Science Museum, making a visit here one that can be enjoyed by all. Exhibits and displays range over the long timescale of man's scientific inquiries, from pre-Christian medical technology to up-to-the-minute computing, nuclear physics, and microbiology. Forty topic areas are spread through seven floors. Some of the most intriguing are described here.

### EAST HALL, GROUND FLOOR

The **Power** exhibition fascinates with the sheer weight and strength of early devices, from Newcomen's beam pumping-engine of 1791 to the gigantic mill engines built by Burnley Ironworks in 1903 and used until the 1970s.

*Young and old are fascinated by the technology on display in the Science Museum, from space exploration (launch pad light pipes, below) to bizarre early flight experiments.*

From here you move into the **Exploration of Space Gallery,** with pride of place given to the Apollo 10 command module "Charlie Brown," which took three astronauts on a dress rehearsal (May 18–26, 1969) for the Apollo 11 pioneer moon landing on July 20.

### LEVEL 3

There are some weird and wonderful early experiments in the **Flight Gallery**—the 1905 Weiss Glider based on the form of an albatross, or the Frost Ornithopter with its feathered wings flapped by a motorcycle engine. Hung from the roof of the gallery are various historic airplanes—Spitfire and Hurricane fighters from World War II, the Vickers Vimy, which first flew the Atlantic in 1919, and Britain's first jet aircraft—the Gloster Whittle E28/39.

### LEVEL 4

**Health Matters** is a portrait of 20th-century medicine in three sections. The **Rise of Medicine** shows the development of medical care through drugs and machines. Expect some surprises: an explanation, for example, of the connection between the Mexican yam and contraceptives.

The **Rise of Health** allows you to explore the way that modern medical statistics have revolutionized our approach to health. **Science in Medicine** looks at how we now turn to science to solve medical problems, and the importance of DNA.

The gallery ends with an audiovisual show focusing on AIDS, cancer, and heart disease, while an "update" area hosts temporary exhibitions. ∎

# Natural History Museum

NO LONGER DOES THE NATURAL HISTORY MUSEUM consist solely of rank upon rank of glass cases (though there are still plenty of these). Exhibitions have been brought up to date and feature a mix of hands-on areas and interactive technology.

### EARTH GALLERIES

From Exhibition Road, across from the Victoria & Albert Museum's "side exit," you pass under an inscription that reads "Geological Survey & Museum" (witness to the building's former use) and enter the **Earth Galleries.** Big statues on crystal bases flank your approach to an escalator rising through a hollowed-out model of the Earth up to the **Power Within** exhibition, full of the rumble and roar of volcanic eruptions and earthquakes.

### LIFE GALLERIES

A different atmosphere prevails in the beautiful Waterhouse building, which houses a successful mixture of traditional look-and-marvel cased exhibits and ultramodern displays. **Gallery 33** has creepy-crawlies (eyelash mites, the intimate body parts of a locust, a spidery "hunt-the-fly" game). **Gallery 32** has a stirring "video wall" demon-

strating the water cycle. From here walkways lead you around a beautifully conceived **Ecology** section through a range of displays explaining how different life systems interconnect. These walkways also give an opportunity to admire the beautiful details that went into the museum's 1873–1881 construction—carved stone animals and foliage under the cast-iron roof girders.

**Gallery 21** contains the ever popular dinosaurs, viewed either from walkways or down at claw level. This is the children's favorite spot, especially the animated tableau of three *Deinonychus* feasting on a *Tenontosaurus* with suitable grunts and squeals. **Galleries 23** and **24** exhibit mammals—brilliantly displayed land mammals from the collared peccary to the Arabian oryx, sea mammals on the balcony, and hanging above them all the gigantic shape of a blue whale. ∎

**Natural History Museum**

🅰 48 B2

✉ Cromwell Rd., South Kensington, SW7

☎ 020-7942 5011

💲 $$$ (free Mon.–Fri. 4:30–5:50 p.m., Sat. & Sun. 5–5:50 p.m.)

🚇 Tube: South Kensington

**Within its ornate Victorian structure of wrought iron and carved stone, the Natural History Museum contains state-of-the-art displays. But it is the old faithfuls, the dinosaurs, that draw the biggest crowds.**

# London's parks

London has a large number of open spaces where everyone is welcome to wander at will. Some of this rich legacy of public parkland harks back to the 17th century, when the Stuart monarchs began to open up portions of hitherto private royal hunting forests for the enjoyment of the populace. Other gardens and parks are remnants of fields or common-land enclosed when buildings were put up, or leftovers from attempts to safeguard springs and wells, or the results of philanthropic endowment in Georgian and Victorian times. Whatever their provenance, nowadays they are very carefully preserved from encroachment or development.

Largest of the central parks north of the Thames are the neighboring **Hyde Park** (*Map 48 C3, tube: Hyde Park Corner; see p. 81*) and **Kensington Gardens** (*Map 48 B3, tube: Lancaster Gate; see p. 81*), with fashionable Knightsbridge to the south. To the west, off

**Picnickers, below, laze by the Serpentine in Hyde Park while at Speaker's Corner, right, others exercise their right to free speech.**

Kensington High Street, rises hilly, wooded **Holland Park** (*Tube: Holland Park*), opened in 1952 on the grounds of Holland House, which had been destroyed during World War II bombing. The park contains an open-air theater and a café, and is surrounded by fine late Victorian houses.

In ultra-exclusive Mayfair, on the eastern border of Hyde Park, 200-year-old plane trees and sculptures stand at the heart of **Berkeley Square** (*Tube: Green Park*):

> …*there was magic abroad in the air;*
> *There were angels dining at the Ritz,*
> *And a nightingale sang in Berkeley Square.*
> —Eric Maschwitz, *A Nightingale Sang in Berkeley Square* (1940)

**A view of Horse Guards Parade from St. James's Park on a spring day**

Only the big traffic circle at Hyde Park Corner separates Hyde Park from **Green Park** (*Map 48 D3, tube: Green Park*), a relatively uncrowded green space in spite of its proximity to Buckingham Palace. This was a noted dueling ground in Georgian times.

Just across the Mall is **St. James's Park** (*Map 48 D3, tube: St. James's Park*), the oldest park in London; it was one of Henry VIII's deer parks. After the Restoration, Charles II opened it to the public. It was landscaped by John Nash (1752–1835) in about 1828, a period when he was redesigning Buckingham Palace (see p. 59) and going through too much of George IV's money. From the beautiful bridge that nips in the waist of the park's lake, there is a good open view east to the Queen Victoria memorial on the traffic circle just in front of Buckingham Palace.

North of Hyde Park is the roughly circular **Regent's Park** (*Map 48 C5, tube: Regent's Park*), also designed by Nash early in the 19th century to provide the Prince Regent with a place of recreation that could be reached from his residence in St. James's via a scenic drive. The terraced houses around the park are some of the finest in London. You can boat on the long lake here, and in summer there are performances in the open-air theater.

On the north side of the park is **London Zoo** (*tel 020-7722 3333, tube: Camden Town*), not so long ago a sad, run-down collection with falling visitor numbers. Recent improvements have seen the zoo, in line with contemporary understanding, adopt more enlightened, conservation-minded policies.

Just north across Prince Albert Road is **Primrose Hill** (*Map 48 C6, tube: St. John's Wood*), with splendid views over the city.

### Less famous parks

A little east and south of Regent's Park, on the eastern borders of Bloomsbury, **Coram's Fields** (*Brunswick Sq., tube: Russell Sq.*) in the St. Pancras district incorporates a pets' corner in a calm playground shaded by plane trees. Only child-accompanied adults are admitted to these delightful gardens, which were once fields around a Foundling Hospital endowed in 1745 by choleric but soft-hearted sailor, Capt. Thomas Coram.

Down in trendy Chelsea, just east of Albert Bridge, **Chelsea Physic Garden** (*66 Royal Hospital Rd., SW3, tel 020-7376 3910, call for hours, tube: Sloane Square*) on Swan Walk is an area of ancient plants and trees founded in 1673 by the Society of Apothecaries. ■

# Knightsbridge & Kensington walk

This walk includes three great museums, Harrods store with all its seductive displays, Hyde Park and Kensington Gardens, and the royal residence of Kensington Palace. A good plan would be to allow a full day for the walk, and to select just one of the three museums, leaving the other two for another day.

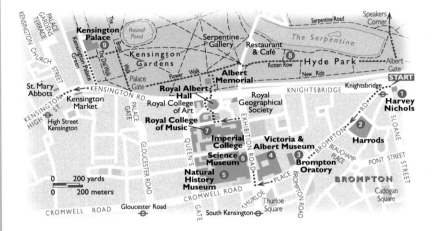

As you emerge from Knightsbridge tube station onto the Brompton Road, **Harvey Nichols** store ❶ (see p. 73) is to your right. Turn left along the Brompton Road and in 300 yards on the left is the fairy-lit emporium of **Harrods** ❷ (see p. 73).

Leave the store by the main exit; turn left along the Brompton Road, window-shopping all the way, to the **Brompton Oratory** ❸ (*tel 020-7808 0900, tube: South Kensington*) on the right, its gray dome rising above a massive pillared portico. Inside, angels recline in elaborate drapery above the arches, while 12 beautiful 17th-century marble statues of the apostles stand in the gloom, far from their original home in Siena Cathedral. The Oratory was opened in 1884, the dome and facade added in the 1890s. It was built in response to a great revival of English Catholicism during the Victorian era, which had been sparked during the 1840s by John Henry Newman, the influential Oxford academic, vicar, and theologian.

Bear right along Thurloe Place to reach the grandiose entrance to the **Victoria & Albert Museum** ❹ (see pp. 74–75) on Cromwell Road. If you ever extract yourself from its

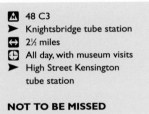

🅼 48 C3

▶ Knightsbridge tube station

⟳ 2½ miles

⊕ All day, with museum visits

▶ High Street Kensington tube station

**NOT TO BE MISSED**

- Harrods
- Victoria & Albert Museum
- Science Museum

tangled mysteries, leave by the Exhibition Road exit to find, opposite, the entrance to the Earth Galleries section of the **Natural History Museum** ❺ (see p. 77). On the left, 200 yards north on Exhibition Road, is the **Science Museum** ❻ (see p. 76).

After sampling one or more of these great museums, continue on Exhibition Road; turn left along Prince Consort Road, passing Imperial College (engraved "Royal School of Mines") and the **Royal College of Music** ❼. The college's **Museum of**

**Instruments** (*Prince Consort Rd., SW7, tel 020-7589 3643, ext. 4346, closed April–May, July–mid-Sept. & Dec.–Feb., closed Thurs.–Tues. rest of year, tube: South Kensington*) is full of strange creations: a beautifully inlaid Parisian hurdy-gurdy, an ophicleide (primitive 1842 saxophone), and fiddles, lutes, lyres, and guitars.

Cross Prince Consort Road and climb the steps past the **Great Exhibition Memorial.** This celebrates Prince Albert's instigation of the "Great Exhibition of the Work and Industry of All Nations," held in 1851 in Hyde Park in the huge glass-and-iron hall called the Crystal Palace (see p. 34). Pass the elliptical **Royal Albert Hall** of 1871 with its frieze of scenes from British history and everyday life, and cross Kensington Gore to reach the **Albert Memorial,** erected in 1861.

Walk beyond the Albert Memorial to turn left along Flower Walk, beautiful at any time of year with its flower beds. **Hyde Park** ❽ (see p. 78) was part of the land belonging to

Westminster Abbey that Henry VIII appropriated during the Reformation. James I opened it to the public, and it soon became a notorious haunt of prostitutes working the thoroughfare called Rotten Row. The Serpentine Lake, that separates Hyde Park from Kensington Gardens to the west, was dug in Georgian times—now a favorite boating spot.

A detour to the northeast corner of the park brings you to **Speaker's Corner,** famous for the soapbox orators who exercise their right to spout whatever opinions they like.

Continue the walk from Hyde Park into **Kensington Gardens,** home of the famous statue of Peter Pan, and near the western end of the parkland bear right along the Broad Walk past the Round Pond to reach **Kensington Palace** ❾ (see p. 82).

From the palace, walk along Palace Avenue to leave Hyde Park on High Street Kensington, then turn right to reach High Street Kensington tube station. ■

**The cathedral-like Natural History Museum is modeled on French Romanesque architecture.**

# Kensington Palace

KENSINGTON PALACE IS WELL KNOWN ALL ROUND THE world as the London home of Charles and Diana, Prince and Princess of Wales, before their marriage broke up in 1991, and as Diana's home thereafter. The palace has become something of a shrine since the princess's death in 1997, with tributes of flowers often to be seen at the gates. Converted from a grand house into a palace between 1689 and 1696 by Sir Christopher Wren, the building has seen three centuries of royal history.

**Kensington Palace**

◩ 48 B3
✉ Kensington Gardens
☎ 020-7937 9561
💲 $$$
Ⓜ Tube: High St. Kensington, Queensway

**The gilded gates of Kensington Palace hint at the sumptuous interior that lies beyond the modest facade.**

Until 1760 and George III's move to Buckingham Palace (see p. 59), this was the principal London residence of the sovereign. William III and Mary II ordered its conversion, and Wren gave the couple separate suites—and separate entrances.

Very grand State Apartments were added inside the building during the 18th century, with beautiful murals and painted ceilings by William Kent, a prime collection of royal portraiture, and a range of exquisite classic furniture. These form part of the visitors' tour that has become one of London's chief tourist draws; the other part consists of a collection of court dresses, costumes, and

uniforms dating from the 1760s to the present day.

On June 20, 1837, the 18-year-old Princess Victoria was woken at the palace very early in the morning to be told that her uncle, William IV, had died, and that she was now sovereign. Outside Kensington Palace, facing the Round Pond, is a touching statue of her as a round-faced and innocent girl-queen.

You can stroll in part of the palace garden, then take tea in the nearby Orangery, which was designed by Wren's pupil Nicholas Hawksmoor and embellished by the Rotterdam-born mastercarver Grinling Gibbons. ■

Fireworks illuminate the fanciful Tower Bridge, opened in 1894 with great ceremony.

# Following the Thames

Although not Britain's longest river, the Thames is the best known, because of its association with London. It provides a really wonderful unrolling panorama of the capital when traveled either by boat or on foot. Walking the Thames has become possible since the 1996 opening of the Thames Path National Trail, while river cruises stopping off near the main attractions have always been a pleasure for Londoners and visitors alike.

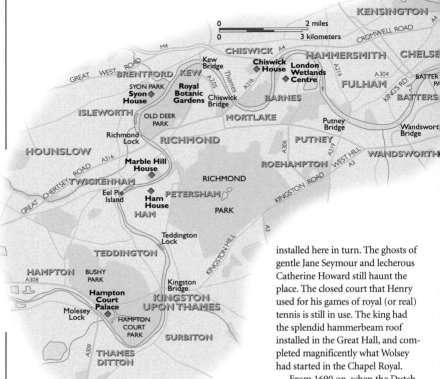

### BOAT TRIPS

Boat trips run west from Westminster Pier to Kew, Richmond, and Hampton Court *(tel 020-7930 2062)*; and east to the Tower of London *(tel 020-7237 5134)*, and Greenwich and the Thames Barrier *(tel 020-7930-4097)*. Several companies operate cruises through central London from Westminster and Charing Cross Piers. ■

### DOWNSTREAM FROM HAMPTON COURT

Going toward central London from Sunbury Lock the river takes a great southward and then northward loop, with **Hampton Court Palace** *(tel 0870-752-7777)*, the finest and grandest Tudor building in Britain, on the left. This extraordinary riverside palace was Cardinal Wolsey's before he gave it to Henry VIII in 1528 in vain hope of buying off his death sentence.

Henry smothered the palace with the carved entwined initials of himself and his second wife, Anne Boleyn; after she had gone to the block, each of the following four was installed here in turn. The ghosts of gentle Jane Seymour and lecherous Catherine Howard still haunt the place. The closed court that Henry used for his games of royal (or real) tennis is still in use. The king had the splendid hammerbeam roof installed in the Great Hall, and completed magnificently what Wolsey had started in the Chapel Royal.

From 1690 on, when the Dutch King William III and Queen Mary II felt themselves secure on the throne of England, they began to improve and extend Hampton Court. The work, overseen by Sir Christopher Wren and continued by Queen Anne, constituted a masterful blending of the baroque with the existing Tudor building. The King's and Queen's Apartments and other State Rooms date from this time, as do the beautifully laid out gardens that include water features and the baffling Maze.

Further on, past the built-up sprawl of Kingston-upon-Thames to the right, the Thames snakes east past Eel Pie Island (a Victorian day-trippers' paradise, and noted 1960s rock 'n' roll venue) to pass the green fields around **Ham House**

St. Paul's Cathedral · Globe Theatre · Tower of London · STEPNEY COMMERCIAL ROAD · POPLAR · A13 · NEW HAM WAY · CANNING TOWN · Somerset House · TateModern · Southwark Cathedral · WAPPING · West India Docks · Blackwall Tunnel · Royal Victoria Dock · London City Airport · MAYFAIR · London Eye · Tower Bridge · Thames · Woolwich Ferry · WESTMINSTER · Clink Exhibition · BERMONDSEY · ISLE OF DOGS · Millennium Dome and Park · Thames Flood Barrier · Big Ben · London Aquarium · Design Museum · Houses of Parliament · OLD KENT ROAD · A200 · MILLWALL · National Maritime Museum · CHARLTON · Tate Britain · Vauxhall Bridge · WALWORTH · Gipsy Moth IV · 2. Cutty Sark · 3. Royal Naval College · GREENWICH · Chelsea Bridge · DEPTFORD · A2 · Old Royal Observatory · Battersea Power Station · A202 · A20 · GREENWICH PARK · A2 · SHOOTERS HILL RD. · LAMBETH · A302

(NT, Han St., tel 020-8940 1950, closed—House: Nov.–March & Thurs.–Fri. April–Oct. Garden: Thurs.–Fri., tube: Richmond, then bus 371). The house, built in 1610, has been beautifully restored. Lord Lauderdale was given the lease of the Ham Estate, and created 1st Earl of Dysart, as compensation for his rather painful childhood role as a "whipping boy," whose duty it was to receive any punishment beatings earned by the young prince who later became Charles I.

## PARKS & GARDENS
Soon the Thames passes the edge of **Richmond Park** on the right,

with Richmond Hill prominent— views down from the hilltop across the river are even better. Richmond Park was a royal hunting ground in the time of Charles I, and fallow deer still graze under its ancient oaks. On the left the river passes **Marble Hill House** (*Richmond Rd., Twickenham, tel 020-8892 5115, closed Mon.–Fri. Nov.–March, tube: Richmond, then bus*), a Palladian villa built 1724–29 by Henrietta Howard, Countess of Suffolk, with £12,000 ($20,000) she received as a present from her young lover, the future George II.

Now the **Royal Botanic Gardens at Kew** (*Kew Rd.,*

**Since Henry VIII first took over and enlarged Hampton Court Palace, successive monarchs have repaired and altered both the palace and its 60 acres of gardens, creating a vivid mix of styles.**

Richmond, tel 020-8332 5655 for recorded information, tube: Kew Gardens) open on the right. These are the yardstick by which all other botanical collections measure themselves. They were started in 1759 on nine acres of ground; the orangery and the pagoda date from that era, when the great botanist and polymath, Joseph Banks, was appointed director and oversaw an enormous influx of exotic species collected from all over the world.

Today the gardens' staff continue their pioneering botanical research, while visitors stroll the site (expanded to fill 300 acres) and enjoy the two great Victorian conservatories (the Palm House with its rain forest species, and the Temperate House), to which the Princess of Wales conservatory has been added with its display of plant adaptation across a spectrum of the climatic zones. Next on the left is **Syon House** (Syon Park, Isleworth, tel 020-8560 0882/3, house closed Nov.–mid-March & Mon.–Tues. & Fri. mid-March–Oct., tube: Gunnersbury, then bus 237 or 267), residence of the Dukes of Northumberland since it was built on a nunnery site in Tudor times. Robert Adam remodeled the interior along Palladian lines in the 1760s. On the grounds, which were landscaped by Capability Brown (1715–1783), are a butterfly house and a collection of historic cars.

**Chiswick House** (Burlington Lane, W4, tel 020-8995 0508, House closed Mon-Tues., & Nov.–March,

**Looking from the balcony down the elegant spiral staircase of the Temperate House, one of two great Victorian conservatories at the Royal Botanic Gardens at Kew**

tube: Turnham Green, then bus E3; Hammersmith, then bus 190), also on the left, with its great colonnaded portico, was built in the 1720s by the 3rd Earl of Burlington as a country retreat in which to show off his art collection.

## HEADING INTO TOWN
From here downstream the houses begin to draw in closer to the leafy banks of the Thames. The river passes the pretty cottages of Chiswick, then the bird-haunted ponds of the **London Wetlands Centre** at Barnes (Queen Elizabeth Walk, tel 020-8409 4400, tube: Hammersmith, BritRail station: Barnes), and then the wharves, works, and reservoirs toward Putney Bridge—a stretch of the river rowed in the annual Boat Race between the crews of Oxford and Cambridge Universities.

The Thames slides past first Wandsworth, then the big pleasure-gardens complex of Battersea Park and the enormous chimneys of the landmark Battersea Power Station, to turn north for its passage through the heart of London. Here are the classic sites and views.

On the north bank **Tate Britain** (see p. 65) slips by, followed by the **Houses of Parliament** and **Big Ben,** the 3,500-year-old obelisk from Heliopolis known as **Cleopatra's Needle,** and the long eastward run of the Victoria Embankment below **Somerset House** (Strand, WC2, tube: Temple, Covent Garden, Holborn). This original headquarters of the Royal Academy of Arts now houses the Courtauld Gallery. The **Courtauld Gallery** (tel 020-7848 2526) contains a wide-ranging collection from Italian Renaissance masters to 20th-century British artists, with an especially notable group of French Impressionists that includes

**The Riverside at Richmond is a neo-Georgian development designed by the architect Quinlan Terry, a favorite of Prince Charles, in the late 1980s.**

### THAMES PATH

The London section of the Thames Path National Trail runs, clearly marked on both banks, between Hampton Court and the Thames Barrier—this London section is 38 miles along the north bank, 36 miles along the south; or shorter sections can be followed. For further details on walking all or some of the Thames Path, visit a tourist information center (see p. 341), where you can pick up a free brochure. ■

work by Renoir, Cézanne, van Gogh, Manet, and Degas.

Approaching Blackfriars Bridge, the dome of **St. Paul's Cathedral** (see pp. 52–53) is seen on this north side.

### DOWNSTREAM FROM WESTMINSTER

On the south bank beyond Westminster Bridge, the river passes the big florid County Hall now containing the **London Aquarium** (*Riverside Building, Westminster Bridge Rd., SE1, tel 020-7967 8000, tube: Waterloo, Westminster*), one of Europe's largest displays of aquatic life. Next comes the giant **London Eye** observation wheel (*County Hall, booking tel 0870-5000 600 or www.londoneye.com., tube: Waterloo, Westminster*), then the **South Bank Centre** (*tel 020-7960 4242*), an arts complex of gray concrete boxes comprising the Hayward Gallery, Royal Festival Hall, Purcell Room and Queen Elizabeth Hall; also here is the **Royal National Theatre** (*see p. 390*).

Then comes Southwark, not so long ago a red-light district. That is what it was in Shakespeare's time, when he part-owned the Globe Theatre in an area of brothels, drinking dens, and bear-baiting pits. The Globe has been superbly reconstructed, **Shakespeare's Globe Theatre** (*New Globe Walk, Bankside, SE1, tel 020-7902 1400, tube: London Bridge, Mansion House*) hosts Elizabethan plays in its outdoor arena (*May–Sept., tel 020-7401 9919*). An exhibition tells the story of its re-creation.

Other attractions here are the giant **Bankside Power Station,** reopened in 2000 as **Tate Modern** (see p. 65); the graceful bow of the **Millennium Footbridge;** the **Clink Prison Museum** (*1 Clink St., SE1, tel 020-7378 1558, tube: London Bridge*), an atmospheric crawl through the miseries of bygone prison life and sexual misdemeanor; and **Southwark Cathedral** (*Montague Close, SE1, tel 020-7367 6700, no tours during services, tube: London Bridge*), which features a memorial to Shakespeare and a very beautiful fan-vaulted retrochoir.

The great steel hoods of the Thames Barrier are raised against a stormy sky. Fears that sea-driven floods might devastate low-lying London caused the barrier to be built.

## TOWARD THE SEA

Standing on the Thames's north bank is the grim and mighty **Tower of London** (see pp. 89–92), near the twin towers of **Tower Bridge** *(SE1, tel 020-7403 3761, tube: Tower Hill)*. This great Gothic lifting bridge began opening to let tall sailing ships up- and downriver in 1894—an operation still carried out several times a week.

Now the Thames passes the **Design Museum** *(Shad Thames, tel 0870-833 9955, tube: Tower Hill),* bends around the fantastic post-modern architecture of Docklands on the **Isle of Dogs,** and passes **Greenwich** on the south, where you will see the tall masts of champion Victorian tea clipper *Cutty Sark (King William Walk, tel 020-8858 3445, DLR: Cutty Sark),* towering over the diminutive, world-navigating *Gipsy Moth IV (Greenwich Pier, King William Walk, DLR: Cutty Sark).*

Nearby, drawn up around their huge Grand Square, are the buildings of the **Royal Naval College** *(King William Walk, tel 020-8269 4747, DLR: Cutty Sark),* founded by William and Mary, designed by John Webb and completed by Sir Christopher Wren, Nicholas Hawksmoor, and Sir John Vanbrugh. Behind lies the **National Maritime Museum** *(Romney Rd., SE10, tel 020-8858 4422, DLR: Cutty Sark),* recounting the history of man's travels by water. The museum is centered on the beautiful Palladian **Queen's House** *(separate admission),* designed by Inigo Jones in 1616.

Above rises **Greenwich Park,** enclosing the **Royal Observatory Greenwich** *(Greenwich Park, SE10, tel 020-8312 6565, DLR: Cutty Sark),* founded in 1675 to fix the exact position of longitude worldwide. Here the prime meridian is marked in the courtyard. Daily at 1 p.m. the Greenwich Mean Time ball drops down its pole to mark the precise measurement of time.

Moving downstream the river passes the futuristic "space tent" shape of the **Millennium Dome,** and reaches the gleaming silver hoods of the **Thames Barrier** *(Unity Way, SE18, tel 020-8854 1373),* opened in 1984 to prevent sea surges from flooding London—its monthly test-raising is a big attraction. ■

# Tower of London

TO NEARLY 30 GENERATIONS OF BRITONS THE TOWER of London was a grim instrument and symbol of harsh judgment, imprisonment, torture, and execution—undoubtedly the chief reasons for its position today as one of the country's top attractions. Add the scarlet-trimmed Beefeaters, the legendary ravens, and all the glamour and glitter of the Crown Jewels, and you can understand its enormous popularity.

The first wooden fortification was built at this site on the north bank of the Thames by William the Conqueror—almost as soon as he was established on the throne of England—to command the vital and vulnerable sea approach to London. The Tower of London (in fact a great stronghold incorporating 19 towers built over the centuries) was named after its first and greatest tower, the 90-foot **White Tower,** built in 1097 of stone and subsequently whitewashed in 1241.

The many hundreds of years of building on and adding to the Tower produced a roughly hexagonal moated stronghold with an enormously thick and high outer wall incorporating six towers and enclosing a narrow Outer Ward (patrolable space). Looking out onto the Outer Ward is an inner wall reinforced at regular intervals with cylindrical drum towers.

Inside this inner wall is the Inner Ward, a broad enclosed area. Here, over the years, soldiers' quarters, houses, chapels, and other buildings have been incorporated, the ancient White Tower rising commandingly in the center to dominate all with its four onion-domed corner turrets.

**Tower of London**
- 49 G4
- Tower Hill, EC3
- 020-7709 0765
- $$$$
- Tube: Tower Hill

**The four pepper-pot turrets of the White Tower, dwarfing the ominous opening of Traitors' Gate, rise to form the centerpiece of the Tower of London.**

ENTRY TO THE TRAITORS GATE

Yeomen Warders of the Tower of London, nicknamed Beefeaters, will cheerfully pose for the camera in their Elizabethan ruffs and hats.

## UNTIMELY DEATHS

Over the course of 900 years, legend and history have woven themselves deep into the fabric of the Tower of London. In the south face of the Outer Wall is the foursquare **St. Thomas's Tower,** with the arched mouth of **Traitors' Gate** giving on to the Thames.

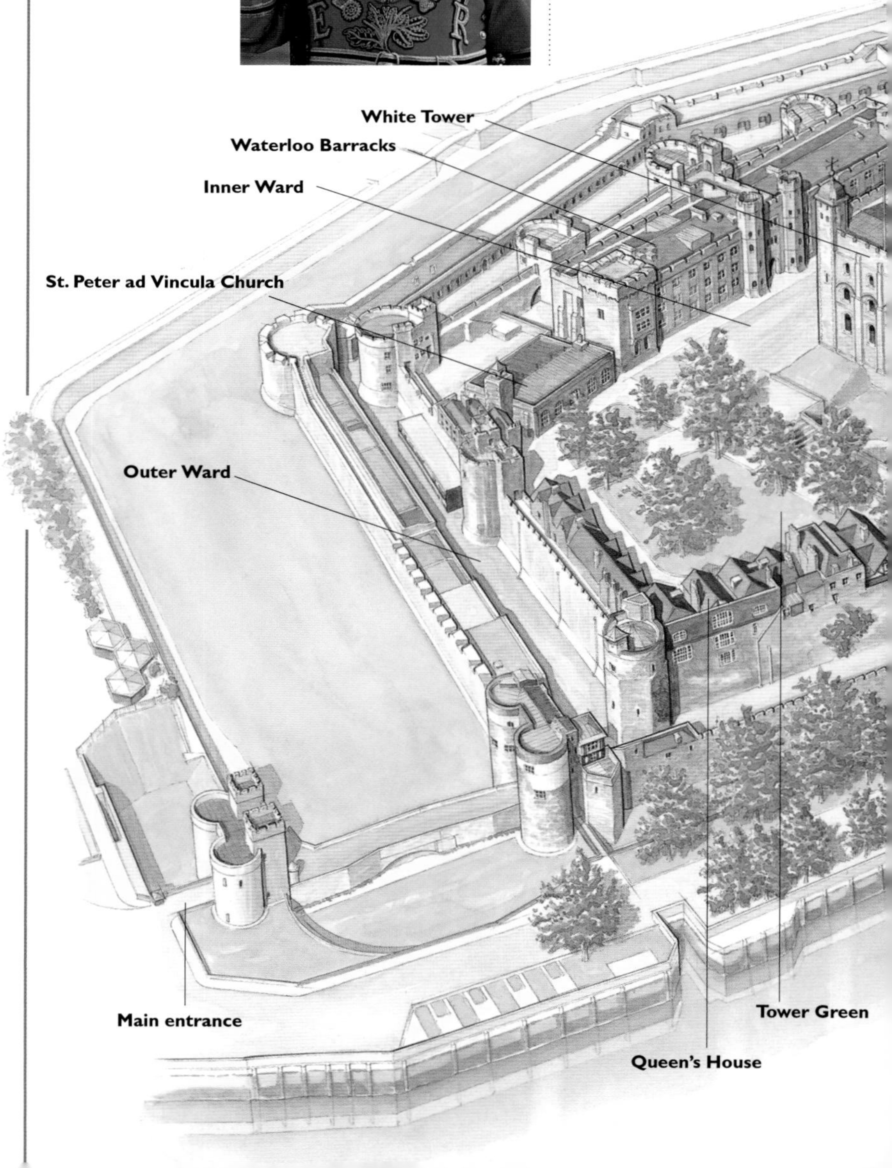

White Tower

Waterloo Barracks

Inner Ward

St. Peter ad Vincula Church

Outer Ward

Main entrance

Tower Green

Queen's House

Those enduring trial in Westminster Hall for high treason were brought by boat downriver in ceremonious ignominy to be taken into the Tower by this entrance.

Just behind Traitors' Gate in the inner wall, facing into the Inner Ward, is the **Bloody Tower.** Here the heir to the throne, Prince Edward, and his younger brother, Prince Richard, were brought in 1483 on the orders of their uncle, Richard, Duke of Gloucester, immediately after the death of their father, Edward IV. No one outside the Tower saw the boys again, and "Crookback Dick" was crowned Richard III before the year was out. In 1674 the skeletons of two boys were unearthed nearby, adding fuel to the general suspicion that the ambitious duke had had his nephews murdered. They were not the only royals to be done to death

Martin Tower

St. John's Chapel

Salt Tower

Moat

Wakefield Tower

St. Thomas's Tower

THAMES

Bloody Tower

Traitors' Gate

**Prisoners were led from the river to the Tower through this eerie medieval entrance, aptly named Traitors' Gate, still visible from the embankment.**

**In the upper chamber of the Bloody Tower is a re-creation of Sir Walter Raleigh's sleeping quarters. He was imprisoned at the Tower of London three times before being beheaded at Westminster in 1618.**

here; their father may well have ordered the killing of his mentally disturbed predecessor, Henry VI, who died in 1471 in **Wakefield Tower** next to the Bloody Tower.

Death, by execution or torture, is an integral part of the Tower of London's story. Traitors were executed in public on Tower Hill outside the fortress; but a "privileged" few were granted the privacy of decapitation on **Tower Green,** in front of the White Tower. These included two of the wives of Henry VIII: wild, six-fingered Anne Boleyn (No. 2), mother of Elizabeth I, beheaded by a French swordsman brought across to London for the job; and the injudicious, adulterous Catherine Howard (No. 5), executed with an ax like most other traitors.

### THE GUARDS

The Beefeaters—42 of them, properly called Yeoman Warders—look after the Tower and its two and a half million visitors a year and pose for photographs in their Tudor uniforms of red and black. At night they lock up ceremonially, an enjoyable ritual. The Ceremony of the Keys is performed nightly at 9:35 p.m. (*to attend write well in advance to The Constable's Office, Tower of London, EC3*). Other residents at the Tower are the ravens, whose continued presence guarantees the survival of the nation—so legend says.

You must line up to pass through the display hall in the **Waterloo Barracks** where the Crown Jewels are kept, but it is worth the wait. These splendidly glittering and gleaming baubles include rings, orbs, swords, and scepters; Elizabeth II's own crown with the famous Koh-I-Noor diamond; and the Imperial State Crown made in 1837 for the coronation of Queen Victoria. This last incorporates the Star of Africa diamond and a sapphire that belonged to Edward the Confessor. ∎

# More places to visit in London

## CHELSEA

Trendy and fashionable Chelsea (*Map 48 B2*), in its superb location on the north bank of the Thames, preserves a bohemian atmosphere and has attracted artists, writers, painters, and pub philosophers down the years. J.M.W. Turner, Henry James, T.S. Eliot, George Eliot, Mick Jagger, Laurie Lee, and Oscar Wilde are just a handful of its famous and infamous residents, whose blue plaques can be seen on houses along riverside Cheyne Walk and elsewhere.

At the other end of the inhabitant spectrum are the 400 Chelsea Pensioners, old soldiers in long red coats (blue in winter) who live in retirement in the Royal Hospital built by Sir Christopher Wren in 1682.

## HAMPSTEAD

Up in the north of London, the hilly green acres of **Hampstead Heath** form a network of woods, meadows, open spaces, ponds, wetland, and grassland. Here you'll find an atmospheric old pub called Jack Straw's Castle, and 17th-century **Kenwood House** (*Hampstead Lane, NW3, tel 020-8348 1286, tube: Archway, Hampstead, Golders Green*), with paintings by Rembrandt, Reynolds, Van Dyck, Vermeer, and Gainsborough.

## SIR JOHN SOANE'S MUSEUM

John Soane was born in 1753, the son of a bricklayer. He proved to be a brilliant architect (the Bank of England was one of his designs), and helped his fortunes along when he married the niece of a well-to-do builder. The museum consists of the many thousands of artifacts he collected and crammed into the house he lived in.

In the Dining Room and Library are Sir Thomas Lawrence's 1828 portrait of Soane, the epitome of reflective sensitivity; Sir Joshua Reynold's "Love and Beauty," with the coquettish subject glancing playfully from behind her rounded white arm; and the Cawdor Vase, a late fourth-century B.C. Italian piece covered in warlike and sportive heroes and gods.

Delicately carved Roman marbles are in the Dressing Room and Study, with more on view from the window in the Monument Court, an internal light well, along with Hogarth's "Oratorio" and a Canaletto street scene.

There is an astonishing array of treasures in the Picture Room, featuring William Hogarth's original series of paintings, "A Rake's Progress" and "The Election." The walls are panels, cunningly hinged to fold out; behind the Hogarths are 18th-century monochromes of Doric temples by Piranesi, and a Turner watercolor, "Kirkstall Abbey."

In the Crypt you'll find the Sepulchral Chamber, housing the enormous, bathlike alabaster sarcophagus of Pharaoh Seti I (died 1279 B.C.), and the Catacombs stacked with decorative Roman funerary urns.

The New Picture Room has three Canaletto waterscapes, including the 1736 "View toward Santa Maria della Salute, Venice," which is considered one of his finest.

Hanging in the first-floor Drawing Rooms are poignant portraits of Sir John Soane as a worried and prematurely old man, and of his two ne'er-do-well sons, George and John.
🅰 49 E4  ✉ 13 Lincoln's Inn Fields, WC2

**A visual reference library—Sir John Soane's Museum, with its labyrinth of rooms, houses a bizarre collection of objets d'art.**

**Terra-cotta and brightly painted flowerpots at the Chelsea Flower Show, held every May.**

☎ 020-7405 2107  🕐 Closed Sun., Mon., &
Tues. (except first Tues. of month)  💲 Guided
tours: $$  🚇 Tube: Holborn

## MARYLEBONE

Three of London's best known visitor attrac-
tions lie at the southwestern corner of Regent's
Park, in the district of Marylebone *(Tube: Baker
Street)*. The theoretical personal belongings,
furniture, and memorabilia of fiction's most
famous private detective, Sherlock Holmes, can
be viewed at the **Sherlock Holmes Museum**
*(221b Baker St., tel 020-7935 8866, open daily)*.
Nearby on Marylebone Road are two attractions
covered by one ticket—**Madame Tussauds**
world-famous waxworks with its pop stars,
celebs, and ghastly murderers, and the **London
Planetarium** where sophisticated special
effects take you deep into space. *(Marylebone
Road, tel 0870-400 3000, open daily)*

## MUSEUM OF LONDON

For a fascinating insight into London's rich
history you can't do better than the Museum of
London. Permanent displays in seven galleries
take you through Roman and Saxon London,
the Middle Ages, and the London of the Tudor,
Stuart, Georgian and Victorian eras, right up to
the start of WWI. Changing exhibitions fill in
the varying facets of the modern age.

A little farther east, in the heart of the now
revamped dock area of the city, you'll find the
**Museum in Docklands** *(No. 1 Warehouse,
West India Quay, Hertsmere Road E14 4AL, tel
0870-444 3857, tube: Canary Wharf; Docklands
Light Railway: West India Quay)*, an outstation
of the Museum of London, telling the ram-
bunctious, riches-to-rags-to-riches story of the
docks and their late 20th-century re-creation as
a showpiece business and residential area. For
the kids there's a hands-on Children's Gallery.
🅰 49 F4  ✉ London Wall, EC2Y 5HN
☎ 0207-600 3699/0870-444 3852  🕐 Open
daily  💲 $$  🚇 Tube: Barbican, St. Paul's

## WALLACE COLLECTION

Displayed in 29 galleries in a fine Italianate
mansion just south of Regent's Park, the
Wallace Collection was bequeathed to the
nation on condition it would be kept in one
piece. Four generations of the Seymour-
Conway family, Marquesses of Hertford,
assembled it during the late 18th and 19th centuries and their legacy forms the richest private
art collection in London. Most notable are the
18th-century French paintings and sculpture
collected by the 4th Marquess and his son,
Sir Richard Wallace (1818–1890).
🅰 48 C4  ✉ Hertford House, Manchester Sq.
W1  ☎ 020-7935 0687  🕐 Closed Sun. a.m.
🚇 Tube: Bond St.  ∎

They encircle the capital—neatly pretty Surrey, Royal Berkshire with Windsor and the Thames, leafy Buckinghamshire and its Chiltern Hills, the long flatlands of Bedfordshire, and Hertfordshire's great houses set in rolling countryside.

# Home Counties

Introduction & map **96–97**
The Thames west of London **98–99**
Royal Windsor **100–105**
Woburn Abbey **106–107**
Stowe **107**
The Chilterns **108–109**
St. Albans Cathedral **110–11**
Hatfield House **112–13**
More places to visit in the
Home Counties **114**
Hotels & restaurants in the Home
Counties **346–49**

**Cottages at Bradenham
near High Wycombe, Bucks**

# Home Counties

THE HOME COUNTIES IS THE NAME GIVEN TO THE RING OF COUNTIES THAT surrounds London. Setting aside Kent (more properly a part of the great chalk barrier that forms the South Country) and Essex (in atmosphere associated more closely with East Anglia), the Home Counties, moving clockwise, are Surrey to the south of London, Berkshire and Buckinghamshire out west, Bedfordshire and Hertfordshire to the north. Naturally these are all commuter counties, but the influence of London culture and atmosphere grows rapidly weaker the farther out from the M25 expressway you travel.

Here are opulent country houses sealed away behind high walls and built by the wealthy for their proximity to London, charming villages, an astonishing amount of woodland, some of the prettiest British river scenery along the Thames in Berkshire and the Wey in Surrey, and everywhere a tangle of footpaths through beautiful countryside.

## SURREY & BERKSHIRE

Lying for the most part in Surrey is the chalk rampart of the North Downs, along which runs a bridlepath, the Pilgrim's Way. There are wonderful high views from this ancient track. Surrey also possesses plenty of scenic villages, and in the west some wide tracts of undeveloped heathland.

**The Queen awards the Order of the Garter in grand style at Windsor Castle.**

Royal Berkshire spreads lush meadows along the River Thames between Windsor and Henley-on-Thames, and boasts the monarch's premier residence of Windsor Castle as its chief landmark.

## BUCKS TO BEDS

"Leafy Bucks" has the glorious Chiltern Hills, mecca for metropolitan riders and walkers, where old beechwoods smother rolling hills; and a great chalk escarpment that looks north and west over enormous plains stretching off into Oxfordshire and Bedfordshire.

Here are some of the prettiest and most historic Home Counties villages—the perfect National Trust village of Hambleden near Henley; Chalfont St. Giles, where Milton finished *Paradise Lost;* and West Wycombe, home of the 18th-century Hellfire Club (see

p. 109). Hertfordshire has Hatfield House (the greatest Jacobean mansion in Great Britain), more excellent walking, and its own clutch of fascinating places such as picture-perfect Aldbury in the west, eccentric and irresistible Ayot St. Lawrence with the home of George Bernard Shaw, and Perry Green in the east, where Henry Moore's unfathomable and beautiful sculptures lie silhouetted on the skyline. ■

# The Thames west of London

FROM THE OXFORDSHIRE LOWLANDS SOUTH OF OXFORD, the River Thames flows by way of Pangbourne and Mapledurham through the outskirts of Reading before swinging north to reach Henley-on-Thames, one of this well-to-do river's most agreeable little towns. Almost all of Henley's interest lies along its river frontage, for this is the venue of the world-renowned Henley Royal Regatta in the first week of July.

**Henley-on-Thames**
🗺 97 B2
**Visitor information**
✉ King's Arms Barn, King's Road
☎ 01491-578034

**Marlow**
🗺 97 B2
**Visitor information**
✉ 31 High St.
☎ 01628-483597

Henley Week (*tel 01491-572153*) is one of those landmarks in the social calendar when the snobbish side of the English character is allowed full play—both on the part of the straw-boater-toting, blazer-wearing, cravat-knotting, champagne-swigging persons who fill the bunting-draped grandstands beside the River Thames, and of the chip-on-shoulder sourpusses who love to moan and complain about them.

The boat racing began in 1829 as a challenge between Oxford and Cambridge Universities. In 1839 it was instituted annually. When Prince Albert became patron in 1851, Henley Regatta received its royal imprimatur—and since then it has never looked back.

White suits, straw hats, cream teas: The once exclusive rituals of the English upper classes are pursued by those who attend the Royal Regatta at Henley.

**MARLOW TO COOKHAM**
**Hambleden** village itself, just off the A4155, contains enough charming flint-and-brick cottages with roses around the door to satisfy any camera wielder. St. Mary's (see p. 27) is a big cruciform church with some fine carving and a wonderful decorated tub font that was probably old when the Normans came to Britain. Beyond Hambleden, the Thames swings east to flow past the photogenic weir, mill, lock, and lockkeeper's cottage at **Marlow.** Soon the river is crossed by a fine 1836 suspension bridge. The Compleat Angler Hotel (1653) has a stained-glass fish window to the memory of Izaak Walton (see p. 129), the London hardware dealer who fished all these waters and wrote a philosophical and piscatorial masterpiece, *The Compleat Angler.*

Now the Thames skirts the meadows at Bourne End and reaches **Cookham,** where during the ceremonial "Swan Upping" each July Her Majesty's Swan Keeper counts the birds. Cookham High Street has the creaky old Bel and The Dragon Inn, and the **Stanley Spencer Gallery** (*High St., tel 01628-471885, closed Mon.–Fri. Nov.–Easter),* which displays many splendidly vigorous, individualistic paintings by local artist Sir Stanley Spencer (1891–1959). Typical of his work is the huge, unfinished "Christ Preaching at Cookham Regatta," in which Christ in a straw boater energetically harangues a crowd of hedonistic merrymakers (see pp. 42–43).

**DOWNSTREAM TO WINDSOR**
Below Cookham, the Thames passes through the beechwoods of Cliveden Reach near the opulent **Cliveden House** (now a hotel, see p. 348, but sympathetic to interested explorers), where the "Cliveden Set" of 1920s and 1930s

politicians and glitterati gathered to chatter and arrange the world with Lord and Lady Astor.

Boulter's Lock and the handsome bridges at Maidenhead are next; then Bray and Monkey Island with its simian-themed hotel. Finally, the Thames slides by Eton and Windsor (see pp. 100–105) to reach the site of **Runnymede** just before passing under the M25 and approaching London proper.

At Runnymede there is a 1953 Commonwealth Air Forces Memorial to 20,000 unburied dead airmen of World War II, and a 1965 memorial to President John F. Kennedy on an acre of ground presented to the United States. Most pertinent to Britain's story, however, is a neoclassic temple donated in 1957 by the American Bar Association in memory of the signing at Runnymede of Magna Carta. The world's first bill of civil rights was forced on a reluctant King John by his own barons in June 1215. ■

### Riverside walk

A lovely 6-mile walk goes downstream from Henley Bridge on the east bank of the Thames. It passes Temple Island mid-river with its 18th-century James Wyatt folly, the starting point for the regatta crews on their 1-mile, 550-yard dash to Henley Bridge, and reaches Hambleden Lock and an exciting crossing of the river on a catwalk bridge to picturesque Hambleden Mill. From the lock, a path goes south to Aston and the delightful Flower Pot Hotel (characterful old bars and shady gardens), then southwest back to Henley by way of Remenham Woods. ■

**The Angel pub in Henley—perfect for spending an afternoon, drink in hand, relaxing by the river**

# Royal Windsor

**Windsor**
◭ 97 C2
**Visitor information**
✉ 24 High St.
☎ 01753-743900

**Windsor Castle**
✉ Windsor
☎ Recorded
information: 01753-
831118
🕐 Closed during State
visits (call to
check). Chapels
closed Sun. except
for services
💲 $$$$

EVERYONE KNOWS WINDSOR FOR ITS GREAT CASTLE, A royal residence for over 900 years. But before visiting the castle, it is worth strolling around Windsor town to see some of its remarkable old buildings—including the Guildhall on High Street, completed in 1689 by Sir Christopher Wren, who installed its ornamental columns under protest. He left a gap between the tops of the columns and the ceiling to show that they were not structurally necessary. The crooked Market Cross House stands alongside. On Church Street is Burford House, where Charles II dallied with Nell Gwynne; also the Old King's Head Tavern which displays a "Warrant to Execute Kinge Charles the First, A.D. 1648."

**Towers, turrets, and busby-clad guards—these are the images that make Windsor Castle, official residence of the Queen and her family, the ultimate in royal castles.**

## WINDSOR CASTLE

The castle's unmistakable shape is an icon to the British; in particular the great Round Tower, from whose summit flies the Royal Standard when the monarch is in residence.

The first castle was built of wood shortly after the Norman Conquest, on a rise of ground commanding the Thames and only a day's march from William I's main residence in the Tower of London. Henry II was the first monarch to live at Windsor, rebuilding the castle in stone from around 1165. The **Round Tower,** centerpiece of the whole ensemble, was likewise converted from wood to stone construction around this time. The castle was laid out in three wards (walled areas), with the Round Tower built in the Middle Ward. The tower's upper works were added from 1828 by George I, in a burst of full-blooded medievalizing. Nowadays it houses the **Royal Archives and Photographic Collection.**

### Upper Ward

This part of the castle contains a 13th-century court with the **Waterloo Chamber,** a state apartment built in 1832 to celebrate the victory at the Battle of Waterloo. Also here is **St. George's Hall,** built in 1362–65. It was very badly damaged in the 1992 fire, but has since been restored. The **State Apartments** are crammed with treasures—Antonio Verrio frescoes on the ceilings, Adam fireplaces, carvings by Grinling Gibbons, paintings by Canaletto, Van Dyck, Hans Holbein, Rembrandt, Rubens, Hogarth, Gainsborough, and Constable. It is a solid assemblage of the masters of various branches of art down the ages. One bit of fun: Queen Mary's Dolls' House, designed in 1923 by Sir Edwin Lutyens to a meticulous 1:12 scale,

with real miniature books, pictures, electric lighting, and running water.

## Lower Ward

Most impressive of the castle's buildings is the late Gothic **St. George's Chapel,** a Tudor creation of 1475–1528 with delicate

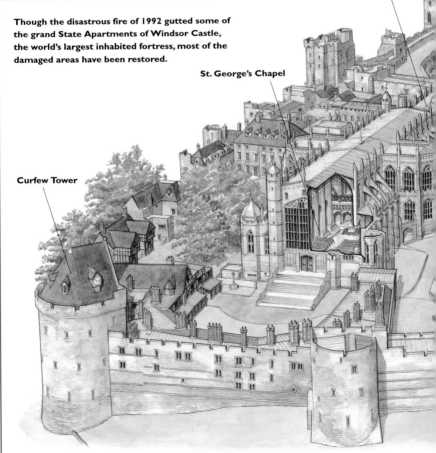

**Albert Memorial Chapel**

Though the disastrous fire of 1992 gutted some of the grand State Apartments of Windsor Castle, the world's largest inhabited fortress, most of the damaged areas have been restored.

**St. George's Chapel**

**Curfew Tower**

stone carving, pride of place going to the elaborate fan vaulting. The Order of the Knights of the Garter, founded by Edward III in 1348, has 26 members, and their tall, carved stalls stand in the chapel under their individual banners and crests. Ten monarchs are buried in St.

George's—they include Henry VIII and his third wife, Jane Seymour, the beheaded Charles I, George V, and George VI.

The castle also contains the 13th-century **Albert Memorial Chapel,** restored from 1861 in memory of Queen Victoria's beloved

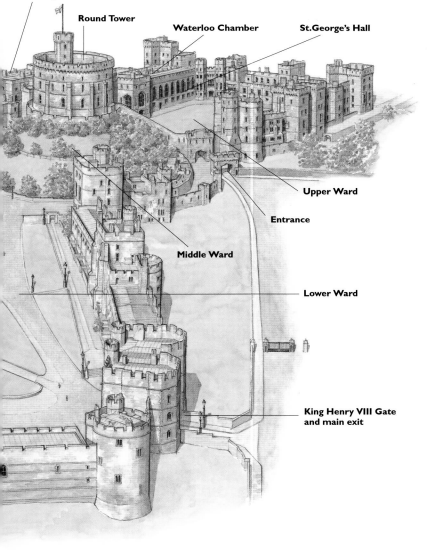

**State Apartments**

**Round Tower**

**Waterloo Chamber**

**St.George's Hall**

**Upper Ward**

**Entrance**

**Middle Ward**

**Lower Ward**

**King Henry VIII Gate and main exit**

**Eton schoolboys participate in the Fourth of June Procession of Boats. During the private ceremony for parents, crews in naval costume stand and shake the flowers from their boaters.**

Prince Consort. Here also are a number of grace-and-favor houses, and the 13th-century Curfew Tower.

### GREAT PARK & ETON

The 4,800 well-wooded acres of **Windsor Great Park** are interlaced with a network of footpaths. **Savill Garden** (*tel 01753-847518*) lies to the southeast of the park. Its 35 acres feature formal rose gardens, perennial borders, and glorious fall foliage.

North of the town a footbridge crosses the Thames to Eton, where you may see top-hatted and tail-coated boys from **Eton College** (*High St., tel 01753-671177, closed Oct.–March. & a.m. during school year*), Britain's most exclusive school, founded in 1440 and source (to date) of 18 prime ministers. ■

## Royal Ascot

The four-day race meeting of Royal Ascot, initiated by horse-loving Queen Anne in 1711, is an indelible entry in the June diaries of exhibitionist or socially exclusive Britons. Huge hats, extravagantly confected, are de rigueur for the ladies. Gentlemen come attired in top hats and tails. The Royal Family give the occasion their seal of approval, some or all of them attending the running of the Ascot Gold Cup on the racecourse (*tel 01344-876876*), just south of Windsor Great Park. ■

# Woburn Abbey

**Woburn Abbey**

- 🗺 97 C3
- ✉ Woburn
- ☎ 01525-290666
- 🕐 Closed Nov.–Dec., Mon.–Fri. Jan.–late March & Oct.
- 💲 $$$

**Woburn Safari Park**

- ✉ Woburn Park
- ☎ 01525-290407
- 🕐 Closed Jan.–early March
- 💲 $$$$ (cheaper after 3 p.m.)

**The Russells, dukes of Bedford, have lived at Woburn Abbey— at first in part of the former monastery, then in the Georgian mansion they built—since Stuart times.**

WOBURN ABBEY, JUST TO THE SOUTHWEST OF THE sprawling new town of Milton Keynes, stands in a 3,000-acre park crisscrossed with beautiful tree-shaded walks. About 350 acres of Woburn land is used as a safari park (Woburn Safari Park), home to white rhino, lions, and other exotic animal species. But Woburn's best known conservation work is connected with the welfare of Chinese deer. The deer park was set up in 1900 by the 11th Duke of Bedford to nurture 18 Père David deer, the remnants of the last known herd of its type, which had been discovered by the eponymous French missionary near Peking (Beijing) in 1865.

At that time the deer were on the verge of extinction. Nowadays you can see the Père Davids contentedly at home in the park, along with many other species of deer, from diminutive humpbacked muntjac and spotted Indian chital, to dark and shaggy Javanese rusa. The painstaking recovery program was so successful that in 1985 the Duke of Bedford was able to return a small herd of Père Davids to their native China, where they are now breeding successfully.

### THE BIG HOUSE

Woburn Abbey itself is a splendid mid-18th-century house built for the Russell family, dukes of Bedford. There had been a Cistercian monastery here since 1145, but at the Dissolution it was handed to the Russells by Henry VIII. It took another hundred years for the family to move to Woburn from their Tudor house of Chenies (a delight to visit in its own right) in south

Buckinghamshire, and they took their time modernizing and rebuilding their new Bedfordshire residence. Henry Flitcroft supervised the start of the work in 1747, and it was completed by Henry Holland around 1788.

A tour through the State Apartments will show you superb gilded ceilings, and a range of paintings that includes work by Reynolds, Gainsborough, and 21 works by Canaletto in the Venetian room. In the Long Gallery hang Tudor portraits.

### BEYOND THE PARK

The village of **Woburn,** just west of the abbey, was largely rebuilt at the same time as the house. You can spot various "B" monograms, capped with coronets, on walls and gables around the place. One phenomenon may strike you as odd. Some of the houses are built with no front doors. The doorlessness was ordered by a former Duke of

Bedford, who was distressed to see his tenants standing gossiping at their front doors.

To the east of Woburn the wide clay lowlands of Bedfordshire sweep up toward the chalk hills of northern Hertfordshire. This is an exhilarating escarpment, whose heights are crossed by the 6,000-year-old track known as the **Icknield Way,** now a long-distance trail. An excellent section of this track crosses the B655 just east of Pegsdon. You can walk it southwest over Telegraph Hill, the site of one of the 18th-century semaphore stations set up by the Admiralty at 10-mile intervals to carry news between London and Great Yarmouth. ■

**Elizabeth I in all her regal splendor as painted by George Gower (circa 1588)**

# Stowe

The Dukes of Buckingham and Chandos were owners of the house at Stowe (now accommodating a public school) in the northwest of Buckinghamshire. But it is **Stowe gardens** (NT) that command attention. All the landscaping luminaries of the 18th and early 19th centuries worked on Stowe—Sir John Vanbrugh, James Gibbs, William Kent, Charles Bridgeman. Capability Brown spent ten years as head gardener here before beginning a freelance career. These grounds capture the transitional period between 17th-century formality and later 18th-century pastoral idyll. Classical ideals are in evidence throughout—Greek temples, Roman columns, a wonderful Palladian bridge over the lake, a "Grecian Valley" designed by Capability Brown (his maiden landscaping achievement), and heroic monuments to British Worthies, to Concord and to Victory. ■

**Stowe**

🅰 97 B4

✉ 2½ miles northwest of Buckingham

☎ Gardens: 01280-822850. House: 01280-813650

🕐 Gardens closed late Oct.–late March; Mon. & Tues. late Mar.–July & Sept.–late Oct.; Mon. July–Sept. House closed school year & winter holidays; other times Sat. & a.m. Opening times vary due to restoration.

💲 Gardens: $$ House: $

# The Chilterns

THE CHILTERN HILLS HOLD A VERY SPECIAL PLACE IN THE hearts of London and Home Counties walkers and countryside lovers. This great rise of chalk and flint, smothered with beechwoods and dotted with quiet open spaces and rough downland slopes, curves for 30 miles as it shadows the western perimeter of London. The Chilterns bend like a bow northeast from the Thames around to the meeting point of Buckinghamshire, Bedfordshire, and Hertfordshire near Ivinghoe Beacon, where the ancient Ridgeway track joins the equally ancient Icknield Way.

**The Chilterns**
🗺 97 B2
**Visitor information**
✉ 6 Cornmarket, High Wycombe
☎ 01494-421892
🕐 Closed Sun.

The range's outer rim, at the top of an impressive chalk escarpment, commands wonderful views. In the beechwoods and on the downland slopes thrive huge numbers of wildflowers—orchids, Chiltern gentian, rockrose, yellow-wort—along with yews, spindle bushes, wild service trees, and ancient holly. Butterflies, songbirds, and hawks thrive. This is some of the best walking territory within 30 miles of London, crisscrossed with footpaths and dotted with village pubs for en-route refreshment.

The hollow golden ball atop St. Lawrence's Church, West Wycombe (right), served as one of the meeting places of the Hellfire Club.

Huge gnarled and twisted trees in the woods of Burnham Beeches (below), south of Beaconsfield, are the result of several centuries of coppicing.

## AROUND WYCOMBE

In the slice of countryside between the M40 London–Oxford freeway and the M1 lies some of the most attractive Chiltern countryside, less frequented than the sometimes overcrowded region farther south around Henley-on-Thames and Hambleden (see p. 98). **West Wycombe,** just northwest of High Wycombe, is a delightful brick and timber village looked after by the National Trust. Here are the **West Wycombe Caves** (*tel 01494-533739, closed Mon.–Fri. Nov.–Feb.*), excavated in Georgian times by local squire Sir Francis Dashwood for stone to surface the roads. He put the caves to more notorious use as the setting for orgies held by his Hellfire Club, a band of wild pranksters that included many of the most eminent men of the day. On the hill above the village, **St. Lawrence's Church** (*West Wycombe, closed Sun. & some Sats.*) is topped with a big hollow, golden globe; it served as a bizarrely sited clubroom where Hellfire members could gamble and drink. Nearby stands the hexagonal shell of a mausoleum built to house their hearts.

## ON THE NORTHERN SLOPES

Farther east on the A413 is the very attractive valley of the River Misbourne, stretching between the Georgian market town of Amersham and the village of **Chalfont St. Giles.** Here the cottage in which the blind poet John Milton finished writing *Paradise Lost* in 1665–66 has been turned into a small museum—**Milton's Cottage** (*Dean Way, tel 01494-872313, closed Nov.–Feb., Mon. March–Oct.*). **St. Giles's Church** has beautiful 14th-century wall paintings, notably the Creation, the Crucifixion, and the beheading of John the Baptist.

Ten miles north, on the far side

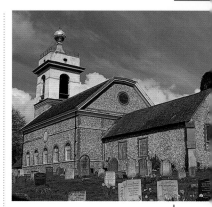

of A41 and the Grand Union Canal, the Ashridge Estate's 4,000 acres of prime National Trust woodland occupies a long north–south ridge. Tucked under its western flank is **Aldbury,** charmingly grouped around its duck pond, village green, and 16th-century manor house. The Pendley Chapel in St. John's Church holds the superbly carved 15th-century effigies of Sir Robert and Lady Whittingham.

A footpath climbs east up the ridge, then follows a sunken track-way north through the beechwoods to the 100-foot column of the **Bridgewater Monument** (*NT, tel 01442-851227, closed Nov.–March & Mon.–Fri., April–Oct. unless by arrangement.*) It was erected in 1832 in honor of the 3rd Earl of Bridgewater, whose pioneering canal building in 18th-century England hastened the coming of the industrial revolution. It also made him rich, and his descendants built the huge Gothic Ashridge House on the ridge opposite. Spiral steps lead up to a spectacular view from the top of the Monument, but an even better one can be had by following the path northward for two miles to join the ancient long-distance path called the **Ridgeway.** From the 755-foot brow of Ivinghoe Beacon you look out over 30 miles of countryside. ■

# St. Albans Cathedral

**St. Albans**

🏔 97 C3

**Visitor information**

✉ Town Hall,
   Market Place

☎ 01727-864511

🕐 Closed Sun. mid-
   Sept.–mid-July

**St. Albans
Cathedral**

✉ Sumpter Yard

☎ 01727-860780

💲 Donation

HAD IT NOT BEEN FOR THE RESTORING ZEAL OF LORD Grimthorpe in mid-Victorian times, St. Albans Cathedral in south Hertfordshire would now be another picturesque ruin left over from the Reformation. For the great Norman abbey church—it was not consecrated as a cathedral until 1877—had been steadily decaying since it was saved from destruction at the Dissolution: The townsfolk had rescued it by buying it for use as their own parish church.

Whether the Victorian restoration was an aesthetic success has been vigorously questioned. The exterior of the cathedral certainly does not compare with Wells, Canterbury, York Minster, or the other soaring masterpieces of medieval church architecture in Britain. There is something crouched and bulky about it. The huge west window overshadows its spindly flanking turrets, and the tower is squat and plain. But inside there are some fine 13th- and 14th-century frescoes on the piers, one showing the Crucifixion, and several areas of beautifully fresh blue and red medieval glass.

**St. Albans
Cathedral is
named after
Britain's first
Christian martyr,
Alban, who was
executed here.**

**Patron saint**

Here, too, is the 14th-century marble shrine of the church's patron saint, St. Alban, carved with scenes from his martyrdom. The shrine was shattered into over 2,000 pieces during the Reformation, but was painstakingly reassembled from the hoarded fragments during the Victorian restoration of the church and has again been re-assembled in the last few years. Alban himself was a Roman soldier-citizen who became Britain's first Christian martyr in A.D. 209, when he was beheaded for giving shelter to Amphibalus, the priest who had converted him to

Christianity. He was canonized in A.D. 429, a time when the exhausted Roman Empire was crumbling in the face of barbarian vigor and appetite for conquest. Offa, the Mercian king who built a mighty dike along the border with Wales (see p. 174), founded St. Albans Abbey in 793 over the spot where the martyrdom was said to have taken place. When the Normans arrived, they quickly built a splendid church here, using many of the bricks that the Romans had made to build their town of Verulamium a thousand years before.

### Early beginnings

The Romans were not the first settlers in the valley of the River Ver. In **Prae Wood,** a couple of miles west of St. Albans, extensive earthworks show where the Belgae tribe of Britons had their stronghold. Verulamium was one of the most important towns in Britain, a social and economic center for the many Roman villas and estates scattered across the Chilterns. Roman and Celtic farmers came into town to have their corn ground at the water mills, and to sell and barter produce. Standing at the crossing place of the two important Roman highways of Watling Street and Akerman Street, Verulamium had its interests and safety guaranteed by a legion that was garrisoned in the town.

On display in St. Albans' excellent **Verulamium Museum** is a variety of finds unearthed from the Roman town. There

are some wonderfully intricate mosaics, particularly one based on a beautiful scallop shell. Embossed, heavily ornamented lead coffins show one mood of Roman culture; delicate and lively paintings of birds on plaster demonstrate another. There are extensive remains of an enormous theater (A.D. 140), big enough to seat up to 6,000 spectators, complete with its stage.

### THE TOWN

The town of St. Albans has been a trading center and staging post since Roman times, and its position on a hill has given it strategic importance, too. You can get an overview of the whole place by climbing the early 15th-century clock tower on High Street.

The **Church of St. Michael** stands on Saxon foundations which are themselves bedded on the basilica and forum of the Roman town of Verulamium. In the nave, a fine Norman structure, a handsome tomb holds the remains of the Tudor statesman, philosopher, and writer Sir Francis Bacon (1561–1626), who lived at nearby Gorhambury.

St. Albans is full of old pubs with character; one of the best-known is **Ye Olde Fighting Cocks** on Abbey Mill Lane. Parts of the building probably date back to Norman times (it started life as the dovecote of St. Albans Abbey); it is said locally to be the oldest pub in Britain. Its octagonal shape, pyramidal roof, and crooked chimneys are certainly striking. Another handsome old building worth looking at is the carefully restored 16th-century **Kingsbury Water Mill,** beside the River Ver. ■

One of the Roman finds unearthed at Verulamium, and now displayed in the Verulamium Museum, is this delicate bronze statuette of Venus dating from the late first or second century A.D.

**Verulamium Museum**

✉  St. Michael's St.

☎  01727-751810

$  $$

# Hatfield House

ROBERT CECIL, 1ST EARL OF SALISBURY, WAS PROBABLY THE most influential man in the kingdom when he started building Hatfield House in 1607. His father, William, 1st Lord Burghley, chief adviser to Elizabeth I, had died nine years before. Subsequently Robert had made himself invaluable to the Queen, and after her death in 1603 his was the voice in the ear of James I, who succeeded to the English throne.

**Hatfield House**

- 🗺 97 C3
- ✉ Hatfield
- ☎ 01707-287025
- 🕐 Closed late Sept.–March
- 💲 $$$; Park only: $

**William Cecil, 1st Lord Burghley: The stiff-looking robes are those of a courtier, the face that of the wise, subtle, and experienced elder statesman upon whose advice Queen Elizabeth I came to depend.**

The house stands squarely on its raised and balustraded terrace, a dignified, E-shaped building of red brick dressed with white stone, its tall, stone-casemented windows topped off by crown motifs—the most magnificent and impressive house of its day. The architect appointed by Cecil was Robert Lyminge, who went on to produce another wonderful Jacobean house, Blickling Hall near Norwich in Norfolk (see p. 219).

The Jacobean **gardens** at Hatfield House were laid out for Robert Cecil by, among others, John Tradescant the Elder and Salomon de Caus. These formal 17th-century knot and scented gardens are one of a few remaining examples.

A descendant of Cecil's, the present Marquess of Salisbury, still resides at Hatfield House today.

### THE OLD HOUSE

Superb though the Jacobean mansion and its gardens are, there is as much history attached to the mellow old early Tudor building by way of which you approach Hatfield House itself. This was Hatfield Palace (known today as the Old Palace), built before the turn of the 16th century. The original palace was far bigger than the single wing that survives, most of it having been dismantled by Robert Cecil while he was building his great house. Queen Elizabeth I spent much of her rather lonely childhood in Hatfield Palace. Her father, Henry VIII, was not much interested in his second daughter as he was desperate for a son to succeed him. He had her mother, Anne Boleyn, executed for treason and adultery before the princess

## William & Robert Cecil

**B**oth Elizabeth I and her successor, James I, had cause to be grateful to the Cecils. It was the good advice and steadying influence of William Cecil (1520–1598), 1st Lord Burghley, and his son Robert (1563–1612), 1st Earl of Salisbury, that kept the country on an even keel through the turbulent waters of the Reformation: This period of unease was whipped up by the anti-Catholicism of Henry VIII and the fervent persecution of Protestants conducted by his Catholic daughter,

Queen Mary. In 1558 William Cecil was appointed adviser to Queen Elizabeth, a post that lasted for 40 years until his death in 1598; Robert followed suit, becoming secretary of state both to Elizabeth and to King James. The exceptional ability and subtlety of this father-and-son political team was highlighted in retrospect by the shortsighted arrogance of Robert Cecil's successor as adviser, the high-handed and much disliked George Villiers, Duke of Buckingham. ∎

was three years old. Elizabeth spent more time penned up out of the way at Hatfield after her half-sister, Mary, came to the throne in 1553. It was in this house in 1558 that Elizabeth first heard of her accession to the throne.

## QUEEN ELIZABETH

Of the various mementoes of Elizabeth I at Hatfield House, the most amusing is a family tree painstakingly concocted to show her descent from—among other more verifiable ancestors—Adam, Noah, and King Lear. There are several portraits of the Queen, whose formative early years were spent here. The Isaac Oliver portrait with its allegorical comparison of Elizabeth to a rainbow, and another by Nicholas Hilliard suggesting all her intelligence and steeliness of character, show a woman marooned in the isolation of absolute power. William and Robert Cecil must have been a formidable pair, to have steered the diamond-hard Gloriana, Queen Elizabeth, the way they managed to do. ∎

**Most of the Old Palace at Hatfield was demolished by Robert Cecil in 1607 to make way for the new house, but the original garden has survived.**

**A footpath leading out of rural Shere village**

## More places to visit in the Home Counties

### AYOT ST. LAWRENCE

Ten miles north of St. Albans, in the quiet south Hertfordshire countryside, is the village of Ayot St. Lawrence, with its fine dark-beamed Brocket Arms pub and its neoclassic Church of St. Lawrence, built in the 1770s in the Palladian style by rich tobacco merchant Sir Lionel Lyde. His tomb and that of his wife are set in pavilions on opposite sides of the church. Sir Lionel left orders that since the church had forced them to stay together in life, he would at least make sure it separated them in death.

Just along the road is **Shaw's Corner** (*NT, Ayot St. Lawrence, tel 01438-820307, closed Nov.–March & Mon.–Tues. April–Oct.*), where George Bernard Shaw, the often controversial Irish-born playwright, lived from 1906 to his death at age 94 in 1950.

While living at Shaw's Corner he wrote, among other works, *Androcles and the Lion, Saint Joan,* and *Pygmalion* (the basis for the successful musical *My Fair Lady*). He was awarded the Nobel Prize for Literature in 1925.

▲ 97 D3 **Visitor information** ✉ Town Hall, Market Place, St. Albans ☎ 01727-864511

### MUCH HADHAM

West of Bishop's Stortford in the east of Hertfordshire, the Church of St. Andrew at Much Hadham contains wonderful medieval carvings. Flanking the west doorway are two heads by modern sculptor Henry Moore (1898–1986), whose house and studio at Perry Green—**The Henry Moore Foundation** (*Map 97 D3, tel 01279-843333, by appointment only, closed mid-Oct.–March*) are surrounded by his enigmatic, large-scale figures.

▲ 97 D3 **Visitor information** ✉ Town Hall, Market Place, St. Albans ☎ 01727-864511

### SURREY

Immediately south of London is Surrey, a commuter county with beautiful and well-cared-for countryside. The heavily wooded country just east of Guildford contains villages with lots of character such as **Abinger Hammer** and **Friday Street,** sunk deep in the trees. **Leith Hill Tower** offers a splendid view, as does the Pilgrim's Way on the chalky escarpment of steep **Box Hill** (*Map 97 C1*). Nearby **Shere** (*Map 97 C1*) features on many "rural England" calendars; its Norman Church of St. James is full of treasures. ■

A landscape of billowing chalk, from Kent—the "Garden of England"—over the cliffs and downs of Sussex and through the meadows and trout streams of Hampshire, by way of Wiltshire's prehistoric monuments, deep into rural Dorset

# The South Country

Introduction & map 116–17
Great houses of Kent 118–21
Canterbury 122–23
Charles Dickens
    & northern Kent 124
Around the Kent coast 125
Brighton 126
Chichester & Fishbourne
    Roman Palace 127
Winchester 128–29
Hampshire's rivers & coast 130
Salisbury Cathedral 131–32
Around Salisbury 133
Stonehenge 134–35
New Forest 138
Hotels & restaurants in the South
    Country 349–53

**Stained glass in Hambledon village church**

# The South Country

THE SOUTH COUNTRY—A TERM COINED BY THE POET AND COUNTRY writer Edward Thomas (1878–1917)—is not one of the portmanteau geographical labels universally used and understood by the British, as are the West Country or East Anglia or the Highlands. But it does suggest a cohesion in the great sweep of rolling countryside, characterized by open downs and lush green valley pasture, that runs west from Kent for 200 miles all the way to Dorset.

It is chalk that knits the South Country together—the smoothly undulating billows of the downs under grain or grass, and the bitten-off walls of the white cliffs that march from Kent into Sussex, decline to a flat sandy coast in Hampshire, and then rise again beyond Bournemouth for a final flourish around the Isle of Purbeck in Dorset.

and smallish castles, and one of the world's great cathedrals at Canterbury; while to the north is the setting for some of Charles Dickens's best known novels.

## SOUTH OF LONDON
Kent, so close to London and so conveniently placed for journeys to the Continent, boasts more than its share of impressive and historic great houses

Sussex has its South Downs that enfold charming flint-and-brick villages, and a splendidly overblown seaside resort in Brighton. Hampshire is for trout fishing in clear chalk streams, and for reading Jane Austen—her house at Chawton is now a museum, and her memorial stands in splendid Winchester Cathedral nearby.

## TO THE WEST

The neighboring county of Wiltshire has two outstanding pieces of architecture as its chief claim to fame. One is the sublime 13th-century cathedral at Salisbury with its immense spire, the tallest in Britain. The other is around 3,000 years older: the enigmatic Bronze Age monument of Stonehenge. The downs and plains of Wiltshire are thickly dotted with prehistoric sites, especially around the mighty stone circle at Avebury.

Dorset is associated with Thomas Hardy, and here are most of the settings of his Wessex novels. The hills hide secret valleys, and the coast is spectacularly beautiful. ■

**Nautical crafts on display inside the Sail and Colour Loft of Chatham Dockyard**

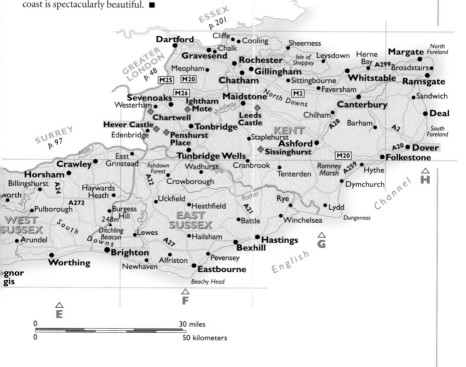

# Great houses of Kent

**Penshurst Place**

117 F3

✉ Penshurst

☎ 01892-870307

🕐 Closed Nov.–Feb. & Mon.–Fri. March

$ $$/$$$

**Ecclesiastical details of architecture show the medieval origins of Penshurst Place, one of Kent's oldest and most historic houses.**

KENT IS SOMETIMES CALLED THE "GARDEN OF ENGLAND," a tribute to its long establishment as a fruit-growing county. Blossom time in the Kentish orchards is beautiful and memorable. In the tall, conical shapes of the old oast houses or hop-drying kilns that are common here, and in the hop fields themselves, you can trace Kent's enduring—and continuing—association with the sticky and odoriferous flower that gives beer its essential bitterness.

"After passing an afternoon with the drier in the kiln," enthused the Victorian rural writer Richard Jefferies, "seated close to a great heap of hops and inhaling the odour, I was in a condition of agreeable excitement....I wanted music, and felt full of laughter.

Like the half-fabled haschish, the golden bloom of the hops had entered the nervous system; intoxication without wine, without injurious after-effect, dream intoxication; they were wine for the nerves." Beware the power of Kentish hops!

Considering the geographical position of the county—conveniently near London, yet far enough removed to be a separate entity, and placed ideally to form the gateway between the capital and the Continent—it is not surprising that so many rich and influential people should have settled here. Kent probably contains, acre for acre, more fine houses than any other county in Britain, some of them dating back to early medieval times or even further.

## PENSHURST PLACE

This is one of the greatest of Kent's great houses, on the western edge of the county. Penshurst is also one of England's oldest country houses, built for the rich London merchant Sir John de Pulteney in 1341. The Barons' Hall—64 feet long and almost as high—still survives with its roof of chestnut beams and its minstrels' gallery, along with the original solar, buttery, and pantry.

Sir Philip Sidney, the very flower of Renaissance manhood, who could fight and sing as well as he could rhyme and reason, was born at Penshurst Place in 1554, two years after his family came into possession of the estate. After his untimely death at the Battle of Zutphen in 1586, the house found a most hospitable owner in his younger brother, Robert. Many early 17th-century visitors commended Penshurst, and especially the beauty of its gardens.

*Then hath thy orchard fruit, thy*
*garden flowers,*
*The early cherry with the*
*later plum,*
*Fig, grape and quince, each in*
*his turn doth come;*
*The blushing apricot and*
*woolly peach*
*Hang on thy walls, that every*
*child may reach.*

That was the view of dramatist Ben Jonson, and the pleasure he took in the Penshurst fishponds was almost as intense:

*Fat, aged carps, that runne*
*into thy net,*
*And pikes, now weary their*
*owne kinde to eat;*
*Bright eeles, that emulate them,*
*and leape on land*
*Before the fisher, or into*
*his hand.*

The Penshurst Place gardens with their tall old beech trees, and the formal Italian gardens around the house itself, are open to all comers these days.

## IGHTHAM MOTE

Ten miles north of Penshurst, the hills are blanketed in the oak, birch, and sweet chestnut of the northern Kentish Weald. Weald meant "woodland" to the Saxons, and much remains of the great forest they knew. Sunk among the trees lies Ightham Mote (NT), a beautiful medieval manor house, moated as its name suggests. Unlike Penshurst Place, Ightham is of modest size, but its history stretches back at least as far. A 14th-century Great Hall and chapel are hidden inside the Tudor exterior of local brick, timber, and ragstone, a harmonious mishmash of materials and architectural styles.

## HEVER CASTLE

Hever Castle, in the rolling countryside just west of Penshurst Place, has a poignant place in the story of the six wives of Henry VIII. Anne Boleyn, the ill-starred second wife, grew up at Hever; and it was here that, as a bewitching young woman, she began to receive visits from the king. Later in Henry's marital saga his fourth wife, Anne of Cleves, was given Hever Castle as part of the

**Ightham Mote**

🅰 117 F3
✉ Ivy Hatch
☎ 01732-810378
🕐 Closed Nov.–March,
   Tues. & Sat.
   April–Oct.
💲 $$

**Delightful sculpted figures fill the Italian garden at Hever Castle.**

**Hever Castle**

🅰 117 F3
✉ Hever
☎ 01732-865224
🕐 Closed Dec.–Feb.
💲 $$$

### Chartwell
 117 F3
☎ 01732-866368
🕐 Closed Nov.–March,
& Mon.–Tues.
April–Oct. (open
Tues. July & Aug.)
$ $$

### Leeds Castle
117 G3
☎ 01622-765400
$ $$$

divorce settlement, when the king divorced her less than a year after their marriage.

The moat and gatehouse at Hever date from around 1270. Within these walls a Tudor manor house was built for the Boleyn family. The interior was restored with notable Edwardian woodwork early in the 20th century, after the American owner of *The Times* newspaper, William Waldorf Astor (1848–1919), took a fancy to Hever Castle and bought it. For good

**This plain-looking wall on the grounds of Chartwell has historical resonance, for it was built by enthusiastic part-time bricklayer Sir Winston Churchill.**

measure he also built an entire neo-Tudor village behind the castle, for the servants and any overspill guests.

In the Inner Hall hangs a Hans Holbein portrait of Henry VIII, looking fat and ruthless. He certainly made his two Annes suffer. Anne Boleyn paid at the execution block for her failure to produce a male heir, and perhaps for sexual misdemeanors, too. But Anne of Cleves—"that Flanders mare," as Henry contemptuously called her—at least got out of it with her life.

### CHARTWELL
Five miles north of Hever, Chartwell (NT), a big Victorian house, is well known as the country

home of Sir Winston Churchill from 1924 until his death in 1965. Here you can see a collection of Churchill memorabilia. The rooms are left as they were in Sir Winston and Lady Churchill's lifetime. The garden studio contains Sir Winston's easel and paintbox; he was a keen artist and several of his paintings are on display here.

### LEEDS CASTLE
Four miles east of Maidstone, Leeds Castle—often named the most beautiful castle in England—rises dreamily above its own reflection in a lake under wooded hills. This Norman castle was given to Edward I in 1278 and remained a royal residence until Tudor times.

The castle was a favorite of Henry VIII, who stayed here often. His first wife, Catherine of Aragon, was sent to live here after their divorce. The castle passed out of royal hands in 1552 when Henry gave it to Anthony St. Leger, his long-serving lord deputy in Ireland. Later, French prisoners were held here during the Napoleonic Wars.

History soaks the building, astutely marketed these days as a center for conferences and cultural and sporting events. Many are held in the Banqueting Hall, with its superb Tudor oak ceiling. Among attractions in the castle's 500 acres of parkland, landscaped by Capability Brown, are a huge maze, an aviary, herb gardens, and a golf course.

## SISSINGHURST CASTLE GARDEN

At Sissinghurst, 10 miles south of Maidstone, is Sissinghurst Castle Garden (NT). Here beautifully designed areas are planted alongside others that grow in rough profusion. It was created in the 1930s in and around the ruin of a moated Elizabethan mansion by Vita Sackville-West and her husband, Sir Harold Nicolson, members of the Bloomsbury Group (see p. 68).

In Vita's study in the four-storied gate tower is the printing press used by Virginia and Leonard Woolf to run off the first volumes produced by their Hogarth Press—including, in 1922, T.S. Eliot's *The Waste Land*. ∎

**Leeds Castle is superbly situated on two islands in a lake formed by the River Len.**

**Sissinghurst Castle Garden**

 117 G3

☎ 01580-710701

🕐 Closed Nov.–late March & Wed.–Thurs. late March–Oct. Due to limited capacity, visit early or late in the season to avoid disappointment. Timed ticket system operates.

 $$$

# Canterbury

**Canterbury**
🅼 117 G3
**Visitor information**
✉ 34 St. Margaret's St.
☎ 01227-766567
🕐 Closed Sun.
Jan.–March

**Canterbury
Cathedral**
✉ Buttermarket
☎ 01227-762862
💲 $$$

**Pilgrims travel to Canterbury to pray at the shrine of St. Thomas à Becket: Detail from a 13th-century stained-glass window in the south aisle of the cathedral, created only a few years after Becket's murder.**

CHIEF OF THE MANY TREASURES IN THE CITY OF Canterbury is the cathedral, Mother Church of the Church of England and seat of its premier archbishop. The main approach to the cathedral is through Christ Church Gate, ornate and brightly painted, with a lugubrious Christ looking gravely down from the center. The twin west towers and central 235-foot Bell Harry Tower are splendidly pinnacled.

## THE CATHEDRAL

The church was started in 1070, very shortly after the Norman Conquest, on the site of an Anglo-Saxon cathedral destroyed by Danish marauders. St. Augustine had arrived on the pope's orders in A.D. 597 to begin converting the locals, and so Canterbury—a few miles inland from his landing place on the east Kent coast—became a place of pilgrimage well before the December 1170 murder of Thomas à Becket in the cathedral.

In the northwest transept is **The Martyrdom,** the spot where Becket—close friend turned critic of Henry II—was killed on his return from a period in exile, by four knights after the king had uttered in hot blood the infamous exclamation: "Will no one rid me of this turbulent priest?" A 15th-century panel shows a reproachful Becket being cut down by his fiendish-looking assassins.

The murder was very swiftly declared a martyrdom (Becket was canonized only three years after his death), and his golden shrine became the object of one of the most popular medieval pilgrimages. A penitent Henry II was one of the first pilgrims, but the most famous are the fictional travelers—the Miller, the Wife of Bath, the Nun's Priest, and all the other companions—in Geoffrey Chaucer's wise and bawdy *Canterbury Tales*, written between 1387 and Chaucer's death in 1400.

In **Trinity Chapel,** at the east end of the cathedral, the Altar of Sword Point stands on the site of the shrine, which was destroyed at the Reformation in 1538 on the orders of Henry VIII after a posthumous "trial" had convicted Becket of high treason. Candles are kept burning in the chapel in memory of the saint, whose life and death are depicted in early medieval stained glass. More moving still are the hollows in the steps that were worn by the friction of countless millions of pilgrims' knees.

Other features at this east end of the church include the splendid brass effigy of the Black Prince (died 1376), with reproductions of his armor hanging above, and the finely sculpted alabaster tomb of Henry IV and his queen, Joan of Navarre. The sky blue and leaf green of the stained glass here shows multiple biblical scenes—Abraham and Isaac with the ram

caught in the thicket, Moses striking water out of the rock, ancient Methuselah in medieval robes and footwear.

Below in the crypt is a stone forest of Romanesque arches and pillars, their capitals carved with foliage and faces. There is 14th-century fan vaulting in the chapter house, and a fine early 15th-century stone screen shielding the choir.

## THE CITY

Medieval city walls extend around three sides of Canterbury, enclosing streets lined with crooked, half-timbered buildings. The monks built in stone; their early 14th-century Fyndon Gateway stands in Monastery Street at an entrance to St. Augustine's Abbey, where the pioneer saint is buried. Charles I and his bride, Henrietta Maria, spent their wedding night in a chamber over the gateway. Of the original gates into the city, only the 1387 West Gate survives; it was once used as the city jail and holds a display of prison hardware (fetters, manacles, and the like), along with arms and armor.

In the former St. Margaret's Church in St. Margaret's Street there is audiovisual and olfactory fun with **The Canterbury Tales** (*tel 01227-479227*), tableaus of some of Chaucer's fruitiest. **Eastbridge Hospital** on High Street (*tel 01227-471688, closed Sun.*), founded in 1190 to care for pilgrims to Becket's shrine, has early 13th-century frescoes of Christ in Majesty.

**Canterbury Heritage Museum** in Stour Street (*tel 01227-452747, closed Sun. Nov.–May*), housed in a superb medieval building, offers a tour through 2,000 years of the city's history. ■

**Dominating Canterbury is its cathedral's great central tower—the Bell Harry Tower. It was completed in 1503 to house a single bell, known as Harry.**

# Charles Dickens & northern Kent

**Rochester**
🅐  117 F3
**Visitor information**
✉  95 High St.
☎  01634-843666

**Gad's Hill Place**
✉  South of Higham
☎  01474-822366
🕐  Open only 1st Sun.
of each month p.m.
& bank holidays
💲  $$

CHARLES DICKENS (1812–1870) USED NORTH KENT AS A setting in many of his novels, including *The Pickwick Papers* (1836–37), *The Uncommercial Traveller* (1860), and the unfinished *Mystery of Edwin Drood* (1870). Dickens knew the county well; he spent several childhood years in Chatham, and lived at Gad's Hill Place near Rochester from 1856 until his death. It was *Great Expectations* (1860–61), written at Gad's Hill Place, that Dickens most fully imbued with the strange, moody presence of this mostly flat and estuarine landscape.

## ROCHESTER

Across from the **Charles Dickens Centre** (*tel 01634-844176*) on Rochester's High Street stands the gabled and timbered building that was pompous Uncle Pumblechook's seed-and-corn shop. In the Bull Hotel (now the **Royal Victoria & Bull Hotel**) Pip in *Great Expectations* had his meeting with Bentley Drummle. Dickens featured the curly gabled Restoration House

*Dickensian characters are brought to life at the Dickens Festival in Rochester, Kent.*

on Maidstone Road as the creepy Miss Havisham's house.

The town has a fine Norman cathedral and an impressive castle with a 125-foot keep—the tallest in England.

## GREAT EXPECTATIONS COUNTRY

The novel has many connections with the marsh country to the north of Rochester. In **Chalk** village, on the A226, the white weatherboard cottage by the road was Joe Gargery's forge and Pip's adoptive home. Farther west, a mile north of Higham village, stands lonely **St. Mary's Church.** In the graveyard, the convict Magwitch jumped out at Pip and swung him upside down so that the steeple flew under his feet.

A footpath leads north for a mile to **Cliffe Fort,** a stark ruin facing the broad River Thames, where Pip ran through the fog on Christmas morning to bring "wittles" and a file to Magwitch.

Just east, in **Cooling church-yard,** are 13 small, lozenge-shaped children's tomb slabs. Dickens used them as the gravestones of Pip's brothers; Pip himself believed, from the shape of the slabs, that his brothers "had all been born on their backs with their hands in their trouser-pockets." ∎

# Around the Kent coast

SEA SURROUNDS KENT ON THREE SIDES, THE COASTLINE
running clockwise from the creeks of the Medway estuary on the
north coast to the wetlands of Romney Marsh, haunt of smugglers
in the 18th century, on the south.

**Chatham,** at the mouth of
the Medway estuary, has a wonderful maritime heritage attraction,
the **World Naval Base** on
Dock Road. Under nearby **Fort
Amherst** (*tel 01634-847747*)
are nearly 6,000 feet of tunnels
hacked out by Napoleonic
prisoners-of-war.

At the estuary's eastern end, the
**Isle of Sheppey** is a wildfowl-
watcher's paradise. Here the tiny
Norman Church of St. Thomas
stands near remote Ferry House Inn.

The north Kent coast runs east
around the Isle of Thanet with its
three shoulder-to-shoulder
resorts—cheap and cheerful
**Margate;** slightly more attractive
**Broadstairs,** where Charles
Dickens wrote *David Copperfield*
(1849–1850) and *Bleak House*
(1852–53); and the faded elegance
of **Ramsgate.**

**Sandwich** and **Deal,** farther
south, are two historic old fishing
and smuggling ports, rich in flint-
and-brick architecture.

Around the curve of the South
Foreland, the famous white chalk
cliffs cradle the ferry port of
**Dover** with its enormous castle,
and the Victorian seaside resort of
**Folkestone,** since autumn 1994
the point of entry to the channel
tunnel railway link with France.

Beyond Folkestone lie the 80
square miles of beautiful **Romney
Marsh,** a dead-flat apron of green
fields and straight watercourses.

On the western edge, just across
the border in East Sussex, the
fascinating old red-roofed town of
**Rye** perches on its hill, as pretty as
a picture with its crooked, steep
little streets, medieval Land Gate,
Mermaid Inn (an old smugglers'
haunt), and **Lamb House**
(*NT, West St., tel 01372-453401,
closed late Oct.–March, also
Sun.–Tues., Thurs. & Fri. April–late
Oct.*), where the American novelist
Henry James (1843–1916) lived
from 1898 until his death. Climb St.
Mary's Church tower to get the best
view of all of this. ■

**Chatham**
 117 F3
**World Naval Base**
✉ Dock Rd., Chatham
☎ 01634-823800
⊕ Closed Dec.–Jan.,
    & Mon.–Tues.,
    Thurs.–Fri.
    Feb.–March & Nov.
💲 $$$

**Rye**
 117 G2
**Visitor
information**
✉ Strand Quay
☎ 01797-226696

Rye's steep
cobbled streets
and red-tiled
roofs and walls
make it magneti-
cally attractive to
visitors—some
of whom put
down roots and
never leave.

# Brighton

**Brighton**

🅰 117 E2

**Visitor information**

✉ 10 Bartholomew Sq.

☎ 0906-711 2255

**Royal Pavilion**

✉ Pavilion Parade

☎ 01273-290900

💲 $$

BRIGHTON IS A PARADOX, AN ATTRACTIVE CONFERENCE center as well as a seaside resort for day-trippers, where superb elegance and glitzy raffishness sit happily side by side. As a vacation destination Brighton has suffered, like many of Britain's seaside resorts, from cheaper and sunnier foreign competition. But there are still enough aesthetically pleasing buildings here, and enough roguish twinkle, to reflect the town's former glory as "old Ocean's Bauble, glittering Brighton."

During the late 18th century, the tiny Sussex fishing village of Brighthelmstone swelled into a seawater spa. There are still reminders of the old Brighthelmstone in the area of narrow streets called **The Lanes,** just behind the seafront.

Inland spread the terraces and crescents of Regency architecture that proliferated when the Prince Regent, George IV-to-be, came to Brighton early in the 19th century to rule as the Prince of Pleasure. In 1815 he had a palace built for himself right in the heart of Brighton—the ostentatiously vulgar and delightful **Royal Pavilion,** an absolute must-see for any visitor, with its enormous onion domes, its minarets, its great ceiling-mounted dragons, and its tree-shaped chandeliers. Contemporary critics enjoyed themselves—"turnips and

**Described by essayist William Hazlitt as "a collection of stone pumpkins and pepperpots,"** the Royal Pavilion, a pastiche of Chinese and Indian styles, has been restored to its former vibrant color.

tulip bulbs" (William Cobbett); "one would think that St. Paul's Cathedral had come to Brighton and pupped" (Sidney Smith).

Down on the seafront are the **Brighton Pier** (1899) and the **Sea Life Centre** *(Marine Parade, tel 01273-604234)* where an underwater tunnel—the longest in Europe—allows you to view sharks and other marine animals at close quarters. Here you can ride in one of the little carriages of **Volks Electric Railway** out east to Marina Station *(tel 01273-292718, closed Oct.–Easter)*, or climb up the hill into elegant **Kemp Town.** The town's designer, local wild boy (and MP) Thomas Read Kemp, died broke before his plans were realized in the 1850s, but his memorial is one of the finest Regency-style developments ever built. ∎

# Chichester & Fishbourne Roman Palace

THOUGH BRIGHTON IS THE FLASHIEST, BIGGEST, AND most prosperous town in Sussex, the county capital of West Sussex is the ancient cathedral city of Chichester, 30 miles west of Brighton along the coast. Its Roman street plan still radiates out from the finely carved Tudor market cross at the town's heart, though the buildings are mostly solid Georgian.

**Chichester**
🅰 117 D2
**Visitor information**
✉ 29A South St.
☎ 01243-775888

## CHICHESTER CATHEDRAL

Begun in about 1075 but rebuilt at the end of the 12th century after a fire, Chichester Cathedral (*tel 01243-782595*) soars in pale, silvery limestone over its red-roofed Deanery. Its slim 277-foot spire is a landmark seen for many miles. Rare early 12th-century stone carvings on the south side of the choir show Lazarus being raised from the dead. At the other end of the age spectrum are Graham Sutherland paintings, a 1966 tapestry by John Piper, and a vivid 1978 stained-glass window by Marc Chagall, full of prancing and skipping figures on a blood red background.

The **Chichester Festival Theatre** (*tel 01243-781312*) is a celebrated venue, with a main season between May and October that is generally booked solid.

## FISHBOURNE ROMAN PALACE

Just west of the city is Fishbourne Roman Palace, the largest Roman villa to be excavated to date in Britain. It was discovered in 1960 during ditch digging. The palace was built in about A.D 75, shortly after the Romans' arrival. More than 100 rooms were disposed around a garden, and remnants include walls, baths, and a hypocaust heating system. Superb mosaic floors feature intricate geometrical designs; a really remarkable one depicts a winged god riding a cavorting dolphin. ■

A carefree god and dolphin—one of the remarkable Roman mosaics excavated at Fishbourne

## The South Downs Way

This national trail runs for 106 miles along the chalk-and-turf crest of the South Downs, the low hills that extend from East Sussex to west Dorset. It starts at Winchester and continues to Eastbourne, in beautiful open countryside all the way. *A Guide to the South Downs Way* by Miles Jebb (Constable) is an excellent companion to the trail. ■

**Fishbourne Roman Palace**
🅰 116 D2
✉ Salthill Rd.
☎ 01243-785859
🕐 Closed Mon.–Fri. mid-Dec.–early Feb.
💲 $$

# Winchester

**Winchester**
▲ 116 D2
**Visitor information**
✉ Guildhall, Broadway
☎ 01962-840500
⏰ Closed Sun.
     Oct.–May

THE CHIEF TOWN IN ENGLAND ONE THOUSAND YEARS ago, capital of the ancient kingdom of Wessex, seat of the Anglo-Saxon kings from Alfred the Great until the Norman Conquest—Winchester is founded upon a deeply rooted rock of history. Twenty kings are buried here. The city is rich in myth, too, swirling around its association with King Arthur and the Knights of the Round Table. This is a place to walk around slowly, savoring the atmosphere.

## CATHEDRAL

At 556 feet, Winchester Cathedral (*The Close, tel 01962-857200*) is the world's longest medieval building, a truly mighty church. It was a long time in construction, started in 1079 and not finished until 1404. Saxon kings who died before the present church was begun are buried around its choir. Among them lies King William II (known

**The Round Table in Winchester's Great Hall is, in fact, a resplendent medieval fake.**

as Rufus), son of the Conqueror, killed—probably accidentally—by an arrow while hunting in the New Forest (see p. 138). The choir stalls are beautifully carved with very early 14th-century misericords, the oldest in Britain.

At the east end of the cathedral is the shrine of St. Swithun, Bishop of Winchester from 852 to 862. Swithun, who once taught Alfred the

Great, was very popular with medieval pilgrims—particularly those keen to negotiate a change in the weather, since superstition held that if it rained on St. Swithun's Day (July 15) it would continue to rain for 40 days and 40 nights.

The cathedral's 12th-century font is especially beautiful, its black marble carved with scenes from the life of the patron saint of seafarers, St. Nicholas. Three memorials stand out among many. One in the north aisle is to Jane Austen, who died at No. 8 College Street, Winchester, in 1817 (*house not open to the public*); another in the south transept honors Izaak Walton (1593–1683), hardware dealer and author of *The Compleat Angler* (1653), who died at No. 7 Cathedral Close. His memorial window shows him sitting reading by a river, his rod and creel by his side. "Study to be quiet" runs the legend. The third memorial, at the east end, is a statue of diver William Walker in his clumsy suit and boots. Between 1906 and 1911 he worked in cold, dark water under the cathedral's east wall, ramming over a million bricks and sacks of concrete into place to shore up the medieval masonry, which was threatening to collapse.

Outside the building, the **Pilgrims' Hall** in the cathedral close was built for devotees of St. Swithun; its beautiful hammerbeam roof of 1290 is the oldest in the country.

In the city, the **Great Hall** (*Castle Avenue, tel 01962-846476*) of 1235 houses the 18-foot-diameter **Round Table,** like a giant dartboard in black-and-white segments, with a red-lipped and curly-bearded King Arthur seated at the top. Experts have dated it to the 13th century—but legend says that Merlin created it by magic for Arthur's court, so that every knight's place would have equal honor.

### THROUGH THE WATER MEADOWS

A lovely walk runs through the water meadows by the River Itchen, passing **Winchester College** (*Kingsgate St., tel 01962-621209, closed Oct.–March & Sun. a.m. April–Sept.*), Britain's oldest school, founded in 1382; the Norman ruins of **Wolvesey Castle** (*College St., tel 01962-854766, closed Nov.–March*); and the nearby Stuart residence of the Bishop of Winchester, to reach the **Hospital of St. Cross** (*St. Cross Rd., tel 01962-851375, closed Sun.*).

St. Cross was founded in 1132 to provide shelter for 13 paupers and sustenance for 100 more. Travelers can still knock on the hatchway in the Porter's Lodge of the Beaufort Tower here to claim "Wayfarer's Dole"—a horn cup of ale and a cube of bread. At St. Cross and around the city, you may still see the hospital's Brethren (senior citizens) in their black-and-purple gowns marked with a silver cross. ■

**Winchester Cathedral, at the heart of the city, is an amalgam of every style of medieval English architecture from Norman to perpendicular.**

## Jane Austen's house

Jane Austen (1775–1817) lived with her mother and sister in a simple redbrick house (*tel 01420-83262, closed Mon.–Fri. Jan. & Feb.*) in Chawton village from 1809 until 1817. Here she revised *Sense and Sensibility* (1811) and *Pride and Prejudice* (1813), and wrote *Mansfield Park* (1814), *Emma* (1816), and *Persuasion* and *Northanger Abbey* (both published posthumously in 1817). The house is full of mementos: first editions, manuscripts, Jane's comb, portrait, and much else. ■

# Hampshire's rivers & coast

THE SOFT LANDSCAPE OF HAMPSHIRE—WATER MEADOWS
and valley pastures threaded by fast-flowing chalk streams, crooked
lanes, and straightbacked downs topped with beechwoods known as
hangers—is the very heart and spirit of the South Country.

This is a county where fishing is
taken seriously; fly-fishing for trout
in shallow rivers, particularly along
the Rivers Itchen and Test, is a popular pastime.

The downs north of the Test
between Overton and Whitchurch
are where Richard Adams set his
classic children's novel *Watership
Down* (1972). Watership Down
itself is reached by walking west for
a mile from White Hill on the B3051.

On Hampshire's south coast lies
**Portsmouth,** the Royal Navy's
home port during the centuries
that Britain ruled the waves. At
**Flagship Portsmouth** in the
Historic Dockyard you can visit
*Mary Rose,* Henry VIII's flagship,
which capsized in the Solent in
1545 and was raised in 1982, and
also see H.M.S. *Warrior,* a magnificently restored Victorian warship.
Nearby is Lord Horatio Nelson's
flagship H.M.S. *Victory,* on which
he was killed on October 21, 1805
at the Battle of Trafalgar.

Other must-see sites are the
**D-Day Museum** (*Clarence
Esplanade, tel 023-9282 7261*) in
Southsea, with its 272-foot
Overlord Embroidery depicting the
Allied landings in Normandy on
June 6, 1944, and **Charles
Dickens Birthplace Museum**
(*tel 023-9282 7261, closed
Oct.–Nov., 1 week in Dec. &
Jan.–March*) on Old Commercial
Road. ■

## Portsmouth

🅰 116 D2

**Visitor information**

✉ The Hard

☎ 023-9282 6722

## Flagship Portsmouth

✉ Historic Dockyard
(entry via Victory
Gate, College Rd.)

☎ 023-9286 1512

💲 Free entrance to
site; \$\$/\$\$\$ for
each ship; \$\$\$\$
combined ticket for
all 3 ships

## Isle of Wight

🅰 116 C1

**Visitor information**

✉ Isle of Wight
Tourism, Westridge
Centre, Brading Rd.,
Ryde

☎ 01983-813818

🕐 Closed Sat.–Sun.

---

## Isle of Wight

The diamond-shaped Isle of
Wight, separated from the
mainland by the Solent Channel, is
a small but distinct world apart.
Chief attractions are **Osborne
House** (*tel 01983-200022, closed
Nov.–March, unless by pre-booked
tour*), where Queen Victoria and
Prince Albert and their family
relaxed; **Carisbrooke Castle** (*tel
01983-523112*), where Charles I
was held from 1647 to 1648 after
the Civil War; and the colored
cliffs of Alum Bay and the tall
chalk blades of The Needles, both
out west. ■

---

**Nelson's flagship
H.M.S. *Victory*
was afloat for
150 years before
it was placed in
dry dock during
the 1920s. The
vessel has since
been restored to
its former glory.**

# Salisbury Cathedral

THERE IS NO MISTAKING SALISBURY CATHEDRAL; ITS PALE gray spire, at 404 feet the tallest in Britain, dominates the medieval city in its hollow among the hills. The views from the Eight Door Level at the base of the octagonal spire are lovely.

The cathedral, built in the Early English Gothic style between 1220 and 1258, is a remarkably unified piece of building work. Unlike most of the great cathedral churches, which took many decades if not centuries to complete and incorporated several consecutive eras of architectural fashion, Salisbury Cathedral was finished in fewer than 40 years.

Richard Poore, Bishop of Salisbury, founded it down in the water meadows by the River Avon after the Norman cathedral

settlement on the heights of Old Sarum (see p. 133) had to be abandoned in 1220. The church was built of chalky limestone quarried nearby at Chilmark, which gives it a silvery sheen in sunlight and a ghostly paleness under cloud.

As for that enormously tall and sturdy-looking spire—it must be one of the country's least solidly founded, for the cathedral foundations go down only four feet into the loose gravelly ground. The top of the spire is actually two feet five inches out of true.

**Salisbury**
◮ 116 C2
**Visitor information**
✉ Fish Row
☎ 01722-334956

**Salisbury Cathedral**
✉ The Close
☎ 01722-555121
⑤ $$

**The 404-foot spire of Salisbury Cathedral, its Chilmark limestone silvered by sunlight, stands reflected in the River Avon.**

### THE SALISBURY GIANT

In the days when guilds marched in procession on civic occasions, a wooden giant was proudly paraded by the merchant tailors, accompanied by a sword-bearer, mace-bearer, Morris dancers, and a hobby horse called Hob-Nob.

Ranks of saints adorn the west front of the cathedral, approached across a tranquil close. Inside, the inverted boat shape of the nave is bathed in a dim pinkish green light. The dark Purbeck marble pillars look too slender for their job—as, in fact, they are. Standing at the crossing and looking up, you can see how their burden of 6,400 tons of stone roof, tower, and spire has bowed them out of the perpendicular.

In the north aisle, under the tattered and faded colors of the Wiltshire Regiment, the cogged wheels and rotor arm of an ancient clock turn with a solemn, heavy ticking. It was built in 1386— and is the oldest working clock mechanism in Britain. Farther along is the 16th-century chantry chapel of Bishop Edmund Audley, a delicate stone box with intricate fan vaulting. Victorian medallions in the choir roof show scenes of medieval rural labor—peasants chopping wood, sowing seed, picking apples. In the south aisle is a 13th-century Tree of Jesse window (circa 1240).

**A modern-day version of the Salisbury Giant is paraded through the city during the St. George's Day festival.**

A stroll through the vaulted cloisters (added in 1263 to 1266, after the cathedral was built) brings you to the octagonal 13th-century chapter house. A big umbrella of vaulting ribs springs from a slender central pillar. Around the walls are lively carvings of the Genesis and Exodus stories. Here is kept one of only a handful of original copies of Magna Carta, the bill of rights reluctantly signed in 1215 by King John.

### IN THE CLOSE

The cathedral close is crammed with beautiful old buildings: the little red-brick Matron's College, built in 1682 for the widows of clergy; **Mompesson House** (NT, tel 01722-335659, closed Nov.– March & Thurs.–Fri. April–Oct.) of 1701, with its carved staircase, glass collection, and garden laid out with perennial borders, all arranged to give the flavor of 18th-century life in the close. The patched and crooked brick and flint of the 13th-century Wardrobe houses the **Salisbury Museum of the Royal Gloucestershire, Berkshire and Wiltshire Regiment** (tel 01722-419419, closed Mon., Feb.–March & Nov.). The Queen Anne facade on the 13th-century **Malmesbury House** and the **Bishop's Palace,** built at the same time as the cathedral, now housing the Cathedral School, are there, too.

### AROUND THE CITY

Salisbury is an excellent strolling and exploring town, centered on the pinnacled **Poultry Cross** on Silver Street. Medieval street names indicate former trades: Butcher Row, Fish Row, Salt Lane. Visit the upstairs display room in **Watsons** china shop on Queen Street to see wonderful 14th-century woodwork. Seek out **St. Thomas's Church** at the turn of High Street, with its carved angel roofs of 1450 and medieval frescoes. Enjoy the creaky old **Haunch of Venison** pub on Minster Street, where in a barred recess they keep a grisly relic—the severed hand of an 18th-century gambler, and the playing cards it was holding when discovered. ■

# Around Salisbury

THE CITY OF SALISBURY LIES IN A HOLLOW, WITH THE Wiltshire countryside undulating in all directions. Tucked into this rolling, chalky landscape are fine country houses, charming small villages, and dozens of prehistoric monuments.

## OLD SARUM

Two miles north of Salisbury rises the flat-topped hill of Old Sarum, its sides corrugated with earthen ramparts. The hilltop is a wonderful spot to look down on Salisbury and its cathedral, established near the river when the former hilltop settlement was abandoned around 1220.

Old Sarum, high above the surrounding country, was always a valuable lookout point. Iron Age tribesmen first fortified Old Sarum; then the Romans strengthened the ramparts of Sorviodunum and ran their Portway road to it from the settlement at Silchester, 40 miles away to the northeast.

The Saxons were here, too, calling it Searoburgh or "dry town," for there was very little water at hand. A cramped, unsanitary township grew up around the cathedral that the Normans completed at Old Sarum in 1092, but lack of water and space to expand drove the inhabitants down to the valley two centuries later, to start again.

## WILTON HOUSE

Just west of Salisbury, Wilton House is a 17th-century Palladian mansion, adapted by Inigo Jones from a Tudor house that was itself a conversion of a convent dissolved at the Reformation. Pride of the house are the Single Cube Room (30 feet in length, width, and height) and the Double Cube Room (same width and height, but 60 feet long) with their painted and gilded plasterwork ceilings, and fine furniture by Chippendale and William Kent (1685–1748).

## LACOCK

In the northwest of Wiltshire, Lacock is a perfectly preserved National Trust village of gray stone houses, where time has stopped in the 18th century. At **Lacock Abbey** you can see the oriel window from which William Henry Fox Talbot took the world's first photograph in 1835. Adjacent to the Abbey a Tudor barn houses the **Fox Talbot Museum**. ∎

**Old Sarum**

🔺 116 C2
☎ 01722-335398
$ $

**Wilton House**

🔺 116 C2
✉ Wilton
☎ 01722-746720
🕐 Closed late Oct.–
   Easter
$ $$$

**Lacock Abbey & Fox Talbot Museum**

🔺 116 B3
✉ Lacock
☎ Abbey: 01249-
   730227, Museum:
   01249-730459
🕐 Abbey: closed
   Nov.–late March &
   Tues. late March–Oct.
   Grounds: closed late
   Oct.–late Feb.
   Museum: closed
   Nov.–Feb.
$ $$

**Colorful flowers adorn the half-timbered cottages in Lacock village, some of which date to the 13th century.**

# Stonehenge

**Stonehenge**

🗺 116 C3

✉ 10 miles north of
Salisbury, 2 miles
west of Amesbury

☎ 01980-624715

💲 $$

**Avebury**

🗺 116 C3

**Visitor information**

✉ Avebury Chapel
Centre, Green Street

☎ 01672-539425

THERE ARE PROBLEMS WITH STONEHENGE—NOT JUST THE age-old problems of interpreting Europe's best known ancient site, but modern problems of security and overwhelming visitor numbers. These mean that, at the time of writing, access to the stones themselves is forbidden. Visitors must keep outside a fence that draws a wide circle around the monument. There's an inadequate interpretive center, and the whole site is cut across by two fast, noisy roads. All these difficulties are soon to be addressed, but, at present, the ambience is not ideal.

None of this, however, should dissuade you from making a pilgrimage to this astonishing structure, whose impact must strike anyone with an ounce of imagination. The doorwaylike silhouettes of Stonehenge's great trilithons, outlined against the sky, are as challenging to the intellect as they have ever been, still provoking questions of when, how, and why.

The "when" of Stonehenge has been reasonably accurately pinned down. In about 2950 B.C. a circular bank was constructed and around 400 years later a double circle of 80 bluestones—dolerite stones carried from the Preseli Hills in southwest Wales, some of them up to 10 feet high—was erected inside the bank. Later the bluestones were rearranged, and sarsen

# Wiltshire's ancient monuments

Two ancient, long-distance trackways cross Wiltshire. One, the well-marked Ridgeway, starts on Overton Hill a mile east of Avebury and goes 85 miles northeast to join the Icknield Way on Ivinghoe Beacon (see p. 107). The other, the even more ancient Harroway—which may be over 6,000 years old—passes Stonehenge.

A notable group of monuments lies around **Avebury** (*NT, tel 01672-539250*), north of Salisbury Plain. From the early Bronze Age stone circle, made up of around a hundred sarsen stones, a ceremonial avenue of standing stones leads to Overton Hill.

Just south of the village are **West Kennet Long Barrow,** the largest chambered communal tomb in England, built around 3250 B.C.;

and enigmatic flat-topped **Silbury Hill,** 130 feet high and 200 yards around the base, constructed around 2600 B.C. for an unknown purpose. As much as can be explained is superbly dealt with in the **Alexander Keiller Museum** in Avebury (*tel 01672-539250*). ■

**Stonehenge (above) appears even more mysterious as sunlight streams through the stones on a winter day.**

**The monumental entrance to West Kennet Long Barrow (above right) leads to a series of stone-lined tomb rooms.**

("saracen" or alien) stones from the Marlborough Downs were put up instead, much as they stand today, in the form of trilithons—pairs of upright stones 14 feet high, joined together by a third laid on top like the lintel of a doorway and held in place with a mortise and tenon joint. An outer ring of 25 of these was set up, enclosing an inner horseshoe shape of five more trilithons. Later on, some of the dismantled bluestones were erected again between the outer and inner trilithons, and the largest bluestone—these days known as the Altar Stone—was placed at the center of the horseshoe. After about 1600 B.C., no further alterations were carried out.

As for how Bronze Age men managed to transport, shape, and erect such enormous stones—in particular the bluestones, which traveled 200 miles—tremendous

organization and disposition of manpower would have been needed. But if the imperative was strong enough, Bronze Age leaders did wield enough authority, and the necessary technology of rafts, rollers, and levers was advanced enough to carry out what must have been decades worth of planning and effort.

Which begs the question—"why?" Once all the New Age theories have been set aside, all that is known for sure is that on Midsummer's Day (June 21) the sun, when viewed from the Altar Stone in the center of the structure, is seen to rise directly over the Heel Stone, 256 feet away at the far end of what now remains of an earthwork avenue. Stonehenge may have been some kind of observatory for seasonal timekeeping; but whether that was its only function, no one can say. ■

# Hardy's Dorset

In Dorset, the westernmost of the South Country counties, the figure of Thomas Hardy (1840–1928) casts a long shadow. What Sir Walter Scott is to the Scottish Lowlands, or William Wordsworth to the Lake District, Hardy is to Dorset. The area of southwest England that he immortalized in his "Wessex novels" covers parts of Hampshire, Berkshire, Oxfordshire, Wiltshire, Somerset, Devon, and Cornwall; but the heart of the region, called by Hardy "South Wessex," is his native county of Dorset.

## Immortalized in print

Many places in Dorset are central to Hardy's life and writing. He was born on June 2, 1840, in a thatched cottage—now called **Hardy's Cottage,** *(NT, tel 01305-262366, closed Nov.–early April & Tues.–Wed. early April–Oct.)* at Higher Bockhampton, a hamlet near the county town of Dorchester. While living at his birthplace, Hardy wrote *Under the Greenwood Tree* (1872) and *Far from the Madding Crowd* (1874). The house features as Tranter Dewy's house in *Under the Greenwood Tree,* in which Higher and Lower Bockhampton and neighboring Stinsford are amalgamated to form "Mellstock."

In Stinsford churchyard, Hardy's heart is buried in the grave of his first wife, Emma Gifford (died 1912), whom he mourned all the more bitterly for having drifted into a cold relationship with her in life. There is a stained-glass window memorial to Hardy in the church, of which he wrote:

> On afternoons of drowsy calm
> We stood in the panelled pew
> Singing one-voiced a Tate-and-Brady psalm
> To the tune of "Cambridge New."
>
> We watched the elms, we watched the rooks,
> The clouds upon the breeze,
> Between the whiles of glancing at our books,
> And swaying like the trees.

**Thomas Hardy (right) and the pretty cottage and gardens at Higher Bockhampton that were his home (below)**

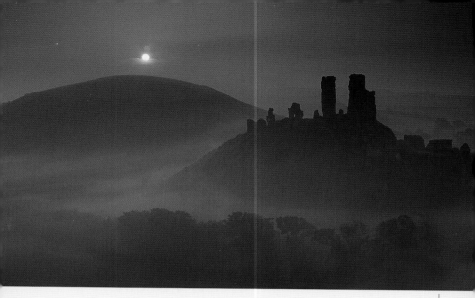

**Corfe Castle in Dorset repelled 600 attackers during the Civil War before it was ruined.**

The heathland south of here, much of it nowadays planted with conifers, is Hardy's somber "Egdon Heath," the ruling feature of *The Return of the Native* (1878).

Three miles east along the A35 is Puddletown, where Hardy's grandfather would play his bass viol in the church orchestra and at village dances. Puddletown was "Weatherbury" in *Far from the Madding Crowd*. Bathsheba Everdene's farmhouse, "Weatherbury Farm," where Gabriel Oak had to endure the sight of Bathsheba married to Sergeant Troy, was probably modeled on handsome Tudor Waterstone Manor, on the B3142 west of Puddletown.

Bere Regis, six miles east of Puddletown, was "Kingsbere-sub-Greenhill" in *Tess of the D'Urbervilles* (1891). In its Saxon church you can see the Turberville tombs, and their lion rampant crest in a 15th-century window.

South of here the River Frome runs east through a lush valley, Tess's "Valley of the Great Dairies." Woolbridge Manor, in the village of Wool on the A352, was transformed by Hardy into "Wellbridge Manor house," where Tess and Angel Clare had their strange, lonely wedding night.

Cranborne Chase—"The Chase," where caddish Alec D'Urberville had his way with Tess—lies off the A354 about 15 miles northeast of Puddletown.

**Other attractions**

One site not to miss is **Max Gate** *(NT, tel 01305-262538, closed late Sept.–early April, Tues. & Thurs.–Sat. early April–late Sept.)* on Arlington Avenue, **Dorchester** *(visitor information, Antelope Walk, tel 01305-267992)*— Hardy's home from 1885 until his death, and where he wrote all his great and late poetry.

Dorset has some wonderful walks among its chalk downs and wooded valleys, and some dramatic coastal scenery—particularly east of the Georgian resort of **Weymouth** *(visitor information, Kings Statue, The Esplanade, tel 01305-785747)*, where the semicircular Lulworth Cove and the cliff-flanked promontory of St. Aldhelm's Head can be enjoyed from the Dorset Coast Path.

Other coast sites include **Lyme Regis** *(visitor information, Church St., tel 01297-442138)* with its fossil beach, ancient massive Cobb breakwater, and Undercliff wilderness (John Fowles's *The French Lieutenant's Woman* was set here); the medieval **Swannery** *(New Barn Rd., tel 01305-871858, closed late Oct.–mid-March)* and the **Sub Tropical Gardens** *(Bullers Way, tel 01305-871387)* at **Abbotsbury;** and oddball **Swanage** *(visitor information, Shore Rd., tel 01929-422885)*, crammed with architectural rarities salvaged by local stonemason George Burt from the Victorian rebuilding of London. ■

# New Forest

EAST OF DORSET'S SPRAWLING SEASIDE RESORT OF
Bournemouth, just across the border into Hampshire, lies the New
Forest, a real forest in the traditional sense of being an interrelated
patchwork of woodland, farmland, common land, and small settlements. At nearly 150 square miles, this is one of the largest stretches
of open, undeveloped country in England.

**New Forest
Museum
& Visitor Centre**

116 C2

High St., Lyndhurst

Museum: 023-8028
3914; Visitor Centre:
023-8028 2269

$$

**Ambiguously
named (the New
Forest is neither
new nor wholly a
forest), this
enclosure of heath
and woodland is
particularly
famous for its
wild ponies.**

In spite of its name, the New Forest
is the oldest of the royal hunting
forests, planted well before the
Norman Conquest. The second
Norman king of England, William
Rufus, was killed while hunting
here on August 2, 1100, transfixed
by an arrow fired by his compan-
ion, Walter Tyrrell.

### ANCIENT CUSTOMS

The many quirky customs and
laws of the New Forest have more
to do with tradition these days than
with the administration of justice.
But they were serious enough back
in the Middle Ages, when to disturb
one of the king's deer carried a
penalty of blinding, to shoot at one
meant losing both hands, and to
kill one condemned the poacher to
death. In spite of the harsh conse-
quences of crossing the king, the
inhabitants or "commoners" of the
Forest applied ongoing pressure to

be allowed to collect wood and
graze their animals. A Verderers
Court has adjudicated on Forest
law for centuries, and still sits; its
green-jacketed "agisters" (agents)
patrol on horseback.

Within the mosaic of habitats
that thrive across the New Forest
are woodland, wetland, ponds and
streams, heaths, and farmland. The
commoners exercise their historic
rights of turbary (peat cutting) and
estover (firewood collecting), as
well as the autumnal mast when
pigs are permitted to forage for
acorns and beechnuts.

### WILDLIFE

The New Forest is a superb wildlife
refuge for deer, foxes, birds,
amphibians, and butterflies, as well
as for the shaggy and appealing
New Forest ponies (descended from
Spanish horses shipwrecked during
the 1588 Armada, some claim). ■

The West Country—lush cider orchards and cattle pastures of Somerset; Devon's cream teas and thatched cottages; quintessential English seaside in the sandy bays and rocky coves of Cornwall—all spiced with Arthurian legends.

# The West Country

Introduction & map 140–41
Exeter & around 142–43
North Devon coast 144
Plymouth & around 145
Cornwall 146–47
Glastonbury & the
    Somerset Levels 150
Wells 151
Bristol 152
Bath 153
A walk around Bath 154–55
Around Bath 156
Great country houses 157
More places to visit in the
    West Country 158
Hotels & restaurants in the West
    Country 353–58

**Fisherman and boats**

# The West Country

THE LONG PENINSULA THAT FORMS THE SOUTHWESTERN CORNER OF Britain is a land of dairy pastures, moors, woodlands, and gentle hills. The coasts of these West Country counties of Somerset, Devon, and Cornwall grow sharper teeth the farther south and west you venture. Down in the western toetip of Cornwall there are craggy headlands and storm-carved cliffs to rival anything elsewhere in England.

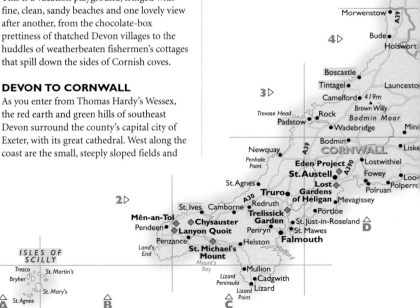

**Locals gather at a pub in St. Ives, Cornwall, to chat and reminisce.**

This is a vacation playground, fringed with fine, clean, sandy beaches and one lovely view after another, from the chocolate-box prettiness of thatched Devon villages to the huddles of weatherbeaten fishermen's cottages that spill down the sides of Cornish coves.

## DEVON TO CORNWALL

As you enter from Thomas Hardy's Wessex, the red earth and green hills of southeast Devon surround the county's capital city of Exeter, with its great cathedral. West along the coast are the small, steeply sloped fields and

woods of the South Hams, and then the city of Plymouth, from which the Pilgrim Fathers set out for the New World in 1620.

Next you cross the River Tamar, the boundary of the civilized world for all right-thinking Cornishmen. The south coast of Cornwall, all high headlands and sandy bays, leads west to the wild and little-frequented Lizard Peninsula, and finally to the rock stacks of Land's End.

Now comes the far bleaker north coast of Cornwall, a 100-mile stretch of granite cliffs and sand-floored, rocky coves relieved by appealing little towns such as St. Ives, Padstow, and Tintagel. Inland are windswept uplands dotted with ancient stone monuments, and

with the shafts and pumping houses of the county's now defunct tin-mining industry.

## SOMERSET & AVON

Three great moors lie at the heart of the southwest peninsula—Bodmin, Dartmoor, and Exmoor. From Exmoor you enter Somerset, the county of cider drinkers and dairy farmers, moving north to the West Country's great maritime city of Bristol, and finally to Bath and its graceful Georgian buildings of cream-colored stone. ■

# Exeter & around

**Exeter**
🅰 141 F3
**Visitor information**
✉ Civic Centre,
   Paris St.
☎ 01392-265700
🕐 Closed Sun. in
   winter

**Exeter Cathedral**
✉ The Close
☎ 01392-214219
💲 Donation

ALTHOUGH BEST KNOWN FOR ITS CATHEDRAL, THE CITY of Exeter has some nice surprises tucked away, including a creepy and fascinating walk beneath the streets through the city's medieval water conduits. Exeter Cathedral, one of the great church buildings of Britain, dominates the close at the heart of the city, its massive bulk somehow emphasized by the lack of a commanding central tower. Two stubby, square Norman towers crown the transepts. The appearance of a crouched beast is enhanced by the flying buttresses that spring out and down to the ground like slender legs.

## THE CLOSE

In the cathedral close are a number of fine buildings. The most striking of these is the late Tudor Mol's Coffee House, dated 1596 on its lion-and-dragon coat of arms of Elizabeth I. Mol's is a handsome timber-framed house with curly gables and a railed gallery high on the third story. A great bay window checkered with panes fills the whole width of the first floor. ■

### THE CATHEDRAL & ITS INTERIOR

The cathedral was begun by the Normans between 1112 and 1206, but most of it was built from around 1270 until the mid-14th century. Of this era are the seated statues, ranked in their hundreds in three tiers, that decorate the pale stone west front: monarchs and prelates, saints and sages, with Christ and his Apostles taking pride of place in the center.

Inside, the eye is drawn immedi-ately up the length of the Purbeck marble pillars to what is reckoned to be the world's longest continu-ous stretch of Gothic vaulting, a run of over 300 feet that covers both nave and choir. Carved bosses, picked out in gold and bright col-ors, stud the vaulting.

A big 15th-century astronomical clock in the north transept traces the cycles of the sun and moon. A great screen, erected in 1325, guards the choir with its battered but still vigor-ous early medieval misericords and

**Beyond the sculptured west front of Exeter Cathedral (among the finest in the country) is the historic Mol's Coffee House.**

its great Bishop's Throne, almost 60 feet high and carved of oak in 1312. Near the entrance to the Lady Chapel is a beautiful fresco of the Coronation of the Virgin Mary, painted in early Tudor times, about 40 years before the Reformation.

### CITY SIGHTS

The Benedictine **St. Nicholas Priory** (*The Mint, off Fore St., tel 01392-271732, open Mon., Wed., & Sat. p.m. Easter–Oct.*) in the Mint has a Norman undercroft and kitchens, a Great Hall from about 1400 with a fine timber roof, and some striking plasterwork ceilings.

Medieval wool paid for the handsome sandstone **Tuckers Hall** (*Fore St., tel 01392-412348, call for hours*) in the 15th century for the newly founded Guild of Weavers, Fullers, and Shearmen.

An even older **Guildhall** (*High St., tel 01392-665500, call for hours*) stands on the pedestrianized High Street: This magnificent building has a Tudor upper story propped on granite pillars; but the oldest part dates from 1330, and the chamber where the council meets is at least 600 years old. And for a look right back into Exeter's distant history, there are sections of a third-century Roman city wall to admire on the west side of Southernhay, in Northernhay, and in Rougemont Gardens.

Down on the Quay is a collection of warehouses and industrial buildings dating from the 17th and 19th centuries, now used for different purposes such as antiques centers, craft shops, offices, and excellent pubs and restaurants.

### OUT OF TOWN

Seventeen miles along the A30 is **Honiton,** famous for producing delicate lace. On the Georgian High Street is the **Allhallows Museum** (*tel 01404-44966, closed late Oct.– March & Sun. March–late Oct.*), where lacemaking is occasionally demonstrated, and the **Honiton Lace Shop** (*44 High St., tel 01404-42416*), where you can buy lace made locally.

Another enjoyable venue close to Exeter is the highly eccentric, 16-sided house called **A La Ronde** (*NT, Summer Ln., Exmouth, tel 01395-265514, closed Nov.–March & Fri.–Sat. April–Oct.*). It was built in 1796 by cousins Jane and Mary Parminter, and decorated with seashells, feathers, and seaweed.

South, on the coast, the small Regency resort of **Sidmouth** hosts a celebrated International Festival of Folk Arts in early August. ∎

**Pretty Sidmouth beach, with fishing boats lining the shore, is flanked by spectacular red cliffs.**

**Sidmouth**
⬛ 141 F3
**Visitor information**
✉ Ham Ln.
☎ 01395-516441
🕐 Closed Sun. Nov.–Feb.

# North Devon coast

THE CLIFFS OF THE NORTH DEVON COAST ARE BEAUTIFULLY rounded, like a succession of green knees presented to the ever widening Bristol Channel. At their feet are pebbly beaches, which become sandier and better for swimming the farther west you go.

**Porlock**
⚠ 141 F5
**Visitor information**
✉ West End, High St.
☎ 01643-863150

**Lynton**
⚠ 141 E5
**Visitor information**
✉ Town Hall, Lee Rd.
☎ 01598-752225

**Dunster** and **Porlock** are, in fact, in Somerset, but these two highly attractive villages, each set a little way inland, belong in character and spirit to this region.

Dunster has a Norman castle, home of the Luttrell family from 1376 until the late 1990s, and its octagonal **Yarn Market** of 1609, where local cloth was once sold, is the centerpiece of its sloping main street. Porlock's thatched houses huddle under steep hills.

eccentric, cramped **Lyn and Exmoor Museum** (*Market St., closed Sat.*), while in the **Exmoor National Park Visitor Centre** (*tel 01598-752509, closed Nov.–March*) down on Lynmouth's Esplanade an exhibition tells the story of an epic overland lifeboat launch. This coast can be deadly dangerous in gale conditions. Lynmouth itself suffered a weather-related tragedy on August 15, 1952, when 34 people were drowned by floodwater rushing downriver.

A beautiful, well-marked cliff walk runs west from Lynton for a couple of miles through the Valley of Rocks.

## WEST OF LYNTON

Farther west on a sandy beach lies the Victorian seaside resort of **Ilfracombe** (*visitor information, The Promenade, tel 01271-863001*). Then the coast turns a sharp corner and runs south, by way of superb sands at **Woolacombe** and a famous surfing bay at **Croyde,** to pass the sand dune nature reserve of **Braunton Burrows** before reaching the great twin estuary of the Rivers Taw and Torridge.

Here are the neighboring towns of **Barnstaple** (*visitor information, 36 Boutport St., tel 01271-375000*) and **Bideford** (*visitor information, The Quay, Kingsley Rd., tel 01237-477676*), with their ancient bridges and narrow byways. Beyond lies **Clovelly,** picturesquely packed around a precipitous cobbled street descending the cliffs; cars are not allowed. ■

**Idyllically set in a gap in the cliffs, Clovelly, with its semicircular little harbor, is one of a few safe havens on the North Devon coast.**

Beyond here, notoriously steep roads switchback westward to **Lynton,** perched on a plateau 500 feet above its sister village of **Lynmouth.** A rattly but safe cliff railway, installed in 1890 and worked by the weight of water, connects the two. Lynton contains the

# Plymouth & around

**Plymouth**
🅜 141 E2
**Visitor information**
✉ 9 The Barbican
☎ 01752-304849

**Buckland Abbey**
🅜 141 E2
✉ ¼ mile south of
Yelverton
☎ 01822-853607
🕐 Closed Thurs.
April–Oct. &
Mon.–Fri.
Nov.–March
💲 $$; grounds only $

ON JULY 31, 1588, THE SEA CAPTAINS, DRAKE, FROBISHER, and Hawkins sailed out from the city of Plymouth to challenge and beat the ships of the Spanish Armada. It was from Plymouth that the Pilgrim Fathers set out for the New World in 1620; and Capt. James Cook embarked here in 1772 at the start of his three-year voyage of discovery through the South Seas. Sir Francis Chichester set sail from Plymouth in 1966 on his pioneering solo sailing voyage around the world, for which he was knighted.

Much of Britain's long and distinguished seafaring story is wrapped up in this historic seaport. Along **Plymouth Hoe,** a broad park with a raised promenade for strolling, is Sir Francis Drake's statue; the green where, although the Spanish galleons had already been sighted, he insisted on finishing his game of bowls; and the leonine Armada monument. The harbor is guarded by the grand **Royal Citadel** (*Marsh Mills Tourist Information Centre, 01752-266030*), built between 1666 and 1670 on the orders of Charles II. In the eastern part of the harbor is the excellent **National Marine Aquarium** (*Rope Walk, Coxside, tel 01752-600301, open daily*).

Opposite the aquarium you'll find the **Mayflower Steps,** a simple arch monument where the imagination pictures the Pilgrims setting off. On August 5, 1620, the Puritan adventurers left Southampton in two ships, *Speedwell* and *Mayflower*.

However, bad weather forced them into Plymouth Sound where they abandoned the storm-damaged *Speedwell,* and set sail for the New World from Sutton Pool, Plymouth, on September 6—102 souls packed into the tiny *Mayflower*.

**NEARBY ATTRACTIONS**
These include the hands-on industrial museum at **Morwellham Quay** (*tel 01822-832766*), north off the A390; **Buckland Abbey** (NT), just north of Plymouth, Drake's home from 1581 to 1596; the cobbled quays and tight streets of **Dartmouth** (*visitor information, Mayors Ave., tel 01803-834224*) east of the city via the A3, the A385, and Totnes; and the preposterous but delightful art deco **Burgh Island Hotel** (*tel 01548-810514*) enjoyed by Noël Coward, Agatha Christie, and the Duke of Windsor—on tidal Burgh Island, off Bigbury-on-Sea near Kingsbridge. ■

**Smeaton's Tower is the third Eddystone Lighthouse to have been built. It was reassembled on Plymouth Hoe in the 1880s. Climb the stairs for a great view over the Hoe.**

## Trelissick Garden

- 140 C2
- Feock
- 01872-862090
- $$

## St. Michael's Mount

- 140 C2
- Marazion
- 01736-710507
- Closed Nov.–March;
  Sat. Sept.–late June
- $$

Pinnacles and stacks of granite mark Land's End, mainland Britain's most south-westerly point.

# Cornwall

GEOGRAPHICALLY ISOLATED FROM THE REST OF THE country at the wildest end of the westernmost peninsula, the self-contained Celts of Cornwall nurtured their own language until 200 years ago, their working tradition of mineral mining until 1998, and their livelihood through sea fishing up until the present day. Visitors return to Cornwall year after year to enjoy the clean seas and beaches, the cave-burrowed cliffs, the spectacularly sited fishing villages, and the narrow flowery lanes.

## FISHING VILLAGES

Thirty miles west of Plymouth lies **Polperro,** a classic Cornish fishing village of steep narrow streets; from the harbor, footpaths lead west over 400-foot cliffs to superb, lonely beaches. Narrow roads shadow the paths to **Fowey** (*visitor information, Post Office, 4 Custom Hill House, tel 01726-833616*), a charming little gray stone town set on a winding estuary; take the foot-ferry

across to Bodinnick and wander along the cliffs, returning by ferry from Polruan.

Then head west again to reach St. Austell, surrounded by the "Cornish Alps," white mountains of china-clay waste. From the B3272 St. Austell–Mevagissey road, brown signs direct you to the **Lost Gardens of Heligan** (*Pentewan, tel 01726-845100, open daily*), a most extraordinary project. Since 1991 the

gardens developed by the Tremayne family over 300 years, subsequently overgrown and forgotten, have been wonderfully restored. Equally striking and ambitious is the nearby **Eden Project** *(Bodelva, signed from the main roads, tel 01726-811911, open daily)*, where exotic climates and vegetation are reproduced inside enormous "biomes" in an old slate quarry.

## DOWN TO LAND'S END

South of **Truro** *(visitor information, Boscawen St., tel 01872-274555)*, capital city of Cornwall, the A3078 approaches **St. Just-in-Roseland,** where the little Norman church in its precipitous graveyard looks across the thickly wooded Fal Estuary. Cross by the thrice-hourly King Harry Ferry to Feock, to visit **Trelissick Garden** (NT), where Mediterranean flowers crowd tree-shaded paths by the river. Pendennis and St. Mawes Castles, opposite each other across the estuary, were built by Henry VIII against the threat of French invasion.

Now comes the winding, secluded River Helford, where Daphne du Maurier (see p. 148) hid her dashing pirate lover in *Frenchman's Creek*, and south of it the **Lizard Peninsula,** which surprisingly few visitors bother to explore. Drink strong home-brewed Spingo beer in the Blue Anchor *(50 Coinagehall St.)* at **Helston** *(visitor information, 79 Meneage St., tel 01326-565431, closed Sun.)*, where in early May the famous Furry Dance winds in and out of the houses. Visit **Lizard Village** on the tip of the peninsula to buy polished green, red, and white serpentine rock, and walk out to **Kynance Cove** (NT) to see it in the cliffs.

**St. Michael's Mount** (NT), a rocky isle in the sea crowned by a Norman abbey, a fort, and a grand house, is reached from Marazion by causeway across the sands at low tide, and by boat *(summer only)* at high water.

Out at **Land's End** avoid the tacky "Experience" and use the coastal footpath to enjoy the stirring views.

## NORTH COAST

Cornwall's north coast is rugged and exposed. On the moors at this western end are ancient relics to make you gasp: **Chysauster Ancient Village;** the Bronze Age burial chamber of **Lanyon Quoit;** and the holed stone of **Mên-an-Tol** near Morvah.

Busy **St. Ives** *(visitor information, Guildhall, Street-an-Pol, tel 01736-796297)* has superb galleries and museums: sculptor Dame Barbara Hepworth (1903–1975) lived here, and her house and garden on Barnoon Hill, packed with her work, form the **Barbara Hepworth Museum and Sculpture Garden;** Bernard Leach's (1887–1979) pottery *(closed Sun.)* is on the western edge of town in Higher Stennack; and a branch of the **Tate Gallery** *(tel 01736-796226, closed Mon. Nov.–Feb.)* on Porthmeor Beach.

At **Padstow** *(visitor information, North Quay, tel 01841-533449)*, on May Day, two fierce Obby Osses (men dressed as horse-faced beasts) dance through jam-packed streets. Commercialized **Tintagel,** higher up the coast, claims its romantic castle is King Arthur's birthplace. **Boscastle** *(visitor information, Cobweb Car Park, tel 01840-250010)*, 5 miles north, is a beautifully preserved village in a narrow cleft of the cliffs. ∎

**Chysauster Ancient Village**
- 🅰 140 C2
- ✉ 2½ miles northwest of Gulval, off B3311
- ☎ 01831-757934
- 🕐 Closed Nov.–March
- 💲 $

**Barbara Hepworth Museum and Sculpture Garden**
- ☎ 01736-796226
- ✉ Barnoon Hill, St. Ives
- 🕐 Closed Mon. (except bank holidays) Sept.–May
- 💲 $$

**Padstow's Obby Oss festival, celebrating the defeat of winter, is believed to be among the oldest dance festivals in Europe.**

# West Country moorland

At the heart of the West Country lie three extensive tracts of moorland. Cornwall's Bodmin Moor is known to few. Devon possesses warm sandstone Exmoor in the north, while in the south of the county broods grim, granite-bedded Dartmoor, famous for fogs and wild legends.

## Bodmin Moor

Of the three great West Country moors, Bodmin *(Map 140 D3, Bodmin tourist information, Shire House, Mount Folly Sq., tel 01208-76616)*, some 15 miles in diameter, is certainly the least well known, although it is sliced in two by the busy A30, traveled every year by millions of vacationers.

Closely associated with the moor is Dame Daphne du Maurier's smuggling romance, *Jamaica Inn,* published in 1936. Du Maurier (1907–1989) was inspired by yarns spun to her when she stayed on Bodmin Moor in 1930 at the pub called Jamaica Inn—no longer lonely and evocative in its location above the roaring A30, but still worth a stop for its grim, slate-hung aspect and atmospheric interior. From here it is only a short walk south to the allegedly bottomless Dozmary Pool, into which Sir Bedevere flung Excalibur after taking the unbreakable sword from the mortally wounded King Arthur. Five miles east of Dozmary Pool stand The Hurlers, three stone circles dating from 2200–1400 B.C., which, stories say, are impious locals turned to stone for playing hurling games on the Sabbath. Nearby is the Cheesewring, a granite tor 30 feet high made of slabs of rock undercut by wind and rain. A couple of miles south is Trethevy Quoit, an ancient burial chamber with a giant capstone poised on massive stones.

Signposted off the A39 along the northern edge of Bodmin Moor, just north of Camelford,

**The Cheesewring (left) on Bodmin Moor is a granite stack weathered by wind and rain. Dartmoor (below) demands to be explored to see features like stone circles.**

**Exmoor is an area of high, wild moorland, striped by drystone walls.**

is the highest point of the moor and Cornwall, the 1,377-foot hummock of Brown Willy. A mile-long footpath connects the peak with neighboring Rough Tor (1,311 feet).

### Dartmoor

**Dartmoor National Park** *(Map 141 E3, Park Authority Headquarters, Parke, Haytor Rd., Bovey Tracy, tel 01626-832093)* covering over 300 square miles of granite tors, heathery cleaves (valleys), and lonely bogs, lies in a great ragged oval to the northeast of Plymouth.

From Postbridge on the B3212, you can walk north along the River East Dart to find the stone circles called the Grey Wethers.

Farther east, at Manaton, there are beautiful walks along the wooded cleft of the River Bovey; while on the western fringe of the moor a dramatic footpath winds deep down in the bottom of Lydford Gorge.

### Exmoor

The third moor, Devon's light and airy **Exmoor National Park** *(Map 141 E5, Park Authority Headquarters, Exmoor House,*

*Dulverton, Somerset, tel 01398-323665),* has none of Dartmoor's oppressive grimness. The warmth of the underlying sandstone seems to pervade the moor, and the combes (wooded valleys) cut deep grooves in the upland flanks. England's largest herd of wild red deer roams freely here. The B3223 and B3224 cut across Exmoor, and from these there are a number of very well-marked walks.

Other celebrated Exmoor locations are scattered around the edges of the moor: **Arlington Court** *(NT, 7 miles northeast of Barnstaple, tel 01271-850296, closed Nov.–March & Sat. April–Oct.)* in the west, with walks through lovely wooded grounds; Dunkery Hill in the north, Exmoor's highest point at 1,703 feet; and the medieval clapperbridge of Tarr Steps, northwest of Dulverton.

The country of R.D. Blackmore's (1825–1900) romantic novel, *Lorna Doone* (1869), lies between Watersmeet and Dunkery. Here is Doone Valley itself (Lank Combe off Badgworthy Water) and St. Mary's Church at Oare, where the jealous Carver Doone shot Lorna during her wedding. ■

# Glastonbury
# & the Somerset Levels

**Glastonbury**

🗺 141 G5

**Visitor information**

✉ The Tribunal,
9 High St.

☎ 01458-832954 or
01458-832949

**Somerset Rural
Life Museum**

✉ Chilkwell St.

☎ 01458-831197

🕐 Closed Mon., also
Sun. Nov.–Easter

💲 $/$$

THE SOMERSET LEVELS—500 SQUARE MILES OF FLATLAND between the Quantock and Mendip Hills—were marshy sea washes until medieval monks built flood defenses and reclaimed them. Straight, narrow roads are lined with pollarded willows, fields are bounded by watercourses called rhynes (pronounced REENS) rather than by hedges, and little knolls protrude from the peat tableland.

**Glastonbury Tor,** just outside Glastonbury, is the best known Levels knoll. Legend, myth, and history cluster thickly around this sleeping-dragon shape, topped by its 14th-century church tower. Some say that King Arthur and his knights lie sleeping under the tor; others assert that the "once and future king" and his tragic, star-crossed queen Guinevere are buried in the sparse but beautiful ruins of **Glastonbury Abbey** (*Magdalene St., tel 01458-832267).*

Saxon monarchs were buried here, two Edmunds and an Edgar, for Glastonbury is the earliest Christian foundation in England. There is a lovely late Norman Lady Chapel on the site of a wattle-and-daub church (burned down in 1184), said to have been built by Joseph of Arimathea.

Nearby is the 14th-century **Abbot's Kitchen** with its octagonal roof, and the **Somerset Rural Life Museum** is housed in the 14th-century Abbey Barn. ■

Legends of King Arthur and other heroes cluster round the strange hummock of Glastonbury Tor with its landmark tower, nowadays a focus for New Age pilgrims.

## Cidermaking

There is sweet, clear, fizzy cider for the commercial market, and then there is scrumpy. The national drink of Somerset is cloudy, sharp, and extraordinarily heady. Ask in a pub or farmyard the whereabouts of the local scrumpy shed; then go and watch apple juice being squeezed by ancient screw presses out of a "cheese" of straw and pomace. Confused? Don't fret—enjoy the matured result of the cidermaker's labor, and lay the rest of the day in the lap of the apple god. ■

# Wells

WELLS IS ENGLAND'S SMALLEST CITY, THOUGH WITH MORE
an air of a small market town. It lies at the foot of the Mendip Hills,
its medieval streets dominated by its great Gothic cathedral. The
limestone hills offer several attractions west of the city—the caves at
Wookey Hole and Cheddar, a beautiful nature trail at Ebbor Gorge
(NT), and the West Mendip Way footpath along the spine of the hills.

**Wells**

  141 G5

**Visitor information**

✉ Town Hall, Market
Place

☎ 01749-672552

**Wookey Hole
Caves**

 141 G5

✉ Wookey Hole, 2
miles northwest of
Wells

☎ 01749-672243

$ $$$

**Cheddar Caves &
Gorge**

 141 G5

✉ Cheddar, 8 miles
northwest of Wells

☎ 01934-742343

$ $$$

## WELLS CATHEDRAL

Approaching Wells Cathedral *(tel
01749-674483)* either through
Penniless Porch from the Market
Place, or through the medieval
gateway in Sadler Street known as
"the Dean's Eye," you are confronted by what many reckon is the
finest west front of any cathedral in
Europe. Between the square-topped
twin towers sit six tiers of 13th-
century statues of priests, kings,
and saints—300 figures in all.

Entering, you are immediately
struck by the futuristic yet entirely
harmonious appearance of the
huge scissor-arches with their spec-
tacle holes, installed between 1338
and 1348 to shore up the unsteady
central tower. The cathedral, begun
in 1180, is rich in treasures of

medieval carving and architecture;
particularly noteworthy are the animated astronomical clock of 1392
in the north transept, on which
jousting knights knock each other
flat every hour, and the early 14th-
century chapter house at the top of
its flight of wide steps, where 32
ribs of fan vaulting spring with
supreme grace from a slender central column.

The moated **Bishop's Palace**
*(tel 01749-678691, closed Nov.–
March, Sat. April–Oct.),* the 14th-
century **Vicars' Close** (the
oldest complete medieval street in
Europe), and the excellent **Wells
Museum** *(8 Cathedral Green, tel
01749-673477, closed Mon.–Tues.
Nov.–Easter)* are all one minute's
walk from the cathedral. ∎

The great
Early English west
front of Wells
Cathedral with
its tiers of seated
figures, now
beautifully
restored, is among
the most splendid
in Europe.

# Bristol

BRISTOL IS AN ANOMALY—A FAMOUS SEAPORT THAT IS not actually on the sea, although the winding, 4-mile Avon Gorge connects the city with the Bristol Channel. Atlantic-facing Bristol enjoyed seaborne prosperity for centuries, through trade with the United States and the West Indies in wine, tobacco—and slaves. John Cabot, the Genoese-born navigator, sailed from the city in 1497 to "discover" Newfoundland and mainland America; his rugged statue sits on Narrow Quay.

**Bristol**

<N> 141 G6

**Visitor information**

<N> The Annexe
Wildscreen Walk

<N> 0117-926 0767

Around the waterfront in the city's center are the shops and cafés of cobbled Narrow Quay; the Wildwalk, Explore, and IMAX cinema attractions at **@t Bristol** *(Harbourside, tel 0845-345 1235);* atmospheric old King Street with the **Theatre Royal** of 1766 and the half-timbered 17th-century **Llandoger Trow;** and above all the superbly graceful 14th-century **Church of St. Mary Redcliffe,** with its tall spire and elaborately carved north porch.

Little yellow-painted water taxis buzz you around all these attractions and down the harbor to **S.S. _Great Britain_** *(Great Western Dock, Gas Ferry Rd., tel 0117-926 0680).* They'll also transport you to Temple Meads Station, where you'll find the fascinating **British Empire & Commonwealth Museum** *(Station Approach, tel 0117-925 4980).*

Then wander around the Regency terraces and crescents of elegant **Clifton,** northwest of the center, before crossing the dizzily high suspension bridge (see box) to enjoy a stroll along the pathways of Leigh Woods above the gorge. ■

**Clifton Suspension Bridge Visitor Centre**

<N> Bridge House, Sion Place

<N> 0117-974 4664

**Isambard Kingdom Brunel** standing in front of the huge launching chains of the *Great Eastern*—until 1899 the largest vessel ever built

## Isambard Kingdom Brunel (1806–1859)

The little genius with the big name epitomized all the swagger, confidence, and inventiveness of the Victorian engineer. He developed steamships, built bridges and docks, and dreamed up a railway that ran on air suction. Bristol displays many of his most brilliant works, including **Bristol Old Railway Station** (1839–1840), the oldest terminus in the world and the end of Brunel's Great Western Railway; **S.S. _Great Britain_** (launched in 1843), the world's first oceangoing steamship with screw propulsion; and the **Clifton Suspension Bridge** (1836–1864) across the Avon Gorge, Bristol's symbol and Brunel's chief monument. ■

# Bath

AS ENGLAND'S SHOWPIECE OF HARMONIOUS GEORGIAN architecture, Bath is an absolute must for any traveler through Britain. And the beautiful, if often overcrowded, city is one of the most enjoyable and rewarding in Europe for strolling around (see pp. 154–55).

**Bath**

🅰 141 G5

**Visitor information**

✉ Abbey Chambers, Abbey Church Yard

☎ 01225-477101

**Bath's Royal Crescent is just one of the many perfectly proportioned Georgian buildings in honey-colored stone that make the city so memorable.**

Britain's premier inland spa town, unmatched for elegance and sophistication during the 18th-century height of its fame, started in a humble way in around 850 B.C. when (according to legend) King Bladud became an outcast swineherd after he contracted leprosy. Watching his itchy-skinned pigs wallowing in the warm muddy springs of these limestone hills, Bladud followed suit and found his complaint was cured.

When the Romans arrived around A.D. 44 they found the locals already using the springs. The Romans built and dedicated a temple to Sulis Minerva, the Romano-Celtic goddess of healing, together with baths and other fine buildings. The extensive remains of most of these lay unexcavated until the 1880s.

## FASHIONABLE SPA

After the Romans left the town, sufferers continued to use the healing waters at Bath. The town became really fashionable after 1704, when Richard "Beau" Nash (1674–1762) was elected Master of Ceremonies—a taste and style arbiter whose word was absolute law. Balls, parties, card sessions, and visits were arranged, and Bath became the most fashionable meeting, greeting, flirting, and marriage-marketing place in Britain.

Ralph Allen opened his quarries in Combe Down, south of the little spa, and the golden Bath stone was fashioned by the two John Woods, father and son, into the incomparably elegant squares, circuses, terraces, and crescents you see today. ∎

# A walk around Bath

This walk takes you on a tour of the highlights of Bath—from the superbly preserved Roman Baths of the first century to the parks, terraces, squares, and the Royal Crescent, the epitome of Georgian elegance.

Begin at the visitor information center on Abbey Church Yard. Here you can pick up a Trail Guide entitling you to a reduced entrance fee at many of the museums along the way.

Outside are the **Roman Baths** ❶ (Stall St., tel 01225-477785), built in about A.D. 65–75. The green waters of the adjacent hot spring feed the baths, at a constant temperature of 115.7°F. In the Baths Museum is a model of the whole bath/temple complex, along with fascinating artifacts excavated here, most striking among them a superb bronze

head of Sulis Minerva, and a giant, staring god's head fashioned in stone, with knotted and writhing hair and beard.

Above is the elegant 18th-century **Pump Room,** where you can take tea to the sound of piano playing, or dare to drink a glass of the health-giving water—tasting faintly of eggs, soap, and metal.

Outside the baths stands the city's **Abbey Church** ❷ (tel 01225-422462), begun by Bishop Oliver King in 1499, on whose west front a host of angels climbs up and tumbles

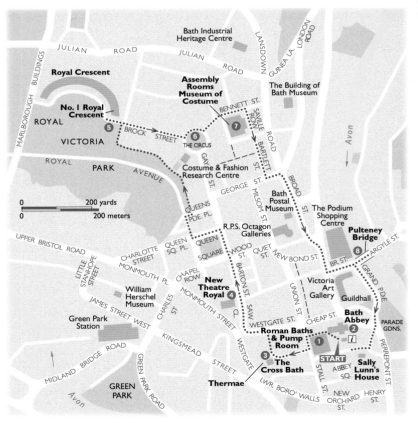

The Roman Great Bath, once covered by a roof, is now exposed to the elements. In the background is the Abbey Church.

down ladders. Inside is much delicate fan vaulting and a clutter of effigies and monuments.

Leaving the jugglers, saxophonists, and performance artists in **Abbey Church Yard,** go between the pillars across Stall Street and along Bath Street to **The Cross Bath** ❸, very elegantly urned and swagged, where James II's wife erected a cross in 1688 in

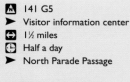

- 🗺 141 G5
- ▶ Visitor information center
- ↔ 1½ miles
- ⊕ Half a day
- ▶ North Parade Passage

**NOT TO BE MISSED**

- Roman Baths
- Abbey Church
- Royal Crescent

gratitude for having at last become pregnant after bathing in this spring. **Thermae,** a contemporary spa bath center, is scheduled to open in the fall of 2004.

Turn right into Saw Close to Barton Street to pass the **Theatre Royal** ❹ *(Saw Close, tel 01225-448844, tours at 11:00 a.m. Wed. & Sat.),* carefully restored and maintained, plush and ornate. Continue on Barton Street into Queen Square, around which John Wood the Elder showed off the Bath stone to best advantage.

From the top left corner of Queen Square, ascend to the lion-guarded entrance into **Royal Victoria Park,** and take the raised gravel walk on the right, which curves around to meet the classic sweep of **Royal Crescent.**

The harmonious frontages were built in the 1760s and 1770s by John Wood the Younger, and speculators ran up the houses behind as they pleased. **No. 1 Royal Crescent** ❺ *(tel 01225-428126, closed Dec.–Jan. & Mon. Feb.–Nov.)* is done up complete with sedan chair in the hall, port and pipes in the study, and a big cheerful kitchen below stairs, to re-create a mid-Georgian atmosphere.

Continue along Brock Street to **The Circus** ❻, John Wood the Elder's masterpiece of circular building, with a weird frieze of masks, foliage, magical symbols, musical instruments, and wildlife running all the way around.

Just beyond, turning right off Bennett Street, are the **Assembly Rooms** ❼ *(tel 01225-477789)* of 1772: A long ballroom lit by 18th-century chandeliers, an octagonal card room with a musicians' gallery, and a pillared and curtained tearoom. Here the fashionable Bathonians of Jane Austen's day would gather to gamble, flirt, and dance. In the basement is Bath's **Museum of Costume** *(tel 01225-477785),* featuring modes of dress from Elizabethan blackwork embroidery to ultra-modern fashion.

Bartlett Street and Broad Street bring you to Robert Adam's beautiful **Pulteney Bridge** ❽ of 1769–1774, just above a broad weir across the River Avon.

Grand Parade, the circular Orange Grove, and elegant Terrace Walk land you close to your starting point in North Parade Passage, where you can relax over a cup of tea and one of Bath's enormous and justly celebrated buns in **Sally Lunn's House.** ∎

## Dyrham Park

🅰 141 G6

☎ 0117-937 2501

🕐 House & garden:
closed Nov.–March,
Wed. & Thurs.
April–Oct. Domestic
rooms: open
Sat.–Sun. Nov.–mid-
Dec. Park: open
year-round

💲 House & garden:
$$$. Garden only:
$$. Park & domestic
rooms: $$. Park: $

## American Museum
in Britain

🅰 141 G5

✉ 2½ miles southeast
of Bath

☎ 01225-460503

🕐 Closed Nov.–March
& Mon. April–Oct.

💲 $$

**See how the early
settlers fared as
you walk through
the meticulously
re-created
historic rooms of
the American
Museum in
Britain at
Claverton Manor.**

# Around Bath

JUST NORTH OF THE A431, 4 MILES WEST OF THE CITY, THE
tiny hillside village of North Stoke is the starting point for a lovely, if
often extremely muddy, walk to the beech clump on the top of
Kelston Round Hill. On a clear day, views from here extend 50 miles
from Wiltshire through Somerset and Gloucestershire to the Severn
Estuary and the Welsh hills.

Farther north, off the A46, 8 miles
north of Bath, the 17th-century
mansion of **Dyrham Park** (NT)
sits at the foot of a great landscaped
slope in a park where deer roam.
South of Bath is a ridge by Beechen
Cliff, giving views over the city.

Two miles out of town to the
southeast is **Prior Park** (*NT, tel
01225-833422, closed Tues., &
Mon.–Thurs. Dec.–Jan.*), the big
house built for Ralph Allen by John
Wood the Elder from 1735 to 1750.
The house is not open, but you can
stroll in the landscaped grounds
(*no parking on grounds*) and admire
one of the finest Palladian bridges
in existence.

Nearby is the **American
Museum in Britain** at Claverton
Manor, which takes you on a journey through American domestic life
from colonial days to the end of the
19th century. It has the simplicity of
early pioneer furnishings, the quiet
elegance of the 18th century, and

the heavy elaborations of the 19th
century—all offset by quilting and
rugmaking, Navajo art, and Shaker
furniture in its pristine severity. You
can snack on Connecticut snicker-
doodles, baked the way Grandma
did it.

South again are secret valleys,
where pleasing villages such as
**Englishcombe, Wellow,** and
**Priston** wait to be discovered.

### BRADFORD-ON-AVON
East of Bath, where Somerset gives
way to Wiltshire, is the charming
stone-built wool town of Bradford-
on-Avon (*Map 141 G5, visitor
information, 34 Silver St., tel 01225-
865797*), with a grim little jail on
the bridge, a great medieval tithe
barn out along the riverside path,
and a rare pre-Norman church,
that stood for centuries unrecog-
nized. Bradford, like Bath, is a town
with many fine houses of Stuart
and Georgian wool merchants. ■

# Great country houses

THE ARCHITECTURE OF SOUTH SOMERSET IS DOMINATED by the glorious, honey-colored hamstone quarried from Ham Hill. Hereabouts the cool chalk of the South Country gives way to the warmth of the West Country limestone and sandstone.

## MONTACUTE HOUSE

Montacute (NT) lies just off the A3088, 4 miles west of Yeovil in south Somerset. This Tudor Gothic mansion, started during the year of the Spanish Armada, was built of honey-colored hamstone for Sir Edward Phelips, Speaker of the House of Commons.

Under the balustraded roofline, sculptured figures stand guard in their niches, looking over formal terraced gardens with trimmed old yew hedges and Tudor rose bushes. Inside are 16th- and 17th-century portraits, Jacobean tapestries and samplers, and huge Elizabethan fireplaces.

## LONGLEAT HOUSE

Just across the northeastern border of Somerset into Wiltshire, between Frome and Warminster, stands Longleat House, a grand Elizabethan mansion. It was built between 1559 and 1580 by Sir John Thynne, who, in 1541, had snapped up the local priory after the Dissolution of the Monasteries, together with 900 acres of prime land, at the bargain price of £53 (about $95).

Inside the symmetrically square-sided house are the original Great Hall with its dark hammerbeam ceiling, a fine collection of Old Master paintings, and nearly 50,000 books in seven library rooms.

In 1948, the 6th Marquess of Bath opened Longleat to the public, and the park now contains a safari park, a big maze, adventure playgrounds, a narrow-gauge railway, a Dr. Who exhibition, and many other delights.

## STOURHEAD

This big Palladian house was built between 1721 and 1724 for rich banker Henry Hoare, and contains furniture by Chippendale and romantic landscape paintings by Poussin and Claude. These French artists were a great influence on Hoare and his son, "Henry the Magnificent," when they were laying out the glory of Stourhead, its superbly landscaped grounds. Grottoes, rotundas, and temples stand by the lake and among fabulously varied trees. Nearby stands a Hoare folly, the 160-foot **King Alfred's Tower** *(tel 01747-841152, closed Nov.–March)*—climb its 206 steps for a 50-mile view. ■

**Montacute House**
- 141 G3
- 01935-823289
- Closed Nov.–March & Tues. April–Oct.
- $$

**Longleat House**
- 141 G5
- 01985-844400
- House: closed Jan.–March Safari Park: closed Nov.–March
- House or Safari Park: $$

**Stourhead**
- 141 G5
- Stourton
- 01747-841152
- Closed Nov.–March & Wed.–Thurs. March–Oct.
- House & garden: $$$. House or garden: $$

**The huge maze at Longleat House**

*Tresco's gardens were the creation of the Isles' 19th-century Lord Proprietor, Augustus Smith.*

## More places to visit in the West Country

### ISLES OF SCILLY

Off the southwestern extremity of Britain lies a scattering of small islands. Remotest of all are the Isles of Scilly, visible from Land's End on a clear day.

Of the five inhabited islands, **St. Mary's** is the biggest. Daffodils grow in tiny walled fields, and the twisty lanes are uncrowded. **Tresco** is a subtropical paradise, planted with exotic species. Roads here, as on all the other islands except St. Mary's, are car free. Neighboring **Bryher** is rugged and tiny; **St. Martin's** is long and spiky-backed, with beautiful beaches: Lonely little **St. Agnes,** the southernmost island, faces the Western Rocks in Cornwall.

140 A1 **Visitor information** ✉ Old Wesleyan Chapel, Well Ln., Hugh Town, St. Mary's ☎ 01720-422536; ✈ Isles of Scilly Skybus ☎ 0845-710 5555; Scotia Helicopter Services ☎ 01736-363871; ⛴ Isles of Scilly Steamship Company ☎ 0845-710 5555

### LUNDY ISLAND

Off the northwestern corner of Devon rises Lundy, 11 miles out into the widening mouth of the Bristol Channel. Three miles long, half a mile wide, isolated and beautiful, the island has a spectacularly indented cliff coastline to flank its rounded back. About 20 people live here all year-round, running the Marisco Tavern, a shop, and a small number of vacation cottages for the Landmark Trust, which owns the island.

140 D5 ⛴ From Bideford, Ilfracombe, and Clovelly ☎ 01271-863636

### STEEP HOLM & FLAT HOLM

Farther upchannel are the hump of Steep Holm and the low-lying pancake of Flat Holm, two bird sanctuaries well worth a day's exploration.

**Steep Holm** 141 F5 ⛴ Tel 01934-632307
**Flat Holm** 141 F5 ⛴ Tel 01466-747661 ■

Wales is the land of the Red Dragon celebrated by poets and singers, with steep borderlands in the east and splendid mountains in the west, studded with mighty castles and bounded by a dramatic coastline.

# Wales

Introduction & map 160–61
Wye Valley 162
Cardiff & the Valleys 163
Pembrokeshire Coast
    & Gower Peninsula 164–65
Central Wales 166–67
A drive from Dolgellau to Conwy
    168–69
Caernarfon Castle 170–71
Snowdonia 172
Portmeirion & the Lleyn Peninsula
    173
Welsh Borders 174
Hotels & restaurants in Wales
    358–62

**Conwy Castle**

# Wales

WALES IS STRIKINGLY ATTRACTIVE, WITH DRAMATIC MOUNTAINS IN THE north, a hilly interior, a coastline of fishing villages among long stretches of cliffs and sandy beaches, and rolling hills and valleys punctuated with castles. The country looks with pride on its artistic heritage of legend, song, and poetry, and on its contribution to British society of so many politicians, thinkers, orators, and social activists. In a 1997 referendum the Welsh voted—narrowly but decisively—to establish their own Assembly, a decision that reflects the country's mood of self-confidence and its strength of national identity.

## FIGHTING FOR INDEPENDENCE

It has not always been this way. Like their fellow Celts in Scotland and Ireland, the Welsh came off second-best in confrontations with the Saxon and Norman English. In the eighth century, Offa, King of Mercia, built an 80-mile defensive bank and ditch along the border. After the Norman Conquest the barons known as the Lords Marcher (Lords of the Border) ruled from their castles like kings.

There were plenty of Welsh uprisings, notably under Prince Llewelyn the Great (1173–1240) and his grandson, Llewelyn the Last (died 1282), but Edward I crushed Welsh autonomy with a mailed fist during two decisive campaigns in 1277 and again in 1282–84. One last great confrontation took place around 1400, when the charismatic Prince Owain Glyndwr set the Borders on fire. After he was defeated and driven to an obscure end in the mountains, the English dominance of Wales was complete.

## STILL ITS OWN COUNTRY

England and Wales were unified under Henry VIII from 1536 to 1543. Evidence of the previous 400 years of occupation and resistance lies all across Wales in the shape of great castles, fortified manor houses, defensive earthworks, and churches built as grimly as fortresses.

In recent years there has been a resurgence in Welsh language and culture, spreading from its stronghold in the north and west of the country. Anyone who travels through this beautiful nation today cannot fail to be struck by the strengthening "Welshness" of Wales. ■

**Hiking in the Brecon Beacons, viewed here from the west of Craig Cwareli toward Pen-y-Fan**

# Wye Valley

**Wye Valley**

🗺 160 D2

**Visitor information**

✉ Chepstow Castle Car
Park, Bridge St.,
Chepstow

☎ 01291-623772

**Chepstow Castle**

✉ Bridge St., Chepstow

☎ 01291-624065

💲 $$

**Tintern Abbey**

✉ 5 miles north
of Chepstow

☎ 01291-689251

💲 $

FOR VISITORS CROSSING THE SEVERN ESTUARY FROM
Bristol by way of the twin bridges, the Wye Valley is their first glimpse
of Wales. This heavily wooded, deeply cut valley, with England on its
eastern bank and Wales on its west, makes a beautiful introduction to
the principality.

It is 18 miles from **Chepstow** at
the mouth of the muddy tidal River
Wye to Monmouth at the head of
the valley, a stretch of country where
you can walk on the ancient rampart
of **Offa's Dyke** (see p. 174) high
up on the English bank, looking
down through beech and hazel
woods to the snakelike river hun-
dreds of feet below. Alternatively,
you can drive along the floor of
the valley on the winding, often
crowded A466.

    **Chepstow Castle,** the earli-
est stone-built Norman castle in
Britain, sprawls along its narrow
ledge above the sheer limestone
cliffs of the Wye. From here the val-
ley curls north through St. Arvans
to Tintern, where the tall gray stone
ruins of **Tintern Abbey,** as fine
and delicate as lacework, stand on
their leveled ground by the river.
Three of the abbey's soaring win-
dows still remain intact.

    Tintern village itself is an unre-
pentant tourist trap, but a little far-

ther up the valley you can cross the
Wye to eat and drink in the friendly
old **Brockweir Inn** *(tel 01291-
689548)* without having your elbow
jogged. Here, in the old days, goods
from Bristol were transferred from
vessels into "trows" (flat-bottomed
barges), to be pulled to Monmouth
over the Wye's weirs by teams of
men known as "bow-haulers,"
whose leather chest-harnesses were
attached to the trows by ropes.

    North of Brockweir the valley
road passes beneath the hanging
white houses of Llandogo, then
crosses the river to the English bank
for its final run up to **Monmouth**
*(visitor information, Shire Hall,
Agincourt Sq., tel 01600-713899).* By
the time you reach the town, the
pale limestone river cliffs have given
way to gentler slopes of red sand-
stone. With its cobbled square and
13th-century gatehouse on the
bridge, Monmouth is a typical
Welsh Borders market town, self-
contained and easy paced. ∎

Turner painted,
and Wordsworth
revered, the ruins
of Tintern Abbey.
Set on a valley
floor, it illustrates
the Cistercian eye
for a fine site.

# Cardiff & the Valleys

CARDIFF, NOW THE CAPITAL CITY OF WALES, WAS A MODEST coastal town until the Marquess of Bute developed its docks at the dawn of the railway era in the 1830s. Within 100 years it had become the busiest coal port in the world, a conduit for the mighty flood of coal pouring out of the mines in the valleys just to the north.

## CARDIFF CITY

The mines are closed now, and Cardiff Bay has taken on a regenerated life as a leisure area of spanking new bars, restaurants, stores, and upscale housing.

In the city, **Cardiff Castle** is a extravagant fantasy of a romantic castle, assembled from 1867 to 1875 by the 3rd Marquess of Bute around the nucleus of a Norman keep. Enjoy the galleried Summer Smoking Room, the handpainted nursery rhyme tiles in the Nursery, the Arab Room with Islamic designs created in marble, lapis lazuli, and gold by imported Arabian craftsmen, and the covered roof garden.

Also worth seeing in the city is the impressively pompous **City Hall** in Cathays Park, with a dragon perched atop its 200-foot dome; and the nearby **National Museum and Gallery** (*Cathays Park, tel 029-2039 7951, closed Mon.*) with its superbly displayed prehistoric collection and its comprehensive coverage of Impressionist art.

On the outskirts of the city at St. Fagans is the **Museum of Welsh Life** (*tel 029-2057 3500*) where you can experience old customs and lifesyles of Welsh people.

## IN THE VALLEYS

North of Cardiff stretch the Valleys, roughly parallel slashes in the landscape where coal and iron were dug and metal ores smelted until the 1980s. To get an idea of what the miners' working lives were like, try the **Big Pit Mining Museum** (*tel 01495-790311, closed Dec.–*mid-Feb.*) at Blaenafon, 27 miles north of Cardiff, or the **Rhondda Heritage Park** (*tel 01443-682036, closed Mon. Oct.–Easter*) at Trehafod where a pit-head tour, guided by ex-miners, leads to a journey through cramped, dank workings 300 feet underground.

Walks in the Valleys are rewarding, from the long, narrow industrial villages on the Rhondda, Ebbw, Sirhowy, and other valley floors, up along old pony tracks onto the high, windy tops of the hills. ■

**Cardiff**

🅰 160 C1

**Visitor information**

✉ The Old Library
The Hayes

☎ 029-2022 7281

**Cardiff Castle**

✉ Castle St.

☎ 029-2087 8100

💲 $$

**Heavily carved foliage smothered in gold leaf is one of the Moorish-influenced motifs that form part of the decoration at Cardiff Castle.**

# Pembrokeshire Coast & Gower Peninsula

**St. David's**

🏛 160 A2

**Visitor information**

✉ The Grove

☎ 01437-720392

**St. David's Cathedral**

✉ The Close

☎ 01437-720202

$ Donation. Tours $$

**St David's Bishop's Palace**

✉ Next to St. David's Cathedral

☎ 01437-720517

$ $

THE PEMBROKESHIRE COAST NATIONAL PARK COMPRISES the wild and storm-sculptured tip of Wales's extreme southwest. Out at the westernmost point of Pembrokeshire's rough and rugged peninsula sits St. David's, the smallest city in the U.K., and one of the most appealing. Its glory and pride is the great cathedral of St. David, which was begun in 1180 on the site of a monastery founded by the saint himself in about A.D. 550. Relics of St. David, patron saint of Wales, were enshrined here and attracted many pilgrims throughout the Middle Ages.

## ST. DAVID'S CATHEDRAL

The cathedral sits surprisingly low, the stumpy central tower seeming less than its actual 125-foot height. At the west end is a big rose window, from which the finely carved early 16th-century oak roof of the nave runs east toward the 14th-century rood screen. Fresh flowers are always placed at the cathedral's crossing to decorate the shrine of St. David, a 1275 replacement of the pre-Norman original, which was stolen. In the choir one stall is reserved permanently for the British monarch. Lift some of the seats to enjoy the 15th-century misericords, which incorporate scenes of hunting and of shipbuilding.

Next to the cathedral stands the grand ruin of the **Bishop's Palace,** with its superb Great Hall rose window, and the private chapel of the Bishops of St. David's. The stories say that Bishop Barlow, the first Protestant bishop to be enthroned here at the Reformation in 1536, had the lead roofs of the palace stripped for sale, so that he could provide dowries for his five daughters who were each betrothed to a bishop.

**Portrait of Dylan Thomas by Augustus John (1878–1961)**

## Dylan Thomas

Dylan Thomas (1914–1953), Wales's national poet, used language as no one else has. His mellifluous voice, reciting one of his flowing poems or reading such rich, dense prose as *A Child's Christmas in Wales,* became well known through his BBC broadcasts. It is his play for voices, *Under Milk Wood,* published posthumously in 1954, by which he is best known. Thomas's last home, known as the **Dylan Thomas Boathouse** (*Dylan's Walk,* tel 01994-427420), stands on a rough pedestrian track beside the Taf Estuary at Laugharne, off the A40 10 miles west of Carmarthen. The Thomas family's living room with its wonderful estuary view is preserved; also the writing table and materials in the garage shed in the lane, where Thomas wrote *Under Milk Wood,* and many other poems and stories.

In November 1953, the poet, whose drinking habits were out of control, died of a "massive insult to the brain" while on a lecture tour of the United States. His grave is in the churchyard at Laugharne.

The **Dylan Thomas Centre** in Swansea (*Somerset Place,* tel 01792-463980) gives a good overview of the life and death of this flawed genius. ∎

## COASTAL WALKS & ISLAND SANCTUARIES

Of the many glorious coastal walks in Pembrokeshire and the **Pembrokeshire Coast National Park,** the 4-mile round-trip from Whitesands Bay around **St. David's Head** (3 miles beyond St. David's) is one of the best—it takes in Iron Age hut circles, Stone Age burial chambers, and the beach from which St. Patrick set off early in the fifth century to convert the Irish.

Another 4-mile walk leads around **St. Govan's Head** (to get there from St. David's, follow the A487 to Haverfordwest; then take the A4076 and the A477 to Pembroke; and the B4319 to Bosherston), visiting the beautiful lily ponds at **Bosherston** and the tiny Chapel of St. Govan, which is built in an extraordinary location, wedged into a crack in the cliffs.

Twenty miles northeast of St. David's is **Dinas Head,** a blunt-nosed promontory with a very enjoyable 3-mile walk around its craggy perimeter.

Offshore islands include **Ramsey Island, Skokholm Island,** and **Skomer Island,** bird and wildlife sanctuaries of beauty and isolation. An overnight stay on these islands is a never-to-be-forgotten experience, but one that should be planned well in advance. For details contact St. David's visitor information center (see p. 164).

## GOWER PENINSULA

Some of the most unspoiled and beautiful scenery in South Wales can be found farther east on the Gower Peninsula, just 18 miles long by 5 miles wide. Its cliffs and beaches are considered to be among the finest in Britain. ∎

**The Gower Peninsula contains dramatic coastal scenery, none more so than the humpbacked promontory of Worm's Head.**

**Pembrokeshire Coast National Park**
- 160 A2
- ✉ Llannion Park Pembroke Dock
- ☎ 0854-345 7275

**Gower Peninsula**
- 160 B1

**Visitor information**
- ✉ Plymouth St., Swansea
- ☎ 01792-468321

# Central Wales

**Brecon Beacons
National Park**
🏔 160 C2
✉ Plas y Ffynnon
Cambrian Way
Brecon
☎ 01874-624437

**Powis Castle**
🏔 160 C3
☎ 01938-551929
🕐 Closed Nov.–late
March, &
Tues.–Wed.
💲 $$$. Garden only
$$

THE CENTRAL HIGHLANDS OF WALES ARE WILD AND lonely—superb walking country with the highest mountains in Britain south of Snowdonia. Towns and villages—ancient settlements quietly brooding in a landscape of standing stones and hill forts—are few and far between.

### BRECON BEACONS
These high hill ranges lie north of the valleys, forming the heart of the **Brecon Beacons National Park.** They are crisscrossed with horseback riding routes, and paths leading to and around the two main summits of Pen-y-Fan (2,907 feet) and nearby Corn Du (2,863 feet). These sandstone peaks look north over impressive sheer cliffs, but their other aspects invite walkers to climb them; the A470 Merthyr Tydfil–Brecon road near Storey Arms is a good starting place, and the path is clearly marked.

### BLACK MOUNTAINS
The Black Mountains, rising northeast of the Brecon Beacons, form a parallel series of four northwest–southeast sandstone ridges with straight, horizontal backs above deep valleys. Take at

**Old Radnor**
 160 D3

**Aberystwyth**
160 B3
**Visitor information**
✉ Terrace Rd.
☎ 01970-612125
🕐 Closed Sun.

On the land-
scaped grounds
of Powis Castle,
statuary lines
a gracefully
arcaded terrace—
typical of the late
17th-century
Italianate style of
garden design.

least a day to explore them, winding up and down the narrow valley roads to find the elegant, soaring 12th-century arches of the ruined **Llanthony Priory** in the Vale of Ewyas. The priory never prospered and fell into private hands at the Dissolution. Also worth a visit are the churches at Michaelchurch Escley and Partrishow, decorated with macabre medieval murals. Don't miss **Hay-on-Wye** *(visitor information, Craft Centre, tel 01497-820144)* north of the mountains, where there is a huge number of secondhand bookshops.

### OLD RADNOR
Just off the A44, 12 miles north of Hay-on-Wye, Old Radnor consists of a few houses, a big church containing a rough, round, eighth-century font that some think might have once been a Bronze Age altar stone, and the dark-beamed old Harp Inn across from the church.

### POWIS CASTLE
Farther north and 1 mile south of Welshpool off the A483, Powis Castle (NT) is one of the country's finest mansions, built up around a 13th-century fortress in Tudor and Stuart times. The Long Gallery and State Bedrooms are gloriously ornate, and the castle's Italianate gardens, landscaped between 1688 and 1722, are the U.K.'s sole remaining design of this type.

### ABERYSTWYTH & AROUND
The seaside town of Aberystwyth stands on the A487 halfway up the enormous curve of the Cardigan Bay coastline. The town itself, with its University College of Wales, its National Library of Wales, and its Welsh Language Society headquarters, is uncompromisingly Welsh.

In Aberystwyth's stores and pubs you will hear more Welsh

than English spoken. Pro-Welsh sentiment is as strong here as anywhere in Wales, given a prominent voice by the presence of so many bastions of Welsh nationalism and cultural identity.

Yet the look of the town, particularly the seafront with its pier and ranks of tall hotels, is of an English Victorian seaside resort—a legacy of the expansion that followed the arrival of the railroad in 1864.

There is a good overview of this lively, self-possessed town from the **Great Aberystwyth Camera Obscura** *(tel 01970-617642, closed Nov.–March)* on Constitution Hill to the north, reached by the little wooden carriages of the **Aberystwyth Electric Cliff Railway** *(tel 01970-617642, closed Nov.–March)* that rises slowly up the bushy face of a 380-foot cliff. From here a path runs for 6 steep and exhilarating miles north to Borth, from which you can journey back to Aberystwyth by train.

Twelve miles inland along the A4120—or half-an-hour's ride on the **Vale of Rheidol Steam Railway** *(tel 01970-625819)*—is **Devil's Bridge,** a spectacular spot where the Afon Mynach (Monk's River) leaps 300 feet downward beneath a triple bridge. The lowest span is Norman; it is said to have been created in a magical flash by the devil, who was trying to outsmart an old Welsh woman. Needless to say, she came off best.

North of Aberystwyth is the wide estuary of the River Dyfi (Dovey), and north of that rises the 2,927-foot peak of Cader Idris, one of Wales's most satisfying mountains to climb.

The steepish path, starting 3 miles southwest of Dolgellau, is clear all the way to the stony cairn at the top. Sleep here, legend claims, and you will awaken either a poet or a madman. ∎

# A drive from Dolgellau to Conwy

In the streets of Dolgellau you will hear plenty of Welsh spoken, for the northwest corner of Wales is the heartland of the national language. Slate and gold were both dug from the surrounding hills, of which there are fine views as you drive west to Barmouth, where a great railway viaduct strides across enormous sands on 114 spindly legs.

From **Dolgellau** (*visitor information, Ty Meirion, Eldon Sq., tel 01341-422888*), take the A496 10 miles west and north to **Harlech Castle** ❶ (*Castle Sq., tel 01766-780552*), one of the Iron Ring fortresses (see p. 170) established by Edward I.

Harlech was built between 1283 and 1289 of dark gritstone, perched on a crag to exude impregnability with its great gatehouse, 40-foot walls, and corner towers.

From Harlech, the A496 crosses the Dwyryd Estuary at Maentwrog; turn left here onto the A487, passing the little steam trains and stations of the **Ffestiniog Railway** ❷ (*Blaenau Ffestiniog, tel 01766-516000, limited service early Nov.–late March*). The line was built to carry slate quarried in the hills at Blaenau Ffestiniog down to the harbor at **Porthmadog** (*visitor information, High St., tel 01766-512981*), 13½ miles away. It closed in 1946, but enthusiasts reopened it for passengers gradually between 1954 and 1982. One day soon the **Welsh Highland Railway** (*tel 01286-830200*)—at present (2004) reopened for half its length—will be steaming the full 25 miles from Porthmadog to Caernarfon.

At Porthmadog bear right on the A498, up over the steep and spectacular pass of Aberglaslyn with mountain views all around, to reach **Beddgelert** ❸. Here you can visit **Gelert's Grave** (see p. 171) by the River Glaslyn, where lies (or so it is said) the faithful hound Gelert, killed by his master, Llewelyn the Great (grandfather of Llewelyn the Last), in a fit of mistaken rage.

## OVER TO ANGLESEY & BACK

The A4085 snakes its way to **Caernarfon** ❹ and the mightiest of the Welsh castles (see pp. 170–71). Here you rejoin the A487 and skirt the Menai Strait, a narrow channel of water with fierce currents spanned by twin bridges, which separates the Welsh mainland from the **Isle of Anglesey.** If you decide to explore this intensely Welsh island, keep off

the unappealing A5 Holyhead highway and wander the back roads across the rolling interior. Make time to see **Beaumaris Castle** ❺ (*Castle St., tel 01248-810361*), the last of Edward I's castles to be built.

Just beside the more westerly of the Menai bridges is **Llanfairpwllgwyngyllgogerychwyrndrobwllllantysiliogogogoch** (*visitor information, Holyhead Rd., tel 01248-713177*), which means the "Church of St. Mary in the hollow of the white hazel near a rapid whirlpool and St. Tysilio near the red cave"—the longest place-name in Britain, generally shortened to Llanfair P.G.

Back on the mainland, the A55 coast road leads east, skirting Bangor and passing **Penrhyn Castle** ❻ (*NT, Llandegai, 1 mile east of Bangor, tel 01248-353084, early Nov.–late March & Tues. April–Oct.*), a fascinating 19th-century extravaganza built around the shell of a Norman castle by local slate baron George Dawkins-Pennant. The A55 leads northward to reach **Conwy** ❼ (*visitor information, Cadw visitor Centre, Castle Entrance, tel 01492-592248*), a truly delightful small town still ringed by its medieval walls.

Walk a circuit of these before exploring the huge **castle** (*Castle St., tel 01492-592358*) that adjoins the walls, another link in Edward I's Iron Ring, which crouches magnificently over the Conwy Estuary, the mountains rising behind. ■

---

🗺 160 C4
► Dolgellau
🔁 85 miles
🕐 2½ hours
► Conwy

**NOT TO BE MISSED**
- Harlech Castle
- Ffestiniog Railway
- Caernarfon Castle
- Penrhyn Castle

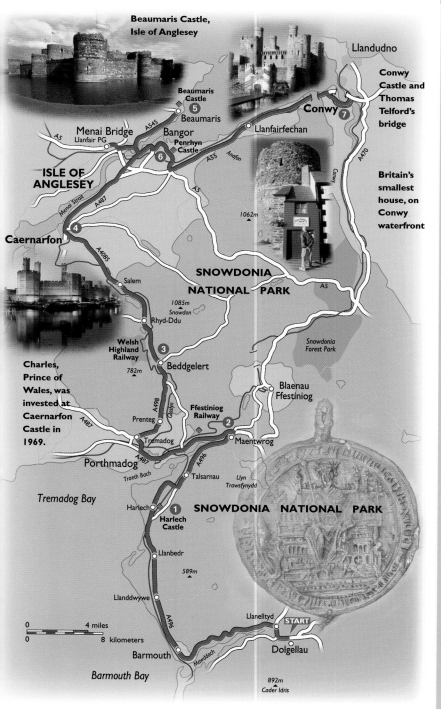

**Beaumaris Castle, Isle of Anglesey**

Llandudno

**Conwy Castle and Thomas Telford's bridge**

Beaumaris Castle **5**

Beaumaris

Conwy **7**

Menai Bridge
Llanfair PG

A545

Bangor

Penrhyn Castle

Llanfairfechan

A5

**6**

A55

Anafon

**Britain's smallest house, on Conwy waterfront**

**ISLE OF ANGLESEY**

A487

Menai Strait

A5

A470

Conwy

1062m

Caernarfon **4**

A4085

**SNOWDONIA**

Salem

**NATIONAL PARK**

1085m
Snowdon

Rhyd-Ddu

A5

Snowdonia Forest Park

**Welsh Highland Railway**

**3**

782m

Beddgelert

Blaenau Ffestiniog

**Charles, Prince of Wales, was invested at Caernarfon Castle in 1969.**

A498

Glaslyn

**Ffestiniog Railway**

Prenteg

**2**

A487

Tremadog

Maentwrog

A487

A496

**Porthmadog**

Traeth Bach

Talsarnau

Llyn Trawsfynydd

**Tremadog Bay**

Harlech

**SNOWDONIA    NATIONAL    PARK**

**1**

**Harlech Castle**

Llanbedr

589m

Llanddwywe

A496

Llanelltyd

START

| 0 | | 4 miles |
|---|---|---|

| 0 | | 8 kilometers |
|---|---|---|

**Dolgellau**

**Barmouth**

Mawddach

**Barmouth Bay**

892m
Cader Idris

# Caernarfon Castle

**Caernarfon Castle**

△ 160 B4
✉ Castle Ditch
☎ 01286-677617
§ $$

CAERNARFON CASTLE, SAID DANIEL DEFOE, WAS "BUILT by Edward I to curb and reduce the wild people of the mountains"— a very succinct summing up of the reason behind the construction of this mighty fortress on the Menai Strait. This is the most famous and impressive castle in Wales, though by no means the most picturesquely sited. Dourly glowering over the water, it conveys today exactly the message of formidable strength that Edward I intended the Welsh to read in its massive walls and towers.

**Caernarfon Castle's massive octagonal towers and crenellated walls represent the statement of authority intended by Edward I.**

## THE IRON RING

Caernarfon was begun in 1283 as the strongest link in the Iron Ring, a loop of eight castles placed around the perimeter of the northern half of Wales. Flint, Rhuddlan, Conwy, Beaumaris, Caernarfon, and Harlech formed a defensive chain hemming in the mountains of Snowdonia, each castle a day's march from the next. Aberystwyth and Builth Wells held the ring farther south.

It was the charismatic Llewelyn ap Gruffydd, "Llewelyn the Last," the last truly Welsh Prince of Wales,

## GELERT'S GRAVE

Llewelyn the Great left his dog Gelert to guard his baby son. On returning he found the cradle overturned and Gelert covered in blood. Thinking the dog had killed his son, Llewelyn slew Gelert. Only after he found his son safe, along with the body of a wolf, did he realize that Gelert had in fact saved the baby. The dog's grave is in Beddgelert (see p. 168). ■

whose drive to regain lost land and establish Welsh autonomy provoked Edward I of England into his decisive all-out drive to crush the Welsh for once and all time (see p. 161). Victorious by 1284, Edward set about stamping his authority on the troublesome mountain people in the form of impregnable-looking castles.

## STRUCTURE

The designer of the magnificent Caernarfon Castle was James of St. George d'Espéranche, the master stonemason and foremost military architect of the late 13th century. His brief was to combine in one building the strongest defenses, and the most civilized and comfortable accommodations.

The great walls of the castle were built in bands of dark sandstone and light limestone, perhaps inspired by the similar design of the city walls of Constantinople. This banding gives the walls an oddly unmilitary, exotic look, compared with those of Conwy, Beaumaris, and Harlech; and the same is true of the octagonal shape chosen for the towers, which themselves are topped by slender, castellated turrets.

The **King's Gate** makes a most impressive entry, with five distinct gateways and six portcullises, sniper slits for bowmen, and murder holes

for the pouring of boiling oil, all impeding any attack. Of the towers, the most interesting to explore are the **Eagle Tower** at the western end, with its weathered eagle sculptures, and the **Queen's Tower** on the south, which contains a museum that gives an enjoyable run-through of the history of the Royal Welch Fusiliers since Stuart times.

You can walk between the towers, through connecting passages built into the width of the walls, and out along the tops of the walls themselves.

## HISTORY

In 1282, Edward I defeated the Welsh and had Llewelyn the Last beheaded. For the sake of security it was essential for him to install an English Prince of Wales. According to the (probably apocryphal) story, he let it be known that the chosen one had been born in Wales, and had not yet learned to speak English. The unsuspecting Welsh agreed to accept the king's nominee sight unseen, believing that one of their own native leaders had been appointed. The wiliness of the king was only revealed when he produced the new Prince of Wales—his own son Edward, who had just been born in Caernarfon Castle.

In the early 1400s the nationalist leader Owain Glyndwr made two unsuccessful attempts to capture the castle; a measure of its strength is that a garrison of just 28 men kept him at bay. In the Civil War of the 1640s, the castle changed hands three times before finally coming under the control of Parliament.

During the 20th century Caernarfon Castle, seat of government for North Wales and the official Welsh residence of the monarch, saw two investitures of a prince of Wales: Prince Edward (later Edward VIII) in 1911, and Prince Charles in 1969. ■

# Snowdonia

**Snowdonia National Park**
🏔 160 C4
✉ Information Section, Snowdonia National Park Authority, Penrhyndeudraeth, Gwynedd LL48 6LS
☎ 01766-770274

**Blaenau Ffestiniog**
🏔 160 C4
**Visitor information**
✉ Isallt, High St.
☎ 01766-830360
🕐 Closed Oct.–March

**Betws-y-Coed**
🏔 160 C4
**Visitor information**
✉ Royal Oak Stables
☎ 01690-710426

**The calm waters of Llynnau Mymbyr reflect Mount Snowdon— Yr Wyddfa.**

SNOWDONIA NATIONAL PARK COVERS NEARLY 840 SQUARE miles of northwest Wales and includes some of the most impressive mountains and moorlands in Britain. This is walkers', climbers', and outdoor enthusiasts' country, a genuine mountain landscape that tops out on Snowdon, the highest mountain in Wales.

There is one curious exclusion zone, the "Hole in the Park," which contains the slate-producing village of **Blaenau Ffestiniog—**this important industrial landscape was considered in 1949 to be insufficiently attractive to be included in the national park. A visit to the village, however, will be rewarded by a fascinating tour of the **Llechwedd Slate Caverns** (*tel 01766-830306*), where you can also watch a demonstration of the highly specialized skills of slate-splitting—and try it yourself.

Eleven miles north is **Betws-y-Coed,** a favorite village with hill walkers. A whole network of paths into the surrounding mountains starts from here.

**Capel Curig,** 5 miles west of Betws-y-Coed, is another great hiking and climbing center, looking north and west to the jagged and rugged Glyders and Carneddau ranges, and southwest into the

**Nant Gwryd Valley** toward Snowdon. Information can be obtained from the Snowdonia National Park Authority.

The jewel in the crown is 3,560-foot **Snowdon,** Yr Wyddfa to the Welsh, meaning "tomb": This is the burial place of the giant Rhita Gawr, who wore a cloak woven of the beards of kings he had killed. This monster was killed here by the hero King Arthur himself.

Climb Snowdon from Pen-y-Pass Youth Hostel (*tel 01286-870428*) on the A4086, midway between Capel Curig and Llanberis (an 8-mile circuit, steep in places, allow five to six hours), or go up on the **Snowdon Mountain Railway** (*tel 01286-870223, closed Nov.–mid-March & other times in bad weather*) from Llanberis. From the summit, in clear weather, you can see Wales, England, Scotland, and Ireland in a 250-mile circle. ■

# Portmeirion & the Lleyn Peninsula

THE FANTASY "VILLAGE" OF PORTMEIRION, SET ON A private peninsula to the southeast of Porthmadog, is a must for any visitor to North Wales. This bizarre confection, a theatrical and exuberantly overblown Italianate village, was assembled here between 1925 and 1972 by the Welsh architect Sir Clough Williams-Ellis (1883–1978).

**Portmeirion**
- 160 B4
- 2 miles southeast of Porthmadog
- ☎ 01766-770000
- $$

Williams-Ellis grabbed pieces of endangered buildings from any-where and everywhere—statues of gods from Hindu temples, a mock-classical colonnade from Bristol, an Italian campanile shaped like an extended telescope.

Entering Portmeirion through the Triumphal Arch, you find build-ings scattered around a central piazza, with more on the slopes and shores around—a castle, a light-house, an Indian hotel bar, and a Town Hall with a 17th-century fresco of Hercules on its ceiling. Little color-washed cottages with red roofs are dotted about. Eucalyptus and cypress trees grow in the landscaped gardens. The widely known Portmeirion pottery, deco-rated with flowers and butterflies, is sold from a shop with a curlicued facade. Visitors may stay overnight in the lavish Portmeirion Hotel, or in one of the vacation cottages.

Portmeirion appealed to Noël Coward: He wrote his play *Blithe Spirit* (1941) while staying at Fountain Cottage. In the 1960s, the surreal surroundings made an ideal setting for the nightmarish cult TV series *The Prisoner*.

## LLEYN PENINSULA

Portmeirion lies at the root of the 30-mile-long Lleyn Peninsula, a narrowing finger drooping south-west from Snowdonia. The peninsu-la is flanked by cliffs and indented with sandy bays; its south coast claims the three seaside resorts of Criccieth, Pwllheli, and Abersoch.

The north coast is quieter, with superb bicycling and walking. Out toward the tip, the south side is torn by the 3-mile gash of **Hell's Mouth** (Porth Neigwl), a bay notorious for shipwrecks.

Beyond lies the rugged little village of **Aberdaron,** and off the very tip of Lleyn the humped shape of **Bardsey Island.** You can visit the lonely island by boat from Pwllheli or Aberdaron, tide and weather permitting, and even stay on it; details from the Bardsey Island Trust (*tel 01758-760667*). ∎

**Prepare for surprises in Portmeirion, where examples of architecture from around the world and across the ages rub shoulders.**

# Welsh Borders

**Offa's Dyke**
🏞 160 D3
**Offa's Dyke Association**
✉ West St., Knighton
☎ 01547-528753
🕐 Closed Sat.–Sun. Nov.–Easter

**Plas Newydd**
✉ Hill St., Llangollen
☎ 01978-861314
🕐 Closed Nov.–March
💲 $/$$

**Forest of Dean**
🏞 160 D2

THE WELSH BORDERS ARE A LAND APART, KNITTED together as one entity by the great 80-mile earth rampart of Offa's Dyke. Although the political border between England and Wales runs nearby, it is the defensive bank built between 778 and 796 by Offa, King of Mercia, that truly marks the boundary. The Offa's Dyke long-distance footpath runs more than twice as far (168 miles), crossing and following the ancient earthwork from Chepstow in the south to Prestatyn in the north.

As you make your way south from the North Wales coast along the Welsh Borders, the **Vale of Clwyd** is well worth a look. Offa's Dyke runs right along the spine of the Clwydian Range on the east (a beautiful walk in its own right), while down in the broad vale are the county town of Denbigh, in the shadow of a ruined castle, and **Ruthin** *(visitor information, Ruthin Craft Centre, Park Rd., tel 01824-703992)*, with its medieval St. Peter's Square and collegiate Church of St. Peter with a very fine, carved Tudor roof.

At the southern end of the Clwydian Range is **Llangollen** *(visitor information, Town Hall, Castle St., tel 01978-860828)*, a trim little town on the A5 with craggy hills all around. Enjoy diesel-driven canalboat rides over the Pontcysyllte aqueduct nearby, and visit black-and-white **Plas Newydd** (NT),

once the home of the eccentric bluestocking "Ladies of Llangollen," crammed full of fantastic oak carvings and tooled-leather fittings.

There is more good, nonspecialist walking southwest of Llangollen in the **Berwyn Mountains,** where at Tan-y-Pistyll (4 miles northwest of Llanrhaeadr-ym-Mochnant) the tremendous **Pistyll Rhaeadr** waterfall (the highest in England and Wales) plunges 240 feet in two mighty leaps.

One more area of the borders not be missed is the **Forest of Dean,** some 24,000 acres of tangled woodland on the eastern (English) flank of the Wye Valley, way down south. "Foresters" are not like other folk, and their secret, tree-smothered kingdom is like nowhere else in Britain. Explore its many beautiful footpaths from the ancient **Speech House Hotel** on the B4226, in the very center of the forest. ∎

**Countryside-lovers enjoy the long-distance walk along wind-swept Offa's Dyke at Springhill, near Knighton.**

Rolling uplands of Cotswold with villages of silvery stone; Oxford and its "dreaming spires"; Shakespeare's Stratford-upon-Avon; and vibrant cities where many cultures mix and match—these are the essence of the South Midlands.

# South Midlands

Introduction & map 176–77
Three cathedral cities 178–80
Two Cotswolds drives 181–83
Warwick Castle 184–85
Stratford-upon-Avon 186–87
Cities of the South Midlands 190
Oxford 191
A walking tour of Oxford 192–94
Around Oxford 195
Blenheim Palace 196–97
Northamptonshire 198
Hotels & restaurants in the South
    Midlands 362–66

**Zodiac clock,
Gloucester Cathedral**

# South Midlands

THE MIDLANDS OF ENGLAND ARE THE COUNTRY'S HEARTLAND, A GREAT circle of mostly low-lying land between what northerners would call the "soft South," and what southerners tend to think of as the "hard North." Their character is made up of of elements from both: the gentleness of oolitic limestone and red sandstone landscapes of fields and woods, and the severity of a clutch of traditionally hardworking cities beginning to face a future shorn of many of their manufacturing industries.

Too often it is these great conurbations—especially Birmingham, sprawling untidily around its tangle of highways—that people picture when they think of the South Midlands. Yet most of this region is pastoral, peaceful countryside, dotted with some of the most appealing cathedral cities, market towns, and villages to be found anywhere in Britain.

**THREE CATHEDRALS**

The western boundary is marked by the Welsh Borders, where the celebrated "Three Cathedrals" of Gloucester, Worcester, and Hereford lie around the ancient Malvern Hills. Farther east, the Cotswold Hills—archetypal English countryside in all its beauty—roll from Gloucestershire away into Oxfordshire.

**The Cotswolds are dotted with Roman treasures, such as this 1,600-year-old mosaic floor.**

The beauty of the villages built of silvery or creamy limestone, the richness of the medieval churches, and the gentleness of the landscape draw visitors by the hundreds of thousands to the Cotswolds.

## MIDLAND TOWNS

Even more popular is Stratford-upon-Avon, birthplace of William Shakespeare and biggest attraction of the county of Warwickshire, though mighty Warwick Castle comes close. North from here again you will find three Midland towns: Coventry, with its showpiece postwar cathedral crammed with modern works of art; Leicester, with a vibrant Asian culture; and much maligned Birmingham—no beauty, for sure, but a friendly and lively city of mixed ethnic groups.

## OXFORD & GREAT HOUSES

Southeast is Oxford, a world away from all of this, where you can stroll around a superb collection of medieval colleges and their churches, halls, and quads—unparalleled, except perhaps by Cambridge.

Blenheim Palace, all pomp and glory, lies just north; and out to the east is Althorp House, where Diana, Princess of Wales, lies buried on a lake island on its grounds. ■

# Three cathedral cities

**Gloucester**

🗺 177 B2

**Visitor information**

✉ 28 Southgate St.

☎ 01452-421188


**Hereford**

🗺 177 A2

**Visitor information**

✉ 1 King St.

☎ 01432-268430

🕐 Closed Sun.
   Oct.–Easter


**Hereford Cathedral**

✉ Cathedral Close

☎ 01432-374200

🕐 Mappa Mundi & Chained Library exhibition closed Sun. Oct.–Easter

💲 Cathedral: donation. Exhibition: $$

THE THREE CATHEDRAL CITIES AND COUNTY CAPITALS OF Gloucester, Hereford, and Worcester form a triangle in the southwest region of the South Midlands, a triangle that encloses the distinctive upthrust spine of the Malvern Hills. This is cattle-grazing and fruit-growing country of red earth and green meadows, well provided with orchards of apples for eating and cidermaking.

## GLOUCESTER

The southernmost of the three cities, Gloucester contains one of the most glorious cathedrals in Britain. Marked by its beautiful 225-foot tower, **Gloucester Cathedral** (*College Green, tel 01452-528095*) stands in a green close secluded from the city's streets. It was started in 1089 and finished within 20 years; the dog-tooth decoration of the rounded arches in the nave shows these early Norman origins. In 1216 Henry III was crowned in the church.

It was the death of Edward II and his burial in Gloucester Cathedral in 1327, that sparked a whole new phase in the life of the building. The allegedly homosexual Edward had been horribly put to death in nearby Berkeley

**Highlights of Gloucester Cathedral include (above) a monument to Thomas Machen, Mayor of Gloucester (died 1614), his wife, and family, and (opposite) the 14th-century cloisters, a setting for the Hogwarts School in the *Harry Potter* films.**

Castle (a heated poker was plunged into his bowels on the orders of his wife, Isabella) and a sympathetic popular cult of pilgrimage to his alabaster tomb in the cathedral brought riches that were used to rebuild and beautify the church.

From this era dates the huge east window of 1352, showing the Coronation of the Virgin Mary and the coats of arms of nobles who had fought at the great defeat of the French at the Battle of Crécy in 1346. Measuring 80 feet by 38 feet, this is an enormous area of

medieval stained glass. The Great Cloister was beautifully fan vaulted between 1370 and 1410.

Outside in College Court is the crooked little house, now a museum, that featured in Beatrix Potter's (1866–1943) *The Tailor of Gloucester*. Down at the docks in Llanthony Warehouse is a big collection of boats in the **National Waterways Museum** (*tel 01452-318200*). Off the A38/B4213, 8 miles north of Gloucester, is the beautiful Saxon church at **Deerhurst.** Two miles on, **Tewkesbury** (*visitor information, Tewkesbury Museum, 64 Barton St., tel 01684-295027*) has one of Britain's finest abbey churches, and some extravagant woodcarving on its medieval houses.

## HEREFORD

The second cathedral city is Hereford, to the northwest of Gloucester. **Hereford Cathedral** is a marvelous Romanesque building of pink-gray sandstone, full of memorably decorated tombs such as those of the fully armored Sir Peter de Grandison (1358), and St. Thomas of Hereford (1320) with his guard-of-honor of sorrowing Knights Templar.

Attached to the 15th-century Southwest Cloister, the **New Library Building** (1996) houses the Mappa Mundi, or map of the world. Drawn in 1289 by Richard of Haldingham, who jammed in every known fact or fantasy about the medieval world—all rendered in his

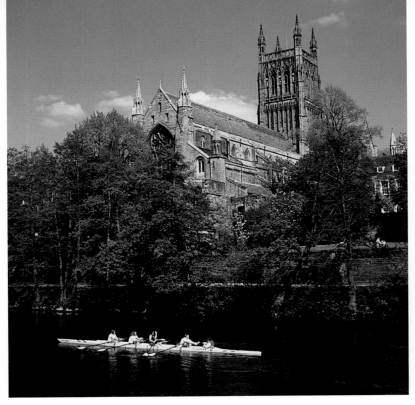

Worcester Cathedral's 14th-century tower is a notable landmark on the bank of the River Severn, though much of the cathedral is, in fact, a Victorian restoration.

**Worcester**

🅜 177 B3

**Visitor information**

✉ Guildhall, High St.

☎ 01905-726311

**Worcester Cathedral**

✉ College Green

☎ 01905-28854

🕐 Tower, call for opening times

💲 Donation

own vigorous draftsmanship—it presents a vivid and moving glimpse into the educated medieval mind. In the same building is the finest **Chained Library** in Britain—1,500 books chained to their original 17th-century book presses, full of exquisitely decorated Dark Ages and medieval monkish work.

## WORCESTER

Worcester, to the northeast, possesses the third of these fine churches. **Worcester Cathedral** occupies a splendid position, with its great east window overlooking the county cricket ground and the looping River Severn. An English king lies buried here, too—King John, whose final resting place in 1216, at his own command, was between the two saints Wulstan and Oswald.

A big Norman crypt of 1084 underlies the church, there is also a

superb ten-sided chapter house of about 1120 and a 14th-century 200-foot-high tower. The cathedral shows many traces of its restoration in Victorian times at the hands of George Gilbert Scott (1811–1878), notably the black-and-white marble nave floor and stained glass.

In town, the **Royal Worcester Porcelain Company** (*Severn St., tel 01905-746000*) has been making beautiful china since 1751. Visitors are welcome in the factory and the museum.

Just southwest of Worcester are the **Malvern Hills** (*visitor information, 21 Church St., Malvern, tel 01684-892289*), a 9-mile succession of ridges and peaks of ancient granite with a high-level footpath running their length. You can see seven counties and the three cathedrals from the 1,394-foot summit of Worcestershire Beacon. ∎

# Two Cotswolds drives

The Cotswold Hills, with their gently rounded pastures and hanging beech and oak woods, their secret little valleys, and, above all, their small towns, villages, churches, and field walls made of silvery limestone, are quintessential rural England, the classic southern English landscape. These two drives, both based on Cheltenham, show off the region's chief attractions.

Cheltenham *(visitor information, 77 Promenade, tel 01242-522878)* has been a spa town since the early 18th century, and contains some of Britain's best Regency architecture. From the green-roofed Rotunda, and the extravagantly curlicued wrought-iron trellises and balconies of **Montpellier,** descend to the town's broad central Promenade, lined with flower beds, trees, a splendid Neptune fountain, and a parade of exclusive stores. The domed **Pittville Pump Room** (1825–1830) in Pittville Park, built for balls, galas, and social intercourse, and now a museum *(tel 01242-523852, closed Tues.),* still contains its fountain of mineral-tasting spa water. The Cheltenham Gold Cup, one of Britain's premier horse races, is held each March at the Prestbury Park racecourse, east of the town. A large and lively Irish contingent usually attends.

## SOUTH COTSWOLDS

From **Cheltenham** ❶, take the A46 south to **Painswick** ❷ *(visitor information, The Library, Stroud Rd., tel 01453-813552),* a pretty ridge-top village with a celebrated churchyard containing 99 yew trees and many ornate 18th-century table tombs.

Continue to **Stroud** *(visitor information, The Subscription Rooms, George St., tel 01453-760960),* where huge old textile mills line the wooded Golden Valley. The A46 continues south, up over the Cotswolds with wide views all around. A left turn 4 miles south of Nailsworth leads to the 600-acre **Westonbirt Arboretum** ❸ *(3 miles south of Tetbury, tel 01666-880220),* one of the world's largest collections of trees, glorious in autumn with blazing maples and other delights.

From the arboretum turn left onto the

**Cheese-rolling—a madcap event that takes place at Cooper's Hill in the Cotswolds**

A433, then right through Shipton Moyne to **Malmesbury** ④ *(visitor information, Town Hall, Market Ln., tel 01666-823748).* The town is built on several levels high above the Avon. Its Norman abbey has a wonderfully carved south porch and a stained-glass window depicting Elmer the Monk, who tried to fly from the tower in 1005 (he broke both legs).

Follow the B4014, which leads northwest to **Tetbury** *(visitor information, 33 Church St., tel 01666-503552),* another charming small town with a Georgian church.

From Tetbury, follow the A433 northeast for 10 miles to **Cirencester** ⑤ *(visitor information, Corn Hall, Market Pl., tel 01285-654180),* capital of the south Cotswolds. The late

**St. Mary's Church in the village of Painswick**

medieval parish church of St. John the Baptist, built of golden stone, has a beautiful fan-vaulted south porch. The **Corinium Museum** on Park Street (*tel 01285-655611, closed Mon. Nov.–March*) contains Roman mosaics unearthed nearby.

The B4425 goes northeast to **Bibury** 6, where you can see charming Arlington Row

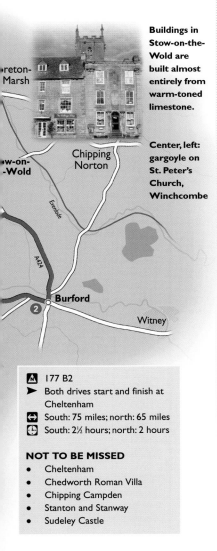

**Buildings in Stow-on-the-Wold are built almost entirely from warm-toned limestone.**

**Center, left: gargoyle on St. Peter's Church, Winchcombe**

177 B2

► Both drives start and finish at Cheltenham

⬌ South: 75 miles; north: 65 miles

🕐 South: 2½ hours; north: 2 hours

**NOT TO BE MISSED**

- Cheltenham
- Chedworth Roman Villa
- Chipping Campden
- Stanton and Stanway
- Sudeley Castle

**Left: Arlington Row in Bibury**

with its 17th-century weavers' cottages, then take the pretty Coln Valley minor road northwest to cross the A429 and reach the superbly preserved **Chedworth Roman Villa** 7 (*NT, Yanworth, tel 01242-890256, closed Dec.–Feb. & Mon. March–Nov.*).

Continue northwest through Withington to Dowdeswell. Pick up the A40 here and turn left to reach Cheltenham.

## NORTH COTSWOLDS

From **Cheltenham** 1, head east on the A40 to **Burford** 2 (*visitor information, The Brewery, Sheep St., tel 01993-823558*), a delightful, small stone-built town with a strong Georgian feel, then take the A424 toward Stow-on-the-Wold. After 6 miles turn left to **Bourton-on-the-Water** 3 (*visitor information, Victoria St., tel 01451-820211*), the "Venice of the Cotswolds," with its tiny footbridges spanning the River Windrush.

The A429 leads north to **Stow-on-the-Wold** 4 (*visitor information, Hollis House, The Square, tel 01451-831082*), high and windswept, with its huge marketplace where sheep are still sold. From here the A424 runs northwest toward Broadway; after 8 miles turn right onto the B4081 to **Chipping Campden** 5, the Cotswold's best-preserved town. In the 15th-century Church of St. James a splendid Doomsday painting broods over the chancel arch. See the Woolstaplers' Hall, where medieval experts assessed the quality of fleeces.

South of elegant **Broadway** 6 (*visitor information, 1 Cotswold Court, tel 01386-852937, closed Jan., Sun. early March–Oct.*) lie **Stanton** and **Stanway,** two gorgeous Tudor/Jacobean villages.

In **Winchcombe** (*visitor information, Town Hall, High St., tel 01242-602925, closed Mon.–Fri. Nov.–March*), 4 miles south, fabulously grotesque 15th-century gargoyles surround the church where Saxon carvings from the former Benedictine abbey are preserved.

From here, walk a mile up the well-marked **Cotswold Way** trail to pre-Tudor **Sudeley Castle** 7 (*tel 01242-602308, castle closed Nov.–March, gardens closed Nov.–Feb.*), with its Elizabethan knot garden and fine paintings; then on to **Belas Knap,** a gigantic neolithic, 5,000-years-old chambered cairn. Return to Winchcombe, and descend into Cheltenham. ■

# Warwick Castle

**Warwick Castle**

🅰 177 C3

✉ Castle Hill, Warwick

☎ 0870-442 2375.
Recorded
information: 0870-
442 2000

💲 $$$

WARWICK IS 7 MILES NORTHEAST OF STRATFORD-UPON-Avon, just beyond the point where the northern Cotswolds run down into the fertile Vale of Evesham and the great plains of the central Midlands. This was one of the natural gateways between northern and southern England, and before the Norman Conquest there was a fortified settlement here beside the River Avon, built early in the tenth century on the orders of Ethelfleda, the daughter of King Alfred the Great. In 1068, only two years after invading Britain, the Normans began building their own castle, whose remains still stand on the landscaped hillock called The Mound.

In 1264, during the Barons' Rebellion against Henry III, the rebels' leader Simon de Montfort captured and destroyed the Norman castle. Between 1350 and 1501 it was largely rebuilt, much as it stands today. The great ramparted outer walls and gray turrets of **Warwick Castle** dominate a curve of the River Avon, reflecting the power and consequence of the incumbent Earls of Warwick.

The most influential of all was Richard Neville, "Warwick the Kingmaker," whose machinations during the Wars of the Roses engineered Edward IV's deposition of Henry VI in 1461.

Then the Kingmaker, having fallen out with the king he had installed, changed camps and oversaw the brief and doomed return of Henry in 1470, before being killed at the Battle of Barnet the following year when Edward staged his own successful comeback.

**Gleaming armor is displayed in the sumptuous Great Hall and other State Rooms in Warwick Castle.**

## CROWN PROPERTY

After the end of the Wars of the Roses the castle was appropriated by the Crown and spent more than a century as the property of the sovereign, until in 1604 the newly enthroned James I gave it to Sir Fulke Greville, one of his allies. Greville, a great friend of Sir Philip Sidney, met a bizarre end in 1628; he was murdered by a servant who thought he had been cut out of his master's will. The murder victim allegedly still walks the castle's Watergate Ghost Tower.

With the final ebbing away of the military power of the nobility, the Earls of Warwick turned their attention over the next 200 years to creating a residence that would reflect their social standing. The Great Hall was remodeled, State Rooms were paneled and furnished with Adam fireplaces and Old Master paintings, and the grounds were landscaped—most strikingly in 1750 by Capability Brown himself. Much of the castle had to be refurbished after a fire in 1871.

## TODAY'S ATTRACTIONS

The castle's aspect of a classically grim medieval fortress makes it one of Britain's most popular visitor attractions and one of the country's finest stately homes. It was taken over in 1978 by the Tussaud Group,

which introduced some top-quality waxwork tableaus.

The enormous **gatehouse,** built in the 1350s has its original portcullis and cleverly concealed murder holes.

Nine **State Rooms** have been arranged with appropriate furnishings. A "Royal Weekend Party, 1898" attraction depicts a party hosted by the earl and countess, with Edward, Prince of Wales (later Edward VII), as guest of honor.

The castle's **Armory** is lined with complete sets and individual pieces of historic armor, including the severe peaked helmet of Oliver Cromwell, complete with cheek and neck guards. There are more suits of armor and weapons on display in the **Great Hall,** with its red-and-white marble tiled floor.

Outside, the grounds are split up into various types of gardens, including the famous and beautiful **Victorian Rose Gardens.**

On some summer weekends there may be jousting tournaments; these are always hugely popular and draw big crowds. ■

**An elegant and lavishly decorated country mansion inside, Warwick Castle nonetheless retains the external appearance of a grimly impregnable medieval fortress.**

# Stratford-upon-Avon

**Stratford-upon-Avon**

⛰ 177 C3

**Visitor information**

✉ Bridgefoot

☎ 0870-160 7930

🕐 Closed Sun. Nov.–Easter

**Shakespeare's Birthplace**

✉ Henley St.

☎ 01789-204016

💲 $$

**Home of the Royal Shakespeare Company, the present Royal Shakespeare Theatre was built in 1932 to replace an earlier building that burned down in 1926.**

STRATFORD-UPON-AVON, ON THE RIVER AVON SOME 20 miles southeast of Birmingham, is England's premier cultural visitor destination outside London, thanks to the genius of the world's most celebrated playwright/poet, William Shakespeare, born here in 1564. The town is best avoided on summer holiday weekends. To get the most out of a visit to Stratford, it is best to focus on a few sites and take time to enjoy them, rather than to arrive unprepared. Luckily, the center of the town, where the chief locations stand close together, is small enough to stroll around in a couple of hours.

## FAMILY HOMES

**Shakespeare's Birthplace** on Henley Street is where the Bard (see pp. 188–89) was born. A Tudor half-timbered building, the birthplace was for many years divided into two houses but is now one. In 1847, after years of use as a pub—the Swan & Maidenhead—the building was bought for the nation, reconstructed, and refurbished. The room styled the "birth-room" is not necessarily the one in which William was born; it was selected extempore by the actor David Garrick in 1769. Names of famous people connected with the literary and theatrical worlds—Thomas Carlyle, Henry Irving, Isaac Watts, Ellen Terry, Walter Scott—can be seen scratched into the glass of the window. Outside, the gardens are planted with the flowers, herbs, and trees mentioned in many of the works of Shakespeare.

At the foot of Henley Street make a right turn onto the High Street. Here on the corner stands **Judith**

**Shakespeare's House** (it had previously been the town prison of Stratford, long before William was born), where his daughter Judith lived; it is now a shop.

Outside the Town Hall is a fine statue of Shakespeare, donated to the town in 1769 by David Garrick, who was instrumental in reviving interest in the national playwright.

Also on High Street is **Harvard House** *(tel 01789-204016, closed Nov.–May)*, a timber-framed house of 1596, where John Harvard's mother was born. Harvard, an early settler in America, bequeathed his estate in 1638 to what later became known as Harvard University. Mark Twain looked around the house in 1907 on the invitation of its then owner, the novelist Marie Corelli, who presented it to Harvard University two years later.

High Street becomes Chapel Street, where **Nash's House** *(tel 01789-204016)*, now a museum of local history, stands on the site of New Place, to which Shakespeare retired in 1610 and where he died in 1616. There is an Elizabethan-style knot garden with low-trimmed box hedges where New Place itself stood; it was demolished in 1759 on the orders of its owner, the Reverend Francis Gatrell, who had had enough of uninvited Shakespeare devotees, inspired by Garrick's enthusiasm, knocking on his door.

## OTHER LANDMARKS

Farther along, where Chapel Street turns into Church Street, is **King Edward VI Grammar School.** Shakespeare may have studied here as a boy, in the timber-roofed room above the **Guildhall.**

On the chancel wall of the adjacent **Guild Chapel,** which dates from the 13th to 15th centuries, is a threatening Doom scene, painted over shortly before Shakespeare was born.

Church Street bears left into Old Town, where stands **Hall's Croft** *(tel 01789-204016)* with its oversailing upper story. Shakespeare's daughter Susanna lived here with her doctor husband, John Hall; the house contains an exhibition on the medical practices of his era.

At the bottom of Old Town is the golden gray **Holy Trinity Church** *(Trinity St., tel 01789-266316),* above the River Avon. Inside the altar rail lies the body of Shakespeare, flanked by his wife, daughter, and son-in-law. You can obtain a copy of the parish register entries of his birth and death, and admire the 19th-century stained-glass window, donated by U.S. enthusiasts, which depicts the Seven Ages of Man from *As You Like It.*

From the church a riverside footpath leads back to the red bulk of the **Royal Shakespeare Theatre,** opened in 1932, where the Royal Shakespeare Company performs the Bard's plays. Turn left on the bridge beyond the theater to get back to the town center. ∎

**The Over Hall in Stratford's 15th-century grammar school, where Shakespeare was thought to have been a pupil.**

**Royal Shakespeare Theatre**
☎ Information: 0870-609 110

# William Shakespeare

There was nothing particularly special about the family into which history's most richly talented wordsmith was born. William Shakespeare's father, John Shakespeare, married somewhat above himself; he was the son of a humble yeoman from the village of Snitterfield, not far from Stratford-upon-Avon, and the playwright's mother, Mary Arden, was the daughter of a well-to-do gentleman farmer at Wilmcote. On her father's death in 1556, Mary found herself well provided for, with a good house and land. Within a year John Shakespeare had married her and embarked on a steady livelihood as a glover and wool merchant, and a climb up the social ladder that would eventually make him a prosperous, middle-class alderman and High Bailiff of Stratford.

William was the third of eight children born to John and Mary Shakespeare. His actual birthdate is unknown, but since he was baptized (as Gulielmus Shakspere) on April 26, 1564, it has become customary—and appropriate—to celebrate his birthday on April 23, feast day of St. George, England's patron saint; it is also the date on which he died, in 1616. Almost nothing is known of William's childhood, although it is assumed that he attended the grammar school on Church Street, and that he was bitten by the stage bug through seeing performances of plays by one of the traveling companies that would have visited his hometown from time to time.

### A prolific writer

In 1582, at the age of 18, Shakespeare married Anne Hathaway, daughter of a yeoman farmer who lived at Shottery, a mile away from Stratford. The couple had a son and two daughters. Some time between 1585 and 1592, William Shakespeare left Stratford (possibly with a troupe of strolling players) to make his way in London as an actor, director, manager, and playwright. He made quick progress; by 1597 he was joint owner of the Globe Theatre (see pp. 39 and 87) on the south bank of the Thames, in the seedy but vibrant red-light area of Southwark. Six years later, already well-known and underwritten by patronage, Shakespeare himself became patron of the royal theater troupe, the King's Men.

Meanwhile, the plays poured out of him, 37 in all, from *Love's Labour's Lost* (about 1590) to *Henry VIII* (about 1611); poems, too, from scores of pungent and brilliant sonnets to a handful of rambling historico-classical epics written to please patrons.

By 1610, Shakespeare had had enough. He sold his share in the Globe Theatre and moved back to Stratford-upon-Avon, where he died six years later. At this time his reputation had probably not spread far beyond the world of the theater, and it was not until 1623 that his collected plays were published in a folio edition. For more than a century after that there was little general appetite for Shakespeare, until in the mid-18th century the actor David

**Bust of William Shakespeare—looking unflatteringly stiff and expressionless—above his tomb in Holy Trinity Church, Stratford**

**OBERON: Ill met by moonlight, proud Titania.**
**TITANIA: What, jealous Oberon! Fairies, skip**
**hence: I have foresworn his bed and company.**
**A Midsummer-Night's Dream, Act 2, Scene 1**

Garrick spearheaded a revival of interest in the life and work of the finest playwright the world has ever seen.

## Other Shakespeare sites
**Mary Arden's House** (*tel 01789-204016*), at Wilmcote, off the A3400, 4 miles north of Stratford, is a superb Tudor farmhouse, where

Shakespeare's mother was born. Displays of country crafts and pursuits, inside and out, make up the Shakespeare Country Museum.

**Anne Hathaway's Cottage** (*tel 01789-204016*), in the hamlet of Shottery on the northwestern outskirts of town, is a thatched farmhouse of some size, timber-framed and brick-built, whose low-ceilinged rooms are filled with Tudor furniture. The lovely garden outside is planted with a representation of each species of tree mentioned in the works of Shakespeare.

Off the B4086, 4 miles east of Stratford, is **Charlecote Park** (*NT, tel 01789-470277, closed Nov.–Feb. & Wed.–Thurs. March– Nov.*), an Elizabethan mansion in whose park—tradition says—Shakespeare was caught in his youth poaching deer by Sir Thomas Lucy, the owner, and flogged. Shakespeare took re-venge by circulating some rude doggerel about Sir Thomas, and fled to London to escape the landlord's wrath. The fact that Charlecote did not have a deer park in Tudor times has not diminished this story's popularity. ■

**Magpie-striped half-timbering frames the walls of Mary Arden's House at Wilmcote.**

# Cities of the South Midlands

**Birmingham**
🅰 177 B3
**Visitor information**
✉ 2 City Arcade
☎ 0121-643 2514

**Coventry**
🅰 177 C3
**Visitor information**
✉ Bayley Ln.
☎ 024-7622 7264

**Leicester**
🅰 177 C3
**Visitor information**
✉ 7/9 Every St., Town Hall Sq.
☎ 0116-299 8888

**The modern art in Coventry Cathedral was considered daring, even shocking, when it was unveiled in 1962.**

ASK MOST BRITONS TO NAME THE ATTRACTIONS OF THE three neighboring cities of Birmingham, Coventry, and Leicester, and you'll get a blank stare. "Ugly" and "boring" are the adjectives you are most likely to hear in relation to these former powerhouses of Midlands industry. But times have changed, and it would be a pity to miss out on their lively, multicultural buzz.

## BIRMINGHAM

Birmingham is loud, energetic, brazen, and enormous fun. The gay quarter, south of New Street Station, stays sharp and trendy till the early hours. Farther south around Balsall Heath is the "Balti Triangle," with 101 excellent, inexpensive Asian restaurants—bring your own drink. Nearby Cannon Hill Park is a green, leafy oasis.

Around **Centenary Square** in the city center, skyscrapers dwarf the Georgian humpbacked bridges and clustered canal boats of **Gas Street Basin.** (Birmingham has more canals than Venice.) Nearby on Curzon Sreet you'll find **Thinktank**

(*tel 0121-202 2222, open daily*), a museum celebrating the city's great industrial heritage. The superb **Birmingham Museum and Art Gallery** (*tel 0121-303 2834*) on Chamberlain Square is rich in pre-Raphaelite art.

## COVENTRY

East of Birmingham is Coventry, horrifically bombed in 1940. The shell of the medieval cathedral, burned out in the raid, stands next to the modern replacement, Britain's most remarkable postwar church building.

**Coventry Cathedral** (*tel 024-7652 1247*), designed by Sir Basil Spence (1907–1976; see p. 37), is a treasure house of modern art, from sculptures such as Sir Jacob Epstein's "St. Michael Subduing the Devil" to the giant west wall of glass etched with angelic figures. Benjamin Britten composed his *War Requiem* for the dedication of this wonderful church on May 30, 1962.

## LEICESTER

Leicester, 17 miles northeast of Coventry, has a very successful and distinctive Asian community life. Visit the Sikh temple and **Guru Nanak Sikh Museum** (*tel 0116-262 8606, open Thurs. p.m.*) in the Holy Bones area, and the intricately decorated **Jain Temple** on Oxford Street; stroll down Belgrave Road to shop for filigree jewelry, silks, and Indian cooking ingredients, and to eat spiced lamb, *bhajias*, and *chana bhatura* in one of the restaurants. ∎

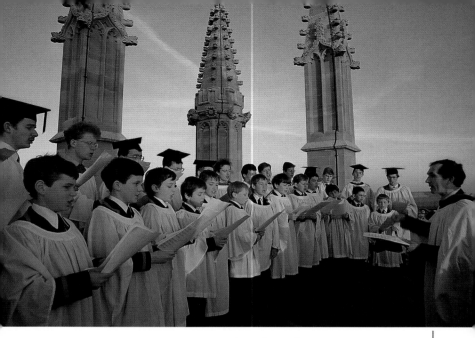

# Oxford

**Oxford**

🅰 179 C2

**Visitor information**

✉ Old School,
Gloucester Green

☎ 01865-726871

🕐 Closed Sun. in
winter

OXFORD, LIKE ITS SISTER UNIVERSITY CITY OF CAMBRIDGE, is all about ambience: a mellow, beautiful mixture of medieval architecture, church spires rising above ancient centers of learning, neat lawns and gardens surrounded by arcaded or gabled quadrangles, and always in the background the sight or sound of a river. Matthew Arnold's "sweet city with her dreaming spires"—though surrounded by all the drab ordinariness of highways and housing developments—still lives on at the heart of Oxford.

**Six o'clock on a May Day morning, and choirboys in their surplices perpetuate one of Oxford's most cherished traditions by hymning the dawn from the top of the Tudor bell tower of Magdalen College chapel.**

Of course, if it were not for **Oxford University** (see pp. 192–93), the "sweet city" would be nothing. This, Britain's oldest seat of learning, was probably already a monastic center of education before 1167, when English scholars ejected from the university at Paris settled here under the protection of a royal residence of Henry II.

The first colleges were founded by religious organizations during the following centuries (Merton traces its origins back to 1264). They were laid out to a monastic pattern: A chapel and a refectory or dining hall forming part of a quadrangle, with the graduates' rooms around it like monks' cells. Ordinary undergraduate students lived out in hostels or lodgings until Tudor times.

These medieval students were far from monkish. Their drunkenness, rowdiness, and frequent confrontations with locals became a byword. But their collective influence was remarkable, with a very high proportion of the most powerful positions in the Church, the City of London, politics, the judiciary and intellectual life filled by Oxford (and Cambridge) graduates. Much the same situation holds true today, though an "Oxbridge" degree is no longer the meal ticket and social imprimatur that it was. ■

# A walking tour of Oxford

In all Europe there is nothing comparable to the richness of Oxford's concentration of religio-academic architecture. This walk lets you taste the cream of it. It can be done at a leisurely pace in a single day, but you might prefer to take a couple of days and divide it up into two sections, one south and the other north of the High Street, known as The High. Note that some of the colleges may charge entrance fees, and any of them may be closed to the public at any time—particularly in term time and in May and June during undergraduate examinations.

**A colorful procession passes under Hertford College's Bridge of Sighs (built in 1913) during the ceremony of Encaenia, when honorary degrees are conferred.**

## SOUTH OF THE HIGH

Carfax is the center of Oxford, the point where the four main roads meet. From the top of **Carfax Tower** ❶ (*tel 01865-792653*), a remnant of the 14th-century Church of St. Martin, there is a superb panoramic view over the whole university and central city.

From Carfax, walk south down St. Aldate's past the Victorian **Town Hall** housing the **Museum of Oxford** (*tel 01865-252761*), a good overview of the city's history from Roman times.

Continue past **Christ Church College** ❷ (*tel 01865-276492*), otherwise known as "The House," founded in 1525 by Cardinal Wolsey. The college chapel is

Oxford's city cathedral, a Saxon foundation with a Norman nave and choir, and 15th-century vaulting. The main quadrangle is **Tom Quad,** arcaded all around; it was to be a cloister, but the builders got no further than raising a terrace. One of its gateways is Sir Christopher Wren's "Tom Tower," from which the Great Tom bell still rings evening curfew for Christ Church undergraduates at 9:05 p.m. —although they ignore it these days.

Turn left along Broad Walk beside Christ Church Meadow to reach the River Cherwell. Bear left up Rose Lane to The High (main street): Turn right here for the **University Botanic Garden** ❸ (*tel 01865-286690*), founded in 1621. It was the first garden in

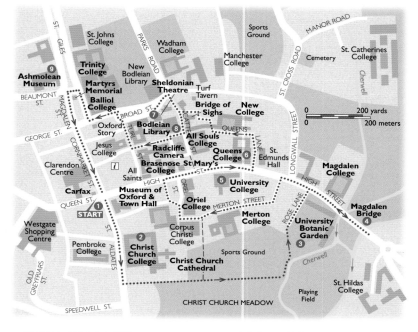

| | |
|---|---|
| ⛰ | 177 C2 |
| ➤ | Carfax |
| ↔ | 2½ miles |
| ⏱ | 6 hours |
| ➤ | Carfax |

### NOT TO BE MISSED

- Botanic Garden
- Sheldonian Theatre
- Ashmolean Museum

Britain dedicated to the scientific study of
plants, and is always beautiful with its herba-
ceous borders, Jacobean formal flower beds,
and big greenhouses.

### Via Magdalen and Merton

Beyond the garden is **Magdalen Bridge** ④,
where you can rent punts (boats) in summer,
and across the road is **Magdalen College**
(*tel 01865-276000*), pronounced MAUDLIN,
founded in 1458 and rich in grotesque
gargoyles. The choir here sings a hymn from
the top of the Tudor bell tower at dawn on
May Day (see p. 191).

Return up The High past Rose Lane, and
turn left along cobbled Merton Street past
**Merton College** (*tel 01865-276310*),
founded in 1264 by the Lord Chancellor of
England. Within is the 14th-century **Mob
Quad,** which contains the oldest library in
England still in use: It holds, among other
treasures, Geoffrey Chaucer's own astrolabe
(star-measurer).

From here bear right onto Oriel Square,
then left past Oriel College along Bear Lane;
take the first right to reach The High. Turn left
if you want to return to Carfax.

### NORTH OF THE HIGH

To continue the walk, turn right along The
High, passing on the left the medieval
**Church of St. Mary the Virgin,** the official church of the university. Continue past
**University College** ⑤ (*tel 01865-276602*),
from which the poet Percy Bysshe Shelley
(1792–1822) was rusticated (sent home) in
1811 for subversive pamphleteering. U.S.
President Bill Clinton was a Rhodes Scholar
here. Now turn left up Queen's Lane, looking
up and around to enjoy the extravagant stone
gargoyles, with **Queen's College** ⑥ (*tel
01865-279120*) on your left (mostly Nicholas

Hawksmoor's work, though Sir Christopher Wren designed the chapel), and on along New College Lane with **New College** (*tel 01865-279555*) on your right. Founded in 1379 by the Bishop of Winchester, to turn out educated priests after their numbers had been decimated by the Black Death, the college has a beautiful quadrangle and gardens, and a chapel with a Nativity by Sir Joshua Reynolds, "St. James" by El Greco, and Sir Jacob Epstein's modern "Lazarus" rising powerfully from the dead.

Pass under the **Bridge of Sighs,** a 20th-century replica of Venice's famous bridge, to reach Catte Street. Bear right onto Broad Street, where the curved rear of the **Sheldonian Theatre** ⑦ (*tel 01865-277299, closed Sun.*) fills the corner. The Sheldonian was built by Wren in 1669, his first design. Balustraded and green-domed, it is used these days for degree ceremonies and concerts. The painted ceiling shows Art and Science banishing Ignorance and Jealousy, two chubby miscreants looking suitably downcast.

Return south on Catte Street to reach **All Souls College** (*tel 01865-279379*), founded by Henry VI in 1438 to commemorate the dead of the Battle of Agincourt. There are no

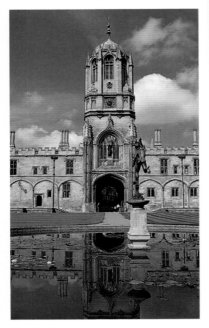

undergraduates here, only Fellows. Opposite All Souls, cross the street to walk between the Bodleian Library and the Radcliffe Camera.

The **Bodleian Library** ⑧ (*Broad St., tel 01865-277161, closed Sat. p.m. & Sun.*) receives a copy of every book published in the U.K. Rarities among its 6,333,000 books and manuscripts are on display in the fan-vaulted, 15th-century Divinity School—the university's oldest lecture room.

The **Radcliffe Camera** (*closed to the public*), just across the way, was built between 1737 and 1749: An eccentric circular building, Italianate in spirit, domed and portholed, it is used as a university reading room.

### Trinity to the Ashmolean

Keep straight on Brasenose Lane, and turn right onto Turl Street. **Trinity College** (*tel 01865-279900*) can be seen opposite at the junction with Broad Street. Founded in 1555, Trinity has Grinling Gibbons carvings in its chapel and a beautiful Lime Walk in its gardens.

Turn left along Broad Street, then go north on Magdalen Street, with **Balliol College** (*tel 01865-277777*) on your right; it was founded in the 13th century by a Scotsman, John Balliol, as a penance for insulting the Bishop of Durham.

Where the street broadens into St. Giles, pass the **Martyrs' Memorial,** designed in 1843 by Sir George Gilbert Scott to commemorate the Reformation martyrdoms of the Protestant bishops Latimer, Ridley, and Cranmer.

Beyond the memorial is the splendid **Ashmolean Museum** ⑨ (*Beaumont St., tel 01865-278000, closed Sun. a.m. & Mon.*), the U.K.'s oldest museum and art gallery (founded in 1683), its eclectic contents from the collection of explorer John Tradescant (1570–circa 1638). Here are Michelangelo's "Crucifixion" and King Alfred's priceless ninth-century jewel, Egyptian mummies and Turner landscapes, Raphael drawings and Pre-Raphaelite paintings, Guy Fawkes's conspiracy lantern and Oliver Cromwell's death mask.

Reel back along Magdalen Street and Cornmarket Street to return to Carfax. ∎

**The bell in the "Tom Tower" of Christ Church is rung 101 times each evening: once for each of the original college members.**

# Around Oxford

THERE ARE BEAUTIFUL WALKS TO BE HAD ALONG THE Thames on both sides of Oxford. A particularly enjoyable upstream walk starts on the western edge of the city at the black-beamed old Trout Inn by Godstow Bridge. You can then follow the river from the pale stone ruin of Godstow Nunnery up to the graceful old toll bridge at Swinford, and on to the little foot-ferry and the Ferryman Inn at Bablockhythe.

**Mapledurham House**

🗺 177 C1

✉ Off A4074, 5 miles northwest of Reading

☎ 0118-972 3350

🕐 Closed Oct.–Easter & Mon.–Fri. Easter–Sept.

💲 House & Mill: $$/$$$. House: $$. Mill: $$.

**The old watermill in the village of Mapledurham is the only remaining working mill on the Thames.**

## LITERARY ASSOCIATIONS

South from Oxford, downstream along the Thames, there is a whole string of attractive and interesting little places to explore. **Sutton Courtenay** is a typical English village around a green; the writer Eric Arthur Blair (pseudonym George Orwell, 1903–1950) is buried in the churchyard.

**Ewelme** is another lovely village, where the 15th-century church, school, and almshouses make a highly photogenic group. Jerome K. Jerome (1859–1927), who wrote the ultimate comic novel about boating on the River Thames, *Three Men In A Boat* (1889), is buried here.

**Mapledurham House** is the big Elizabethan mansion built for the Blount family; also in the village is another waterside grouping of lock, mill, and weir, which inspired

Ernest Shepherd while he was composing his illustrations for Kenneth Grahame's 1908 children's classic, *The Wind in the Willows*. Grahame himself, born in 1859, lived in Church Cottage at **Pangbourne,** just upriver from Mapledurham, from 1924 until his death in 1932.

## BERKSHIRE DOWNS

Some 20 miles southwest of Oxford lies **Lambourn,** famous racehorse-training center on the Berkshire Downs. From here take either the B4000 Ashbury or the B4001 Childrey road to bisect the course of the ancient **Ridgeway** track along the crest of the Downs.

On the Ridgeway, between the two crossing points, lies the famous **White Horse,** its outline cut into the chalk in the Bronze Age, and the vast Neolithic burial chamber of **Wayland's Smithy.** ■

# Blenheim Palace

AT THE END OF PARK STREET, ON THE EDGE OF Woodstock, you pass through the Triumphal Arch to enter the grounds of the old royal hunting lodge, where Henry II and his mistress "Fair Rosamund" Clifford dallied and were discovered by Queen Eleanor. The lodge was said to have been built like a maze, with 150 doors and such labyrinthine twists and turns that only those who knew the secret could enter. However, legend says that this did not prevent the jealous queen from hunting down the Gloucestershire girl. Rosamund was poisoned, or done to death in some other way. The distraught Henry had a cross erected at every place at which the bier-carriers stopped during their journey with her body to Godstow Nunnery.

### HISTORY

By the beginning of the 18th century, when the Royal Manor of Woodstock, which included Woodstock Park, was granted to John Churchill, 1st Duke of Marlborough, there were only a few traces left of the lovers' lodge. The land at Woodstock was the nation's gift to the Duke, a thanksgiving for leading Queen Anne's troops to victory over the French at the Battle of Blenheim in 1704. Parliament also voted the hero an enormous sum of money—in the end it came to £240,000 ($400,000)—to build himself a palatial mansion that would properly reflect the scale of the nation's gratitude. As the building of this house gradually pro-

The Saloon (right), lavishly furnished like all Blenheim Palace's State Rooms, enshrines the handiwork of Louis Laguerre and Grinling Gibbons.

Architects Sir John Vanbrugh and Nicholas Hawksmoor de-signed Blenheim Palace (below)—the grandest of baroque houses—to reflect the nation's gratitude to the Duke of Marlborough, its military hero.

gressed—it took almost 20 years, from 1705 until 1724—the project became ever more expensive and troublesome, and Parliament proved reluctant to come up with the necessary funds. The Duke of Marlborough died in 1722, and his widow, Sarah, had to finish off the enormous baroque structure.

### GRAND PLANS

This really is a palace, the only non-royal one in the country. The designer was Sir John Vanbrugh (1664–1726), essentially a self-taught architect, and he planned on the grandest of scales with the help of Sir Christopher Wren's star pupil, Nicholas Hawksmoor. There are said to be more than 200 rooms in the palace, whose entrance porti-co is impressively colonnaded. From the central block, wings stretch forward to flank the Great Court. The impression one gets—as was intended—is of viewing a national monument as well as the dwelling of a successful general.

Of the many very splendid rooms, the 183-foot **Long Library** is particularly impressive with its arched ends, richly stuc-coed ceiling, and collection of paintings. The **Great Hall's** painted ceiling shows the Duke of Marlborough explaining his plans for the Battle of Blenheim to Britannia. In other **State Rooms** are elaborate murals by Louis Laguerre, and tapestries depicting the duke's military triumphs in his campaigns. His heroic marble mon-ument, sculpted in 1733 by Michael Rysbrack, stands in the **chapel** in the West Wing.

### GREAT LANDSCAPING

Near the house are superb rose gar-dens, a formal Italian garden, and a water terrace garden with sinuous ponds, fountains, and statues. Farther out in the 2,100-acre park,

landscaped by Capability Brown between 1764 and 1774, are a beau-tiful Temple of Diana, a great posthumous Victory Column topped by the Duke dressed as a Roman general, and a Grand Bridge with a 100-foot span, which was installed shortly after building work began on the house. Brown planted trees that are now in their full pomp, and he dammed the River Glyme to create a lake on which today's visitors can idle in a rented boat.

Sir Winston Churchill, a descen-dant of John Churchill, the Duke of Marlborough, was born in the palace on November 30, 1874—several rooms are given over to a display about him. Churchill died in 1965 and lies buried in the churchyard at **Bladon** on the southern edge of the park. ∎

# Northamptonshire

NORTHAMPTONSHIRE, A LONG AND NARROW COUNTY ON the eastern edge of the South Midlands, is often overlooked by visitors, perhaps because of the unremarkable character of Northampton as a county town. However, there is plenty to explore here.

**Althorp House**

📍 177 C3

✉ Off the A428,
6 miles northwest
of Northampton

☎ 01604-770170 (24
hours)

🕐 Closed Oct.–June

💲 $$$/$$$$

**The house at the center of the beautiful Althorp estate conceals a Tudor core that is well worth a visit.**

## ALTHORP HOUSE

The county's best-known house is undoubtedly the Spencer family's seat of **Althorp,** on whose grounds Diana, Princess of Wales, lies buried on an island in a lake. The house itself, an 18th-century remodeling of a Tudor country house, contains fine furniture and portraits (Van Dyck, Gainsborough, Reynolds), but the Diana burial site and museum are the chief attractions.

Northamptonshire is bisected by the M1 expressway, and the **Grand Union Canal,** connecting London with Birmingham. There is a good towpath walk along the canal.

## STOKE BRUERNE

At Stoke Bruerne, off the A508 3 miles south of Northampton, the whole community is focused on the canal, its brightly painted narrowboats, shops, and the delightful waterside **Boat Inn** where impromptu singalongs can occur.

## OUNDLE

Some 25 miles to the northeast of Northampton is **Oundle** (*visitor information, 14 West St., tel 01832-274333*), a very handsome old town built of pale limestone.

The 13th-century **Church of St. Peter** is worth inspection. Its 203-foot spire was climbed in 1880 by a boy from Oundle School; when he reached the ground again his headmaster thrashed him soundly for insubordination, and gave him a golden sovereign for his daring.

A beautiful 3-mile circular walk by the River Nene starts from the church by way of the Market Place, South Road, and Bassett Ford Road. The riverbank path loops from south to north to reach pretty Ashton Mill, before returning into town. Beside the Nene just north of Oundle stands the mound of **Fotheringhay Castle,** where Mary Queen of Scots was imprisoned and executed. ■

England's great treasure of beautiful old churches, handsome Elizabethan country houses, and medieval villages is at its best in easygoing East Anglia, skirted by un-crowded coasts where wildfowl throng in the millions.

# East Anglia & Lincolnshire

Introduction & map **200–201**
Cambridge **202-203**
A walk around Cambridge **204–206**
Newmarket & Ely **207–208**
Saffron Walden & around **209–211**
Suffolk's wool towns **212**
Essex coast **213**
Norwich **216**
Norfolk Broads **217**
Architecture of Norfolk **218–19**
Fenland **220**
Lincolnshire **221**
More places to visit in East Anglia & Lincolnshire **222**
Hotels & restaurants in East Anglia & Lincolnshire **366–79**

**Horsey Mere, Norfolk**

# East Anglia & Lincolnshire

EAST ANGLIA IS ANOTHER OF THOSE NEBULOUS AREAS OF BRITAIN WHOSE exact boundaries remain unfixed. The counties of Suffolk and Norfolk are its heartland; Essex fringes it to the south, Cambridgeshire to the west, Lincolnshire to the north. Its chief characteristic is a lack of dramatic hills, though the East Anglian landscape is not all as flat as its reputation would have you believe. During the Middle Ages, between the 13th and 15th centuries, it was the wealthiest and most populous part of Britain, thanks to the quality of its woolen textiles and the skills of Flemish weavers who settled here when religious persecution drove them from their own countries.

Since those high days, East Anglia has been out of the mainstream of British commerce and fashion, a region with no main through-roads and (apart from Cambridge) only one significant city, Norwich. Agriculture has been its mainstay: grain grown on heavy clay lands, and vegetables on superb silty coastal soil.

Recently East Anglia has been "discovered" by escapees from city pressures who have moved out from London to live the good life here, attracted by the moderate pace of life.

The county of Essex is often overlooked, but its coasts contain hidden marshlands and creeks ideal for bird-watching, while in Saffron Walden and Thaxted in the northwest are some of East Anglia's finest medieval buildings. Suffolk and Norfolk are the real architectural treasure-houses of the region; the

**Horning Water, a man-made lake in the Norfolk Broads, is a prime boating center.**

A

5▷

Barton-upon-
Humber

S.YORKS.
*p. 263*

●Immingham

●Scunthorpe

**M180**

●Grimsby ● ●Cleethorpes

Brigg
●Epworth Caistor

B

*North
Sea*

●Gainsborough

Market
Rasen ●Louth

NOTTS.
*p. 225*

●Scampton

●Mablethorpe

LINCOLNSHIRE

**Lincoln** ●Horncastle

4▷ Old ●
Bolingbroke ●Ingoldmells
●Skegness
●Coningsby
●Leadenham ●Sibsey

LEICS.
*p. 177*

●Sleaford

**Grantham**

A52

Holkham
Hall Wells-next-
the-Sea Felbrigg
Hall ●Cromer

D

▷

Colsterworth

The
Wash

Boston Hunstanton●
Burnham
Market ●Binham
Houghton
Hall ●Fakenham Blickling
Hall ●North Walsham

Sandringham

RUTLAND
*p. 177*

Bourne●

Castle
Rising Salle● Aylsham
●Wroxham Horning

3▷ Stamford **Burghley**

The Fens

Spalding Long Sutton Castle
Acre NORFOLK
Ranworth● The
Broads

Market
Deeping Wisbech
Crowland Dereham
Swaffham **Norwich** Brundall **Great
Yarmouth**

**Peterborough** Upwell Downham
Market ●Watton ●Wymondham A146 Loddon

●Whittlesey March Welney A134 ●Attleborough **Lowestoft**

**A1(M)** Chatteris Little Ouse **Thetford** Diss Bungay ●Beccles

●Sawtry ●Ely Waveney

NORTHANTS.
*p. 177*

●Huntingdon CAMBRIDGESHIRE Stretham ●Mildenhall ●Ixworth Eye● Blythburgh● Southwold

2▷ St.Ives A14 **Wicken Fen** Newmarket **Bury St. Edmunds** Framlingham **Minsmere** ●Dunwich

BEDFORD-
SHIRE
*p. 97*

●St.Neots A428 **Cambridge** Stowmarket Saxmundham
Thorpeness
Snape Aldeburgh

●Melbourn Great Shelford Clare Cavendish Lavenham Woodbridge ●Orford
Orford Ness

Haverhill Long● Kersey **Ipswich** Shingle Street

HERTFORD-
SHIRE
*p. 97*

**Audley End** Saffron
Walden Sudbury●Melford
Stoke-by-Nayland● East Bergholt Felixstowe

●Thaxted Nayland● Dedham **Flatford** Harwich
The Naze

**M11** Great
Dunmow **Braintree** **Colchester** Walton on the Naze
Frinton-on-Sea

A120 **Cressing Temple** ●Coggeshall **Clacton-on-Sea**

**Harlow** ●Witham West
●Mersea **St. Peter's-at-the-Wall**

●Epping **Chelmsford** Chipping
Ongar ●Maldon Dengie
Peninsula

1▷ Greensted Blackwater ●Burnham-on-Crouch

**Chigwell** Foulness

GREATER
LONDON
*p. 48* **Basildon** A13 **Southend-on-Sea**
**Canvey Island**

M25 ●Tilbury

KENT
*p. 116*

0 _____ 30 miles
0 _____ 50 kilometers

Area of map detail

★London

medieval wool
merchants spent
their riches on build-
ing elaborately carved
timber-frame houses
and the finest collec-
tion of parish churches
in Britain, while 16th-
and 17th-century
landowners built them-
selves magnificent
redbrick mansions.

Cambridgeshire, of course, is famous for
the beauty of its great university city. North of
Cambridge the countryside smooths out into
the dead-flat spaces of fenland—rich farmland
cut by straight watercourses, where church

spires and pylons spear into huge skies.
Beyond here rise the Lincolnshire Wolds, a
limestone upland that stretches north to the
old cathedral city of Lincoln. ■

# Cambridge

**Cambridge**

◪ 201 B2

**Visitor information**

✉ Old Library,
Wheeler St.

☎ Inside the UK:
0906-586 2526.
Outside the UK:
44-1223-464 732

CAMBRIDGE IS JUST AS BEAUTIFUL AS OXFORD—SOME think it more so, because it has not been built up and urbanized in the way that Oxford has. The beauty of Cambridge is of a subtle and dreamy order. There is often a misty thickening of the air here on the borders of Fenland, which softens the towers and pinnacles.

**One of the pleasures of strolling around Cambridge is noticing the myriad details of decorative stone carving—in this case the coat of arms (above right) of Magdalene College.**

**Punting on the River Cam at Cambridge (left) is one of the time-worn rituals for undergraduates and visitors alike in this dreamy, watery city.**

## HISTORY OF THE UNIVERSITY

There were already monastic houses and seats of learning along the River Cam hereabouts when lay scholars arrived from Oxford in about 1209. Religious disagreements and a certain amount of trouble between the scholars and the Oxford townsfolk had prompted them to move here. At first the Cambridge scholars—in many cases only in their early teens—lived out in the town, each selecting his own tutor. In 1284 Peterhouse, the oldest and smallest Cambridge college, was founded to bring tutors and pupils together in one community. Dozens of colleges were endowed over the following centuries by academics, religious orders, rich men hoping to pay for a ticket to heaven, and trades unions or guilds. The layout of the Cambridge colleges was the same as at Oxford, with cloisters, dining hall or refectory, chapel, and accommodations laid out around an open square after the general monastic pattern.

There were the usual "town-and-gown" confrontations as privilege and poverty lived side by side. When riots broke out in Cambridge during the Peasants' Revolt of 1381, some of the colleges were plundered and there were several arson attempts. After the dust settled, five locals were hanged for their impudence.

At the Reformation, Cambridge became one of the hotbeds of Protestant thought. Archbishop Cranmer (Jesus College), and bishops Latimer (Clare) and Ridley (Pembroke) were all educated here. A century later Oliver Cromwell (Sidney Sussex) became Member of Parliament for Cambridge. The university continued to have a radical edge and has maintained its position as a spearhead of learning and research. James Watson and Francis Crick discovered the structure of the DNA double helix here, and Ernest Rutherford split the atom in the Cavendish Laboratory. ∎

# A walk around Cambridge

This walk around the compact center of Cambridge can easily be done in a day; or it can be split into north and south Cambridge, with a day allotted to each to allow thorough exploration of one of the finest assemblies of medieval buildings in Europe. Some colleges now charge admission fees. Any of them may be closed to the public at any time, especially during May/June examinations. Telephone first to avoid disappointment.

## NORTH CAMBRIDGE

Leave the visitor information center on Wheeler Street and turn right to reach King's Parade. Bear right to find **Great St. Mary's Church** ➊ on your right. Climb the tower of this 15th-century church for superb views over the city; foolhardy undergraduates have been known to make the ascent up the outside of the tower. Farther along on the left is **Gonville & Caius College** (pronounced KEYS), founded in 1348, with its three Gates of Humility, Virtue, and Honour representing stages on the path to academic fulfillment.

**Lush, willow-fringed meadows line the River Cam—the famous Backs in the city itself, and farther south Grantchester Meadows.**

### Trinity to the Round Church

Keep straight ahead along Trinity Street, with **Trinity College** ➋ (tel 01223-338400) on your left. It was founded in 1546; witness the statue of Henry VIII over the gateway. He holds a chair leg, substituted for his scepter in the 19th century either by a student prankster or by a college porter tired of replacing the oft-pilfered symbol of sovereignty. Trinity's two courts—Cambridge's equivalents of Oxford's quads—are famous. **Great Court**

is the scene of a well-known race in which undergraduates try to run around its perimeter while the clock is striking 12. In the other court, **Nevile's Court,** Isaac Newton (1642–1727) calculated the speed of sound by stamping and timing the echo.

Trinity Street becomes St. John's Street, leading to Bridge Street, where the **Round Church (Church of the Holy Sepulchre)** ➌, with its fine Norman doorway, stands at the intersection. Its circular nave was built in imitation of Jerusalem's church of the same name.

### Magdalene to St. John's

Bear left along Bridge Street and cross Magdalene Bridge, where punts (boats) can be rented, to find the tall brickwork walls and chimneys of **Magdalene College** ➍ (tel 01223-332100) on the right. In Second Court the 17th-century **Pepys Building** contains Samuel Pepys's library, including his famous diary written in his own shorthand. It took 19th-century scholars three years to decode, after which they discovered Pepys's key lying unnoticed among the books.

Retrace your steps down St. John's Street and turn right into **St. John's College** ➎ (tel 01223-338600), a Tudor foundation, through the turreted and tabernacled gateway. This was William Wordsworth's college (1787–1790). He wrote of Cambridge in *The Prelude*: "Gowns grave or gaudy, doctors, students, streets/Courts, cloisters, flocks of churches, gateways, towers," which pretty well sums up today's scene, too.

### Along The Backs to King's

Walk through St. John's to cross the River Cam by Kitchen Bridge (also called St. John's Bridge); look downstream to see the **Bridge of Sighs,** a covered bridge, pinnacled and

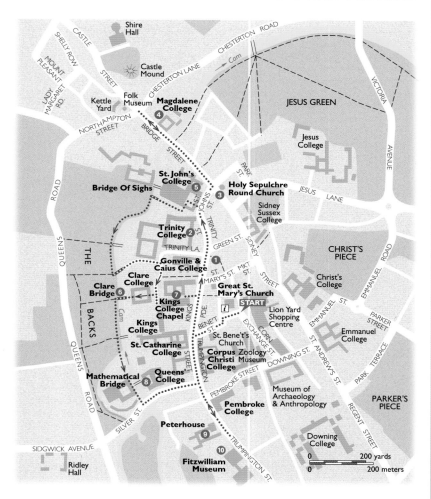

Shire Hall

Castle Mound

CASTLE STREET

CHESTERTON LANE

CHESTERTON ROAD

Cam

SHELLY ROW

CASTLE STREET

MOUNT PLEASANT

LADY MARGARET RD

Kettle Yard

Folk Museum

**Magdalene College** ④

NORTHAMPTON STREET

BRIDGE STREET

JESUS GREEN

Jesus College

VICTORIA AVENUE

ROAD

**St. John's College**

**Bridge Of Sighs**

⑤

PARK ST.

ST. JOHN'S ST.

TRINITY ST.

**Holy Sepulchre Round Church** ③

Sidney Sussex College

JESUS LANE

GREEN ST.

SIDNEY ST.

**Trinity College** ②

TRINITY LA.

CHRIST'S PIECE

QUEENS ROAD

THE

**Gonville & Caius College** ①

ST. MARY'S ST.

MKT ST.

Christ's College

Christ's College

EMMANUEL ROAD

**Clare College**

**Clare Bridge** ⑥

Cam

**Kings College Chapel** ⑦

**Great St. Mary's Church**

**START**

ℹ

Lion Yard Shopping Centre

EMMANUEL ST.

ST. ANDREW'S ST.

PARKER STREET

**Kings College**

KINGS PARADE

BENE'T ST.

ST. BENE'T ST.

CORN EXCHANGE ST.

St. Bene't's Church

Emmanuel College

**St. Catharine College**

TRUMPINGTON STREET

**Corpus Christi College**

Zoology Museum

DOWNING ST.

PARK TERRACE

BACKS

QUEENS ROAD

**Mathematical Bridge** ⑧

**Queens' College**

PEMBROKE STREET

Museum of Archaeology & Anthropology

PARKER'S PIECE

SILVER ST.

**Pembroke College**

REGENT STREET

**Peterhouse** ⑨

TRUMPINGTON ST.

Downing College

SIDGWICK AVENUE

Ridley Hall

**Fitzwilliam Museum** ⑩

0 _____ 200 yards

0 _____ 200 meters

crenellated, built in 1831. Across the Cam, bear left along **The Backs,** Cambridge's famous green spaces that fringe the river.

At Garret Hostel Lane recross the Cam, noting upstream the lovely balustraded **Clare Bridge** ⑥ of 1639, the oldest bridge in Cambridge.

Continue ahead to turn right along Trinity Lane to the buttresses and turreted white stone walls of **King's College Chapel** ⑦, one of the best known churches in the world thanks to its annual radio and television broadcast of the Christmas service of Nine Lessons and Carols.

🅰 201 B2

▶ Tourist information center

↔ 2 miles

🕐 5 hours

▶ Tourist information center

**NOT TO BE MISSED**

- Trinity College
- The Backs
- King's College Chapel
- Queens' College
- Fitzwilliam Museum

Probably Britain's finest example of perpendicular Gothic architecture, the chapel was begun in 1446 and finished in 1515. The fan-vaulted nave, the vivid Tudor glass, the huge baroque organ, and the Rubens altarpiece all lend grandeur and fascination to this wonderful church, where at 5:30 p.m. daily *(except Mon.)* you can enjoy the red-cassocked choir's celestial singing at Evensong.

**King's College** *(tel 01223-331100)* faces onto King's Parade, from where you can return to the visitor information center.

Fan vaulting high above the nave of King's College Chapel leads the eye forward to the carved screen around the organ case.

## SOUTH CAMBRIDGE

From **King's College Chapel** return to Trinity Lane, bearing left through the Jacobean courts of **Clare College** *(tel 01223-333200)* to recross the Cam by Clare Bridge. Turn left and follow the path along The Backs (behind King's College), bearing left along Silver Street

down the side of **Queens' College** **8** *(tel 01223-335511)*, one of Cambridge's most beautiful colleges, with wonderful Tudor courts and the half-timbered **President's Lodge.** Recross the river over Silver Street Bridge from where you can see the **Mathematical Bridge,** built using coach screws in 1749 by James Essex the Younger and subsequently rebuilt in 1866 and 1905.

Continuing up Silver Street to the intersection, turn right along Trumpington Street. **Peterhouse** **9** *(tel 01223-338200)*, founded in 1284, is on the right, the oldest and smallest college in Cambridge, retaining its 13th-century hall. The poet Thomas Gray, a fellow here in the 1740s, was terrified of fire and had iron bars (still there) fixed to his window to support an escape ladder. Unsympathetic students roused him one night by shouting "Fire!" and watched him drop in his nightshirt into a tub of water they had placed under his window. Mortally offended, Gray quit Peterhouse forthwith.

### Back via the Fitzwilliam

Beyond Peterhouse are the granite and marble halls of the **Fitzwilliam Museum** **10** *(Trumpington St., tel 01223-332900, closed Mon.)*, one of Europe's best museums. The Lower Galleries hold a classical collection; the ceramics and English pottery are well known; and there are numerous illuminated medieval and Dark Ages manuscripts. The Upper Galleries' art collection is breathtaking, from Titian and Hans Hals through English masters to Pre-Raphaelites, Impressionists, and 20th-century stars including Modigliani and Picasso.

Return along Trumpington Street, passing **Pembroke College** *(tel 01223-338100)*. Beyond Silver Street you will find **Corpus Christi College** *(tel 01223-338000)*, on the right. Corpus Christi was founded in 1352 to give gifted men of humble birth the chance of a decent education.

On the north side a gallery links the college to St. Bene't's Church, whose Saxon tower is the oldest structure in this ancient town.

Continue along King's Parade, and turn right up Bene't Street to reach the visitor information center. ■

# Newmarket & Ely

IN THE MID-18TH CENTURY, THE JOCKEY CLUB WAS founded in Newmarket to regulate the unbridled and dissolute sport of horse racing, and since then Newmarket has been the very heart of British racing, training, and bloodstock breeding. In the flattish, open country around the town are some 50 stud farms, several dozen training stables ranging from world-famous names with hundreds of horses to unknown hopefuls with a handful of also-rans, and nearly 50 miles of gallops on which the horses can be seen exercising at any time of year.

**Jockeys train for their big day on the gallops at Newmarket.**

## Sport of kings

Newmarket has been a favorite with horse-racing enthusiasts ever since James I stopped on his way through to enjoy a little hare-coursing on the great sandy heaths around the town.

In 1622 the first recorded horse race was run, and within 50 years King James's grandson had made Newmarket one of the most fashionable places in the land.

The Merry Monarch, Charles II, not only shifted his whole court each spring and summer to a palace he had built for himself in Newmarket, he once risked his own neck riding in the 4-mile Newmarket Town Plate race—and came in first. At night Charles would go adventuring incognito under the name of his favorite stallion, Old Rowley.

Nowadays the sport is influenced by immensely rich Arab owners, but still takes place in much the same way as of old—public days out in summer on the July Course, and a more serious form in spring (e.g. the two Classics, 1,000 and 2,000 Guineas) and fall (the Champion Stakes) on the Rowley Mile nearby. ∎

**Newmarket**

🗺 201 B2

**Visitor information**

✉ Palace House, Palace St.

☎ 01638-667200

**Ely**

🗺 201 B3

**Visitor information**

✉ Oliver Cromwell's House, 29 St. Mary's St.

☎ 01353-662062

**Ely Cathedral's great central octagon, topped with its wooden lantern, stands as a landmark visible over 20 miles of flat Fenland country.**

## NEWMARKET

The trim little town of Newmarket lies 13 miles east of Cambridge off the A45. On High Street, a handsome avenue of Georgian and Victorian buildings, is **The National Horseracing Museum** *(tel 01638-667333, closed Nov.–Easter; Mon. Easter–June & Sept.–Oct.)*, with many fascinating trophies and racing exhibits.

Nearby is the headquarters of the **Jockey Club** (visits possible as part of a tour organized by the National Horseracing Museum), where racing's rules are reviewed, and errant jockeys and owners are hauled over the coals.

Along The Avenue, just below the museum, is **Tattersalls** *(tel 01638-665931, call for dates of sales)*, Britain's most famous venue for bloodstock sales. Nearby are the buildings of the **National Stud** *(Tours by appointment, tel 01638-666789, closed Oct.–Feb.)*.

## ELY

Fifteen miles north of Cambridge, on the edge of the great flat region of Fenland, the small cathedral city of Ely stands on a low rise of ground. In 1083 building work began on **Ely Cathedral** *(tel 01353-667735)*; it was completed in 1189. In 1322, after the original Norman tower had collapsed, a great octagon of wood weighing 400 tons was raised to a central position over the building, topped off in 1348 with a graceful 62-foot lantern held in place by enormous trunks of oak. This crownlike structure, together with the 217-foot tower at the west end of the church, gives Ely Cathedral an unmistakable and entirely dominant profile in the level landscape.

Inside, the wooden roof of the nave was painted during Queen Victoria's reign with scenes from the Bible. At the east end are two elaborately carved Tudor chantry chapels, and in the roofs of the two transepts the medieval carvers left wonderful bosses—best seen with a pair of binoculars.

Examples of the glasspainter's skill, dating back through the centuries to 1240, are displayed in the **Stained Glass Museum** *(South Triforium, tel 01353-660347)* in the cathedral. ∎

# Saffron Walden & around

"THE BEST-LOOKING SMALL TOWN IN EAST ANGLIA" IS A title claimed for Saffron Walden, and with some justification. Around Gold Street, High Street, Church Street, and King Street the half-timbered, color-washed houses crowd the sidewalks of this prosperous and beautifully preserved town in the northwest corner of Essex. The visitor information center has an excellent Town Trail leaflet, and sells bulbs of the mauve saffron crocus flower that gave the town both its name and—used in the manufacture of yellow dye—its prosperity from late Tudor times onward, when woolen textile wealth was beginning to drift northward away from East Anglia.

**Saffron Walden**

▲ 201 B2

**Visitor information**

✉ 1 Market Pl.

☎ 01799-510444

There are effigies of the crocus on Saffron Walden's coat of arms, in an aisle carving opposite its church's south door, and on the sides of its old houses in the form of pargetting—the art of ornamental plasterwork. Pargetting reaches its apogee on the walls of the 14th-century **Sun Inn** (now an antique shop) on Church Street, where, tangled up in a riot of foliage and wildlife, some strange symbols are seen, among them a stockinged foot, and the Giant of Wisbech doing battle with local hero Tom Hickathrift. Across Church Street and up Museum Street, under a 193-foot spire, stands the big **Parish Church of St. Mary;** angels support its medieval roof, and the organ has a phenomenally loud extra set of pipes known as a *trompeta real.*

Parallel with Church Street is Castle Street, with the remains of Walden Castle and the excellent **Saffron Walden Museum** *(Museum St., tel 01799-510333)* at

**Saffron Walden is one of Essex's most appealing small towns, its streets lined with eccentrically shaped, medieval buildings.**

its northern end. Across from St. Mary's on Castle Street is the narrow entrance to **Bridge End Gardens** (tel 01799-510444, *Victorian maze open by appointment*)—some formal, some informal, all grown around with roses. **Bridge Street,** at the foot of Castle Street, is an attractive huddle of medieval houses looking west into open country, while **Myddylton Place** off the High Street is crammed with lovely old buildings. Perhaps the best view of

the town, showing the dominance of St. Mary's clerestory windows and spire, is from **Gold Street.**

East Street leads out to Saffron Walden's big open common, into which someone cut a circular **turf maze** some 800 years ago.

### AUDLEY END

One mile west of Saffron Walden, Audley End (tel 01799-522399, *closed Nov.–March & Tues. April–Sept. Select openings, March & Oct. Call for times*) is a monument to the pride and ambition of Thomas Howard, 1st Earl of Suffolk and Lord Treasurer to James I, who spent a quarter of a million pounds on building this superb mansion house between 1605 and 1614.

What you see today is only one-third of the original house; the rest was demolished in the 1720s under the direction of Sir John Vanbrugh to make it more habitable. During the 18th century Robert Adam redesigned the drawing and dining rooms, and Capability Brown landscaped the grounds.

### THAXTED

Six miles southeast of Saffron Walden on the B184 is Thaxted (*visitor information, Clarance House, Watling St., tel 01371-831641*), another town that became rich on the medieval wool trade, and also on the manufacture of cutlery, quite a novel concept in pre-Tudor times. This wealth paid for the slow building, during the 14th and 15th centuries, of the big **Parish Church of St. John the Baptist,** with its 181-foot spire. Gustav Holst (1874–1934) composed parts of his "Planets Suite" while he was organist here.

In the marketplace stands a 14th-century Guildhall (tel 01371-831641, *closed Oct.–Easter & Mon.–Sat. Easter–Sept.*), its three stories overhang the sidewalks. Along Mill Lane, John Webb's Windmill (tel 01371-830285, *call for opening times*) houses a rural museum.

### COGGESHALL

Coggeshall is a notable town with more than 200 medieval buildings. The **Woolpack Inn** near the church is gorgeous; so is the elaborately carved **Paycocke's House** (NT, West St., tel 01376-561305, *closed mid-Oct.–early April, Mon., Wed., Fri.–Sat. early April–mid-Oct.*). **Coggeshall Grange Barn** (NT, Grange Hill, tel 01376-562226, *closed same as Paycocke's*), a reputedly haunted cathedral of the harvest, dates back to 1140, the oldest barn in Europe. ■

# Suffolk's wool towns

**Sudbury**

🅰 201 C2

**Visitor information**

✉ Town Hall, Market Hill

☎ 01787-881320

**Lavenham**

🅰 201 C2

**Visitor information**

✉ Lady St.

☎ 01787-248207

🕐 Closed Jan.–Easter, & Mon.–Fri. Nov.–Dec.

THE GENTLY ROLLING VALLEYS OF SOUTH SUFFOLK ARE particularly rich in small towns beautified by wealth from the medieval wool trade. The River Stour forms the boundary between Suffolk and Essex, and along the Stour Valley lies a whole string of these wool towns, the focus of a few days' rewarding exploration.

**Clare** and **Cavendish** are twin towns to the northwest of Sudbury. Clare has a number of half-timbered houses and the active Nethergate Brewery; Cavendish is all pink-faced charm around a broad green.

Farther downstream, **Long Melford** has one of East Anglia's most splendid parish churches in Holy Trinity, two fine Elizabethan mansions in **Melford Hall** *(NT, tel 01787-880286, closed Nov.–March., Mon.–Fri. April & Oct., & Mon.–Tues. May–Sept.)* and **Kentwell Hall** *(tel 01787-310207, closed Jan., reservations only Feb.–March & Nov.–Dec., call for summer hours)*, a long main street lined with timbered houses, and a superabundance of antique shops.

South lies **Sudbury**, dotted with more medieval houses; **Gainsborough's House** *(46 Gainsborough St., tel 01787-372958)*

is the birthplace of the artist, now a museum of his work.

Southeast again are **Nayland** in the valley and **Stoke-by-Nayland,** with its striking church tower on the ridge.

North of Stoke is half-hidden **Kersey** in its dip of ground, a tumble of medieval houses.

Next is **Lavenham,** the showpiece wool town of Suffolk, with its superb **Guildhall of Corpus Christi** *(NT, Market Place, tel 01787-247646, closed Dec.–Feb., Mon.–Fri. March & Nov., Mon.–Tues. April)*, now a local history museum; the 15th-century **Little Hall** *(Market Place, tel 01787-247179, closed Nov.–March, also Mon.–Tues.& Fri. April–Oct.)*; the Angel Hotel, with 14th-century murals; the great church (1480–1520) buttressed by a big tower; and the crazily half-timbered **Swan Inn** with the medieval Wool Hall swallowed up inside. ∎

Built by the Guild of Corpus Christi in the 16th century, Lavenham Guildhall has had many uses over the centuries and now houses a museum showcasing 500 years of local history.

# Essex coast

ESSEX HAS A RAGGED, INDENTED COAST SLICED INTO marshy creeks and tidal mudflats. Three well-known seaside resorts lie shoulder to shoulder along its northern reach: Clacton-on-Sea (brash and commercial), Frinton-on-Sea (clean and upscale), and Walton-on-the-Naze (quirky and old-fashioned). But there are subtler pleasures to be enjoyed.

## AROUND THE DENGIE PENINSULA

Northeast of London the Rivers Crouch and Blackwater fringe the lonely **Dengie Peninsula;** out on its northeast tip is **St. Peter's-at-the-Wall,** the oldest Saxon church (A.D. 654) in use in Britain. On the Blackwater lies **Maldon,** an atmospheric little port where sea salt is processed and red-sailed veteran barges lie up at The Hythe. North of the Blackwater is **Tollesbury,** with wooden sail-drying lofts and a big red lightship moored in the salt marshes; **Mersea Island,** where you can eat oysters caught locally; and **Old Hall Marshes bird reserve,** wardened by the Royal Society for the Protection of Birds, superb for watching wildfowl.

## THE NAZE & HARWICH

North again are the crumbling red cliffs of **The Naze,** yielding prehistoric sharks' teeth; and, sheltered behind them, **Hamford Water** (also known as Walton Backwaters), a tidal inland sea where a few people live on little marsh islands.

Finally, where Essex looks at Suffolk across the estuary of the River Stour, stands **Harwich,** a medieval port packed on a headland that contains lighthouse museums, one of the oldest cinemas in the country, the house where the *Mayflower*'s captain lived, and the Redoubt fort built by French prisoners-of-war to keep their own Napoleon Bonaparte at bay. ∎

## Colchester

The Colchester Town Trail leaflet, available from the Tourist Information Centre *(1 Queen St., tel 01206-282920),* shows you Britain's oldest recorded town in a two-hour stroll. Highlights include the **Roman city wall;** the Norman **St. Botolph's Priory;** the Saxon tower of **Holy Trinity Church** (now a museum); the Roman **Balkerne Gate; Jumbo,** the Victorian water tower; medieval weavers' houses in the **Dutch Quarter;** and the **Colchester Castle Museum** *(tel 01206-282939).* ∎

**Maldon**
🅰 201 C1
**Visitor information**
✉ Coach Lane
☎ 01621-856503

**Harwich**
🅰 201 C2
**Visitor information**
✉ Iconfield Park, Parkeston
☎ 01255-506139
🕐 Closed Sun. Oct.–March

**The Punch and Judy show—traditional seaside fun**

# Constable Country

Following the River Stour for a couple of miles through the lush meadows of John Constable's Dedham Vale, this 3-mile walk presents you with one famous view after another from Constable's best known landscapes. Remarkably little has changed here in the century and a half since the painter died.

John Constable was born in 1776 at East Bergholt, 2 miles northeast of Dedham where your walk begins at the river bridge. For a time the young painter was apprenticed to his father, Golding Constable, a well-to-do miller who owned the water mill at **Flatford** *(visitor information, Flatford Lane, tel 01206-299460, closed Nov.–mid-Dec., Mon.–Fri. Jan.–Feb., Mon.– Tues. March)*, a mile or so downriver, and also the mill here at Dedham. "Dedham Lock and

Mill," painted in 1820, shows the old brick-built mill (later replaced by the present one), its mill pond, sluice, and the lock that admitted barges to the upper reaches of the Stour. Dedham's late 15th-century church and wide, tree-lined High Street of half-timbered medieval houses make a typically East Anglian ensemble.

### Along the river

From Dedham bridge walk toward the village along the B1029, turning left past the mill by a redbrick house onto a lane to reach a little ford. Go over the stile on the right and pass through the grounds of elegant **Dedham Hall.** Bear left at the top of the drive onto a footpath, dropping diagonally down through fields and trees to reach the southern bank of the Stour, where you bear right along the river.

The broad stretch of river between here and Flatford is, in fact, a canal, cut when the Stour was being altered to take barge traffic early in the 18th century. Its original course is marked by a narrow channel that wriggles through the fields on your right-hand side.

## Famous landscapes

Handsome trees shade these broad meadows where sheep and cows graze. The path winds beside the river among gnarled old willows to reach Flatford by a bridge, where you can compare the view with the one painted by John Constable in "Flatford Mill" (1817). The impatient lad whom the artist placed astride a huge, placid barge horse has his present-day counterpart in the local boys who wait by the bridge with baited lines and bated breath. This is the same tranquil scene of water, trees, and mellow old buildings that Constable painted. There is a superb photogenic view of the mill, seen across the mill pond, from a point a few yards farther down the south bank. To reach the mill, cross the bridge and turn right down the lane by the thatched, 16th-century **Bridge Cottage** *(NT, tel 01206-298260, closed mid-Dec.–early Jan., Mon.–Fri. Jan.–Feb., Mon.–Tues March–April & Nov.–mid-Dec.)*, with teas, boat rental, a Constable exhibition, a shop, and guided walks. Just beyond, on the right, is the dry dock depicted in "Boat-building near Flatford Mill" (1815), rediscov-

ered a few years ago along with the skeleton of one of the Constable family's barges.

At the end of the land stands Golding Constable's Mill, given to the National Trust in 1943 and now a field studies center. Across the mill pond is Willy Lott's House, which overlooks the carters, horses, and laden wagon depicted in the "Hay-wain" of 1821, the most famous Constable landscape of all.

## More classic views

From Flatford Mill, retrace your steps up the lane past Bridge Cottage to the top of the large parking lot on the hillside above, and turn left onto a narrow lane (uncomfortably busy on summer weekends). This climbs in half a mile to a right-angle bend. A stile on the left here brings you onto a path descending a field slope, from which you can enjoy the wonderful view that Constable celebrated in "The Valley of the

**The National Trust maintains Willy Lott's House (above) exactly as John Constable depicted it in the sun-splashed "Hay-wain" (left)—standing among trees with its tapering brick chimney stack facing the pool of Flatford Mill.**

Stour, with Dedham in the Distance" (1805).

Continue down to the bottom of the slope then turn left to cross a wooden footbridge and continue to the River Stour. On reaching the river, bear right and follow the north bank which returns you to Dedham bridge. ∎

# Norwich

NORWICH, CAPITAL OF EAST ANGLIA, IS A BEAUTIFUL medieval city of manageable size. Twelfth-century Flemish settlers brought it prosperity as a weaving center; the industrial revolution of the 18th and 19th centuries largely sidelined it. Here life runs at an agreeably relaxed pace.

**Norwich**
🗺 201 C3
**Visitor information**
✉ The Forum
 Millennium Plain
☎ 01603-727927
🕐 Closed Sun.

**Brightly striped "tilts" (awnings) cover the stalls and labyrinthine alleys of Norwich's permanent market, beyond which stand the Guildhall of 1407–1413 and Norwich City Hall.**

## NORWICH CATHEDRAL

By far the most striking building in the city is its magnificent Norman cathedral *(tel 01603-218321)* of pale Caen limestone, the nave's height enhanced by superb 15th-century fan vaulting and more than 700 individually carved roof-bosses (which can be inspected with the help of special wheeled mirrors). A slender spire soars 315 feet into the sky—only Salisbury's is taller (see pp. 131–32)—and delicate flying buttresses set the east end of the building sailing like the prow of a great stone ship. Chapels bulge from this end, their interiors decorated with 14th-century frescoes.

## AROUND THE CLOSE

Tudor buildings, made of stone from the demolished monastery, surround the cathedral green, which is entered by the tall and imposing **Erpingham Gate,** built in 1420 by Sir Thomas Erpingham. The knight, whose effigy adorns the gateway, directed the archers' deadly arrow fire at the Battle of Agincourt in 1415.

The River Wensum encloses the cathedral, and footpaths run along the bank to the east and north past attractive **Pull's Ferry,** the cathedral's 15th-century watergate, or riverport, and the bottom of Wensum Street.

Southwest of the cathedral is the busy and lively **Market Place.** Here stands the beautiful 15th-century **Church of St. Peter Mancroft,** with a roof of carved angels and an east window showing biblical scenes in the stained glass.

Above is **Norwich Castle** *(tel 01603-493625, recorded information 01603-493648),* its Norman keep now a museum notable for its early 19th-century East Anglian landscapes by the Norwich school and its huge collection of teapots. ■

# Norfolk Broads

THERE ARE NEARLY 50 OF THE SHALLOW LAKES KNOWN AS the Norfolk Broads, spread out in a great arc to the north and east of Norwich between the city and the Norfolk coast. This area is threaded by wriggling, snakelike rivers—the Yare, Bure, Waveney, Ant, and Thurne—and bedded on solid peat.

It was the peat that brought the Norfolk Broads into being, for the broads are flooded pits that were excavated by peat-diggers during medieval times to feed the tremendous appetite for fuel of the quickly expanding city of Norwich. The Norfolk marshmen dug channels to join up the water-filled pits; reeds and sedges were cut for thatching from shallow boats; and wild ducks and fish were trapped and netted.

## MANAGING THE LAND

This entire landscape of broads, fen, reeds, carr woodland, pasture, and watercourses is known as Broadland, nowadays a playground for amateur sailors and motorboaters, fishermen, and vacationers. Discovery by the outside world has brought problems of erosion, pollution, noise, and waterside development. The Broads Authority is having fair success at tackling these issues; its schemes include creating many thousands of acres of nature reserves, reinstating traditional ways of Broadland management, pumping out polluted mud, and encouraging the growth of new plant life in broads whose water had become a sterile, algal soup. The area was designated a national park in 1989, which brought it under much needed statutory protection.

## BOATING & WILDLIFE

Broadland, in its healthy and properly managed state, is a delicately balanced jigsaw in which each element contributes to the whole. It is a spellbinding place, particularly away from the main tourist area around Hoveton, Horning, and Wroxham. Sailing *(boats are for rent from these places, and elsewhere)* is by far the best way to enjoy the Norfolk Broads, along with a walk along the duckboard trails of such reserves as Hickling Broad and Ranworth Broad. The **Broadland Conservation Centre** is at Ranworth, 8 miles east of Norwich.

Wildlife includes reed buntings and marsh tits, grasshopper warblers and spotted flycatchers, marsh harriers and barn owls, and, among the reed beds, the shy booming bittern and the dramatic yellow swallowtail butterfly. ■

**Broadland Conservation Centre**

🗺 201 D3

✉ Ranworth, off the B1140; 4 miles southeast of Wroxham

☎ 01603-270479

🕐 Closed Nov.–March

**Windmills such as this one at Horsey Mere were built to help drain the surrounding marshes.**

# Architecture of Norfolk

**Sandringham**

🅰 201 B3

☎ 01553-772675

🕐 Closed early Oct.–Easter & late July–early Aug.

💲 $$

**Houghton Hall**

🅰 201 C4

☎ 01485-528569

🕐 Closed late Sept.– Easter & Mon.– Wed. & Fri.–Sat. Easter–late Sept.

💲 $$/$$$

THE GENTLY ROLLING FLINT, CHALK, AND CLAY LANDSCAPE of north Norfolk, thickly wooded and wonderfully peaceful, is remarkably well endowed with notable buildings, signposting a thousand years of history. Ecclesiastical architecture of the Middle Ages, which reached its English rural apogee in East Anglia, is also well represented.

## CASTLE RISING & CASTLE ACRE

Over in the westernmost part of the region at **Castle Rising,** 4 miles northeast of King's Lynn, stands a splendid late Norman **castle** *(tel 01533-631330, closed Mon.– Tues. Nov.–March)* built inside Roman ramparts by William d'Albini in 1138, its great stone staircase losing itself in a warren of vaulted rooms and galleries.

Fifteen miles east is **Castle Acre,** where a tree-lined village street of great charm runs from the ruined walls and massive earth-works of the castle to the impressive remains of an early Norman Cluniac **priory** *(tel 01760-755394, closed Mon.–Tues. Nov.–March),* founded around 1090. The arcaded west front with its expressive grotesques is striking, as is the all-but-intact Prior's Lodging.

## BINHAM & SALLE

Another very fine Norman priory church of the same date survives at **Binham,** off the A148 8 miles northeast of Fakenham. The west front with its round window is one of the very earliest examples of

The Sandringham estate, one of the Royal Family's country homes

Early English architecture. Perhaps the finest example among literally hundreds of lovely and memorable parish churches in north Norfolk is that of **St. Peter and St. Paul** at **Salle,** a tiny hamlet off the B1145, 12 miles northwest of Norwich. The church's great 111-foot tower dwarfs the houses in its shadow. There are strangely feathered angels swinging censers over the west door, ragged wild men (woodwoses) guarding the north porch with clubs, and, inside the church, a great deal of remarkable work from memorial brasses to woodcarving. But it is the supreme dignity and harmony of the interior, the sense of great space flooded with clear light, that gives Salle its preeminence among north Norfolk churches.

## SANDRINGHAM

Of the great country houses that are the glory of north Norfolk, Sandringham, 10 miles north of King's Lynn, is the best known by virtue of its use since 1862 by the Royal Family as their East Anglian vacation hideaway.

There is a museum of field sports and a collection of vintage royal vehicles, but the attraction of looking around this Georgian house is the opportunity to touch (figuratively) the hem of the robe of the House of Windsor.

## HOUGHTON & HOLKHAM

Before purchasing Sandringham in 1862 for her son Edward, Prince of Wales, Queen Victoria had considered buying, but turned down, **Houghton Hall,** 7 miles to the east, a splendid Palladian pile built in the 1730s for England's first prime minister, Sir Robert Walpole (1676–1745). The William Kent-designed State Rooms and Stone Hall qualify Houghton as one of England's most impressive country houses.

The same can also be said of **Holkham Hall** *(tel 01328-710227, closed Oct.– May, except Bank Holiday weekends, and Tues.–Wed. June–Sept.),* another Kent design, with grounds designed by Capability Brown. Holkham, 8 miles north of Fakenham. Huge and sprawling, its State Rooms

contain paintings by English and Dutch masters and classical Roman sculpture.

## BLICKLING & FELBRIGG

The north Norfolk house best known on its own merit is **Blickling Hall** *(NT, tel 01263-738030, closed Nov.–late March, Mon.–Tues. late March–Oct.),* 15 miles north of Norwich. This wonderful redbrick Tudor mansion with its curly Dutch-style gables, where Anne Boleyn lived as a child, was largely redesigned in Jacobean times. Plasterwork ceilings ornamented with allegorical figures, and splendid tapestries are among the attractions of Blickling.

As an antidote to grandeur, visit **Felbrigg Hall** *(NT, tel 01263-837444, closed Nov.–March, Thurs.–Fri. April–Oct.),* 2 miles southwest of Cromer, a 17th-century gentleman's residence with an orangery and a fine walled garden. ■

Felbrigg Hall's stylish dining room, with its prominent rococo plasterwork, Georgian table, and fine china dessert service

# Fenland

**The Fens**

△ 201 B3

**Wicken Fen**

✉ Lode Ln., Wicken

☎ 01353-720274

🕐 Visitor center
closed Mon.

💲 $$

**King's Lynn**

△ 201 B3

**Visitor information**

✉ The Custom House,
Purfleet Quay

☎ 01553-763044

FENLAND IS A MAN-MADE LANDSCAPE, A HUGE 700-SQUARE-mile saucer of peat and silt bounded by the uplands of Lincolnshire, Cambridgeshire, Suffolk, and Norfolk. Most of it lies flat, at or below sea level, drained of its water during the 17th century by Dutch engineers, protected by sea walls and flood banks, and converted from waterlogged marsh and fen to some of the richest farmland in the world.

## WICKEN FEN & STRETHAM

A taste of old predrainage Fenland can be had at **Wicken Fen** (NT), 17 miles northeast of Cambridge, where 600 acres of undrained, unimproved fen is traditionally managed with sedge- and reed-cutting for the benefit of dragon-flies, butterflies, owls, songbirds, and waterbirds such as the great crested grebe.

At **Stretham,** 3 miles away off the A10 Ely road, a huge 1831 steam-driven beam pumping engine powers a 37-foot wheel to show how water was lifted into drainage channels from the fields, which are still sinking as their underlying peat dries and shrinks.

## UP TO THE WASH

To the west run the twin Bedford Rivers, cut in the 17th century; halfway up their 20-mile, dead-straight course is the **Wildfowl & Wetlands Trust's** bird reserve *(tel 01353-860711)* at Welney, where you can see dramatic flights of wild-fowl in winter months.

The A1101 runs north from Welney to **Upwell,** a pretty village with curly-gabled houses along the banks of the Old River Nene.

Five miles north of Upwell on the A1101, the New (straightened) Nene divides the town of **Wisbech** *(visitor information, 2–3 Bridge St., tel 01945-583263, closed Sun.),* which stands among fields of strawberries, daffodils, and roses. The Georgian houses of North and South Brinks shadow the curve of the river. The Nene runs north to empty into the great Fenland estu-ary of **The Wash.** Here stands **King's Lynn,** another dignified old port with medieval churches and guildhalls. ∎

**The Bedford River, near Newport in Cambridgeshire, was dug in the 17th century to help drain the marshy fens.**

## Lincolnshire Wolds

The Lincolnshire Wolds are a 40-mile-long range of unfrequented, rolling limestone hills, rising between Lincoln and the coast. Prettiest among the villages they shelter is **Old Bolingbroke** in the south, where Henry IV was born in 1367. **Louth,** to the east, is an attractive Georgian market town with a tall church steeple. ∎

# Lincolnshire

**Stamford**

🏰 201 A3

**Visitor information**

✉ Stamford Arts
Centre,
29 St. Mary's St.

☎ 01780-755611

**Boston**

🏰 201 B4

**Visitor information**

✉ Market Pl.

☎ 01205-356656

**Lincoln**

🏰 201 A4

**Visitor information**

✉ 9 Castle Hill

☎ 01522-873213

**Many of Lincoln's
finest buildings,
clustered around
the castle and
cathedral on the
hill, date from
medieval times.**

IN THE EXTREME SOUTHWEST OF LITTLE-VISITED
Lincolnshire lies Stamford, one of England's most attractive Georgian
towns. Barn Hill gives the best overall view of the town's winding
medieval street plan and its cluster of church spires.

## BURGHLEY HOUSE

Just south of Stamford is Burghley
House *(tel 01780-752451, closed
Nov.–March)*, a giant Elizabethan
mansion built between 1565 and
1587 for Queen Elizabeth I's
favorite and counselor, William
Cecil, 1st Lord Burghley (1520–
1598), and altered and improved
during the following century.
Pepperpot cupolas, chimney
stacks like runs of classical colon-
nading, side towers, and buttresses
are all dominated by the great
central gatehouse.

Inside are 240 rooms: Star sights
are the fantastic double Hell
Staircase, whose ceiling by Antonio
Verrio (1639–1707) shows sinners
being devoured by a demonic cat,
and the equally exaggerated Heaven
Room, with its frolicking Verrio
nymphs and gods. Burghley's
splendid deer park was landscaped
in about 1766 by Capability Brown.

## BOSTON

Northeast of Stamford is Boston,
whence came the religious dissenters
who sailed from Southampton in
1630 to found Boston in America.
Boston's beautiful 14th-century
**Church of St. Botolph** is
crowned by the Boston Stump, a
272-foot tower that commands a
vast prospect over Lincolnshire.

## LINCOLN

The city of Lincoln, 35 miles northwest of Boston, has medieval streets,
a Norman castle, and a superb
triple-towered Norman cathedral
high above the River Witham.
Especially notable are the 13th-
century rose windows with original
glass, the rood screen carvings and
14th-century choir stall misericords,
the chapter house, and the angels of
1280 supporting the choir roof, with
the mischievous little Lincoln Imp
(the city's emblem) among them. ■

**Beach huts at Southwold, a delightful old-fashioned resort on the shingly Suffolk coast**

# More places to visit in East Anglia & Lincolnshire

At **Cressing Temple** (*tel 01376-584903, closed Nov.–Feb., Mon.–Sat. March–April & Oct., Mon.–Tues. & Sat. May–Sept.*), south of Braintree, are two enormous, very early medieval barns, beautifully restored.

## BURY ST. EDMUNDS
This is Suffolk's spiritual capital, where a shrine for the body of St. Edmund (martyred in A.D. 870) was built. Medieval houses are incorporated into the striking west front of the 11th-century abbey ruins. The **Cathedral of St. James** (begun 1438, completed 2004 with a new tower) stands next to the abbey in beautiful gardens. Charles Dickens had Mr. Pickwick staying at **The Angel** on Angel Hill, reached from the abbey through a 14th-century gateway.
🅜 201 C2  **Visitor information**  ✉ 6 Angel Hill  ☎ 01284-764667

## IPSWICH
Ipswich is an old port on the River Orwell. Worth seeing here are the extravagantly par-getted **Ancient House** in the Buttermarket; the local landscape paintings, including some Constables, in **Christchurch Mansion Museum and Art Gallery** (*Soane St., tel 01473-433554, closed Mon.*); and the copies of the Sutton Hoo Treasure, superb funerary paraphernalia excavated in 1939 from a nearby Anglo-Saxon ship burial—in **Ipswich Museum** (*High St., tel 01473-433550, closed Sun. & Mon.*).
🅜 201 C2  **Visitor information**
✉ St. Stephens Church, St. Stephens Lane
☎ 01473-258070

## SUFFOLK COAST
The lonely Suffolk coast, a crumbling, shingle-lined shore, stretches north from the Stour Estuary across from **Harwich** (see p. 213). Between Stour and Orwell lies the Shotley Peninsula; the Butt & Oyster, on its north shore at Pin Mill, is a superb sailing pub.

Other coastal pleasures include the Napoleonic Martello Tower at Shingle Street; the little shingle-choked port of **Orford;** Benjamin Britten's grand concert hall at **Snape;** the eccentric House In The Clouds at **Thorpeness;** the Royal Society for the Protection of Birds bird reserve at **Minsmere** (*tel 01728-648281, closed Tues.*); and the seaside resort of **Southwold,** where Adnams brew their beer. ■

The North Midlands is a region of contrasts, from historic Nottingham and the border towns of Ludlow and Shrewsbury to the limestone dales of Derbyshire, where great houses stand on magnificent parkland.

# North Midlands

Introduction & map **224–25**
Nottingham & around **226–27**
Southwell Minster **228**
A drive around the Peak District **229–31**
Chatsworth House **232–33**
Hardwick Hall **234–35**
Ludlow **238**
Shrewsbury **239**
Around Shrewsbury **240**
Chester **241**
More places to visit in the North Midlands **242**
Hotels & restaurants in the North Midlands **369–73**

**Detail on the Feathers Hotel, Ludlow**

# North Midlands

THE NORTH MIDLANDS REGION COMPLETES THE UPPER HALF OF THE GREAT ragged circle, of which the South Midlands is the lower segment, that lies at the heart of England. Nottinghamshire, in the east, neighbor of Lincolnshire, has no real East Anglian feel. It is a true Midlands county, rural in the east where it slopes to the River Trent, industrial in the west where the great manufacturing and historic city of Nottingham lies south of the tattered remnants of Robin Hood's Sherwood Forest and a wide scatter of coal mines and pit villages.

## THE PEAK DISTRICT

West of Nottinghamshire is Derbyshire, again a county of contrasts, with an industrial southern belt around the county town of Derby. North and west lies one of Britain's best loved and most frequented national parks, the Peak District. This is high, exciting country. In the south—known as the White Peak—are deep, water-cut limestone gorges and small villages of dove gray stone. Farther north the pale limestone gives way to sparkling, dark gritstone, the grass to heather moorland, and the light White Peak atmosphere to the brooding moodiness of the Dark Peak. Both White and Dark Peaks are superb walking country.

Derbyshire contains two of England's grandest and most enjoyable country houses, Chatsworth House and Hardwick Hall, both of which are bound up with the story of the imperious, egocentric, dynamic Elizabethan woman Bess of Hardwick.

**Chester's famous two-storied Rows, with their black-and-white timbered facades**

## CHESHIRE AND SHROPSHIRE

The Peak District spills over into Cheshire, a broad county of plains and low hills. Its ancient capital city of Chester, full of medieval, Tudor, and Stuart buildings, lies on the eastern border near the wide Dee Estuary. Staffordshire, neighbor of southwest Derbyshire, also catches some of the best limestone fringes of the Peak District, and has a fascinating industrial history to explore around Stoke-on-Trent, home of the world's finest china for 200 years.

The western flank of the North Midlands is shaped by the long, whaleback heights of Shropshire's great hill ranges—Wenlock Edge, the Long Mynd, the Clee Hills—all wonderful for walkers and back-road explorers. Jewel of the Welsh border country is black-and-white Ludlow, on its ridge. ∎

**Oak Apple Day in Castleton, Derbyshire: Ancient customs such as these are still very much a feature of the county.**

# Nottingham & around

**Nottingham**

🅰 225 D3

**Visitor information**

✉ 1–4 Smithy Row

☎ 0115-915 5330

🕐 Closed Sun.
Oct.–Feb.

**Sherwood Forest
Country Park**

🅰 225 D3

**Visitor Centre**

✉ Edwinstowe

☎ 01623-824490

FOR THOSE VISITORS WHO THINK THAT ALL MIDLANDS cities are unremittingly grim and industrial, Nottingham comes as a very pleasant surprise. The city lies well to the northeast of the industrial heartland sprawl of Birmingham and Coventry, with the M1 expressway on its western flank and the looping River Trent to the east. Nottingham's many light engineering works made it a target for bombing during World War II, and the bomb sites became targets for ugly planning decisions during the 1950s and '60s. Notwithstanding these patches of modern blight, Nottingham is definitely the North Midlands' prime city for historical interest and visitor attractions.

## CASTLE AREA

Nottingham Castle has a history packed with drama. It stands on a high rock honeycombed with caves and passages. The Norman castle was twice destroyed and rebuilt during the 1135–1154 civil war between King Stephen and his cousin Matilda. In October 1330, so stories say, Edward III and his men sneaked in through a tunnel more than 300 feet long to capture his mother, Isabella, and her lover Roger Mortimer, who had ordered the murder of his father Edward II three years before. You can inspect the underground passages in the Castle Rock as part of the **Castle Caves Tour** (*tel 0115-915 3700, no tour Sat. & Sun.*).

It was from Nottingham Castle that Charles I rode out in August 1642 to set up his standard and signal the opening of the English Civil War. After the war was over, the castle was partly destroyed by Parliament. From 1674 to 1679, the Duke of Newcastle converted the grand shell into an even grander Italianate residence; this was torched in 1831 by rioting factory workers. Forty years later, the castle was restored once more; now it houses **Nottingham Castle Museum and Art Gallery** (*tel 0115-915 3700*), with some fine Pre-Raphaelite and modern paintings, and a display of late medieval alabaster sculpture.

## Robin Hood

Outside the 13th-century gatehouse is a statue of Robin Hood. His incarcerations and escapes, and his besting of the wicked Sheriff of Nottingham in archery contests held at the castle, make irresistible tales. In adjacent Maid Marian Way there is an effects-enhanced exhibition called **Tales of Robin Hood** (*tel 0115-948 3284*). For a long, exciting weekend in October each year, the "Merrie England" of Robin Hood springs back to life during the Robin Hood Pageant, held on the grounds of Nottingham Castle.

## City of Lace

In Castle Road stands the **Lace Centre** (*tel 0115-941 4058*), housed in a beautiful 1350 building crammed with examples of the machine-made lace for which Nottingham has been famous for centuries; lace is still made in several of the city's factories.

In nearby Castle Gate is the **Museum of Costume and Textiles** (*tel 0115-915 3500, closed Mon.–Tues.*), with examples of lace, textiles, and the early machines that revolutionized their manufacture.

Below the castle, **Ye Olde Trip to Jerusalem** inn is tucked into the rock. This 17th-century building is founded on an inn built in 1189 where crusaders setting off for

the Holy Land would toast success. Another area worth exploring is the old **Lace Market,** beyond the Broadmarsh Shopping Centre. Victorian warehouses stand along narrow little roadways around the 15th-century St. Mary's Church.

### SHERWOOD FOREST

Sherwood Forest, the ancient royal hunting forest where Robin Hood and his Merry Men had their hideout, once covered a vast area of the east Midlands. At the time when Robin Hood may actually have lived, around the 12th century, the forest stretched nearly 30 miles north of Nottingham. But foresting, coal mining, agriculture, industrialization, and the expansion of towns have decimated Sherwood.

The most atmospheric remnant of the forest lies around the village of **Edwinstowe** (where Robin married Maid Marian in St. Mary's Church), about 20 miles north of Nottingham on the A6075, and all the woodland northward, to the west of the A614. Here is the entrance to the **Sherwood Forest Country Park,** near the ancient Major Oak, with its 33-foot girth. Footpaths lead off among the oaks and bracken. ∎

**Although primarily used for recreation today, Britain's waterways—including the Nottingham Canal (above)—still carry nearly four million tons of goods every year.**

## D. H. Lawrence

The coal-mining village of Eastwood, 7 miles northwest of Nottingham, was the birthplace of the novelist D. H. Lawrence (1885–1930).

Lawrence, fourth son of a miner, was born in a "two-up, two-down" (four-room) row house at 8A Victoria Street, now the **D. H. Lawrence Birthplace Museum** (tel 01773-763312). Its cramped little rooms have been evocatively furnished in the sparse manner of any miner's house in 1885. A heritage center depicts the origins of Eastwood itself and its links with Lawrence. ∎

# Southwell Minster

"BY MY BLUDE," EXCLAIMED JAMES I WHEN HE FIRST SET eyes on Southwell Minster, "this Kirk shall justle with York or Durham, or any other kirk in Christendom!" The king's enthusiasm was understandable, for the great Norman church at Southwell (pronounced SUTH´-LL) has a rare beauty.

**Southwell Minster**
🅰 225 D3
✉ Church St., Southwell
☎ 01636-812649
💲 Donation

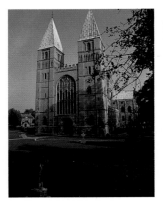

The minster shows the twin towers of its west end to the approach path, while the inside is flooded with dusky light reflected from old, pale pink sandstone. The 18th-century **chapter house** is decorated with superb stone carving: a riot of sharply detailed foliage, out of whose leaves peep pigs, hounds, a hare, and a Green Man. The 14th-century chancel screen is wonderfully carved, too, with nearly 300 figures. Far older carving decorates a door lintel.

On the south wall of the minster is older artwork still, in the form of fragments of a fresco of Cupid and attendant fish, reassembled from the bathroom wall of a Roman villa excavated just beyond the church's east end.

In the great east window are scenes from the stained-glass workshops of Flemish artists, full of lively, expressive faces under extravagant medieval headgear.

The brass **eagle lectern** nearby, another medieval piece, has its own strange story: It was dredged from a pond where it had been thrown during the Dissolution of the Monasteries. Inside the lectern were the deeds to Newstead Abbey, still in place where the monks had hidden them 300 years before. ■

**Expressions of the stonecarver's art do not come much finer than the work in the chapter house (above) of Southwell Minster (left).**

**Two distinct landscapes form the Peak District: a central area of limestone known as the White Peak, and a surrounding horseshoe of moorland called the Dark Peak. This view (right) is from Mam Tor, looking northwest toward the Dark Peak.**

# A drive around the Peak District

Crossing the wild moorland and rolling limestone dales of the Peak National Park, this drive passes through the charming Georgian towns of Buxton, Ashbourne, and Matlock, and visits two of the Peak's great country houses, medieval Haddon Hall and stately Chatsworth House.

Best of the sights in **Buxton** ❶ *(visitor information, The Crescent, tel 01298-25106)* are the elegant sandstone **Crescent** of 1780–1790, modeled on Bath's Royal Crescent (see pp. 153 & 155); the **Edwardian Opera House** (the Theatre in the Hills) with its rich golden interior; the **Victorian Pavilion** of iron-and-glass in its beautiful gardens; the great dome on the Duke of Devonshire's palatial stables, now the **Devonshire Royal Hospital;** and the **Old Baths.** Across from the baths, **St. Ann's Well** still pours a stream of mineral water at 82.4°F, collectible for free.

### BUXTON TO ILAM
From Buxton, take the A54 west for 10 miles, then bear left on a minor road through the village of Wincle. Continue southward from the bridge below the Ship Inn to the town of **Leek** ❷ *(visitor information, 1 Market Pl., tel 01538-483741)*, with **Brindley Mill,** a 1752 water mill devised by the famous (and semi-literate) engineering genius James Brindley. Now bear east across high, lonely moors, through Warslow and Alstonefield to **Ilam,** whose 19th-century hall is now a youth hostel. The village churchyard contains the decorated shafts of two Saxon crosses.

**Ashbourne** ❸ *(visitor information, 13 Market Pl., tel 01335-343666, closed Sun. Oct.–Feb.)*, just south of Ilam, is a Georgian town and a good base for exploring the **White Peak.** The 13-mile **Tissington Trail** starts here, running north along a disused railroad line, and joining up at Parsley Hay with the **High Peak Trail,** another railroad path of 17 miles.

### TO ALTON TOWERS & BACK
A detour of 20 miles there and back (signposted) takes you out of Ashbourne along the A52 Stoke-on-Trent road, then left on the B5032 at Mayfield, to reach **Alton Towers** ❹ *(Alton, tel 0870-444 4455, closed Nov.–March)*, a brash, white-knuckle ride theme park.

### ON TO BAKEWELL
From Ashbourne, the B5035 runs through Kniveton and on to Wirksworth and Matlock Bath, picturesquely tucked down in the bottom of Derwent Gorge.

Bakewell Pudding, a pastry tart that has been made in the town since about 1860

Well dressing honors pagan water gods.

| | |
|---|---|
| ⊠ | 225 B3 |
| ► | Buxton |
| ⟷ | 80 miles |
| ⏱ | 2½ hours |
| ► | Buxton |

**NOT TO BE MISSED**
- Leek
- Matlock
- Haddon Hall
- Chatsworth House
- Bakewell

**Matlock** **5** *(visitor information, Crown Square, tel 01629-583388)*, just beyond, along the A6, is a late Georgian spa with a mammoth 1853 hydro-health-center bulkily squatting on the hill above. The B5057 and the B5056 run west and north in beautiful upland country through Winster to the A6, passing **Haddon Hall** **6** *(tel 01629-812855, closed Nov.–March, Mon.–Wed. Oct.)*, with a Tudor Long Gallery, and a 14th-century Great Hall.

Turn right on the A6 to Rowsley, then left on the B6012 to **Chatsworth House** **7** (see pp. 232–33), and on to **Bakewell** *(visitor*

*information, Old Market Hall, tel 01629-813227)*, where you can sample the local delicacy, Bakewell Pudding. From here, the A6 leads west for 12 miles back to Buxton. ∎

The fine Georgian buildings of
fashionable Buxton

**START**

**Buxton**

A515

Taddington

A6

Ashford in
the Water

Pilsley

B619

B6012

**Chatsworth House** **7**

**Bakewell**

Wye

**Haddon Hall**

**6**

Beeley

Rowsley

B5056

Derwent

**Chatsworth behind its Emperor Fountain**

B5057

**Winster**

**Matlock**

**5**

A6

Matlock Bath

Warslow

Dove

A5012

Cromford

**PEAK DISTRICT NATIONAL PARK**

**Wirksworth**

Alstonefield

Milldale

Hope

Manifold

Hopton

Carsington Water

Dove Dale

Ilam Park

Ilam

Thorpe

A515

B5035

Kniveton

Mapleton

**3**

**Ashbourne**

**4**

Ellastone

B5032

Dove

**Alton Towers**

Gothic Ilam
Cross, erected
in 1840

0        4 miles

0        8 kilometers

# Chatsworth House

TO THE WEST OF NOTTINGHAMSHIRE LIES DERBYSHIRE, whose northwestern area contains the beautiful and very varied Peak National Park. Of the many fine country houses within the national park, the best known and most impressive is the home of the Duke and Duchess of Devonshire: Chatsworth House, some 35 miles northwest of Nottingham. A thorough exploration of the house and gardens makes a very full day's excursion.

**Chatsworth House**

- 225 C3
- 8 miles north of Matlock, off the B6012
- 01246-556300
- Closed mid-Dec.– mid-March
- $$$. Garden only: $$

## A COUNTRY PALACE

Driving through the deer park toward the house, you are struck by the tremendous orderliness of the beautifully kept grounds, and by the symmetry of the enormous mansion of honey-colored sandstone that stands squarely on the far side of a gently landscaped valley. This must be one of Britain's best approaches to a historic house, and the carefully planned message of

**The succession of open-ended perspectives is a feature of Chatsworth's interior.**

grandeur and condescension is still conveyed effectively.

Chatsworth is a country palace, a baroque mansion with a harmonious Palladian facade, built from 1687 to 1707 for the immensely

rich 1st Duke of Devonshire. The duke had a solid foundation to build on, for the house that his Chatsworth replaced was a splendid early Elizabethan mansion built by his imperious and egocentric great-great-grandmother, Bess of Hardwick (see pp. 234–35).

The tragic and lonely Mary, Queen of Scots stayed here several times on the orders of Queen Elizabeth I, under more or less stringent house arrest as the "guest" of Bess of Hardwick's fourth husband, the Earl of Shrewsbury. Bess, suspecting that the Earl and the still alluring Mary were getting on a little too well, soon walked out on him.

## TREASURES WITHIN

You walk between tulip trees to the house door. In the entrance hall hangs Sir Edwin Landseer's painting of Bolton Abbey. Marble is used to great effect on the ornate floors and short flights of stairs. The **State Rooms** have beautifully painted ceilings by Verrio and Louis Laguerre. In the **Music Room** you see what you will swear is a real violin hanging up behind a door, but it is a trompe l'œil painting, a little joke by Jan Van der Vaart (1651–1727).

Pictures vary from formal Van Dyck and Rembrandt portraits to a charming painting of the schoolgirls who were billeted here during World War II. The **chapel** (1693), tall and subdued, contains a giant,

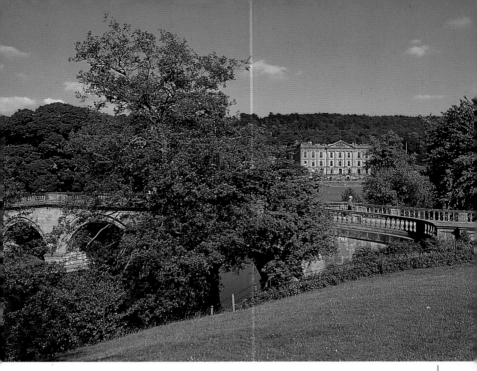

elaborate altarpiece. The **Great Dining Room** is immaculately and formally laid out as it was for the 1933 visit of George V and Queen Mary.

By contrast, the **Oak Room,** with its baroque wooden sculptures and bizarre twisty columns recalling those above the shrine in St. Peter's in Vatican City, is a freakishly oppressive and eccentric kind of bachelor smoking room.

Tall vases of highly polished Blue John, or fluorspar, a mineral retrieved from nearby caves in the limestone, glitter and wink from pedestals as you wander through Chatsworth House and out by way of the cold white marble beasts and human figures in the **Sculpture Gallery.**

### PARK & GARDENS

Chatsworth is set in a vast park of 1,000 acres. The garden near the house was created with an orangery and wonderful rose gardens from 1826 onward by Joseph Paxton, whose name was made by his design for the Crystal Palace, built in London's Hyde Park to house the Great Exhibition of 1851. It was based on Paxton's since-demolished Great Conservatory at Chatsworth, whose site is now filled by a maze. But the garden designer's **Conservative Wall** of glass still climbs the slope to the east of the house.

Capability Brown (who else?) landscaped the park in the 1760s. The park is rich in grottoes, summerhouses, vistas across shallow valleys, and walks through the rhododendron groves.

To the southeast of the house a grand cascade of 1696 tumbles from a domed temple down a flight of spillway steps; while the south front itself looks out over the long, narrow Canal Pond, where Joseph Paxton's **Emperor Fountain** spurts 100 feet into the air—only a third of its original height. ∎

**The grand west front of Chatsworth House, at first seen far off and apparently small, stays in view and steadily grows during the long approach to the house, until it towers over and dominates the visitor.**

# Hardwick Hall

WHILE CHATSWORTH HOUSE SITS RIGHT AT THE HEART OF the Peak District, the other great house built by Bess of Hardwick lies in the extreme east of Derbyshire, only a mile across the county border from the coal-mining area of western Nottinghamshire. Coming west, you pass from grim pit villages into rolling parkland near junction 29 of the M1 expressway. As you follow the long approach drive and get your first good look at Hardwick Hall (NT), you see the monumental letters "ES" carved repeatedly along the gold stone balustrades, and realize that Elizabeth, Countess of Shrewsbury, builder of Hardwick Hall and the original Chatsworth House, was the possessor of a healthy—not to say rampant—ego.

**Hardwick Hall**

🅰 225 C3

✉ Doe Lea, 9 miles southeast of Chesterfield

☎ 01246-850430

🕐 Hall: closed Nov.–March, also Mon., Tues. & Fri. April–Oct. Old Hall: Nov.–March, Tues. & Fri. April–Oct. Park open year-round

💲 Hall & Old Hall $$$. Garden only $$

## BESS OF HARDWICK

"Hardwick Hall, more glass than wall," ran the jingle, and the most striking aspect of the exterior of Hardwick Hall is the high proportion of glass to stone or brick in its walls. Hardwick's lattice-paned windows are enormous, inserted regardless of cost at a time when windows tended to be built small because of the exorbitant expense of glass. This display of glazing amounted to ostentation, in Tudor terms: a sign that Bess of Hardwick had plenty of money, and would spend it how she pleased. Bess was canny, however; it was her own glassworks and her own quarry that supplied the raw materials.

The appearance and atmosphere of Hardwick Hall, inside and out, is entirely bound up with the hard, flamboyant, practical, and ego-centric character of the woman who built it. Four centuries have softened and mellowed the house, but not the memory of the firebrand Bess.

She was born in 1527; her father, John Hardwick, was a modest gentleman farmer. Bess, however, grew up ambitious and determined to better herself. She married four husbands, each time raising herself a notch on the social scale. There were six offspring of these marriages, three sons and three

daughters. Contemporary likenesses (no shortage of these in the house) show her red-haired, dark-eyed, hawk-faced: as purposeful and implacable as that other Tudor Bess, her sovereign.

When she left her last husband, the Earl of Shrewsbury (see p. 232), Bess was in her mid-50s. She bought Hardwick Old Hall from her brother and began to refurbish it. The extensive ruins of the **Old Hall** (owned by English Heritage), still standing near Hardwick Hall, contain ornate plasterwork and other additions ordered by Bess during the 1580s.

Then, in 1590, the Earl of Shrewsbury died, and Bess set out to spend his money between 1591 and 1597 on mirroring her own pride and consequence in the stone and glass of her brand-new Hardwick Hall.

## A GRAND HOUSE

Hardwick was never really intended to be a home; it was more of a grand reception center in the country, a place to entertain royalty and the aristocracy. Hence, perhaps, its poignant air of coolness, of empty grandeur.

The walls of most rooms are smothered with tapestries, mile upon mile of woven pictures, which are only allowed a few hours of light each day for fear of fading. These fragile hangings, their original bright colors dimming, make for a claustrophobic atmosphere in many of the rooms. Intricate needlework applied to soft furnishings is on display, mostly the work of Bess and her servants, men included. Everyone was expected to chip in some sewing time. Their obscure lives are brought a little closer by the 1601 inventory of the hall's contents, which reveals many of the original furnishings—an inlaid wooden table, beds, and painted hangings—still present.

## A TOUR OF THE HALL

A tour of Hardwick begins in the **Main Entrance Hall** and shifts through to the **Great Hall.** A strikingly wide Tudor staircase rises to the **High Great Chamber** with its painted frieze.

In the **Long Gallery** hangs an impish portrait of Mary, Queen of Scots—catalyst, innocent or otherwise, of the breaking up of Bess's fourth marriage. The tour ends in the cavernous **kitchens.** The housebuilder herself died in 1608, in her 81st year. The self-referential portraits, the carved initials, the broken marriages all speak of an appalling arrogance allied to an appealing insecurity—part of Bess's enduring fascination. ■

Hardwick lifts on high its crowning motifs, the initials "ES" (below). Bess is seen here in a portrait attributed to Rowland Lockey (1592).

# Wedgwood & the potteries

During the 1960s, the North Midlands conurbation of Stoke-on-Trent *(visitor information, Quadrant Rd., Hanley, tel 01782-236000),* up in the northwesternmost corner of Staffordshire, had a greater proportion of derelict land than any city in Europe: more marl holes per square mile, more slag banks, scraff heaps, pit heads, and kiln yards. Stoke was one of the most polluted places in the world. Since then there has been a green revolution. Industrial excavation holes have been turned into athletics stadiums, coal-mine spoil hills converted to grassy uplands, flooded clay pits metamorphosed into fishing lakes.

The companies that produce the fine china for which Stoke is world renowned have eagerly opened their doors to the inquisitive public. It has been a remarkable turnaround in the fortunes of postindustrial Stoke-on-Trent, a city whose foundations, prosperity, and traditions were all bedded for centuries on the coal and clay that underlie the region.

The pottery that was made in and around the area from Neolithic times onward was plain, utilitarian stuff. Most of what has been excavated is workaday earthenware in brown or red. Then, in Stuart times, there was a social revolution when ships began to bring tea back to Britain. Tea drinking became de rigueur at fashionable gatherings. The gentry desired fine and fancy crockery for the tea ceremony, and stoneware was developed to meet the demand—it was hard, nonporous, and

**Traditionally, pottery was fired in distinctive, bottle-shaped kilns known as "potbanks."**

translucent. But fine tableware had to be produced locally, for local consumption. The rough surfaces of the roads, and the jolting suffered by goods being transported in horse-drawn goods wagons, meant that delicate ceramics could not travel far.

## Wedgwood and others

Josiah Wedgwood (1730–1795), destined to become one of Britain's most successful and celebrated pottery manufacturers, was born in Burslem, one of the "Six Towns"—the others are Tunstall, Hanley, Stoke, Fenton, and Longton—that make up the conurbation of present-day Stoke-on-Trent.

Wedgwood learned his trade in Burslem, and opened his first factory there in 1759. Two years later, the Duke of Bridgewater's pioneering canal opened near Manchester, and a new transport age had dawned.

When the Trent & Mersey Canal opened in 1777, the breakable products of the potteries could be transported smoothly and safely to the coast, from where ships could take them anywhere in the world. China-clay and other raw materials could be brought into the potteries in bulk. It meant a huge expansion in business for Josiah Wedgwood, as for the other Six Towns potters: Josiah Spode (1754–1827), with his willow-patterned bone china; the transfer-printed earthenware of Thomas Minton (1765–1836); Toby jugs made by Ralph Wood of Burslem; and, later in the railway age, the Parian ware statuettes from Copeland of Stoke; and Henry Doulton's superb Doulton ware (to become Royal Doulton in 1901).

## Etruria—a new town

By 1769 Wedgwood was in business at Etruria nearer Hanley, based in a newly built factory. He had bolstered his reputation with the production of cream-colored tableware which the Queen adored, and which by Royal Assent became known as Queen's Ware; and he had also begun to produce his trademark "Jasper," fine stoneware items in blue, green, lavender, black, and yellow, with a white design, often a classical scene, applied in relief.

The new factory and its attendant workers' cottages formed a sizable industrial township. There was excitement at that time over the excavations at Herculaneum and Pompeii near Rome, and the exquisite quality of the highly decorated Etruscan vases that were being unearthed. Wedgwood named his new town "Etruria" in homage and began producing his own "basalt" vases of black stoneware with classical designs. But he, like the other master potters of the Potteries, also turned out mass-produced tableware. ■

**Wedgwood is famous for its classically inspired white figures in relief on blue.**

## Manufacturers visitor centers

You can admire (and buy) the products and learn the fascinating stories of Wedgwood and the other great potteries on a trip round the museums/showrooms that are operated nowadays; some also offer factory tours.

**Wedgwood Story**
✉ Barlaston, Stoke-on-Trent
☎ 01782-204218

**Etruria Industrial Museum**
✉ Lower Bedford St., Etruria, Stoke-on-Trent
☎ 01782-233144
🕐 Closed Thurs.–Fri., and Thurs.–Sun. Jan.–Feb.

**The World of Spode Visitor Centre**
✉ Spode Works, Church St., Stoke-on-Trent
☎ 01782-744011

**Royal Doulton Visitor Centre**
✉ Nile St., Burslem, Stoke-on-Trent
☎ 01782-292434
🕐 Factory closed Sat.–Sun.

# Ludlow

JUST SOUTHWEST OF STOKE-ON-TRENT YOU SLIP OVER THE boundary, by way of the A53, from industrial Staffordshire into Shropshire, one of the most rural, green, and pleasant counties in England. Shropshire runs cheek by jowl with Wales along its entire western border, and here there are round-backed hills with hidden valleys. Farther south and east the hills become rougher in profile, the Clee Hills in particular, under whose southwestern spurs sits Ludlow.

Ludlow is one of those small country towns that people fall instantly in love with. It perches on a long spine of high ground,

**The Feathers Hotel (1603), on Old Street in Ludlow, is a splendid example of the ornate timberwork that characterizes the area's buildings.**

cradled in the arms of the Rivers Corve and Teme. The walls of **Ludlow Castle** stand high at the western end of the crest, enclosing Norman fortified buildings and later additions. Edward IV's two young sons, Edward and Richard, were held here until their father died in 1483; then they were taken to the Tower of London and murdered (see pp. 91–92).

A market under striped awnings takes place in Castle Square (*Mon.,*

*Fri.–Sat., & Wed. Easter–Sept.*).
**St. Laurence's Church** (to the left of the square), built high and mighty during the 14th and 15th centuries by rich Ludlow wool merchants, contains beautiful stained glass, and the church's misericords are among the finest in central England. In the churchyard lie the ashes of A.E. Housman (1859–1936), whose slim book of poems *A Shropshire Lad* is on sale in the town's bookshops.

> *Into my heart an air that kills*
> *From yon far country blows:*
> *What are those blue*
> *    remembered hills,*
> *What spires, what farms*
> *    are those?*

These were the poignant words that the Worcestershire-reared Housman wrote about his sentimental yearning for neighboring Shropshire.

There are many finely carved, half-timbered old buildings in Ludlow. Showiest among them is the 17th-century **Feathers Hotel,** its black-and-white frontage crawling with faces, foliage, and checkerboard and diamond timber patterns.

**Bridgnorth** (*visitor information, The Library, Listley St., tel 01746-763257, closed Sun. Oct.–Feb.*), 20 miles northeast across the Clee Hills by the B4364, is a historic town on the River Severn. It is well worth exploring for its old houses and pubs, steep river-steps, Norman castle, and little cliff railway. ■

# Shrewsbury

THE OLDEST PART OF SHREWSBURY, COUNTY TOWN OF Shropshire, sits on a bulbous peninsula in a tight loop of the River Severn, toward the northwestern corner of the county.

### A BORDER STRONGHOLD

Blood and conquest are inextricably bound up with the story of Shrewsbury, plugging as it does one of the important river gaps in the border between England and Wales. The town changed hands with fire and slaughter many times during the three centuries of fighting between the two countries. Prince Dafydd, brother of Llewelyn the Last, was hanged, drawn, and quartered at Shrewsbury's High Cross in 1283. Harry "Hotspur" Percy was killed at the Battle of Shrewsbury in 1403, having thrown in his lot with the Welsh rebel leader Owain Glyndwr. In *Henry IV Part I*, Shakespeare has Falstaff claiming to have slain Hotspur after fighting an hour by Shrewsbury clock. Hotspur's body was displayed at the High Cross and pieces of it dispatched around the country.

Early Norman **Shrewsbury Castle,** built on the narrow neck of the peninsula, was added to over the centuries; much of what stands today (housing the **Shropshire Regimental Museum**) dates from the wild years of Edward I's great offensive against the Welsh at the turn of the 13th century.

### MEDIEVAL STREETS

On nearby St. Mary's Street, the beautiful medieval **Church of St. Mary** (*tel 01743-357006, closed some Sun.*) contains the finest display of medieval stained glass anywhere along the Welsh borders. Among many treasures, the entire east window is filled with a vivid 14th-century Tree of Jesse, and there is a wonderfully compassionate Crucifixion scene of roughly the same date in the south aisle.

Elsewhere, Alkmond's Square is surrounded by narrow streets lined with medieval buildings. **Ireland's Mansion** (1575) and **Owen's Mansion** (1592) are a pair of magnificent timber-framed Tudor houses on High Street. There are good walks beside the River Severn all around the medieval town. ■

**Shrewsbury**

🅰 225 A2

**Visitor information**

✉ The Square

☎ 01734-281200

🕓 Closed Sun.
Oct.–Feb.

**Shrewsbury Castle & Shropshire Regimental Museum**

✉ Castle St.

☎ 01743-358516

🕓 Closed Oct.–mid-Feb., Sun.–Tues. mid-Feb.–March, Sun.–Mon. April–May.

**The Greek Revival style of St. Chad's Church (1790–92), on St. John's Hill, contrasts with Shrewsbury's mainly medieval buildings.**

# Around Shrewsbury

**Church Stretton
Visitor information**

✉ Church St.

☎ 01694-723133

🕐 Closed Oct.–Feb. &
   Sun.

**Stokesay Castle**

🅰 225 Al

✉ 1 mile south of
   Craven Arms, off the
   A49

☎ 01588-672544

🕐 Closed Mon.–
   Thurs. Nov.–Feb.,
   Tues.–Wed. April
   & Sept.

💲 $$

THE HILLY COUNTRY SOUTH OF SHREWSBURY, BISECTED BY the A49 road to Ludlow, contains some nooks and corners well worth seeking out. To the east rises the 16-mile-long double ridge of Wenlock Edge, a green wooded barrier with a hollow heart. Tucked away between the two spines of the Edge is the hidden valley of Hopedale, where stands the supposedly haunted Wilderhope Manor, now a youth hostel.

## THE LONG MYND

To the west of the A49 looms the rounded, rolling whaleback of the Long Mynd, a grassy limestone upland whose flanks are cut by steep stream valleys known as "batches" on the south and east, and "beaches" on the north and west of the range. **Church Stretton** lies on the A49 at the feet of the Long Mynd, a neat, orderly, small town full of cozy tea shops. At the Burway Bookshop on Beaumont Road you can buy a paperback edition of *A Night In The Snow* by the Reverend Donald Carr, before climbing up the beautiful **Cardingmill Valley** (signposted) and its tributary batch of Lightspout Hollow to the top of the Long Mynd. Here, on January 29, 1865, Carr survived an epic night wandering in a ferocious blizzard. The account he wrote of his terrify-

ing and almost fatal ordeal reads as snappily as any thriller.

From Church Stretton a narrow moor road snakes west over the Long Mynd, by way of Ratlinghope, to reach the quartzite outcrops of the **Stiperstones,** weird shapes against the sky with demonic reputations and the Devil's Chair itself in their midst. A path connects the five chief outcrops.

## STOKESAY CASTLE

Seven miles north of Ludlow is Stokesay Castle, England's oldest and finest moated manor house, founded in Norman times and fortified against the Welsh in 1296 on the order of Edward I. Beyond the half-timbered, stone-roofed gatehouse stands the Great Hall with its timbered roof and original upper chamber. A beautiful garden follows the moat. ■

**A handsome view across the moat to the sunlit walls of Stokesay Castle, whose origins go back to Norman times**

# Chester

CHESTER IS THE COUNTY TOWN OF OFTEN OVERLOOKED
Cheshire in the northwest of England on the border with North
Wales. The Romans were here from A.D. 79 onward, establishing a
fortress—Castle Deva by the River Dee, a natural deepwater harbor.
During the 19th century, the early Norman castle overlooking the
river was rebuilt in grand style from a ruin.

A 2-mile walk around the city's red sandstone walls—the best preserved and most complete medieval city walls in Britain—leads to the castle, and also to the partly unearthed first-century **Roman Amphitheatre,** the largest in Britain, on Little John Street. Opposite is the **Chester Visitor & Craft Centre** (*Vicar's Lane, tel 01244-402111),* which should be your first port of call in the city. From the **King Charles Tower** (*tel 01244-321616, closed Nov.–March*), in the northeast corner of the walls, Charles I watched his beaten army straggle into Chester after their defeat on Rowton Moor in September 1645. It was the death knell of the Royalist cause in the English Civil War.

The four main streets of Chester converge at the 15th-century **High Cross,** from which the stentorian town crier shouts the news at noon Tuesday to Saturday, May through August. Along these streets are Chester's famous **Rows,** covered galleries of shops built at second-floor level during the 13th and 14th centuries. Above the Rows are mock-medieval frontages, all Victorian reproductions. But there are dozens of genuinely Stuart, Tudor, and older buildings around, too. **Bishop Lloyd's House** is on Watergate Street, as is the splendid Tudor **Stanley Palace,** and there are more half-timbered houses beyond the ornate Victorian Jubilee archway and clock in Eastgate.

In **Chester Cathedral** (*tel 01244-324756*), on St. Werburgh Street, there is fine Norman stonework, rich 14th-century carving in the choir stalls and pew ends, and some good grotesque-beast misericords under the seats.

## MALPAS
In the market town of Malpas, 15 miles south of Chester, the **Church of St. Oswald** contains two Tudor husband-and-wife effigies: the snooty-looking Sir Randle and Lady Eleanor Brereton, and the half-smiling Sir Hugh and Lady Mary Cholmondeley. ■

**Chester**
⚑ 225 A3
**Visitor information**
✉ Town Hall, Northgate St.
☎ 01244-402111

**Chester's
Eastgate clock
commemorates
Queen Victoria's
Diamond Jubilee.**

Every August a ceremony is held to remember Eyam's plague victims.

## More places to visit in the North Midlands

### CASTLETON

The great attraction here is the number of caves. The half-mile-long **Peak Cavern** *(tel 01433-620285, closed Mon.–Fri. Nov.–March)*, with its 100-foot opening, lies just southwest of the village; all the others are northwest under the "shivering mountain," Mam Tor. Here are the **Speedwell Cavern** *(Winnats Pass, tel 01433-620512)* with stalactites, boat trips, and a bottomless pit; the **Blue John Cavern** *(Buxton Rd.)*; and the **Treak Cliff Cavern** *(tel 01433-620571)*, where fluorspar was retrieved—some used for decoration at Chatsworth House (see pp. 232-33).
225 C3  Peak National Park Information Centre  ✉ Castle St.  ☎ 01433-650345  🕐 Call for opening information

### EYAM

The village of **Eyam** (pronounced EEM) in Derbyshire, just north of the A623, is famous for its self-sacrifice during the Great Plague of London in 1665. The bubonic plague arrived in Eyam on September 7, 1665, via infected fleas in a bolt of cloth brought from London by tailor George Viccars. The rector, William Mompesson, ordered self-imposed quarantine for Eyam. Food was left at the parish boundaries and paid for with coins left in bowls of disinfectant vinegar. In all, the disease claimed the lives of 250 of the 350 inhabitants.

The Eyam History Trail map in the church guides you around Mompesson's Well, his grave, plague-struck sites, and the Riley graves where, in August 1666, a mother buried three sons, three daughters, and her husband within eight days.
225 C3

### IRONBRIDGE

Ironbridge *(visitor center: tel 01952-884391)*, on the River Severn 5 miles south of Telford, was the cradle of the Industrial Revolution. A range of fascinating museums tells the story, and from a number of footpaths you can view the graceful, semi-circular bridge of 1779, the world's first cast-iron bridge.
225 B2  ■

M ake time to enjoy the
lively atmosphere and
historic buildings of Liverpool
and Manchester, classic northern cities, before plunging in
among the lakes and mountains
of William Wordsworth's
beloved Lake District.

# Northwest England

Introduction & map 244–45
Liverpool 246–47
Manchester 248–49
Lancashire moorlands 250
Southern Lakeland
  & the coast 251
Lake District National Park 252-53
A drive around the Central Lakes
  256–57
The Pennines 258–59
Northeast Pennines 260
Hotels & restaurants in Northwest
  England 373–76

**Sailing, Thirlmere and Helvelyn**

# Northwest England

NORTHWEST ENGLAND CONTAINS ONE OUTSTANDING JEWEL OF LAND-scape—the Lake District, far famed thanks to William Wordsworth and the Romantic poets, writers, and painters. Yet there is very much more to this otherwise rather over-looked region of England, whose character derives largely from the massive industrial complexes that weigh down its southerly border from Liverpool to Manchester, and from the great bleak uplands of the Pennine Hills, which fill most of its northern width.

The mill hands and factory workers of Sheffield, Manchester, Bradford, and the Lancashire cotton-spinning towns have always looked to the high bare Pennine moors for their leisure time, walking, and cycling. These enormous vistas of rolling moors and deep-cut valleys are lent extra drama by the tightly huddled towns with their black houses, facto-ries, chapels, and public buildings made of gritstone (hard crystalline rock) that lie below the hillsides.

The cities of Liverpool and Manchester are well worth exploring in their own right. Each has suffered economic decline, Liverpool in its 7-mile stretch of docks, Manchester in its vast textile industry. Both have fought back by sensitively restoring once derelict areas. Visitors are encouraged to explore the streets with their great overblown Victorian temples of Mammon—warehouses, spinning mills, dockside offices, factories—that made the prosperity of these great and still lively commercial cities.

The once grimy industrial towns of east Lancashire—Rawtenstall, Bacup, Todmorden, Blackburn, and others—have also lost their palls of smoke since the virtual shutdown of the northwest's textile industry. Here, too, the architecture reflects Victorian prosperity. Today these towns make good bases for exploring the packhorse trails and green lanes across the high moors that surround them.

**"The Bandstand," L.S. Lowry's grittily realistic depiction of his hometown, Salford**

London
Area of map detail

SCOTLAND p.289

NORTHUMBERLAND p.263

0 — 20 miles
0 — 30 kilometers

Bowness-on-Solway
Longtown  Hadrian's Wall
Brampton  A69  Haltwhistle
**Carlisle**
Silloth  Allendale
Wigton  Thursby  Blanchland
Maryport  A596 Aspatria  Caldbeck
Alston
Cockermouth  931m Skiddaw  A66  **Penrith**  Dufton  Wearhead  Stanhope
**Workington**  Keswick  893m Cross Fell  **DURHAM** Wear  Middleton-in-Teesdale
**Whitehaven**  Appleby-in-Westmorland  Barnard Castle
St. Bees  Buttermere  Patterdale  Shap  Brough  A66  Bowes
Egremont  978m Scafell Pike  **CUMBRIA**  Kirkby Stephen
Gosforth  West Water  LAKE DISTRICT NATIONAL PARK  Tebay  A685
Ravenglass  Hawkshead  Grasmere  Ambleside  Windermere  Thwaite
Coniston  **Kendal**  Hawes
Broughton-in-Furness  Bowness-on-Windermere  Sedbergh  YORKSHIRE DALES NATIONAL PARK
Bootle  Newby  Dent  693m Pen-y-Ghent
Ulverston  Bridge  **Cartmel Priory**  Kirkby Lonsdale  Horton-in-Ribblesdale
**Furness Abbey**  Grange-over-Sands  Ingleton  A65  Settle
**Barrow-in-Furness**  Carnforth  Malham
Isle of Walney  **Morecambe**  **Lancaster**
Heysham  Bowland Forest
Overton  M6  Slaidburn
**Fleetwood**
Cleveleys  **LANCASHIRE**  Barnoldswick
Longridge  Clitheroe
**Blackpool**  Ribble  Burnley
**Lytham St. Anne's**  M55  **Preston**  M65  **Burnley**
**Southport**  **Leyland**  A677  **Blackburn**
**Ormskirk**  Rawtenstall  Bacup
**Chorley**  **Rochdale**
Formby  M6  M61  M66  **Bury**
**Crosby**  M58  **Wigan**  **Bolton**  **Oldham**
**Kirkby**  GREATER  **MANCHESTER**
**LIVERPOOL**  M57  **St. Helens**  Salford  **Stockport**
**Birkenhead**  MERSEYSIDE  Altrincham  **Cheadle**
Bebington  DERBYSHIRE p.225

Irish Sea

Isle of Man
Point of Ayre
Kirk Michael  Ramsey
Peel  620m Snaefell  Laxey
rt Erin  Douglas
Castletown
f of Man

WALES p.160  CHESHIRE p.225  DERBYSHIRE p.225
Dee

M6  Eden  Settle–Carlisle Railway  Lune  Ribble  A565  Dee

NORTH YORKSHIRE p.263  WEST YORKSHIRE p.263

## CUMBRIA

Compressed into the westward bulge of the county of Cumbria are the glories of the Lake District—endlessly exciting and inspirational, however many times you may have admired and walked along these rounded or sharp-edged mountains that enfold a spatter of bright little lakes. It's worth exploring Cumbria beyond the lakes, too: Take time for a railway ride all around the forgotten Cumbrian coastline to the historic city of Carlisle; and leave a day or two to walk those moody, starkly beautiful Pennines around Weardale and Teesdale. ■

# Liverpool

**Liverpool**
🄰 245 B1
**Visitor information**
✉ Queen Sq.
✉ Atlantic Pavilion, Albert Dock
☎ 0906-680 6886

LIVERPOOL'S RISE TO BECOME THE BRITISH EMPIRE'S second most important port after London began in the 17th and 18th centuries, with the misery of the three-cornered slave trade between West Africa, the New World ports and plantations, and the western English ports. Liverpool got its first dock in 1715; soon the wharves had sprawled 7 miles along the Mersey. During the 19th century, transatlantic liners and emigrant ships brought rich and poor alike to the city. A cosmopolitan population formed—Irish, Scots, Indians, Chinese, Americans, and Eastern Europeans—who, for one reason or another, never got any farther than the great port on the Mersey Estuary.

**The Liver Birds perch atop the pinnacles of the Royal Liver Building at Liverpool's Pier Head.**

These days, Liverpool can be a poignant place. Grand 19th-century waterfront buildings rise eerily above a silent river shore. The wharves and warehouses along the River Mersey are being redeveloped for housing and leisure activities.

Down on the waterfront at the Pier Head, the Mersey Ferries embark passengers for Birkenhead across the water and run several excellent themed cruises *(tel 0870-608 2608)*. These are enjoyable rides, worth taking for the view back to Liverpool's grand Merseyside threesome: the domed **Port of Liverpool Building,** the great bulk of the **Cunard**

**Building,** and the soaring clock towers of the **Royal Liver Building** with their spreadwinged twin Liver Birds.

Generically known as Scousers, the Liverpudlians have developed an instant wit and skill in repartee that makes any conversation here an enjoyable entertainment.

**Albert Dock** *(tel 0151-708 7334)* near the Pier Head, is the city's contemporary showpiece, a conversion of early Victorian warehouses into museums, shops, and cafés. The **Merseyside Maritime Museum** *(tel 0151-478 4499)* tells the story of Liverpool's shipyards and ocean liners, and its earlier prosperity on the back of the slave trade, as well as outlining its key role during the World War II Battle of the Atlantic. This is not to be missed. Likewise, the contemporary art in Tate Britain's northern outstation: **Tate Gallery Liverpool** *(The Colonnades, tel 0151-702 7400, closed Mon., except Bank Holiday Mon.).* The **Museum of Liverpool Life** *(tel 0151-478 4080)* and **The Beatles Story** *(Britannia Vaults, tel 0151-709 1963)* exhibition make enjoyable introductions to the city.

Beatles' fans can get some mild kicks at 8–10 Mathew Street, site of the **Cavern Club** *(tel 0151-236 1965),* where the Beatles made their reputation in 1961–62. The original "Cellarful of Noise" was thoughtlessly destroyed in the 1970s; but a faithful reproduction exists, a venue for live music and much nostalgia. The Beatles phenomenon is better celebrated and explained on one of the guided tours of Beatles sites, on foot or by bus, organized by **Cavern City Tours** *(tel 0151-709 3285),* or on a minibus visit to the National Trust-owned childhood homes of John Lennon **(Mendips, 251 Menlove Avenue)** and Paul McCartney at **20 Forthlin Road** *(tel 0870-900 0256, info; 0151-708 8574, morning reservations; 0151-427 7231, afternoon reservations).*

Elsewhere in the city, the **Walker Art Gallery** *(William Brown St., tel 0151-478 4199)* ranges from very early Italian Renaissance painting up to David Hockney, by way of Bellini, Rembrandt, Rubens, Constable, Cézanne, and Matisse. Liverpool's two modern cathedrals, both worth a visit, are built on high ground overlooking the city. ∎

**The Beatles were Liverpool's most famous sons, and numerous sites across the city claim an association with the Fab Four.**

## The Mersey Beat

For anyone growing up in Britain in the early 1960s, Liverpool was the Scene. Few youngsters knew or cared about the illustrious and murky history of the foggy northern port; all that mattered was the Mersey Beat, a sound stolen from American R&B records that were brought into Liverpool by stewards, stokers, and sailors on the transatlantic liners and cargo ships. Somehow, recycled on cheap clanging guitars, filtered through the hoarse voices of the untutored Scouse bands, toughened by repeated plays during marathon residencies in the red-light clubs of Hamburg, these perky, cymbal-driven three-minute songs took on a Mersey Beat flavor that seemed entirely fresh. Gerry and the Pacemakers, The Searchers, Kingsize Taylor and the Dominoes, the Big Three, and the Merseybeats themselves—they never reached the creative or musical heights so often scaled by their precocious, once-upon-a-time Liverpool mates and rivals, the world-dominating Beatles. But they were all great. ∎

# Manchester

**Manchester**
⛰ 245 C1
**Visitor information**
✉ Town Hall Extension, Lloyd St.
☎ 0161-234 3157

A CENTURY AGO, THE GREAT NORTHERN METROPOLIS OF Manchester was Britain's—and therefore the world's—premier textile city. Richard Arkwright's spinning machines, steam power, a damp climate, and proximity to the coalfields and to the port of Liverpool had all made Manchester's cotton trade huge business. Georgian cotton barons, and later Victorian traders and merchants, made enormous fortunes and filled the city with giant, overbearing warehouses and offices. They endowed art galleries, public parks, and civic buildings. Meanwhile, the mill hands lived in increasingly desperate and insanitary conditions, crowded into reeking, close-packed slums.

**A carpenter's bench and tools and other evidence of Manchester's industrial past can be found in the Saddleworth Museum in the village of Uppermill.**

## FROM THE ASHES

Cheap textiles from the colonies and world recessions put the skids under Manchester's business in the 20th century. World War II bombing tore big holes in the city, then postwar clearance of slums and derelict sites opened up the face of Manchester. Civic buildings were cleaned of grime as the Clean Air Act took a grip. These days, with Manchester United established as one of the world's top soccer teams, and a very active and trendy nightclub scene (the rave revolution of the late 1980s was rooted here), there is a new confidence about Manchester.

Booklets and maps, available from the Manchester Tourist Information Centre on Lloyd Street, steer you around most of the sights in a day. You can also get a good vivid impression of this great redbrick and terra-cotta industrial city from one of the Metrolink trams that ply the streets.

## VICTORIAN MAGNIFICENCE

Behind the visitor center is Albert Square, dominated by the giant Gothic **Town Hall** with its 280-foot clock tower. The first-floor Great Hall has Pre-Raphaelite murals by Ford Madox Brown.

On the corner of Peter Street, across from the circular Central Library and Theatre, is the florid purple **Midland Hotel** (officially the Crowne Plaza Manchester—The Midland), excellent for taking English afternoon tea on the terrace.

## CANALS, CLUBS, & CHINATOWN

The **G-Mex Centre** (tel 0161-834 2700) is on Watson Street, housed under the soaring, arched iron-and-glass roof of the former Central Station. The G-Mex metro station is just beyond; cross the tracks and bear left down a ramp and steps to the Rochdale Canal. Opposite, on the corner of Whitworth Street West, its curved wall stuck with blue- and red-glazed tiles, is the **Hacienda Club,** seedbed of the rave scene (now closed).

Follow the canal towpath west to **Castlefield Urban Heritage Park** (Liverpool Rd., Castlefield, tel 0161-234 3157), a mix of canals and boats, heavy Victorian bridges and architecture. The excellent **Museum of Science & Industry in Manchester** (tel 0161-832 2244) on Liverpool Road, Castlefield, has hot oil and hissing engines in the Power Hall, ramshackle early gliders, and huge reconnaissance planes in the Air and Space Gallery.

Where Liverpool Road meets Deansgate, turn left. Off Deansgate

to the right is Brazenose Street with its Abraham Lincoln statue and nearby **St. Mary's Church,** with its stained-glass cupola and swirly marble pillars.

Farther up Deansgate is St. Ann's Street and Square (off to the right), with the dignified **St. Ann's Church** (1712). Nearer the Victorian cathedral, drop into the **Crown & Anchor** pub for a pint among middle-aged men loudly declaiming to each other—a real taste of Manchester's character.

Other enjoyable sites are **Chinatown,** between Princess Street and York Street, with its ornamental archway, Ho's Bakery, excellent restaurants, and the lively **Gay Village** around Princess Street and Sackville Street. Also visit

the **City Art Galleries** (tel 0161-235 8888) on Mosley Street/Princess Street, with its collections of early medieval religious paintings, Canalettos and Gainsboroughs, Pre-Raphaelites, and L. S. Lowry's "matchstick men" depictions of Manchester folk walking bowed in the shadow of oppressive factories.

In Lowry's birthplace of Salford, near Manchester United football club's famous **Old Trafford** stadium, the **Salford Quays** complex (tel 0161-84 8601) offers bars, theaters, galleries, and two main attractions—the **Imperial War Museum North** (tel 0161-836 4000), and **The Lowry Arts Centre** (tel 0161-876 2000), which holds the world's largest collection of works by Lowry. ■

**Gladstone stands on Albert Square, one of Manchester's many statues that extol the city's local politicians and philanthropists who worked to alleviate the grim conditions of the factory hands.**

# Lancashire moorlands

BETWEEN MANCHESTER AND THE LAKE DISTRICT LIE the remote Lancashire moorlands of the Forest of Rossendale and Bowland Forest, with a superb network of walks on old packhorse trails, high above the valleys dotted with former textile towns.

**Rawtenstall**

🅰 245 C2

**Visitor information**

✉ 41–45 Kay St.

☎ 01706-244678

🕐 Closed Sun.

**Lancaster**

🅰 245 B3

**Visitor information**

✉ 29 Castle Hill

☎ 01524-32878

**Lancashire's Bowland Forest, despite its name, has very little tree cover. Instead, this former royal hunting ground offers huge areas of open moorland and lonely, alluring hills.**

## RAWTENSTALL

This has been the most successful of the region's mill towns at sprucing itself up for visitors, and the **Weaver's Cottage** loom shop in Fall Barn Fold introduces you to preindustrial textile manufacture.

East of here along the A681, through Bacup to Todmorden, a whole run of huge mill buildings, terraced houses, factory chimneys, and Methodist chapels under precipitous hillsides recall the gritty nature of life in these communities until the decline of the textile industry in the 1950s and 1960s.

## BOWLAND FOREST

North of Burnley, narrow roads straggle north and west over the empty moorland of Bowland Forest, Lancashire's wildest region. **Slaidburn,** on the B6478 in the middle of the moors, has several ancient stone houses, the cheerful Hark To Bounty Inn, and some fine footpaths leading onto the surrounding moorland hills.

## LANCASTER

The Trough of Bowland road leads northwest through Dunsop Bridge and Abbeystead to Lancaster, a handsome old riverport built in black-and-pink sandstone, full of narrow medieval lanes and solid Georgian merchants' houses. A grim battlemented castle crowns the knoll above the city, and the restored quays and warehouses below, along the tidal River Lune, are Georgian industrial architecture at its most dignified.

The **Maritime Museum** (*tel 01524-64637*) in the Custom House on St. George's Quay tells the tale of Lancaster's seaborne prosperity.

South is **Sunderland Point,** a huddle of houses on a windswept point cut off at high tides, where the first bale of cotton from the New World was landed.

Across the point (signposted) lies the grave of Sambo, a West Indian slave who died here in 1736 of a broken heart at being taken from his homeland. ■

# Southern Lakeland
# & the coast

TO ENJOY A CORNER OF THE LAKE DISTRICT THAT IS NOT
inundated with visitors, make for the three broad peninsulas that
push south from the coastal fringe of Lakeland into Morecambe Bay's
vast 117-square-mile saucer of tidal sands.

This beautiful, wide-open coastline
holds many attractions: **Furness
Abbey** and **Cartmel Priory
Gatehouse** (NT); seals, orchids,
hen harriers, and natterjack toads
in the nature reserves on the **Isle
of Walney** *(tel 01229-471066);*
and a guided Sands Crossing
over Morecombe Bay *(Grange-
over-Sands Tourist Information
Centre, Victoria Hall, Main St.,
tel 015395-34026),* through rivers
and swaths of sand—a most
unusual expedition.

Built by the old Furness Railway
Company to carry iron ore out of
the hills, the Cumbrian coast railroad snakes and loops on skeletal
viaduct legs across the three great
estuaries of the Rivers Kent, Leven,
and Duddon. It is over 100 miles by
this rattling coastal railroad from
Carnforth right around to Carlisle.

**Whitehaven** *(visitor information, Market Hall, Market Place,
tel 01946-852939, closed Sun.*

*Oct.–Feb.),* halfway up, is a planned
Georgian town refurbishing itself
after decades of decay. **St. Bee's
Abbey** is a fine example of Norman
architecture. **Carlisle** *(visitor information, Old Town Hall, Green
Market, tel 01228-625600, closed Sun.
Oct.–Feb.),* at the end of the journey
is a solidly handsome city, with a
grim and massive sandstone castle.
The Norman cathedral contains
medieval stained glass, woodcarving, and sandstone sculpture. ■

**Furness Abbey**
✉ Barrow-in-Furness
☎ 01229-823420
⊕ Closed Mon.–Tues.
  Oct.–Easter
💲 $$

**Cartmel Priory
Gatehouse**
✉ Cavendish St.,
  Cartmel
☎ 015395-36874
⊕ Closed Mon.–Fri.
  Nov.–March,
  Mon.–Tues.
  April–Oct.
💲 Self-guided tour: $

## Isle of Man

It takes about 3½ hours to reach
the Isle of Man by ferry from
Heysham on the Lancashire coast
and 2 hours by Seacat *(tel 08705-
523523)* from Liverpool. The
humpbacked island in the Irish Sea,
30 miles long and 10 wide,
possesses its own parliament,
customs, and special atmosphere.
By far the best way to see the
island is to walk the 25-mile
Millennium Way footpath, which

runs from Ramsey to Castletown
all down the hilly spine of Man. The
best view is from the 2,036-foot
summit of Snaefell (also attainable
by mountain railway).

Each year the island plays host
to the leather-clad bikers of the
world during its famous T.T. Races.

Contact the visitor information
center at Sea Terminal Building
*(Douglas, tel 01624-686766, closed
Sat.–Sun. Oct.–Feb.).* ■

**Cartmel Priory's
monks guided
medieval travelers
across the treach-
erous sands of
Morecambe Bay.
Poignant inscrip-
tions in St. Mary's
Church record
the fate of those
who attempted
solo crossings.**

# Lake District National Park

THE LAKE DISTRICT HOLDS A SPECIAL PLACE IN ENGLISH hearts. For it is here that cultivation and wilderness—landscape features much prized in this orderly yet individualistic country—are best seen in juxtaposition, the one in the greenly fertile valley bottoms, the other around the upper regions of the fells (hills).

The 900-square-mile Lake District National Park, set up in 1951, includes 16 natural lakes and several reservoirs, and 180 fells over 2,000 feet high—four over 3,000 feet. Scafell Pike is the highest mountain in England at 3,210 feet.

These statistics say nothing of the glorious beauty of England's best loved, most jealously guarded and most frequented piece of landscape, nor of the overcrowding in the little towns, erosion of fell paths, and noise pollution of lakes that such popularity inevitably brings. Yet you can easily avoid these annoyances, for the vast majority of visitors stick to the main roads, to the well-known

beauty spots, to Windermere, Bowness, Grasmere, and Keswick, to the low-level trails, and to the summer and bank (public) holidays. The fells out on the fringes of the Lake District are still remarkably uncrowded. Do exercise sensible caution, though, when you are walking (see p. 320), and check the weather forecast *(tel 017687-75757)* before you set out.

In the southwest corner of Lakeland there are several excellent walks from the stations of the **Ravenglass & Eskdale Railway** *(tel 01229-717171),* whose miniature steam and diesel locomotives draw the tiny carriages up from Ravenglass on the coast to the foot of the hills at Dalegarth.

## WASTWATER

This is a wonderful spot for lovers of unadorned, uncompromising lake and fell scenery. Wastwater is the darkest, deepest, and moodiest of the lakes, its southeast slopes one long curtain of loose scree. The little church and inn at Wasdale Head lie tucked down under the slopes, backed by the hunched, pyramid shape of Great Gable.

## COCKERMOUTH

This market town was where the Wordsworths were born—William on April 7, 1770, Dorothy on Christmas Eve 1771—in what is now called **Wordsworth House** (NT). Their father, John, is buried in the shady little churchyard. ■

**Lake District National Park**

A 245 B4

**Visitor information**

✉ Lake District National Park Visitor Centre, Brockhole, Windermere

☎ 015394-46601

🕐 Closed Nov.–March

**Cockermouth**

A 245 B4

**Visitor information**

✉ Town Hall, Market St.

☎ 01900-822634

🕐 Closed Sun. Oct.–Feb.

**Wordsworth House**

✉ Main St., Cockermouth

☎ 01900-824805

🕐 Closed Sun. Nov.–May

💲 $$

**Board one of the Ravenglass & Eskdale Railway steam trains (left) to take in the scenic beauty of Lakeland.**

**Derwent Water at dawn (right) epitomizes the majestic scenery of northern England's Lake District.**

# Wordsworth & the Romantics

William Wordsworth (1770–1850) is not the only poet to have extolled the drama and beauty of England's Lake District, but it was he who first focused and expressed the feelings of awe, delight, and magnetic fascination that these 900 square miles of mountain, moor, and lake spark in almost everyone who comes to see them. Wordsworth celebrated the attractions of Lakeland, but he also wrote of how the fells could inspire fear, as in this incident on Esthwaite Water:

> …I struck and struck again,
> And growing still in stature the grim shape
> Towered up between me and the stars,
>     and still,
> For so it seemed, with a living purpose of
>     its own
> And measured motion like a living thing

> Strode after me. With trembling oars
>     I turned,
> And through the silent water stole
>     my way…
> —William Wordsworth, *The Prelude*, Book I

### Early visitors

Before the late 18th-century picturesque movement "discovered" the area, the big, bare fells (hills) were generally seen as an abomination. In 1698, Celia Fiennes rode through and spared only a brief, disapproving glance for "those inaccessible high rocky barren hills which hangs over ones head in some places and appear very terrible." In the 1720s Daniel Defoe thought Lakeland "a country eminent only for being the wildest, most barren and frightful of any that I have passed over…frightful appearances to the right and

**Wordsworth House (above) in Cocker-mouth, birthplace of William (above left) and his sister, Dorothy.**

**Sunshine casts its light over the Lake District (left), highlighting the fall beauty of Grasmere's larches.**

left…this terrible aspect of the hills.…" It was the poet Thomas Gray (1716–1771) with his *Journal* (1775) who suggested that the fells and lakes might be worth looking at, rather than hiding from (though Gray himself would pull down his carriage blind to shut out the sight of particularly terrifying hills). Thomas West's *Guide to the Lakes* (1778) recommended "viewing stations" and gave road directions, while employing the purplest of prose to encourage visitors. The waterfall above Ambleside "is precipitated with a horrid rushing noise into a dark gulph, unfathomable to the eye.…It is dashed with a thundering noise headlong down a steep craggy channel…this scene is highly awful and picturesque."

## Tourism begins

A number of factors combined to set up the Lake District as an earthly paradise for early 19th-century visitors. The disfiguring effects of the industrial revolution upon the countryside were sharpening people's appreciation of "unspoiled" landscape, at the same time as revolution in France and the Napoleonic Wars had shut off access to the Continent for the customary horizon-expanding Grand Tour.

Thomas Gainsborough came to paint the fells and lakes in 1783, John Constable in 1806. Turner was a frequent visitor. The Lake District, around the time that Wordsworth began writing about it, was established by the Romantics as the "English Switzerland."

The Lake District homes in and near Grasmere (see p. 256) that Wordsworth shared with his sister, Dorothy, and later with his wife, Mary Hutchinson, and their children, became magnets for visiting and resident poets and men of letters. Samuel Taylor Coleridge (1772–1834) came to Keswick in 1800, the year after William and Dorothy had taken up their life of "plain living and high thinking" at Dove Cottage. Robert Southey arrived in 1802, Thomas De Quincey in 1808. Wordsworth himself became a Romantic tourist attraction. His curiously undetailed *A Description of the Scenery of the Lakes in the North of England*, published in 1810, was a roaring success. By the time he died in 1850—poet laureate, and full of honors—the Lake District was on the railroad, and well and truly on the vacationers map.

## Over the hills

In the ensuing century, unguided walking over the Lakeland fells (with an eye on the weather) became the norm. Far and away the best companion on the hills has proved to be Alfred Wainwright, with his quirky, hand-drawn, seven-volume *Pictorial Guide to the Lakeland Fells*. Wainwright was another Romantic admirer of the fells, his bluff style only a thin veneer over a true Lakeland lover's heart.  ∎

# A drive around the Central Lakes

This drive starts at Windermere, the Lake District's chief visitor center and railhead, and heads north via the Kirkstone Pass up to Keswick. The southern return goes through Borrowdale and Newlands Valley to Grasmere, passing Buttermere and Crummock Water along the way.

The A592 leaves Windermere and Bowness, two towns given over to tourism, and runs south along **Lake Windermere** ❶ (*visitor information, Victoria St., tel 015394-46499*) to Newby Bridge. Cross the River Leven here, and turn right onto the minor road up the lake's heavily wooded western shore. The **Lakeside & Haverthwaite Steam Railway** (*Haverthwaite–Lakeside, tel 015395-31594, not running Nov.–Easter*) makes short trips along here.

At Near Sawrey is **Hill Top** ❷ (*NT, tel 015394-36269, closed Nov.–late March & Thurs.–Fri. late March–Oct.*), the gray stone, 17th-century farmhouse where Beatrix Potter lived from 1905 to 1913 and wrote her much loved children's tales.

In Sawrey village turn left on the B5285 beside Esthwaite Water to reach **Hawkshead** ❸ (*visitor information, tel 015394-36525, closed Mon.–Fri. Nov.–Feb.*). Here are the grammar school that Wordsworth attended from 1779 to 1787 (he carved his name on his desk lid), and the **Beatrix Potter Gallery** (*NT, Main St., tel 015394-36355, closed late Oct.–early April & Thurs.–Fri. early April–late Oct.*) in the former office of the writer's lawyer husband. The road continues to **Ambleside** (*visitor information, Central Buildings, Market Cross, tel 015394-32582*), a place of dark-stone houses with gables and bargeboards.

## OVER THE FELLS

Follow the A591 Grasmere and Keswick signs out of town; in a quarter of a mile take the steep, narrow road on the right signed "Kirkstone 3." Soon you are up among bare fells. Turn left onto the A592 as the road snakes over the 1,489-foot Kirkstone Pass, the highest in the Lake District. "Who comes not hither ne'er shall know/How beautiful the world below" (*The Pass of Kirkstone*, 1815). Wordsworth was right; the forward view into Patterdale is breathtaking, down between the sweeping arms of the fells to Little Brother Water and the crinkled humps of Angletarn Pikes and Place Fell.

Beyond Glenridding, the A591 turns left for Troutbeck. Just past the junction, on the A592, a signed path goes left above beautiful Ullswater to the fine 70-foot waterfall of **Aira Force** ❹. Beyond Troutbeck turn left on the A66 for **Keswick** (*visitor information, Moot Hall, Market Sq., tel 017687-72645*), through a broad green valley with first Blencathra and then the rounded slate shoulder of 3,054-foot Skiddaw to the north.

## KESWICK & BACK

From the busy town of Keswick the B5289 runs south into dark and rugged Borrowdale, alongside the beautiful oval of **Derwent Water** ❺. From the road a signed path climbs to **Lodore Falls.**

The steep, brackeny road climbs at a 1:4 gradient from Seatoller over the Honister Pass, then plunges down to **Buttermere** and **Crummock Water,** twin lakes under the slopes of Red Pike and High Stile, and the bulky block of Haystacks. Just before the Bridge Hotel, turn right up a narrow mountain road, over the spectacular pass of **Newlands Hause,** and down into the Newlands Valley.

The A591 leads back to Windermere through **Grasmere** (*visitor information, Red Bank Rd., tel 015394-35245, closed Mon.–Fri. Nov.–March*), prime attraction for Wordsworth fans. Here is **Dove Cottage** ❻ (*tel 015394-35544*), William and Dorothy's home from 1799 to 1808. Alongside stands the **Jerwood Collection Centre,** which houses over 50,000 Wordsworth documents. Farther along the A591, **Rydal Mount** ❼ (*tel 015394-33002, closed Tues. Nov.–Feb.*), where the Wordsworth ménage settled from 1813 onward. Their graves are in St. Oswald's churchyard. ∎

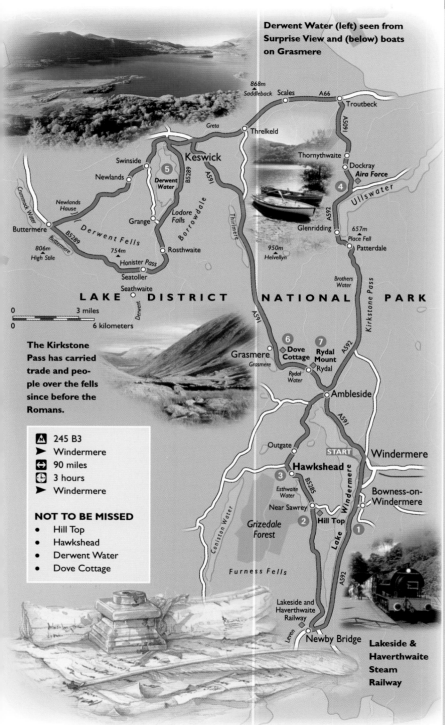

**Derwent Water (left) seen from Surprise View and (below) boats on Grasmere**

868m
Saddleback · Scales · A66 · Troutbeck
Greta
Threlkeld
Thornythwaite
Keswick
Swinside
Newlands
Derwent Water · 5
Newlands Hause
Grange
Lodore Falls
Rosthwaite
Buttermere
Derwent Fells
806m High Stile
754m
Honister Pass
Seatoller
Seathwaite

Dockray · 4 · Aira Force
Ullswater
Glenridding
657m · Place Fell · Patterdale
950m · Helvellyn
Brothers Water
Kirkstone Pass

LAKE DISTRICT NATIONAL PARK

0 —— 3 miles
0 —— 6 kilometers

**The Kirkstone Pass has carried trade and people over the fells since before the Romans.**

Grasmere · 6 · Dove Cottage
Grasmere · 7 · Rydal Mount · Rydal
Rydal Water
Ambleside

A591

Outgate
START
Hawkshead · Windermere
3 · Esthwaite Water
Near Sawrey
Bowness-on-Windermere
Grizedale Forest
2 · Hill Top
1
Lake Windermere

245 B3
Windermere
90 miles
3 hours
Windermere

**NOT TO BE MISSED**
- Hill Top
- Hawkshead
- Derwent Water
- Dove Cottage

Furness Fells
Coniston Water

Lakeside and Haverthwaite Railway
Leven
Newby Bridge

**Lakeside & Haverthwaite Steam Railway**

# The Pennines

THE PENNINE HILLS, BACKBONE OF ENGLAND, RUN FROM the north Midlands through the great industrial conglomeration around Manchester, Sheffield, and Leeds, and on northward for another 100 miles to Hadrian's Wall and the Scottish border. The Derbyshire Dales surround their southern extremity, the Yorkshire Dales penetrate their eastern flanks, and the Lake District outlies them on the west; but the more northerly Pennines have a character all to themselves.

These are high, bleak uplands, dark gritstone in the south and lighter limestone and sandstone farther north, with extensive stretches of peat moorland and huge swaths of high grassland—really exhilarating walking country, under skies that can deliver rain, hail, mist, and sunshine within the space of an hour.

You can appreciate this lonely grandeur from the 70-mile **Settle–Carlisle Railway** line, whose best known feature, the 24-arch Ribblehead Viaduct, is regularly cited as too expensive to maintain. Luckily the line has always been given a reprieve, up to now.

**Settle, Brough, Appleby,** and **Penrith** are northern country towns on or just off the railroad line—solid, stone-built, windswept places, often cut off by winter snow.

As for road routes, the M6 freeway cuts up the western flank of the range, closely shadowed by the far more atmospheric A6 which it superseded. The A6 over Shap Fell in winter is still a snowy, slippery, and adventurous journey.

Other, quieter, roads to give you a taste of Pennine wildness are the A684 (Sedbergh–Hawes), the A683 (Sedburgh–Kirkby Stephen), and the A686 (Penrith–Alston).

Alfred Wainwright devised a west–east **Coast-to-Coast Walk** from the Cumbrian to the North Yorkshire coast. The 35-mile section between Bampton Grange, northeast of Haweswater, and Keld on the Pennine Way offers some very fine northern upland walking.

From strung-out Shap, a wide-built village on the old A6, the path crosses the fells by ancient settlements and reedy ponds, mine-scarred fellsides, and stone-walled green pastures—all beautiful, harsh, and lonely.

## THE PENNINE WAY

The 259-mile **Pennine Way National Trail,** one of Britain's longest and toughest long-distance paths, takes about three weeks to complete at a reasonable pace (though it has been run in under three days). There are all kinds of circular detours off the main route.

### Practical considerations

If you want to sample a couple of days—say Malham to Hawes, or Middleton-in-Teesdale to Dufton— remember that the Pennine Way is extremely popular, and in high summer accommodations en route may be full. Weather can be wet, cold, windy, and misty, so take suitable hiking clothing and equipment. For all its eccentricity and occasional inaccuracy, and the fact that it was written over 30 years ago, Alfred Wainwright's *Pennine Way Companion* (revised edition) is still the best guidebook. When soaked and lost in failing light, you can always get comfort and a laugh from the author's acerbic little

Rugged rock outcrops and wind-tattered trees are typical upland features of the Yorkshire Dales; in the distance looms the round brown shoulder of Ingleborough.

comments on dreary or tricky sections of the Way: "A wet and weary trudge," "Mostly muck and manure,"—even "You will question your own sanity."

### Heading northward

The southernmost portion of the Way, from Edale in Derbyshire's Peak District to Hebden Bridge in Yorkshire's Calder Valley, is mostly a heavy upland slog through sodden peat. Then come the Brontë moors (see p. 272; the Way goes right past Top Withens farm— Wuthering Heights), **Malham's** spectacular limestone cove, and superb hills and dales in open, breezy country, descending to the charming small towns of **Hawes,** **Horton-in-Ribblesdale,** and **Middleton-in-Teesdale.**

North of Middleton lies **Upper Teesdale** with its rich flora, including royal blue spring gentians and other fragile survivals from post-Ice Age Britain. The Way passes **High Force,** a thunderous fall of water over the lip of the Whin Sill, and climbs to more open moorland.

From peaceful little Dufton you hurdle the 2,930-foot summit of **Cross Fell,** highest point of the Way, then descend through the South Tyne Valley to Hadrian's Wall (see pp. 284–85). Last come the Northumbrian forestry plantations, and very wild and lonely moors to journey's end at Kirk Yetholm, just across the Scottish border. ■

# Northeast Pennines

A LESS WELL-KNOWN SECTION OF THE PENNINE HILLS is where northwest County Durham meets Northumberland, around Weardale and Allendale. This is an uncrowded corner of England, with its own harsh beauty. The wild moors of Weardale show signs of past lead- and iron-mining; the A689 runs up the length of the valley, with several intriguing detours.

**Barnard Castle**
🗺 245 C4
**Visitor information**
✉ Woodleigh,
 Flatts Rd.
☎ 01833-690909

**Josephine and John Bowes Museum**
✉ Newgate, Barnard
 Castle
☎ 01833-690606
💲 $$

The ruined drum towers and curtain walls of the Norman castle stand dramatically on their wooded crag above the River Tees at Barnard Castle.

## BARNARD CASTLE

Just beyond Stanhope, the B6278 runs south across remote moors into Teesdale, where Barnard Castle makes an enjoyable stopping place. Charles Dickens stayed here in 1838 at the King's Head Hotel while researching his setting for Dotheboys Hall in *Nicholas Nickleby*. Steep little streets run below the big ruined Norman **Barnard Castle** *(tel 01833-638212, closed Mon.–Tues. Nov.–March)*. Just outside town is the **Josephine and John Bowes Museum,** a splendid French château built in 1869 as a museum by local coal-owner John Bowes. Art works include paintings by Canaletto, Goya, and El Greco; porcelain, silver, and tapestries. Try and be here when the curator operates the fascinating automated silver swan in the lobby.

## AROUND WEARDALE

From Westgate in Weardale a steep side road zigzags north to **Blanchland** in the Derwent Valley, an ancient village with remnants of a medieval monastic settlement, including a superb 15th-century gatehouse and the Abbots Lodge (now the Lord Crewe Arms Hotel), where there is a bar in the vaulted undercroft, a priest's hiding hole, and huge medieval fireplaces.

Another good side road is the B6295, which leaves Weardale at Cowshill and runs north for ten wild miles beside the River East Allen to the small market town of **Allendale.** Every New Year's Eve the "tar-barrelers" take over the streets of Allendale, carrying blazing containers of tar on their heads. Trails lead off across the moors in all directions from the town. ■

Yorkshire boasts lovely York and its famous Minster; Durham offers Britain's finest Norman cathedral; while Northumberland can show a memorable Roman monument in Hadrian's Wall.

# Northeast England

Introduction & map **262–63**
York **264–69**
York Minster **266–67**
A walk around the city walls **268–69**
Around York **270–71**
A drive in the West Riding **272–73**
Yorkshire Dales **274–75**
North York Moors drive **276–77**
Durham Cathedral **278–79**
Durham **280–81**
Newcastle & the Northumbrian coast **282–83**
Hadrian's Wall **284–85**
More places to visit in Northeast England **286**
Hotels & restaurants in Northeast England **376–89**

**Detail from the York Story**

# Northeast England

THE THREE NORTHEASTERN COUNTIES OF YORKSHIRE, DURHAM, AND Northumberland contain some of the most beautiful pastoral countryside in England, some of the wildest and bleakest moorland, and nearly 200 miles of spectacular cliff-edged coastline. They also encompass some depressed towns and villages, and pockets of postindustrial blight; for until the recessions and reorganizations of the 1980s, South and West Yorkshire, eastern County Durham, and the Northumbrian capital city of Newcastle upon Tyne were steeped in strong traditions of heavy work in textiles, coal-mining, steel-making, mineral extraction, and shipbuilding. The legacy of industrial dereliction has largely been swept away, with the disused industrial areas now landscaped or turned into factory or office developments.

### YORKSHIRE

Yorkshire, as all its true-born sons and daughters will loudly tell you, has more and better of everything. There are three national parks in England's biggest county: the Yorkshire Dales, with their wide gritstone and limestone valleys and pretty villages; the North York Moors, with a superabundance of unfrequented peat moors and a splendid craggy coastline dotted with fishing villages; and the Peak District, whose northern tip encroaches into Yorkshire.

Pride of all Yorkshire is York itself, the city that gave its name to the whole county, snug and appealing under the eye of its great Minster church inside a tight ring of medieval walls. To the south are the great manufacturing centers of Sheffield, Leeds, and Bradford, thinning out westward into revitalized and cleaned-up textile towns that shelter under the moors where the Brontë sisters lived and received their inspiration.

### DURHAM & NORTHUMBERLAND

County Durham, farther north, has its share of former mining villages and industrial towns stripped of their raison d'être. But the western moors are wonderfully wild, and the great cathedral city of Durham is a magnet for

**Newcastle upon Tyne's award-winning "Blinking Eye" bridge rotates to allow shipping to pass.**

any visitor. Here, perched dramatically on a river peninsula, is the castle of the medieval prince bishops, sharing the ridge with Durham's crowning glory, the finest Norman cathedral in Britain.

The northernmost county in England, Northumberland fills a triangular space bounded by the Scottish border and the beautiful, brisk Northumbrian coast. In the southeastern corner is the county capital of Newcastle upon Tyne, sharp and lively by day or night. England's wildest national park, Northumberland, fills the interior with hills blanketed in forestry or covered in moor grass and heather. Along the Scottish border roll the high Cheviot Hills, a walker's paradise. ■

0    30 miles
0    50 kilometers

SCOTLAND p. 289

Berwick-upon-Tweed
Northumberland Coast
Holy Island
Beal   Lindisfarne Castle
Bamburgh   Farne Islands
Wooler   Seahouses
816m   Dunstanburgh Castle
The Cheviot   Craster
Alnwick   Alnmouth
Alwinton   Warkworth Castle
Rothbury
NORTHUMBERLAND NATIONAL PARK   Longframlington
Otterburn
NORTHUMBERLAND
Kielder Water   Morpeth   Ashington
A696   Blyth

Housesteads Fort
Birdoswald Fort   Hadrian's Wall
Greenhead   Chesters Fort   TYNE
Vindolanda   Corbridge
Bowness-on-Solway   Haltwhistle Hexham   Newcastle upon Tyne
& WEAR
Stanley   Sunderland
Consett   Washington
Beamish
Durham   Peterlee
Stanhope   DURHAM
Middleton-in-Teesdale   Sedgefield   Hartlepool
Bishop Auckland
Barnard Castle   Middlesbrough
Bowes   Darlington   Stockton-on-Tees   Staithes
Keld   Scotch Corner   Guisborough   Whitby
Thwaite   Reeth   Richmond   Stokesley   Robin Hood's Bay
Swaledale   Grosmont   Ravenscar
Wensleydale   Northallerton   Goathland
Ellerbeck   Rosedale   NORTH YORK   North Yorkshire
YORKSHIRE DALES NATIONAL PARK   Leyburn   Rievaulx   Abbey   Hutton-le-Hole   MOORS   Moors Railway
Aysgarth   Bedale   NORTH   NAT. PARK
693m   Buckden   Masham   Lastingham   Scarborough
Thirsk   YORKSHIRE   Helmsley Pickering   Thornton le Dale
Pen-y-Ghent   704m   Studley   Filey
Ingleton   Arncliffe   Great Whernside   Royal   Ripon   Easingwold   Malton   Flamborough Head
Settle   Grassington   Fountains Abbey   Castle   Flamborough
Malham   Brimham   Ripley   Knaresborough   Howard   Bridlington
Bolton   Rocks   A59   York   Driffield   Skipsea
Skipton   Abbey   Harrogate   EAST RIDING   Hornsea
Ilkley   Wharfe   Tadcaster   OF YORKSHIRE
Keighley   Wetherby   Market   Beverley
Haworth   Bingley   Weighton   Hull   Hedon
Bradford   LEEDS   Selby   Withernsea
Hebden Bridge   WEST   A63   Goole   Easington
Todmorden   Halifax   Wakefield   Spurn Head
Huddersfield   YORKSHIRE
Holmfirth   Barnsley
GREATER MANCHESTER   SOUTH YORKSHIRE   Doncaster
PEAK DISTRICT NATIONAL PARK   Rotherham
SHEFFIELD

North Sea

CUMBRIA p. 245
LANCASHIRE p. 245
GREATER MANCHESTER p. 245
LINCOLNSHIRE p. 201
NOTTINGHAMSHIRE p. 225
DERBYSHIRE p. 225

London ★
Area of map detail

# York

YORK IS THE FINEST SMALL CITY IN THE NORTH OF England. Other places have ancient town walls, narrow old streets, good museums, and fine big churches, but none has them in quite such a concentration of excellence as does York.

## WITHIN THE WALLS

The circular walk around the walls of York (see pp. 268–69) is the best of its kind in Britain. The tangle of medieval streets (called "gates" in York) and alleyways inside those walls draws you in and along, from one oversailing, timbered, or stonework corner to the next, down Gillygate and Davygate; Fossgate and Goodramgate; Stonegate, where a skinny red printer's devil sits chained by the waist high over the crowds; and narrow little Whip-ma-whop-ma-gate, whose name has never quite been satisfactorily translated. The Shambles, once the medieval butchers' quarter, is now stuffed with bookshops and knick-knackeries, but with the original meat hooks still jutting out where they were driven in above the ground-floor windows.

## FINE MUSEUMS

The main focus of interest, of course, is the magnificent **York Minster** (see pp. 266–67), but there are also a number of excellent museums.

The **Yorkshire Museum** *(tel 01904-551800)* on Museum Gardens and the **York Castle Museum** *(tel 01904-650333)* on *The Eye of York* are two further attractions, with superb treasures from Roman times to the present day.

The ever popular **Jorvik Viking Centre** in Coppergate, with its time car travel and "authentic" sounds and smells, shows Viking York (Jorvik) and its excavations in a way you would not otherwise see.

The **York Dungeon** on Clifford Street *(tel 01904-612602)* takes you on a spine-chilling tour round the plague-infested streets of 14th-century York. You can follow Dick Turpin to the gallows and be introduced to ghostly reincarnations of Roman legionnaires.

**National Railway Museum** on Leeman Road, outside the city walls, which holds a host of gleaming behemoths of steam. ∎

**York**
🗺 263 C2
**Visitor information**
✉ Exhibition Square
☎ 01904-621756

**Jorvik Viking Centre**
✉ Coppergate
☎ 01904-643211
💲 $$

**National Railway Museum**
✉ Leeman Rd.
☎ 01904-621261
💲 $$/$$$

**Floodlighting by night draws attention to the twin towers (completed in 1474) that flank the west end of York Minster (left). It took almost 250 years to build the great church.**

**Walk about Victorian York with its cobbled streets in the York Castle Museum (right).**

# York Minster

BEGUN IN 1220 AND FINISHED IN 1472, YORK MINSTER IS the largest medieval church in northern Europe, a great storehouse of fine artistic treasures—chief among them being the 120-odd stained-glass windows. Its official title is The Cathedral and Metropolitan Church of St. Peter in York.

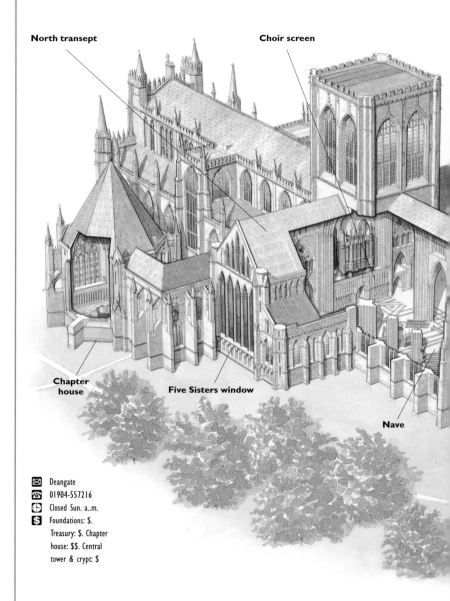

**North transept**

**Choir screen**

**Chapter house**

**Five Sisters window**

**Nave**

✉ Deangate
☎ 01904-557216
🕐 Closed Sun. a..m.
💲 Foundations: $.
   Treasury: $. Chapter
   house: $$. Central
   tower & crypt: $

**The beautiful 16th-century rose window**

South transept

Rose window

Main entrance

West window

## WEST END

The enormous **west window,** 54 feet high, is filled with 14th-century glass, its fine traceried stonework formed in the shape of a heart. The **nave** (1291–1360), with its slender pillars, soars almost 100 feet to a delicately rib-vaulted roof studded with gilt bosses. One shows the Virgin Mary feeding Jesus with a bottle—a Victorian bowdlerization of the more natural medieval original. Halfway along on the north side notice a curious golden dragon—a pivoted crane most likely used to lift a font cover—sticking out of the clerestory.

The **north transept** contains an **astronomical clock** and the five-lancet **Five Sisters window** of 1250, filled with over 100,000 pieces of grisaille (gray) glass—go close to appreciate its muted beauty. Off this transept, leading to the octagonal chapter house (1260–1307), is an area lined with wonderful examples of stonework.

## EAST END

The octagonal late 13th-century **chapter house** is edged with stone carvings—a monkey making a face, a cat and a ram, a falconer—and some splendid irreverent grotesques of priests and prelates.

There are more finely carved bosses in the roof of the crossing, and some wildly coiffed and bearded kings in the 1461 **choir screen.** Across in the south transept is the minster's famous **rose window,** filled kaleidoscopically with Tudor glass. Below, in the **crypt,** are pillars from the original Norman church.

At the east end rises the great **east window,** as big as a modern tennis court, the largest area of medieval stained glass in the world. Creation and Doomsday are its themes, best admired with binoculars to savor their glorious color and detail. ∎

# A walk around the city walls

Unlike many other British cities whose medieval city walls survive only in half-eroded bits and pieces, York has an almost complete ring of about 3 miles of sturdy wall—15 or 20 feet high in most places. An excellent booklet, *Walking The Walls,* is available from the Tourist Information Centre.

From the footway you enjoy a succession of good views across the tight-packed roofs of the city to the great towers and walls of York Minster, and also out across the streets and parks that have grown over the centuries outside the constricted huddle of the medieval city.

The Roman city of Eboracum was defended by a stout wall, earth banks, and ditches, but by the Norman Conquest these had almost disappeared. The medieval strengthening and rebuilding was of a different order, a full moated defensive wall with strong towers, its entrance gates (called bars) guarded by barbicans—gateways with out-thrusting fortified courtyards. The one at Walmgate Bar still exists in good condition, but the others were all pulled down in the 1820s and '30s, in spite of protests. One such protester was Sir Walter Scott, who offered in vain to walk from

Edinburgh to York if the city's corporation would agree to spare Micklegate Barbican.

What is remarkable about the city walls of York is how much has survived nearly eight centuries of assault by siege and aerial bombardment (the city was bombed in a "Baedeker Raid" in 1942), as well as the ravages of neglect and the rapacity of developers.

### BRIDGES & BARS

Starting from the castle parking lot you pass the bulging stone walls of **Clifford's Tower ❶** *(Tower St., tel 01904-646940).* It was completed in 1313 to replace a wooden keep in which 150 Jews killed themselves during a pogrom in 1190, rather than fall into the hands of the rioting mob outside.

**Skeldergate Bridge** takes you across the River Ouse, up and down steps and along the walls to reach **Micklegate Bar,** where medieval traitors' heads were impaled on spikes as a public warning.

Beyond the bar the wall starts to bend and snake north to recross the Ouse by **Lendal Bridge ❷,** with a good view over to the Minster. Across the river the wall disappears at **Lendal Tower;** you continue through the lovely **Museum Gardens ❸,** beside the ruins of St. Mary's Abbey and the Roman masonry of the big **Multangular Tower,** to the squat and solid medieval gateway of **Bootham Bar,** which straddles the Roman road into Eboracum.

Now **York Minster ❹** (see pp. 266–67) looms close alongside, dwarfing the trees, flowers, and vegetable patches in the Deanery gardens below the wall.

The next gateway on the circuit is **Monk Bar,** tall and grim, topped by stone statues making threatening gestures toward the outside world.

**Monk Bar is the tallest and starkest of York's four old city gates.**

Beyond here, just outside the walls, is the domed brick roof of the city's **Ice House** ⑤, built in about 1800. Ice was collected from ponds each winter and stored here between layers of straw until needed for cooling and refrigeration purposes the following summer.

The route leads to a break in the defenses caused by the creation of a fishpool during William the Conqueror's reign. You walk beside the River Foss along Foss Islands Road to the stumpy Tudor brick lookout post called the **Red Tower**. Here the wall reappears and brings you to **Walmgate Bar** ⑥, with its jutting, castellated, and turreted barbican, the only complete example left in England. The spiked portcullis hangs in its slot above the gateway, and the great oaken doors still stand, pierced with a tiny wicket gate. There are bullet and cannonball scars in the stonework, inflicted during the Civil War siege of York in 1644. Curiously, given its military

purpose, the barbican softens and diminishes the grim effect of the gateway behind it, which is so noticeable at York's other bars.

Beyond Walmgate Bar comes the tall outlook tower of **Fishergate Postern Tower,** just before the circuit ends at the castle. ■

🗺 263 C2
➤ Castle
↔ 3 miles
🕐 2 hours
➤ Castle
Visitor information:
20 George Hudson St.
tel 01904-554488

**NOT TO BE MISSED**
- Clifford's Tower
- Museum Gardens
- York Minster

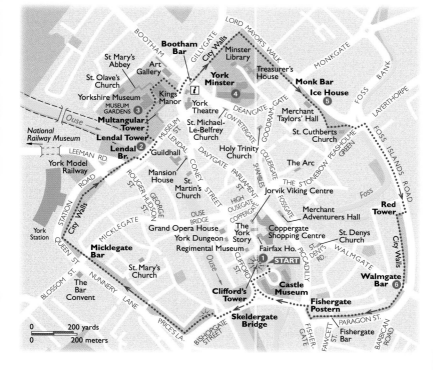

# Around York

**Beverley**
263 C2
**Visitor information**
✉ Guildhall,
   Register Sq.
☎ 01482-867430
🕐 Closed Sun. Oct.–Feb.

**Castle Howard**
✉ 6 miles southwest
   of Malton
☎ 01653-648444
🕐 Closed late
   Oct.–mid-Feb.
💲 $$$

ALTHOUGH THE CITY OF YORK ITSELF IS THE CHIEF JEWEL in the crown of this region, there are many other delights in the Vale of York, as well as farther to the west where the land begins to rise toward the Yorkshire Dales. And the flat, green farming country out eastward toward the fast-crumbling coast of southeast Yorkshire—an area known as Holderness, with Beverley at its heart—is too often overlooked by visitors.

## BEVERLEY

Thirty miles east of York lies Beverley, whose chief glory is its 13th-century **Minster** (*Minster Yard, tel 01482-868540*). King Athelstan (*R.924–939*) gave the Minster the Saxon "frith," or sanctuary stool, kept beside the altar, as a thank-you to St. John of Beverley for answering his prayers by helping him to beat the Scots.

There are some enjoyable grotesque medieval carvings of musicians in the north aisle, including a madly grinning lute player, puff-cheeked woodwind blowers, and a hurdy-gurdy man with a Zapata moustache.

Beverley has one fortified gateway, **North Bar,** and plenty of cobbled medieval streets and lanes to explore. **St. Mary's Church** is a good place to wield your binoculars on the bright chancel ceiling paintings of kings, and on the finely carved nave roof bosses. There are chubby-cheeked Tudor minstrels on a nave pillar, and at the entrance to the **Chapel of St. Michael** a cartoonish sculpture of a rabbit with a pilgrim's scrip slung across one shoulder, which is said to have inspired the illustrator Sir John Tenniel in his famous depiction of the White Rabbit in Lewis Carroll's *Alice's Adventures in Wonderland* (1865).

## CASTLE HOWARD

Northeast of York is Castle Howard, the Palladian mansion used in the television adaptation of Evelyn

*Right: John Jackson, the Yorkshire artist, completed this painting of Lady Mary Howard in 1828 when she was age five years.*

Waugh's snobbery-and-decadence novel *Brideshead Revisited.* Designs for a great palace of a house were commissioned from Sir John Vanbrugh in 1692 by the 3rd Earl of Carlisle, Charles Howard. Vanbrugh, only 28 and with no track record as an architect, was delighted. He took seven years to finish the plans, and Sir Christopher Wren's pupil Nicholas Hawksmoor oversaw the building of the house, which was largely completed by 1712.

The big cupola above the enormous north-facing facade shelters a Great Hall with a vast acreage of tiled floor. Other state rooms include the Long Gallery, with portraits by Van Dyck and Holbein, among others. There is a fine collection of historical costumes, too.

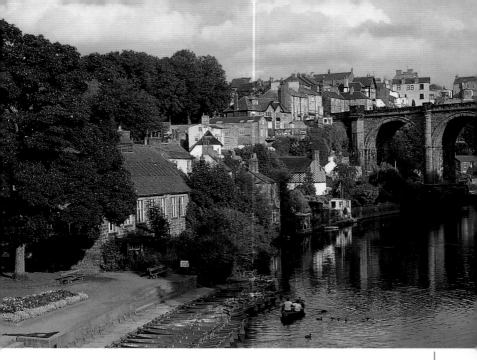

Two-thirds of the house is currently open to the public, with the remaining third, the East wing, occupied by the Howard family.

Outside in the grounds are follies, towers, and obelisks to enhance the views. Here stands a beautifully balanced **Temple of the Four Winds,** with its dome and porticos. This was Vanbrugh's last throw—he died shortly after the temple was completed in 1726.

## KNARESBOROUGH

West of York is Knaresborough, above the gorge of the River Nidd, with the castle ruins rising above all. Chief attraction is **Mother Shipton's Cave** *(Prophesy House, tel 01423-864600),* where you can learn the story of local seer Ursula Sontheil, born in 1488 in a riverside cave. She predicted all manner of events and discoveries such as the launch and defeat of the Spanish Armada, and the invention of cars and airplanes.

In the nearby well, everyday objects hang under streams of limestone-filtered water, slowly "turning to stone"—i.e., becoming coated with a thick calcified layer.

## HARROGATE

Just down the road is elegant, gray stone Harrogate. Between the late Victorian era and World War I, sufferers and society-seekers would come to drink the sulfurous water under the dome of the octagonal **Royal Pump Room** *(Crown Place, tel 01423-556188),* nowadays mostly given over to a museum. Its stained-glass window shows a Pre-Raphaelite angel rising in a puff of steam from the town's healing springs; these were discovered in 1571 on The Stray, a grassy common area south of the town.

Stroll in Valley Gardens to the west of the town center, where "temples" stand over wells; and try a genuine Victorian Turkish bath at the 1897 **Royal Baths Assembly Rooms** *(Crescent Rd., tel 01423-556746).* ∎

**Piled up one above another along steep streets, the houses of Knaresborough make a picturesque and often painted ensemble on their cliff overlooking the River Nidd.**

**Knaresborough**
 263 B2
**Visitor information**
✉ 9 Castle Courtyard
☎ 01423-866886
🕐 Closed Nov.–Easter

**Harrogate**
🄰 263 B2
**Visitor information**
✉ Royal Baths
   Assembly Rooms,
   Crescent Rd.
☎ 01423-537300
🕐 Closed Sun.
   Oct.–March

# A drive in the West Riding

**The industrial southwest of Yorkshire might strike anyone not in the know as a surprising area to visit. All mill towns, textile factories, and bleak moors—that has been the reputation of what was known as the West Riding of Yorkshire. But here today, as in so much of postindustrial Britain, it is all change.**

The textile trade has gone, and the small industrial towns have rediscovered the lovely silvery stone that has been hidden for more than a century under coats of sooty grime and skins of oxidized black. The wholesale demolition of mills, factories, and row houses that went on in the 1960s and '70s has slowed, if not halted, as their significance to Britain's industrial and social heritage is recognized.

## UP ON THE MOORS

As for the moors—bleak they certainly can be in dour weather. But they are also beautiful, striped with gritstone walls, rising steeply above the manufacturing towns that huddle in the depths of the valleys. Methodist and Baptist chapels are scattered everywhere: The West Riding was one of the most fertile seedbeds for John Wesley, William Darney, and the other founding fathers of militant nonconformist religion.

The West Riding moors are lonely, moody places, often swept by wind and rain. The Brontë sisters lived and wrote in the hilltop village of Haworth, and the landscape seems full of their spirit—particularly the wild, brooding spirit of Emily Brontë, who set her masterpiece *Wuthering Heights* here.

## HAWORTH TO HEBDEN BRIDGE

Start at **Haworth** *(visitor information, tel 01535-642329).* The **Brontë Parsonage Museum** ❶ *(tel 01535-6423234)* is at the top of the village street, a sandstone Georgian house in whose dining room the Brontë sisters wrote their astonishing novels. Study, dining room, kitchen, bedrooms. All are spotless, quiet, and sober, unlikely ground for the growth of such vivid, self-assertive minds.

A 7-mile round-trip walk from Haworth takes you across **Haworth Moor,** passing the Brontë Waterfalls and the rock called the "Brontë Chair," and along the Pennine Way (see pp. 258–59) to the ruin of **Top Withens**

farmhouse—Emily's model for Heathcliff's house, Wuthering Heights. A walk booklet can be bought at Haworth visitor information center.

From Haworth, the A629 leads south for 10 miles into **Halifax** *(visitor information, tel 01422-368725),* a northern textile town to the backbone and one that is unjustifiably overlooked by many visitors. The **Shibden Hall Folk Museum** ❷ *(Lister's Rd., tel 01422-352246, closed Dec.–Feb.)* demonstrates rural traditions and crafts, while the **Piece Hall** ❸ of 1779 is a massive monument to Georgian wool trading—it contains over 300 merchants' rooms around a vast cobbled, arcaded, Italianate courtyard. A visitor information center is also sited here. In the 19th-century mill next door is the **Calderdale Industrial Museum** *(Square Rd., tel 01422-358087, closed Mon.)* with working textile machinery and exhibits telling the history of mining.

Two detours worth taking are to Bradford (M26, Jct. 26), where the **1853 Gallery** *(tel 01274-531163)* in Salt's Mill, Saltaire, houses Europe's largest collection of works by Bradford-born artist David Hockney; and Wakefield (M26, Jct. 29 or 30) with its splendid **National Coal Mining Museum** *(tel 01924-848806).*

Cut west along A58 and the A646 to **Hebden Bridge** ❹ *(visitor information, tel 01422-843831)* to see how beautiful cleaned-up gritstone mills and terraces can be.

The A6033 from Hebden Bridge leads you back across the moors to Haworth. ∎

---

🗺 263 B2
▶ Haworth
🔁 34 miles
🕐 1½ hours
▶ Haworth

**NOT TO BE MISSED**
- Brontë Parsonage Museum
- Piece Hall

Shops on Haworth's Main Street

KEIGHLEY
MOOR

443m

Brontë Parsonage
Museum

**Haworth**    ①    Barcroft

Stanbury

**START**

Penine Way

459m

WADSWORTH
MOOR

Oxenhope

A629    Denholme    **BRADFORD**
1853 Gallery

Keelham    Hardcastle Crags rise
above Hebden Dale.

A6033    447m

Ogden

Hardcastle
Crags    Pecket
Well    **Queensbury**

Illingworth

**Hebden
Bridge**    ④

A629

Shibden Hall
Museum    ②

A646    Midgley

**Mytholmroyd**    Luddenden
Foot    **HALIFAX**

Calder    Calderdale
Industrial Museum

A58    ③    **Piece
Hall**

National Coal
Mining Museum

**Sowerby
Bridge**

0                          3 miles

0                          6 kilometers

M62

**HUDDERSFIELD**

Mills along the Rochdale Canal in Hebden Bridge

# Yorkshire Dales

NORTH OF KEIGHLEY AND WEST OF HARROGATE STRETCH-es Yorkshire Dales National Park, hundreds of square miles of wild upland moors, grasslands, and hills, cut by broad valleys with shallow rushing rivers where some of the lushest pasture in Britain makes everything green. Dales folk are extremely proud of their small, neat villages, cozy little pubs, green fields seamed with drystone walls, and far-ranging views.

## WHARFEDALE

Wharfedale runs northwest from the lower edge of the Yorkshire Dales, with the village of Bolton Abbey at the entry to the national park. **Bolton Priory** *(tel 01756-710238)* was built in the mid-12th century; the great east window still stands flanked by tall arches, while the nave is used as the parish church. Two miles north at **The Strid,** the River Wharfe crashes in white water between narrow rocky jaws. Many have drowned attempting to jump across.

The B6160 runs up Wharfedale to **Grassington** *(visitor information, Colvend, Hebden Rd., tel 01756-752774, closed Mon.–Fri. Oct.–Feb.),* the dale's chief village, where the **Upper Wharfedale Folk Museum** *(6 The Square, tel 01756-753059, closed Mon.–Fri. Oct.–March)* gives a good idea of the area and its history. Four miles north, a side road to the left leads up Littondale to **Arncliffe,** where the **Falcon Inn** is unspoiled and serves excellent beer.

Back in Wharfedale, the B6160 continues through pretty Kettlewell and Buckden to **Hubberholme** and its striking grouping of George Inn, humpbacked bridge, and little church, which contains a rare Tudor rood loft.

## NIDDERDALE & AROUND

Strictly speaking outside the national park, **Ripley,** on the eastern edge, is an Alsatian village re-created around a cobbled square. It was built in the 1820s by one of the Ingilby family, who have lived at **Ripley Castle** for seven centuries (28 generations and counting). The churchyard has a remarkable "kneeling cross," with hollows scooped by penitents' knees. **Nidderdale** goes northwest from here, strung with reservoirs but still lovely.

The B6265 leaves to the right of the dale road, passing the bizarrely shaped gritstone outcrops of **Brimham Rocks** on its way over to **Fountains Abbey** (NT), set in a lovely wooded valley. Founded by Benedictines in 1132, taken over by Cistercians three years later, within a generation Fountains was the richest abbey in Britain through wool, lead, quarrying, and agricultural interests. The refectory, infirmary, abbot's house, dormitory, cloister, chapter house, and giant vaulted undercroft (300 feet long) remain. In 1720, John Aislabie bought the ruins and land. He and his son William created **Studley Royal** (NT) water garden and 1,800 acres of landscaped grounds—grottoes, cascades, temples, lakes, bowers and alcoves, deer parks, woods, and wide open spaces—a treat not to be missed.

Two miles east, **Ripon** *(visitor information, Minster Rd., tel 01765-604625)* has the late Norman **Cathedral of Saints Peter and Wilfrid,** showing a beautiful 13th-century west front with twin towers, but concealing a seventh-

**Yorkshire Dales National Park**

🅰 265 A3

**Ripley Castle**
☎ 01423-770152
✉ Ripley
💲 $$ (gardens only $/$$)

**Fountains Abbey & Studley Royal**
✉ Fountains, Ripon
☎ 01765-608888
💲 $$

century Saxon crypt. In the Market Square, at 9 p.m., the Wakeman in his scarlet-trimmed coat and black hat blows curfew on a great curved horn—the original, of Saxon date, is in the Town Hall.

At **Masham**, 10 miles to the northwest, a tour of **Theakston's Brewery** will introduce you to their pale and potent bitter, and to the celebrated Old Peculier ale—treacle-dark and very strong.

## WENSLEYDALE

The A6108 and A684 travel west beside the River Ure along Wensleydale, famous for cheese and pastoral beauty. At **Aysgarth** *(National Park Centre, tel 01969-663424)* the river tumbles spectacularly in two long falls over limestone steps.

## SWALEDALE

North of Wensleydale runs Swaledale, the most northerly and most rugged of the Yorkshire Dales (save **Arkengarthdale,** which swings off northwest). Keld, Thwaite, Muker, and Gunnerside are hamlets under the moors. **Richmond** *(visitor information, Friary Gardens, Victoria Rd., tel 01748-850252),* at the eastern foot of the dale, has a massive Norman castle perched on a knoll, its great curtain walls enclosing a 100-foot-high keep with walls 11 feet thick. Scolland's Hall, inside, dates from 1080 and may be the oldest domestic building in Britain.

The town itself has the biggest cobbled marketplace in Britain, steeply sloping with many narrow, medieval alleys leading off it. ■

**Characteristic landscape of the Yorkshire Dales, the lower pasture fields of Swaledale are separated by drystone walls, which run on up into the uncultivated, heathery upland moors.**

**Theakston's Brewery**

✉ Red Lane, Masham
☎ 01765-689057
🕐 Closed mid-Dec.–March
💲 $$

# North York Moors drive

**North York Moors National Park holds harshly beautiful moorland, lonely hills, and spectacular coastal cliffs. This is an area of country with little of the soft green pastorality of the Yorkshire Dales, but with its own wild and exciting character.**

This tour begins at **Pickering** ❶ *(visitor information, tel 01751-473791)*. Situated near the southern edge of the national park at the junction of the A170 and the A169, it makes a good base for touring the moors. It is a compact town, whose Parish Church of Sts. Peter and Paul contains 15th-century frescoes, including Thomas à Becket at the moment of his martyrdom, and St. George dealing with a rather weedy dragon.

Running 18 miles from Pickering north to Grosmont, the **North York Moors Railway** *(Pickering Station, Park St., tel 01751-472508, call for schedule)* gives superb views throughout the journey. The line closed in 1965, but since 1973 it has operated as a steam railway. There are good walks from the intermediate stations; one from the moorland village of **Goathland** descends to Mallyan Spout, a 70-foot waterfall.

Just west of Goathland you can explore **Wade's Causeway,** a remarkable paved road dating from the later stages of the Roman occupation, although modern researchers suggest it may pre-date the Romans altogether.

## FROM PICKERING TO THE COAST

Take the A170 east to Thornton Dale, then a side road on the left to reach the **Dalby Forest Drive** ❷, looping and winding for 9 miles from one viewpoint to the next, emerging at Hackness.

Continue east to **Scarborough** *(visitor information, tel 01723-373333)*, Yorkshire's premier seaside resort. North Bay beyond the castle-topped headland is quieter than the central South Bay.

The A165 or the A171 leads north to Cloughton, where the coast road switchbacks north to Staintondale and Ravenscar. From Ravenscar you can follow on foot the abandoned railway track or the cliff-top path to reach Robin Hood's Bay, 3 miles north.

Take the A171 north from Ravenscar and a short, steep right turn down a minor road

(B1447) will bring you to **Robin Hood's Bay** ❸ *(Information from Whitby visitor information center)*, a red-roofed fishing village very picturesquely piled in its narrow cleft.

The B1447 and the A171 continue north to **Whitby** ❹ *(visitor information, tel 01947-602674)*, charm encapsulated, with its 13th-century abbey ruins on the cliff. At the top of the 199 Church Stairs stands the Norman Church of St. Mary, its interior woodwork reputedly the creation of ships' carpenters. Bram Stoker set part of *Dracula* (1897) in the graveyard. James Cook (1728–1779), explorer and global circumnavigator, lodged as an apprentice on Grape Lane—the house is now the **Captain Cook Memorial Museum** *(tel 01947-601900, closed late Oct.–Feb. & Mon.–Fri. March)*. From Whitby the A174 leads in 10 miles to **Staithes** ❺, a pretty cliff village where Cook served as assistant to a grocer until, legend says, he stole a shilling from his master and ran away to Whitby.

## OVER THE MOORS

Continue to Easington on the A174. Take a side road on the left to turn right onto the A171. In a mile turn left on minor roads through Danby, Castleton, and Westerdale. South of Westerdale pass **Ralph Cross,** where medieval travelers left coins for "those less fortunate"; then bear left past Fat Betty, or White Cross, to Rosedale Abbey set in the lovely valley.

Side roads connect Rosedale Abbey with **Hutton-le-Hole** ❻ *(Pickering visitor information, The Ropery, tel 01751-473791)*, a very popular village with a collection of restored local buildings in the **Ryedale Folk Museum** *(tel 01751-417367, closed early Nov.–mid-March)*.

Two miles east is **Lastingham** ❼, where St. Mary's Church shelters a Norman crypt full of earlier stonework. On the A170, south of Hutton-le-Hole, turn right for the

*Rye*

**Rievaulx Abbey** ❽

*Ryedale*  B1257

Helmsle

Staithes offers shelter from the icy North Sea.

*Robin Hood's Bay*

**NORTH YORK MOORS**

**NATIONAL PARK**

*Dalby Forest Drive*

South Beach, Scarborough

**Right: North Yorkshire Moors Railway, Goathland**

market town of **Helmsley** and nearby **Rievaulx Abbey** ⑧ *(Rievaulx, tel 01439-798228)*. This 12th-century Cistercian building, had to be orientated north–south rather than the conventional east–west because of its constricted site. The A170 returns you to Pickering. ∎

263 C3

Start and finish at Pickering

120 miles

5 hours. Making a few overnight stops (see pp. 376–79) along this route will help you get the most out of your visit to this national park.

# Durham Cathedral

**The classic view of Durham Cathedral—finest Norman cathedral in Britain— whose twin west towers loom over Jesus Mill on the inner bank of the River Wear**

THE MEDIEVAL PRINCE BISHOPS OF DURHAM RULED the northeast of England as the authorized delegates of the king. Mandated as they were by the Crown to use any and every means to keep the Scots at bay and the rule of law secure, they possessed power, wealth, and influence of an order unimaginable today. They had their own army, their own mint, and their own courts of law. Their palace at Durham was a fully fortified castle, and the cathedral where their spiritual influence was centered, sharing its narrow eminence above the River Wear with the castle, was—and still is—reckoned to be the finest and most spectacularly sited church that the Normans built in Britain.

## NORMAN MASTERPIECE

From the center of the great railroad viaduct that strides across the northern half of the city, you are struck with the impression of castle and cathedral as a single temporal and spiritual stronghold. Close up, the size of the cathedral makes an unforgettable impact when viewed from Palace Green. This is building to a grand design, an impression reinforced as you step past the replica lion's head sanctuary knocker on the north door, and enter the dusky interior.

Durham's Romanesque cathedral was started in 1093 and completed in 1274, but almost all of it is high Norman, 12th-century work—solid, bulky, everything on the massive scale. The cylindrical piers, and both round and pointed arches in the **nave,** are geometrically carved with dogtooth, chevron, and lozenge patterns, a Byzantine or perhaps Moorish effect as a reminder that experiences on Crusade had expanded many 12th-century minds in England. The 11- to 12th-century **choir** soars high; its aisle roofs are seamed with stone rib vaulting installed some time shortly after the Conquest.

At either end of the cathedral is a chapel containing the remains of a Dark Ages saint. The beautiful **Galilee Chapel** at the west end, built in the 1170s, echoes the Moorish influence seen in the nave; but here everything is done with a light, delicate touch. Slender Purbeck marble columns support the roof over the simple **tomb** of the Venerable Bede. The monkish scribe from Jarrow on the River Tyne, who died in 735, was a historian of the early Christian church in England, and biographer of the north of England's favorite saint, Cuthbert, the shepherd and Bishop of Lindisfarne.

## HERMIT SAINT

St. Cuthbert lies under a plain slab marked "Cuthbertus" at the cathedral's eastern end in the **Chapel of the Nine Altars.** The chapel was built from 1242 to 1280 so that the dozens of monks in the Durham community could all receive communion more or less simultaneously. Cuthbert preferred to live alone with the seals and seabirds on the windswept and rocky Farne Islands (see p. 282), but his restless fate, wisdom, and skill as an orator forced him into high office and responsibility.

He died in A.D. 687, but had no peace in death. In order to preserve his body from the attacking Vikings, the Lindisfarne monks removed it from the island in 875. They wandered with it for over 100 years, until in 995 a vision told them to lay Cuthbert to rest at Dun Holme—now Durham. Legend says that William I ordered the tomb to be opened so that he could see for himself if the saint's body was, as the monks insisted, perfectly preserved. Whatever the Conqueror saw scared him so badly that he ran for his horse and galloped off, never drawing rein until he had crossed the Tees, 20 miles away.

In 1104, Cuthbert's body was buried behind the easternmost altar. His shrine, focus of countless medieval pilgrimages, was broken up at the Reformation, and the saint's bones reburied. In 1827 he was exhumed again, a skeleton in a silken shroud with a jeweled pectoral cross on its breast.

St. Cuthbert's cross and his wooden coffin, carved with the images of the apostles, along with treasures of the cathedral of Durham, can be seen in the cathedral **Treasury,** where you can also view a copy of the fabulously illustrated 7th-century Lindisfarne Gospels. ■

### Durham Cathedral
- ✉ The College
- ☎ 0191-386 4266
- 🕐 Tower closed Sun.
- 💲 Donation for cathedral.
  Monk's Dormitory: $.
  Tower: $. Treasury: $

**The lion's-head sanctuary knocker on Durham Cathedral's northwest door is a copy of the original 12th-century knocker (now in the cathedral Treasury), which hunted criminals would grasp to claim protection.**

# Durham

DURHAM HAS COME A LONG WAY SINCE THE 1950s, WHEN coal mines all around this university city gave it a gritty, working-class aura. Now the pits are all closed, and the place has been spruced up. The medieval quarter of Durham is a compact area of not much more than half a mile, squeezed into a narrow, southward-pointing peninsula. The River Wear is forced into a tight loop around this high-knuckled finger of land; only a couple of hundred yards prevents it from being severed at the root to form an island. A tour around this fascinating city center on foot is short on distance, therefore, but long on interest, and at least a couple of hours should be set aside for it—more if you want to make a thorough exploration of the cathedral and castle.

**Durham**
🅰 263 B4
**Visitor information**
✉ 2 Millennium Place
☎ 0191-384 3720
🕐 Closed Sun.
Oct.–Feb.

**Durham University Museum of Archaeology**
✉ Old Fulling Mill, The Banks
☎ 0191-334 1823
🕐 Closed Tues.–Thurs. Nov.–March
💲 $

**Durham Castle**
✉ Palace Green
☎ 0191-334 3800
🕐 Closed late April–June & Oct.–mid-March Functions at the castle may cause closure at other times.
💲 $$

A good place to start exploring the city of Durham is the pedestrianized **Market Place,** with its 1861 equestrian statue of Charles William Vane Stewart, 3rd Marquis of Londonderry and Lord Lieutenant of Durham, a splendid figure in a frogged uniform and plumed shako astride a proudly pawing stallion.

From here, curving Silver Street leads across the 14th-century **Framwellgate Bridge,** from where you enjoy the first of a succession of wonderful views across the river to the castle walls and twin cathedral towers rising above the wooded banks of the Wear.

### ALONG THE RIVERBANK

At the far end of the bridge, steps to the left lead down to the riverside path. Soon a slanting weir—a favorite spot for white-water canoeists—crosses the river to Jesus Mill (mostly 18th-century, but on medieval foundations) on the far bank. The profits of this former fulling mill (where cloth was beaten and thickened) were used to build the cathedral's altar—hence the name. Nowadays the building houses the excellent **Durham University Museum of Archaeology.** This view of weir, mill, castle walls, and cathedral

towers is a photographers' favorite.

On the other side of the River Wear, across the three slender arches of Prebend's Bridge (built in 1776 to replace a timber bridge washed away in floods), the path turns right to continue around the inner curve of the peninsula. Just beyond the bridge is "The Upper Room," an ingenious piece of modern sculpture assemblage using carved tree trunks.

A short way along the bank, half hidden under the trees, is a curious little stone structure like a summerhouse. Its entrance is flanked by fluted pillars. They once formed part of a house built on this spot for one of Durham's most celebrated citizens, the Polish émigré Count Boruwlaski. The count settled in Durham early in the 19th century, and died here in 1837, at the age of 97. His fame came from his diminutive size, for he was just 3 feet 3 inches tall—a wise and generous man, according to reputation.

Farther on, the riverside footpath passes under modern Kingsgate Bridge, with Durham University's students' union building and some lecture rooms along the far bank. Soon the narrow, pointed arches of 12th-century

**Elvet Bridge**—Durham's oldest bridge—appear ahead. Beyond lies **Brown's Boathouse,** where in summer you can rent a punt (boat).

## UP TO THE CASTLE

Just before the bridge, the narrow steps of Drury Lane Vennel climb away on the left to emerge through a low archway on the spine of the promontory in North Bailey. To the left, cobbled Owengate leads right to Palace Green, surrounded by 17th-century buildings, with **Durham Cathedral** (see pp. 278–79) ahead and the castle on your right.

**Durham Castle,** begun in 1072, retains some older features—notably a Tudor chapel with some beautiful misericords, and a 15th-century kitchen. Most of it, though, is an 18th-century Gothic rebuild for the bishops of Durham, who remained in residence until 1836 when the castle was given to the university (founded in 1832 by Bishop van Mildert).

After visiting the cathedral, you can leave the Treasury to reach South Bailey. The winding street leads down past the university colleges of St. John's, St. Chad's, and St. Cuthbert's Society. The roadway then passes through the 1778 Watergate arch. Before Prebend's Bridge, a path bearing right leads along the east bank of the River Wear past Jesus Mill to return to Framwellgate Bridge, Silver Street, and the market square. ■

**Market Place, Durham: The city's downhill streets and steep and winding alleys, known as vennels, form one of the best townscapes in Britain.**

# Newcastle & the Northumbrian coast

NEWCASTLE UPON TYNE, FORMER CAPITAL CITY OF England's northernmost county of Northumberland, is a vibrant, lively place. It has seen its shipbuilding and heavy engineering fade away, but the Geordies (Newcastle natives) have lost neither their strong local accent nor their quick-fire wit in the city's recent scramble for a consumerist good-time image.

**Newcastle upon Tyne**

🅰 263 B4

**Visitor information**

✉ 132 Grainger St.

☎ 0191-277 8000

🕐 Closed Sun.

**Warkworth Castle**

✉ Warkworth, 30 miles north of Newcastle

☎ 01665-711423

🕐 Closed Tues.–Fri. Nov.–March

💲 $$

**Bamburgh Castle**

✉ Bamburgh

☎ 01668-214515

🕐 Closed Nov.–late March (unless by appointment)

💲 $$

Highlights of the city are the bridges across the River Tyne, especially the graceful bow-girder **Tyne Bridge** of 1928 and its ingeniously-opening neighbor, the so-called **Blinking Eye,** built in 2000 to celebrate the Millennium. Nearby on the south, or Gateshead, bank of the Tyne stands **BALTIC, the Centre for Contemporary Art** (tel 0191-478-1810). Youngsters make for **Bigg Market,** the setting for Newcastle's nighttime hangout-cum-street-party.

## NORTHUMBRIAN COAST

From Newcastle the Northumbrian coastline stretches 70 miles north to the Scottish border. Windswept, with cold water and beautifully clean beaches, this superb run of low rocky cliffs and sandy bays would be as crowded as Cornwall if it were not for the far colder climate here.

Leading north along the coast from Newcastle you come first to the 12th- to 14th-century **Warkworth Castle,** the setting in Shakespeare's *Henry IV Part I* for Harry Hotspur's distracted leave-taking of his exasperated wife. Next comes **Alnmouth,** a handsome little red- and gray-roofed coastal town behind extensive sandbanks, and at **Craster** (visitor information, tel 01665-576007, closed Mon.–Fri. Oct.–Feb.) you can eat locally smoked herring, and walk the cliffs for 1½ miles to the impressive ruins of **Dunstanburgh Castle** (tel 01665-576231, closed Mon.–Tues. Nov.–March).

**Bamburgh Castle** frowns out from its shoreline crag toward the 28 low rock ledges of the **Farne Islands**. Boats from nearby **Seahouses** (visitor information, car park, Seafield Rd., tel 01665-720884, closed Nov.–March) visit the islands to see the seals and birds, the lighthouse home of Grace Darling (the lightkeeper's daughter, heroine of an epic 1838 rescue), and the monastic ruins on Inner Farne, where St. Cuthbert fasted and prayed A.D. 676–684.

Passing the causeway to **Holy Island** at Beal (see box p. 283), you reach **Berwick-upon-Tweed** (visitor information, 106 Marygate, tel 01289-330733, closed Sun. Oct.–Feb.), an ancient border town often bloodily disputed between England and Scotland.

## NORTHUMBERLAND

**Northumberland National Park** is the wildest, remotest, and least visited of the national parks. Much of its bare, peat-bedded upland area has been planted with Forestry Commission woodland, especially around **Kielder Water reservoir**—there are 250 square miles of close-packed conifers here. Yet Kielder has its own beauty, around the lake and along the footpaths of the peaceful, endlessly wind-stirred **Kielder Forest.**

## Off the beaten track

Fast cross-border roads streak

northwest through this landscape between Newcastle and Edinburgh, but to catch a more intimate flavor of Northumbrian forest and hill farmland, take the side road east from Saughtree (on the B6357 Carlisle–Jedburgh road) for 30 miles, through the heart of the Kielder Forest and north by Lanehead to Otterburn.

An alternative approach to the heart of Northumberland is from its eastern flank at Longframlington (on the A697 Morpeth–Edinburgh road), coming west through **Rothbury** with its old fortified defensive tower, and on up the B6341 through the villages of Thropton, Sharperton, and Harbottle to Alwinton.

This is wonderful empty country, deep in the flanks of the rolling Cheviot Hills, with a cul-de-sac road winding on for a dozen miles past lonely hill farms. You can take your pick of a number of green lanes here—challenging or easy walking routes across the hills, following ancient tracks such as Salter's Road and Clennell Street, or sticking to the well-beaten national trail of the Pennine Way (see p. 258).

### Musical tradition

Northumberland's traditional music, played on the Northumbrian small-pipes, is wild and distinctive, music to make you want to dance or play. The local organization Folkworks *(tel 0191-443 4666)* has helped revitalize it with concerts, dances, and workshops where all are welcome. It's a good way to catch the real spirit of this elusive and beautiful area. ■

## Holy Island

**D**rive over the causeway from Beal (check tide times) to visit Holy Island village, the church and priory (founded A.D. 635), the castle, and the seabirds of St. Cuthbert's Holy Island of Lindisfarne—a magical experience. ■

**Perched atop Beblowe Crag on the south side of Holy Island, Lindisfarne Castle was built in the 1550s as a border fortification against the Scots, and still retains a grim air of defiance.**

**Northumberland National Park Authority**
✉ Eastburn, South Park, Hexham
☎ 01434-605555

**Lindisfarne Castle**
✉ Lindisfarne (Holy Island)
☎ 01289-389244
🕐 Closed Nov.–March, Mon. April–Oct.
💲 $$

# Hadrian's Wall

**Hadrian's Wall**
 263 B4

**Chesters Roman
Fort & Museum**
✉ 1½ miles west of
Chollerford
☎ 01434-681379
$ $$

**Housesteads
Roman Fort
& Museum**
✉ 2¼ miles northeast
of Bardon Mill
☎ 01434-344363
$ $$

**Vindolanda Fort
& Museum**
✉ 1¼ miles southeast
of Twice Brewed
☎ 01434-344277
🕐 Call for winter
closing hours
$ $$

**Roman Army
Museum**
✉ Near Greenhead
☎ 01697-747485
🕐 Closed mid-
Nov.–mid-Feb.
$ $$

**Birdoswald
Roman Fort**
✉ Gilsland
☎ 01697-747602
🕐 Interior closed
Dec.–Feb.
$ $/$$

HADRIAN'S WALL IS FAR AND AWAY THE MOST IMPORTANT relic of Roman rule in Britain. Its sheer size (73 miles in length) means that huge numbers of archaeologically priceless items have been excavated on, under, or near it. Its unbroken westward run from Wallsend in Newcastle upon Tyne to Bowness on the Solway Firth gives it a coherence and solidity that helps bring the 400 years of Roman occupation alive across two millennia. Though tumbledown or obliterated in places, the impact of the wall is stunning—particularly where it rides the rim of the great dolerite cliffs of the Whin Sill like the crest of an enormous, northward-breaking wave.

About 50 years after the Romans had arrived in Britain, the northern limit of their presence—and the northern boundary of their entire empire—was the ground between the Tyne and the Solway. North of here was barbarian land, the country of the Caledonians. In A.D. 120 Emperor Hadrian ordered the building of the wall, both as a defensive position for soldiers in case of barbarian attack, and as a physical expression of the boundaries of Roman law and order. In 122 the emperor came to see for himself how the work was coming along.

As it finally stood, Hadrian's Wall was stone-built, eight feet thick and 15 feet high, with six-foot battlements on top. Every Roman mile (1,620 yards) there was a milecastle,

garrisoned by troops; between each milecastle stood two signal and observation turrets. Every 5 miles was a fort, like a barracks. A deep ditch ran along the front, except where there were natural defenses such as cliffs. The garrison soldiers were mostly recruits from outlying Roman provinces.

By the early fifth century, Hadrian's Wall had been abandoned. Much of the stonework was

## Hadrian's Wall Path

The **Hadrian's Wall Path National Trail** runs for 84 miles from Newcastle to Bowness-on-Solway, passing through outstanding scenery along the way and taking in all the forts, museums, and existing sections of the wall. The *Hadrian's Wall Path National Trail Guide* by Anthony Burton (Aurum Press) is the official guidebook. ∎

taken by locals over the ensuing centuries, and sharp eyes may spot the shaped blocks, some inscribed, in the walls of farm buildings, houses, and churches all over the area.

## WHAT REMAINS

Running west from Newcastle, there is a stretch of wall and remains of a turret at **Low Brunton.** The cavalry fort at **Chesters,** in parkland in the Tyne Valley, has a museum full of inscriptions and sculpture, and a well-preserved regimental bathhouse layout with steam rooms and chilling-out chambers. The best section of the wall begins here, and runs for 20 miles to Greenhead.

Best known of all the wall sites is **Housesteads Roman Fort** (NT), very well preserved and complete, set in a superbly dramatic position right on the edge of the Whin Sill cliffs with a marvelous view out north.

The museum is small and rather disappointing, but the fort makes

up for it with its gate thresholds worn down by the soldiers' feet, the north gate cornerstones scarred with the scraping of wagons, and a commanding officer's house with black slag still lumped around the bathroom's furnace hearth. There are also communal latrines, cheerless barrack blocks, a chilly stone-built hospital—there is atmosphere and despair here.

At **Vindolanda,** just west, extensive military and civilian settlement remains are on show, along with a helpful reconstruction of a stone turret and length of wall, and a timber milecastle gate. The museum here is excellent.

Beyond, at **Cawfields,** is a clear section of wall ribboning up and down; and at Walltown Crags are more spectacular views and a good **Roman Army Museum,** next to Magnis Roman fort. At **Birdoswald** you'll find a well-preserved fort and bridge abutment. ∎

Hadrian's Wall, astonishingly complete and nowadays well maintained, dips from Cuddy's Crag (below) before ascending the cliff of the Whin Sill to reach Housesteads Roman fort.

**Edward Burne-Jones executed these panels in Hexham Abbey.**

## More places to visit in Northeast England

### BEAMISH, THE NORTH OF ENGLAND OPEN AIR MUSEUM

To get a flavor of what the northeast was like before the coal mines closed, visit this open air museum in northern County Durham. Here, set in 300 acres, is a reconstructed pit village complete with pithead buildings, chapel, school, a mine with underground tours guided by ex-miners, and a row of pit cottages with their own vegetable plots (allotment gardens).

A tram ride away is "The Town," complete with cooperative store, candy factory, working pub, dentist's surgery, printworks, and its own railroad station. There is also a working farm and Pockerley Manor and gardens, which recreates life in the early 1800s and 1900s.

🅰 263 B4 ☎ 0191-370 4000 🕒 Closed Mon. & Fri. Nov.–March & last 2 weeks in Dec. 💲 $$$

### CORBRIDGE

Corbridge is a handsome little town with a fine Roman site just outside at **Corstopitum** *(tel 01434-632349, closed Mon.–Fri. Nov.–March).* Here is the outline of a garrison town, and a museum with pottery, weaponry, and superb Roman stonemasonry, including the famous Corbridge Lion crouched over a deer, grinning through its curly beard.

🅰 263 B4 **Corbridge visitor information**

✉ Hill St. ☎ 01434-632815 🕒 Closed Oct.–Feb.

### HEXHAM

Three miles along the valley by road or train is Hexham, another old town close to the wall that has seen plenty of bloodshed and strife. In **Hexham Abbey** *(Wentworth Car Park, Hexham, tel 01434-652220, closed Sun. Oct.–Feb.),* perched high above the river, are fascinating historical relics, including the elaborately carved pagan memorial slab of Flavinus, a standard-bearer in a Roman cavalry regiment. Ask a steward to be taken down into the dark, cold crypt; here are inscribed stones from Hadrian's Wall and pagan altar slabs.

🅰 263 B4

### HULL

The old fishing port on the River Humber in southeast Yorkshire is a fascinating place often bypassed by visitors. It's a town with a strong flavor—literally, when the wind blows from the docks! At the tourist office you can pick up walking guide leaflets to Hull's **Fish Trail** and **Ale Trail.** Well worth visiting is **The Deep** aquarium and sea museum *(tel 01482-381000).*

🅰 263 D2 **Visitor information** ✉ 1 Paragon St. ☎ 01482-381000 ∎

From the tumbled Border country of Robert Burns and Sir Walter Scott with its scattering of abbeys and fortified castles, to lively Glasgow and dignified Edinburgh, the Scottish Lowlands are both diverse and beautiful.

# Scottish Lowlands

Introduction & map **288–89**
Scottish Borders **290–91**
Burns country **292–93**
Glasgow & around **294–97**
Edinburgh **298–303**
Two Edinburgh walks **300–303**
A drive from Glasgow to
   St. Andrews **306–307**
More places to visit in the
   Scottish Lowlands **308**
Hotels & restaurants in the
   Scottish Lowlands **379–84**

**Entrance gates to the
Palace of Holyroodhouse**

# Scottish Lowlands

*Out through the Crichtons Willie he ran,*
*And dang them down baith horse and man;*
*O but the Johnstones were wondrous rude,*
*When the Biddes-burn ran three days blood!*
—Sir Walter Scott "The Lads of Wamphray," *The Border Minstrelsy* (1802–1803)

It was not just the Crichtons and the Johnstones who fought, feuded, and raided across the rolling landscape of the Scottish Borders. Armstrongs, Charltons, Maxwells, and dozens of other local families were at it, too.

## BORDER STRIFE

During medieval times these rounded hill ranges, which form the southernmost region of Scotland, were savagely disputed between neighbor and neighbor. Cattle-thieving, raiding, and opportunistic killing were a way of life. As for cross-Border relations, a Scots defeat by the English army of Edward I at the Battle of Dunbar in 1299, and another by the army of Henry VIII at Flodden Field in 1513, bookended more than two centuries of international warfare and bloodshed throughout the region. Incursion and counterthrust went on until the mid-17th century, and a more settled—though not entirely happy—atmosphere only really descended after the 1707 Act of Union between the two countries.

## VARIOUS STRONGHOLDS

Four great Border abbeys were founded within a short distance of each other during the reign of the Scots king, David I (*R.*1124–1153), partly bankrolled by the king as a statement of his would-be authority among these lawless hills: Kelso, Melrose, and Dryburgh along the Tweed Valley southeast of Edinburgh, and Jedburgh 10 miles farther south.

The most powerful local lords, who actually wielded the influence that counted hereabout, built themselves castles and fortified tower-fortresses such as the Douglases' 15th-century Tantallon Castle on the East Lothian coast, and the 16th-century Smailholm Tower near Kelso, where Sir Walter Scott spent boyhood vacations, or less celebrated strongholds such as the 14th-century Neidpath Castle, and 15th-century Barns Tower on the River Tweed, near Peebles.

For all the area's grim history, this is one of Scotland's most beautiful regions. Among the hills are small characterful market towns, each a center for walking, horseback riding, and exploring the great houses of the Borders, from Sir Walter Scott's Abbotsford and the old

## Sir Walter Scott

Sir Walter Scott (1771–1832), though rarely read nowadays, is undoubtedly Scotland's best known and most influential novelist. As a delicate and imaginative boy, he became passionately attached to Jacobite, Highland, and Border history and legend.

Scott's 1802–1803 poetical collection *The Border Minstrelsy* sparked tremendous interest in the bloody Border feuds, and his Waverley series of novels (produced at yearly intervals from 1814 onward—*Waverley, The Antiquary, Rob Roy, The Heart of Midlothian*, and others) romanticized and popularized Scottish legend as history, especially the Jacobite Rebellions of 1715 and 1745. The great 19th-century revival of interest in tartans, kilts, and Scottish music and dance was largely due to Scott's influence.

In spite of his enormous fame and success, Scott's finances were always in poor shape because of unlucky business moves and overspending on his beloved house of Abbotsford. He wrote his great novels under pressure, to stave off debt, and ruined his health with overwork. This son of the Borders, who did so much to restore the pride of Scotland, lies buried in Dryburgh Abbey (see p. 290). ■

0 ____ 30 miles
0 ____ 50 kilometers

1. RENFREWSHIRE
2. E. DUNBARTONSHIRE
3. FALKIRK
4. CLACKMANNANSHIRE
5. PERTH & KINROSS

ANGUS
p. 311

PERTH & KINROSS p. 311

STIRLING p. 311

ARGYLL & BUTE p. 311

Newport-on-Tay
Leuchars
Newburgh
Auchtermuchty
Cupar
St. Andrews
Fife Ness
Crail
Anstruther

FIFE

Loch Lomond and The Trossachs National Park
Dunblane
Castle Campbell
Glenrothes
Kippen
Balmaha
STIRLING
Stirling
Alloa
Cowdenbeath
Kirkcaldy
Drymen
Campsie Fells
Strathblane
Falkirk
Bo'ness
Dunfermline
Aberlady
North Berwick
Tantallon Castle
Dunbar
Helensburgh
Balloch
Dumbarton
EDINBURGH
Haddington
Cockburnspath
St. Abb's Head
Greenock
GLASGOW
Musselburgh
Livingston
Dalkeith
EAST LOTHIAN
Paisley
Coatbridge
MIDLOTHIAN
Eyemouth
Chirnside
West Linton
Lauder
Duns
Largs
Great Cumbrae
NORTH AYRSHIRE
E. RENS.
Motherwell
Penicuik
Gordon
Greenlaw
West Kilbride
Stewarton
East Kilbride
Strathaven
Peebles
Traquair
Galashiels
Kelso
Coldstream
Ardrossan
New Lanark
Lanark
SOUTH LANARKSHIRE
Biggar
Traquair House
Melrose
Floors Castle
Irvine
Kilmarnock
Neidpath Castle
Abbotsford House
Selkirk
Dryburgh
Troon
Tarbolton
Mauchline
Drumelzier
Upper Tweeddale
BORDERS (SCOTTISH)
Prestwick
EAST AYRSHIRE
Abington
Jedburgh
Burns Cottage
Ayr
Alloway
Cumnock
Grey Mare's Tail
Hawick
Culzean Castle
Maybole
Sanquhar
Moffat
Teviothead
Turnberry
Kirkoswald
Dalmellington
Eskdalemuir
Girvan
Carsphairn
Thornhill
Ailsa Craig
SOUTH AYRSHIRE
Langholm
NORTHUMBERLAND p. 263
Ballantrae
Galloway Forest Park
DUMFRIES AND GALLOWAY
Lockerbie
New Galloway
Dumfries
Kirkcolm
Caerlaverock Castle
Annan
Gretna Green
Cairnryan
Newton Stewart
Castle Douglas
CUMBRIA p. 245
Stranraer
Creetown
Dalbeattie
Glenluce
Gatehouse of Fleet
East Stewartry Coast
Portpatrick
Wigtown
Kirkcudbright
Fleet Valley
Whithorn
Wigtown Bay
Drummore
Luce Bay
Solway Firth
Mull of Galloway

Maxwell Stuart seat of Traquair, to the 18th-century Floors and Culzean Castles. And on the west coast, around Alloway, lie the birthplace and lifetime haunts of Scotland's national poet, Robert Burns. ∎

**Painted wooden figures, such as this one now displayed at the Museum of Edinburgh, served as shop signs in 19th-century Scotland. They advertised snuff—a product of Glasgow's tobacco trade.**

London
Area of map detail

**Jedburgh Abbey**

▲ 289 D2

☎ 01835-863925

🕐 Closed Sun. a.m.
Oct.–March

$ $$

**Dryburgh Abbey**

▲ 289 D2

✉ 5 miles southeast of
Melrose on B6404

☎ 01835-822381

$ $/$$

**Kelso Abbey**

▲ 289 D3

🕐 Closed Sun. a.m.

**Fine remains
show the power
and prestige of
Jedburgh Abbey.**

# Scottish Borders

IT IS WORTH PUTTING ASIDE A COUPLE OF DAYS AT LEAST
to explore the country between England and Scotland. Here are great
pine forests and heather moors, giving way as you go north to a
greener and more pastoral landscape along the valley floors and
around the little Scottish Border towns. And don't forget to venture
south and west, to discover the hills and coasts of Galloway.

### JEDBURGH ABBEY

Heading north from Hadrian's Wall
(see pp. 284–85), the first of the
four great 12th-century abbeys is
Jedburgh (1138). The garth (monk's
garden) at the abbey is evocatively
complete behind its cloister wall,
and there are some ornate tombs
of medieval bishops and abbots.

The abbey museum contains
early Christian carvings and a 12th-
century walrus-tusk comb with
both fine and coarse teeth.

### DRYBURGH ABBEY

North of Jedburgh, in the wide val-
ley of the River Tweed, is Dryburgh
Abbey (1150), where you can admire
monastic buildings in excellent
condition, including the vaulted
chapter house and the refectory
with its rose window. The abbey's
north transept holds the tombs of
two famous Scots: Field Marshal
Earl Haig, architect of many of
Britain's World War I triumphs and
disasters, and the poet and novelist
Sir Walter Scott (see p. 288).

### KELSO ABBEY

At Kelso, to the east of Dryburgh,
not much remains of the ruined
Benedictine abbey (1128), but the
north transept's great facade, beau-
tifully carved, is worth the detour.

Just outside the town is **Floors
Castle** *(tel 01573-223333, closed
late Oct.–Easter)*, a huge castle-style
mansion designed by William
Adam in the early 1720s.

### MELROSE ABBEY

The fourth of this cluster of monas-
tic foundations is Melrose Abbey
(1136), charmingly sited below the
Eildon Hills just north of Dryburgh.
Arches set the keynote here; soaring
window arches (Robert the Bruce's
heart is said to be buried below the
great east window), arches to the
eight side chapels off the south aisle
of the nave, arches of the cloisters
and monastic quarters, and the
arched vaulting of the presbytery.

Two miles west on the bank
of the River Tweed is **Abbotsford**

**House** (tel 01896-752043, closed Nov.–mid-March), built by Sir Walter Scott between 1811 and 1822 complete with romantic towers, peaked roofs, and castellations. Inside, you can see the desk at which Scott wrote the Waverley novels, the chair he sat in, the bed he died in, and the collection of memorabilia celebrating his life.

## TRAQUAIR HOUSE
West again is Innerleithen and Traquair House, the oldest continuously inhabited house in Scotland. Traquair looks every inch the dwelling of an ancient Border family, and inside the house the ups and downs of that family through the centuries are touchingly apparent in the assortment of Jacobite mementoes, Tudor relics, and secret holes and corners where priests, villains, and heroes hid in various states of extremity.

## DUMFRIES
Southwest is the county town of Dumfries (Map 289 B2, visitor information, 64 Whitesands, tel 01387-253862), where the poet Robert Burns (see pp. 292–93) died in 1796. Here you can visit **Burns House** (Burns St., tel 01387-255297, closed Sun.–Mon. Oct.–March), where he died, now a museum; the **Burns Mausoleum,** where he lies in St. Michael's Churchyard; the **Burns Statue** by Greyfriars Church; and the **Robert Burns Centre** (Mill Rd., tel 01387-264808, closed Sun.–Mon. Oct.–March), which tells of his life here.

The north coast of the Solway Firth is superb bird-watching territory, especially the **Wildfowl and Wetlands Trust Centre** (Caerlaverock, tel 01387-770200). Nearby is moated **Caerlaverock Castle** (tel 01387-770244). ∎

The facade of Kelso Abbey's north transept is a poignant reminder of the church's beauty before it was sacked in 1545.

**Melrose Abbey**
- 289 C3
- 01896-822562
- Closed Sun. a.m. Oct.–March
- $$

**Traquair House**
- 289 C3
- Innerleithen
- 01896-830323
- Closed Nov.–Easter
- $$

# Burns country

ROBERT BURNS (1759–1796), THE "HEAVENTAUGHT PLOUGH man," is a towering figure in the national psyche of Scotland. Born in a poor clay cottage, sketchily educated, and with a deep-rooted aversion to authority and the high-and-mighty, fond of high jinks in bed and bar, Burns lived fast (by the standards of a small-time rural Scots farmer) and died comparatively young.

**Ayr**

🗺 289 A2

**Visitor information**

✉ 22 Sandgate

☎ 01292-290300

🕐 Closed Sun.
Nov.–Feb.

**Brig o'Doon in Alloway, the setting for one of Burns's most famous poems, *Tam O'Shanter***

He used his quick-witted poetic gift to excoriate the rich and wellborn, satirize politicians, glorify the nation's heroes, and make epic comic verse out of the drunken adventures of his friends.

Burns Night Suppers are celebrated with haggis, turnips, whisky, and a kilted piper on January 25, the poet's birthday, not only in Scotland itself but in every corner of the world where members of the Scottish diaspora are found.

### Early years

Burns was brought up in a plain-living household among rural-dialect speakers, and that earthy atmosphere informs all his best poetry. The family moved about from farm to farm around the Ayr district until Burns's father, William, died in 1784. Two years later Burns produced his first volume, *Poems Chiefly in the Scottish Dialect*, which was an immediate hit with Scots of all classes. A head-turning winter in Edinburgh followed, with the young farmer often camouflaging his awkwardness by playing up his lack of polish and sophistication.

The next few years saw Burns's best work; a comic masterpiece in *Tam O'Shanter*, socialist polemic in *A Man's a Man for a' That*, and a flood of songs still passionately sung by Scots today, including

"Auld Lang Syne," "Green Grow the Rashes-O," "Scots wha hae wi Wallace bled," and dozens more. Toward the end of his life Burns achieved financial stability with a job as an exciseman. But he had burned himself out, and died of rheumatic fever in Dumfries at age 37, his future status as a Scottish icon assured.

## ALLOWAY

The very heart of Burns country is undoubtedly Alloway (*Map 289 A2*), just to the south of Ayr. On the main road through the village is **Burns Cottage and Museum,** the house where Robert Burns was born on January 25, 1759.

Nearby are the heroic **Burns Monument** of 1823, and two places featured in Burns's comic epic poem *Tam O'Shanter*—the roofless shell of **Alloway Old Kirk** (burial place of the poet's father), where drunken Tam saw the devil playing bagpipes for a wild witches' and warlocks' dance, and below it the early medieval **Brig o' Doon,** the bridge across which Tam's mare, Meg, "brought off her master hale/But left behind her ain grey tail."

## AYR & AROUND

In Ayr town stands the 13th-century **Auld Brig,** Burns's "poor narrow footpath of a street/Where two wheel-barrows tremble when they meet." **The Tam O'Shanter** pub on High Street is decorated with quotations from the poet.

Five miles northeast of Ayr is **Tarbolton** village, with the thatched house, now a National Trust for Scotland museum, where Burns learned to dance, became a Freemason, and formed a Bachelors' Club. Burns lived at nearby **Lochlea Farm** (signposted) from 1777 until his father's

death. East at Mauchline are **Burns House Museum** (*Castle St., tel 01290-550045, closed Nov.–Easter & Sun.–Mon. Easter–Oct.*), where in February 1788 the poet rented a room for his mistress Jean Armour; **Gavin Hamilton's House** (*private residence*), next to Mauchline Tower, where he married her; **Poosie Nansie's Tavern,** one of his haunts; and **Mauchline Church** (*closed Sept.–May & Thurs.–Mon. June–Aug.*), since rebuilt, where Burns had to do public penance for fornication, and in whose churchyard four of his children are buried.

Twelve miles south of Ayr, Kirkoswald has a Burns museum in **Souter Johnnie's Cottage** (*NTS, Main Rd., tel 01655-760603, closed Oct.–March*), the thatched house of "souter" (cobbler) John Davidson. Burns featured him in *Tam O'Shanter* as the "ancient, trusty, drouthy cronie" of the poem's hero, Tam, who was also based on a local man, Douglas Graham of nearby Shanter Farm. ■

**Burns Cottage and Museum**

✉ Burns National Heritage Park, Murdoch's Lane, Alloway

☎ 01292-443700

💲 $$

Charles Lucy's (1814–1873) painting shows the parting of a youthful Robert Burns and his love, Mary Campbell; she died before they could be married.

# Glasgow & around

**Glasgow**

🅰 289 B3

**Visitor information**

✉ 11 George Sq.

☎ 0141-204 4400

**Tenement House**

✉ 145 Buccleuch St., Garnethill

☎ 0141-333 0183

🕐 Closed Nov.–Feb.

💲 $$

**The Glasgow School of Art represents Charles Mackintosh's finest example of interior design.**

GLASGOW'S RECENT SHEDDING OF A LONG-ESTABLISHED grim image has been something of a modern miracle. Only 20 years ago, the Cultural Capital of Europe 1990 and U.K. City of Architecture and Design 1999 was notorious for unemployment, violence, and slum housing. But Glasgow owes much to its prosperous industrial heritage, not least the superb art collections donated to the city over the years by the sons of Glasgow, such as Sir William Burrell, who made it big.

In the 18th century Glasgow merchants, enriched by trans-atlantic trade in cotton, rum, and tobacco, established a merchant city of fine dwellings, grand offices, and warehouses. Victorian bankers and insurance brokers built handsome squares and terraces.

During the 19th century, the city's population grew tenfold. Shipyards lined the River Clyde, and iron foundries and heavy engineering works proliferated. Some of the worst city slums in Europe developed, persisting until long after World War II. It has taken some typically bold and aggressive self-promotion, a very Glaswegian attitude, to turn things around.

## GEORGE SQUARE

Grand civic buildings dominate the square, chiefly the enormous 1888 City Chambers. St. Vincent Street leads west, lined with elaborate Victorian pomp-and-circumstance: unicorns above the Old Post Office Building door, Ionic columns propping up the Old Bank of Scotland (now a pub), and the towering pink sandstone Royal Chambers and Liverpool & London & Globe Insurance buildings. Compare these sonorous temples of commerce with the modern lines of the Prudential offices, or the stylish adventurousness of Nos. 151 to 155.

North of Vincent Street, and parallel to it, runs famous Sauchiehall Street, once the rowdiest thoroughfare in the city. North again, at 145 Buccleuch Street, the **Tenement House** (NTS) is a Glasgow apartment block, built in 1892. The upstairs is crammed with the possessions of Miss Agnes Toward, a typist who lived here from 1911 until 1965. When she moved out and into hospital, she left the apartment frozen in time.

## GLASGOW SCHOOL OF ART

On the corner of Scott Street and Renfrew Street is the Glasgow School of Art *(167 Renfrew St., tel 0141-353 4526, closed Sun. Sept.–June)*, reckoned to be the architectural masterpiece of pioneering art nouveau designer Charles Rennie Mackintosh (1868–1928), and designed by him while still in his mid-20s. This is still a working school of art, but guided tours introduce visitors to Mackintosh's revolutionary ideas— maximizing space, simple, dark wood paneling to emphasize light from above, bold bow shapes in ceiling joists, and the use of worked metal and stained glass.

## ST. MUNGO'S CATHEDRAL

The interior of the medieval St. Mungo's Cathedral *(tel 0141-552 6891)* descends from the tall west end by steps to the much lower east end, which is the cathedral's crypt. In the crypt's vaulted chapel lies the tomb of St. Mungo, who founded a chapel here in the sixth century.

Nearby in Castle Street is the **St. Mungo Museum of Religious Life and Art** *(tel 0141-553 2557)*, an intriguing mishmash that includes Hindu gods, Taoist chinaware, animist fetishes, Islamic prayer rugs, Egyptian mummies, and Christian stained-glass images. Across the road stands the tall **Provand's Lordship** *(tel 0141-552 8819)*, Glasgow's oldest house,

**Towering above the statues in George Square is the late Victorian bulk of the City Chambers.**

### TEA IN STYLE

Take a cup of tea in the Willow Rooms at 217 Sauchiehall Street (above Henderson The Jewellers), a 1903 Mackintosh creation with tall ladderbacked chairs, long thin window panes, and characteristic colored glass hearts and rosebuds. ■

built in 1471 for one of the canons of St. Mungo's. Later in its life, the house became—among other things—a common tavern, as an exhibition upstairs points out. Outside is a well-tended garden, planted with medicinal herbs.

## KELVINGROVE PARK

In Glasgow's leafy West End is a cluster of four good galleries and museums centered on beautiful Kelvingrove Park. The **Art Gallery and Museum,** *(currently closed for major renovations)* situated in a vast sandstone pseudo-castle of 1901, contains collections of British and Continental paintings; these feature a gallery of Scottish works (dark and gloomy Glencoes by McCulloch and Hamilton are noteworthy), Constable's "Hampstead Heath," Turner's "Modern Italy," some beautiful Flemish landscapes, and French works from Corot to Monet.

Other sections of the museum include natural history, archaeology, and a magnificent display of arms and armor.

The **Museum of Transport** *(1 Bunhouse Rd., tel 0141-287 2720),* in Kelvin Hall across from the gallery, contains enough locomotives, cars, trams, and ship models to gladden any child's heart.

On the other side of the park are the dour Victorian buildings of Glasgow University; here is the **Hunterian Art Gallery** *(82 Hillhead St., tel 0141-330 5431, closed Sun.),* with paintings, drawings, and prints by such artists as Pissarro and Corot, Rembrandt and Whistler, as well as a reconstruction of principal rooms from the town house of art nouveau design genius Charles Rennie Mackintosh. The **Hunterian Museum** *(University Ave., tel 0141-330 4221, closed Sun.),* whose zoological and archaeological displays are the longest established in Scotland (since 1807), is also here.

Farther north, at 870 Garscube Road, **Queens Cross Church** is the only example of a complete Mackintosh-designed church, a curious-looking sandstone construction, tapered outside and full of images of light and dark within. The church is the headquarters of the **Charles Rennie Mackintosh Society** *(closed Sat.);* ring the bell to be admitted or call 0141-946 6600.

## BURRELL COLLECTION

Three miles to the southwest of the center of Glasgow is Scotland's finest individual collection of art and artifacts. This was the delight and obsession of Glaswegian ship owner Sir William Burrell (1861–1958), who gave it to his native city in 1944 and then continued to add to it.

Housed in an outwardly uninspiring modern building (though a winner of design awards for architecture) within the leafy acres of Pollok Country Park, the collection is superbly laid out for unplanned wandering, by far the best way to appreciate the 8,000 exhibits. Elaborately carved medieval doorways lead from Rodin bronzes to Etruscan mirrors, Persian carpets, a Greek scent bottle, Tang dynasty tomb guardians, suits of armor, and 16th-century German religious carvings in limewood. Hogarth, Rembrandt, Reynolds, Romney, and Sir Henry Raeburn are among the portrait painters; Lucas Cranach the Elder's "Judith" (1530) smiles smugly over her bloody sword at the severed head of Holofernes; Millet, Sisley, Cézanne, Degas, and Manet represent the French Impressionists. This is a truly fascinating and intriguing peep through the keyhole of one rich man's remarkably catholic taste.

## AROUND GLASGOW

South of Glasgow on A73 you'll find the tall cotton mills of **New Lanark** *(visitor center: tel 01555-*

**Kelvingrove Park: Art Gallery and Museum**
✉ Aryle St., Kelvingrove
☎ 0141-287 2699

**Burrell Collection**
✉ 2060 Pollokshaws Rd., Pollok Country Park
☎ 0141-287 2550

661345), a workplace that in the 19th century became a model of good practice, humane treatment, and education. Explore this UNESCO World Heritage site, take the New Millennium Experience ride, and walk the path to the spectacular Falls of Clyde.

North of the city are the **Campsie Fells** *(Map 289 B3),* the nearest piece of upland walking country for Glaswegians. The Campsies rise to 1,800 feet, a hummock of moorland, farmland, and rolling hills with deeply scored sides.

### Loch Lomond

By far the best known countryside recreation area north of Glasgow is **Loch Lomond** *(Map 289 A4),* still—despite the fame of its "bonny, bonny banks"—a place enjoyable for its peaceful beauty at all times of the year except crowded summer weekends. In 2002 the whole area of Loch Lomond and the neighboring Trossach Hills was designated **Loch Lomand and The Trossachs National Park,** the first National Park in Scotland.

The A82, narrow and winding, shadows the west bank of the loch and gives the best views; the even narrower and far less frequented east bank road is too often among the trees for consistently good views, but takes you north for 6 miles from Balmaha to the Rowardennan Hotel. Here it ends.

You can continue all the way up the loch on the West Highland Way footpath. Or, if you're feeling lazy, take a boat trip among Loch Lomond's islands from Balloch at the south end, but get there early to avoid the lines. ■

**Glasgow's nearest beauty spot, Loch Lomond, glows in autumn colors. Beyond rises the rugged bulk of Ben Lomond.**

# Edinburgh

SOLID, DIGNIFIED, COMPLACENT: TRADITIONAL EDINBURGH as it appears through its monumental architecture and superb location on and among rugged volcanic crags. Lively, outgoing, unstuffy: modern Edinburgh, as its citizens think of it. In spite of Glasgow's pretensions, Edinburgh is unquestionably the capital city of the Scots.

This is an outstanding city. The dark courts and cobbled streets of the medieval Old Town contrast with the grand Georgian squares, circuses, and crescents of the New Town. These two distinct areas are explored in the walks that follow (see pp. 300–303), starting with **Edinburgh Castle,** with which the city's history is so closely bound.

Here are castle walls that give views over nearly a hundred miles of Lowland Scotland; dank cells and dungeons for both military and civilian prisoners; the great siege cannon Mons Meg, forged in 1457; military museums; and the shrine of the **Scottish National War Memorial.** The royal palace of the Scottish monarchs contains a line-up of its incumbents' portraits, among which the dour, dark Stewarts stand out in sulky pride.

Also here are displayed the ancient regalia (Ceremonial Honours of Scotland)—jeweled sword, scepter, and crown—which were discovered in 1818 as the result of a search initiated by Sir Walter Scott, sealed in the Crown Room where they had lain forgotten for over a century. Alongside lies the Stone of Destiny (sometimes called the Stone of Scone, after Scone Palace where it was kept from A.D. 838 onward), on which all Scots kings were crowned from the sixth century until the English king, Edward I, took it south to Westminster Abbey in 1296. The stone was ceremonially returned to Scotland in November 1996. ■

**Edinburgh**

🅰 289 C3

**Visitor information**

✉ 3 Princes St.

☎ 0131-473 3800

**Edinburgh Castle**

✉ Castle Hill

☎ 0131-225 9846

$ $$$

## Edinburgh festivals

The **Edinburgh International Festival** (*tel 0131-473 2000*), the world's biggest arts festival,

takes over the city during the last two weeks in August and the first week in September; it comprises theater, classical music, opera, and dance. An epic **Military Tattoo** (*tel 0870-555 1188*) takes place at night in front of the floodlit castle for three weeks in August. Complementing the official festival is the **Edinburgh Fringe Festival** (*tel 0131-226 0026*), where artists from jugglers to comedians perform. Simultaneous events are the **International Film Festival;** the **International Jazz and Blues Festival;** and the **International Book Festival.** ■

**Edinburgh Military Tattoo at the castle (right): The city is at its most exhilarating during the renowned International Festival in late summer.**

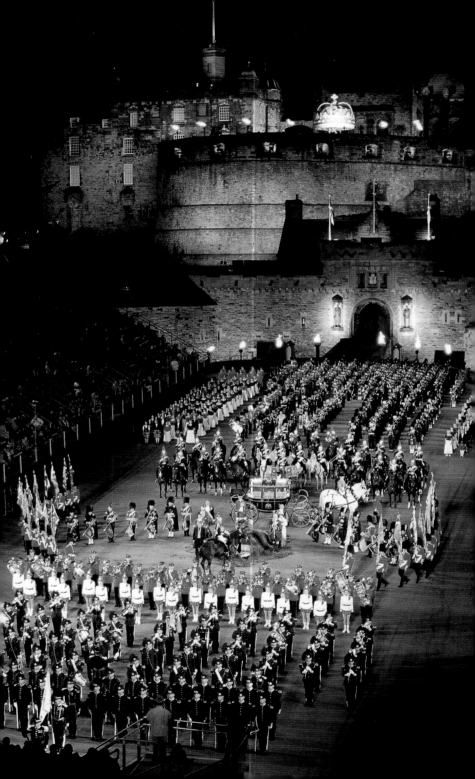

# Two Edinburgh walks

Two very distinct Edinburghs stand side by side—Old Town and New Town. Allow at least a day to walk slowly about each. The Edinburgh and Scotland Information Centre (see visitor information p. 298) provides all kinds of background and arranges walking tours of the city with themes ranging from architecture to ghosts and crime.

## OLD TOWN WALK

This is essentially a medieval walk, for Edinburgh is remarkable for the way in which so many of its oldest and most interesting buildings have survived and are still in use. "Auld Reekie," the stinking and smoky old city crammed upon a ridge, lives on (though it is now more salubrious) along the flanks of the Royal Mile, the sloping thoroughfare that connects the grim military castle on its high crag and the Royal Palace of Holyroodhouse at the foot of the hill. **Edinburgh Castle** (see p. 298) commands the city from its height, and is the place to start your walk.

From the esplanade in front of the castle, the **Royal Mile** descends as Castlehill, Lawnmarket, High Street, and then Canongate between the tall houses of the **Old Town.** The Royal Mile is packed with bagpipe-makers, whisky-sellers, kiltmakers, Highland crafts shops and weavers, and also with excellent museums and other attractions.

Chief among these, in order of encounter walking down from the castle, are the self-explanatory **Scotch Whisky Heritage Centre ❶** (354 Castlehill, tel 0131-220 0441); **Gladstone's Land ❷** (NTS, 477b Lawnmarket, tel 0131-226 5856, closed Nov.–March), a restored six-story land (tenement house) built for an Edinburgh merchant in 1620 and featuring colorful painted ceilings and astonishingly cramped accommodations; the **Writers' Museum** dedicated to Scott, Stevenson, and Burns in **Lady Stair's House ❸** (Lady Stair's Close, Lawnmarket, tel 0131-529 4901, closed Sun.), built in 1622, turreted and elaborately carved; **St. Giles Cathedral,** below the Lawnmarket, the High Kirk of Edinburgh where John Knox was minister (1559–1572); and **John Knox's House ❹** (43–45 High St., tel 0131-556 9579, closed Sun.), elbowing into High Street, a beautifully carved and painted 16th-century town house where the fiery preacher and spearhead

Granite cobblestones depicting the Heart of Midlothian mark the former site of the city jail on High Street.

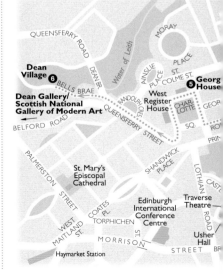

of the Scottish Reformation lived toward the end of his life.

Below this are **The People's Story Museum** (tel 0131-529 4057, closed Sun.), housed in Edinburgh's old Tolbooth (city jail) on the left of Canongate, which explores the work, fights, fun, and suffering of the city's citizens through the centuries; and the **Museum of Edinburgh** 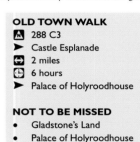 (142 Canongate, tel 0131-529 4143, closed Sun.) on the right, three 16th-century houses grouped together to contain the city museum, full of Edinburgh's history—a contemporary copy of the original 1638 National Covenant is here.

### Taverns & kirks

Along the route, in between these museums, are numerous wynds (narrow alleys) and closes (enclosed courts), hemmed in by the tall lands that were built ever higher during the cramped Middle Ages. The 17th-century **Milne's Court,** on the left above Gladstone's Land, gives a good idea of a close.

There are various characterful pubs to enjoy along this walking route. In **Deacon Brodie's Tavern** on the Lawnmarket, you get not only a cozy bar, but also the story, in mural paintings, of William Brodie. This respectable Edinburgh councillor by day and burglar by night designed the gallows he was

himself hanged on in 1788. Robert Louis Stevenson is believed to have based his novel *The Strange Case of Dr. Jekyll and Mr. Hyde* (1886) on the double life of Deacon Brodie.

Across from Deacon Brodie's Tavern, George IV Bridge leads off to the right. A five-minute walk along here leads to **Greyfriars Kirk,** in whose graveyard dissenting Presbyterians signed the National Covenant in 1638—some in their own blood. Under pink granite headstones lie "Auld Jock" Gray (1858) and his faithful terrier Bobby (1872). The dog mourned by his master's grave for 14 years and became an international celebrity. A memorial drinking fountain, topped with a statue of Greyfriars Bobby, stands outside the churchyard.

On Chambers Street, just opposite the Greyfriars Bobby memorial, two great

### OLD TOWN WALK

- ⊠ 288 C3
- ► Castle Esplanade
- ⬌ 2 miles
- ⏱ 6 hours
- ► Palace of Holyroodhouse

### NOT TO BE MISSED

- Gladstone's Land
- Palace of Holyroodhouse

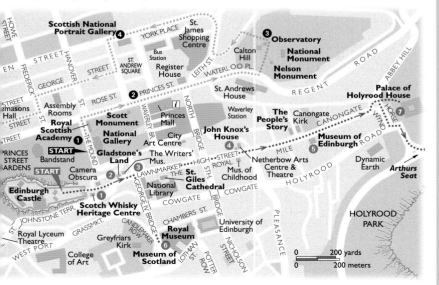

museums stand side by side. The history of Scotland unrolls in the fortress-like modern **Museum of Scotland** ⑥ *(tel 0131-247 4422)*; while next door in the iron and glass halls of the **Royal Museum** *(tel 0131-247 4217)* is a fine collection representing the art, science, and industry of the world.

### A royal palace

At the bottom of Canongate, beyond gates of intricate ironwork and a splendid overblown fountain, is the handsome **Palace of Holyroodhouse** ⑦ *(tel 0131-556 5100, closed when the Queen is in residence)*, the British monarch's official residence when staying in Edinburgh. Holyrood Abbey was founded here in 1128 by David I of Scotland; from about 1500 on, James IV and James V built a royal palace around the abbot's guest quarters. Burned in the mid-16th century, it was rebuilt more than once. In the 1670s, the old northwest tower was incorporated into the present palace.

Tours begin just inside the front door, and you are moved fairly briskly up the Grand Stair, through the Household Dining Room with its portrait of Bonnie Prince Charlie, and then through the State Apartments—drawing room and bedrooms with fabulous, elaborate 17th-century ceilings plastered with a mixture of horsehair, plaster, and egg white. Jacob de Wet the Younger was extensively employed, to great effect with his painted ceilings ("Hercules gaining entry to Heaven" in the King's Bedroom is superb), and to grotesque purpose in the Great Picture Gallery where, between 1684 and 1686, he turned out, at great speed, 89 portraits depicting a Stuart lineage retreating 2,000 years into the mists of time. This was a barely sustained effort of guesswork in which the excruciating difficulty of making each picture different from all the others, while still containing recognizable Stuart traits, is all too ludicrously clear.

A darker note is struck when you reach the Historical Apartments and climb the twisting staircase from Lord Darnley's rooms to those of his wife, Mary, Queen of Scots—as the jealous Darnley and his henchmen did on March 9, 1566. They dragged Mary's Italian secretary and close adviser David Rizzio from the little cabinet room off the Queen's bedroom, where he and Mary were at supper together, and stabbed him 56 times. Rizzio bled to death under the window in Mary's bedroom; at one time, visitors were shown fake bloodstains on the floorboards.

South of Holyroodhouse hangs the long gray curtain of **Salisbury Crags,** the buttress of Edinburgh's own mini mountain of **Arthur's Seat** (822 feet). An enjoyable walk leads counterclockwise along Queen's Drive into **Holyrood Park's** green acres.

Set against the breathtaking backdrop of Salisbury Crags and opposite the Palace of Holyroodhouse is Scotland's newest and most exciting attraction, **Dynamic Earth** *(tel 0131-550 7800, closed Mon.–Tues. Nov.–March)*, which tells the story of the planet using state-of-the-art interactives and dramatic effects.

### NEW TOWN WALK

Edinburgh's New Town was planned in 1767, on a spine of three great parallel streets to the north of the medieval city, in order to relieve the congestion and insanitary conditions of Auld Reekie. It is one of the most complete—certainly the most spacious and dignified—Georgian townscapes in Britain.

The walk begins across from **The Mound** adjoining **Princes Street,** Edinburgh's famous chief thoroughfare, bordered on the south by a steep drop to gardens. Here stands the imposing **National Gallery of Scotland** ① *(off Princes St., tel 0131-624 6200)*, with works from the 15th to the 19th centuries, informatively labeled, which include most of the major European artists from

## Around Edinburgh

Other suggestions close to Edinburgh are: **Blackford Hill** in the southern suburbs, 2½ miles from Princes Street, with a walk south up to the **Royal Observatory** *(tel 0131-668 8405)*; **Leith Docks** north of the city center, recently revived as a good restaurant area; **Aberlady Bay,** on the railroad 12 miles east, superb for bird-watching and coastal walks; the **Pentland Hills** just south of the city, threaded by footpaths; and the magnificent 13th-century St. Colm's Abbey on the gull-haunted **Inchcolm Island** in the Firth of Forth *(Boat from South Queensferry, tel 0131-331 4857, not sailing mid-Oct.–March)*. ∎

**Visiting the National Gallery of Scotland, repository of fine works spanning four centuries**

Raphael, Titian, and Veronese through Rubens, Rembrandt, and Van Dyke to Turner, Gainsborough, and Constable. Next door is the heavily pillared frontage of the **Royal Scottish Academy** (built 1823–1836).

Turn east to pass the dramatic Gothic spire of the **Scott Monument** ❷ (1840–1844), which commemorates Scotland's great writer and publicist (see p. 288), then **Waverley Station** under the huge clock tower of the Balmoral Hotel. At the top of the street, climb the steps up **Calton Hill** ❸ to enjoy its clutch of bizarre neoclassic monuments: the fluted columns of the never finished **National Monument** (begun in 1822, it is also known as "Edinburgh's Disgrace"); the **City Observatory;** obscure philosophy don **Dugald Stewart's Monument** of 1837; the Corinthian temple of a memorial to Burns (1830); and the extended-spyglass-on-end that is the **Nelson Monument** (1807–1815). Climb this last for another splendid city, sea, and mountain prospect.

### City of contrasts

A footpath northward around the hill leads via Royal Terrace onto **York Place.** Here is celebrated Georgian painter Sir Henry Raeburn's house, No. 32, with a palette-shaped plaque, and the excellent **Scottish National Portrait Gallery** ❹ (*1 Queen St., tel 0131-624 6200*) is farther along.

George Street runs parallel with Queen Street, wide and dignified; Rose Street, between George and Princes Streets, is packed with Victorian pubs—try the Abbotsford at No. 3 or the Rose Street Brewery.

**Charlotte Square,** at the end of George Street, is the New Town's finest square, designed in 1791 by architect Robert Adam. No. 7, the **Georgian House,** ❺ (*NTS, tel 0131-225 2160, closed Jan.–Feb.*) accurately reproduces a furnished town house.

A ten-minute walk westward via Queensferry Street brings you steeply down Bell's Brae into **Dean Village** ❻, a hidden area of restored cottages, mills, and warehouses crammed into the secluded wooded valley of the Water of Leith in the heart of the city—one of Edinburgh's best-kept secrets. Just above Dean Village the **Dean Gallery** and the **Scottish National Gallery of Modern Art** (*tel 0131-624 6200*) face each other across Belford Road. ∎

---

**NEW TOWN WALK**

🗺 288 C3
➤ The Mound, Princes Street
⟷ 2½ miles
🕓 6 hours
▶ Dean Village

**NOT TO BE MISSED**
- National Gallery of Scotland
- Georgian House
- Dean Village

# The game of golf

The worldwide fame of St. Andrews rests squarely on its status as the Home of Golf. It was here, on the flat grass that covers the St. Andrews sand dunes, that medieval Scots began banging a ball about with a stick. Three Scots kings in succession—James II in 1457, James III in 1471, and James IV in 1491—banned the "unprofitable sporte of golfe," which was distracting young men from going to church and from practicing their archery. James IV must have thought better of his decree—or maybe he was himself bitten by the bug—because in 1502 he legitimized the game. By 1567, the year that Mary, Queen of Scots, played golf at St. Andrews, the sport had become the ruling passion of Scots from all walks of life.

first time, and since then it has regularly been held at St. Andrews.

## Great golfers

Most of the greatest names in the history of golf have had strong connections with St. Andrews, and revolutionary developments in the equipment, rules, and conduct of the game have emanated down the years from this small Fife seaside town.

In 1845 the first gutta-percha ball was made here, replacing the old-style ball with its core of feathers. Allan Robertson (1815–1859), recognized as the world's first professional golfer, won a championship match here with a feathery ball in 1842, and another with a gutta-percha ball in 1858. Robertson was so

**Mary, Queen of Scots, trying her hand at the newly fashionable game at St. Andrews**

## Royal approval

In 1754 a group of "22 noblemen and gentlemen of Fife" established the Society of St. Andrews Golfers in order to run an annual competition. The seal of royal approval was granted in 1834 when William IV accepted the patronage of the Society, which renamed itself the Royal and Ancient Golf Club (R&A). Twenty years later the R&A built itself a handsome stone clubhouse, which still stands in its superb position overlooking the Old Course and the wide West Sands. In 1873 the British Open Championship took place here for the

good at the game that after his feather-ball triumph he was banned from other contests by his brother golfers, "it being their impression that they would have no chance in any competition in which Allan took part."

Another great character was Old Tom Morris (1821–1908), who became the R&A's first professional golfer in 1865. He won the Open in 1861, 1862, 1864, and 1867, and laid out the New Course, which was opened in 1895.

Tom's son, Young Tom Morris (1851–1875), was a golfer as redoubtable as his father, winning the Open in 1868, 1869, 1870, and 1872. Young and Old Tom, along with Allan Robertson and a dozen more golfing greats, lie in the precincts of St. Andrews Cathedral burial ground; a leaflet *(available from St. Andrews visitor center, 70 Market St., tel 01334-472021)* shows the location of their graves.

### A round or two

Each year tens of thousands of golfers come to St. Andrews with the intention of playing a ceremonial round on the Old Course. The wise ones make reservations months ahead, turn up well in advance of their tee time, and allow four or five hours to complete the 6,566-yard course (par 72). Bunkers with names such as Pulpit, Principal's Nose, Cat's Trap, Lion's Mouth, and Hell lie in wait for the unwary.

Deacon Sime's Bunker contains the ashes of the eponymous cleric; he declared that since he'd spent half his life in the bunker, he should spend eternity there, too. Other courses in St. Andrews are New (par 71), Jubilee (par 72), Bronze (par 69), Eden (par 70), Strathtyrum (par 69), and the 9-hole Balgrove (par 30). ∎

**Keen players enjoy a round of golf on the course at St. Andrews.**

A DRIVE FROM GLASGOW TO ST. ANDREWS

# A drive from Glasgow to St. Andrews

This pleasant drive takes you north from central Glasgow, passing the rolling Camspie Fells, to Stirling with its magnificent castle. From here, you follow a rural route south of the Ochil Hills before reaching St. Andrews, the home of golf.

From junction 17 of the M8 motorway in Glasgow (see pp. 294–97), follow the A82 Dumbarton road, then turn right onto the A81, heading due north out of the city. Ten miles north of Strathblane, turn right onto the A811 to descend the wide Forth Valley to Stirling.

The town of **Stirling** ❶ *(visitor information, tel 08707-200620)* rises up the spine of a long volcanic crag, culminating in the famous castle perched dramatically at the 250-foot summit.

Among the attractions along the cobbled streets are the 15th-century **Church of the Holy Rude** (Rood), where James VI (James I of England, see p. 30), the 13-month-old son of Mary, Queen of Scots, was crowned in 1567 as successor to his deposed mother; a 1632 town house, residence for the Dukes of Argyll,

known as **Argyll's Lodging** *(tel 01786-450000);* and the ornate 16th-century facade of **Mar's Wark,** a grand residence planned but never completed by the 1st Earl of Mar, hereditary Keeper of Stirling Castle and Regent of Scotland during James VI's infancy.

Pride of the town, though, is **Stirling Castle** ❷ *(tel 01786-450000),* used by James IV (*R.*1488–1513), James V (*R.*1513–1542), Mary, Queen of Scots (*R.*1542–1567), and James VI (*R.*1567–1625) as their Royal Court.

Inside are spacious State Rooms, most of them empty, though one contains the Stirling Heads—56 beautifully carved oak medallions commissioned by James V when he converted the grim fortress into a comfortable dwelling.

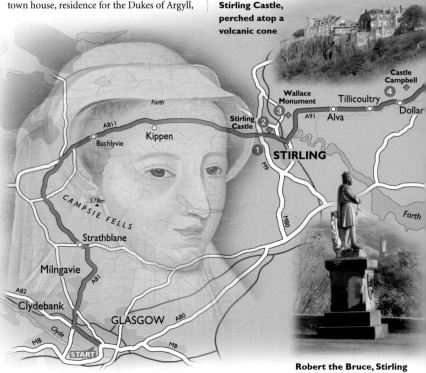

**Stirling Castle, perched atop a volcanic cone**

**Robert the Bruce, Stirling**

The Chapel Royal contains a 17th-century frieze and a trompe-l'œil west window; and the sumptuous Great Hall echoes all the kingly pride of James IV, its creator.

In the higher part of the castle are the King's Old Buildings, housing the excellent **Regimental Museum** of the Argyll and Sutherland Highlanders, with ceremonial dress, mementoes from the regiment's service around the world, and remarkable photographs of the Crimean War.

Two miles north of the town stands the **National Wallace Monument** ③ *(Abbey Craig, tel 01786-472140)*, erected to the Scots hero executed by the English in 1305. There are superb views from the top.

### ON TO ST. ANDREWS

From Stirling, the A91 leads east under the green-and-brown rampart of the Ochil Hills.

At Dollar, turn left (signposted) to ascend (a 2-mile walk there-and-back) the steep, narrow, and beautiful **Dollar Glen.** High on

**Castle Campbell in Dollar Glen**

DUNDEE

Firth of Tay

A92

Guardbridge

Dairsie

**St. Andrews** ⑤

**Cupar**

A91

Auchtermuchty

Eden

Gateside

Lomond Hills

OCHIL HILLS

M90

Milnathort

A91

Loch Leven

Kinross

Glenrothes

Devon

| 0 | 4 miles |
| 0 | 8 kilometers |

A92

M90

**St. Andrews Cathedral**

the hillside at the top is the stark, atmospheric ruin of **Castle Campbell** ④ *(tel 01259-742408, closed Thurs.–Fri. Oct.–Dec. & Fri. Jan.–March).*

The A91 continues into the flatter farming country of Fife, eventually reaching **St. Andrews** ⑤ *(visitor information, tel 01334-472021)*, a charming little town set above broad sands and rocky bays, and a mecca for golf enthusiasts (see p. 304). Well worth visiting are the cathedral ruins on their headland; the castle with its 16th-century mine tunnels; and the two university college quadrangles of St. Salvator (endowed in 1450), off the Scores, and St. Mary's (endowed in 1537), on South Street. ■

---

🗺 289 B3
➤ Glasgow
🔄 95 miles
🕐 3 hours
➤ St. Andrews

### NOT TO BE MISSED
- Mar's Wark
- Stirling Castle
- Castle Campbell
- St. Andrews castle

**The charming East Neuk village of Crail, subject of many an amateur painter's canvas**

## More places to visit in the Scottish Lowlands

### EAST NEUK OF FIFE

On the north shore of the Forth, along the A917 east of Kirkcaldy, the East Neuk (eastern "corner") of Fife has a string of attractive small fishing harbors, notably **Anstruther** *(Map 289 C4)*, with its excellent **Scottish Fisheries Museum,** and tiny, picturesque **Crail,** 4 miles east of Anstruther.

**Scottish Fisheries Museum** ✉ St. Ayles, Harbour Head, Anstruther ☎ 01333-310628

### FIRTH OF FORTH

From Edinburgh take the train or follow the A198 along the coast to **North Berwick** *(Map 289 C3, visitor information, Quality St., tel 0845-225 5121, closed Sun. Oct.–Feb)*, where you can climb the 613-foot cone of **Berwick Law** to the whale's jaw-bone-arch at the top. Boats from the harbor visit the **Bass Rock**, in the Firth of Forth, a lump of volcanic rock smothered with 50,000 gannets. **Tantallon Castle,** a 600-

year-old Douglas fortress spectacularly sited on the cliffs, stands 3 miles east.

**Tantallon Castle** 🏔 289 D3 ☎ 01620-892727 🕐 Closed Thur.–Fri. Oct.–Dec., Fri. Jan.–March

### SOUTH OF EDINBURGH

In the rolling Border country south of Edinburgh, the beautiful **Tweed Walk** footpath takes you from the snug, gray stone town of **Peebles** *(Map 289 C3, visitor information, High St., tel 0870-608 0404, call for opening hours)* past the romantic ruin of 13th-century **Neidpath Castle** and on beside the wide River Tweed. To the southwest, 5 miles north of Moffat, the A701 runs along the lip of the **Devil's Beef Tub,** a cavernous hollow. In *Redgauntlet,* Sir Walter Scott had a character roll into the Beef Tub to escape from soldiers—as a real-life Jacobite did in 1746.

**Neidpath Castle** 🏔 289 C3 ☎ 01721-720333 🕐 Closed Sept.–mid-June ∎

From the lochs, glens, and great mountain ranges to the wild, indented coastline and far-flung magical islands, the Scottish Highlands and Islands is a region of breathtaking landscapes and one that is steeped in history, too.

# Highlands & Islands

Introduction & map **310–11**
Southwestern Highlands **312–13**
Central Scotland **314–15**
A drive through Royal Deeside **316–17**
Grampians & Cairngorms **318–19**
Inverness & the north **322–24**
**Scottish Islands 325–34**
Isle of Skye **326–327**
Inner Hebrides **330**
Outer Hebrides **331**
Orkney **332**
Shetland **333**
More islands to visit **334**
Hotels & restaurants in the Highlands & Islands **384–87**

St. John's Cross, Iona Abbey

# Highlands & Islands

ALTHOUGH NO ONE KNOWS FOR SURE EXACTLY WHERE THE HIGHLANDS of Scotland start, everyone knows when they have reached them. The landscape lifts, loses its lowland roll, and gains a Highland roughness and cragginess. The air smells sharper, water tastes sweeter, and evenings and mornings are mistier and chillier. Rural houses become small and white; accents soften and begin to dance. Geologically, perhaps, the Highlands lie north and west of the Highland Boundary Fault; geographically, maybe, beyond that great southwest-to-northeast slash of the geological sword known as the Great Glen. But the Highlands, like Scotland itself, are partly a state of mind.

One could certainly debate the Highland status of southwestern Argyll, Perthshire, and Angus; likewise the flat farmlands along the Aberdeenshire coast. But no one has any doubts about the Grampian Mountains in all their grandeur, the huge empty glens and hills of Wester Ross, the high ranges of the far northwest, and the great peat bog of the Flow Country up in the northeast corner of Scotland. As for the islands, each is a world apart, where time and perceptions tend to run differently from the way they do on the mainland.

## ARGYLL & INVERNESS

The power of Atlantic wind and waves has clawed deep rips in the southwestern flank of the Highlands. Narrow, winding sea inlets such as Loch Fyne, Loch Linnhe, and Loch Sunart penetrate far into the Argyll and Inverness coasts. Lonely peninsulas have been left isolated between the sea lochs of Kintyre, Morvern, Ardnamurchan, Moidart, Morar, and Knoydart. These are remote, hilly places where roads are few and narrow, walking and boating are superb, and the coastal bays and hidden beaches warmed by the Gulf Stream seem to stretch forever. They are also the cradle of Scottish culture, for it was here that Irish Celts settled during the first few centuries A.D. In early medieval times the Macdonalds were hugely powerful in the region, but they lost power to their bitter rivals, the Campbells.

## NORTH & SOUTH OF THE GRAMPIANS

It was a Campbell who led the massacre of Macdonalds in 1692 at Glencoe, the savage glen bordering wild Rannoch Moor and the approaches to Angus and Perthshire.

Below these are the Trossachs, the Highlands in Miniature, as this range of hills and lakes is often called: Rob Roy country, with a romantic skein to it that Sir Walter Scott wove into several of his books.

Farther northeast the long and beautiful glens of Angus—Glen Esk, Glen Clova, Glen Doll, and Glen Isla—push up into the southern flanks of the Grampians, topped by the many high peaks of the central Cairngorm range at over 4,000 feet. This is classic skiing and mountain sporting country.

Running in from the "granite city" of Aberdeen on the east coast is the handsome valley of the River Dee, Royal Deeside, so beloved of the Royal Family.

North again, bounding the southern shores of the Moray Firth, is a region often overlooked by visitors, a gentle farming countryside edged by a dramatically rough coastline dotted with sturdy, granite-built fishing villages.

## NORTHERN HIGHLANDS

To the north and west of Inverness and the Great Glen (where Loch Ness and the monster lie) are the Highlands proper, where the clan system survived and flourished for a thousand years.

Increasing demands by monarchs, at first Scots and then English, for loyalty that overrode clan allegiance culminated at the Battle of Culloden, just east of Inverness, in 1746, the last warlike gathering of the clans under Bonnie Prince Charlie. The clans were smashed, their way of life deliberately and

0 ___ 30 miles
0 ___ 50 kilometers

Westray
Rousay  Eday  Sanday
Mainland  Skara Brae  Stronsay
Maes Howe
Ring of Brodgar  Kirkwall
Stromness
ORKNEY
Hoy  Burwick

Herma Ness
Haroldswick  Unst
Gutcher  Fetlar
Sullom  Yell  Out
Voe  Muckle  Toft  Skerries
Papa  Roe  Whalsay
Stour
SHETLAND
Mainland  Lerwick
Scalloway  Isle of
West  Noss
Burra  Bressay
Jarlshof  Mousa
Broch
Sumburgh
Head

Pentland Firth
Cape Wrath  Duncansby Head
Durness  Thurso  John
Kinlochbervie  Tongue  Melvich  O'Groats
Scourie  927m  Wick
Unapool  Ben Hope  Latheron
Lochinver  998m  Helmsdale
Inchnadamph  Ben More  Lairg  Brora
Assynt  Dornoch
Laide  Ullapool  Tain
Inverewe  Invergordon  Lossiemouth  Cullen
Garden  Dingwall  Nairn  Elgin  MORAY  Banff  Fraserburgh
The  Shieldaig  Kinlochewe  Culloden  Dufftown  Huntly  Macduff
Quiraing  Glen Carron  Inverness  Battlefield  Peterhead
Dunvegan  Portree  Kyle of Lochalsh  Strathspey  ABERDEENSHIRE
Castle  Eilean Donan Castle  Steam Railway
Shiel Bridge  Aviemore  CAIRNGORMS  Aberdeen
Armadale  HIGHLAND  Kingussie  NAT.  Balmoral
Castle  Glen  Invergarry  PARK  Castle  Drum Castle
Kinloch  Ardvasar  Garry  Lochy  Ballater  Crathes Castle
Glenfinnan  Fort William  Braemar
Lochailort  Linn of Dee
Inverbervie
Ben Nevis  Blair Castle  Killiecrankie  ANGUS
Strontian  Pitlochry  Brechin
Glencoe  Aberfeldy  Forfar
Lochaline  PERTH &  Dundee
Duart Castle  KINROSS
Oban  Balquhidder  Scone  Arbroath
Fingal's Cave  Inveraray  Palace  Perth
Fionnphort  Castle  The Trossachs  M90
Crinan  Callander
Lochgilphead  Aberfoyle  SCOTTISH LOWLANDS
Port Askaig  BUTE  LOCH LOMOND
Dunoon  AND THE  p. 289
Craighouse  TROSSACHS
Port Ellen  Kildalton  Rothesay  NAT. PARK
Cross  Claonaig
Machrie
Campbeltown
Firth of Clyde

Area of map detail
London

ruthlessly demolished by force and by statute, and the vast majority of their people cleared from the land during the late 18th and the whole of the 19th century by incoming land-lords—or by the clan chiefs themselves—to make way for lucrative sheep farming. Hence the emptiness of the superbly beautiful and awe-inspiring mountains and glens of Wester

Ross and Sutherland, the wild peatlands of Caithness, and many of the Hebridean islands.

North Sea oil has brought an economic boom to Shetland in recent years; most of the other islands, all of which are enormously hospitable and magical places, still struggle against depopulation. Beauty and sadness, hand in hand. ■

# Southwestern Highlands

FROM TARBET ON LOCH LOMOND, THE A83 LEADS WEST-ward to Inveraray, a planned town built in its superb position (reflected in Loch Fyne) in 1745 by the Duke of Argyll. He built Inveraray Castle at the same time. Victorian additions have rendered it a Gothic dream of candlesnuffer roofs and turrets.

**Inveraray**
🗺 311 B2
**Visitor information**
✉ Front St.
☎ 0870-720 0616

**Inveraray Castle**
☎ 01499-302203
✉ Inveraray
🕐 Closed Nov.–March, Fri. April–May & Oct.
💲 $$

From here you can continue south on the A83 for nearly 100 miles down the Kintyre Peninsula to the **Mull of Kintyre** (fine views of the Antrim Mountains in Northern Ireland), or turn north on the A819 and the A85 to **Oban** (33 miles), then on north via the A828 and the A82 to **Invergarry** (75 miles), where the A87 runs west to **Kyle of Lochalsh** (50 miles). West of these long roads lie the lonely, under-populated peninsulas that make up the beautiful southwestern coast of the Highlands. To reach them you have to work your way west from Fort William on the A830 Mallaig road, along Loch Eil to Glenfinnan.

## GLENFINNAN

Here a Highlander stands in monu-mental statue form against the mountains of Lochaber, commem-orating the raising of Bonnie Prince Charlie's standard on this spot on August 19, 1745. Prince Charles Edward Stuart (1720–1788)—the Young Pretender, grandson of the exiled James VII of Scotland (II of England)—had been in Scotland for a month after landing from France, in the hope of raising enough Highland support to march on London, overthrow George II, and have his father James Stuart—the Old Pretender—crowned king. Donald Cameron of Lochiel threw in his lot (and 700 men) with the prince, and others then began to join. It was all the encouragement Charles needed to proclaim his father King James VIII and to start the doomed Jacobite uprising that would end so disastrously at Culloden, eight months later.

From Lochailort, 10 miles west of Glenfinnan, the A861 snakes south on a 70-mile circuit of **Moidart, Sunart,** and **Ardgour.** At Salen (22 miles), the B8007 strikes off west into the heart of **Ardnamurchan,** a long finger of

hills, cliffs, and sandy coves.

Just beyond Strontian (33 miles), the A884 threads through bleak and beautiful **Morvern**. But these southerly peninsulas, wild as they are, are tame compared with the northern face of **Morar** and the whole of **Knoydart**.

**Inverie** on Loch Nevis in South Knoydart can be reached by boat from Mallaig; Barrisdale on the northern side, on Loch Hourn, from Arnisdale, itself a tiny settlement on the nearly-as-remote peninsula of Glenelg.

**Kyle of Lochalsh** *(visitor information, car park, tel 01599-534276, closed Nov.–March)* at the end of the A87, was the ferry port for the Isle of Skye until the expensive and not altogether popular toll bridge was opened in 1995. Here the spectacular Kyle Railway line from Inverness (see p. 323) comes to an end.

## EILEAN DONAN CASTLE
The drive back toward Glasgow along the A87 (8 miles) brings you to Eilean Donan Castle *(Dornie, tel 01599-555202, closed Nov.–March)*, picturesquely sited, perched on its rock where lochs Duich, Aish, and Long all meet. Built in 1230 as a defense against Viking raids, it was blown up by a Hanoverian frigate in 1719 after Jacobite Spaniards had occupied it in support of the Old Pretender's last and futile uprising. Later restored, it has become a prime attraction.

## FORT WILLIAM
The A87 runs east through spectacular mountain scenery to Invergarry. From here the A82 leads in 25 miles to Fort William *(visitor information, Cameron Sq., tel 0845-225 5121)*, an unprepossessing town from which Glen Nevis curves southeast under the bulky, shapeless mass of **Ben Nevis,** at 4,406 feet the highest mountain in Britain. Rangers at **Glen Nevis Visitor Centre** *(Glen Nevis Rd., tel 01397-705922, closed Nov.–March)* can advise on mountain climbs and on walks in the glen.

## GLEN COE
Eighty miles north of Glasgow, the A82 passes Glencoe village and climbs through the truly dramatic and dark pass of **Glen Coe,** overhung with upswept rocky slopes.

From Altnafeadh the **Devil's Staircase,** a zigzag 17th-century track built by soldiers, climbs to cross the moors to Kinlochleven. ■

The awesome scenery of Loch Shiel and the surrounding mountains (with the Glenfinnan monument in the foreground) typifies the beauty of the Highlands.

**THE MASSACRE**
The notorious massacre of February 13, 1692, took place near Glencoe village: Campbell of Glenlyon and his soldiers murdered 38 of the local Macdonalds. The reason given was that Macdonald had missed a deadline for swearing allegiance to William III and Mary II, but the orders given to Campbell show how determined the authorities were to stamp out this troublesome sept (segment of a clan). ■

# Central Scotland

**Aberfoyle**
🏔 311 C2
**Visitor information**
✉ Main St.
☎ 0870-720 0604
🕐 Closed Mon.–Fri.
   Nov.–March

**Queen Elizabeth
Forest Park
Visitor information**
✉ I mile north
   of Aberfoyle on
   the A821
☎ 01877-382258
🕐 Call for opening
   hours
$ $ (parking)

**Sir Walter Scott**
✉ Trossachs Pier,
   Loch Katrine
☎ 01877-376316
🕐 Not operating
   Nov.–March
$ $$

**Killiecrankie
Visitor Centre**
✉ Killiecrankie
☎ 01796-473233
🕐 Closed Nov.–March
   (site open year-
   round)
$ $ (parking)

THE A81 LEADS NORTHWARD FROM GLASGOW TO THE
Trossach Hills, which rise on the southernmost fringe of the Scottish
Highlands. Aptly nicknamed "Highlands in Miniature," the Trossachs
form part of Loch Lomand and The Trossachs National Park,
Scotland's first national park.

## ISLE OF INCHMAHOME

**Aberfoyle,** at the heart of the
Trossachs, does not offer much of
an incentive to stop, but the beautiful calm **Lake of Menteith,**
5 miles to the east on the A81, shelters the wooded **Inchmahome
Island,** reached by boat from just
beyond the Lake of Menteith Hotel.
On the "Isle of Rest" are the striking
ruins of a **priory** *(tel 01877-
385294, closed Oct.–March)*
founded in 1238, where five-year-
old Mary, Queen of Scots, was hidden from the English in 1547 before
being spirited away to France.

North of Aberfoyle the A821
winds its way through wild, thickly
forested mountains to the 50,000-
acre **Queen Elizabeth Forest
Park Visitor Centre,** which has
details of superb walks and forest
drives—in particular the **Achray
Forest Drive** *(A821, 3 miles
north of Aberfoyle).*

## LOCH ACHRAY

At Loch Achray, a left turn (follow
the sign) brings you in half a mile to
the parking lot at the eastern end of
**Loch Katrine,** made famous by
Sir Walter Scott in *The Lady of the
Lake.* Ellen's Isle can be seen near
the landing stage (in real life the
MacGregor clan grazed stolen cattle
on the island), and the antique
steamcruiser *Sir Walter Scott* will
take you and a rented bicycle up the
lake to Stronachlachar, from where
you can walk or ride back along the
quiet and pretty north bank track.

Back beside Loch Achray, the
A821 continues east to the popular

holiday town of **Callander** *(Rob
Roy and Trossachs Visitor Centre,
Ancaster Sq., tel 0870-720 0628,
closed Mon.–Fri. Jan.–Feb.),* from
where the **Trossachs Trundler**
*(tel 01786-442444, not operating
Oct.–April)* minibus makes
a delightful Callander–Loch
Katrine–Aberfoyle circuit.

## BALQUHIDDER

Twelve miles north of Callander
on the A84, the churchyard at
Balquhidder holds the **grave** of
another Scott hero, Rob Roy
MacGregor (1671–1734). Rob Roy
(Red Robert) made a reasonably
honest living as a cattle dealer
until, at about age 30, his chief
drover absconded with £1,000
(approximately $1,800) that
belonged to MacGregor's patron,
the Duke of Montrose.

The duke impoverished Rob Roy,
who turned to plundering his former boss under the protection
of Montrose's enemy, the Duke of
Argyll. Whether the outlaw ever performed the Robin Hood-type deeds
postulated by Scott in *Rob Roy*
(1817) is unclear. He surrendered to
General Wade in 1722, was imprisoned in London, pardoned in 1727,
and returned to Balquhidder for the
last seven years of his life.

## PERTH

The A85 runs east through fine
Highland scenery to Perth, the Fair
City *(visitor information, Lower
City Mills, West Mill St., tel 01738-
450600, closed Sun. Oct.–Feb.).* Set
by the River Tay, the city is full of

interesting old buildings. On North Inch, 60 warriors of Clan Chattan and Clan Quhale (Kay) fought in 1396 a bloody combat to decide who should have pride of place in battle. Scott tells the tale in *The Fair Maid of Perth* (1828).

Two miles north is the medieval sandstone **Scone Palace,** where the **Stone of Destiny** stayed from 838 until 1296 (see p. 298).

### PITLOCHRY

The A9 starts its long run north to Inverness, in 27 miles passing **Pitlochry** *(visitor information, 22 Atholl Rd., tel 01796-472215)* among its hills. Here the renowned **Festival Theatre** *(tel 01796-484626)* puts on a season of drama and music between late July and late October. Down at the foot of nearby Loch Faskally is a **salmon pass,** where people watch the silver fish climb the ladder.

Above Pitlochry the hills press in to form the very dramatic Pass of Killiecrankie, where the deposed James II's Highlanders under Graham of Claverhouse ("Bonnie Dundee") charged and defeated King William's troops on July 27, 1689. The **Killiecrankie Visitor Centre** (NTS) recounts the story.

Beyond the pass is **Blair Castle,** a striking white edifice—turreted and gabled—dating from 1296. Here a piper from the Duke of Atholl's private army still serenades his master. ∎

*Every inch the romantic Highland castle, this fantastic pile is in fact the Hydro Hotel at Pitlochry, set in the valley of the River Tummel.*

**Blair Castle**
- ✉ Blair Atholl
- ☎ 01796-481207
- 🕐 Call for opening hours
- 💲 $$/$$$

# A drive through Royal Deeside

This drive takes you west from Aberdeen for 60 miles to reach Braemar beyond Balmoral Castle, and in that distance the landscape alters entirely from the low pastoral meadows and cornlands of the Aberdeenshire coast to the full rugged splendor of the Cairngorm Mountains.

Royal Deeside has everything—woodlands, a noble river, high mountains, castles, small, neat villages. No wonder Queen Victoria fell in love with this "chocolate-box" valley and persuaded Prince Albert to buy the Balmoral Estate in 1852.

The 195-foot steeple of St. Nicholas's Kirk dominates the pale granite buildings of **Aberdeen ❶** *(visitor information, tel 01224-632727, closed Oct.–Feb.)*, a town that sparkles and shimmers on a sunny day. Aberdeen is a good place to explore on foot, with the turreted and many-windowed 16th-century **Provost Skene's House** *(tel 01224-641086)* the chief attraction, if you can spot it cowering in Guestrow under the monstrous, modern multistory block of St. Nicholas House—along with the superb **Mercat Cross** (1686) on Castle Gate, decorated with likenesses of ten Stuart monarchs.

Ten miles west of Aberdeen along the A93 stands **Drum Castle ❷** *(NTS, tel 01330-811204, closed Oct.–March)*, followed shortly by **Crathes Castle ❸** *(NTS, tel 01330-844525, closed Nov.–March)*. These are two wonderful twins—Drum, a 13th-century keep with a 1619 mansion tacked on, and Crathes, a late 16th-century tower house (altered later) with several turrets jutting from a solid base.

The road goes through Banchory and Aboyne to reach snug **Ballater ❹** *(visitor information, tel 013397-55306, closed Oct.–Feb.)* among its rounded, conifer-clad hills. Ballater came into being when the water

| ▲ | 311 D3 |
| ➤ | Aberdeen |
| ⟷ | 60 miles |
| ⏱ | 2 hours |
| ➤ | Braemar |

**NOT TO BE MISSED**
- Provost Skene's House, Aberdeen
- Drum Castle
- Crathes Castle
- Balmoral Castle

**Clunie Water at Braemar**

**Balmoral, a baronial castle**

from a local well was found to cure scrofula, and it became a popular spa resort.

Next comes the royal bit of Royal Deeside. The simple **Parish Church of Crathie** *(tel 013397-42208, closed Nov.–March),* on the right, is used for worship by the Royal Family when they are staying at **Balmoral Castle** ⑤ *(tel 013397-42334, closed Aug.–early April).* The big Scottish baronial castle, glimpsed through trees from the A93, is largely what

Queen Victoria and Prince Albert built. The grounds are open for walks, and some rooms are occasionally shown.

In 8 miles is **Braemar** ⑥ *(visitor information, tel 013397-41600),* whose annual Highland Gathering (see p. 14) sees strong men toss cabers and hurl hammers.

Follow "Linn of Dee" signs for 6 miles on a narrow backroad to the **Linn of Dee** ⑦, where the river foams through a rocky defile. ∎

# Tartans

The House of Windsor, so often seen and photographed in tartan kilts around Royal Deeside, has done a lot to popularize this traditional Highland cloth.

Plaids of tartan have been worn by Scots since Roman times, their checkered patterns (setts) referred to by visiting or invading commentators time and again down the years. At first only chiefs had tartans vegetable dyed with multicolored grid patterns; then ordinary people began to sport setts that distinguished their home district, and then their clan—very handy in the confusion of a raid or skirmish.

Until Jacobite times, plaids contained up to 16 yards of tartan and doubled as sleeping

blankets. Then the short philibeg (knee-length kilt) became popular. The tartan kilt was adopted throughout Scotland as a Jacobite symbol, and as such was stringently outlawed after the Battle of Culloden.

The ban was lifted in 1782, and with Sir Walter Scott's enthusiastic promotion tartan became high fashion during the 19th century. The sett patterns became prescribed and fixed.

Nowadays there are setts for individual clan bigwigs, for families, for regions, and for units of the armed services. Huge sentiment attaches to these post-Culloden tartans, but somewhere along the line the essential beauty of the sett's original aptness has been obscured. ∎

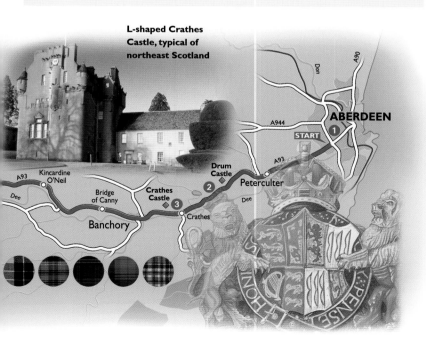

L-shaped Crathes Castle, typical of northeast Scotland

# Grampians & Cairngorms

**Banff**
🔺 311 D3
**Visitor information**
✉ Collie Lodge
☎ 01261-812419
🕐 Closed Sun.
   Oct.–Feb.

**Aviemore**
🔺 311 C3
**Visitor information**
✉ Grampian Rd.
☎ 0845-225 5121
🕐 Closed Sun.
   Oct.–Feb.

*The River Spey—*
*one of the best*
*salmon-fishing*
*rivers in*
*Scotland—is*
*wide, shallow, and*
*fast flowing.*

THE GRAMPIAN RANGE OF MOUNTAINS FORMS THE central spine of Scotland—a spine with curvature, a bent bow springing from southwest Argyll, curving northeast until it dips toward the North Sea coast near Aberdeen. The beautiful glens of Angus furrow the southern flank of the Grampians at this eastern end.

Abutting the great Grampian massif on the north are the gray granite Cairngorm Mountains (designated Scotland's second national park in 2003), six of the craggy peaks rising over 4,000 feet, their central platform the highest, wildest, and coldest place in Britain. Ptarmigan, mountain hare, wild cat, red deer, and golden eagle are all present, particularly in the 100 square miles of the **Cairngorms National Nature Reserve** *(Glenmore Forest Park Visitor Centre, Glenmore, Aviemore, tel 01479-861220).*

The A93 from Ballater to Spittal of Glenshee, the A939 from Ballater to Tomintoul, and the B970 from Aviemore to Feshiebridge and on up Glen Tromie to Gaick Lodge give an idea of the mountains' grandeur.

### COASTAL HINTERLAND
Northeast of the Cairngorms, a rocky, rough coast curves west between Aberdeen and Inverness along the Moray Firth.

The twin towns of **Banff,** with its fine Georgian domestic architecture and splendid William Adam-designed baroque **Duff House** *(tel 01261-818181, closed Nov.–March)* and **Macduff,** with its small lively fish market are worth exploring; while **Cullen,** west along the coast, is a delightful small town dominated by its handsome old railroad viaduct. It is possible to walk along the former track.

## SPEY VALLEY

The western flank of the Cairngorm Mountains is defined by the wide and extremely beautiful Spey Valley. **Aviemore** is the "capital"; **Kingussie,** 12 miles southwest, is lower-key, older, and better looking. The **Strathspey Steam Railway** puffs the 5 miles from Aviemore to Boat of Garten (to be extended to Grantown on Spey 2001–2002), and a mile away is the **Loch Garten Nature Reserve** *(8 miles northeast of Aviemore, off the B970, tel 01479-821409),* where you can observe ospreys feeding and nesting from April to August. The seven distilleries and one cooperage that comprise the **Malt Whisky Trail** *(brochure from any visitor information office)* are strung out along the Spey, one of the best fly-fishing rivers in Britain *(information about permits available from Aviemore visitor center).* The **Speyside Way** gives 30 miles of superb walking from Spey Bay to Ballindalloch, with a spur to Tomintoul. ■

**Kingussie**
🅰 311 C3
**Visitor information**
✉ King St.
☎ 01540-661307
🕐 Closed Oct.–April

**Strathspey Steam Railway**
✉ Aviemore Station, Dalfaber Rd., Aviemore
☎ 01479-810725
🕐 Diesel service only Nov.–March (except some services in Dec.)
💲 $$ (3rd class round-trip), $$$ (1st class round-trip)

**Speyside Way Ranger Service**
✉ Boat o'Fiddich, Craigellachie
☎ 01340-881266
🕐 Call to confirm times

## Whisky

**U**isge beatha, the Water of Life—inspiration for dancing and musicmaking, greetings and farewells, solo evenings and the communal visits called *ceilidh.*

Most whisky is now a blend of malted spirit (made in a pot-still from malted barley) and grain spirit (made from a mixture of malted and unmalted barley and grain). Soft water from a burn (brook) and a good yeast are other essentials. Single malt or unblended whisky is the connoisseur's choice—either a lighter and sweeter Speyside variety such as Glenlivet or Glenfiddich, or the oily whiskies of the islands (such as the Islay-distilled Laphroaig and Lagavulin), whose malt is smoked over peat to produce a rich, tarry, and smoky tang.

The golden color develops gradually over years of maturing in oak casks—these are often bought secondhand for flavor from American bourbon distilleries. Up to 30 percent can be lost through evaporation during this aging process, and this upward-drifting and invisible spirit is known as "the angels' share."

Almost any distillery, given a little notice, will be happy to let you look around and sample the Water of Life. ■

As their temperature rises, the copper stills produce first "low wines" (weak spirit), then the proper whisky spirit. Last appears a deadly liquid known as "feints," as potent and poisonous as paint stripper.

# Outdoor Scotland

Scotland's scenery, from the rolling Border hills, through the Lowlands and up to the dramatic Highlands and islands, is as varied as it is beautiful. Snowcapped mountains, heather moorland, fast-flowing rivers, sparkling lochs, desolate beaches, and endless tidal estuaries each hold their own particular charm and offer numerous outdoor pursuits, as well as some of the most wonderful opportunities for observing the country's wildlife.

**Fishing on the River Tweed**

## Outdoor activities

Golf is a democratic game in Scotland and public golf courses are plentiful and inexpensive. You'll need your handicap certificate to play at the best known courses, which include **St. Andrews** *(tel 01334-475757);* **Carnoustie** *(tel 01241-853789),* near Dundee; **Gleneagles** *(tel 01764-694469),* near Auchterarder; **Royal Dornoch** *(tel 01862-810219),* north of Inverness; and **Turnberry** *(tel 01655-331000),* south of Glasgow. See also pp. 304–305.

You can walk and climb anywhere within reason, though it's wise to ask permission if you meet a private landowner—especially during the deer-stalking season *(mid-Aug.–mid-Oct.),* when stray bullets may be flying. The best known and most challenging walking areas are the Cairngorms, the mountains in the West Highlands, and the formidable Cuillin Hills on the Isle of Skye.

For skiing and other snow sports, try the **Nevis Range** near **Fort William** *(tel 01397-705825),* with snow from December to April and a dry slope from July to October; **Cairngorm Chairlift Company** *(tel 01479-861261),* near Aviemore; or **The Lecht** *(tel 01975-651440)*

---

## Mountain safety

In 1992–93, a particularly bad year, more than 50 people died in the Scottish mountains, most of them through ignorance and poor preparation. Every year hundreds have to be rescued by volunteers risking their own lives. The Scottish mountains are small stuff compared with the world's great ranges, but they can be extremely dangerous if not treated with proper respect.

### The basic rules are:

1. Seek local advice; find out the local weather forecast.
2. Be realistic about your fitness and experience, and go in parties of three or more.
3. Be suitably equipped—boots, bad-weather gear, food and drink, an emergency whistle, and a survival bag if going high or far.
4. Take a large-scale map and a compass, and know how to use them.
5. If things look bad, be prepared to call off the expedition, or turn around.
6. Tell someone where you are going, and what time and where you intend to finish. Keep to your planned route and report in when you reach your destination.
7. If bad weather or darkness threatens on the hills, get down fast.
8. If things do go wrong, stay calm. If someone is hurt or exhausted, one person stays with the casualty, others go for help. Keep warm, dry, and optimistic. ∎

**Scottish mountains provide superb terrain for the experienced and well-equipped hiker.**

near Tomintoul. The **Ice Factor** at Kinloch-leven near Glencoe village *(tel 01855-831100)* offers ice, rock, and boulder climbing and many more activities—indoor and out.

Coarse fishing thrives in the Lowlands, and is generally organized through local clubs; the Highlands are likely to offer game fishing for salmon (expensive) or trout (reasonable). Sea fishing is available all round the coast.

For information about these activities, contact any local visitor information center.

### Wildlife

In the south, the Solway Firth is a vast natural larder of tidal muds and merses (salt marshes) lying between the Cumbrian and Galloway coasts. Here the entire population of barnacle geese from Spitzbergen in the Arctic Circle (about 20,000 birds) spends the winter, a truly memorable sight and sound, best appreciated from the Wildfowl and Wetlands Trust Centre, Caerlaverock (see p. 291).

The farther north you go, and the higher the landscape, the better your chances of see-ing the wildlife so typical of the Scottish Highlands. On the lower slopes, especially around pine woods, you may see pine marten, red deer, black grouse, wildcat (extremely wary), the still declining red squirrel, and, if you are lucky, the turkey-size capercaillie flouncing away among the trees. On the moors the ubiquitous red grouse, preserved for sport, whirs away croaking out "Go-back, go-back!"

In remote places such as Wester Ross are the noble, red-trunked, native Scots pines, remnants of the great Wood of Caledon that once covered Scotland. Deer and wildcat are still present high up, and in the Cairngorms you may spot the herd of reintroduced rein-deer. Mountain hare and ptarmigan turn white for camouflage in the winter snows here, and ravens are often seen doing acrobatics over the mountains. The greatest wildlife thrill for most visitors, however, is to catch sight of a golden eagle in soaring flight.

The islands provide refuge for the reintro-duced white-tailed sea eagle (Rum), whimbrel, and red-necked phalarope (Fetlar in Shetland), corncrakes (Coll and the Western Isles), and many other threatened species. Sandy machair—a grassy sward built up on lime-rich shell sand, rich in orchids, lady's bedstraw, bird's-foot trefoil, and huge clovers—is a distinctive feature. ■

# Inverness & the north

**Inverness**

🅰 311 C3

**Visitor information**

✉ Castle Wynd

☎ 0845-225 5121

🕐 Closed Sun.
Oct.–Feb.

**Inverness Museum
and Art Gallery**

✉ Castle Wynd

☎ 01463-237114

🕐 Closed Sun.

**Culloden
Battlefield (NTS)**

✉ Culloden Moor

☎ 01463-790607

🕐 Visitor center closed
Jan. Battlefield open
year-round

💲 $$ (Visitor center)

**Ullapool**

🅰 311 B4

**Visitor information**

✉ Argyle St.

☎ 0845-225 5121

🕐 Closed Oct.–Feb.

THE GREAT GLEN, RUNNING NORTHEAST FROM FORT William for 70 almost straight miles to Inverness, in effect slices Scotland in two with a string of long, narrow stretches of water— Loch Linnhe, Loch Lochy, and Loch Ness. The A82 follows the glen all the way. Whether Nessie, the Loch Ness monster, really exists is all down to speculation based on old legends, dubious photographs, and sighting claims.

**Inverness,** known as the Capital of the Highlands, is a compact little place just the right size for exploring on foot. Behind the tourist information center is **Inverness Museum and Art Gallery,** with carved Pictish stones, Celtic jewelry, Jacobite relics, and much else.

Across the river from the gallery is **St. Andrew's Cathedral,** its polished pillars made of speckled Peterhead granite, with a beautiful angel font and unexpectedly subtle Victorian stained glass.

**Church Street,** across from the tourist office, is full of interesting old buildings; on the left is the **High Church,** in whose churchyard is a gravestone with a notch said to have been used by marksmen shooting Jacobite prisoners after the Battle of Culloden.

### CULLODEN BATTLEFIELD

The battlefield lies 5 miles east of Inverness on the B9006 (follow the signs). On its exposed, heathery moorland, well marked, are the positions where 5,000 Highlanders —exhausted after a four-month retreat from Derby in England, hungry, and short of sleep—lined up on April 16, 1746, to charge nearly twice as many English soldiers. They were slaughtered on the battlefield, and butchered in scores in the surrounding countryside by the victorious dragoons for days afterward.

Bonnie Prince Charlie escaped and began his months of fugitive

wandering before leaving Scotland for the Continent, where he spent nearly half a century in drunken, degraded exile. The clans he left behind sadly lost their coherence, their leadership, and their way of life.

### ACROSS TO THE WEST

The spectacular **Kyle Railway Line** (*tel 08457-484950*) runs southwest from Inverness to Kyle of Lochalsh on the west coast, down savagely beautiful Glen Carron—a good way to enjoy the scenery of Wester Ross.

From here, the A832 loops round the necks of remote western peninsulas to **Ullapool** (ferry to Stornoway on Lewis), on the way passing **Inverewe Garden** (*tel 01445-781200*), with its acres of lush subtropical plants.

It is 80 long, winding, mountainous, and extremely lonely but beautiful miles north from Ullapool to **Cape Wrath,** the granite headland over 500 feet tall at Britain's northwestern extremity. At **Inchnadamph,** on the A837 (25 miles), a footpath runs east from the Inchnadamph Hotel toward the striking 3,273-foot Ben More Assynt, through remote **Glen Dubh,** notable for wildflowers of both peat bog and limestone.

In 2 miles you reach a number of sinkholes, through which the river can be seen and heard rushing underground.

**Once one of Scotland's largest castles, Urquhart, on the banks of Loch Ness, was blown up in 1692 to prevent it from being taken over by the Jacobites.**

**A piper wrings every nuance from his set of bagpipes.**

## Traditional music

There is music for war: stirring marches played on the bagpipes to summon clans to gatherings, battles, and mourning. Then there is music for peace: leaping strathspeys, tearing reels, and tender slow airs played on the fiddle and accordion for dancing, celebrating, and lovemaking. You can hear it at formal gatherings and competitions, in the massed accordion and fiddle clubs, in bars at informal sessions where anyone can join in, at village dances in remote rural community halls, and on city street corners from lone pipers with a hat out on the ground for public donations. Visit www.skyelive.com for gig news; and the **National Piping Centre**, 30-34 McPhater Street, Glasgow *(tel 0141-353-0220)* for all things bagpipe. ∎

**John O'Groats**
◪ 311 C4
**Visitor information**
✉ County Rd.
☎ 01955-611373
⏱ Closed Oct.–Feb.

### UP THE EASTERN COAST

Back on the east coast, 90 miles northeast of Inverness on the A9, the **Strath of Kildonan** is good, wild, walking country. The A897 follows the strath (valley), then leads through the bleak and beautiful **Flow Country** (a million acres of peat, loch, and mountain) to reach the north coast in 40 miles.

The A9 runs from **Helmsdale** along the dramatic Caithness coast for 55 miles to **John O'Groats,** "northernmost point" of mainland Britain (Dunnet Head to the east actually has that honor). John O'Groats is 876 miles as the crow flies from Land's End at the southern tip of Britain. There's nothing much here except a big hotel, but try visiting the **Last House Museum,** which explains the area's history.

From **Duncansby Head,** 2 miles east, there are spectacular views across to Orkney. ∎

# Scottish Islands

THE OFFSHORE ISLANDS OF SCOTLAND ARE GENERALLY DIVIDED INTO three main groups: the Inner Hebrides, a loose scatter of islands just off the west coast, whose largest and best known component is beautiful Skye; the Outer Hebrides, or Western Isles, a ragged island chain 130 miles long that lies farther west and roughly parallel; and the sister archipelagoes of Orkney and Shetland, known as the Northern Isles, that stretch northward from the John O'Groats coast.

## A WAY OF LIFE

History lies thickly on the islands' stones, prehistoric settlements, Pictish brochs (defensive stone towers), burial chambers, corrugated cultivation ridges called "lazybeds," and villages left abandoned during the Highland Clearances. And many island practices and traditions—nonmechanical cultivation of hay fields in the Western Isles, for example, or the *ceilidhing* and dancing of the Northern Isles, or the way islanders greet and welcome strangers—closely echo the customs of past generations.

Yet the islands are not static museums to the distant past, nor self-conscious theme parks portraying some idyllic way of life. Making a living out there, in the face of wind, frequently harsh weather, and isolation is still hard, requiring considerable determination and adaptability.

## WINDS OF CHANGE

In recent years there have been big changes. North Sea oil, with its economic benefits and social upheaval, has come to Shetland. There has been a measure of self-government for the Western Isles through Comhairle nan Eilean (the Council of the Islands) and the Co-Chomunn (island cooperatives). The islands as a whole have benefited from European Union grants and other subsidies. Incomers have begun to settle in ever increasing numbers, bringing change to the social structure of the islands, some of it for the better, some not.

The islands remain magical: There is no better word for the spell they cast on visitors. Except in extreme weather conditions, they are readily accessible. Don't make too many plans, though: If the weather does not slow you down, then the hospitality, the beauty, and the dreaminess of the islands certainly will. ∎

Skara Brae, an entire Neolithic settlement, lay preserved in Orkney's sand dunes until 1850.

# Isle of Skye

SKYE, ONE OF THE INNER HEBRIDES, IS FAMOUS FOR ITS
spectacular mountain scenery and beautiful transitions of rain, cloud,
sun, and mist. Portree, the capital town, is strung around its bay, 35
miles from the mainland bridge at Kyleakin. Just south on the A850,
the Aros Experience (Skye's heritage center) displays the island's history.

**Portree**
⚑ 311 B3
**Visitor information**
✉ Bayfield House,
    Bayfield Rd.
☎ 0845-225 5121
🕓 Closed Sun.
    Oct.–Feb.

**Aros Experience**
✉ Viewfield Rd.,
    Portree
☎ 01478-613649
💲 $$

**Skye Museum of
Island Life**
✉ Hungladder, Kilmuir
☎ 01470-542206
🕓 Closed Nov.–March
💲 $

**Museum of the
Isles**
✉ Clan Donald Centre,
    Armadale Castle,
    Sleat
☎ 01472-844305
🕓 Closed Nov.–March
💲 $$

To appreciate Skye to its fullest,
you need to penetrate the hidden
corners of its five far-flung peninsulas: Counterclockwise from Portree,
these are Trotternish, Vaternish,
Duirinish, Strathaird, and Sleat.

## NORTHERN SKYE
The spine of **Trotternish** is a dramatic curtain of basalt cliffs 30
miles long, with superb walking
around the **Quiraing** outcrops at
1,700 feet. **Flora Macdonald's
house** (see box) now forms part of
the accommodations offered by the
Flodigarry Hotel below the
Quiraing. Her grave lies near the
**Skye Museum of Island Life** at
Kilmuir in western Trotternish.
    In the northwest of Skye, where
Vaternish and Duirinish meet, is
**Dunvegan Castle** (tel 01470-
521206), ancient and grim stronghold of the Macleods.
    In Duirinish you can explore
the art of bagpiping in **Borreraig
Park Piping and Heritage
Centre** (tel 01470-511311).

## SOUTHERN SKYE
From **Elgol** in south-facing
**Strathaird** a spectacular footpath
leads to Camasunary Bay and
superb mountain views.
    The **Museum of the Isles**
at Armadale Castle in Sleat gives
real insight into the history and
heritage of clans.
    Skye's landscape is dominated
by the centrally placed **Cuillin
Hills,** formed from volcanic rock;
20 of their crests are over 3,000 feet.
Their wilder heights provide

climbing for experts, but for lower
and less hazardous walking, contact
the Portree information center. ■

## Flora Macdonald

Flora Macdonald was 23 when, in June 1746, two months after the Battle of Culloden, she escorted the fugitive Bonnie Prince Charlie—disguised as her maid—from her native South Uist in the Outer Hebrides, "over the sea to Skye" in an 18-foot rowing boat. After Charles's escape, she was captured and imprisoned for a year in the Tower of London.

In 1750, Flora married a Skye man, Allan Macdonald. In 1774 the family emigrated to America but Flora returned with her seven children six years later after her husband was captured in the Revolutionary War. She died in 1790. ■

**Torrin village looks across Loch Slapin toward the Cuillin Hills.**

# Islanders

Although every island has its own land-scape, character, and history, Scottish islanders have more in common with each other than they do with mainlanders. The first thing that strikes every visitor is the tremendous island hospitality, which finds expression in a polite greeting on the road, the offer of a lift, an invitation to a *ceilidh* (social gathering), a courteous switch from Gaelic into English if a nonspeaker joins the conversation, and practical and immediate help given in any difficulty or emergency.

This habit of hospitality and good manners, so deeply ingrained in islanders, is born—like most island characteristics—out of the hard reality of life in a small, isolated community, the absolute necessity not to tread on your neighbor's toes, but to give him the space you hope to be given. Together with the hospitality, and for exactly the same good practical reason, goes a modesty and reserve that hold back intimacy.

### Treading carefully

Newcomers can easily misinterpret both hospitality and reserve, especially when they have witnessed another prominent side of the island character: wild abandon in celebration, at dances in village halls or late-night musical sessions in bars or back kitchens. It is tempting to trespass too far on the islanders' good nature or to take their hospitality for granted; equally, their reserve can be mistaken for indifference, even hostility.

By far the best way to appreciate the islanders, and to ensure that they appreciate you, is to be yourself, but to be sensitive, carefully measuring your level of familiarity against theirs.

Don't be frightened to accept an invitation, though, to join in wholeheartedly with fun and celebrations, to go to church and the pub and the village dance. And leave yourself plenty of lazy, unplanned days, empty pools of time into which unexpected but invariably welcome fish may swim.

**The face of Skye changes from craggy peaks to bleak moorland, wooded valleys to farmland.**

**Two island industries—small-scale inshore fishing and peat-cutting. Nowadays peat for commercial use is cut by machine, but islanders handcut turfs for domestic use.**

### A workaday place

Island life is demanding. Weather is harsher, soil poorer, communications more uncertain, everything more expensive and more time-consuming than on the mainland. Some islanders hide from these challenges behind the bottle, or cocoon themselves in laissez-faire. But most are hard workers, endurers who have learned to be adaptable. The man who pulls your pint also drives the bus and trawls for lobsters. The woman running the shop also organizes the island dances and raises sheep on a croft. These are practical people, whose houses more often than not stand in seas of flotsam and jetsam—fish boxes, lobster creels, lengths of wire, plastic tubs, fence stakes, tractor tires—things they may never need, but are squirreling away in case they do. Their business is not to make their community as pretty as a picture, but to make it work and last. And how exactly do you get rid of a broken-down Ford, or an old bedstead, when you live on a tiny island? You slide it down the cliffs as far away as possible from the village, and turn a blind eye.

### New ways

In recent years newcomers—generally known to the natives as "white settlers"—have abandoned mainland life in increasing numbers to settle in the islands. Strangely, these new faces have often been instrumental in preserving aspects of traditional island life—good neighborliness, visiting the elderly, communal care of children—which were dying out as young native islanders gradually left for the mainland bright lights and the island population began to age.

The "blow-ins" have pushed for things that born-and-bred islanders never got around to demanding—reliable electricity supplies, decent health care, improved shops, better ferry and plane services, better schools, better political representation.

Human nature being what it is, though, these new brooms have sometimes generated resentment through their breezy clean sweeping. They are vocal, in a way that native islanders seldom allow themselves to be, about the very many delights that island life has to offer—the unpolluted air, the absence of crime and violence, and the freedom from nine-to-five stress.

The islands are there to enjoy for all these things, and for their fabulous, unspoiled beauty and variety. The islanders, once befriended, will remain friends for life—take your time among them; you are sure to return. ∎

# Inner Hebrides

**Arran**

⚐ 311 B1

**Visitor information**

✉ The Pier, Brodick

☎ 01770-303774/6

🕐 Closed Sun. Oct.–Feb.

**Bute**

⚐ 311 B1

**Visitor information**

✉ 15 Victoria St., Rothesay

☎ 0870-720 0619

🕐 Closed Sat.–Sun. Oct.–Feb.

**Mull**

⚐ 311 B2

**Visitor information**

✉ The Pier, Craignure

☎ 0780-720 0610

**Staffa's extraordinary basalt formation**

THE INNER HEBRIDEAN ISLANDS LIE IN A JUMBLE OFF THE west coast. Arran, Bute, and Mull are well known; the others less so, and all the more rewarding and seductive for that.

**Arran,** in the Firth of Clyde, is spectacularly mountainous in the north, with wonderful walking around 2,866-foot Goatfell, and more pastoral toward the south end. There are ancient stone circles and burial chambers around Machrie in the west.

**Bute,** northeast of Arran, is a soft green island for gentle walks and golfing.

**Islay** lies isolated at the south end of the Hebridean chain. Its chief treasure is Kildalton High Cross, carved about A.D. 800 and miraculously preserved. The bird-watching is notable; likewise the famous peaty Islay whiskies.

**Jura,** just east of Islay, is wild and empty. George Orwell lived at Barnhill from 1946 to 1949, and wrote *1984* there. Climb the 2,000-foot Paps of Jura; watch the 5,000 red deer; enjoy peace and quiet.

**Colonsay,** north of Islay, is tiny, remote, and tranquil.

**Mull** boasts superb sea coasts on its three west-facing peninsulas. Enjoy a morning's exploration of 13th-century **Duart Castle** (*tel 01680-812309, closed early Oct.–March, Fri.–Sat. April* ), and an evening's drama at the tiny **Mull Little Theatre** (*tel 01688-302828*).

From Fionnphort a foot ferry crosses to **Iona,** cradle of the Celtic church in Scotland; here, in sublimely peaceful surroundings, are the restored abbey and chapels, and the gravestones of ancient kings. Boats sail from Fionnphort and Iona to **Staffa,** whose magical Fingal's Cave (227 feet by 66 feet) inspired Felix Mendelssohn's *Hebridean Overture.*

The so-called Cocktail Isles include wedge-shaped **Eigg** (climb the 1,292-foot Sgurr, walk Cleadale's inland cliffs, and discover the Massacre Cave); tiny round **Muck;** mountainous **Rum** (Scottish Natural Heritage looks after red deer, sea eagles, mountains, and the eccentric Kinloch Castle); and low, green, peaceful **Canna.**

Coll and Tiree, farthest west, possess wonderful windy beaches. **Coll** has a Royal Society for the Protection of Birds (RSPB) corncrake sanctuary at Totronald (*tel 01879-230301*), its western end, while **Tiree** offers glorious flowery machair (see p. 321) and exciting windsurfing. ■

# Outer Hebrides (Western Isles)

IF YOU ARE LOOKING FOR WONDERFULLY WILD AND beautiful scenery, and people who retain hospitality and courtesy as second nature, the remote Western Isles will provide a few days you will never forget.

**Barra**'s *(Map 311 A3)* airstrip is a white cockleshell beach. Compton Mackenzie, author of the famous Western Isles romp, *Whisky Galore,* is buried at Eoligarry. At Castlebay, Kisimul Castle (mostly dating from the 11th century) stands dramatically out in the bay. Here you can get a boat (inquire locally) to off islands **Pabbay** (Pictish, Celtic stones) and romantic **Mingulay.**

Flora Macdonald's birthplace (see p. 327) is at Milton, toward the middle of **South Uist** *(Map 311 A3),* marked by a memorial. There is a museum and heritage center at Kildonan, and good hill-walking and climbing up to Bein Mhor (2,033 feet).

Take the passenger ferry from Ludag in the south to **Eriskay,** the island where the freighter *Politician* was wrecked in 1941 with 20,000 cases of whisky. Bonnie Prince Charlie's first landing was here on July 23, 1745.

**Benbecula** is flat, watery, windswept, and lonely, if you discount the soldiers billeted here.

**North Uist** *(Map 311 A3)* has stone circles, cairns, fine western beaches, and excellent loch fishing; also bird-watching at Balranald reserve out west and the Uist Animal Visitor Centre in Bayhead.

**Harris** *(Map 311 A3)* has superb beaches in the west, superb mountains in the north. Harris Tweed manufacture is coordinated by the Harris Tweed Association.

A passenger ferry from Leverburgh runs to **Berneray,** whose west coast is one long beach.

**Lewis** *(Map 311 B4)* is the largest and most northerly of the Western Isles. In summer, the 12th-century walrus-ivory Uig chessmen are displayed in **Museum nan Eilean** *(tel 01851-709266),* Stornoway.

Across on the west is **Carloway Broch,** 70 feet high and 2,000 years old, the most complete Hebridean broch (stone tower); and the famous **Callanish Standing Stones,** an impressive array of circles, rows, and other Neolithic megaliths beside a bleak and beautiful loch. ■

**Western Isles Visitor information**

✉ 26 Cromwell St., Stornoway, Isle of Lewis

☎ 01851-703088

🕐 Closed Sun. all year, Sat. Oct.–Feb.

**Callanish Standing Stones, one of the most haunting prehistoric sites in Britain**

## Gaelic

The Gaelic language came from Ireland around A.D. 400, was almost extinguished after Culloden, and is in reasonable shape today thanks to its teaching in schools. In the Western Isles it is widely spoken and sung—beautiful and mellifluous to hear, hard to read, harder still to learn and understand. ■

# Orkney

THE ORKNEY ARCHIPELAGO IS FOUNDED ON WARM
sandstone, which gives these islets a pastoral, green fertility. Here you will
find some of Scotland's most awe-inspiring prehistoric monuments.

**Orkney**
🗺 311 C5
**Visitor information**
✉ 6 Broad St., Kirkwall
☎ 01856-872856
🕐 Closed Sun.
Oct.–Feb.

**Star attraction of
the island of Hoy,
the towering rock
stack known as
the Old Man of
Hoy is part of the
North Hoy
Nature Reserve.**

**Mainland** is the chief island, and
Kirkwall the capital. Eight centuries
have blurred and smoothed the
sandstone of the magnificent St.
Magnus's Cathedral; the nearby
Earl's Palace (1600–1607) is
encrusted with turrets.

**Stromness** in the west is a
close-built little seaport, hosting
a lively folk festival in May. In this
area are four astonishing prehistoric sites: the grassy mound of
**Maes Howe** burial chamber, the
finest in Britain; the neighboring
**Standing Stones of Stenness**
and **Ring of Brodgar;** and the
buried Stone Age settlement of
**Skara Brae.**

To the south, **Hoy's** 1,000-foot
cliffs play host to peregrine falcons,
Arctic skuas, and a host of seabirds,
while offshore rises the famous Old
Man of Hoy, a sandstone rock stack
450 feet high.

The A961 runs south from
Mainland between **Lamb Holm,
Burray,** and **South Ronaldsay**
on wartime causeways built by
Italian prisoners, who also created
the poignant **Nissen Hut
Chapel** on Lamb Holm.

**Shapinsay** has the baronial
**Balfour Castle** (*tel 01856-711282,
tours Sun., Wed. 2:15 p.m., May–
Sept. Reservations at Kirkwall Tourist
Information Centre, tel 01856 -
872856*) and **Rousay,** the Great
Ship of Death, has a Stone Age
chambered cairn where 24 seated
skeletons were discovered in 1932.

On **Egilsay** is the round
towered, 12th-century St. Magnus's
Church; on **Wyre,** Cubbie Roo's
Castle, stronghold of 12th-century
Norse warlord Kolbein Hruga; on
**Eday,** the 15-foot Stone of Setter.

There are remote early Christian
hermit cells off **Stronsay,** a big
chambered cairn 5,000 years old at
Quoyness on **Sanday,** old churches
and a Jacobite cave on **Westray,**
and on **Papa Westray** prehistoric
farmhouses at the Knap of Howar.

**North Ronaldsay,** farthest
north, has beautiful, empty beaches
and a wonderfully tranquil feel.

To travel to Orkney, contact
P&O Scottish Ferries (*tel 01224-
572615*) or John O'Groats Ferries
(*tel 01955-611353*); or fly with
Loganair (*tel 0870-850 9850*) from
any main Scottish airport. ■

# Shetland

THE SHETLAND CHAIN OF ISLANDS, BRITAIN'S REMOTEST and most northerly, is a ragged archipelago 70 miles long, windswept, and almost treeless. Here are harsh beauty, tremendous hospitality, and the most energetic music anywhere in the British Isles.

**Shetland**

🅰 311 D4

**Visitor information**

✉ Market Cross, Lerwick

☎ 01595-693434

🕐 Closed Sat.–Sun Oct.–Feb.

**Bronze Age huts, Iron Age wheel houses, a Norse longhouse, and medieval farms make up Jarlshof Prehistoric and Norse Settlement.**

The capital of Shetland is Norse-flavored Lerwick, on **Mainland,** one of the three main islands. This harbor town hosts a folk festival in April. Off the southeast coast **Mousa Broch** on Mousa Island *(For ferries call 01950-431367),* is a 45-foot high broch (stone tower). At **Jarlshof Prehistoric and Norse Settlement** *(tel 01950-460112, closed Oct.–March),* on Sumburgh Head, five periods of occupation covering about 3,000 years are represented.

The east coast of windy **Yell** is moodily attractive. The Fishermen's Memorial at Gloup in the north commemorates 58 locals lost in a storm on July 20, 1881—a grim reminder of the reality of Shetland weather. **Fetlar** is for bird-watching; red-necked phalaropes are among the rarities on the **RSPB reserve** *(tel 01597-733246).*

**Unst,** bare and beautiful, has the wildly windblown headland seabird reserve of Hermaness *(tel 01595-693345),* looking down on Britain's Most Northerly Point.

To travel to Shetland contact P&O Scottish Ferries *(tel 01224-572615);* Loganair *(tel 0870-850 9850)* operates flights from Sumburgh. ∎

## Up Helly Aa'

**O**n the last Tuesday in January each year, over 40 bearded Vikings in full battle dress stamp and roar their way through the streets of Lerwick under command of their chief, the Guizer Jarl. With them they drag a full-size longship, which they have spent the whole previous year preparing. The Guizer Jarl, Lord of Misrule during this midwinter ceremony of Up Helly Aa' (see p. 13), officiates during the evening's spectacular torchlit procession, which culminates when the longship, piled high with blazing torches, burns to ashes. ∎

# More islands to visit

## BRESSAY

Bressay lies just across the water from the Shetland capital, its 350 people mostly involved in fish processing.

On the east side, reached by inflatable boat, is the National Nature Reserve of **Noss Island,** with enormous cliffs at The Noup where thousands of seabirds breed.

311 D4 🚢 Car ferry from Lerwick

## FAIR ISLE

Fair Isle is owned by the National Trust for Scotland. The bird observatory is world famous; so is the Fair Isle knitwear still produced by the 60-odd inhabitants, some incomers and some Fair Isle families established for many generations.

Twenty miles south of Mainland, the same distance north of Orkney, Fair Isle is the most isolated island community in Britain. That does not stop the islanders having fun; the Fair Isle dances, with music by the island band, are irresistible all-join-in affairs.

off map 311 D5 🚢 Passenger ferry from Sunburgh/ Lerwick; air service from Tingwall

## OUT SKERRIES

With a population of around 80, Out Skerries is a group of three islands northeast of Whalsay, with a sheltered communal harbor.

311 D4 🚢 Car ferry from Lerwick/Vidlin; air service from Tingwall

## PAPA STOUR

Papa Stour, lying off the northwest Mainland coast, has about 40 inhabitants. The coast of this Great Island of the Priests, a pilgrimage center during the Middle Ages, is spectacularly sea-cut into stacks, caves, and arches.

311 D4 🚢 Boats from West Burrafirth; air service from Tingwall

## WHALSAY

Off the northeast coast of Mainland, Whalsay has a population of around 1,000, doing well through fishing and fish processing. The 17th-century Bremen Böd on the quay at Symbister is a store built during the later days of the Hanseatic League, when all kinds of outlanders came to fish and trade in Shetland.

311 D4 🚢 Car ferry from Laxo/Symbister ■

**Waves tirelessly pound the feet of the mighty basalt cliffs at Eshaness, on Shetland Mainland.**

# Travelwise

**Travelwise information 336–41**
Planning your trip **336**
How to get to Britain **336**
Getting around **336–38**
Practical advice **338–41**
Emergencies **341**
**Hotels & restaurants 342–87**
**Shopping in Great Britain**
   **388–89**
**Entertainment 390**

**London bus**

# TRAVELWISE INFORMATION

## PLANNING YOUR TRIP

### CLIMATE

Britain is a temperate country, warmed by the Gulf Stream and by a southwestern airflow, cooled by its northerly latitude. Winter and spring are mostly mild, though it gets noticeably colder the farther north you go, and in winter there can be significant snowfall on the hills of northern England and in the mountains of Wales and Scotland. A temperature below freezing is reckoned a cold snap. In summer, anything above 80°F is described as a heat wave. Recent years have seen a general rise in temperature.

### WHAT TO TAKE

Pack warm and waterproof clothing at any time of year, just in case the British climate springs one of its surprises. If visiting in winter you will need a heavy coat. A folding umbrella is also a good idea at all times. Jeans are acceptable in most establishments (even the theater now) though most nightclubs stipulate "no jeans." More formal attire (jacket and tie; dress or skirt and blouse) is the norm if dining out in better-class restaurants and for an evening at the opera, ballet, or classical concert. Also bring some sturdy, but comfortable, shoes—even if only visiting London, as you will be doing a lot of walking to see the sights—as well as one pair of more formal footwear. If visiting a church, dress respectably (a scarf or shirt is a useful cover-up) and remove your hat on entering.

Bring a light pair of binoculars to enjoy wildlife and landscape, and especially for details of architecture and decoration high up in churches, stately homes, etc.; a small medical kit; basic hiking gear if you are venturing into the mountains; and a camera.

## HOW TO GET TO BRITAIN

### PASSPORTS

For European Union citizens a valid passport or national identity card is required to enter the U.K. Nationals of other countries including the U.S., Canada, Australia, and New Zealand can also enter on only a passport (no visa is required).

### AIR

Scheduled services on all the world's major airlines fly into one of London's two main airports—Heathrow, just west of the capital, tel 0870-0000 123, or Gatwick, just south, tel 0870-0002 468. These are connected to central London by tube (Heathrow), rail (Gatwick), and bus services, as is the third and smallest of London's airports at Stansted, tel 0870-0000 303, in Essex. Journey times from these airports to central London are between 30 and 75 minutes.

British Airways is the national airline. For reservations in the U.K., tel 0870-850 9850; for reservations in the U.S., tel 800/403-0882.

Most sizable cities in Britain have their own regional airport not far away, with adequate transportation into town—often by taxi.

### SEA

It is still possible to cruise from the United States to Britain aboard a luxury liner. Most sea passengers, however, arrive from the Continent—chiefly France, Belgium, and Holland, with some service from Spain, Germany, and Scandinavia—to Plymouth, Poole, Southampton, Portsmouth, Newhaven, Folkestone, or Dover on the south coast. Services also run to Harwich (Essex) from the Hook of Holland, Hamburg (Germany) and Esbjerg (Denmark) to Hull (Humberside) from Zeebrugge (Belgium) and Rotterdam (Holland); to Newcastle upon Tyne from Ijmuiden (Holland), Hamburg (Germany), Gothenburg (Sweden), and Kristiansand, Stavanger and Bergen (Norway).

### RAIL

Trains run through the Channel Tunnel: Le Shuttle, tel 08705-353535, takes cars and passengers between Calais (France) and Folkestone (Kent) in 35 minutes, while the fast Eurostar passenger service, tel 08705-186186, connects Paris (3 hours), Lille (2 hours), and Brussels (2 hours, 40 minutes) with London's Waterloo Station.

## GETTING AROUND

### TRAVELING AROUND BRITAIN

**BY CAR**

**Renting a car**
Car rental in Britain can be on the expensive side, so you are well advised, if possible, to rent as part of an overall vacation package. To drive in Britain you need a current national driver's license, held for a minimum of one year. Many car-rental firms insist on a minimum driver age of 21.

The major international car-rental firms are all represented in Britain, with desks at the main airports and the biggest rail stations:

**Reservations**
Avis, tel 08705-900500
Budget, tel 0800-181181
  (toll-free)
Europcar, tel 08457-222525
Hertz, tel 08705-996699
Holiday Autos, tel 08705-300400
Thrifty, tel 08705-168238

**Motoring information**
Driving is on the left side of the

road. Remember to yield at roundabouts (traffic circles) to traffic coming from your right.

**Breakdown assistance** 24-hour breakdown coverage is offered by the Automobile Association (AA), tel 0800-887766, and the Royal Automobile Club (RAC), tel 0800-828282. You might consider joining either—their reasonably modest annual fee is a small price to pay for peace of mind while driving in Britain. Check first with your own motoring organization, as both AA and RAC have reciprocal agreements with many other organizations throughout the world. For advice on what to do in a traffic accident, see p. 341.

**Drink-driving** Drinking and driving is frowned upon both legally and socially, and the penalties for driving while over the limit are severe. The limit is currently 80mg of alcohol to 100ml of blood (about 1½ pints of medium-strength beer, one measure of spirits, or two glasses of medium-strength wine); but it's best to avoid alcohol entirely if you are driving.

**Parking** In Britain's crowded city centers parking is a problem. Where a "Park & Ride" plan has been established, you will have a more enjoyable and less anxious visit if you use it. This involves leaving your car in a parking lot on the outskirts of the town and taking a cheap, frequent bus service into the center. If you do take your own car into a major city, park in a designated parking lot; it's better to pay a small charge than risk having your car broken into, having to pay a fine, or being booted or even having your vehicle towed away if you park illegally. Double yellow lines at the side of the road forbid parking; single yellow lines restrict parking (see the notice displayed nearby for specific times of prohibition).
**Peak periods** In cities and larger towns the peak rush

hours (between 8 and 9:30 a.m. and 5 and 6:30 p.m. on weekdays) are best avoided.

**Road types** For getting around a good touring map is essential. On route maps, B roads are secondary roads; A roads (often two-lane) are main routes; roads marked with "M," followed by an identifying number, are motorways (freeways); while small, unclassified roads criss-cross rural areas.

**Seat belts** Front seat belts must be worn, and rear belts if they are fitted to the car.

**Speed Limits**
Speed limits (increasingly enforced by speed cameras) are 30 mph in built-up areas, 60 mph on highways, and 70 mph on two- to four-lane highways and freeways.

**Motorcyclists**
Motorcyclists are obliged to wear a helmet.

## BY TRAIN
Now privatized into 25 separate companies, the railroads are a worry-free and fast way to get around. There are two classes of travel: standard class and first class, which costs about one-third more. Generally round-trip (particularly same-day round-trip) fares are cheaper than two one-way tickets. Many saver tickets are available—the further ahead you book, the cheaper they are. Travel is cheaper after 9:30 a.m. Mon.–Fri. Ask about discounts for young, for elderly, and for travelers with disabilities, as well as full-time students.

Telephone 08457-484950 for all train information. A BritRail Pass saves money if you are traveling extensively, but can only be bought by non-Europeans in their own country. Contact your local British Tourist Authority (BTA) office (see p. 341) for details.

## BY BUS
Travel by long-distance express

bus is half the cost of rail travel, and can take up to twice as long on busy routes (especially into and out of London). National Express, tel 08705-808080 is the national company. There are also literally hundreds of small, private bus companies running vehicles all over Britain. Ask at the local visitor information center for details; or buy the *Great Britain Bus Timetable*, published twice a year by Southern Vectis, Nelson Road, Newport, Isle of Wight, Hampshire PO30 1RD, tel 01983-522456. Transport Marketing, 15 Station Road, Knowle, Solihull, West Midlands B93 0HL, tel 01564-771901 produces the free *Scenic Britain by Bus* providing information on bus services in holiday locations.

## BY TAXI
Taxis will take you from provincial towns out to any obscure corner of the land. Expect to pay a little over £1 (approx. $1.50) per mile, and double it for the taxi's empty journey back home after dropping you off. For journeys of more than about 20 miles, you can negotiate a fare. Don't forget the obligatory ten percent tip.

## BY AIR
Britain's size means that internal air travel is only worth considering over longish distances, for example from London to Scotland, or for easier access to many of the offshore islands. British Airways, tel 0870-850 9850, and several smaller airlines compete for business between regional airports—for example, Birmingham, Bristol, Cardiff, Edinburgh, Glasgow, Inverness, Liverpool, Manchester, and Newcastle. Small planes serve the numerous Scottish islands that possess an airstrip. Always shop around for the best ticket deal, as the cheapest can be several times cheaper than the most expensive.

## ORGANIZED TOURS & SIGHTSEEING

Organized tours around the chief visitor attractions do not do justice to a country as small and diverse as Britain, where it is the odd corners that contain the best secrets. Better to explore for yourself, by car or public transportation. But you might consider joining one of the guided walks that visitor information centers organize around their historic town centers.

## WALKING

Britain is superb walking territory. There are several National Trails that introduce you to wide tracts of country—these include the 256-mile Pennine Way up the spine of northern England, the South West Coast Path that runs approximately 600 miles around the toe-tip of Britain, the 110-mile Cleveland Way around North Yorkshire's moors and coasts, the Thames Path that follows the River Thames for 175 miles from source to mouth, the Offa's Dyke path running 168 miles along the beautiful Welsh borders, and the 95-mile West Highland Way from Milngavie, near Glasgow, north into the Scottish mountains. In addition, there are scores of less well-marked trails, and hundreds of thousands of miles of walking on designated rights of way.

### Recommended books

Bookstores around the country stock a huge array of walking guide books. The most comprehensive selections can be obtained from:
**Stanfords** 12–14 Long Acre, Covent Garden, London WC2E 9LP, tel 020-7836 1321.
**Ramblers' Association** 2nd Floor, Camelford House, 87–90 Albert embankment, London SE1 7TW, tel 020-7339 8500. This 100,000-strong association provides comprehensive information and advice on walking in Britain.

A recommended selection of guidebooks includes:

*Country Walks Near London* by Christopher Somerville (Simon & Schuster)
*Discovering Walks in the Cotswolds* by Ronald Kershaw and Brian Robson (Shire Publications)
*Walks in the Country Near London* by Christopher Somerville (New Holland)
*The Thames Path* by David Sharp (Aurum Press)

## GETTING AROUND LONDON

Forget driving a car around London—you would be quicker walking. The famous black taxi-cabs and red buses, allied to the very comprehensive underground rail network known as "the Tube," will get you everywhere you want to go. Each tube station is clearly identified by its distinctive circular red-and-blue logo. The 12 tube lines are color-coded and maps are posted at every station. The system is divided into six zones (zone 1 is central London). Fares depend on how many zones you cross and can be expensive. Good value if you have several journeys to make is a One Day Travelcard offering unlimited travel after 9:30 a.m. Monday to Friday and all day weekends and public holidays on bus, train, and tube services within chosen zones. It can be bought at tube stations, National Rail stations in the London area, information centers, and newsstands. For information on times, fares, and journey planning of bus, tube, train and riverboat services call 020-7222 1234 (24 hours). Arm yourself with the *London A–Z* street map guidebook, widely available from newsstands.

# PRACTICAL ADVICE

## COMMUNICATIONS

### POST OFFICES

Open 9 a.m.–5:30 p.m. Mon.–Fri. and 9 a.m.–1 p.m. Sat. In villages, they are often operated on the same premises as a general store. Buy postage stamps here: One price sends a letter to all European destinations outside of the UK. Rates to the United States are a little more. Within Britain, first class arrives the next day, second class takes two or three days.

### MAILBOXES

Mailboxes are red and may be freestanding or attached to a wall. Details of collection times are displayed on the mailbox.

### TELEPHONES

Calls are relatively cheap, and cheaper still between 6 p.m. and 8 a.m., and on weekends. Phone booths may be old scarlet beauties, or new plastic uglies. Coin phones take 10p, 20p, 50p, and £1 coins (20p is the minimum to make a call). Unused coins will be refunded, though if you insert a large-value coin and do not use up the money you will not get any money back—for this reason it is better to have several smaller denomination coins at hand and keep "feeding" the phone. Many phones though are now equipped for phonecards (buy them from post offices, and stores displaying a green 'phonecard' sign). Avoid the hotel room telephone: The markup is ludicrously high.

**Useful telephone numbers**
U.K. Operator 100
International Operator 155
U.K. Directory Inquiries 118500 (free from public phone booths)
International Directory Inquiries 118866 (free from public phone booths)

**Using the telephone**
To telephone the U.K. from the U.S.: Dial 011, then drop the first 0 of the area code, followed by the number.

To telephone abroad from the U.K.: Dial the international code 00, then the national code (1 for the U.S. and Canada; 61 for Australia; 64 for New Zealand), then the area code (minus any initial 0), followed by the sub-scriber's number.

Numbers prefixed by 0800 and 0808 are free calls.
Numbers prefixed by 0845 are cheap, local-rate calls.
Numbers prefixed by 0870 are national-rate calls.
Numbers prefixed by 0900, 0901, 0906, 0907 and 0909 are expensive, premium rate calls.

## CONVERSIONS

Britain, though officially metricated with the rest of Europe, has many imperial measures still in common use. Road distances, for example, are in miles and beer is sold by the pint (the imperial pint is 20 percent larger than the U.S. measure). The major concessions are that gas is now sold in liters (1 liter = 0.2624 U.S. gallon) and loose food is sold in kilograms (2.2 pounds).

**Women's clothing**

| U.S. | 6 | 8 | 10 | 12 | 14 | 16 |
|------|---|---|----|----|----|----|
| U.K. | 8 | 10 | 12 | 14 | 16 | 18 |

**Men's clothing**

| U.S. | 36 | 38 | 40 | 42 | 44 | 46 |
|------|----|----|----|----|----|----|
| U.K. | 36 | 38 | 40 | 42 | 44 | 46 |

**Women's shoes**

| U.S. | 6 | 6½ | 7 | 7½ | 8 | 8½ |
|------|---|----|---|----|---|----|
| U.K. | 4½ | 5 | 5½ | 6 | 6½ | 7 |

**Men's shoes**

| U.S. | 8 | 8½ | 9½ | 10½ | 11½ | 12 |
|------|---|----|----|-----|-----|----|
| U.K. | 7 | 7½ | 8½ | 9½ | 10½ | 11 |

## ELECTRICITY

Britain's electrical current is 240V, 50-cycle A/C. U.S. appli-ances require a voltage trans-former (unless dual-voltage capable) and an adapter.

## ETIQUETTE & LOCAL CUSTOMS

Britain brings together three very different countries: England, Scotland, and Wales—each with its own very different

cultural heritage. Be careful never to refer to England if you mean all of Britain, or worse still, speak of everywhere else in Britain as if it were a suburb of London—you will offend those living outside England or London if you do. The British (the English especially) have a reputation for being reserved. While a generalization it has a basis in truth. This is not to say that they are unfriendly, just that they take more time to warm up! Some visitors find that people get more friendly the farther north they go—this may be true. In general the British need more personal space around them than, say, Americans, but if you respect this you should fit in well.

## MEDIA

### NEWSPAPERS
Daily tabloid papers are small, cheap, and scandal-rich. Low-level are *The Sun*, *The Mirror*, *Daily Star*, and *The Sport*. In the middle ground are the tabloids *Daily Mail* and *Daily Express*. Broadsheets contain weightier matter: *The Daily Telegraph*, *The Times*, *The Independent*, and *The Guardian*. Most of these papers have special Sunday editions.

### TELEVISION
Britain offers five terrestrial channels: the two BBC channels (BBC1 and BBC2), and the commercials (ITV, Channel 4, and Channel 5). The BBC continues to lead the field in quality. Best viewing are docu-mentaries, news and current affairs, wildlife programs, cos-tume drama and modern plays, and alternative comedy. Cable has arrived or is on its way; satellite has already landed.

### RADIO
Here, too, the BBC leads the field with Radio 1 (pop music on 97.6–99.8 MHz FM), Radio 2 (easy listening on 88–91 MHz FM), Radio 3 (classical music and serious talks on 90.2–92.4 MHz

FM), Radio 4 (features, conversation, discussion, plays, news on 92.4–94.6 MHz FM, 198 kHz LW and 909 kHz), and Radio 5 (light news and sports on 693 and 909 kHz MW). Many commercial and local stations are on air, too.

## MONEY MATTERS

British currency is figured in pounds sterling (£) and pence (p): £1=100p. Coins come in denominations of 1 and 2 pence (bronze), 5, 10, 20, and 50 pence (silver), and 1 and 2 pounds and the rare 5 pounds (gold-colored); banknotes in amounts of 1 (Scotland only), 5, 10, 20, and 50 pounds. Scotland's bank notes differ from those of England and Wales, but they are legal tender throughout the U.K. Avoid any chance of difficulties by changing these before you cross the border coming south.

Most major credit cards are accepted in main centers, but always carry some cash with you, especially in the more remote areas and smaller towns. Cashpoints (Automatic Teller Machines, or ATMs) are installed in the outer walls as well as the inside of most banks and building societies.

Traveler's checks are the safest alternative to carrying around large amounts of cash. They can be exchanged at most banks, bureaux de change, and larger travel agencies such as American Express and Thomas Cook. If you have traveler's checks in pounds sterling they can also be used like cash at most hotels, restaurants, and large stores.

Rates of exchange are posted in all banks and main post offices (for general opening times, see p. 340), and at bureaux de change, which are at airports, major railroad stations, good travel agents, and the bigger hotels.

## NATIONAL HOLIDAYS

Also known as Public or Bank Holidays—on these days banks, offices, and most shops, restaurants, museums, and attractions close:
January 1 (New Year's Day)
January 2 (Bank Holiday in Scotland only)
Good Friday
Easter Monday (not Scotland)
May Bank Holiday (1st Mon. in May)
Spring Bank Holiday (last Mon. in May)
Summer Bank Holiday— Scotland (1st Mon. in Aug.)
Summer Bank Holiday—England and Wales (last Mon. in Aug.)
December 25 (Christmas Day)
December 26 (Boxing Day)

### OTHER DAYS OF NATIONAL CELEBRATION

On these days places do not close:
**Britain** November 5 (Guy Fawkes Day, or Bonfire Night)
**England** April 23 (St. George's Day, patron saint)
**Scotland** January 25 (Burns Night); November 30 (St. Andrew's Day, patron saint)
**Wales** March 1 (St. David's Day, patron saint)

## NATIONAL TRUST

Many of Britain's historic buildings, parks, gardens, and expanses of countryside and coastline are administered by the National Trust (NT) or the National Trust for Scotland (NTS). Many NT and NTS properties have special architectural or historical interest and are protected from alteration or demolition. NT and NTS properties are identified within the main text.

## OPENING TIMES

Opening times may vary from place to place, but a general indication is given below:
**Stores** 9 or 10 a.m.–5:30 p.m. or 6 p.m. Mon.–Sat., Sun. 10 a.m.– 4 p.m.

**Large supermarkets** 8 a.m.–8 p.m. Mon.–Sat.; 10 a.m.–4 p.m. Sun.
**Pubs** 11 a.m.–11 p.m. Mon.–Sat. (some close 3 p.m.–5:30 p.m.); noon–3 p.m. and 7 p.m.–10:30 p.m., Sun. (some open noon– 10:30 p.m.), in Scotland 12:30 p.m.–2:30 p.m. and 6:30 p.m.– 11 p.m.
**Post offices** 9 a.m.–5:30 p.m. Mon.–Fri.; 9 a.m.–1 p.m. Sat.
**Banks** 9:30 a.m.–3:30 p.m. Mon.–Fri.; some also 9:30 a.m.– 12:30 p.m. Sat., and Mon.–Fri. until 4:30 or 5:30 p.m. in bigger towns.
**Gas stations** Most big cities have at least one 24-hour station; most freeway service stations are open 24 hours.
**Parish churches** Places of worship are often kept locked to guard against theft.

## THE PET SCHEME

The PETS (Pet Travel Scheme) allows owners of cats and dogs from certain countries (including most European countries, USA, Canada, Australia, New Zealand, and others) to bring their pets into UK without quarantine, provided they have been microchipped, vaccinated, blood-tested, treated against tapeworms and ticks, and issued with official documentation. Pets must enter UK from another PETS country by an authorized route and with an approved transport company.

Full details of the scheme are available on the PETS helpline, tel 00-44 (0)870 241 1710, or at www.defra.gov.uk/animalh/ quarantine.

## PLACES OF WORSHIP

The Church of England and the Church of Scotland (equating to the American Episcopalian and Presbyterian churches respectively) have historically been the predominant religions in Britain—essentially Protestant. In today's multicultural society, religious observance is probably

stricter and keener among other groups. Inquire at the local visitor information center to find which denominations are represented in the area and for times of services.

## REST ROOMS

Rest rooms can be found in train stations, on main streets of towns, in big stores, and hotels; also in all pubs and restaurants. Standards are usually good. (Ten or twenty pence entrance may be charged.)

## TIME DIFFERENCES

Greenwich mean time (GMT) operates from the last Sunday in October to the last Sunday in March; British Summer Time (BST)—for which the clocks are put forward by one hour—for the rest of the year.

## TIPPING

Add ten percent to the bill in restaurants, if a service charge has not already been added. Taxi drivers expect a ten percent tip. Do not tip bar staff in a pub, although the offer of a drink instead is appreciated. Hairdressers should be tipped ten percent and luggage porters 50p to £1. Do not tip theater or movie ushers.

## TRAVELERS WITH DISABILITIES

In general, modern buildings, taxis, trains, and buses (post-1985) are wheelchair friendly. Many historic attractions such as castles and stately houses present problems to wheelchair users. There are reserved seats for travelers with disabilities on buses, tube trains, and rail cars; there is also reserved parking near the entrance of most supermarkets and many public buildings and visitor attractions.

Hearing-impaired travelers will find audioloop facilities in banks, telephone booths, and other places where the ear logo is displayed.

Reduced fares on public transportation are available. For advice on all matters connected with vacationing in Britain, contact:
**RADAR** (Royal Association for Disability and Rehabilitation), 12 City Forum, 250 City Road, London EC1V 8AF, tel 020-7250 3222
**Holiday Care Service,** 2nd Floor, Imperial Buildings, Victoria Road, Horley, Surrey RH6 7PZ, tel 01293-774535

Visitor information centers can advise on local conditions.

## VISITOR INFORMATION

BTA (British Tourist Authority) maintains several offices abroad. These include:
**Australia** Level 16, Gateway, 1 Macquarie Place, Sydney, NSW 2000, tel 02-9377 4400
**Canada** 5915 Airport Road, Suite 120, Mississauga, Ontario L4V 1T1, tel 905/405-1840 or 888/847-4885
**Ireland** 18–19 College Green, Dublin 2, tel 01-670 8000
**Japan** Akaska Twin Tower 1F, 2-17-22 Akaska, Minato-ku, Tokyo, tel 03-5562 2546
**Netherlands** Aurora Gebouw (5e), Stadhouderskade 2, 1054 ES Amsterdam, tel 020-689-0002
**New Zealand** 17th floor, Fay Richwhite Building, 151 Queen Street, Auckland 1, tel 09-303 1446
**Sweden** Klara Norra Kyrkogata 29, S-111 22 Stockholm (visitors); Box 3102, 103 62 Stockholm (mail), tel 08-4401 700
**United States** 7th Floor, 551 Fifth Avenue, Suite 701, New York, New York 10176-0799, tel 212/986-2200 or 800/462-2748

## NATIONAL TOURIST BOARDS
**Britain and England**
VisitBritain, Thames Tower, Black's Road, Hammersmith, London W6 9EL, tel 020-8846 9000

Also try the Britain and London Visitor Centre, 1 Regent Street, London SW1Y 4XT (no telephone inquiries).
**Scotland** VisitScotland, 23 Ravelston Terrace, Edinburgh EH4 3TP, tel 0131-332 2433
**Wales** VisitWales, Brunel House, 2 Fitzalan Road, Cardiff CF24 0UY; mailing address Department GE1, PO Box 1, Cardiff CF24 2XN, tel 0870-121 1251

BTA produces a map guide with the location, address, and telephone number of every local visitor information center in Britain.

# EMERGENCIES

## CRIME & POLICE

Britain is a safe place to visit, given the precautions that travelers anywhere need to take against being alone in isolated places after dark. Pickpockets and car thieves are the chief problem, and the remedies are obvious: Guard your wallet and open bags in crowded places, and don't leave valuables in your car. The police in their characteristic dark blue helmets (police-women in caps) are unarmed and helpful with any inquiry.

**Emergency phone numbers** 999 for police, ambulance, fire, and coastguard

## WHAT TO DO IN A TRAFFIC ACCIDENT

If you are involved in a road traffic accident with another vehicle in which no one has been injured, simply exchange names, telephone numbers, and insurance details. If you are driving a rented vehicle, phone the rental company and explain what has happened.

In the event of an accident that involves injury, call the police (tel 999) immediately.

## LOST PROPERTY

Report any lost property to the nearest police station (don't forget to obtain a report signed by the duty officer if you intend to make a claim on your insurance company); or to the appropriate company if the loss occurs on public transportation.

## LOST OR STOLEN CREDIT CARDS

You should cancel any lost or stolen credit cards by calling the following emergency numbers:
American Express, tel 01273-696933
Diners Club, tel 0800-460800 (toll-free)
MasterCard/Eurocard, tel 0800-964767 (toll-free)
Visa, tel 0800-891725 (toll-free)

## HEALTH

Valid travel and health insurance is advised. No vaccinations are needed for entry to Britain. National Health Service (N.H.S.) health care is free to all EU nationals, and N.H.S. care is available to all in an emergency. A qualifying form (available from health departments of EU countries) enables EU nationals to claim back their expense. Other nationals should take out insurance to cover medical expenses. Emergency dental treatment may be chargeable—some dentists are N.H.S., most are not.

Tap water is safe to drink everywhere.

## PHARMACIES

Known as chemists, pharmacies stock standard remedies and dispense doctors' prescriptions; pharmacists can give advice. In larger towns chemists operate a late-evening roster system.

# HOTELS & RESTAURANTS

Accommodations in Britain come in all shapes and sizes to suit every taste, from mansion hotels to tiny cottages with only a few rooms; facilities and standards are reflected in the prices.

During the last 20 years or so, food in Britain has improved enormously, and wherever you go you will find a wide variety of restaurants, particularly in the cities, where the choice is far more cosmopolitan. Many hotels have their own restaurants and some restaurants also have rooms to rent.

The following is a recommended selection of the most comfortable, interesting, and welcoming places in which to stay and eat in Britain, from a luxury hotel in London to a country inn in the Lake District, and from foie gras to fish and chips.

### Hotels

Many hotels offer "half-board" accommodations, which includes breakfast and dinner, while "full board" includes lunch as well. Wherever possible the hotels chosen are both individual and typical, perhaps with notable local or historic associations. Always try to reserve in advance, particularly in high season; you may be asked for a deposit or credit card. The hotels listed in this guide are graded from two to five stars, according to the Automobile Association (AA) rating system. This is what you might expect:

★★ May be group- or proprietor-owned. Rooms are small to medium in size and at least half the bedrooms will have a private bath/shower. There may also be telephone and television.

★★★ Usually more spacious rooms with a greater range of facilities and services, including full reception facilities as well as a more formal restaurant and bar. All bedrooms have private bathrooms.

★★★★ Accommodations are more spacious, offering high standards of comfort and food. All bedrooms will have private facilities (both bath and shower).

★★★★★ Large luxury hotels offering the highest international standards.

Red Stars (★), ranging from one to five, are awarded to hotels recognized for excellence within their star rating for consistent, outstanding levels of hospitality, service, food, and comfort.

Please note that, **unless otherwise stated:**
1. Breakfast is included in the price.
2. The hotel has a restaurant.
3. All rooms have a telephone and television.
4. Room prices are given only for guidance and do not take into account seasonal variations.
5. Prices given are per (double) room.

### Bed & Breakfast (B&B)

These types of accommodations are a specialty in Britain. They are usually small, informal establishments, generally inexpensive and well run, and may also suit travelers who want to get more of a feel of local life. As the name suggests, prices include a room and breakfast (served in a communal room at a fixed time in the morning).

The B&Bs included in this directory are high-quality establishments. They may be a guesthouse, farmhouse, or inn with outstanding levels of accommodations and service, with the emphasis on quality and a friendly, hospitable atmosphere.

### Restaurants

The following selection aims to recommend good regional restaurants offering typical local dishes, as well those featuring inventive fare reflecting foreign influences. Most restaurants offer a fixed-price menu, sometimes including wine. Otherwise (and usually more expensively) you order separate items à la carte.

---

## PRICES

**HOTELS**
An indication of the cost of a double room with breakfast is given by **$** signs.

| | |
|---|---|
| **$$$$$** | Over $300 |
| **$$$$** | $220–$300 |
| **$$$** | $160–$220 |
| **$$** | $100–$160 |
| **$** | Under $100 |

**RESTAURANTS**
An indication of the cost of a three-course dinner without drinks is given by $ signs.

| | |
|---|---|
| **$$$$$** | Over $80 |
| **$$$$** | $50–$80 |
| **$$$** | $35–$50 |
| **$$** | $20–$35 |
| **$** | Under $20 |

Restaurants are awarded from one to five rosettes, according to the AA rating system. In this selection, where a restaurant has rosettes, this is indicated by the ❀ symbol. You should expect the following:

❀ Chefs must be able to produce good quality meals using fresh ingredients.

❀❀ Dishes must reflect technical skill, ability in balancing ingredients, and make use of seasonal produce.

❀❀❀ Cuisine must be of the highest standard, imaginative, accurately cooked, demonstrating well-developed technical skills and flair.

❀❀❀❀ At this level the cooking must be innovative, highly accomplished, and achieve noteworthy standards of consistency, accuracy, and flair.

❀❀❀❀❀ Superb standards of cuisine at an international level. Faultlessly presented dishes cooked to perfection with intense, exotic flavors and using luxurious ingredients (with imaginative flair of experienced and accomplished chefs).

L = lunch, D = dinner
Please note that awards and ratings may change during the currency of the guide.

---

**KEY**  🏨 Hotel  🍴 Restaurant  🛏 No. of bedrooms  💺 No. of seats  🚇 Tube  🅿 Parking  🕐 Closed  ⬆ Elevator

**HOTELS & RESTAURANTS**

## Dining hours in Britain
Lunch usually starts around noon and continues until 2 p.m. Dinner may be eaten any time between 7 p.m. and 9 p.m. In peak season, or if you have a special place in mind, do make a reservation.

## Credit cards
Most larger hotels and restaurants accept all major credit cards; smaller ones may only accept one or two, and bed-and-breakfast establishments may require checks or cash. The abbreviations used in this section are: AE–American Express; DC–Diner's Club; MC–Mastercard; and V–Visa

## Tipping
In a restaurant or hotel a service charge is normally included in the bill. Where it is not, you are expected to leave a tip of between 10 and 15 percent, although this is at your own discretion and depends on the quality of service.

## Travelers with disabilities
Facilities for visitors with special needs can vary considerably. If you have special requirements it is always best to check by telephoning in advance.

**LONDON**

**THE CITY**

🏨 **MALMAISON CHARTERHOUSE SQUARE**
$$$ ★★★ ⊛
18-21 CHARTERHOUSE SQ.
CLERKENWELL
EC1M 6AH
TEL 020-7012 3700
FAX 020-7012 3702
A fine, comfortable hotel in a completely refurbished, elegant old building on a quiet square.
🛏 97 🚇 Barbican 🔁 🅂
🅰 🅆 🅂 All major cards

🍴 **RESTAURANT TWENTYFOUR**
$$$ ⊛
TOWER 42 OLD BROAD ST.
EC2N 1HQ
TEL 020-7877 7703/2424

FAX 020-7877 7742
You can enjoy views of Tower Bridge and the Millennium Dome from this modern restaurant located in the heart of the city. Try the breast of cannette duck with red onion Tatin.
🍴 70 🚇 Bank/Liverpool Street 🕐 Closed Sat. & Sun.
🅂 🅰 All major cards

**WESTMINSTER & THE WEST END**

🏨 **BROWN'S**
$$$$$ ★★★★⊛⊛
ALBEMARLE ST.
MAYFAIR
W1X 4BP
TEL 020-7493 6020
FAX 020-7493 9381
Closed for major refurbishment until spring 2005
Exclusive English elegance in the heart of London's Mayfair, with a traditional country-house feeling. Restaurant offers innovative menus using the best seasonal ingredients.
🛏 118 🍴 70 🚇 Green Park 🔁 🅂 All major cards

🏨 **DORCHESTER**
$$$$$ ★★★★★ ⊛⊛⊛
PARK LANE
W1A 2HJ
TEL 020-7629 8888
FAX 020-7409 0114
One of the world's finest hotels, sumptuously furnished. Traditional British food in The Grill, exotic Cantonese dishes in The Oriental. Discreet, friendly management and staff provide exceptional service.
🛏 250 🍴 81 (Grill) 🍴 51 (Oriental) 🚇 Hyde Park Corner 🅿 21 🔁 🅂 🅆
🅂 All major cards

🏨 **GORING**
$$$$$ ★★★★★ ⊛⊛
BEESTON PLACE
GROSVENOR GARDENS
SW1W 0JW
TEL 020-7396 9000
FAX 020-7834 4393
Personal hospitality and service by the Goring family, owners since 1910. Bedrooms

are comfortable and have modern facilities. The restaurant features well-loved traditional British dishes such as grilled Dover sole, lobster thermidor, skate with capers, roast rump of lamb, and steak and kidney pie.
🛏 74 🍴 60 🚇 Victoria 🅿 8 🔁 🅂 🅂 All major cards

🏨 **HALKIN**
$$$$$ ★★★★ ⊛⊛⊛
HALKIN ST.
BELGRAVIA
SW1X 7DJ
TEL 020-7333 1000
FAX 020-7333 1100
Individualistic hotel with classically influenced, modern Italian design. Bedrooms are designed with the principles of Feng shui foremost. Attentive and professional service in a relaxed atmosphere.
🛏 41 🍴 45 🚇 Hyde Park Corner 🔁 🅂 🅆 🅂 All major cards

🏨 **LE MERIDIEN PICCADILLY**
$$$$$ ★★★★★ ⊛⊛⊛
21 PICCADILLY
W1V 0BH
TEL 0870-400 8400
FAX 020-7437 3574
Well-established, French-influenced hotel close to Piccadilly Circus. Splendid food in Marco Pierre White's The Oak Room restaurant. Pampering in style at Champney's Health Club.
🛏 267 🍴 80 🚇 Piccadilly Circus 🔁 🅂 🈁 🅆
🅆 🅂 All major cards

🏨 **RITZ**
$$$$$ ★★★★★ ⊛⊛
150 PICCADILLY
W1V 9DG
TEL 020-7493 8181
FAX 020-7493 2687
A legend among great hotels with magnificent decor. This hotel has one of the most romantic dining rooms in the country—murals of swooning maidens, gilt ornamentation

**HOTELS & RESTAURANTS**

everywhere, waiters gliding to music from the grand piano. Fixed-price L.

**(i)** 131 **(seats)** 120 **(Tube)** Green Park **(Elevator)** **(s)** **(closed)** **(s)** All major cards

## SOMETHING SPECIAL

### 🏨 SAVOY 🍴

One of the country's leading hotels. High standards of comfort and quality; famous art deco design features. The bathrooms at the Savoy are wondrous to behold in gleaming marble and white, dazzling chrome—and even better to use, with their huge tubs and famous thunderstorm showers. Renowned River Restaurant with executive chef Anton Edelmann; afternoon tea a highlight for both hotel residents and visitors. Tennis at the Vanderbilt Club.

$$$$$ ★★★★★
🌢🌢
STRAND
WC2R 0EU
TEL 020-7836 4343
FAX 020-7240 6040

**(i)** 263 **(seats)** 150 **(Tube)** Charing Cross **(P)** 65 **(Elevator)** **(s)** **(s)** **(s)** All major cards

### 🏨 SHERATON PARK 🍴 TOWER

$$$$$ ★★★★★ 🌢🌢🌢
101 KNIGHTSBRIDGE
SW1X 7RN
TEL 020-7235 8050
FAX 020-7235 8231

Unique circular modern hotel with splendid London views. No need to tie up your own shoelaces or fix your own drink here. In return for a (considerable) supplement, you can enjoy the luxury of a full butler service. *Cuisine de mer* by chef Pascal Proyart at 101 restaurant. Health facilities at affiliated club.

**(i)** 280 **(seats)** 64 **(Tube)** Knightsbridge **(P)** 67 **(Elevator)** **(s)** All major cards

### 🏨 STRAND PALACE

$$$$$ ★★★
STRAND
WC2R 0JJ
TEL 020-7836 8080
FAX 020-7836 2077

Well placed for theaters and the City. Club-floor bedrooms have added luxuries and use of an exclusive lounge. Bars and restaurants include Italian bistro and café-bar, also 372 The Strand (international menu and buffet).

**(i)** 783 **(Tube)** Charing Cross/Covent Garden **(Elevator)** **(s)** All major cards

### 🏨 WASHINGTON MAYFAIR

$$$$$ ★★★★
5–7 CURZON ST.
MAYFAIR
W1J 5HE
TEL 020-7499 7000
FAX 020-7495 6172

Classy hotel, attractively furnished in burred oak, marble, and wood paneling.

**(i)** 173 **(Tube)** Green Park **(Elevator)** **(s)** **(s)** All major cards

### 🏨 RUBENS AT THE PALACE

$$$$ ★★★★ 🌢🌢
BUCKINGHAM PALACE RD.
SW1W 0PS
TEL 020-7834 6600
FAX 020-7233 6037

Enviable location overlooking the Royal Mews behind Buckingham Palace. Well appointed, comfortable hotel. Two restaurants, extensive lounge menu.

**(i)** 173 **(Tube)** Victoria **(Elevator)** **(s)** **(s)** All major cards

### 🏨 THISTLE LANCASTER GATE

$$$$
75 LANCASTER GATE
W2 3NN
TEL 0870-333 9115
FAX 0870-333 9215

Busy hotel in a Victorian row. Suite available; interconnecting family rooms, and ground-floor accommodations for guests with disabilities. Summer barbecues in gardens.

**(i)** 390 **(Tube)** Queensway/ Lancaster Gate **(Elevator)** **(s)** All major cards

### 🍴 LINDSAY HOUSE RESTAURANT

$$$$ 🌢🌢🌢
21 ROMILLY ST.
W1V 5TG
TEL 020-7439 0450

Diners can expect cutting-edge cuisine in an elegant Georgian townhouse.

**(seats)** 50 **(Tube)** Leicester Square **(closed)** Closed L Sat.–Sun., 1 week Easter, 1 week Christmas **(s)** All major cards

### 🍴 LA PORTE DES INDES

$$$$ 🌢🌢
32 BRYANSTON ST.
W1H 7AE
TEL 020-7224 0055
FAX 020-7224 1144

A beautiful, extravagantly decorated restaurant serving high quality Indian cuisine. Set on two magnificent floors it features a 40-foot-high marble waterfall cascading down between carved stone balustrades. Fixed-price L & D

**(seats)** 300 **(Tube)** Marble Arch **(closed)** Closed Sat. L, Dec. 25 L. **(s)** **(s)** All major cards

### 🍴 MIRABELLE

$$$$ 🌢🌢🌢
56 CURZON ST.
W1Y 8DL
TEL 020-7499 4636
FAX 020-7499 5449

This Mayfair restaurant boasts a stylish bar, old parquet flooring and stone-colored vases full of flowers. Try the roast duck Montmorency, fumet of vin de Banyals. Very good wine list.

**(seats)** 110 **(Tube)** Green Park **(s)** All major cards

### 🍴 THE IVY

$$$$ 🌢🌢
1 WEST ST.
COVENT GARDEN
WC2H 9NQ
TEL 020-7836 4751

Immaculate service, unpretentious, with a lively atmosphere. The cooking, influenced by French brasserie style, reveals a welcome directness and includes English favorites among other global dishes. Fixed-price L.

🔢 100 🚇 Covent Garden/ Leicester Square 🕐 Closed Dec. 24–26, Jan. 1 🔲
🔲 All major cards

## 🍴 THE SQUARE
**$$$$** 🟢🟢🟢
6–10 BRUTON ST.
MAYFAIR
W1X 7AG
TEL 020-7495 7100
Exciting cooking—short but well-balanced modern French menu. Luxury ingredients, and all produce is of exceptional quality. Fixed-price D.
🔢 70 🚇 Green Park 🕐 Closed Sat. L, Sun. L, Dec. 24–26 🔲 🔲 All major cards

## 🍴 CHEZ MAX
**$$$** 🟢🟢
3 YEOMAN'S ROW,
BROMPTON RD.
SW3 2AL
TEL 020-7590 9999
Wears its Gallic heart on its sleeve. Although discreet, there is a definite bistro atmosphere, but the cooking is consistently a few notches above that level. Fixed-price D.
🔢 50 🚇 Earl's Court 🕐 Closed L & Sun. 🔲 All major cards

## 🍴 COTTO
**$$** 🟢
44 BLYTHE ROAD
W14 0HA
TEL 020-7602 9333
Placed as it is on a quiet back street, this restaurant has a pleasant local atmosphere. Interesting modern British menu at a reasonable price.
🔢 65 🚇 Kensington (Olympia) 🕐 Closed L Sat. & Sun. 🔲 All major cards

BLOOMSBURY

## 🏨 THE BONNINGTON IN BLOOMSBURY
**$$$$** ★★★
92 SOUTHAMPTON ROW
WC1B 4BH
TEL 020-7242 2828
FAX 020-7831 9170
This Late Edwardian hotel is centrally located with easy access to the West End theaters. Rooms are comfortable and well equipped; some are suitable for families. Air-conditioned Waterfalls Restaurant.
🛈 215 🚇 Russell Square/ Holborn 🔲 🔲 🔲 All major cards

## 🍴 HAKKASAN
**$$$$$** 🟢🟢🟢
8 HANWAY PL.
W1T 9DH
TEL 020-7929 7000
Don't be put off by the exterior; inside it is stylish and very chic. Try a perfect cocktail before a Chinese meal of rare delicacy.
🔢 130 🚇 Tottenham Court Road 🔲 All major cards

KNIGHTSBRIDGE & KENSINGTON

## 🏨 ROYAL GARDEN
## 🍴 HOTEL
**$$$$$** ★★★★★ 🟢🟢🟢
2–24 KENSINGTON HIGH ST.
W8 4PT
TEL 020-7937 8000
FAX 020-7361 1991
This modern hotel, with views over Kensington Gardens and Hyde Park, offers very high levels of service and comfort. The bright, contemporary restaurant serves International cuisine.
🛈 398 🔢 100 🚇 Kensington High Street 🅿 160 🔲 🔲 🔲 🔲 All major cards

## 🏨 THE MILLENNIUM
## 🍴 KNIGHTSBRIDGE
**$$$$$** ★★★★ 🟢🟢🟢
17 SLOANE ST.
KNIGHTSBRIDGE

SW1X 9NU
TEL 020-7235 4377
FAX 020-7235 3705
Sloane Street hotel near world-famous Harrods and Harvey Nichols stores. The restaurant serves modern, cleverly crafted, confident dishes.
🛈 222 🔢 100 🚇 Knightsbridge 🅿 7 🔲 🔲 🔲 All major cards

## 🏨 HOGARTH
**$$$$** ★★★
33 HOGARTH RD.
KENSINGTON
SW5 0QQ
TEL 020-7370 6831
FAX 020-7373 6179
Modern hotel with resident manager and genuinely friendly and helpful staff.
🛈 85 🚇 Earl's Court 🅿 20 🔲 🔲 All major cards

## 🏨 VENCOURT
**$$$** ★★★
255 KING ST.
HAMMERSMITH
W6 9LU
TEL 020-8563 8855
FAX 020-8563 9988
Modern hotel on 12 floors; great views over the city. Lounge/bar and restaurant.
🛈 120 🚇 Hammersmith/ Ravenscourt Park 🅿 27 🔲 🔲 All major cards

## 🍴 BIBENDUM
**$$$$$** 🟢🟢
MICHELIN HOUSE
81 FULHAM RD.
SW3 6RD
TEL 020-7581 5817
The best brasserie food of its kind in the capital. The atmosphere fizzes with life, tables are often turned around three times in a session, and you need to make reservations weeks ahead. Fixed-price L.
🔢 72 🚇 South Kensington 🔲 🔲 All major cards

## 🍴 THE CAPITAL
**$$$$$** 🟢🟢🟢🟢
BASIL ST.
KNIGHTSBRIDGE
SW3 1AT

TEL 020-7589 5171
Discreet and elegant restaurant, styled by Nina Campbell and Lord Linley. Dishes are eye-catching, imaginative, and display a vibrant freshness and clarity of flavor. Service is professional and friendly. Fixed-price L & D.
🔲 35 🚇 Knightsbridge
🕐 Closed Dec. 25 D 🈯
🈯 All major cards

## 🍴 BOXWOOD CAFÉ
**$$$$** ✸✸✸
THE BERKELEY HOTEL
WILTON PLACE
KNIGHTSBRIDGE
SW1X 7RL
TEL 020-7235 1010
FAX 020-7235 1011
Overseen by celebrity chef Gordon Ramsay, this place is great fun; friendly, knowledgeable staff, excellent fish, and heavenly pudding.
🔲 140 🚇 Knightsbridge
🅿 52 🈯 🈯 All major cards

## 🍴 THE GATE
**$$$** ✸
51 QUEEN CAROLINE ST.
W6 9QL
TEL 020-8748 6932
Wonderful vegetarian cooking with plenty of organic and wild ingredients fresh from the country.
🔲 50 🚇 Hammersmith
🕐 Closed L Sat., Sun., Dec. 23–Jan. 3, Easter Mon., Bank Holidays 🈯 All major cards

### ALONG THE THAMES

## 🏨 CONRAD LONDON
**$$$$$** ★★★★★ ✸
CHELSEA HARBOUR
SW10 0XG
TEL 020-7823 3000
FAX 020-7351 6525
Overlooking a small marina at Chelsea Harbour; the modern accommodations are full suites only, most with furnished balconies. A harborside terrace completes the waterfront feel. Exceptionally well-appointed

meeting and function rooms.
🛈 160 🚇 Fulham Broadway
🅿 80 🛗 🈯 🈯 📺
🈯 All major cards

## 🏨 HOTEL IBIS
**$$**
STOCKWELL ST.
SE10 9JN
TEL 020- 8305 1177
FAX 020-8858 7139
A modern hotel in the heart of Greenwich. Public areas are limited to snack facilities, but a brasserie restaurant provides a self-service breakfast.
🛈 82 🚇 Greenwich 🅿 40
🛗 🈯 All major cards

## 🍴 BUTLERS WHARF CHOP HOUSE
**$$$** ✸
THE BUTLERS WHARF BUILDING, 36E SHAD THAMES
SE1 2YE
TEL 020-7403 3403
Terence Conran's beautiful jolly room overlooks the Thames and Tower Bridge, where you can enjoy the best of traditional fare.
🔲 110 🚇 Tower Hill or London Bridge 🕐 Closed Sun. D 🈯 All major cards

## 🍴 RANSOME'S DOCK
**$$$** ✸✸
BATTERSEA
SW11 4NP
TEL 020-7223 1611
FAX 020-7924 2614
This small, stylish restaurant on the south side of the Thames (overlooking a dry dock, no view of the river) offers friendly service, first class ingredients and a good wine list. Bold decor features contemporary art and the cooking is modern European in style. Fixed-price L.
🔲 55 🚇 Sloane Square
🕐 Closed Sun. D 🈯 All major cards

### HOME COUNTIES

## ASPLEY GUISE

## 🏨 MOORE PLACE
**$$$/$$$$** ★★★
THE SQUARE
MK17 8DW
TEL 01908-282000
FAX 01908-281888
A Georgian mansion on its own grounds with rooms. The Victorian-style conservatory restaurant offers English and French cuisine. Friendly and efficient service.
🛈 39 (15 annex) 🅿 70
🈯 Restaurant 🈯 All major cards

## AYLESBURY

## 🏨 HARTWELL HOUSE
**$$$$$** ★★★★ ✸✸✸
OXFORD RD.
HP17 8NL
TEL 01296-747444
FAX 01296-747450
Elegant building on 90-acre estate dates from 1600. Features include delicate ceiling plasterwork and a Jacobean great staircase. Characterful bedrooms, some in a converted stable block. Tennis, fishing, and croquet

lawn. No children under eight.
🛈 30 (16 annex) 🅿 91 ⊟
🚫 Restaurant 🌊 🏋
🚫 All major cards

### 🍴 LA CHOUETTE
**$$$$** 🚫
WESTLINGTON GREEN
DINTON
HP17 8UW
TEL 01296-747422
Cottagelike little restaurant,
with echoes of the owner's
native Belgium on the sensibly
short menu. Plenty of fish and
simple but skillfully prepared
vegetables. Fixed-price L.
🍴 35 🕐 Closed Sat. L &
Sun. 🚫 All major cards

## BEACONSFIELD

### 🏨 GEORGE
**$$$$**
WYCOMBE END
OLD TOWN
HP9 1LZ
TEL 01494-673086
FAX 01494-674034
Delightfully restored Tudor inn,
in picturesque old town near
Windsor. Bedrooms furnished
with antiques and paintings.
🛈 10 🚫 🚫 All major
cards

## BRAY

### 🍴 MONKEY ISLAND
### HOTEL
**$$$$** 🚫
OLD MILL LANE.
SL6 2EE
TEL 01628-623400
Enjoy imaginative food or a
dish of afternoon tea in this
restaurant on an island in the
middle of the River Thames.
🍴 80 🅿 100 🚫

### 🍴 WATERSIDE INN
**$$$$$** 🚫🚫🚫🚫
FERRY RD.
SL6 2AT
TEL 01628-620691
Long windows overlooking
the Thames, the perfect setting
for dinner on a summer
evening, oozing quality in the
most relaxed kind of way. The
service is highly polished,

discreet, and unfailingly helpful.
The cooking is French to the
core. Fixed-price L & D.
🍴 75 🕐 Closed Mon.,
Tues. L, Tues. D (Sept.–May),
late Dec.–Feb. 🚫 All major
cards

## FLITWICK

### 🍴 MENZIES FLITWICK
### MANOR
**$$$$** 🚫🚫
CHURCH RD.
MK45 1AE
TEL 01525-712242
FAX 01525-718753
Elegantly decorated in
gracious, classical style, with
windows overlooking the
grounds. Menus are complex,
founded on classic tradition,
yet experiment with oriental
seasoning and Mediterranean
flavors. Fixed-price L.
🍴 55 🅿 55 🚫 🚫 All
major cards

## HASLEMERE

### 🏨 LYTHE HILL
**$$$$** ★★★★ 🚫🚫
PETWORTH RD.
GU27 3BQ
TEL 01428-651251
FAX 01428-644131
Historic buildings on 20 acres
of grounds. Bluebell wood,
several lakes. Central courtyard garden. Some separate
garden suites; some rooms in
the original 15th-century
black-and-white timbered
house. Henry VIII Suite
features four-poster bed
dating from 1614. Oak-
paneled Auberge de France
Restaurant, and another restaurant in main building. Tennis,
fishing, and croquet lawn.
🛈 41 🅿 202 🚫 Restaurant
🚫 All major cards

## HORLEY

### 🏨 LANGSHOTT MANOR
### 🍴 $$$$ 🚫🚫
LANGSHOTT LA HORLEY.
RH6 9LN
TEL 01293-786680
Spirited modern cuisine

enjoyed in a half-timbered
Tudor house only a few
minutes from Gatwick airport.
🛈 22 🍴 42 🅿 25 🚫 All
major cards

## MAIDENHEAD

### 🏨 FREDRICK'S
**$$$$$** ★★★★ 🚫🚫🚫
SHOPPENHANGERS RD.,
SL6 2PZ
TEL 01628-581000
FAX 01628-771054
Family run hotel and acclaimed
restaurant where the emphasis
is on exceptionally high
standards of food, comfort,
service, and hospitality. Quiet
location, close to Heathrow.
🛈 37 🅿 90 🕐 Closed
Christmas & New Year
🚫 All major cards

SOMETHING
SPECIAL

### 🏨 CLIVEDEN
One of England's great
country houses, set on a
376-acre National Trust
estate. Cliveden was the most
famous political house in
England between the wars,
when Nancy Astor (1879–
1964), Britain's first female
M.P., held court here for all
the star politicians and major
names in finance and the arts.
Visitors are treated as "house
guests." Superb view across
the formal garden from the
Terrace Restaurant; or try
Waldo's for serious dining in
discreet, well-upholstered
luxury. Tennis, fishing, squash,
snooker, Canadian hot bath,
river cruises. Fixed-price L
& D.
**$$$$$** ★★★★★ 🚫🚫🚫
TAPLOW
SL6 0JF
TEL 01628-668561
FAX 01628-661837
🛈 38 (& Spring Cottage)
🍴 Waldo's 24, Terrace 100
🅿 60 🚫 Restaurant 🚫
🌊 🌊 🏋 🚫 All major
cards

---

HOTELS & RESTAURANTS

### 🏨 BEEHIVE MANOR
**$$**
COX GREEN LANE
SL6 3ET
TEL 01628-620980
FAX 01628-621840
Charming 16th-century house
with warm and friendly
atmosphere. No children
under 12.
🛏4 🅿6 ⬛ 🕐 Closed
Christmas & New Year ⬛
⬥ MC, AE, V

## MARLOW

### 🍴 DANESFIELD HOUSE
**$$$$** ★★★★ ⚜⚜
HENLEY RD.
SL7 2EY
TEL 01628-891010
FAX 01628-890408
Formal dining in the grand
Oak Room with its ornate
plaster ceiling and oak panel-
ing. Menus follow the seasons,
blending classical French and
traditional English dishes. The
wine list is an excellent
selection of quality bins. Bar
food. Fixed-price L & D.
🔷45 ⬛ ⬥All major
cards

## REIGATE

### 🏨 BRIDGE HOUSE
**$$$** ★★★
REIGATE HILL
RH2 9RP
TEL 01737-246801
FAX 01737-223756
On top of Reigate Hill, with
panoramic views. Bedrooms
with furnished balconies.
Mediterranean-style
restaurant; live entertainment
and dancing two nights a
week.
🛏39 🅿110 ⬥All major
cards

## ST. ALBANS

### 🏨 SOPWELL HOUSE
**$$$$** ★★★★ ⚜⚜
COTTONMILL LANE
SOPWELL
AL1 2HQ
TEL 01727-864477
FAX 01727-844741

Once owned by the
Mountbattens, relatives of the
Royal Family. Many bedrooms
have four-poster beds. Drinks
in the Library Lounge,
followed by dinner in the
Magnolia Conservatory
Restaurant where the cooking
is technically polished,
confident, and imaginative. The
original magnolia tree grows
through the conservatory.
Less formal dining in the
brasserie. Bar food. Fixed-
price L & D.
🛏122 (16 annex) 🅿360
⬛Restaurant ⬛ 📷 ⬛
⬥All major cards

## SHERE

### 🍴 KINGHAMS
**$$$** ⚜⚜
GOMSHALL LANE
GU5 9HE
TEL 01483-202168
A relaxed and cheerful
atmosphere in this charming
17th-century cottage
restaurant. The menu is
interesting, the cooking
modern British in style. Fixed-
price L & D.
🔷48 🕐 Closed Sun. D,
Mon., Dec. 25–Jan. 4 ⬥All
major cards

## SONNING

### 🍴 FRENCH HORN
**$$$$** ⚜⚜
SONNING
RG4 6TN
TEL 0118-969 2204
FAX 0118-944 2210
This long established
restaurant is superbly located
on the bank of the River
Thames. Guests can enjoy the
classical French cuisine, fine
river views, and lovely village
setting. The signature dish is
half a duck, spit roasted in
front of the fire in the bar and
carved at the table. Fixed-
price L & D. No children
under three.
🛏60 🕐 Closed Good
Friday & New Year's Day
⬥All major cards

## SULHAMSTEAD

### 🏨 OLD MANOR
**$$**
WHITEHOUSE GREEN
RG7 4EA
TEL 0118-983 2423
The owners treat everyone as
their personal guests. Four-
poster bed and spa bath in
one of the bedrooms. No
children under eight.
🛏2 🅿8 🕐 Closed Dec.
23–Jan. 2 ⬛

## WARE

### 🏨 MARRIOTT HANBURY MANOR
**$$$$** ★★★★★ ⚜⚜
WARE
SG12 0SD
TEL 01920-487722
FAX 01920-487692
Marriott group's U.K. flagship,
a Jacobean-style mansion on
200 acres of grounds and
gardens. Wood paneling,
crystal chandeliers, antiques,
wood fires. Bedrooms
comfortably furnished in
country-house style. Zodiac
Restaurant serves modern
French dishes of the highest
standard. Vardons restaurant
offers international cuisine. Bar
food. Golf, tennis, and snooker.
Fixed-price L & D.
🛏134 🅿200
⬛Restaurant ⬛ 📷 ⬛
⬥All major cards

## YATTENDON

### 🍴🏨 ROYAL OAK
**$$$$** ★★ ⚜⚜
THE SQUARE
RG18 0UG
TEL 01635-201325
FAX 01635-201926
Wisteria-clad country inn with
an Anglo/French feel. Carefully
prepared dishes are cooked
with style and confidence
and served in the pretty
restaurant. The wine list is
extensive and desirable, with
some wines by the glass. Old
beams, comfortable
furnishings, and a pretty
garden all complete the

country-house feel. Rooms are richly furnished and guests are well looked after.
**(i)** 5 **[++]** 24 **[P]** 20 **(S)** Restaurant **(S)** All major cards

## THE SOUTH COUNTRY

## AMBERLEY

### SOMETHING SPECIAL

### 🏛 AMBERLEY CASTLE
Eleventh-century castle complete with gatehouse, working portcullis, high curtain walls, gardens, and peacocks. The ancient walls also conceal an oubliette where enemies would be sealed in and forgotten. The Queen's Room restaurant offers several menus, including Castle Cuisine, based on old English recipes. No children under 12.
**$$$$** ★★★ 🍽🍽
AMBERLEY
BN18 9ND
TEL 01798-831992
FAX 01798-831998
**(i)** 15 (5 annex) **[P]** 50 **(S)** Restaurant **(S)** All major cards

## ASHFORD

### 🏛 EASTWELL MANOR
### 🍴 $$$$$ ★★★★ 🍽🍽
EASTWELL PARK, BOUGHTON LEES
TN25 4HR
TEL 01233-213000
FAX 01233-35530
From the moment guests enter the magnificently paneled reception they are promised "quality without compromise." The dining room is dominated by a baronial fireplace and overlooks immaculate gardens. The menu is classically inspired, and the wine list is excellent.
**(i)** 62 **[++]** 80 **(S)** All major cards

## BOURNEMOUTH

### 🏛 ROYAL BATH
**$$$$** ★★★★★ 🍽🍽
BATH RD.
BH1 2EW
TEL 01202-555555
FAX 01202-554158
Large Victorian hotel with fine views out to sea. Health club in a pavilion on the grounds. Choice of restaurants—either the Garden Restaurant or the celebrated Oscars.
**(i)** 140 **[P]** 70 🔲 🏊 🎾 **(S)** All major cards

## BRIDPORT

### 🍴 RIVERSIDE
**$$$** 🍽🍽
WEST BAY
DT6 4EZ
TEL 01308-422011
Lively restaurant specializing in fresh local seafood. The kitchen relies on the day's catch for its repertoire.
**[++]** 80 🕐 Closed Sun. D, Mon., Dec.–Feb. **(S)** All major cards

## BRIGHTON

### 🏛 GRAND
**$$$$$** ★★★★★
KINGS RD.
BN1 2FW
TEL 01273-224300
FAX 01273-224321
Traditional luxury hotel, a well-known landmark on Brighton seafront. Leisure center, beautician, seaview conservatory, weekend nightclub.
**(i)** 200 **[P]** 65 🔲 🏊 🎾 **(S)** All major cards

## CANTERBURY

### 🏛 FALSTAFF
**$$$** ★★★
ST. DUNSTANS ST.
WESTGATE
CT2 8AF
TEL 0870-609 6102
FAX 01227-463525
Sixteenth-century inn next to the Westgate Tower. Attractive restaurant serving English and French cuisine.

**(i)** 26 (22 annex) **[P]** 41 **(S)** Restaurant **(S)** All major cards

### 🍴 CANTERBURY
**$$** 🍽
71 NEW DOVER RD.
CT1 3DZ
TEL 01227-450551
FAX 01227-780145
With plain-spoken simplicity and pleasingly accommodating staff, the Canterbury serves classical French cuisine with an emphasis on techniques and sauces. Bar meals. No children under six.
**[++]** 40 🕐 Closed L (except by arrangement) **(S)** All major cards

## CASTLE COMBE

### 🏛 MANOR HOUSE
### 🍴 $$$$ ★★★★ 🍽🍽🍽
CASTLE COMBE
SN14 7HR
TEL 01249-782206
FAX 01249-782159
Extended 14th-century house on 26 acres of gardens and parkland. Accommodations in the main house and cottage bedrooms. Log fires and floral arrangements in lounges. There is flair and imagination in the menu as well as a range of classic dishes. Bar food. Golf, tennis, and fishing are available. Fixed-price L & D.
**(i)** 21 (24 annex) **[++]** 75 **[P]** 100 **(S)** Restaurant 🏊 **(S)** All major cards

## CHICHESTER

### 🏛 MILLSTREAM
**$$$** ★★★ 🍽
BOSHAM LANE
BOSHAM
PO18 8HL
TEL 01243-573234
FAX 01243-573459
Attractive village hotel and restaurant. Cocktail bar opens out onto the garden. Candlelit restaurant offers fresh local produce and impressive wine list. Bar food. Fixed-price L & D.
**(i)** 33 **[P]** 44 **(S)** Restaurant **(S)** All major cards

---

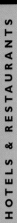

🍴 **WHITE HORSE**
$$$ ✿
CHILGROVE
PO18 9HX
TEL 01243-535219
Thatched 17th-century oak-beamed inn serving hearty French and British cooking. Game is regular, in season. Wine list impressive. Bar food.
🍴 80 🕑 Closed Sun. D, Mon. 🗠 All major cards

### COWES

🏨 **NEW HOLMWOOD HOTEL**
$$ ★★★
QUEENS RD., EGYPT POINT, ISLE OF WIGHT
PO31 8BW
TEL 01983-292508
FAX 01983-295020
A very comfortable and stylish hotel with superb views from its position at the water's edge.
🛏 26 🅿 20 🗠 All major cards

### DORCHESTER

🍴 **YALBURY COTTAGE**
$$$ ✿✿
LOWER BOCKHAMPTON
DT2 8PZ
TEL 01305-262382
Thatched cottage restaurant with oak beams, inglenook fireplaces, and the original bread ovens. Thoughtful and reasonably priced wine list. Fixed-price D.
🍴 30 🕑 Closed L 🗠 All major cards

### DOVER

🍴 **WALLETT'S COURT**
$$$ ✿✿
WEST CLIFFE
ST. MARGARETS-AT-CLIFFE
CT15 6EW
TEL 01304-852424
FAX 01304-853430
Based on a classic, traditional approach and built around bold flavors, the dishes are individual, created from the finest

ingredients. No children under eight.
🍴 60 🛏 15
🗠 Restaurant 🗠 All major cards

### EVERSHOT

🏨 **SUMMER LODGE**
🍴 $$$$$ ★★★ ✿✿✿
EVERSHOT
DT2 0JR
TEL 01935-83424
FAX 01935-83005
Country-house hotel in charming walled gardens, personally owned and run. Tennis. An imaginative, daily set menu is offered, as well as a seasonal menu strong on the modern repertoire. Fixed-price L & D.
🛏 11 (6 annex) 🍴 42
🅿 40 🗠 Restaurant 🏊
🗠 All major cards

### FAVERSHAM

🍴 **READ'S**
$$$$ ✿✿✿
PAINTERS FORSTAL
ME13 0EE
TEL 01795-535344
One of the best restaurants in Kent. Refined cooking style is carefully considered, fresh local produce well found. Fixed-price L & D.
🍴 40 🕑 Closed Sun., Mon. 🗠 All major cards

### FORDINGBRIDGE

🍴 **THE THREE LIONS**
$$$ ✿✿✿
STUCKTON
SP6 2HF
TEL 01425-652489
Homely, family-friendly restaurant with tip-top French and English cooking.
🍴 60 🕑 Closed Sun. & Mon. D, mid-Jan.–mid-Feb.

### FOREST ROW

🏨 **ASHDOWN PARK**
Very well run hotel with an extremely willing and friendly team of staff. Splendid, sprawling building was once home to a community of nuns. Features include a chapel with fine stained-glass windows and a working organ. Bedrooms decorated in a comfortable "homey" style. Restaurant offers classical dishes with modern influences. Golf, tennis, snooker.
$$$$/$$$$$ ★★★★ ✿✿
WYCH CROSS
FOREST ROW
RH18 5JR
TEL 01342-824988
FAX 01342-826206
🛏 107 🅿 200 🔧 🏊 🎾
🗠 Restuarant 🗠 All major cards

### HORSHAM

🍴 **SOUTH LODGE HOTEL**
🏨 $$$$ ★★★★ ✿✿✿
BRIGHTON RD.
LOWER BEEDING
RH13 6PS
TEL 01403-891711
FAX 01403-891766
Splendid restored Victorian mansion featuring the Camellia Restaurant, with its views of the South Downs. The restaurant serves enthusiastic cooking and makes use of both local game and some fine organic beef to create a menu that is a convincing blend of both traditional and modern cuisine. Bar food also available. Fixed-price L & D.
🛏 41 🍴 40 🅿 80
🗠 Restaurant 🗠 All major cards

### LACOCK

🏨 **AT THE SIGN OF THE ANGEL**
$$$
6 CHURCH ST.

SN15 2LB
TEL 01249-730230
FAX 01249-730527
A characterful 15th-century
former wool merchant's
house situated in a National
Trust village. Good home-
cooked traditional food is
served in the lovely beamed
dining rooms which are
warmed by open fires.
**[1]** 6 (4 annex) **[P]** 1
**[1]** Closed Christmas **[S]** All
major cards

## LEWES

### **[1]** SHELLEYS
$$$ ◉◉
HIGH ST.
BN7 1XS
TEL 01273-472361
FAX 01273-483152
The style here is elegant yet
relaxed. A selection of seasonal
specialties is offered to
supplement the fixed-price
menu. There is a serious attitude
to the food, which does not
stray too far from recognized
combinations. Bar food is also
available. Fixed-price D.
**[1]** 30 **[S]** **[S]** All major cards

## LITTLEHAMPTON

**SOMETHING
SPECIAL**

### **[1]** BAILIFFSCOURT
Hotel built in the 1930s
using materials salvaged
from redundant medieval
buildings, with old stone
windows, heavy iron-studded
doors, and ancient arches.
Bedrooms equipped with
antique oak furniture and
embroidered fabrics. Soundly
cooked dishes in the beamed
restaurant. Tennis.
$$$$/$$$$$ ★★★ ◉◉
CLIMPING
BN17 5RW
TEL 01903-723511
FAX 01903-723107
**[1]** 9 (22 annex) **[P]** 60
**[S]** Restaurant **[S]** **[S]** All
major cards

## LYMINGTON

### **[1]** GORDLETON MILL
$$$ ★★
SILVER ST.
HORDLE
SO41 6DJ
TEL 01590-682219
FAX 01590-683073
A 300-year-old converted
watermill complete with its
original sluice gates and weir, a
lily pond, and water gardens.
Good range of dishes at lunch
and dinner. Attractive
bedrooms and bathrooms
featuring whirlpool baths. No
children under eight.
**[1]** 9 **[P]** 60 **[S]** Restaurant
**[S]** All major cards

## MAIDSTONE

### **[1]** MARRIOTT TUDOR
### PARK HOTEL &
### COUNTRY CLUB
$$$ ★★★★
ASHFORD RD.
BEARSTED
ME14 4NQ
TEL 01622-734334
FAX 01622-735360
In the heart of Kent, this is a
country hotel with friendly
and helpful staff and a good
restaurant which always serves
well-prepared and flavored
meals. Golf and tennis facilities
are also available.
**[1]** 120 **[P]** 250
**[S]** Restaurant **[S]** **[S]** **[S]**
**[S]** All major cards

## MIDHURST

### **[1]** ANGEL HOTEL
$$$ ◉
NORTH ST.
GU29 9DN
TEL 01730-812421
FAX 01730-815928
A mellow atmosphere at this
old inn with Tudor origins and
Georgian additions. Dinner in
the classy Cowdray Room
emphasizes light sauces,
maximizing full flavors without
the need for overpowering
garnishes.
**[1]** 60 **[P]** 35 **[S]** **[S]** All
major cards

## MILFORD ON SEA

### **[1]** WESTOVER HALL
$$$ ◉◉
PARK LANE
SO41 0PT
TEL 01590-643044
FAX 01590-644490
An elegant and sophisticated
Victorian hotel dining room,
featuring Jacobean ceiling
molds and pre-Raphaelite
stained glass windows. Dishes
range from Country-house
style to modern, all make
good use of locally sourced
produce. Bar food. Fixed-price
L & D. No children under
seven.
**[1]** 40 **[S]** **[S]** All major
cards

## NEWBURY

### **[1]** DEW POND
$$$ ◉◉
OLD BURGHCLERE
RG20 9LH
TEL 01635-278408
The whole place is imbued
with a charm one would
expect from good English
hospitality. Modern English
and French dishes come from
a classic repertoire based on
fine ingredients and clear
flavors. Fixed-price D. No
children under five.
**[1]** 45 **[1]** Closed L,
Sun.–Mon., 2 weeks Jan., 2
weeks Aug. **[S]** **[S]** MC, V

## NEW MILTON

### **[1]** CHEWTON GLEN
### **[1]** $$$$$ ★★★★★ ◉◉◉
CHRISTCHURCH RD.
BH25 6QS
TEL 01425-275341
FAX 01425-272310
A luxurious and hospitable
retreat with many thoughtful
touches and excellent house-
keeping. Superior of cooking,
using finest raw ingredients;
impressive wine list. Golf and
tennis. No children under six.
**[1]** 53 (2 annex) **[1]** 120
**[P]** 100 **[S]** Restaurant **[S]**
**[S]** **[S]** **[S]** All major cards

### 🏨 COTTAGE
**$**
APPLEDORE
HOLMSLEY RD.
WOOTTON
BH25 5TR
TEL 01425-629506
Delightful cottage in a peaceful New Forest setting. Hearty home-cooked breakfasts are served in the dining room, overlooking the attractive garden. Relaxing atmosphere, and warm and friendly service.
ⓘ 3   🅿 5   🅢

### ROYAL TUNBRIDGE WELLS

### 🍴 THACKERAYS
**$$$** ⊛⊛⊛
TN1 1EA
TEL 01892-511921
Clever but delicious modern French cuisine, particularly good with fish and seafood.
🔢 54   🕐 Closed Sun. & Mon. D

### RYE

### 🏨 MERMAID
**$$$$** ★★★ ⊛
MERMAID ST.
TN31 7EY
TEL 01797-223065
FAX 01797-225069
Famous medieval smugglers' inn, full of character with ancient beamed ceilings, linen-fold paneling, huge old fireplaces. The restaurant serves classic Anglo-French dishes; friendly staff. Bar food. Fixed-price L & D.
ⓘ 31   🅿 25   🅢 Restaurant
🃏 All major cards

### 🏨 JEAKE'S HOUSE
**$$/$$$**
MERMAID ST.
TN31 7ET
TEL 01797-222828
FAX 01797-222623
This 16th-century house on a pretty cobbled street was formerly a wool store, Friends Meeting House, and Baptist Chapel. Shelves full of books, parlor with piano, galleried

breakfast room. Vegetarian breakfast available. No children under 12.
ⓘ 12   🅿 20   🅢 Restaurant
🃏 MC, V

### SALISBURY

### 🏨 ROSE AND CROWN
**$$$$** ★★★
HARNHAM RD.
HARNHAM
SP2 8JQ
TEL 0870-609 0163
FAX 01722-339816
Set on the banks of the River Avon, with fine views of the Cathedral. Pavilions Restaurant virtually on the water's edge. Bar meals. Fixed-price L & D.
ⓘ 28   🅿 42   🅢 Restaurant
🃏 All major cards

### 🍴 OLD MILL
**$$**
TOWN PATH
WEST HARNHAM
SP2 8EU
TEL 01722-327517
FAX 01722-333367
A reliable restaurant built in an historic former papermill with a cascading mill race, set on the peaceful River Nadder on the edge of Salisbury. Careful cooking and a range of bar meals. Fixed-price D.
🔢 50   🕐 L   🅢   🃏 AE, MC, V

### SHAFTESBURY

### 🍴 WAYFARERS
**$$$** ⊛⊛
SHERBORNE CAUSEWAY
SP7 9PX
TEL 01747-852821
Short seasonally changing menu in this 18th-century building. Fixed-price L & D. No children under eight.
🔢 35   🕐 Closed Sun. D, Mon., Sat. L, 2 weeks after Dec. 25   🃏 AE, MC, V

### STOCKBRIDGE

### 🍴 FIFEHEAD MANOR
**$$$** ⊛⊛
MIDDLE WALLOP

SO20 8EG
TEL 01264-781565
FAX 01264-781400
Dining room occupies original main hall of this Saxon manor house. Kitchen displays a repertoire of deftly crafted modern British dishes based on quality ingredients. Bar food. Fixed-price L & D.
🔢 40   🅢 Restaurant   🃏 all major cards

### SUTTON (W. SUSSEX)

### 🏨 WHITE HORSE
**$$**
THE STREET
RH20 1PS
TEL 01798-869221
FAX 01798-869291
An 18th-century inn in the Sussex countryside at the foot of the South Downs. Good range of real ales. Informal, barrel-vaulted dining area.
ⓘ 5   🅿 10   🅢 Bedrooms
🃏 All major cards

### SWAY

### 🏨 NURSE'S COTTAGE
**$$$**
STATION RD.
SO41 6BA
TEL/FAX 01590-683402
Former district nurse's cottage.

Fresh fruit, flowers, chocolates, and fridge in bedrooms. Home-cooking in the attractive Garden Room restaurant. Respectable wine list. No children under ten.
🅘 3 🅿 8 🕒 Closed 2 weeks March & 3 weeks Nov. 🚭 All major cards

## WARMINSTER

### 🏨 BISHOPSTROW HOUSE
$$$$ ★★★★ 🅐🅐
WARMINSTER
BA12 9HH
TEL 01985-212312
FAX 01985-216769
Georgian house furnished with English antiques and 19th-century paintings. Four-poster room; several suites with whirlpool baths. The Mulberry Restaurant and the Wilton Room have traditional English fare. Tennis, fishing, archery, cycling, and croquet lawn.
🅘 32 🅿 60 🚭 Restaurant 🔲 🔳 🌊 🅐 All major cards

## WINCHESTER

### 🏨 ROYAL
$$$ ★★★ 🅐
SAINT PETER ST.
SO23 8BS
TEL 01962-840840
FAX 01962-841582
Popular hotel tucked away on a quiet street and within easy reach of historic city center. Conservatory dining room has an interesting menu of well-prepared modern British dishes, and in the summer months guests can enjoy a barbecue lunch in the walled garden. Bar meals. Fixed-price D.
🅘 75 🅿 80 🚭 Restaurant 🌊 All major cards

### 🍴 HOTEL DU VIN
### 🏨 & BISTRO
$$$ ★★★★ 🅐🅐
14 SOUTHGATE ST
SO23 9EF
TEL 01962-841414
FAX 01962-842458
Centrally located bistro and 18th-century town house. The bistro, filled with wine memorabilia, is stylishly informal with Mediterranean menu.

Bedrooms are comfort-able, each sponsored by a different wine house.
🛏 65 🅘 23 🅿 45 🌊 All major cards

### 🍴 THE CHESIL RECTORY
$$$$ 🅐🅐🅐
1 CHESIL ST.
SO23 0HU
TEL 01962-851555
This classy, understated restaurant in Winchester's oldest house offers great unfussy cooking.
🛏 40 🕒 Closed Sun.–Fri. L & Christmas week

## ASH MILL

### 🏨 KERSCOTT FARM
$
ASH MILL
SOUTH MOLTON
EX36 4QG
TEL 01769-550262
Working farm in beautiful Devon countryside. The house has exposed beams, flagstone floor, inglenook fireplaces. Home-cooking includes crusty bread and hearty soups. No children under 14.
🅘 3 🅿 4 🕒 Closed Nov.–Jan. 🚭

## BARNSTAPLE

### 🍴 HALMPSTONE MANOR
$$$ 🅐🅐
BISHOP'S TAWTON
EX32 0EA
TEL 01271-830321
FAX 01271-830826
Fish, fresh from Bideford Quay, features regularly on the handwritten, five-course dinner menu at this charming, small manor house. Fixed-price D. No children under 12.
🛏 24 🕒 Closed L, Christmas week & Feb. 🚭 🌊 All major cards

## BATH

### 🏨 APSLEY HOUSE
$$$
NEWBRIDGE HILL
BA1 3PT
TEL 01225-336966
FAX 01225-425462

Friendly hotel on the edge of showpiece Georgian city. No children under five.
🅘 9 🅿 10 🕒 Closed Christmas 🚭 Restaurant 🌊 All major cards

### 🍴 THE OLIVE TREE
$$$ 🅐🅐
QUEENSBURY HOTEL RUSSEL ST.
BA1 2QF
TEL 01225-447928
Bold European food in the stylish basement restaurant of a very smart city centre hotel. Fixed-price L & D.
🛏 60 🕒 Closed Sun. L, bank holidays, 4 days at Christmas

### 🍴 MOODY GOOSE
$$$ 🅐🅐
7A KINGSMEAD SQUARE
BA1 2AB
TEL 01225-466688
Basement restaurant with breezily fresh decor and visibly enthusiastic staff. Large pottery goose lords over diners. Cooking, displaying vitality but elegantly under-stated, is based on mainly local ingredients. Fixed-price L & D.
🛏 30 🕒 Closed Sun. & 2 weeks Jan. 🌊 All major cards

## BRISTOL

SOMETHING SPECIAL

### 🏨 AVON GORGE
Commanding position overlooking Avon Gorge and Brunel's famous suspension bridge. Popular hotel in the heart of fashionable Clifton. Well-equipped bedrooms, many with glorious views, a choice of bars (one with a popular terrace), and attractive restaurant. Prompt, efficient service is carried out by a friendly team.
$$$ ★★★
SION HILL
CLIFTON
BS8 4LD
TEL 0117-9738955
FAX 0117-9238125
🅘 76 🅿 23 🔲 🌊 All major cards

HOTELS & RESTAURANTS

## 🍴 GLASS BOAT

$$$ ❀
WELSH BACK
BS1 4SB
TEL 0117-9290704
Moored alongside Bristol Bridge, the converted vessel has a glass-paneled dining room. The modern British menu has Mediterranean influences, and the kitchen works to a consistently high standard. Fixed-price L & D.
🍽 100 ⊕ Closed Sat. L & Sun. 🅂 ⊠ All major cards

## CHAGFORD

## 🏨 GIDLEIGH PARK

🍴 $$$$$ ★★★
❀❀❀❀
CHAGFORD
TQ13 8HH
TEL 01647-432367
FAX 01647X-432574
Mock-Tudor house set on 45 acres of grounds within Dartmoor National Park. The grounds contain rivers, forests, peaceful retreats, and a choice of sporting pursuits. The restaurant offers ambitious and outstanding dishes based on French cuisine, many using local ingredients. The wine list is more than a match for the food. Service is both friendly and professional. Tennis, fishing, and croquet lawn available. Fixed-price L & D.
🛏 12 (3 annex) 🍽 35
🅿 25 ⊠ Restaurant ⊠ All major cards

## CRACKINGTON HAVEN

## 🏨 MANOR FARM

$$
CRACKINGTON HAVEN
EX23 0JW
TEL 01840-230304
Charming manor house dating back to the Domesday Book, with views over countryside. Dinner by prior arrangement. Imaginative set meal from local produce, eaten family-style around one magnificent table. No children.
🛏 2 (1 annex) 🅿 6 🅂

## DARTMOUTH

## 🍴 CARVED ANGEL

$$$$ ❀❀
2 SOUTH EMBANKMENT
TQ6 9BH
TEL 01803-832465
Magnificent waterfront views. Freshness of supplies and a natural, simple approach are what distinguish the food. This is a setup that understands its materials, but is prepared occasionally to adventure. Fixed-price L & D.
🍽 55 ⊕ Closed Sun. D, Mon. & 2 weeks Jan.
⊠ Restaurant ⊠ DC, MC, V

## DUNSTER

## 🏨 DOLLONS HOUSE

$$
CHURCH ST.
TA24 6SH
TEL 01643-821880
FAX 01643-822016
Historic property in medieval village. Two bedrooms have views of the castle, the other overlooks lovely walled gardens. No children under 16.
🛏 3 ⊕ Closed Dec. 25–26
🅂 ⊠ MC, V

## EXETER

## 🏨 BUCKERELL LODGE

$$$ ★★★ ❀
TOPSHAM RD.
EX2 4SQ
TEL 01392-221111
FAX 01392-491111
Privately owned hotel in own gardens. Cocktail bar, and Raffles Restaurant or more informal Lodge Bar.
🛏 53 🅿 100 ⊠ Restaurant
⊠ All major cards

## FALMOUTH

## 🏨 ROYAL DUCHY

$$$$ ★★★★ ❀
CLIFF RD.
TR11 4NX
TEL 01326-313042
FAX 01326-319420
Elegant Victorian seafront hotel just a short walk from the center of town.

Swimming pool complex contains sauna, solarium, and spa bath; separate game room. Fresh local produce on menus.
🛏 43 🅿 50 ⊟ ⊠ ⊠ All major cards

## 🍴 HARBOURSIDE RESTAURANT, GREENBANK HOTEL

$$$ ❀
HARBOURSIDE
TR11 2SR
TEL 01326-312440
FAX 01326-211362
Unrivaled views of Falmouth harbor from the restaurant, whose interior achieves a classic, elegant look. Seafood figures prominently on the menu. Bar food.
🍽 50 🛏 59 ⊠ Restaurant
⊠ All major cards

## FOWEY

## 🏨 FOWEY HALL

🍴 $$$$ ★★★ ❀❀
HANSON DRIVE
PL23 1ET
TEL 01726-833866
FAX 01726-834100
A splendid mansion, built in 1899, looking out over the English Channel. Stunning dining room, candlelit at night, with ceilings, pillars and wood-paneling. Imaginative and accomplished cuisine. Fixed-price D.
🛏 17 (8 annex) 🍽 40
🅿 40 ⊠ ⊠ Restaurant
⊠ All major cards

## 🍴 FOOD FOR THOUGHT

$$$ ❀❀
THE QUAY
PL23 1AT
TEL 01726-832221
A waterside setting, estuary views, wooden beams, and a wood fire create just the right warm atmosphere. Fresh seafood features prominently, depending on the day's catch. Fixed-price D.
🍽 38 ⊕ Closed L, Sun. & Jan.–March ⊠ MC, V

## GULWORTHY

### 🍴 HORN OF PLENTY
$$$$ 🏵🏵🏵
TAVISTOCK
GULWORTHY
PL19 8JD
TEL/FAX 01822-832528
Lovely view from the dining
room over the Tamar Valley.
Excellent canapés, then a
dinner that fulfills all expec-
tations. Fixed-price L & D.
🔲 60 🕐 Closed Mon. L, &
Christmas 🚭 🔲 AE, MC, V

## HAYTOR VALE

### 🏨 ROCK INN
$$ 🏵
TQ13 9XP
TEL 01364-661305
Charming old Dartmoor Inn
where the fresh moorland air
gives an edge to your appetite.
🔲 45

## KINGSBRIDGE

### 🏨 COMBE FARM
$
LODDISWELL
TQ7 4DT
TEL 01548-550560
Beautiful Georgian farmhouse
at the bottom of a small valley
surrounded by sheep-grazed
hills. Warm family atmosphere
and good cooking with home-
grown produce.
🛏 6 🕐 Closed Dec.–Feb.
🚭 No credit cards

## LANGPORT

### 🏨 MUCHELNEY HAM FARM
$$
MUCHELNEY HAM
TA10 0DJ
TEL 01458-250737
This is a lovely old farmhouse
on a working farm in a
charming and restful rural
setting. No children under
seven.
🛏 3 🅿 10 🚭

## LISKEARD

### 🏨 WELL HOUSE
$$$ ★★ 🏵🏵🏵
ST. KEYNE
PL14 4RN
TEL 01579-342001
FAX 01579-343891
Charming small hotel in a
peaceful valley setting between
Liskeard and Looe, offering
personal hospitality and
service. Afternoon tea with
homemade cookies is served
on the terrace, which
overlooks pretty gardens and
hills. Tennis and croquet.
🛏 9 🅿 30 🏊
🚭 Restaurant 🔲 All major
cards

## LIZARD

### 🏨 LANDEWEDNACK HOUSE
Seventeenth-century rectory
in a peaceful setting
overlooking the sea. Bedrooms
are beautifully furnished with
antiques. Look on the interior
surface of one of the
bathroom doors to find the
deeply incised signatures of
Isabella and Rebecca Creagh,
daughters of a 19th-century
rector of nearby St.
Wynwalloe's Church. Evening
meal by arrangement, either at
communal table or individual
tables. No children.
$$$
CHURCH COVE
TR12 7PQ
TEL 01326-290909
FAX 01326-290192
🛏 3 🚭 🏊 🔲 MC, V

## LOOE

### 🏨 COOMBE FARM
$$
WIDEGATES
PL13 1QN
TEL 01503-240223
FAX 01503-240895
Set on ten acres of lawns,
meadows, and woodland

this hotel extends a warm
welcome to its guests.
Game room available. The
four-course dinner provided
makes use of local produce
whenever possible.
🛏 7 🅿 20 🏊 🔲 All
major cards

## LYDFORD

### 🏨 MOOR VIEW
$$
VALE DOWN
EX20 4BB
TEL/FAX 01822-820220
Welcoming house on the
edge of Dartmoor. The
bedrooms all feature family
furniture and many thoughful
touches.. Home-cooked food.
No children under 12.
🛏 4 🅿 15 🚭

## LYNMOUTH

### 🏨 RISING SUN
$$$ ★★ 🏵
HARBOURSIDE
EX35 6EQ
TEL 01598-753223
FAX 01598-753480
Fourteenth-century inn on
the harborfront of historic
Lynmouth. No children under
eight. Fishing offered.
🛏 11 (5 annex)
🚭 Restaurant 🔲 All major
cards

## LYNTON

### 🍴 CHOUGH'S NEST
$$
NORTH WALK
EX35 6HJ
TEL 01598-753315
Spectacular coastal views
accompany your meal here.
Thoroughly cosmopolitan
cooking is the mainstay of the
innovative menu, which is
served in a bright, airy dining
room. Fixed-price D.
🔲 20 🔲 MC, V

## MOUSEHOLE

### 🍴 OLD COASTGUARD HOTEL
$$$ 🏵🏵

HOTELS & RESTAURANTS

THE PARADE
TR19 6PR
TEL 01736-731222
FAX 01736-731720
Fish prepared in a variety of different ways is the order of the day at this relaxing old inn whose gardens run right down to the sea. Bar meals. Fixed-price D.
🛏 50 Ⓢ 🖎 All major cards

## NEWQUAY

🏨 **HOTEL BRISTOL**
**$$$ ★★★**
NARROWCLIFF
TR7 2PQ
TEL 01637-875181
FAX 01637-879347
Personally run and owned hotel with fine views over the sea. Cocktail bar and elegant restaurant.
🛏 74 🅿 105 🖬 🖀
Ⓢ Restaurant 🖎 All major cards

## PADSTOW

🏨 **OLD CUSTOM HOUSE**
**$$/$$$ ★★★ ✿**
SOUTH QUAY
PL28 8BL
TEL 01841-532359
FAX 01841-533372
Situated alongside the harbor, with lovely sea views. Restaurant uses locally caught fish. Real ales and bar meals.
🛏 24 🅿 9 Ⓢ 🖎 All major cards

🍴 **THE SEAFOOD RESTAURANT**
**$$$$ ✿✿✿**
RIVERSIDE
PL28 8BY
TEL 01841-532700
FAX 01841-533574
Rick Stein's TV fame has put the fishing village of Padstow on the map, and brought people from far and wide to visit his seafood restaurant. The hallmark of the cooking is tip-top freshness plus simplicity of technique; desserts are a particular delight, and the wine list is

adventurous. Fixed-price L & D. No children under three.
🛏 104 Ⓢ 🖎 All major cards

## PENZANCE

🏨 **CHY-AN-MOR**
**$**
15 REGENT TERRACE
TR18 4DW
TEL/FAX 01736-363441
An elegant Georgian house, now restored to its former glory. The beautiful and individually decorated bedrooms vary in size. No children under ten.
🛏 10 🅿 10 🕁 Closed Dec.–Jan. Ⓢ 🖎 DC, MC, V

## POLPERRO

🏨 **TRENDERWAY**
**$$**
PELYNT
PL13 2LY
TEL 01503-272214
FAX 01503-272991
Luxurious accommodations in 16th-century farmhouse amid beautiful surroundings. The traditional English breakfasts use only free-range eggs from the farm's own chickens. No children.
🛏 2 (2 annex) 🕁 Closed Christmas 🅿 4 Ⓢ 🖎 MC, V

## PLYMOUTH

🏨 **PLYMOUTH HOE MOAT HOUSE**
**$$$ ★★★★**
ARMADA WAY
PL1 2HJ
TEL 01752-639988
FAX 01752-673816
Modern hotel overlooking The Hoe and Plymouth Sound. Panoramic views of the city from restaurant and bar.
🛏 212 🅿 180 🖬
Ⓢ Restaurant Ⓢ 🖀 🖵 🖎 All major cards

🍴 **CHEZ NOUS**
**$$$$ ✿✿**
13 FRANKFORT GATE

PL1 1QA
TEL/FAX 01752-266793
Genuine warmth and intimacy. French decor, and a daily handwritten menu that follows the market, with fish from Plymouth showing up strongly. Fixed-price L & D. No children under ten.
🛏 28 🕁 Closed L, Sun.–Mon., 3 weeks Feb. & 3 weeks Sept. 🖎 All major cards

## ST. IVES

🍴 **PORTHMINSTER BEACH RESTAURANT**
**$$$ ✿**
PORTHMINSTER
TR26 2EB
TEL 01736-795352
There is a nautical twist to the decor and a strong maritime flavor to the food in this bright and breezy restaurant set right on the beach.
🛏 60 🕁 Closed Nov.–Mar.

🍴 **MERMAID SEAFOOD**
**$$ ✿**
21 FISH ST.
TR26 1LT
TEL 01736-796816
The emphasis is on fresh fish at this lively restaurant carved

out of a former sail loft and awash with old Chianti bottles, local memorabilia, and bric-a-brac. Fixed-price L & D.
🔢 50 🕐 Closed Jan. 🚭
🛗 🏧 MC, V

## SHEPTON MALLET

### 🏨 CHARLTON HOUSE
$$$$ ★★★ ❀❀❀
CHARLTON RD.
BA4 4PR
TEL 01749-342008
FAX 01749-346362
Sixteenth-century house on pretty grounds, sympathetically restored. Warm, relaxed atmosphere. Imaginative cuisine. Fishing, croquet, archery, clay-pigeon shooting, and hot-air ballooning.
ℹ️ 12 (5 annex) 🅿️ 41
🚭 Restaurant 🏊 🏧 All major cards

## STAVERTON

### 🍴 SEA TROUT INN
$$ ❀❀
STAVERTON
TQ9 6PA
TEL 01803-762274
FAX 01803-762506
Fishing theme evident throughout. Praiseworthy cooking in this very busy restaurant and bar. Bar food. Fixed-price D.
🔢 35 🕐 Closed L, Sun. D & Dec. 25–26 🚭 🏧 All major cards

## STON EASTON

### 🏨 STON EASTON PARK
🍴 $$$$$ ★★★★ ❀❀
STON EASTON
BA3 4DF
TEL 01761-241631
FAX 01761-241377
Eighteenth-century Palladian mansion on extensive grounds featuring river and lake. Antique pieces and little personal touches in bed-rooms. Aperitifs and canapés in the elegant saloon, dinner in dining room, after-dinner drinks, coffee, and petits fours in

library. Excellent afternoon teas. Tennis, hot-air ballooning, archery, clay-pigeon shooting, croquet, and horseback-riding. No children under seven. Bar food. Fixed-price L & D.
ℹ️ 18 (2 annex) 🔢 40
🅿️ 52 🚭 Restaurant 🏧 All major cards

## TAUNTON

### 🍴 CASTLE
$$$ ❀❀❀
CASTLE GREEN
TA1 1NF
TEL 01823-272671
An immediate sense of style throughout, with menus that prove imagination is far from lacking in the kitchen. Carefully sourced local ingredients are used to create the impressive, modern British dishes. Fixed-price L & D.
🔢 60 🚭 🏧 All major cards

## THURLESTONE

### 🏨 THURLESTONE
$$$/$$$$ ★★★★ ❀
THURLESTONE
TQ7 3NN
TEL 01548-560382
FAX 01548-561069
Family-owned hotel on beautifully kept gardens and grounds with fine views of the South Devon coast. Golf, tennis, and croquet.
ℹ️ 64 🅿️ 119 🛗
🚭 Restaurant 🏊 🏊 💼
🏧 All major cards

## TORQUAY

### 🏨 IMPERIAL
$$$$ ★★★★★ ❀
PARK HILL RD.
TQ1 2DG
TEL 01803-294301
FAX 01803-298293
Grand hotel with harbor and coastal views. Friendly service. Sundeck, brasserie, Regatta Restaurant. Tennis.
ℹ️ 153 🅿️ 140 🛗
🚭 Restaurant 🏊 🏊 💼
🏧 All major cards

## TWO BRIDGES

### 🏨 PRINCE HALL
$$$$ ★★ ❀❀
TWO BRIDGES
PL20 6SA
TEL 01822-890403
FAX 01822-890676
Local ingredients are used regularly on the short, nightly changing menu at this comfortable country-house hotel in the heart of the spectacular Dartmoor National Park. Fishing. No children under ten. Fixed-price D.
ℹ️ 8 🅿️ 13 🕐 Closed Jan.
🚭 Restaurant 🏧 All major cards

## VERYAN

### 🏨 NARE
$$$$ ★★★★ ❀
CARNE BEACH
TR2 5PF
TEL 01872-501111
FAX 01872-501856
Unobtrusive country-house atmosphere in seaside setting. Easy access to beach. Choice of restaurants with excellent local seafood. Tennis and windsurfing.
ℹ️ 38 🅿️ 80 🛗 🚭 Restaurant 🏊 🏊 💼 🏧 MC, V

## WELLINGTON

### 🏨 BINDON COUNTRY
🍴 HOUSE
$$$$ ★★★ ❀❀
LANGFORD BUDVILLE
WELLINGTON
TA21 0RU
TEL 01823-400070
FAX 01823- 400071
A wonderful country-house hotel, facing the Blackdown Hills. Each splendid bedroom is named after a battle fought by the Duke of Wellington. The Wellesley Restaurant makes a strong designer statement, and the cooking is full of style with herbs cleverly used. Tennis and croquet. Fixed-price L & D.
ℹ️ 12 🔢 35 🅿️ 30 🚭 🏊 🏧 All major cards

## WELLS

### 🏨 BEACONSFIELD FARM
$
EASTON
BA5 1DU
TEL/FAX 01749-870308
Farmhouse set in lovely countryside with a good level of comfort and hospitality. No children under eight.
🛏 3 🅿 10 🕐 Closed mid-Nov.–March 🚫

## WITHYPOOL

### 🍴 ROYAL OAK
$$$ ⚘
WITHYPOOL
TA24 7QP
TEL 01643-831506
FAX 01643-831659
Welcoming atmosphere at a traditional village inn dating back 300 years. Cooking uses quality local ingredients. Bar meals. Fixed-price D.
🍽 30 🃏 All major cards

## WOOLACOMBE

### 🏨 WATERSMEET
$$$$ ★★★ ⚘
MORTEHOE
EX34 7EB
TEL 01271-870333
FAX 01271-870890
Perched above a rocky inlet with sea views from restaurant. Professional and friendly service. Tennis and croquet.
🛏 22 🅿 30 🕐 Closed Jan. 4–Feb. 10 🚫 Restaurant 🦽 🃏 All major cards

---

## WALES

## ABERYSTWYTH

### 🍴 CONRAH
$$$ ⚘⚘
FFOSRHYDYGALED
CHANCERY
SY23 4DF
TEL 01970-617941
FAX 01970-624546
The kitchen rightly favors good regional produce, and the quality of ingredients, cooking, and presentation skills come through in the traditional Welsh and modern International cuisine. Bar food. Fixed-price L & D.
🍽 50 🕐 Closed Christmas week 🚫 🃏 All major cards

## BETWS-Y-COED

### 🍴 TAN-Y-FOEL
$$$ ⚘⚘⚘
CAPEL GARMON
LL26 0RE
TEL 01690-710507
A relaxed ambience and breathtaking views of the mountains of Snowdonia make this a distinctive restaurant. First-class ingredients skillfully cooked in classic style, often with Oriental touches. Reservations are essential. Fixed-price D.
🍽 16 🕐 Closed L, Dec.-mid Jan. 🚫 🃏 All major cards

## BONTDDU

### 🏨 BORTHWNOG HALL
$$$
BONTDDU
LL40 2TT
TEL 01341-430271
FAX 01341-430682
Seventeenth-century country house adjoining Garth Gell nature reserve on Mawddach Estuary. Superb views toward Cader Idris. Library Art Gallery contains original watercolors and oils; also pottery and sculpture for sale. Spacious bedrooms.
🛏 3 🅿 6 🚫 Dining Room 🃏 All major cards

## BRECON

### 🍴 LLANGOED HALL
$$$$ ⚘⚘
LLYSWEN
LD3 0YP
TEL 01874-754525
Imaginative use of local ingredients with Mediterranean and Provençal influences. Fixed-price L & D.
🍽 50 🚫 🃏 All major cards

## CAERNARFON

### 🏨 SEIONT MANOR
$$$$ ★★★ ⚘⚘
LLANRUG
CAERNARFON
LL55 2AQ
TEL 01286-673366
FAX 01286-672840
Snowdon looms just a few miles from this country house on 150 acres of parkland. Hotel cuisine often features regional specialities. Bar food. Fixed-price L & D.
🛏 28 🅿 150 🚫 Restaurant 🦽 🃏 All major cards

## CAPEL CURIG

### 🏨 COBDENS
$$ ★★
CAPEL CURIG
LL24 0EE
TEL 01690-720243
FAX 01690-720354
Long-established hotel with lovely views, a famous center for outdoor pursuits in the heart of Snowdonia. Two bars, one with impressive, exposed rock face. Enthusiastic help, advice, and service.
🛏 16 🅿 60 🚫 Restaurant 🃏 All major cards

## CARDIFF

### 🏨 ST. DAVID'S HOTEL AND SPA
$$$$$ ★★★★★ ⚘⚘
HAVANNAH ST.
CF10 5SD
TEL 029-2045 4045
FAX 029-2048 7056
Views over Cardiff Bay outside and a seven story atrium inside make this a stylish and popular hotel to stay in.
🛏 132 🅿 80 🛗 🚫 🦽 🦽 🃏 All major cards

### 🍴 HANOVER INTERNATIONAL
$$ ⚘
SCHOONER WAY
ATLANTIC WHARF
CF10 4RT
TEL 029-2047 5000
FAX 029-2048 1491

Fine cooking at Halyard's Restaurant draws you to this hotel, housed in a converted Victorian warehouse in the heart of Cardiff's revitalized waterfront. The food is based on traditional European combinations. Fixed-price L.
🍴 110 🕐 Closed Sat. L 🚭 🚫 All major cards

## METROPOLIS
$$ ✿
60 CHARLES ST.
CF1 4EG
TEL 029-2034 4300
Fashionable restaurant in the center of the Welsh capital city, with striking modern decor. Eclectic brasserie-style cooking with simple combinations and fresh flavors. Bar meals. Fixed-price L.
🍴 45 🕐 Closed Sun. & Dec. 25–26 🚭 🚫 All major cards

## CHEPSTOW

## MARRIOTT ST. PIERRE
$$$$ ★★★★
ST. PIERRE PARK
NP16 6YA
TEL 01291-625261
FAX 01291-629975
Hospitable old golf and leisure hotel with own championship golf course and tennis courts. Bedrooms in main house, at lakeside, or in cottage suites.
🛏 148 🅿 430 🚭 Restaurant 🏊 💪 🚫 All major cards

## CONWY

## OLD RECTORY COUNTRY HOUSE
$$$$ ★★ ✿✿✿
LLANRWST RD.
LLANSANFFRAID GLAN CONWY
LL28 5LF
TEL 01492-580611
FAX 01492-584555
Peaceful small hotel set in terraced gardens overlooking the Conwy Estuary and the hills of Snowdonia. Family suite available. Attractively presented cooking using an

interesting combination of ingredients. No children under five. Fixed-price D.
🛏 4 (2 annex) 🅿 10 🕐 Closed Dec.–Jan. 🚭 Restaurant 🚫 All major cards

## CRICKHOWELL

## BEAR
$$$ ★ ✿✿
CRICKHOWELL
NP8 1BW
TEL 01873-810408
FAX 01873-811696
Venerable and cozy inn more than six centuries old, full of beams and tankards. Local produce is used to telling effect for both bar and restaurant menus that draw on influences from far and wide. Good selection of wines. Bar food. No children under six.
🛏 70 🅿 38 🕐 Closed L. & Sun. 🚫 All major cards

## DOLGELLAU

## PENMAENUCHAF HALL
$$$ ★★★ ✿✿
PENMAENPOOL
LL40 1YB
TEL 01341-422129
FAX 01341-422787
Impressive country hideaway, dating from 1860, with breathtaking views. Each of the elegant bedrooms is individually styled. The restaurant serves fresh produce, cooked in a modern style. Game room. Fishing. No children under six.
🛏 14 🅿 30 🚭 Restaurant 🚫 All major cards

## TYDDYNMAWR FARMHOUSE
$
ISLAWRDREF
LL40 1TL
TEL 01341-422331
Eighteenth-century farmhouse at the foot of Cader Idris. Home baking and cooking,

including hearty farmhouse breakfasts that are most enjoyable. Fishing. No children.
🛏 3 🅿 8 🚭

## GREAT ORMES HEAD

**SOMETHING SPECIAL**

## LIGHTHOUSE
Former lighthouse on northern edge of Great Orme, Llandudno's spectacular headland. It was built in 1862 by the Mersey Docks and Harbour Board, and shone a light until 1985 for shipping approaching the treacherous sandbanks of the Dee Estuary and Liverpool Bay. Many original features preserved. Two bedrooms have their own lounge areas; one is the lighthouse's glazed dome. Stunning views; each bedroom equipped with a pair of binoculars. Solid-fuel stove for cold weather.
$$$
MARINE DRIVE
LLANDUDNO
LL30 2XD
TEL 01492-876819
🛏 3 🅿 6 🚭 🚫 MC. V

## HARLECH

## HOTEL MAES Y NEUADD
$$$$ ★★ ✿✿
TALSARNAU
LL47 6YA
TEL 01766-780200
FAX 01766-780211
Set on beautiful grounds with views over Snowdonia. Admirable use of fresh local produce—curly kale, laverbread, wild fungi, and much more besides—with home-baked breads, home-grown fruit and vegetables. Fixed-price D.
🛏 12 (4 annex) 🍴 65 🅿 50 🚭 Restaurant 🚫 All major cards

---

🚭 Non-smoking 🚬 Air-conditioning 🏊 Indoor/🏊 Outdoor swimming pool 💪 Health club 🚫 Credit cards　　KEY

**HOTELS & RESTAURANTS**

## 🍴 CASTLE COTTAGE
$$$ ⊛
PEN LLECH
LL46 2YL
TEL 01766-780479
The menu is not particularly large, but it changes every week and features local produce whenever possible. Fixed-price D.
🔁 45 🕐 Closed L & 3 weeks Feb. 🚫 🚭 All major cards

## GOWER

## 🏨 THE BRITANNIA INN
$
LLANMADOC
SWANSEA
SA3 1DB
TEL 01792-386624
The Britannia is a well-preserved 17th-century inn. The pub still has its original fireplace and bread oven. Some of the beams were taken from shipwrecks.
ℹ 3 🅿 60 🚭 All major cards

## HAY-ON-WYE

## 🏨 SWAN-AT-HAY
$$/$$$ ★★★
CHURCH ST.
HR3 5DQ
TEL 01497-821188
FAX 01497-821424
A coaching inn built in 1821, close to the center of this quaint border town. Choice of bars, lounge, and pleasant restaurant. Fishing.
ℹ 16 (3 annex) 🅿 18 🚭 All major cards

## 🍴 OLD BLACK LION HOTEL
$$$ ⊛
26 LION ST.
HR3 5AD
TEL 01497-820841
Award-winning local produce and imaginative vegetarian dishes in a nice historic setting.
🔁 24 🚭 All major cards

## LAUGHARNE

## 🍴 CORS
$$$

NEWBRIDGE RD.
SA33 4SH
TEL 01994-427219
Chef/proprietor Nick Priestland displays his talent for abstract painting and his green-fingered gift for gardening, as well as providing a menu with a strong Mediterranean slant. Presentation is all primary colors, flavors are undiluted. The short wine list bubbles with character.
🔁 24 🕐 Closed L, Mon.–Wed. D & Dec. 25 🚫 Restaurant

## LLANDRILLO

## 🏨 TYDDYN LLAN
## 🍴 COUNTRY HOUSE HOTEL & RESTAURANT
$$$ ★★ ⊛⊛
LLANDRILLO
CORWEN
LL21 0ST
TEL 01490-440264
FAX 01490-440414
Georgian house set on landscaped gardens. Sharp, imaginative cooking. Well-judged dishes with vibrant natural flavors and not too much complication. Bar food. Fixed-price D.
ℹ 10 🔁 65 🅿 30 🚫 Restaurant 🚭 All major cards

## LLANDUDNO

## 🏨 BODYSGALLEN HALL
$$$$$ ★★★★ ⊛⊛
LLANDUDNO
LL30 1RS
TEL 01492-584466
FAX 01492-582519
Seventeenth-century house with fine views over Snowdonia and Conwy Castle. About 200 acres of parkland and formal gardens, mullioned windows, oak paneling, log fire. Some cottage accommodations; some private sitting rooms and gardens. Tennis and croquet. No children under eight.
ℹ 19 (16 annex) 🅿 50 🚫 Restaurant 🚘 🚭 🚭 All major cards

## LLANGAMMARCH WELLS

## 🏨 LAKE COUNTRY HOUSE
$$$$ ★★★ ⊛⊛
LLANGAMMARCH WELLS
LD4 4BS
TEL 01591-620202
FAX 01591-620457
Comfortable and friendly Victorian house in beautiful countryside. Outdoor pursuits include lakeside and river walks, tennis, golf, and fishing.
ℹ 19 🅿 72 🚫 Restaurant 🚭 All major cards

## LLANGEFNI (ISLE OF ANGLESEY)

## 🏨 TRE-YSGAWEN HALL
$$$
CAPEL COCH
LL77 7UR
TEL 01248-750750
FAX 01248-750035
Georgian mansion on wooded grounds. Drawing room, bar, brasserie, and main restaurant.
ℹ 19 🅿 100 🚫 Restaurant 🚭 All major cards

## LLANGYBI

## 🏨 CWRT BLEDDYN
## 🍴 HOTEL & COUNTRY CLUB
$$$/$$$$ ★★★★ ⊛⊛
LLANGYBI
NP5 1PG
TEL 01633-450521
FAX 01633-450220
Victorian building on parkland in Welsh Borders countryside. Four-posters and carved oak furniture in some bedrooms. Capable cooking, using local ingredients, in Jesters Restaurant. Tennis, squash, and a fine leisure complex.
ℹ 29 (4 annex) 🔁 45 🅿 100 🚫 Restaurant 🚘 🚭 🚭 All major cards

## LLANWDDYN

## 🏨 LAKE VYRNWY
$$$$ ★★★ ⊛⊛
LAKE VYRNWY
SY10 0LY

TEL 01691-870692
FAX 01691-870259
Victorian country house on
26,000 acres of mature
woodland above Lake Vyrnwy.
Many bedrooms have four-
poster beds and balconies;
superb lake views. Restaurant
and Tavern Bar provide a
good variety of meals. Fishing,
shooting, and other outdoor
pursuits. Hotel holds license
for performing civil marriages.
🏠 35 🅿 70 Ⓢ Restaurant
Ⓢ All major cards

## LLYSWEN

🏨 **LLANGOED HALL**
🍽 **$$$$/$$$$$** ★★★★ ✿✿
LLYSWEN
LD3 0YP
TEL 01874-754525
FAX 01874-754545
Imposing Edwardian country
house on Wye Valley parkland,
with tennis and fishing. Inside is
a splendid balance between
comfort and grandeur in
dayrooms, corridors, and
library. Pretty bedrooms
furnished with antiques and
smart bathrooms. Welsh menu
with a Mediterranean and
Provençal twist. No children
under eight.
🏠 23 🍴 50 🅿 85
Ⓢ Restaurant Ⓢ All major
cards

## MACHYNLLETH

🍽 **YNYSHIR HALL**
**$$$$** ★★★ ✿✿✿
EGLWYSFACH
SY20 8TA
TEL 01654-781209
Creative menus with a real
feel for ingredients, scouring
the region for what is best
and appropriate and, in the
kitchen, treating what is
served with respect. Service is
smooth, cheery, and intelligent.
Bar food. Fixed-price L & D.
No children under nine.
🍴 30 🕐 Closed Jan. Ⓢ
Ⓢ All major cards

## MONMOUTH

🍽 **CROWN AT
WHITEBROOK**
**$$$** ✿✿
WHITEBROOK
NP25 4TX
TEL 01600-860254
FAX 01600-860607
Genuine welcome, tranquil
atmosphere. Ingredients are
from sound Welsh sources and
the quality is generally high,
with plenty of good ideas.
Extensive and very well chosen
wine list. Fixed-price L & D. No
children under eight.
🛏 32 🕐 Closed Mon. L, 2
weeks Jan. & 2 weeks Aug.
Ⓢ Ⓢ All major cards

## NEWCASTLE EMLYN

🍽 **EMLYN ARMS**
**$$**
BRIDGE ST.
SA38 9DU
TEL 01239-710317
FAX 01239-710792
National pride is stamped all
over the menu at this historic
18th-century inn. Fresh local
produce is used wherever
possible, and Welsh influences
are apparent in many dishes.
Bar meals.
🛏 45 Ⓢ Restaurant Ⓢ All
major cards

## NEWTOWN

🏨 **DYFFRYN**
**$$**
DYFFRYN
ABERHAFESP
SY16 3JD
TEL 01686-688817
FAX 01686-688324
Carefully restored 17th-
century half-timbered barn.
Children welcome; play area,
many country walks, stream,
abundant wildlife. Sitting
room. Family-style dining.
🏠 2 🅿 3 Ⓢ

## PENYBONT

🏨 **FFALDAU COUNTRY
HOUSE**
**$/$$**

LLANDEGLEY
LD1 5UD
TEL/FAX 01597-851421
Beautifully preserved, early
16th-century house with
beams and stone-flagged
floors. Children welcome.
🏠 3 🅿 25 Ⓢ Ⓢ All
major cards

## REYNOLDSTON

🏨 **FAIRYHILL**
🍽 **$$$$** ★★ ✿✿✿
REYNOLDSTON
SA3 1BS
TEL 01792-390139
FAX 01792-391358
Eighteenth-century mansion
on 24 acres of wooded
grounds on Gower peninsula.
Warm hospitality. Log fires,
fresh flowers. Imaginative
cuisine featuring Welsh dishes.
Fixed-price L & D. No
children under eight.
🏠 8 🛏 60 🅿 50
🕐 Closed two weeks Jan.
Ⓢ Restaurant Ⓢ All major
cards

## RUTHIN

**SOMETHING
SPECIAL**

🏨 **RUTHIN CASTLE**
Characterful early 19th-
century pile with own
castle ruins, which mostly
date from the 13th century, on
30-acre grounds. The castle
withstood an attack by Welsh
rebel leader Owain Glyndwr
in 1400. During the Civil War
it fell to the Roundhead
General Mytton in 1646 after
an 11-week siege, and was
then dismantled. Paneling,
carved ceilings. Medieval
banquets in restored hall.
**$$$** ★★★ ✿
RUTHIN
LL15 2NU
TEL 01824-702664
FAX 01824-705978
🏠 58 🅿 200 🍴 Ⓢ All
major cards

## ST. DAVID'S

### 🏨 WARPOOL COURT
**$$$/$$$$** ★★★ 🌸🌸
ST. DAVID'S
SA62 6BN
TEL 01437-720300
FAX 01437-720676
Former cathedral choir
school overlooking St.
Bride's Bay. Over 3,000
handpainted tiles on display.
Imaginative cuisine.
🛏 25 🅿 100 🕐 Closed
Jan. 🍴 Restaurant 🎡 🐴
🗝 All major cards

### 🍴 MORGAN'S BRASSERIE
**$$$** 🌸🌸
20 NUN ST.
SA62 6NT
TEL 01437-720508
Pleasant little brasserie serving
fresh fish and seasonal Welsh
ingredients. Other dishes are
modern European in style.
🪑 32 🕐 Closed L, Sun. &
Jan.–Feb. (restricted winter
opening times) 🍴 🗝 All
major cards

## SKENFRITH

### 🍴 BELL AT SKENFRITH
**$$$** 🌸🌸
SKENFRITH
NP7 8UH
TEL 01600-750235
FAX 01600-750525
A welcoming coaching inn by
the bridge and near the castle;
very friendly, young, local staff,
clean, uncluttered decor; local
produce with a modern
approach.
🪑 40 🅿 40 🗝 All major
cards

## TENBY

### 🏨 ATLANTIC
**$$$** ★★★
THE ESPLANADE
SA70 7DU
TEL 01834-842881
FAX 01834-842881 EXT 256
Family-run hotel with views
over the sea. Restaurant
menus offer classic French
and English cooking; light
meals served all day in

basement bistro. Fixed-
price D.
🛏 42 🅿 30 🔗 🐴
🗝 All major cards

---

## SOUTH MIDLANDS

## BIRMINGHAM

### 🏨 THE BURLINGTON
**$$$** ★★★★
BURLINGTON ARCADE
126 NEW ST.
B2 4JQ
TEL 0121-643 9191
FAX 0121-628 5005
Situated in the heart of
Birmingham, this elegant hotel
blends together its original
Victorian design with modern
facilities. Imaginative, carefully
prepared cuisine in the Berlioz
Restaurant.
🛏 112 🔗 🐴 🗝 All
major cards

### 🍴 SHIMLA PINKS
**$$** 🌸
214 BROAD ST.
B15 1AY
TEL 0121-6330366
FAX 0121-6433325
Familiar dishes, tikkas and
tandooris especially, using
fresh herbs and spices, and
the evening help-yourself
buffet attracts crowds of
diners to this unusual and
stylish Indian restaurant
housed in a converted car
showroom. Children are
welcomed with their own
menu. Fixed-price L & D.
🪑 350 🕐 Closed Sat L., Sun.
L, Christmas & New Year's
Days 🔗 🗝 All major cards

## BROADWAY

### 🏨🍴 LYGON ARMS
**$$$$$** ★★★★ 🌸🌸
HIGH ST.
WR12 7DU
TEL 01386-852255
FAX 01386-858611
Sixteeenth-century inn
around courtyard. Log fires,
wood paneling. Great Hall
restaurant has heraldic panels
and Minstrels' Gallery; Goblets

Restaurant is less formal.
Tennis and croquet lawn.
Fixed-price L & D.
🛏 65 🪑 90 🅿 152
🍴 Restaurant 🎡 🐴
🗝 All major cards

### 🍴 BUCKLAND MANOR
**$$$$** ★★★ 🌸🌸🌸
BUCKLAND
WR12 7LY
TEL 01386-852626
FAX 01386-853557
Medieval, honey-colored
stone building in lovely
gardens. Country-house
cooking with variations.
Seasonal vegetables, herbs,
fruit from manor's garden.
Remarkable wine list. Fixed-
price L. No children under
eight.
🪑 40 🍴 🗝 All major
cards

## BURFORD

### 🏨 BURFORD HOUSE
**$$$**
99 HIGH ST.
OX18 4QA
TEL 01993-823151
FAX 01993-823240
Hotel with enclosed garden in
the center of Burford. Four-
poster beds, bathrooms with
old-fashioned tubs. Lunch, or

---

tea with a tempting array of homemade cakes.

🚭 7 ❄ 💳 All major cards

## CHELTENHAM

### 🏨 CLEEVE HILL
**$$$**
CLEEVE HILL
GL52 3PR
TEL 01242-672052
FAX 01242-679969
In a commanding position looking over the Severn Valley to the Malvern Hills beyond. Friendly and attentive service from enthusiastic staff. The modern bedrooms, bar, and spacious lounge are furnished to a high standard. No children under 12.

🛏9 🅿10 ❄ 💳 All major cards

### 🍴 LE CHAMPIGNON SAUVAGE
**$$$$** ❄❄❄❄
24 SUFFOLK RD.
GL50 2AQ
TEL/FAX 01242-573449
Great food in an unassuming atmosphere. A restaurant where people enjoy eating civilized French cooking. Fixed-price L & D.

🪑 28 ⏰ Closed Sun., Mon., Easter, 2 weeks June & Christmas ❄ 💳 All major cards

## CHIPPING CAMDEN

### 🏨 COTSWOLD HOUSE
**$$$$** ★★★ ❄❄
THE SQUARE
GL55 6AN
TEL 01386-840330
FAX 01386-840310
Seventeenth-century hotel in the center of this typical Cotswolds town. The relaxed Hicks Brasserie is open all day; Garden Room Restaurant more formal.

🛏15 🅿15 ❄ 🏥
💳 All major cards

## CHURCH ENSTONE

### 🍴 THE CROWN INN
**$$** ❄
MILL LANE
OX7 4NN
TEL 01608-677262
A real Oxfordshire village local made of Cotswold stone and serving good, solid pub fare.

🪑 42 🅿8 ⏰ Closed Mon. L, Sun. D.

## CIRENCESTER

### 🏨 CROWN OF CRUCIS
**$$$** ★★★ ❄
AMPNEY CRUCIS
GL7 5RS
TEL 01285-851806
FAX 01285-851735
A charming hotel made up of two buildings. A 16th century coaching inn houses the bar and pine-adorned restaurant. Bedrooms are in a modern block surrounding a courtyard. Bar food. Fixed-price D.

🛏25 🅿82 ⏰ Closed Dec. 24–30 ❄ Restaurant
💳 All major cards

## CLAVERDON

### 🏨 ARDENCOTE MANOR HOTEL & COUNTRY CLUB
**$$$$** ★★★ ❄
LYE GREEN RD.
CV35 8LS
TEL 01926-843111
FAX 01926-842646
Small hotel with good range of facilities. Bedrooms are decorated with pretty fabrics. Formal dining in the Oak Room; informal snacks and meals in members' bar and at lakeside. Tennis, golf, and fishing.

🛏18 🅿120 ❄ Restaurant
🏊 🏥 💳 All major cards

## DAVENTRY

### 🍴 HELLIDON LAKES
**$$$** ❄
HELLIDON
NN11 6LN
TEL 01327-262550
Spectacular views over

landscaped grounds and lakes. Modern British cooking. Fixed-price D.

🪑 90 ❄ 💳 All major cards

## GREAT MILTON

SOMETHING SPECIAL

### 🏨 LE MANOIR AUX
### 🍴 QUAT' SAISONS
Raymond Blanc's mellow stone 15th-century manor house in immaculately maintained gardens with famous and very busy restaurant. Beautifully appointed bedrooms and suites, some have with own private terrace garden. Outstanding cuisine is enhanced during summer by herbs and vegetables grown in the walled kitchen garden. Croquet lawn. Children welcomed with their own menu. Fixed-price L & D.
**$$$$$** ★★★★ ❄❄❄
CHURCH RD.
GREAT MILTON
OX44 7PD
TEL 01844-278881
FAX 01844-278847

🛏32 🪑120 🅿60
❄ Restaurant 💳 All major cards

## HENLEY-ON-THAMES

### 🏨 RED LION
**$$$$** ★★★ ❄
HART ST.
RG9 2AR
TEL 01491-572161
FAX 01491-410039
Sixteenth-century redbrick and ivy-clad inn with fabulous views of River Thames where the Royal Henley Regatta races end. The competing crews row from Temple Island, 1 mile 550 yards downriver, past packed grandstands to Henley Bridge near the inn. Wood paneling, flagstone floors. Regatta Brasserie offers freshly prepared dishes.

🛏27 🅿25 💳 All major cards

## LEAMINGTON SPA

### 🏨 MALLORY COURT
### 🍴 $$$$$ ★★★ 🏵🏵🏵
HARBURY LANE
BISHOP'S TACHBROOK
CV33 9QB
TEL 01926-330214
FAX 01926-451714
English country house with
friendly and attentive service.
Wood-paneled restaurant
offers light, innovative cuisine.
Homemade canapés, breads,
and petits fours; fresh vegeta-
bles and herbs from the
garden. Tennis and croquet.
Fixed-price L & D. No
children under nine.
🛈 18 🛏 50 🅿 52
🍽 Restaurant 🏊 🏧 All
major cards

## LEOMINSTER

### 🏨 HEATH HOUSE
### $$
STOKE PRIOR
HR6 0NF
TEL/FAX 01568-760385
Surrounded by beautiful
countryside and pretty
gardens, this 17th-century
farmhouse retains many
original interior features such
as exposed beams and open
fireplaces. Bedrooms are
spacious and of excellent
quality, and the hospitality is
warm and welcoming. No
children under six.
🛈 3 🅿 2 🕐 Closed
Oct.–Mar. 🍽

## MALVERN WELLS

### 🏨 COTTAGE IN THE WOOD
### $$$/$$$$ ★★★ 🏵🏵
HOLYWELL RD.
WR14 4LG
TEL 01684-575859
FAX 01684-560662
Former haunt of the
composer Sir Edward Elgar.
There are magnificent views
from the Malvern Hills.
Talented and innovative chef.
🛈 8 (23 annex) 🅿 40 🍽
🏧 All major cards

## OUNDLE

### 🏨 TALBOT
Hospitable 17th-century
hotel in the historic town
of Oundle. Partly built using
material from the ruins of
nearby Fotheringhay Castle
where Mary, Queen of Scots,
was imprisoned and executed.
A painting in the bar of the
hotel shows her descending a
staircase, surrounded by
solemn courtiers and wardens
and followed by weeping
women. Spacious, attractive
bedrooms; many of which
have exposed beams. The cozy
bar and lounge are in keeping
with the hotel's Old World
charm.
**$$ ★★★**
NEW ST.
OUNDLE
PE8 4EA
TEL 01832-273621
FAX 01832-274545
🛈 39 🅿 50 🍽 Restaurant
🏧 All major cards

## OXFORD

### 🏨 LINTON LODGE
### $$$$ ★★★
LINTON RD.
OX2 6UJ
TEL 01865-553461
FAX 01865-310365
Peaceful hotel in residential
area north of the city center.
Wood-paneled restaurant; bar
overlooking croquet lawn.
🛈 71 🅿 40 🛗 🍽 Rest-
aurant 🏧 All major cards

### 🏨 RANDOLPH
### 🍴 $$$$ ★★★★ 🏵
BEAUMONT ST.
OX1 2LN
TEL 0870-400 8200
FAX 01865-791678
Fine landmark Victorian hotel
across from the Ashmolean
Museum. Afternoon teas in
drawing room. Formal dining
in Spires Restaurant.

🛈 119 🛏 60 🅿 64 🛗
🍽 Restaurant 🏧 All major
cards

### 🏨 EASTGATE
### $$$ ★★★
THE HIGH
MERTON ST.
OX1 4BE
TEL 0870-400 8201
FAX 01865-791681
Relaxing hotel with a friendly,
informal atmosphere, close to
Magdalen Bridge with views of
the famous Examination Hall.
🛈 64 🅿 27 🛗 🏧 All
major cards

### 🏨 GABLES
### $
6 CUMNOR HILL
OX2 9HA
TEL 01865-862153
FAX 01865-864054
Charming Victorian house
with large rear garden and
conservatory. Warm, friendly
welcome.
🛈 6 🅿 6 🕐 Closed Dec.
24–Jan. 1 🍽 🏧 MC, V

### 🍴 LE PETIT BLANC
### $$$ 🏵🏵
71–72 WALTON ST.
OX2 6AG
TEL 01865-510999
Raymond Blanc's busy, popular,
sparkling brasserie in a former
piano shop, has a something-
for-everyone menu featuring
regional French food. Fixed-
price L & D.
🛏 136 🍽 🏧 All major
cards

## PAINSWICK

### 🏨 PAINSWICK
### $$$/$$$$ ★★★ 🏵🏵
KEMPS LANE
GL6 6YB
TEL 01452-812160
FAX 01452-814059
Elegant hotel in beautiful
Cotswold village. Rural views
from the garden terrace. The
restaurant uses quality
ingredients, including local
game, gloucestershire cheeses,
lobsters and other shellfish
from the hotel's own tank.

HOTELS & RESTAURANTS

Croquet. Fixed-price L & D.
🚭 19 🅿 25 🅂 Restaurant
🖘 All major cards

## SOLIHULL

### 🍴 NUTHURST GRANGE
$$$ ❀❀❀
NUTHURST GRANGE LANE,
HOCKLEY HEATH
B94 5NL
TEL 01564-783972
Surrounded by landscaped
gardens and woodlands, this
elegant dining room serves
modern British cuisine. Varied
and interesting menus change
seasonally. Fixed-price L & D.
🪑 60 🕐 Closed Sat. L 🅂
🖘 All major cards

## STRATFORD-UPON-AVON

SOMETHING SPECIAL

### 🍴 THE BOATHOUSE
A part from being a
fashionable waterside
restaurant, this is a working
boathouse in its own right,
where guests can rent punts
and rowboats—and it offers a
gondola service to and from
the theater. Balcony dining
room looks out on river.
Earthy food with strong Thai
influence. Fixed-price L & D.
$$$
SWAN'S NEST LANE
STRATFORD-UPON-AVON
CV37 7LS
TEL 01789-297733
🪑 90 🕐 Closed Sat. L,
Christmas & New Year
🖘 AE, MC, V

### 🏨 BILLESLEY MANOR
$$$$$ ★★★★ ❀❀
BILLESLEY
ALCESTER
B49 6NF
TEL 01789-279955
FAX 01789-764145
Sixteenth-century manor
house on peaceful grounds
which include a topiary
garden. Many original features
such as oak paneling and

magnificent fireplaces.
Interesting, carefully prepared
menus. Tennis and croquet.
🚭 41 🅿 85 🅂 Restaurant
🖘 🖘 All major cards

### 🏨 SHAKESPEARE
$$$$$ ★★★★ ❀❀
CHAPEL ST.
CV37 6ER
TEL 0870-400 8182
FAX 01789-415411
Charming gabled central
hotel, with a profusion of
exposed beams, creaking
staircases, and wood fires.
Restaurant menus or
courtyard bistro.
🚭 74 🅿 34 🖪 🅂 Rest-
aurant 🖘 All major cards

### 🏨 ALVESTON MANOR
$$$$ ★★★★
CLOPTON BRIDGE
CV37 7HP
TEL 0870-400 8181
FAX 01789-414095
Warm brick and timber
facade, gable ends, and well-
tended grounds make a
striking building that dates to
the 16th century. The kitchen
is up-to-date with its ideas.
🚭 114 🅿 200 🅂 Rest-
aurant 🖘 All major cards

## SUTTON COLDFIELD

### 🏨 THE THISTLE
### 🍴 NEW HALL
$$$$ ★★★★ ❀❀
WALMLEY RD.
B76 1QX
TEL 0121-3782442
Reputedly the oldest sur-
viving moated manor house
in England. The lovely grounds
include a walled rose garden
and a yew tree walk. Rooms
retain many original features
and have delightful decor.
High quality, imaginative
cuisine. Golf, fishing and
croquet. Fixed-price D.
🚭 60 🪑 60 🅿 70
🕐 Closed Sat. L
🅂 Restaurant 🖘 All major
cards

## TETBURY

### 🏨 SNOOTY FOX
$$$ ★★★ ❀
MARKET PLACE
GL8 8DD
TEL 01666-502436
FAX 01666-503479
Sixteenth-century Cotswold
stone inn; warm and friendly
staff. Restaurant with ornately
carved wall paneling and
impressive ceiling.
🚭 12 🅂 Restaurant 🖘 All
major cards

## THAME

### 🏨 DAIRY
$$$
MORETON
OX9 2HX
TEL 01844-214075
Peaceful and comfortable.
King-size beds, hair dryers,
writing desks, remote-control
TV, fresh flowers. No children
under 12.
🚭 3 🅂 🅿 8 🖘 AE, MC, V

## TOWCESTER

### 🍴 VINE HOUSE
$$$ ❀❀
100 HIGH ST.
PAULERSPURY
NN12 7NA
TEL 01327-811267
Relaxing country cottage
restaurant. Menu changes
daily; repertoire is seasonal,
style modern British. Fixed-
price L & D.
🪑 45 🕐 Closed Sat.–Wed.
L, all Sun., & 2 weeks after
Christmas 🅂 🖘 MC, V

## WALLINGFORD

### 🍴 BEETLE AND WEDGE
$$$$
FERRY LANE
MOULSFORD
OX10 9JF
TEL 01491-651381
This Thames-side restaurant
has literary links (former
home of Jerome K. Jerome,
author of classic Thames farce
*Three Men In A Boat*), river
views, and fine cooking of tip-

**HOTELS & RESTAURANTS**

top freshness on a daily changing menu that follows the seasons.
🍴 25 (dining room), 60 (boathouse) 🅢 Dining room 🅢 All major cards

## WARWICK

### 🏨 CAMBRIDGE VILLA HOTEL
$$
20A EMSCOTE RD.
WARWICKSHIRE
CV34 4PP
TEL 01926-491169
A well-kept hotel converted from two Victorian properties.
ⓘ 14 🅿 10 🅢 All major cards

## WHITNEY-ON-WYE

### 🏨 RHYDSPENCE INN
$$ ★★
WHITNEY-ON-WYE
HR3 6EU
TEL 01497-831262
FAX 01497-831751
Privately owned, personally run 14th-century inn on boundary of England and Wales. Attractive restaurant; two quaint bars with low-beamed ceilings and log fires.
ⓘ 7 🅿 30 🕒 Closed 2 weeks Jan. 🅢 Restaurant 🅢 All major cards

## WISHAW

### 🏨 THE DE VERE BELFRY
$$$$$ ★★★★ ❀❀
B76 9PR
TEL 01675-470301
FAX 01675-470256
Set in peaceful, beautiful countryside, this well known Ryder Cup venue offers three golf courses and a choice of five restaurants. Friendly and helpful staff.
ⓘ 324 🅿 1000 🔁 ☎ 📺 🅢 All major cards

## BLAKENEY

### 🏨 MORSTON HALL
$$$$ ★★ ❀❀❀
MORSTON
NR25 7AA
TEL 01263-741041
FAX 01263-740419
Seventeenth-century house in small village on beautiful and wildlife-rich north Norfolk coast. Conservatory overlooks pretty gardens. Restaurant is full of fresh flowers and paintings. Fixed-price, four-course menu (no choice until dessert), is both well-balanced and skillfully executed; superb produce, wine list, and presentation.
ⓘ 6 🅿 40 🕒 Closed Dec. 25–26 🅢 Restaurant 🅢 All major cards

## BURNHAM MARKET

### 🏨 HOSTE ARMS
$$$ ★★ ❀❀
THE GREEN
PE31 8HD
TEL 01328-738777
FAX 01328-730103
Pub, restaurant, and hotel, upscale and stylish in appearance, yet down-to-earth and unpretentious. Art exhibitions, a splendid atmosphere, and excellent cooking that features local fish.
ⓘ 24 (6 annex) 🅿 60 🅢 All major cards

## BURY ST. EDMUNDS

### 🏨 CHANTRY
$$
8 SPARHAWK ST.
IP33 1RY
TEL 01284-767427
FAX 01284-760946
Splendid Georgian house standing in the site of a former 12th-century Chantry Chapel. Warm hospitality and friendly service.
ⓘ 13 (3 annex) 🅿 16 🅢 Restaurant 🅢 All major card

## CAMBRIDGE

### 🏨 CAMBRIDGE GARDEN HOUSE MOAT HOUSE
$$$$$ ★★★★
GRANTA PLACE
MILL LANE
CB2 1RT
TEL 01223-259988
FAX 01223-316605
Set on own grounds overlooking River Cam. Fishing. Smartly kept modern bedrooms. Stylish restaurant and bar meals. Fixed-price L & D.
ⓘ 117 🅿 180 🔁 🅢 Restaurant ☎ 📺 🅢 All major cards

### 🏨 ARUNDEL HOUSE
$$/$$$ ★★
CHESTERTON RD.
CB4 3AN
TEL 01223-367701
FAX 01223-367721
Town house hotel close to River Cam and Jesus Green parkland. Victorian conservatory for all-day meals; restaurant serves interesting and varied dishes. Attractively decorated modern bedrooms.
ⓘ 83 (22 annex) 🅿 70

🚭 Closed Dec. 25–26
🅰 Restaurant 🅰 All
major cards

## 🍴 MIDSUMMER HOUSE
**$$$$** ⊛⊛⊛
MIDSUMMER COMMON
CB4 1HA
TEL 01223-369299
A bright and airy conser-
vatory is the main focus of
this restaurant that goes
from strength to strength.
Clever use of color and
style reflected in the
seasonal menu. Earthy,
robust ingredients are
refined to great effect.
Fixed-price L & D.
🪑 65 🚭 Closed Sun.–
Mon., 2 weeks Christmas,
Easter, 2 weeks Aug.–Sept.
🅰 🅰 All major cards

## CASTLE ACRE

### 🏨 LODGE FARM
**$$**
CASTLE ACRE
PE32 2BS
TEL 01760-755506
FAX 01760-755103
Large old farmhouse on
20 acres of paddocks and
gardens. The bedrooms are
spacious and traditionally
furnished. No children
under two.
🛏 3 🅿 6 🚭 Christmas
🅰

## COLCHESTER

### 🏨 OLD MANSE
**$**
15 ROMAN RD.
CO1 1UR
TEL 01206 545154
FAX 01206 545153
Family run bed-and-
breakfast situated close to
the town center and
Norman Castle. Historic
Roman wall running along
bottom of the garden.
Warm hospitality. No
children under six.
🛏 3 🅿 1 🚭 Closed
Dec. 23–31 🅰

## DEDHAM

### 🏨 MAISON TALBOOTH
Overlooking tranquil
Dedham Vale, this
pretty Georgian hotel gives a
warm welcome. Stylish
bedrooms equipped with
thoughful touches, such as
fruit baskets. Le Talbooth
Restaurant is a little under a
mile away from the Maison
Talbooth. The hotel has a
courtesy car for diners, but
in fine weather most guests
enjoy the 15-minute stroll to
and from their dining place
on the banks of the River
Stour. The restaurant—the
16th-century weaver's
cottage and toll house
overlooking the river that
John Constable featured in
his famous landscapes—has
good cooking balanced
between traditional and
modern.
**$$$$** ★★★ ⊛⊛
STRATFORD RD.
DEDHAM
CO7 6HN
TEL 01206-322367
FAX 01206-322752
🛏 10 🪑 75 🅿 20 🅰 All
major cards

## DISS

### 🍴 FOX AND GOOSE
The Fox and Goose was
built in Tudor times, say
its deeds, "for the more
reverence of God, in avoiding
eating and drinking necessary
to the profits of the church."
Not an easy intention to
interpret; possibly the idea
was to prevent the locals from
eating in church. The parish
church still owns the inn and
benefits from its rents. A place
of great character with bare
boards, brickwork, oak
beams, log fires, and a lovely
view of the church. Good
solid cooking. Bar meals.
Fixed-price L & D.
**$$$** ⊛⊛
FRESSINGFIELD
IP21 5PB
TEL 01379-586247
🪑 40 🚭 Closed Mon. 🅰
🅰 All major cards

## ELY

### 🏨 LAMB
**$$$** ★★★ ⊛
2 LYNN RD.
CB7 4EJ
TEL 01353-663574
FAX 01353-662023
Privately owned and
personally managed 15th-
century inn. Modern British
cooking in the Octagon
Restaurant.
🛏 32 🪑 40 🅿 20
🅰 Restaurant 🅰 All major
cards

### 🍴 THE ANCHOR INN
**$$** ⊛
SUTTON GAULT, SUTTON
CB6 2BD
TEL 01353-778537
This clean and friendly
riverside inn is notable for its
well-cooked food and
cheerful staff—a little treasure
in the back of beyond.
🪑 70 🅿 16

## GRIMSTON

### 🏨 CONGHAM HALL
**$$$$/$$$$$** ★★★ ⊛⊛
LYNN RD.
PE32 1AH
TEL 01485-600250
FAX 01485-601191
Georgian manor house on
extensive grounds, which
include a herb garden, walled
flower garden, cricket ground,
and tennis courts. The
Orangery Restaurant over-
looks the garden. Appealing
dishes feature produce from
the garden and focus on
Mediterranean and North

HOTELS & RESTAURANTS

European flavor combinations. No children under seven.

🛏 14 🅿 50 🄢 Restaurant
🖃 🖲 All major cards

## HARWICH

### 🏨 PIER AT HARWICH
🍴 **$$$ ★★★** 🌑🌑
THE QUAY
CO12 3HH
TEL 01255-241212
FAX 01255-551922
Excellent small harborfront hotel. Renowned for its cooking, specializing in seafood: choose from the informal, family oriented Ha'penny Pier—try the fish and chips; you won't find a more delicious example of Britain's national fast food dish—or more serious dining in the Pier at Harwich Restaurant, which overlooks the quay and harbor and comes complete with ship's wheel and bell, lots of shipping prints, and maritime murals. Fixed-price L & D.

🛏 6 (7 annex) 🍴 80 🅿 10
🖲 All major cards

## HINTLESHAM

### 🏨 HINTLESHAM HALL
🍴 **$$$/$$$$$ ★★★★** 🌑🌑🌑
HINTLESHAM
IP8 3NS
TEL 01473-652334/652268
FAX 01473-652463
Tudor country house with magnificent Georgian facade. Both the pine-paneled parlor and The Salon restaurant—a magnificent high-ceilinged room that oozes luxury—offer menus that follow the seasons and include precise and razor-sharp cooking. Noted for classical cuisine. Golf, tennis, riding, clay-pigeon and game shooting.

🛏 33 🍴 100 🅿 100
🕐 Closed Sat. L
🄢 Restaurant 🖃 🖲
🖲 All major cards

## HOLKHAM

### 🍴 THE VICTORIA AT HOLKHAM
**$$$** 🌑
PARK RD.
NR23 1RG
TEL 01328-711008
Meat and game from the Holkham Estate, fish from the nearby sea, and a weird but welcoming British colonial decor.

🍴 50 🅿 50

## LAVENHAM

### 🏨 SWAN
**$$$$ ★★★★** 🌑🌑
HIGH ST.
CO10 9QA
TEL 0870-400 8116
FAX 01787-248286
Delightful half-timbered hotel in quintessentially picturesque English town. Minstrels' Gallery, wood fires, and beautiful courtyard gardens add to the atmosphere and enhance the enjoyment of the fresh, seasonal cooking. Bar food.

🛏 51 🅿 60 🄢 Restaurant
🖲 All major cards

## LINCOLN

### 🏨 WHITE HART
**$$$ ★★★★**
BAILGATE
LN1 3AR
TEL 0870-400 8117
FAX 01522-531798
In a delightful central location between the castle and the cathedral with good views of the city. Informal eating in the Orangery; quietly elegant dining room.

🛏 48 🅿 57 🖲
🄢 Restaurant 🖲 All major cards

### 🍴 WIG AND MITRE
**$$$** 🌑
30 STEEP HILL
LN2 1TL
TEL 01522-535190
Marvelously renovated medieval building. Popular bar

downstairs, and smart upstairs restaurant serving modern British cuisine. Bar food. Fixed-price L.

🍴 60 🄢 Restaurant 🖲 All major cards

## NORWICH

### 🏨 SPROWSTON MANOR HOUSE
**$$$ ★★★★** 🌑
SPROWSTON PARK,
WROXHAM RD.
SPROWSTON
NR7 8RP
TEL 01603-410871
FAX 01603-423911
Nineteenth-century manor house on ten acres of parkland on outskirts of city. Modern European cooking and vegetarian dishes in Manor Restaurant. Family and four-poster rooms. Health Spa and golf.

🛏 94 🅿 150 🖲
🄢 Restaurant 🖃 🖲
🖲 All major cards

### 🍴 ADLARD'S
**$$$$** 🌑🌑🌑
79 UPPER ST. GILES ST.
NR2 1AB
TEL 01603-633522
A touch of big city flair, comfort, and easygoing informality in this French-style storefront restaurant. Stripped pine floors, emerald walls hung with modern abstracts and conventional watercolors. Dishes can be combined, either as a set meal or individually. Fixed-price L & D.

🍴 40 🕐 Closed Sun., Mon. L, 1 week after Christmas
🄢 🖲 All major cards

### 🍴 BRUMMELS SEAFOOD RESTAURANT
**$$$$** 🌑🌑
7 MAGDALEN ST.
NR3 1LE
TEL 01603-625555
The menu here is mostly fish, and wholly delicious.

🍴 30

## SOUTHWOLD

### ⊞ SWAN

Handsome old hotel on
Southwold's market-
place. Some bedrooms
surround an old bowling
green. Appetizing, imag-
inative cooking; excellent
wine list. The Swan backs
onto the Sole Bay Brewery of
Adnams. Adnams bitter is
justly famed as one of the
tastiest beers in Britain.
**$$$/$$$$** ★★★ ⊛⊛
MARKET PLACE
SOUTHWOLD
IP18 6EG
TEL 01502-722186
FAX 01502-724800
🛈 26 (17 annex) 🅿 35
🔁 🚭 Restaurant 🐾 All
major cards

## STAMFORD

### ⊞ GARDEN HOUSE
**$$$** ★★★
ST. MARTIN'S
PE9 2LP
TEL 01780-763359
FAX 01780-763339
Charming 18th-century
house. Friendly service and
good, varied menus.
🛈 20 🅿 30 🐾 All major
cards

## STOKE-BY-NAYLAND

### ⊞ ANGEL INN
**$$**
POLSTEAD ST.
CO6 4SA
TEL 01206-263245
FAX 01206-263373
Deservedly popular 16th-
century inn, surrounded by
lovely countryside. Exposed
brickwork, beams, fireplaces,
gallery overlooking dining
room. The emphasis here is
on quality and with
exceptionally good bar meals,
things can get very crowded
on sunny weekends. No
children under eight.

🛈 5 (1 annex) 🅿 25
🚭 Closed Dec. 25–26
🚭 Bedrooms 🐾 All major
cards

## SUDBURY

### 🍽 THE BLACK LION
⊞ **$$$** ⊛
CHURCH WALK, THE GREEN,
LONG MELFORD
CO10 9DN
TEL 01787-312336
FAX 01787-374557
Individually furnished rooms
and an excellent restaurant in
a Tudor hotel on the green of
this village famous for its
antique shops.
🛈 10 🍴 50 🅿 10

## WINTERINGHAM

### 🍽 WINTERINGHAM FIELDS
⊞ **$$$$$** ★★ ⊛⊛⊛⊛
DN15 9PF
TEL 01724-733096
FAX 01724-733898
An oasis of comfort, good
food, and hospitality. Quality is
impeccable, much of it from
the walled garden. Guests
from Europe fly in just to dine
here. Cooking style is based
on traditional methods,
applied with a light touch and
a modern twist. Fixed-price L
& D. No children under eight.
🍴 42 🛈 4 (6 annex) 🅿 17
🚭 Closed Sun., Mon., 2
weeks Christmas, last week
March 1st week Aug. 🚭
🐾 All major cards

## ACTON TRUSSEL

### 🍽 MOAT HOUSE
**$$$** ⊛⊛
ACTON TRUSSEL
ST17 0RJ
TEL 01785-712217
Restored 17th-century
timbered building overlooking
canal. Busy pub/restaurant
offering consistently high
standards of cooking and
efficient service. Fixed-price L.

🍴 120 🚭 Closed Dec.
25–26 & Jan. 1 🚭 🚭
🐾 All major cards

## ASHBOURNE

### 🍽 CALLOW HALL
The family-run kitchen
produces not only breads
but preserves, home-cured
bacon, and sausages as well.
Fresh fish from the market
features strongly. The Spencer
family, who live at Callow
Hall, have long roots in the
area: Their ancestors opened a
bakery in Ashbourne as far
back as 1724. Fixed-price L
& D.
**$$$$** ⊛⊛
MAPPLETON RD.
DE6 2AA
TEL 01335-300900
FAX 01335-300512
🍴 60 🚭 Closed L, Sun. D &
Dec. 25–26 🚭 🐾 All
major cards

## BAKEWELL

### ⊞ HASSOP HALL
**$$$** ★★★
HASSOP
DE45 1NS
TEL 01629-640488
FAX 01629-640577
Fine historic house, family run.
Walks in gardens and woods,
and tennis. Bright dining room.
🛈 13 🅿 80 🚭 Closed Sun.
D, Dec. 24–25 🔁 🐾 All
major cards

### 🍽 FISCHER'S
BASLOW HALL
**$$$$** ⊛⊛⊛
BASLOW HALL
CALVER RD.
DE45 1RR
TEL 01246-583259
This Derbyshire manor house
exudes warmth and comfort.
The cooking is worth traveling
for, but it is not in the mold of
country restaurants; innova-
tive without being outlandish.

**HOTELS & RESTAURANTS**

Fixed-price L & D.
**H** 40 **C** Closed Mon. L, Sun. D **S** **&** All major cards

**H RENAISSANCE**
**$$$** ✦
BATH ST.
DE45 1BX
TEL 01629-812687
Converted barn, now a comfortably appointed restaurant that overlooks a small walled garden. Home-grown herbs and fresh produce are used to create some imaginative dishes. Bar meals. Fixed-price D.
**H** 40 **C** Closed Sun. D, Mon., 2 weeks Jan., 2 weeks Aug. **S** Restaurant
**&** MC, V

## BUXTON

**H LEE WOOD**
**$$$** ★★★ ✦✦
THE PARK
SK17 6TQ
TEL 01298-23002
FAX 01298-23228
Friendly Georgian hotel with two bars, lounge, and conservatory restaurant. An extensive menu with a wide choice of vegetarian dishes. Fixed-price D.
**(I)** 35 (5 annex) **P** 50 **S**
**&** All major cards

**H CONINGSBY**
**$$**
6 MACCLESFIELD RD.
SK17 9AH
TEL/FAX 01298-26735
Carefully restored Victorian house, a short walk from town center and Pavilion gardens. Home cooking. No children.
**(I)** 3 **P** 6 **S** **&** MC, V

## CHESTER

**H CHESTER GROSVENOR**
**$$$$$** ★★★★★ ✦✦✦
EASTGATE
CH1 1LT
TEL 01244-324024
FAX 01244-313246
Inside the Roman walls of the

city. Horsey pictures and lots of polished wood, silver, and oversized glasses in the formal Arkle Restaurant. Experienced and discreetly professional tuxedoed staff. Good ingredients, fancy desserts, lots of extras, tremendous wine list. Fixed-price L & D.
**(I)** 85 **H** 45 **C** Closed Dec. 25–26 **S** **S** **V**
**&** All major cards

**H CRABWALL MANOR**
**$$$$** ★★★★ ✦✦
PARKGATE RD.
MOLLINGTON
CH1 6NE
TEL 01244-851666
Views of the city skyline make a meal at Crabwall Manor something special. The same menu, a mixture of French and English, modern and classical influences, is offered both at lunch and dinner, and all dishes are cooked in a simpler way on request.
**H** 80 **(I)** 48 **P** 120
**C** Closed Mon. L
**S** Restaurant **S** **S** **V**
**&** All major cards

## CHURCH STRETTON

**H MYND HOUSE**
**$$** ★★
LITTLE STRETTON
SY6 6RB
TEL 01694-722212
FAX 01694-724180
Friendly Edwardian-style hotel. Cooking includes regional specialties using local ingredients. No children under ten.
**(I)** 7 **P** 8 **S** **&** MC, V

## GRINDLEFORD

**H MAYNARD ARMS**
**$$$** ★★★
MAIN RD.
S32 2HE
TEL 01433-630321
FAX 01433-630445
Handsome old hotel with fine views of Peak District hills and dales. Visitors' lounge, lounge bar, cocktail bar, restaurant overlooking gardens.

**(I)** 10 **P** 80 **S** Restaurant
**&** All major cards

## HOPE

**H UNDERLEIGH HOUSE**
**$$**
OFF EDALE RD.
S33 6RF
TEL 01433-621372
FAX 01433-621324
Sympathetic barn conversion with award-winning garden. Freshly prepared menu. No children under 12.
**(I)** 6 **P** 6 **C** Closed Christmas & New Year **S**
**&** MC, V

## LUDLOW

**H OVERTON GRANGE**
**$$$** ★★★ ✦✦✦
HEREFORD RD.
SY8 4AD
TEL 01584-873500
FAX 01584-873524
Edwardian house with views across the Shropshire hills. Wood-paneled restaurant; fresh ingredients.
**(I)** 14 **P** 80 **S** Restaurant
**&** All major cards

**H NUMBER TWENTY EIGHT**
**$$**
28 LOWER BROAD ST.
SY8 1PQ
TEL 01584-876996
FAX 01584-876860
Combination of three separate houses, all with original features and quality period furnishings. Warm welcome.
**(I)** 6 **S** **&** AE, MC, V

**H HIBISCUS RESTAURANT**
**$$$** ✦✦✦✦
17 CORVE ST.
SY8 1DA
TEL 01584-872325
Impressive 17th-century inn with much original character; a warm, relaxing atmosphere, and hosts who play their part with enthusiasm. Good modern French cooking. Fixed-price D.

🛏 30 🕐 Closed Sun.,
Mon. & Tues. L, 2 weeks Jan.,
I week Aug. 🚭 🖼MC, V

## 🍴 MERCHANT HOUSE
$$$ 🖼🖼🖼
62 LOWER CORVE ST.
SY8 IDU
TEL 01584-875438
Simple but impressive
cooking; ingredients are very
well chosen and married.
Fixed-price L & D.
🛏 42 🕐 Closed Sun., Mon.,
Tue.–Thurs. L, I week
Christmas & I week spring
🚭 🖼AE, MC, V

## MELTON MOWBRAY

## 🏨 STAPLEFORD PARK
🍴 $$$$$ ★★★★ 🖼
STAPLEFORD
LE14 2EF
TEL 01572-787522
FAX 01572-787651
Stately home on 500 acres of
woods and parkland; fishing
lake, stables, church, and
Capability Brown gardens.
Tennis, riding, shooting,
falconry, off-road driving.
Elegant dining room with
17th-century carvings by
Grinling Gibbons. Quality and
skill are evident throughout the
menu. Bar food. Fixed-price D.
No children under nine.
🛈 44 (7 annex) 🛏 45
🅿 120 ⊟ 🚭Restaurant
🏊 🏋 🖼All major cards

## MUCH WENLOCK

## 🍴 RAVEN
$$$ 🖼
30 BARROW ST.
TF13 6EN
TEL 01952-727251
Characterful inn with original
features, courtyard, kitchen
herb garden, and a deter-
mined effort to provide good
contemporary cooking. Bar
food. Fixed-price L.
🛏 40 🕐 Closed Dec. 25
🚭 🖼All major cards

## ORTHWICH

## 🏨 NUNSMERE HALL
🍴 $$$$ ★★★ 🖼🖼
TARPORLEY RD.
OAKMERE
CW8 2ES
TEL 01606-889100
FAX 01606-889055
Immaculate country-house
hotel, with a careful and
attentive version of modern
cooking. Friendly and
professional staff. Fixed-price L.
🛈 36 🛏 60 🅿 80 ⊟
🚭 Restaurant 🖼All major
cards

## NOTTINGHAM

## 🏨 NOTTINGHAM ROYAL
MOAT HOUSE
$$$$ ★★★
WOLLATON ST.
NG1 5RH
TEL 0115-9369988
FAX 0115-9475888
Centrally placed hotel
featuring a covered arcade
with trees and plants, several
bars and restaurants.
🛈 210 🅿 605 ⊟
🚭 Restaurant 🚭 🏊 🏋
🖼All major cards

## 🍴 SONNY'S
$$$ 🖼🖼
3 CARLTON ST.
HOCKLEY
NG1 INL
TEL 0115-9473041
Bright, airy brasserie with
informal but attentive service;
a stridently modern menu, but
enough of a local accent to
give a sense of individuality.
Fixed-price L.
🛏 80 🚭 🖼AE, MC, V

## OAKAMOOR

## 🏨 BANK HOUSE
$$
FARLEY LANE
ST10 3BD
TEL/FAX 01538-702810
A carefully restored farmhouse
and gardens. Guests dine
family style with the owners.
Warm and friendly hospitality.

Brochures on a range of local
walks available.
🛈 3 🅿 6 🕐 Closed
Christmas week 🚭
🖼MC, V

## RUTLAND

## 🍴 HAMBLETON HALL
$$$$$ 🖼🖼🖼🖼
HAMBLETON
OAKHAM
LE15 8TH
TEL 01572-756991
Archetypal country-house
hotel. Clubby bar, drawing
room with stunning views
over the lake; opulent
restaurant complete with
silk wall coverings. Mature,
restrained, and assured
cooking, full of flavor. Staff
is superb and offers really
skilled service. Fixed-price
L & D.
🛏 60 🚭 🖼All major
cards

## SHEFFIELD

## 🍴 RICHARD SMITH AT
THYME
$$$$ 🖼🖼🖼
34 SANDYGATE RD.
S10 5RY
TEL 01142-666096
Deservedly popular modern
restaurant; exceptionally fair
prices for bright, new-look
International cuisine. Open for
dinner only.
🛏 60 🕐 Closed Sun. D
🚭 🖼AE, MC, V

## 🍴 RAFTERS
$$$ 🖼🖼
220 OAKBROOK RD.
NETHERGREEN
S11 7ED
TEL 0114-2304819
A friendly suburban restaurant
with an unpretentious
modern atmosphere.
🛏 38 🅿 15 🕐 Closed
Mon.-Sun. L, Sun. & Tues.,
I week Jan., 2 weeks Aug.

## SHREWSBURY

### 🏨 ALBRIGHTON HALL
$$$ ★★★★
ALBRIGHTON
SY4 3AG
TEL 01939-291000
FAX 01939-291123
Seventeenth-century country
house on 14 acres of grounds,
that include an ornamental
lake. Oak-paneled rooms;
some with four-poster beds.
ⓘ 29 (42 annex) 🅿 120
🔁 🄢 Restaurant 🄪 📺
🃟 All major cards

### 🍴 ALBRIGHT HUSSEY
$$$ 🕸🕸
ELLESMERE RD.
SY4 3AF
TEL 01939-290571/290523
FAX 01939-291143
Black swans swim in the moat
of this timber-framed Tudor
house. Food is served in the
fine beamed restaurant, where
the fixed-price menus
supplement a menu that is in
the modern British mold. Bar
food. No children under four.
🔳 84 🄢 🃟 All major
cards

### 🍴 COUNTRY FRIENDS RESTAURANT
$$$ 🕸🕸
DORRINGTON
SY5 7JD
TEL 01743-718707
This venerable black and
white half-timbered restaurant
offers a traditional British
menu, featuring beautifully
cooked dishes sourced locally
wherever possible, and very
friendly service.
🔳 35 🅿 30 🕒 Closed
Sun.–Tues., 2 weeks in mid
July

## SOUTHWELL

### 🏨 SARACEN'S HEAD
$$ ★★★
MARKET PLACE
NG25 0HE
TEL 01636-812701

FAX 01636-815408
Half-timbered inn, with rich
historical links. On a May
morning in 1646 the Scottish
Commissioners entered the
Saracen's Head and arrested a
pale-faced man with a pointed
beard—Charles I. It was the
act that signaled the end of
the English Civil War. Sedate
atmosphere in the bar and
restaurant. Bedroom styles
vary, but all are well equipped.
Large restaurant.
ⓘ 27 🅿 80 🄢 Restaurant
🃟 All major cards

## STAFFORD

### 🏨 THE MOAT HOUSE
🍴 $$$$ ★★★★ 🕸🕸
LOWER PENKRIDGE RD.
ACTON
TRUSSELL
ST17 0RJ
TEL 01785-712217
This stylish and comfortable
hotel has been created around
a handsome old fifteenth-
century house, all great thick
chimney stacks and stripy
black and white timber-framed
gables. The hotel lies in a
peaceful location on the banks
of the restored Staffordshire &
Worcestershire Canal. Service
is very friendly and there is
fine dining in the restaurant.
ⓘ 32 🅿 200 🃟 All major
cards

## THORPE

### 🏨 PEVERIL OF THE PEAK
$$ ★★★
THORPE
DE6 2AW
TEL 0870-400 8109
FAX 01335-350507
Named after one of Sir
Walter Scott's heroic novels,
this hotel is surrounded by
beautiful scenery. Comfort-
able bedrooms, cocktail bar
and restaurant overlooking
the pretty gardens.
ⓘ 46 🅿 65 🄢 Restaurant
🃟 All major cards

### 🍴 IZAAK WALTON
$$$ 🕸
THORPE
DE6 2AY
TEL 01335-350555
FAX 01335-350539
Ideally placed as a base for
walks in Dovedale, one of
the Peak District's classic
beauty spots where the
shallow River Dove rushes
through a limestone gorge
under weirdly shaped and
named pinnacles of rock. Bar
meals or restaurant. Fishing
on River Dove. Fixed-price
L & D.
🔳 80 🅿 80 🕒 Closed
Mon.–Sat. L 🄢 🃟 All
major cards

## WORFIELD

### 🏨 OLD VICARAGE
$$$/$$$$ ★★★ 🕸🕸🕸
WORFIELD
BRIDGNORTH
WV15 5JZ
TEL 01746-716497 &
0800-0968010
FAX 01746-716552
Delightful hotel in the
Shropshire countryside,
comfortably furnished and
thoughtfully equipped.

🚭 10 (4 annex) 🅿 30 🚭
🔶 All major cards

## NORTHWEST ENGLAND

### ALTRINCHAM

**🍴 JUNIPER**
$$$$ ⚜⚜⚜
21 THE DOWNS
WA14 2QD
TEL 0161-9294008
A restaurant in tune with the times, relaxed and unstuffy. Fruits of the sea a specialty. Enthusiastic cooking, deft and thoroughly contemporary.
🔲 40 🕐 Closed Sat. L, Sun., Mon. L, 1 week Jan., 2 weeks summer 🚭 🔶 AE, MC, V

### AMBLESIDE

**🏨 GREY FRIAR LODGE**
$$
CLAPPERSGATE
LA22 9NE
TEL/FAX 015394-33158
Country house with warm, relaxing atmosphere, and views over the Brathay river. The set menu makes good use of local produce. No children under 12.
🚭 8 🅿 12 🕐 Closed Dec. 11–Feb. 9 🚭 🔶 MC, V

**🍴 DRUNKEN DUCK INN**
$$$ ⚜
BARNGATES
LA22 0NG
TEL 01539-436347
A four-hundred-year-old coaching inn with log fires and wooden beams that offers imaginative modern cooking and beers from its own brewery.
🔲 42 🅿 40

### APPLEBY-IN-WESTMORLAND

**🏨 BONGATE HOUSE**
$
BONGATE
CA16 6UE
TEL 017683-51245
FAX 017683-51423
A friendly welcome and warm

hospitality await at this charming guest house. Hearty breakfasts and dinners, by arrangement, served in the dining room. No children under seven.
🚭 8 🅿 10 🚭

### BLACKPOOL

**🏨 SAVOY**
$$$ ★★★
QUEENS PROMENADE
NORTH SHORE
FY2 9SJ
TEL 01253-352561
FAX 01253-595549
Located on the North Promenade this hotel offers modern, comfortable bedrooms and stunning sea views. The attractive wood-panelled restaurant features a stained glass ceiling.
🚭 131 🅿 40 🔲
🚭 Restaurant 🔶 All major cards

### BRAMPTON

**🏨 FARLAM HALL**
$$$$$ ★★★ ⚜⚜
HALLBANKGATE
CA8 2NG
TEL 016977-46234
FAX 016977-46683
Family-run country house in landscaped gardens; warm welcome. Elegant dining room for daily changing four-course dinner. No children under five.
🚭 11 (1 annex) 🅿 35 🕐 Closed Christmas 🔶 MC, V

### BURY

**🏨 BOLHOLT COUNTRY PARK**
$$ ★★★
WALSHAW RD.
BL8 1PU
TEL 0161-762 4000
FAX 0161-762 4100
This former mill owner's house is peacefully situated in 50 acres of parkland. Choice of lounges, friendly service

and modern, comfortable bedrooms.
🚭 66 🅿 300
🚭 Restaurant 🔶 🔶 All major cards

### BUTTERMERE

**🏨 BRIDGE**
$$$ ★★
BUTTERMERE
CA13 9UZ
TEL 017687-70252
FAX 017687-70215
Long-established family-run hotel, surrounded by mountains. Home-baked afternoon teas. Bedrooms are comfortable and offer stunning views.
🚭 21 🅿 60
🚭 Restaurant 🔶 MC, V

### CARLISLE

**🏨 BESSIESTOWN FARM COUNTRY GUEST HOUSE**
$$ ★★★★★
CATLOWDY
CARLISLE
CA6 5QP
TEL 01228-577219
FAX 01228-577019
One of the best bed-and-breakfast establishments in Britain—an absolute gem, set in beautiful countryside, with a warm welcome guaranteed.
🚭 5 🅿 10 🚭 🔶
🔶 All major cards

### GRANGE

**🏨 BORROWDALE GATES**
$$$$ ★★★ ⚜⚜
GRANGE
KESWICK
CA12 5UQ
TEL 017687-77204
FAX 017687-77254
Family-run hotel with spectacular views of surrounding fells. Cooking uses local produce.
🚭 31 🅿 40 🕐 Closed Jan. 🚭 Restaurant 🔶 AE, MC, V

HOTELS & RESTAURANTS

## GRANGE OVER SANDS

### 🏨 OLD VICARAGE
### 🍴 COUNTRY HOUSE
**$$$ ★★ 🌸**
WITHERSLACK
LA11 6RS
TEL 015395-52381
FAX 015395-52373
A Georgian country house with an air of away-from-it-all comfort and gentility, surrounded by enchanting mature gardens and grounds. In the Victorian-style restaurant, homemade breads set the tone and the kitchen puts great store by British regional ingredients. Reservations essential. Fixed-price L & D.
🛏 8 (5 annex)  🪑 35
🚫 Restaurant  🚫 AE, MC, V

## KESWICK

### 🏨 WHITE MOSS
### 🍴 HOUSE
One of the most captivating of country-house hotels, in a lakeland setting. Dinner is served in the quaint dining room and offers a five-course menu in keeping with the atmosphere. Ingredients used in the traditional English dishes are chosen with loyalty to the region and the seasons. William Wordsworth bought White Moss House for his son, Willy, a not-very-diligent chap who scratched around looking for a job for much of his life. In 1812, when he was a toddler, his elder brother and sister died, and his parents reacted by spoiling him. Fixed-price D only.
**$$$ ★ 🌸**
RYDAL WATER
LA22 9SE
TEL 015394-35295
🛏 7 (2 annex)  🪑 18
🕐 Closed Sun. L, Dec.–Jan.
🚫 Restaurant  🚫 MC, V

### 🏨 THWAITE HOWE
**$$ ★★**
THORNTHWAITE
CA12 5SA
TEL 017687-78281
FAX 017687-78529
Relaxed, personally run hotel surrounded by magnificent views. A five-course dinner is served at 7 p.m. Although there is no choice, this is good country-house cooking. Fixed-price D only. No children under 12.
🛏 8  🚫  🚫 DC, MC, V

### 🏨 CRAGLANDS
**$**
PENRITH RD.
CA12 4LJ
TEL 017687-74406
Cozy Victorian house. A five-course dinner is served, to which guests should bring their own wine. No children under eight.
🛏 5  🅿 6  🚫

## LANCASTER

### 🏨 ROYAL KINGS ARMS
**$$$ ★★★**
MARKET ST.
LA1 1HP
TEL 0500-636943
FAX 01773-880321
Central hotel retaining many Victorian features. Eat in Magellan's Restaurant.
🛏 55  🅿 20  🚽  🚫 Restaurant  🚫 All major cards

## LANGHO

### 🏨 NORTHCOTE MANOR
**$$$ ★★★  🌸🌸🌸**
NORTHCOTE RD.
BB6 8BE
TEL 01254-240555
FAX 01254-246568
Comfortable and characterful hotel situated in the Ribble Valley. The tempting menus include local Lancashire fare.
🛏 14  🅿 50  🚫 Restaurant
🚫 All major cards

## LIVERPOOL

### 🏨 THISTLE LIVERPOOL
The architect of the modern Atlantic Tower Thistle came up with a curved shape like the bow of a trans-atlantic liner, in homage to the maritime heritage of the Liverpool waterfront where the hotel stands. Stateroom Restaurant, Club Car Diner, cocktail bar, Tradewinds Bar.
**$$$**
CHAPEL ST.
L3 9RE
TEL 0151-227 4444
FAX 0151-236 3973
🛏 226  🚫  🚽  🚫 All major cards 🍴

### 🍴 TAI PAN
**$$ 🌸**
WH LUNG BUILDING, GREAT HOWARD ST.
L5 9TZ
TEL 0151-20738888
Authentic Chinese food with a modern twist in a friendly restaurant on top of a Chinese supermarket in Liverpool's long established Asian quarter.
🪑 250  🅿 120

## LONGRIDGE

### THE LONGRIDGE RESTAURANT
**$$$$ 🌸🌸🌸**
104–106 HIGHER RD.
PR3 3SY
TEL 01772-784969
A very traditional restaurant with a split-level dining room, heavily draped tables, and a comfortable lounge with deep sofas. Staff is correctly drilled, but the ingrained northern sense of hospitality cuts through. This is among the finest cuisine in Lancashire. Fixed-price L & D.
🪑 60  🕐 Closed Sat. L, Mon., & Jan. 1  🚫 All major cards

## MANCHESTER

### 🏨 LE MERIDIEN VICTORIA & ALBERT
**$$$$** ★★★★
WATER ST.
M3 4JQ
TEL 0870-400 8585
FAX 0161-834 2484
An interesting hotel created
from former warehouses, with
exposed bricks, iron pillars,
wooden beams. Café Maigret
Brasserie.
🛏 156 🅿 120 🆒 🔽
🅒 All major cards

## NEAR SAWREY

### 🏨 SAWREY HOUSE COUNTRY HOTEL
**$$$$** 🏵🏵
NEAR SAWREY AMBLESIDE.
LA22 0LF
TEL 01539-436387
FAX 01539-436010
Just along the road from
Beatrix Potter's house at
Far Sawrey, this charming
Victorian country house
hotel stands in beautifully
landscaped gardens
overlooking Esthwaite Water.
🛏 12 🅿 25 🕒 Closed Jan.

## POOLEY BRIDGE

### 🏨 RAMPSBECK
**$$$/$$$$** ★★★    🏵🏵🏵
WATERMILLOCK
NEAR PENRITH
CA11 0LP
TEL 017684-86442/86688
FAX 017684-86688
A wonderful lakeside setting,
18 acres of grounds, warm
hospitality, and skillful cooking.
They do things in style here.
Choice of three menus—veg-
etarian, table d'hôte, and à la
carte. Ingredients are treated
with respect, allowing authen-
tic flavors to shine through.
Bar food. Fixed-price L & D.
🛏 20 🅿 30 🕒 Closed
end-Jan.–early Feb.
🅢 Restaurant 🅢 All major
cards

## SHARROW BAY
**$$$$** ★★★ 🏵🏵🏵
SHARROW BAY
HOWTOWN
CA10 2LZ
TEL 017684-86301/86483
FAX 017684-86349
Lakeside country-house hotel
with a worldwide reputation.
Superb views across Ullswater.
Some accommodations in
cottages and an Elizabethan
farmhouse. Public rooms
furnished with bric-a-brac,
antiques, and paintings. Anglo/
French dishes based around
Lakeland produce. Fixed-price
L & D. No children under 13.
🛏 10 (16 annex) 🅿 35
🕒 Closed Dec.–March
🅢 Restaurant 🅢 DC, MC, V

## ROMALDKIRK

### 🏨 ROSE AND CROWN
🍴 **$$$** ★★ 🏵🏵
ROMALDKIRK
DL12 9EB
TEL 01833-650213
FAX 01833-650828
Lovingly nurtured pub at the
hub of Romaldkirk village, with
a huge stone fireplace, old oak
beams, and shuttered windows.
In the oak-paneled dining room
the daily four-course dinner
menu shows a fondness for
North Country produce. The
locally-produced Cotherstone
cheese is excellent. Fixed-
price D. No children under six.
🛏 12 🍽 24 🅿 24
🕒 Closed Mon.-Sat. L,
Christmas

## ROSTHWAITE

### 🏨 HAZEL BANK
**$$$**
ROSTHWAITE
CA12 5XB
TEL 017687-77248
FAX 017687-77373
Victorian house on four acres
of lawns and woodland, with
fine views of Borrowdale and
surrounding fells. Welcoming
atmosphere; home cooking.
No children under ten.
🛏 8 (1 annex) 🅿 12 🅢
🅢 MC, V

## WASDALE HEAD

### 🏨 WASDALE HEAD INN
**B**eautifully situated, hotel
at the road's end, in
magnificent mountain
scenery. Popular base for
climbers and walkers, and
good advice is always on tap.
**$$$**
WASDALE HEAD
CA20 1EX
TEL 019467-26229
FAX 019467-26334
🛏 9 🅿 50 🅢 Restau-rant
🅢 AE, MC, V

## WINDERMERE

### 🏨 HOLBECK GHYLL COUNTRY HOUSE
**$$$$/$$$$$** ★★★ 🏵🏵🏵
HOLBECK LANE
LA23 1LU
TEL 015394-32375
FAX 015394-34743
Charming country house.
Breathtaking views from
terrace restaurant and
magnificent oak-paneled
dining room, which both offer
excellent, imaginative cooking.
Fixed-price D.
🛏 14 (6 annex) 🅿 30
🅢 Restaurant 🎗 🅢 All
major cards

### 🏨 GILPIN LODGE COUNTRY HOUSE HOTEL
**$$$$** ★★★ 🏵🏵🏵
CROOK RD.
LA23 3NE
TEL 015394-88818
FAX 015394-88058
Exceptionally nice hotel with
an endearing mood of honest
friendliness. Flexible light
lunch menu. The four-course
dinner menu is an ambitious
affair providing plenty of
choice across the board. Bar
food. Fixed-price D. No
children under seven.
🛏 14 🅿 30 🅢 Restaurant
🅢 All major cards

## NORTHEAST ENGLAND

### ARNCLIFFE

🏨 **AMERDALE HOUSE**
**$$$$ ★★** 🌑🌑
ARNCLIFFE
BD23 5QE
TEL 01756-770250
FAX 01756-770266
Manor house with delightful garden views. Careful home cooking.
🛈 10 (1 annex) 🍴 22
🅿 30 🕐 Closed mid-Nov.–mid-March 🍽 Restaurant
🎴 MC, V

### ASENBY

🍴 **CRAB AND LOBSTER**
**$$$** 🌑🌑
DISHFORTH RD.
YO7 3QL
TEL 01845-577286
From the outside the Crab and Lobster looks like a dyed-in-the-wool traditional North Yorkshire thatched pub, but inside the decor is an extravagant clutter of wicker baskets, fishing rods, old fairground slot machines, jockey caps, and crab and lobster pots dangling from the ceiling. The atmosphere fizzes. Fresh fish is the thing to eat here, although the repertoire is a real bonanza of dishes spooned out of the global melting pot. Bar food. Fixed-price L & D. No children under 12.
🍴 120 🍽 🎴 AE, MC, V

### BEVERLEY

🏨 **TICKTON GRANGE**
**$$$ ★★★** 🌑
TICKTON
HU17 9SH
TEL 01964-543666
FAX 01964-542556
Georgian house set on four acres of grounds and gardens, with much of the original charm and character retained. The bedrooms are individually decorated, and one has a four-poster bed. The resident

owners provide a friendly service, and there is a restaurant menu.
🛈 18 🅿 65 🕐 Closed Dec. 25–29 🍽 Restaurant
🎴 All major cards

🍴 **MANOR HOUSE**
**$$$** 🌑🌑
NORTHLANDS
WALKINGTON
HU17 8RT
TEL 01482-881645
FAX 01482-866501
Fine views over the East Riding countryside from the conservatory; otherwise you can eat in the more formal atmosphere of the dining room, where both the fixed-price menus and the à la carte menu are based around supplies of top-notch local ingredients. Fixed-price D. No children under 12.
🍴 50 🕐 Closed Sun., 1 week Christmas & New Year
🎴 MC, V

### BLANCHLAND

#### SOMETHING SPECIAL

🏨 **LORD CREWE ARMS**

Historic hotel in a preserved village. In medieval times it was the lodging of the Abbot of Blanchland, and still retains plenty of atmospheric features, including a priest's hole for fugitive clerics in times of persecution, and enormous old fireplaces that bear witness to the chilliness of winter weather on these moors. Flagstone floors, vaulted ceilings, original stonework. Menu for restaurant and crypt bar.
**$$$ ★★** 🌑
BLANCHLAND
DH8 9SP
TEL 01434-675251
FAX 01434-675337
🛈 9 (10 annex) 🎴 All major cards

#### PRICES

**HOTELS**
An indication of the cost of a double room with breakfast is given by **$** signs.
**$$$$$** Over $300
**$$$$** $220–$300
**$$$** $160–$220
**$$** $100–$160
**$** Under $100

**RESTAURANTS**
An indication of the cost of a three-course dinner without drinks is given by **$** signs.
**$$$$$** Over $80
**$$$$** $50–$80
**$$$** $35–$50
**$$** $20–$35
**$** Under $20

### DEWSBURY

🍴 **HEALDS HALL HOTEL**
**$$$** 🌑
LEEDS RD., LIVERSEDGE
WF15 6JA
TEL 01924-409112
A mill owner built this foursquare house, and the same no-nonsense air invests the short, traditionally British menu.
🍴 40 🅿 90 🕐 Closed Sat. L, Sun. D

### DURHAM

🏨 **ROYAL COUNTY**
**$$$$ ★★★★** 🌑🌑
OLD ELVET
DH1 3JN
TEL 0191-3866821
FAX 0191-3860704
Long-established hotel beside the River Wear with views of both the castle and the cathedral. Magnificent carved oak staircase. Informal meals in the brasserie; formal dining in the County Restaurant.
🛈 151 🅿 80 🛗 🚇 📺
🎴 All major cards

## GRASSINGTON

### ⊞ GRASSINGTON HOUSE
**$$ ★★**
5 THE SQUARE
BD23 5AQ
TEL 01756-752406
FAX 01756-752135
Friendly village center hotel;
popular bar and restaurant
meals.
ⓘ 9 🅿 20 🕒 Closed Dec.
25–26 🚫 Restaurant
🚫 MC, V

## HARROGATE

### ⊞ RUDDING PARK HOTEL AND GOLF
**$$$$ ★★★★ ⊛⊛**
RUDDING PARK
FOLLIFOOT
HG3 1JH
TEL 01423-871350
FAX 01423-872286
Elegant modern hotel
surrounded by a beautifully
landscaped park with a golf
course designed with
environmental friendliness in
mind.
ⓘ 50 🅿 150 🚫 All major
cards

### 🍴 BOAR'S HEAD
**$$$ ⊛⊛**
RIPLEY
HG3 3AY
TEL 01423-771888
Rather patrician country-
house hotel, whose fixed-price
menus are full of invention and
vivid modern ideas. Owned by
Sir Thomas Ingilby, a member
of the Ingilby dynasty who
have lived at the nearby castle
for seven centuries. Fixed-
price L & D.
🍴 40 🚫 🕒 🚫 All major
cards

### ⊞ HOTEL DU VIN
**$$$ ★★★★ ⊛⊛**
PROSPECT PLACE
HG1 1LB
TEL 01423-856800
FAX 01423-856802
A very smart, modern hotel
with a French-style bistro, well
placed overlooking the grassy
sward of the Stray.

ⓘ 43 🅿 30 ⬛ 📺
🚫 All major cards

## HAWORTH

### 🍴 WEAVERS
**$$$ ⊛**
15 WEST LANE
HAWORTH
BD22 8DU
TEL 01535-643822
This likable restaurant near
the Brontë Parsonage was
originally a cluster of weavers'
cottages. Cooking is a mix of
homespun northern food and
dishes that are in tune with
today's gastronomic mood.
There's a refreshing lack of
pretension about the whole
set-up, helped along by
genuine personal service.
Fixed-price D.
🍴 65 🕒 Closed L, Sun.,
Mon., 1 week Christmas &
1 week June 🚫 🕒
🚫 All major cards

## HEBDEN BRIDGE

### ⊞ REDACRE MILL
**$$**
REDACRE
MYTHOLMROYD
HX7 5DQ
TEL 01422-881569
Converted canal-side cotton
warehouse, with wood
paneling and winching
equipment. Dining room
meals around communal
table. Fishing.
ⓘ 4 🅿 8 🚫 🚫 MC, V

## HELMSLEY

### ⊞ BLACK SWAN
**$$$$ ★★★ ⊛**
MARKET PLACE
YO62 5BJ
TEL 01439-770466
FAX 01439-770174
Characterful hotel made up of
a Tudor rectory, an
Elizabethan inn, and a
Georgian house, overlooking
the market square.
ⓘ 45 🅿 50
🚫 Restaurant 🚫 All
major cards

## HEXHAM

### ⊞ DENE HOUSE
**$**
JUNIPER
NE46 1SJ
TEL/FAX 01434-673413
Former farmhouse in
attractive gardens and nine
acres of meadows. Aga-
cooked break-fasts in
farmhouse kitchen.
ⓘ 3 🅿 4 🚫

## HOLMFIRTH

### ⊞ HOLME CASTLE
**$$**
THE VILLAGE
HOLME
HD7 1QG
TEL 01484-680680
FAX 01484-686764
Victorian house with
superb views. Oak
paneling, parquet flooring,
wood fire. Evening meals
by arrangement.
ⓘ 8 🅿 12 🚫 🚫 MC, V

## ILKLEY

### ⊞ ROMBALDS
**$$ ⊛**
11, WEST VIEW, WELLS RD.
LS29 9JG
TEL 01943-603201
FAX 01943-816586
A Georgian house full of style
and comfort, attractively set
on the edge of town.
ⓘ 15 🅿 28 🕒 Closed
New Year

## LASTINGHAM

### ⊞ LASTINGHAM GRANGE
Traditional Yorkshire
hospitality in a family-
run 17th-century farmhouse.
Good home cooking; sunken
rose garden. At neary St.
Mary's Church with its tiny,
ancient crypt, stone carvings
date back to the Dark Ages.
During the 18th century the
crypt was used for cockfights,

and for parties hosted by the curate Jeremiah Carter, at which he played the fiddle.

**$$$$ ★★★**
LASTINGHAM
YO62 6TH
TEL 01751-417345/417402
FAX 01751-417358
**①** 12 **P** 32 **⊖** Closed Dec.–Feb. **⑤** Restaurant

## LEEDS

**Ⅱ FOURTH FLOOR CAFE AT HARVEY NICHOLS**
**$$** ❀
107-111, BRIGGATT
LS1 6AZ
TEL 0113-204 8000
This minimalist and friendly café is in the Harvey Nichols department store—very handy after you've shopped till you've dropped.
**⚏** 80 **⊖** Closed Sun.–Wed. D, Christmas

**Ⅱ BRASSERIE FORTY FOUR**
**$$$** ❀❀
44 THE CALLS
LS2 7EW
TEL 0113-234 3232
FAX 0113-234 3332
Popular brasserie, located in a former grainstore, serving youthful, cosmopolitan cuisine. Colorful chairs, black wooden floors and glass-encased cookery books in the walls. Fixed-price L. & D.
**⚏** 110 **⊖** Closed Sat. L., Sun. **⑤** **⑥** All major cards

**Ⅱ POOL COURT AT 42**
**$$$** ❀❀❀
44 THE CALLS
LS2 7EW
TEL 0113-2444242
French-inspired food, with just enough experimentation to keep customers on their toes. A choice of menus, from set lunches to a six-course "Classics" extravaganza, bristles with ideas, flair, and an instinct for marrying flavors. Fixed-price L & D.
**⚏** 38 **⊖** Closed Sat. L, Sun. **⑤** **⑥** AE, MC, V,

## MORPETH

**Ⅱ LONGHIRST HALL**
**$$**
LONGHIRST
NE61 3LL
TEL 01670-791348
Country mansion set on 75 acres which include a lake. Menus are peppered with lively ideas. Bar meals. Fixed-price L & D.
**⚏** 80 **⊖** Closed Sat. L **⑥** All major cards

## NEWCASTLE

**🏨 VERMONT**
**$$$$ ★★★★** ❀❀
CASTLE GARTH
NE1 1RQ
TEL 0191-2331010
FAX 0191-2331234
Former county hall next to the castle; fine views across River Tyne. Choice of bars and restaurants; brasserie; live music in the evening.
**①** 101 **P** 100 **⊜** **🔽** **⑥** All major cards

**Ⅱ THE FISHERMANS LODGE**
**$$$** ❀❀❀❀
JESMOND DENE, JESMOND
NE7 7BQ
TEL 0191-282 3281
Set in lovely parkland 3 miles from Newcastle city center, this restaurant specializes in high-quality northern British ingredients such as prime Orkney scallops, Loch Fyne oysters, and Highland venison.
**⚏** 60 **⊖** Closed Sun., Bank Holidays

## RIPON

**🏨 RIPON SPA**
**$$$ ★★★**
PARK ST.
HG4 2BU
TEL 01765-602172
FAX 01765-690770
Traditional service, in modern surroundings; lovely grounds, including croquet lawns. Bar, Turf Tavern, restaurant.
**①** 40 **P** 60 **⊜** **⑥** All major cards

## SEAHAM

**🏨 SEAHAM HALL HOTEL**
**$$$$ ★★★★** ❀❀❀
LORD BYRON'S WALK
SR7 7AG
TEL 0191-5161400
FAX 0191-5161410
Lord Byron was married and spent his honeymoon in this imposing house on the Durham coast, now a highly acclaimed hotel that cleverly marries old world dignity and comfort to classy modern conveniences. Dine in style in the restaurant, or enjoy the informal fun of the Thai Brasserie.
**①** 19 **P** 122

## SKIPTON

**🏨 DEVONSHIRE ARMS**
**Ⅱ COUNTRY HOUSE**
**$$$$/$$$$$ ★★★**
❀❀
BOLTON ABBEY
BD23 6AJ
TEL 01756-710441
FAX 01756-710564
Hotel owned by the Duke and Duchess of Devonshire and decorated with many of their pieces of furniture and art. The Burlington Restaurant uses local produce, some of it grown in the hotel garden. Bar food at lunchtime. Tennis, fishing, laser-pigeon shooting, and falconry. Fixed-price D.
**①** 41 **⚏** 80 **P** 150 **⑤** Restaurant **⊠** **🔽** **⑥** All major cards

## WHITBY

**🏨 SEACLIFFE**
**$$**
NORTH PROMENADE
WEST CLIFF
YO21 3JX
TEL/FAX 01947-603139
Cliff-top hotel with fine sea views. Waterbed; family suite. Patio catches the sun.
**①** 19 **⑤** Restaurant **⑥** All major cards

## YORK

### 🏨 MIDDLETHORPE HALL
$$$$/$$$$$ ★★★
🌼🌼🌼
BISHOPTHORPE RD.
YO23 2GB
TEL 01904-641241
FAX 01904-620176
Magnificent country house
less than 2 miles from the
center of York. Peaceful walks
in the restored gardens. Fine
paintings, furniture, and
antiques. Gourmet and daily
menus; vegetarian alternatives.
No children under eight.
Fixed-price L & D.
🚪 30 🅿 70 ⬆ Ⓢ Rest-
aurant 🈳 🗑 Ⓢ MC, V

### 🏨 THE GRANGE
$$$ ★★★ 🌼🌼
1 CLIFTON
YO30 6AA
TEL 01904-644744
FAX 01904-612453
A very friendly and
immaculately kept Georgian
house a few minutes' stroll
from the center of York, where
you can dine in style or enjoy a
more informal brasserie meal.
🚪 30 🅿 26

### 🍽 MELTON'S
$$$ 🌼🌼
7 SCARCROFT RD.
YO23 1ND
TEL 01904-634341
Restaurant in a converted
shop with a bright, cheery
face. Value for money with
plenty of flexible deals
(including an early-evening
offer for anyone prepared
to leave by 7:45 p.m.).
Vegetarians handsomely
provided for. Fixed-price
L & D.
🍴 30 🕐 Closed Mon. L,
Sun., 3 weeks Christmas,
1 week Aug. Ⓢ MC, V

## SCOTTISH LOWLANDS

## ABERFOYLE

### 🏨 FOREST HILLS
$$$ ★★★★
KINLOCHARD
FK8 3TL
TEL 01877-387277
FAX 01877-387307
Popular and friendly hotel
with a choice of lounges and
comfortable bedrooms. Some
rooms have Loch views.
Formal dining in the Garden
Restaurant or try Bonspiel for
a more informal atmosphere.
Tennis, fishing and squash.
🚪 56 🅿 80 🈳 🗑
Ⓢ All major cards

## ANSTRUTHER

### 🍽 CELLAR
$$$ 🌼🌼🌼
24 EAST GREEN
KY10 3AA
TEL 01333-310378
A restaurant full of character
and completely devoid of
pretentiousness. Seafood is
the main theme; what is
offered is totally dependent
on the catch from the local
fishing boats. Fixed-price D.
🍴 30 🕐 Closed
Mon.–Tues. L, Mon. D in
winter, Christmas Ⓢ
Ⓢ AE, MC, V

## BALLOCH

### 🍽 CAMERON HOUSE
$$$$ 🌼🌼🌼
LOCH LOMOND
G83 8QZ
TEL 01389-755565
FAX 01389-759522
Commands a magnificent
Highland setting on a glorious
strip of land jutting into Loch
Lomond. The cooking is shot
through with technical
thoroughness and complex
elaboration. A combination of
both local and seasonal
produce is put to good use for
a range of menus that brim
over with imagination and
finesse. Fixed-price D.

🍴 42 🕐 Closed Tue.–Sat. L,
Mon. Ⓢ Ⓢ All major cards

## CUPAR

### 🍽 OSTLERS CLOSE
$$$ 🌼🌼🌼
BONNYGATE
KY15 4BU
TEL 01334-655574
This restaurant has a
well-deserved, loyal following
of local people who
appreciate good Scottish
cooking that is modern
without being trendy. The
quality of the ingredients is
paramount.
🍴 28 🕐 Closed Sun.–Mon.,
Tue.–Fri. L, Christmas, 2 weeks
Oct. Ⓢ Ⓢ AE, MC, V

### 🍽 PEAT INN
$$$ 🌼🌼
CUPAR
KY15 5LH
TEL 01334-840206
The kitchen at this charming
small restaurant in rural Fife
has an enviable reputation.
Consistency is the hallmark,
ingredients are of irreproach-
able quality, and the accomplished cooking has a good
reputation. Fixed-price L & D.
🍴 48 🕐 Closed Sun., Mon.,
Christmas and New Year's
Day Ⓢ Ⓢ All major cards

## DALBEATTIE

### 🏨 AUCHENSKEOCH LODGE
$$
DALBEATTIE
DG5 4PG
TEL/FAX 01387-780277
Victorian shooting lodge on 20
acres of grounds. Vegetable
garden, croquet lawn, small
fishing loch, and a maze.
Antique and period furniture.
Four-course dinner served
house-party-style at 8 p.m.—
drinks in billiard room, home-
cooked dishes with garden
vegetables. Fishing, snooker, and
croquet. No children under 12.
🚪 3 🅿 22 🕐 Closed
Nov.–March Ⓢ Restaurant
Ⓢ MC, V

**HOTELS & RESTAURANTS**

## EDINBURGH

### 🏨 SHERATON GRAND
### 🍽 $$$$$ ★★★★★ ❀❀❀
1 FESTIVAL SQUARE
EH3 9SR
TEL 0131-229 9131
FAX 0131-228 4510
The hotel's own tartan adorns The Grill Room of this imposing, purpose-built hotel, whose skilled cooking is classical French. Buffet-style menu in The Terrace restaurant. Fixed-price L.
🛏 260  🍴 Grill Room 40, Terrace 100  🅿 80  ⮃  Ⓢ
🏊  🛗  🏧 All major cards

### 🏨 BALMORAL
### $$$$/$$$$$ ★★★★★
❀❀
1 PRINCES ST.
EH2 2EQ
TEL 0131-556 2414
FAX 0131-557 8740
Elegant Edwardian luxury hotel. Afternoon tea in the Palm Court; club ambience in Lobby Bar; lively atmosphere in NB's Bar. Brasserie menu, or serious dining and polished service in Restaurant No. 1 Princes Street.
🛏 186  🅿 100  Ⓢ  ⮃  🏊
🛗  🏧 All major cards

### 🏨 THE BONHAM
### $$$$/$$$$$ ★★★★ ❀❀
35 DRUMSHEUGH GARDENS
EH3 7RN
TEL 0131-226 6050
FAX 0131-226 6080
One of the classiest and most comfortable hotels in Edinburgh, a lovely Victorian house equipped with all modern conveniences. This is a real getaway gem for those in the know.
🛏 48  🅿 20  🏧 All major cards

### 🏨 NORTON HOUSE
### $$$$ ★★★★ ❀❀
INGLISTON
EH28 8LX
TEL 0131-333 1275
FAX 0131-333 5305
A fine handsome "Scottish Baronial" house in its own parkland, very convenient to the airport.
🛏 47  🅿 200  🏧 All major cards

### 🏨 CHANNINGS
### $$$$ ★★★★ ❀❀
SOUTH LEARMONTH GARDENS
EH4 1EZ
TEL 0131-332 3232
FAX 0131-332 9631
Edwardian town house hotel with clublike feel. Imaginative modern menu in the conservatory restaurant.
🛏 46  🕐 Closed Dec. 24–28  ⮃  Ⓢ Restaurant
🏧 All major cards

### 🏨 GEORGE INTER-CONTINENTAL
### $$$$ ★★★★ ❀
19–21 GEORGE ST.
EH2 2PB
TEL 0131-225 1251
FAX 0131-226 5644
Centrally located hotel with magnificent classical facade, marble-floored foyer with Corinthian pillars, a popular, clubby bar, and a choice of eating options; 18th-century Carvers Restaurant or Le Chambertin Restaurant.
🛏 195  🅿 24  ⮃
🛗 Nearby  🏧 All major cards

### 🏨 SANDAIG
### $/$$
5 HERMITAGE PLACE LEITH LINKS
EH6 8AA
TEL 0131-554 7357
FAX 0131-467 6389
Sandaig is a family-run guest house occupying two mid-terraced Victorian villas. It overlooks historic Leith Links park.
🛏 9  🏧 All major cards

### 🏨 MALMAISON
### $$$ ★★★ ❀
1 TOWER PLACE
EH6 7DB
TEL 0131-468 5000
FAX 0131-468 5002
Stylish hotel conversion from former Seaman's Mission in

rejuvenated Leith port and harbor area. Understated bedrooms offer mini-bar, and stereo system. French-style vegetarian buffet in bar; Mediterranean cuisine in brasserie.
🛏 60  🅿 50  ⮃  🛗
🏧 All major cards

### 🏨 GROSVENOR GARDENS
### $$/$$$
1 GROSVENOR GARDENS
EH12 5JU
TEL 0131-313 3415
FAX 0131-346 8732
Elegant, Victorian guesthouse on quiet central cul-de-sac. Bedrooms thoughtfully include a mini decanter of Scotch whisky.
🛏 8  Ⓢ Dining room & lounges  🏧 MC, V

### 🍽 IGGS
### $$$ ❀
15 JEFFREY ST.
EH1 1DR
TEL 0131-557 8184
Latin personality is stamped on this popular addition to the Edinburgh scene, and the menus offer an intriguing blend of Spanish and Scottish dishes based around regional produce. Fixed-price L.

50 Closed Sun.
All major cards

### MARTIN'S
$$$
70 ROSE ST.
NORTH LANE
EH2 3DX
TEL 0131-225 3106
This restaurant champions the
cause of organic produce and
wild foods; the quality of the
raw materials is beyond
reproach, and menus change
daily. Fixed-price L & D. No
children under eight.
30 Closed Sat. L, Sun.,
Mon., 1 week May/June,
1 week Oct. & Dec. 24–3rd
week Jan. All major
cards

### ATRIUM
$$/$$$
CAMBRIDGE ST.
EH1 2ED
TEL 0131-228 8882
The bullish face of cooking in
Edinburgh. The decor is sharp;
the approach is casual,
cosmopolitan, and friendly.
Dazzling modern cuisine
that tingles the senses.
70 Closed Sat. L
(excluding Aug.), Sun.
(excluding Aug.), 1 week at
Christmas and New Year's
AE, MC, V

## ELIE

### GOLF HOTEL
$$$ ★★★
BANK ST.
KY9 1EF
TEL 01333-330209
FAX 01333-330381
Family-run hotel, particularly
popular with visiting golfers
due to its location beside the
splendid links course. The
imaginative and enjoyable
cuisine makes good use of
fresh local produce.
22 50 Restaurant
All major cards

## GALASHIELS

### KINGSKNOWES
$$$ ★★★

SELKIRK RD.
TD1 3HY
TEL 01896-758375
FAX 01896-750377
Victorian turreted mansion
set on own grounds near the
River Tweed, now a family-run
hotel. Tennis. Bar meals and
restaurant.
11 72 Restaurant
All major cards

## GLASGOW

### LANGS HOTEL
$$$ ★★★★
2 PORT DUNDAS PLACE
G2 3LD
TEL 0141-333 1500 OR
0141-352 2452
FAX 0141-333 5700
Nice big bedrooms and a
relaxed but warm welcome at
this stylish city center hotel.
100 All
major cards

### SOMETHING SPECIAL

### MALMAISON
Contemporary hotel
conversion with stylish
rooms. Carved Greek letters
over the entrance translate as
"Christ, Head of the Church."
Together with the vaulted
crypt and the ecclesiastical
pillars and arches of the
interior, they are clues to the
hotel's former incarnation—as
an Episcopalian church. All-
day Café Mal; upbeat cuisine
in brasserie. Exceptionally
friendly, helpful staff.
$$$ ★★★
278 WEST GEORGE ST.
G2 4LL
TEL 0141-5721000
FAX 0141-5721002
72 All
major cards

### ONE DEVONSHIRE
GARDENS
$$$$ ★★★
1 DEVONSHIRE GARDENS
G12 0UX
TEL 0141-339 2001
FAX 0141-337 1663

Very individual hotel in three
adjoining row houses. Bed-
rooms have bold, striking
decor, sumptuous fabrics,
subdued lighting, luxurious
bathrooms, music systems,
and supply of CDs. In one
house, stylish lounge and bar;
in another, elegant cocktail
lounge. Consistently high stan-
dard of cooking, seasonally
changing menus. Attentive
service. Fixed-price L. Dinner
reservations required.
27 12 Restaurant
All major cards

### THE BUTTERY
$$$$
652 ARGYLE STREET
G3 8UF
TEL 0141-221 8188
FAX 0141-204 4639
Modern Scots cooking with a
seasonal bias, served in a
beautiful room with paneled
walls and colored glass
windows.
50 30 Closed
Sun–Mon., L Sat, Dec. 25–26
& Jan. 1–2 All major
cards

### UBIQUITOUS CHIP
$$
12 ASHTON LANE
G12 8SJ
TEL 0141-3345007
Simple city suburb diner with
stone floors, lots of greenery,
and a lively, informal atmosphere. Offers a short, appealing bistro menu.
150 All major cards

## GULLANE

### GREY WALLS HOTEL
$$$/$$$$
MUIRFIELD, GULLANE
EH31 2EG
TEL 01620-842144
Fresh ingredients, skillful
cooking, and a splended wine
list, all to be enjoyed in a
Lutyens-designed house,
overlooking Gertrude Jekyll-
designed gardens and the
celebrated Muirfield golf
course.
45 60

HOTELS & RESTAURANTS

## HUMBIE

### 🏨 THE JOHNSTOUNBURN HOUSE
**$$$$ ★★★**
HUMBIE
EH36 5PL
TEL 01875-833696
FAX 01875-833626
Seventeenth-century country house in the rolling Lammermuir Hills. Wood fires, fine wood paneling, ornate plasterwork. Friendly and relaxed. Good local produce in restaurant. Fishing, clay-pigeon shooting, and croquet lawn.
🛈 11 (9 annex) 🅿 100
🚫 Restaurant 🌐 All major cards

## JEDBURGH

### 🏨 SPINNEY
**$**
LANGLEE
TD8 6PB
TEL 01835-863525
FAX 01835-864883
Attractively furnished converted cottage. Two lodges on grounds also available for B&B rental.
🛈 3 (2 annex) 🅿 8
🕒 Closed Dec.–Feb. 🚫
🌐 MC, V

## KELSO

### 🍴 ROXBURGHE HOTEL
### 🏨 $$$$ ★★★ 🏵🏵
HEITON
TD5 8JZ
TEL 01573-450331
FAX 01573-450611
Bonnie Prince Charlie planted a white rose bush here in 1745. The cooking is well worth a detour. Using the best local ingredients, the kitchen produces sound modern British dishes. Fixed-price D. Golf, fishing and tennis.
🛈 16 (6 annex) 🪑 35
🅿 150 🚫 Restaurant
🌐 All major cards

## LANGBANK

### 🏨 GLEDDOCH HOUSE
**$$$$ ★★★★ 🏵🏵**
LANGBANK
PA14 6YE
TEL 01475-540711
FAX 01475-540201
Set on a 360-acre estate high above the River Clyde with spectacular views across to Ben Lomond, this historic house offers an ambitious modern menu. Fixed-price L & D. Golf, fishing and clay-pigeon shooting.
🛈 39 🅿 200 🌐 All major cards

## LINLITHGOW

### 🍴 CHAMPANY INN
**$$$$ 🏵🏵**
NEAR LINLITHGOW
EH49 7LU
TEL 01506-834532
Housed in an old mill that dates from the time of Mary, Queen of Scots, this plush circular restaurant offers good cooking of local supplies. Vast wine list. Fixed-price L. No children under eight.
🪑 50 🕒 Closed Sat, L, Sun. & Dec. 24–26, 🌐 All major cards

## MELROSE

### 🏨 BURT'S
**$$$ ★★ 🏵🏵**
THE SQUARE
TD6 9PL
TEL 01896-822285
FAX 01896-822870
Long-established, family-run hotel on market square. Elegantly decorated restaurant takes fishing and shooting as its theme, with old rods, flies, and prints dotted around the room. The kitchen handles Scottish ingredients effectively for a modern menu that pulls together many strands and influences. Lounge bar meals. Fixed-price L & D.
🛈 20 🅿 40 🕒 Closed Dec. 24–26 🚫 🌐 All major cards

## MOFFAT

### 🏨 WELL VIEW
**$$/$$$ ★ 🏵🏵**
BALLPLAY RD.
DG10 9JU
TEL 01683-220184
FAX 01683-220088
Small Victorian house, immaculately maintained; friendly, cozy atmosphere. Six-course dinner in a light, contemporary style; flavors, not fussiness.
🛈 6 🅿 8 🕒 Closed 2 weeks Feb. & 1 week Oct.. 🚫 🌐 All major cards

## NEWTON STEWART

### 🏨 KIRROUGHTREE HOUSE
**$$$/$$$$ ★★★ 🏵🏵🏵**
MINNIGAFF
DG8 6AN
TEL 01671-402141
FAX 01671-402425
Seventeenth-century mansion in landscaped gardens and woodland; tennis. Relaxed, friendly staff. Imaginative cooking with local produce. No children under ten. Fixed-price L & D.
🛈 17 🅿 50 🕒 Closed Jan. 4–mid Feb. 🚫 Restaurant 🌐 All major cards

## NORTH BERWICK

### 🏨 THE OPEN ARMS
**$$$ ★★★ 🏵**
DIRLETON, EAST LOTHIAN
EH39 5EG
TEL 01620-850241
FAX 01620-850570
A very welcoming, well-established, and exceptionally friendly hotel overlooking the village green.
🛈 10 🅿 30 🌐 MC, V

## ST. ANDREWS

### 🏨 OLD COURSE
### 🍴 $$$$$ ★★★★★ 🏵
ST. ANDREWS
KY16 9SP
TEL 01334-474371
FAX 01334-477668

Internationally renowned hotel overlooking the world-famous golf course. Magnificent flower displays in lobby. Friendly staff. Informal summertime dining in conservatory. Rooftop Road Hole Grill provides spectacular views of the course, West Sands, and the town.
**[i]** 125 **[bed]** 70 **[P]** 150 **[clock]** Closed Christmas **[↕]** **[S]** Restaurant **[A]** **[Y]** **[C]** All major cards

### FOSSIL HOUSE
**$$**
12–14 MAIN ST.
STRATHKINNESS
KY16 9RU
TEL/FAX 01334-850639
Two bedrooms in converted cottage, two in main house. Lounge, conservatory, books, board games. Home-cooked evening meals can be arranged.
**[i]** 2 (2 annex) **[P]** 5 **[S]** **[C]** MC, V

## STIRLING

### STIRLING HIGHLAND
**$$$$** ★★★★ ❀❀
SPITTAL ST.
FK8 1DU
TEL 01786-272727
FAX 01786-272829
Imaginative conversion of old school with superb city views. School features retained. Scholars Restaurant; Rizzios Restaurant (Italian theme). Squash courts.
**[i]** 94 **[P]** 96 **[↕]** **[S]** Restaurant **[A]** **[Y]** **[C]** All major cards

### CASTLECROFT
**$**
BALLENGEICH RD.
FK8 1TN
TEL 01786-474933
FAX 01786-466716
Friendly family-run establishment in a splendid position on the hillside, under the shadow of the castle. Lovely views of the surrounding countryside. Hearty breakfasts served in the dining room.

**[i]** 6 **[P]** 9 **[clock]** Closed Christmas & New Year **[S]** **[C]** MC, V

### LAKE
**$$$** ❀❀
PORT OF MENTEITH
FK8 3RA
TEL 01877-385258
FAX 01877-385671
Art deco-style conservatory restaurant has splendid views across the Lake of Menteith to the island of Inchmahome and the Trossachs. The short, well-priced menu changes daily. No children under six. Fixed-price L & D.
**[bed]** 32 **[S]** **[clock]** Closed 2 weeks Jan. **[C]** AE, MC, V

## STRANRAER

### GLENAPP CASTLE
**$$$$$** ★★★ ❀❀
BALLANTRAE
KA26 0NZ
TEL 01465-831212
FAX 01465-831000
A beautifully restored, grand Scottish Baronial castle in a fine location looking out to the Isle of Arran. Antiques in the bedrooms, classic furnishings, and stylish presentation of locally-sourced food.
**[i]** 17 **[clock]** Closed Nov.–Mar.

## TROON

### LOCHGREEN HOUSE
**$$$$** ★★★ ❀❀
MONKTONHILL RD.,
SOUTHWOOD
KA10 7EN
TEL 01292-313343
FAX 01292-318661
This is one of Scotland's best hotels, offering an appealing blend of the stylish and the warmly welcoming, with attentive and friendly staff and a chef who knows all about local and seasonal ingredients.
**[i]** 40 **[P]** 50

## TURNBERRY

### WESTIN TURNBERRY
**$$$$$** ★★★★★ ❀❀
TURNBERRY

KA26 9LT
TEL 01655-331000
FAX 01655-331706
Famous hotel on over 800 acres of stunning countryside; spectacular views of the Firth of Clyde. Golf courses host several Open Championships; the Ailsa is considered one of the best in the world. Spa for health and beauty treatments, 65-foot pool. Clubhouse and two restaurants—the Bay (light Mediterranean cuisine) and the main hotel restaurant (traditional atmosphere, classical cuisine). Friendly and professional staff. Golf, tennis, squash, riding.
**[i]** 132 **[P]** 200 **[↕]** **[A]** **[Y]** **[C]** All major cards

## ABERDEEN

### MARCLIFFE AT PITFODELS
**$$$$** ★★★★
NORTH DEESIDE RD.
AB15 9YA
TEL 01224-861000
FAX 01224-868860
Set on eight acres of mature grounds. Informal conservatory restaurant; formal Invery Room. Scottish cuisine. Snooker and croquet lawn.
**[i]** 42 **[P]** 160 **[↕]** **[C]** All major cards

### EWOOD HOUSE
**$$**
12 KINGS GATE
AB15 4EJ
TEL/FAX 01224-648408
Granite-built Victorian home in award-winning gardens. Guests welcomed with tea and home-baking. One room suitable for travelers with disabilities; one has a four-poster bed. No children.
**[i]** 5 **[P]** 10 **[S]** **[C]** MC, V

### ARDOE HOUSE
**$$$/$$$$** ❀❀
SOUTH DEESIDE RD.
BLAIRES

AB12 5YP
TEL 01224-860600
FAX 01224-861283
Built in 1878 for a soap manufacturer, the house has many original features including an oak-panelled staircase and an oak fireplace in the dining room. Menus are well balanced and offer an excellent choice of dishes. Bar Food. Fixed-price D.
🛏 80 ⊗ ⊗ All major cards

## AUCHTERARDER

### 🏨 GLENEAGLES
🍴 $$$$$ ★★★★★ ⊛⊛
AUCHTERARDER
PH3 1NF
TEL 01764-662231
FAX 01764-662134
Renowned Edwardian luxury hotel in beautiful countryside, surrounded by its own golf courses and extensive grounds. Afternoon tea, cocktails in drawing room. Formal but friendly service and piano music in Strathearn Restaurant; modern Scottish cooking. Many other dining options. Outstanding range of sporting activities. Fixed-price D.
🛏 222 🛏 240 🅿 200 ⬍
🚇 🎦 ⊗ All major cards

## BALLACHULISH

### 🏨 BALLACHULISH HOUSE
🍴 $$$ ⊛⊛
BALLACHULISH
PH49 4JX
TEL 01855-811266
FAX 01855-811498
Absolutely glorious Loch Linnhe setting, backed by mountains; after a long day wandering on the hill or lazing by the loch, you'll enjoy this stunning scenery—occasionally to the sound of the pipes played by a local musician—while waiting for a sumptuous dinner of traditional Scottish fare given a modern polish by the chef.
🛏 8 🛏 35 🅿 6

## BALLATER

### 🏨 DARROCH LEARG
$$$$ ★★★ ⊛⊛⊛
BRAEMAR RD.
AB35 5UX
TEL 013397-55443
FAX 013397-55252
Friendly, family-run country house with panoramic views across the Dee Valley toward the Grampian Mountains from both the dining room and conservatory. Dinner menus are short and to the point, with highly accomplished cooking from start to finish. Children welcome, and have their own special menu. Fixed-price D.
🛏 13 (5 annex) 🅿 25
🕐 Closed Christmas & Jan., excluding New Year (these times refer only to the restaurant) ⊗ Restaurant
⊗ All major cards

### 🏨 BALGONIE COUNTRY HOUSE
$$$ ★★ ⊛⊛
BRAEMAR PLACE
AB35 5NQ
TEL/FAX 013397-55482
Charming small country house in Edwardian style, set on four acres of mature gardens. Bedrooms are well maintained and named after fishing pools on the River Dee. The elegant dining room is a perfect setting for the well-produced food, based on French cuisine, which is strong in local produce.
🛏 9 🅿 12 🕐 Closed Jan.–Feb. ⊗ Restaurant
⊗ All major cards

## BLAIRGOWRIE

### 🏨 KINLOCH HOUSE
🍴 $$$$$ ★★★ ⊛⊛⊛
BLAIRGOWRIE
PH10 6SG
TEL 01250-884237
FAX 01250-884333
Set on 25 acres of wooded grounds, this country house offers personal hospitality and service. Good Scottish fruit and vegetables a grown in the

hotel's own gardens. Imaginative cooking with a particularly light touch; ingredients are of a high standard, textures and flavors come through clearly. Fixed-price D.
🛏 20 🛏 55 🅿 40
🕐 Closed Christmas
⊗ Restaurant 🚇 🎦
⊗ DC, MC, V

### 🏨 DUNCRAGGAN
$
PERTH RD.
PH10 6EJ
TEL 01250-872082
FAX 01250-872098
Two bedrooms are pine-furnished, while the third has a four-poster bed and a private bathroom. Guests can choose between light suppers or more substantial dinners.
🛏 3 🅿 6 ⊗

## BRAEMAR

### 🏨 THE INVERCAULD ARMS
$$$ ★★★
BRAEMAR
AB35 5YR
TEL 013397-41605
FAX 013397-41428
This traditional Victorian Highland hotel set amidst

spectacular scenery is justly popular for its attentive and friendly staff.

🛈 68  🅿 80  🖃  🚭
🅢 All major cards

## BRODICK

### 🏨 KILMICHAEL
**$$$** ★★ ✿
GLEN CLOY
ISLE OF ARRAN
KA27 8BY
TEL 01770-302219
FAX 01770-302068
This is a friendly house with a welcoming atmosphere. The accommodations are furnished with a selection of fresh flowers, books, and a variety of items collected from around the world. Modern European cooking. No children under 12.

🛈 5 (3 annex)  🅿 12
🕘 Closed Christmas  🚭
🅢 MC, V

## CRAIGELLACHIE

### 🏨 CRAIGELLACHIE
**$$$** ★★★ ✿✿
CRAIGELLACHIE
AB38 9SR
TEL 01340-881204
FAX 01340-881253
Craigellachie has been attracting visitors from all over the world since 1893 to this lovely part of Speyside. It is an impressive Victorian hotel complete with sitting room, drawing room and library. There is a famously broad range of malt whiskies available in the Quaich Bar. Three dining areas; local ingredients are used in cooking.

🛈 26  🅿 50  🅢 Restaurant
🔽  🅢 All major cards

## DORNOCH

### 🏨 DORNOCH CASTLE
**$$** ★★
CASTLE ST.
IV25 3SD
TEL 01862-810216
FAX 01862-810981
Dating back to the 16th

century, this friendly family-run hotel was once the Palace of the Bishops of Caithness. Enjoy the comfortable lounge overlooking the gardens, the cocktail bar and a choice of dining options.

🛈 4 (13 annex)  🅿 16  🖃
🅢 All major cards

### 🏨 FOURPENNY COTTAGE
**$$**
SKELBO
IV25 3QF
TEL/FAX 01862-810727
Overlooking the Dornoch Firth, this hotel commands glorious views toward Golspie from the dining room. A spacious and well appointed guest house which offers guests a friendly, family welcome.

🛈 4  🅿 10  🚭  🕘 Closed Christmas

## DUNKELD

### 🏨 KINNAIRD
🍴 **$$$$$** ★★★ ✿✿✿
KINNAIRD ESTATE
DUNKELD
PH8 0LB
TEL 01796-482440
FAX 01796-482289
Unashamedly luxurious private country-house hotel on a 9,000-acre estate overlooking the Tay Valley. The bedrooms are provided with antique furnishings and king-size beds. Enjoy the wood fires and fresh flowers. Two dining rooms serve assured and imaginative cooking. Sporting pursuits. are catered for. Fixed-price L & D. No children under 12.

🛈 9  🛏 35  🅿 22
🕘 Closed Mon., Tues., Wed. in Jan. & Feb.  🖃
🅢 Restaurant  🅢 All major cards

## DUNVEGAN

### 🏨 ROSKHILL
**$$**
ROSKHILL
IV55 8ZD

TEL 01470-521317
FAX 01470-521761
Cottage-style croft house offering a warm welcome. The comfortable bedrooms are furnished with antiques and pine. No children under ten.

🛈 4  🅿 12  🕘 Closed Dec.– Jan.  🚭  🅢 All major cards

## ERISKA

### 🏨 ISLE OF ERISKA
🍴 **$$$$$** ★★★★ ✿✿✿
ERISKA
PA37 1SD
TEL 01631-720371
FAX 01631-720531
This granite and sandstone baronial mansion stands in splendid isolation on its own picturesque island (which has vehicular access to the mainland). Dinners here feature a daily roast, as well as a selection of fish, and seafood. Fixed-price D.

🛈 17  🛏 40  🅿 40
🕘 Closed Jan.
🚭 Restaurant  🖃  🔽
🅢 All major cards

## FORT WILLIAM

### 🏨 INVERLOCHY CASTLE
🍴 **$$$$$** ★★★★ ✿✿✿
TORLUNDY
PH33 6SN
TEL 01397-702177
FAX 01397-702953
Victorian pile beneath Ben Nevis on 500 acres of grounds; superb display of rhododendrons. Tennis and fishing. Don't confuse the 19th-century Inverlochy Castle with the square, turreted ruins nearby. These belong to Old Inverlochy Castle, a 13th-century stronghold where at least three battles were fought. Great Hall with frescoed ceiling and crystal chandeliers. Two dining rooms; cooking shows traditional skills and modern ideas, using good local ingredients. Fixed-price L & D.

HOTELS & RESTAURANTS

**↑** 17 **+** 34 **P** 18
**⊕** Closed Jan., Feb.
**Ⓢ** Restaurant **⌂** All
major cards

## 🍴 THREE CHIMNEYS

A 100-year-old crofter's cottage a stone's throw from the sea. You can eat virtually any time of day, although the greatest pleasures are reserved for the evening. Fresh seafood is the star attraction. Just down the road are two museums that should not be missed: the Colbost Folk Museum, which gives a good idea of traditional crofting life, and the Boreraig Piping Centre where you can learn all about—and try your hand (and lungs) at—bagpipe music.
**$$$$** ⊛⊛⊛
COLBOST, ISLE OF SKYE
IV55 8ZT
TEL 01470-511258
**+** 30 **⊕** Closed Sun. L &
3 weeks Jan. **Ⓢ** **⌂** MC,

## INVERNESS

## 🏨 CULLODEN HOUSE

Historic Adam-style Georgian mansion on 40 acres of wooded grounds and parkland. Bonnie Prince Charlie's army of Highland clansmen spent the night of April 15, 1746 sleeping on the ground in the parks here. Next morning they marched out to be cut to pieces by the English dragoons on Drummossie Moor, the bloody end to the second Jacobite Rebellion. Marble fireplaces, ornate plasterwork, chandeliers. Period suites, master rooms, contemporary bedrooms. No-smoking suites. Daily changing five-course menu. Tennis,

croquet, boules, and badminton.
**$$$$$** ★★★★ ⊛⊛
CULLODEN
IV2 7BZ
TEL 01463 790461
FAX 01463 792181
**↑** 23 (5 annex) **P** 50
**Ⓢ** Restaurant **⌂** All major
cards

## ISLE ORNSAY

## 🏨 KINLOCH LODGE

**$$$$** ★★ ⊛⊛
ISLE ORNSAY
ISLE OF SKYE
IV43 8QY
TEL 01471-833214
FAX 01471-833277
The mood inside Lord and Lady Macdonald's converted 300-year-old lodge is one of a family home. Drawing rooms have log fires and comfortable sofas; family portraits and photographs are displayed throughout. Dinner is a fixed-price affair running to four courses and dishes are based resolutely on what the local region can provide.
**↑** 9 (5 annex) **⊕** Closed
Christmas **Ⓢ** **⌂** AE, MC, V

## JOHN O'GROATS

## 🏨 POST OFFICE HOUSE

**$**
CANISBAY
KW1 4YH
TEL/FAX 01955-611213
Views over Pentland Firth. Hostess makes her guests feel welcome and well cared for. Cozy sitting room where tea and dinners are served. Extensive breakfast menu including salmon, smoked haddock, fresh fruit. No children under 12.
**↑** 3 **P** 5 **⊕** Closed
Oct.–Easter **Ⓢ**

## KINGUSSIE

## 🍴 THE CROSS

**$$$$** ★★ ⊛⊛⊛
TWEED MILL BRAE,
ARDBROILACH RD.

PH21 1TC
TEL 01540-661166
FAX 01540-661080
Converted tweed mill run as a friendly restaurant-with-rooms offering lovely accommo-dations. Superbly comfortable beds and many thoughtful touches. Menu features local ingredients. Fixed-price D. No children under 12.
**↑** 9 **+** 28 **⊕** Closed
Christmas, New Year, Jan.
**Ⓢ** Restaurant **⌂** MC, V

## 🏨 SCOT HOUSE

**$$** ★★ ⊛
NEWTONMORE RD.
PH21 1HE
TEL 01540-661351
FAX 01540-661111
Small family-run hotel; genuine warmth of welcome. Fresh local produce in restaurant.
**↑** 9 **P** 30 **⊕** Closed
3 weeks Jan. **Ⓢ** Restaurant
**⌂** All major cards

## KIRKWALL

## 🏨 THE AYRE HOTEL

**$$$** ★★★
AYRE ROAD
KIRKWALL
ORKNEY
KW15 1QX
TEL 01856-873001
FAX 01856-876289
This welcoming hotel overlooks Kirkwall's harbor, jumping off point for the northern Orkney Islands, and is only a few minutes' walk from the charming and historic center of town. Modern rooms and accommodating staff make for a comfortable and pleasant stay at the only 4-star hotel on Mainland Orkney. Also houses a restaurant and a popular local bar. Surcharge for rooms with a sea-view.
**↑** 33 **P** 18 **⊕** Closed
Christmas Day and New
Year's Day **⌂** AE, MC, V

## KYLESKU

### 🏨 KYLESKU
**$$**
KYLESKU
IV27 4HW
TEL 01971-502231/502200
FAX 01971-502313
Pleasant small waterside hotel with good reputation for very fresh seafood. Fishing.
🛏 7 (1 annex)  🅿 50
🕐 Closed Nov.–Easter
🍽 Restaurant  💳 MC, V

## PORT APPIN

### 🏨 AIRDS
🍽 **$$$$$** ★★★ ❀❀❀
PORT APPIN
PA38 4DF
TEL 01631-730236
FAX 01631-730535
The scenery is stunning with views across Loch Linnhe, scattered with islands, to the Morvern mountains beyond. Skillful cooking that shows lots of creativity and finesse. Superb wine list. Fixed-price D.
🛏 12  🍽 36  🅿 15
🕐 Closed Dec. 23–27 & Jan. 6–26  🍽 Restaurant
💳 All major cards

## PORTREE

### 🏨 CUILLIN HILLS
**$$$** ★★★ ❀
PORTREE
ISLE OF SKYE
IV51 9QU
TEL 01478-612003
FAX 01478-613092
Superb views over Portree Bay to the Cuillin Hills. Highland specialties in restaurant.
🛏 21 (9 annex)  🅿 56
🍽 Restaurant  💳 AE, MC, V

## ST. MARGARET'S HOPE

### 🍽 CREEL
**$$$** ❀❀
FRONT RD.
ST MARGARET'S HOPE
ORKNEY
KW17 2SL
TEL 01856-831311
Set in the center of the village right beside the bay, Creel Restaurant

has a sound reputation with visitors and islanders alike. The focus is on fresh Orkney produce. Advance reservations are advisable.
🍽 34  🕐 Closed L, Jan.–March, Nov.  💳 MC, V

## TOBERMORY

### 🏨 WESTERN ISLES
**$$$/$$$$** ★★★
TOBERMORY
PA75 6PR
TEL 01688-302012
FAX 01688-302297
Victorian hotel high above the pier, with picture-postcard view of bay, sea, and hills. Conservatory bar. Eastern cuisine in Spices Restaurant; more traditional main dining room.
🛏 28  🅿 20  🕐 Closed Christmas  🍽 Restaurant
💳 All major cards

# SHOPPING

In the main cities and towns of Britain shops usually open at 8:30 or 9 a.m., and many now stay open until 6 p.m. or later (supermarkets until 8 p.m. or later, some on Sundays, too). "Early closing day" is largely a thing of the past, though in the smaller and sleepier provincial towns and in many villages you will find certain stores shut from 1 p.m. on Wednesday or Thursday.

During the past 20 years, national chain stores and out-of-town supermarkets have posed an increasing threat to the traditional family-run town center store. The stores recommended here still retain their local or individual character.

## LONDON

### BOOKS
Charing Cross Road is home to some of Britain's best-known bookstores, including:
**Foyles** (Nos 113–119) Tel 020-7437 5660
**Sportspages** (Nos 94–96) Tel 020-7240 9604

### DESIGNER CLOTHING
Good places to start looking are the **Hype DF** mall, Kensington High Street for contemporary British fashions.
**Paul Smith,** 43–46 Floral Street, Covent Garden, Tel 020-7379 7133. British designer clothing.

### FOOD & DRINK
**Berry Bros. & Rudd,** 3 St. James's Street, Tel 020-7396 9600. Wine merchant selling everything you would want from a London setting.
**Fortnum & Mason,** 181 Piccadilly, Tel 020-7734 8040. Fabulous chocolates to luxurious hampers.
**Harrods,** 87–135 Brompton Road, Knightsbridge, Tel 020-7730 1234. Lavish Food Halls.
**Neal's Yard Dairy,** 17 Shorts Gardens, Covent Garden, Tel 020-7379 7646. The finest British and Irish cheeses.

### MARKETS
**Camden** (Thurs.–Sun.) is London's busiest market, with a carnival-like atmosphere and everything from street fashion to secondhand clothes.
**Greenwich** (daily; Thurs.—antiques, Fri.–Sun.—arts and crafts) has a more sedate feel but is still full of local character.
**Petticoat Lane** (Mon.–Sat.) is London's best-known market and attracts many visitors and the associated souvenir stalls.
**Portobello Road** (Mon.–Sat.) is over a mile long and is a traditional East End street market.

### TRADITIONAL CLOTHING
**Bates the Hatter,** 21a Jermyn Street, Tel 020-7734 2722. Supplier of top hats, trilbies, and panama hats since 1902.
**Burberrys** 18–22 Haymarket, Tel 020-7930 3343.
**Gieves & Hawkes,** 1 Savile Row, Tel 020-7434 2001. One of the best-known gentlemen's out-fitters of high quality tailor-made clothing on world-famous Savile Row.
**Thomas Pink,** 85 Jermyn Street, Tel 020-7930 6364. Fine shirts.

## HOME COUNTIES & SOUTH COUNTRY

### CLOTHING
Classic clothing is available in many South Country towns, where smaller stores still cater to country gentlefolk:
**County Clothes,** 19 Saint Margarets Street, Canterbury, Tel 01227-765294. Menswear.
**Sam Gordon,** 24 North Street, Brighton, Tel 020-7379 7646. Menswear.

### TEA
**Whittards of Chelsea,** 97 High Street, Guildford, Tel 01483-449393. Specialist teas and coffees.

## WEST COUNTRY

### ART/DESIGN
**Tate Gallery St. Ives**
Porthmeor Beach, St. Ives, tel 01736-796226.

### CHEESE
Cheddar cheese is known throughout the world and is still made in the traditional way at:
**House of Cheese,** Church Street, Tetbury, tel 01666-502865. For a wide range of fine cheeses.

### CIDER
**Burrow Hill Cider,** Pass Vale Farm, Burrow Hill, Kingsbury Episcopi, Martock, tel 01460-240782.

### GLASS
**Bristol Blue Glass,** Visitor Center, Unit 7, Whitby Road, Brislington, Bristol, tel 0117-972 0818.

## WALES

### GOLD
**Pickwicks,** 5 Crosby Buildings, Eldon Square, Dolgellau, Tel 01341-422018. For jewelry and other products made from Welsh gold.

### POTTERY
**Portmeirion Pottery Seconds Warehouse,**
Portmeirion Village, Gwynedd, Tel 01766-770774. Seconds of distinctive pottery are sold here.

## SOUTH MIDLANDS

### ETHNIC FABRICS
There are large populations of people of Asian origin all over Britain. Shops selling ethnic fabrics are often found in towns with large Asian communities.
**Saree Mandir,** 117–129 Belgrave Road, Leicester, Tel 0116-266 8144. This shop selling beautiful fabrics is the largest in the world outside India.

## JEWELRY

Hundreds of jewelry workshops in **Birmingham's Jewellery Quarter** produce much of Britain's finest handcrafted jewelry. For more information visit the Museum of the Jewellery Quarter, 77–79 Vyse St. Tel 0121-554 3598.

## MARKETS

| | |
|---|---|
| Birmingham | Mon.–Sat. |
| Coventry | Mon.–Sat. |
| Hereford | Wed., Sat. |
| Leicester | Mon.–Sat. |
| Moreton-in-Marsh | Tues. |
| Northampton | Mon.–Sat. |
| Oxford | Wed., Thurs. |
| Worcester | Mon.–Sat. |

### EAST ANGLIA & LINCOLNSHIRE

## MUSTARD

**The Mustard Shop,** 15 Royal Arcade, Norwich, Tel 01603-627889. Norwich is synonymous with fine mustard.

### NORTH MIDLANDS

## BEER

Burton-on-Trent is the center of the British brewing industry. As well as many fine pubs in the town you can buy bottled ale at: **The Bass Museum Shop,** Horninglow Street, Burton-upon-Trent, Tel 01283-511000.

## POTTERY

Many factory shops in the Potteries sell famous brands manufactured in the area. **The World of Spode Factory Shop,** Church Street, Stoke-on-Trent, Tel 01782-744011. **Waterford Wedgwood Factory Shop,** King Street., Fenton, Stoke-on-Trent, Tel 01782-316161.

### NORTHWEST ENGLAND

## MARKETS

| | |
|---|---|
| Ashton-under-Lyne | Mon.–Sat., not Tues. |
| Blackburn | Wed., Fri., Sat. |
| Chester | Mon.–Sat. |
| Kendal | Sat. |
| Lancaster | Mon., Tues., Thurs., Fri. |
| Manchester | Mon., Wed., Sat. |
| Preston | Mon., Wed., Fri., Sat. |
| Stockport | Fri., Sat. |

## OUTDOOR CLOTHING

**George Fisher,** 2 Borrowdale Road, Keswick, Tel 017687 72178. This is the most famous of over 25 specialist shops selling outdoorwear in the small Lake District town of Keswick.

## POTTERY

**Wetheriggs Country Pottery,** Clifton Dykes, Penrith, Tel 01768-892733. Traditional earthenware pottery produced in restored Victorian steam pottery.

### NORTHEAST ENGLAND

## CHEESE

Wensleydale cheese is a crumbly, white, hard cheese produced in the Yorkshire dale of the same name. **Wensleydale Dairy Products Ltd.,** Visitor Centre, Gayle Lane, Hawes, Tel 01969-667664.

## JEWELRY & DESIGN

West Yorkshire has produced many fine craftspeople and is still a center of design. **Crafts and Design Shop,** City Art Gallery, The Headrow, Leeds, Tel 0113-247 8241.

## MARKETS

| | |
|---|---|
| Bradford | Mon.–Sat. |
| Doncaster | Mon.–Sat. |
| Darlington | Mon.–Sat. |
| Durham | Tues., Fri., Sat. |
| Halifax | Fri. |
| Hexham | Tues. |
| Huddersfield | Mon. |
| Hull | Tues., Fri., Sat. |
| Leeds | Tues., Fri., Sat. |
| Sheffield | Mon.–Sat. except Thurs. |
| Wakefield | Mon., Fri., Sat. |

## TEA

**Betty's of Harrogate,** 1 Parliament Street, Harrogate, Tel 01423-502746. Tea is sold here by the ounce, or drink it in their world-famous tea rooms.

### SCOTTISH LOWLANDS

## KILTS

**Hector Russell Kiltmakers,** 95 Princes Street, Edinburgh, Tel 0131-225-3315. Both shops sell authentic kilts. **The Kilt Centre,** Units 3, 4, & 5, The Dyeworks, New Lanark, New Lanark Road, Lanark, Tel 01555-666009.

## MARKETS

| | |
|---|---|
| Dumfries | Wed. |
| Dundee | Tues. |
| Edinburgh | Tues. |
| Glasgow, The Barras | Sat., Sun. |

## WOOLENS

**Woollen Mill,** 179 High Street, Edinburgh, Tel 0131-225 8023. Traditional knitwear.

### HIGHLANDS & ISLANDS

## TRADITIONAL MUSIC

You will find recordings of traditional Highlands music at: **The Ceilidh Place,** 14 West Argyle Street, Ullapool, Tel 01854-612103. **Record Rendezvous,** 14A Church Street, Inverness, Tel 01463-231219.

## WHISKEY

Among the distilleries open to the public are: **Dalwhinnie Distillery Visitor Centre,** Dalwhinnie, Tel 01540-672219. **Glenfiddich Whisky Distillery,** Dufftown, Keith, Tel 01340-820373.

# ENTERTAINMENT

In the smaller towns, nightlife tends to be concentrated in the pub or restaurant, with perhaps a more or less mediocre nightclub or provincial theater. The biggest centers, though, have greatly improved the scope and quality of their nightlife in recent years, with a huge number of pubs, clubs, theaters, bars, and halls to choose from. Major cities publish their own listings magazines with reviews, comment, and full details of what's on. These are available from newsdealers, bookstores, and visitor information centers. Following is a selection of some of the main theaters and concert venues in Great Britain.

## LONDON

### CONCERT HALLS
**Royal Albert Hall,** Kensington Gore SW7 2AP, Tel 020-7823 7725, Tube: South Kensington, High Street Kensington. London's circular concert hall, venue for the Proms (see p. 44).
**Royal Festival Hall,** Belvedere Road SE1 8XX, Tel 020-7960 4242, Tube: Waterloo, Embankment. Concert hall designed for the 1951 Festival of Britain.

### OPERA
**Royal Opera House,** Covent Garden WC2E 9DD, Tel 020-7304 4000, Tube: Covent Garden. Britain's premier ballet and opera venue.

### THEATER
**Royal National Theatre,** South Bank SE1 9PX, Tel 020-7452 3400, Tube: Embankment, Waterloo. Three theaters offering classic to experimental pieces.
**Shakespeare's Globe Theatre,** New Globe Walk, Bankside, Southwark, SE1 9DT, Tel 020-7401 9919, Tube: London Bridge, Mansion House. Outdoor Elizabethan plays May through September.

## HOME COUNTIES

### THEATER
**Theatre Royal,** Thames Street, Windsor, Tel 01753-853888. Mainstream drama.

## THE SOUTH COUNTRY

### THEATERS
**Chichester Festival Theatre,** Oaklands Park, Chichester, Tel 01243-781312. Venue for a summer performing-arts festival.
**Salisbury Playhouse,** Malthouse Lane, Salisbury, Tel 01722-320117. Drama, musicals, opera, ballet.
**Theatre Royal,** New Road, Brighton, Tel 01273-328488. Drama, musicals, opera, ballet.

## THE WEST COUNTRY

### THEATERS
**Theatre Royal,** Sawclose, Bath, Tel 01225-448844. One of Britain's oldest and most beautiful theaters.
**Theatre Royal,** King Street, Bristol, Tel 0117-987 7877. The country's oldest theater.

## WALES

### OPERA
**Welsh National Opera,** Tel 029-2046 4666. Superb Welsh singing voices.

### THEATER
**Sherman Theatre,** Senghennydd Road, Cardiff, Tel 029-2064 6900. Unconventional and challenging productions.

## SOUTH MIDLANDS

### CONCERT HALL
**Symphony Hall,** Intl. Conference Centre, Broad St., Birmingham, Tel 0121-780 3333. Concerts by the City of Birmingham Symphony Orchestra.

### THEATER
**Oxford Playhouse,** Beaumont Street, Oxford, Tel 01865-798600. Drama, dance, music,

and opera presented within a Georgian building.
**Royal Shakespeare Theatre,** Stratford-upon-Avon, Tel 01789-403403. Home to the Royal Shakespeare Company.

## NORTHWEST

### CONCERT HALLS
**Bridgewater Hall,** near G-Mex Centre, Manchester, Tel 0161-907 9000. Home of the Hallé Orchestra.
**Philharmonic Hall,** Hope Street, Liverpool, Tel 0151-709 2895. Home of the Royal Liverpool Philharmonic Orchestra.

### THEATERS
**Empire Theatre,** Lime Street, Liverpool, Tel 0151-709 1555. Major touring companies visit here: ballet, opera, drama, musicals, and concerts.
**The Royal Exchange,** St. Ann's Sq., Manchester, Tel 0161-833 9833. Plays ranging from Ibsen to Shakespeare.

## NORTHEAST

### THEATER
**Theatre Royal,** Grey Street, Newcastle upon Tyne, Tel 0191-232 2061. Seasonal performances by the Royal Shakespeare Company.

## SCOTLAND

### CONCERT HALL
**Glasgow Royal Concert Hall,** 2 Sauchiehall Street, Glasgow, Tel 0141-332 6633. Home of the Royal Scottish National Orchestra.

### THEATERS
**Citizens Theatre,** 119 Gorbals Street, Glasgow, Tel 0141-429 0022. One of the most respected theaters in Britain; adventurous productions.
**Edinburgh Playhouse,** 18–22 Greenside Place, Edinburgh, Tel 0131-557 2590. Big shows.

**INDEX**
Bold page numbers
indicate illustrations.

**A**

A La Ronde 143
Abbotsbury Swannery 137
Abbotsford House 290–91
Aberdeen 316, 384
  Provost Skene's
    House 316
Aberfoyle 314, 379
Aberlady Bay 302
Aberystwyth 167, 358
  Camera Obscura 167
  Cliff Railway 167
Abinger Hammer 114
Achray Forest Drive 314
Acton Trussel 369–70
Adam, Robert 32, 86, 210
Air travel 336, 337–8
Aira Force 256
Aldbury 97, 109
Alfriston 26
  Clergy House 26
Allendale 15, 260
Alloway 293
  Alloway Old Kirk 293
  Brig o'Doon **292**, 293
  Burns Cottage
    and Museum 293
  Burns Monument 293
Almouth 282
Althorp 177, 198, **198**
Alton Towers 230
Altrincham 373
Amberley Castle 349
Ambleside 256, 373
American Museum 156,
  **156**
Angus 310, 318
Anstruther 308, 379
  Scottish Fisheries
    Museum 308
Appleby 14, 258, 373
Architecture
  Georgian 32
  industrial 33–4
  medieval 26, 27–8
  postwar 37
  Tudor 29
Ardnamurchan 312–3
Argyll 310
Arisaig 384
Arkengarthdale 275
Arlington Court 149
Arncliffe 274, 376
Arran 330
Art 41–3
Arthur, King 24, 129, 147,
  150
Arts 38–46
Ascot 11, 105, 346
Asenby 376
Ash Mill 353
Ashbourne 230, 370
Aspley Guise 346
Auchterarder 384
Audley End 210, **211**

Austen, Jane 38, 40, 117,
  129
Avebury 135
  Alexander Keiller
    Museum 135
Avebury Stone Circle 22
Aviemore 319
Aylesbury 346–7
Ayot St. Lawrence 97, 114
  Shaw's Corner 114
Ayr 293
Aysgarth 275

**B**

Bakewell **230**, 231, 370
Ballater 316–7, 384–5
Balloch 379–80
Balmoral Castle 317
Balquhidder 314
Balranald 331
Bamburgh Castle 282
Banff 318
  Duff House 318
Banks 340
Bardsey Island 173
Barnard Castle 260, **260**,
  376
  Bowes Museum 260
Barnstaple 144, 353
Barra 331
  Kisimul Castle 331
Bass Rock 308
Bath 24, 141, 153–5, **153**, 353
  Abbey Church 154–5
  Assembly Rooms 155
  The Circus 155
  The Cross Bath 155
  Museum of Costume 155
  No. 1 Royal Crescent 155
  Pulteney Bridge 155
  Pump Room 154
  Roman Baths 154, **155**
  Royal Crescent **153**, 155
  Sally Lunn's House 155
  Theatre Royal 155, 390
  Thermae 155
Battle of Killiecrankie
  Visitor Centre 315
Beaconsfield 347
Beamish Open Air Museum
  286
Beatrix Potter Gallery 256
Beaumaris Castle 168
Bed and breakfast 342
Beddgelert 168
  Gelert's Grave 168, 171
Belas Knap 22, 183
Belton House 46
Ben Nevis 313
Benbecula 331
Bere Regis 137
Berkshire 97
Berneray 331
Berwick Law 308
Berwick-upon-Tweed 282
Berwyn Mountains 174
Bess of Hardwick 232, 234,
  235, **235**
Betws-y-Coed 172, 358

Beverley 270, 376–7
Bibury 183
Bideford 144
Big Pit Mining Museum 163
Binham 218
Birdoswald Fort 284, 285
Birmingham 177, 190, 362
  Museum and Art
    Gallery 190
  Gas Street Basin 190
  Thinktank 190
Black Mountains 166–7
Blackness Castle 46
Blackpool 373
Bladon 197
Blaenau Ffestiniog 172
  Llechwedd Slate
    Caverns 172
Blair Castle 315
Blairgowrie 385
Blakeney 366
Blanchland 260, 377
Blenheim Palace 32, 177,
  196–7, **196–7**
Blickling Hall 219
Bloomsbury Group 68
Blue John Cavern and Mine
  242
Bodmin Moor 10, 148–9,
  **148**
Boleyn, Anne 84, 119, 120,
  219
Bolton Priory 274
Bonnie Prince Charlie 31,
  312, 323, 327, 331
Bontddu 358
Borders 290–91
Boscastle 147
Bosherston Lily Ponds 165
Boston 221
Bournemouth 349
Bourton-on-the-Water 183
Bowland Forest 10, 250, **250**
Bradenham **95**
Bradford 33, 377
Bradford-on-Avon 156
Braemar 14, 317, 385
Brampton 373
Brathay 373
Braunton Burrows 144
Bray 99, 347
Brecon 358
Brecon Beacons **161**, 166
Bressay 334
Bridgewater Monument 109
Bridgnorth 238
Bridport 349
Brighton 32, 117, 126, 349
  Kemp Town 126
  Royal Pavilion 126, **126**
  Sea Life Centre 126
  Volk's Electric Railway 126
Brimham Rocks 274
Bristol 141, 152, 353–4
  @t Bristol 152
  Arnolfini Gallery 152
  Bristol Old Railway
    Station 152
Clifton 32, 152

Clifton Suspension
    Bridge 152
  S.S. *Great Britain* 152
  Theatre Royal 152, 390
British Museum 69–72, **69**,
  **72**
Broadland Conservation
  Centre 217
Broadstairs 125
Broadway 183, 362–3
Brodick 385
Brontë sisters 40, 272
Brown, Capability 32, 107,
  121, 184, 197, 210, 219,
  221, 233
Brunel, Isambard Kingdom
  152, 152
Bryher 158
Buckinghamshire 97
Buckland Abbey 145
Burford 183, 363
Burgh Island Hotel 145
Burghley House 29, 221
Burnham Market 366
Burns, Robert 13, 291,
  292–3, **293** 38
Burray 332
Burslem 237
Bury 374
Bury St. Edmunds 222, 366
Bus travel 337
Bute 330
Buttermere 256, 374
Buxton 230, 370
  Crescent 230
  Edwardian Opera House
    230
  St. Ann's Well 230

**C**

Caerlaverock Castle 291
  Wildfowl and Wetlands
    Trust Centre 291, 321
Caernarfon 168, 358
  Castle 170–71, **170–71**
Cairngorms 310, 318, 320,
  321
Caithness 311
Callander 314
  Rob Roy and Trossachs
    Visitor Centre 314
Cambridge 202–206, **202**,
  **203**, 367
  The Backs **204**, 205
  colleges 204, 205–206
  Fitzwilliam Museum 206
  Great St. Mary's Church 204
  Holy Sepulchre Round
    Church 204
  King's College Chapel 28,
    205–206, **206**
  Mathematical Bridge 206
  Pepys Building 204
  St. Bene't's Church 206
Cambridgeshire 201,
  202–206
Campsie Fells 297
Canna 330
Canterbury 122–3, 349

Canterbury Heritage Museum 123
Canterbury Tales 123
Cathedral 122–3, **122**, **123**
Eastbridge Hospital 123
Cape Wrath 323
Capel Curig 172
Car rental 336
Cardiff 163, 358–9
Castle 163, **163**
Museum of Welsh Life 163
National Museum and Gallery of Wales 163
Cardingmill Valley 240
Carlisle 251
Cartmel Priory 251, **251**
Castle Acre 218, 367
Castle Campbell 307
Castle Combe 349
Castle Howard 46, 270–71, **270**
Castle Rising 218
Castle Tioram 46
Castleton **225**, 242
Cavendish 14–15, 212
Cawfields 285
Central Scotland 314–5
Chagford 354
Chalfont St. Giles 97, 109
Chalk 124
Charlecote Park 189
Charles I 30, **30–31**, 62, 63, 103, 123, 226
Charles II 31, 62, 100, 207, 241
Chartwell 120, **120**
Chatham 125
Historic Dockyard **117**, 125
Chatsworth House 224, 232–3, **232**, **233**
Chawton 117, 129
Chedworth Roman Villa 24, 183
Cheltenham 32, 181, 363
Pittville Pump Room 181
Chepstow 162, 359
Chepstow Castle 162
Cheshire 225
Chester **224**, 225, 241, **241**, 370
Cathedral 241
King Charles Tower 241
Roman Amphitheatre 241
Rows **224**, 241
Chesters Fort and Museum 284, 285
Cheviot Hills 263, 283
Chichester 127, 349
Cathedral 127
Festival Theatre 127
Chilterns 97, 108–109
Chipping Campden 183, 363
Chipping Norton 363
Chiswick House 86
Church Stretton 240, 370
Churchill, Sir Winston 62, 63, 120, 197
Chysauster Ancient Village 22, 147

Cidermaking 150
Cirencester 182–3, 363
Corinium Museum 183
Civil War 30, 241
Clacton-on-Sea 213
Clare 212
Claverdon 363
Clee Hills 225
Cliffe Fort 124
Climate 336
Clinton, Bill 193
Clitheroe 374
Cliveden House 98–9, 347
Clovelly 144, **144**
Coast-to-Coast Walk 258
Cockermouth 252
Wordsworth House 252, 255
Coggeshall 210
Grange Barn 210
Paycocke's 210
Colchester 213, 367
Castle Museum 24, 213
Coleridge, Samuel Taylor 255
Coll 321, 330
Colonsay 330
Communications 338–9
Constable, John 42, 212, 214–5, 255
Conversion tables 339
Conwy 168, 359
Conwy Castle 168
Cookham 98
Stanley Spencer Gallery 98
Cooling 124
Cooper's Hill 14, **181**
Corbridge 286
Cornwall 141, 146–9
Cotswolds 176–7, 181–3
Coventry 177, 190
Cathedral 37, 190, **190**
Crackington Haven 354
Craigellachie 385
Crail 308, **308**
Cranborne Chase 137
Cranbrook 350
Craster 282
Crathes Castle 316
Crathie 317
Credit cards 339, 343
lost or stolen 341
Cressing Temple 222
Crickhowell 359
Crime 341
Croyde 144
Crummock Water 256
Cullen 318
Culloden 310, 323
Cumbria 245
Cupar 380
Currency 339

**D**
Dalbeattie 380
Dalby Forest Drive 276
Dark Peak 224, **229**
Dartmoor National Park **148**, 149
Dartmouth 145, 354

Daventry 363–4
Deal 125
Deben estuary 10
Dedham 214, 367
Deerhurst 178
Dengie Peninsula 213
Dental treatment 341
Derbyshire 224
Derwent Water 253, 256
Devil's Beef Tub 308
Devil's Bridge 167
Devon 140–41, 142–5, 149
Diana, Princess of Wales 177, 198
Dickens, Charles 34, 38, **40**, 68, 116, 124, 125, 222, 260
Dinas Head 165
Disabilities, travelers with 341, 343
Dolgellau 168, 359–60
Dollar Glen 307
Domesday Book 25
Doone Valley 149
Dorchester 350
Max Gate 137
Dornoch 385
Dorset 117, 136–7
Dorset Coast Path 137
Dover 125, 350
Drake, Sir Francis 30, 145
Drinking and driving 337
Drinking water 341
Driving 336–7
Drum Castle 316
Dryburgh Abbey 290
Du Maurier, Daphne 147, 148
Dufftown 385
Dumfries 291
Burns House 291
Burns Mausoleum 291
Robert Burns Centre 291
Duncansby Head 324
Dundee 385
Dungeness 10
Dunnottar Castle 46
Dunstanburgh Castle 282
Dunster 144, 354
Dunvegan 385
Durham 14, 262–3, 280–81, **281**, 377
Castle 281
Cathedral 28, 278–9, **278**, **279**
University Museum of Archaeology 280
Dynamic Earth 302
Dyrham Park 156

**E**
East Anglia & Lincolnshire 10, 199–222
hotels and restaurants 366–9
map 201
East Bergholt 214
East Neuk of Fife 308
Eastwood 227
D.H. Lawrence Birthplace Museum 227

Eday 332
Eden Project 147
Edinburgh 298–303, 380–81
Calton Hill 303
Deacon Brodie's Tavern 301
Dean Gallery 303
Dean Village 303
Edinburgh Castle 298, **299**
Edinburgh Festival 298
Edinburgh Tattoo 298, **299**
The Georgian House 303
Gladstone's Land 300
Greyfriars Kirk 301
John Knox House 300
Lady Stair's House 300
Museum of Edinburgh **289**, 301
Museum of Scotland 302
National Gallery of Scotland 302, **303**
The People's Story 301
Royal Mile 300
Royal Museum 302
Royal Observatory 302
Royal Scottish Academy 302
St. Giles Cathedral 300
Scotch Whisky Heritage Centre 300
Scott Monument 303
Scottish National Gallery of Modern Art 303
Scottish National Portrait Gallery 303
Writers' Museum 300
Edward I 26, 170, 171
Edward II 178
Edward III 26, 226
Edwinstowe 227
Egilsay 332
Eigg 330
1853 Gallery 273
Eilean Donan Castle 313
Electricity 339
Elie 381
Elizabeth I 29–30, 58, **107**, 112–13
Ely 208, 367–8
Cathedral 208, **208**
Stained Glass Museum 208
Emergencies 341
Englishcombe 156
Entertainment 390
Eriskay 331, 386
Essex 200, 209–210, 213
Eton College 104
Evershot 350
Ewell 347
Ewelme 195
Exchange rates 339–40
Exeter 142–3, **142**, 354
Cathedral 28, 142–3, **142**
Guildhall 143
Mol's Coffee House 142
Priory of St. Nicholas 143
Tuckers Hall 143
Exmoor National Park 149, **149**

Eyam 242, 242

**F**

Fair Isle 334
Falmouth 354–5
Farne Islands **20–1**, 282
Faversham 350
Felbrigg Hall 219, **219**
Fenland 220
Fetlar 321, 333
Ffestiniog Railway 168
Film industry 46
Firth of Forth 308
Fishbourne Roman Palace 24, 127, **127**
Fishing **320**, 321
Flat Holm 158
Flatford 214, **214**, 215, **215**
   Bridge Cottage 215
   Willy Lott's Cottage **214**, 215, **215**
Flitwick 347
Floors Castle 290
Flow Country 324
Folkestone 125, 350
Food and drink 16–17
   see also Hotels and restaurants
Forest of Dean 174
   Speech House Hotel 174
Fort William 313, 386
Fountains Abbey 274
Fowey 146, 355
Friday Street 114
Frinton-on-Sea 213
Furness Abbey 251

**G**

Gaelic language 331
Gainsborough, Thomas 212, 255
Galashiels 381
Galloway 10
Gas stations 340
George IV 126
Gibbons, Grinling 67, 82, 194
Glasgow 13, 294–6, **294**, **295**, 381–2
   Burrell Collection 296
   Glasgow School of Art **294**, 295
   Hunterian Art Gallery 296
   Hunterian Museum 296
   Kelvingrove Park Art Gallery and Museum 296
   Museum of Transport 296
   Provand's Lordship 295–6
   Queen's Cross Church 296
   St. Mungo Religious Life and Art Museum 295
   St. Mungo's Cathedral 295
   Tenement House 294
   Willow Rooms 295
Glastonbury
   Abbot's Kitchen 150
   Glastonbury Abbey 150
   Somerset Rural Life Museum 150
Glastonbury Tor 150, **150**

Glen Dubh 323
Glen Nevis 46
Glencoe 310, 313
Glenfinnan 312
Gloucester 178
   Cathedral 28, 178, **178**, 179
   National Waterways Museum 178
Golf 304–305, 320
Gower peninsula 165, **165**
Grahame, Kenneth 195
Grampians 310, 318
Grand Union Canal 198
Grange 374
Grange over Sands 374
Grasmere 256, 374
   Dove Cottage 256
Grassington 274, 377
   Upper Wharfedale Museum 274
Great Britain
   British character 10, 12
   etiquette and local customs 339
   history 22–37
   landscape 18
   local customs and festivities 12–15
Great Glen 323
Great Orme 360
Grimes Graves 22
Grimston 368
Grindleford 370–71
Gullane 382
Gulworthy 355

**H**

Haddon Hall 231
Hadrian's Wall 22, 24, 284–5, **284–5**
Hadrian's Wall Path National Trail 284
Halifax 272
   Calderdale Industrial Museum 272
   Piece Hall 272
   Shibden Hall Museum 272
Ham House 84–5
Hambleden **27**, 97, 98
Hamford Water 213
Hampshire 117, 130, 138
Hampton Court Palace 29, 46, 84, **85**
Hardwick Hall 29, 224, 234–5, **235**
Hardy, Thomas 40, 117, 136–7, **136**
Harlech 360
   Harlech Castle 168
Harris 331
Harrogate 271, 377
   Royal Baths Assembly Rooms 271
   Royal Pump Room 271
Harroway 135
Harwich 213, 368
Haslemere 347
Hastings 350
Hatfield House 97, 112–3

Hawes 259
Hawkshead 256
Hawksmoor, Nicholas 32, 57, 197, 270
Haworth 272
   Brontë Parsonage Museum 272
Hay-on-Wye 167, 360
Health 341
Hebden Bridge 272, 378
Helmsley 277, 378
Helston 14, 147, 355
Henley-on-Thames 98, **98**, **99**, 364
Henry II 25, 122, 196
Henry IV 26, 220
Henry VII 29, 58
Henry VIII 29, **29**, 84, 103, 112–3, 119–20, 121
Hereford 178, 180
   Cathedral 178
   Chained Library 180
   Mappa Mundi 178, 180
Hertfordshire 97
Hever Castle 119–20, **119**
Hexham 286, 378
   Abbey 286, **286**
High Force 259
Higher Bockhampton 136
   Hardy's Cottage 136, **136**
Highlands and Islands 309–34
   hotels and restaurants 384–7
Hill Top 256
Hintlesham 368
Holkham Hall 219
Holmfirth 46, 378
Holy Island 283, **283**
Home Counties 95–114
   hotels and restaurants 346–9
   map 97
Honiton 143
   Allhallows Museum 143
Hope 371
Hopedale 240
Horning Water **200**, 217
Horseracing 207
Horsey Mere **199**, 217
Horsham 350–51
Horton-in-Ribblesdale 259
Hotels and restaurants 342–87
Houghton Hall 218
Housesteads Fort and Museum 284, 285
Housman, A.E. 238
Hoveton 217
Hoy 332
Hubberholme 274
Hull 286
Humbie 382
Hutton-le-Hole 276
   Ryedale Folk Museum 276

**I**

The Ice Factory 321
Icknield Way 107, 135

Ightham Mote 119
Ilam 230
Ilfracombe 144
Ilkley 378
Inchcolm Island 302
Inchmahome Island 314
Inner Hebrides 325, 330
Inveraray Castle 312
Inverewe Gardens 323
Inverness 310, 323
   Balnain House 324
   Museum and Art Gallery 323
   St. Andrew's Cathedral 323
Iona **309**, 330
Ipswich 222
   Christchurch Mansion Museum and Art Gallery 222
   Ipswich Museum 222
Ironbridge Gorge 33, 242
Islay 330
   Kildalton High Cross 330
Isle of Anglesey 168
Isle of Lewis 22
Isle of Man 251
Isle Ornsay 386
Isle of Sheppey 125
Isle of Walney 251
Isle of Wight 130
   Alum Bay 130
   Carisbrooke Castle 130
   Osborne House 130
Isles of Scilly 158

**J**

Jamaica Inn 148
James I 30, 58, 207, 228, 306
James II 31
Jedburgh 382
   Abbey 290, **290**
John O'Groats 324, 386
   Last House Museum 324
Johnson, Samuel 38, 55
Jones, Inigo 32, 88
Jura 330

**K**

Keighley 378
Kelso 382
   Abbey 290, **291**
Kent 116, 118–25
Kersey 212
Keswick 256, 374–5
Kielder Forest 282
Kielder Water 282
King's Lynn 220, 368
Kingussie 319, 386–7
Kirkoswald 293
   Souter Johnnie's Cottage 293
Kirkwall 332
Knaresborough 271, **271**
   Mother Shipton's Cave 271
   Prophesy House 271
Kyle of Lochalsh 312, 313

Kyle Railway 313, 323
Kylesku 387

## L

Lacock 133, **133**, 351
  Fox Talbot Museum 133
  Lacock Abbey 133
Lake District 251–7
Lake of Menteith 314
Lake Windermere 256
Lakeside & Haverthwaite
  Steam Railway 256
Lamb Holm 332
Lambourn 195
Lancaster 250, 375
  Maritime Museum 250
Land's End 141, **146**, 147
Langbank 382
Langho 375
Langport 355
Lanyon Quoit 147
Lastingham 276, 378
Laugharne 164, 360
  Boat House 164
Lavenham 29, 212, 368
  Guildhall 212, **212**
  Little Hall 212
Lawrence, D.H. 41, 227
Leamington Spa 364
Leeds 33, 378
Leeds Castle 120–21,
  **120–21**
Leek 230
Leicester 177, 190
  Jain Temple 190
  Museum of Guru Nanak
  Gurdwara 190
Leominster 364
Lewes 15, 351
Lewis 331
  Callanish Standish Stones
  331, **331**
  Dun Carloway 331
Lincoln 221, **221**, 368
Lincolnshire see East Anglia
  and Lincolnshire
Lincolnshire Wolds 201, 220
Lindisfarne 283, **283**
Linlithgow 382
Linn of Dee 317
Liskeard 355
Literature 38–41
Littlehampton 351
Liverpool 244, 246–7, 246,
  **375**
  Albert Dock 247
  The Beatles Story 247
  Cavern Club 247
  Merseyside Maritime
  Museum 247
  Museum of Liverpool Life
  247
  Tate Gallery Liverpool
  247
  Walker Art Gallery 247
Lizard Peninsula 10, 141,
  147, 355
Llandrillo 360
Llanfair P.G. 168

Llangammarch Wells 361
Llangefni 361
Llangollen 174
  Plas Newydd 174
Llangybi 361
Llanthony Priory 167
Llanwddyn 361
Lleyn Peninsula 10, 173
Llyswen 361
Loch Achray 314
Loch Garten Nature
  Reserve 319
Loch Katrine 314
Loch Lomond 297, **297**
Loch Lomond and
  TheTrossachs
  National Park 297
Loch Shiel **312–3**
London 13, 47–94
  Albert Memorial 81
  Bank of England **51**, 54
  Bankside Power Station
  87
  Banqueting House 32, 63
  Big Ben 56, 62
  Bloomsbury 68–72
  British Library 71
  British Museum 69–72,
  **69, 72**
  Brompton Oratory 80
  Buckingham Palace 59,
  **59**
  Cabinet War Rooms 63
  Cenotaph 63
  Changing of the Guard
  59
  Chelsea 94
  Chelsea Physic Garden 79
  Chinatown 66
  Church of St. Lawrence
  Jewry 55
  the City 51–5
  Clink Exhibition 87
  Coram's Fields 79
  Courtauld Gallery 86
  Covent Garden 66–7
  Cutty Sark 88
  Design Museum 88
  Dickens House Museum
  68
  Downing Street 63
  Dr. Johnson's House 55
  Gipsy Moth IV 88
  Globe Theatre **39**, 87
  Great Exhibition
  Memorial 81
  Green Park 79
  Greenwich 88
  Guildhall 55
  Hampstead 94
  Harrods 73
  Harvey Nichols 73
  Holland Park 78
  hotels and restaurants
  343–6
  Houses of Parliament **56**,
  62
  Hyde Park 78, **78**, 81

Kensington Gardens 78,
  81
Kensington Palace 82, **82**
Kenwood House 94
Knightsbridge and
  Kensington 73–82
Leadenhall Market 54
Lincoln's Inn 55
Lloyd's Building 37, 54
London Aquarium 87
London Eye 87
London Planetarium 94
London Transport
  Museum 67
London Wetlands
  Centre 86
London Zoo 79
  maps 48–9, 54–5, 62–3,
  66–7, 80–81, 84–5
Madame Tussauds 94
Millennium Dome 88
Millennium Bridge 87
Monument 54
Museum of Instruments
  80–81
National Gallery 60–61,
  **60, 61**
National Maritime
  Museum 88
National Portrait Gallery
  64, **64**
Natural History Museum
  77, **77, 81**
Nelson's Column 63
Old Curiosity Shop 55
Old Royal Observatory
  88
  parks 78–9
Queen's Gallery 59
Queen's House 88
Regent's Park 79
River Thames 83–8
Rock Circus 66
Royal Albert Hall 81
Royal College of Music 80
Royal Mews 59
Royal Naval College 88
Royal Opera House 66–7
St. Botolph Church 55
St. James's Palace 59
St. James's Park 63, 79, **79**
St. Margaret's Church 62
St. Martin-in-the-Fields
  **50**, 63
St. Paul's Cathedral 51,
  52–3, **52–3**
St. Paul's Church 67
St. Stephen Walbrook
  54–5
Science Museum 76, **76**
Sherlock Holmes
  Museum 94
Shopping 388
Sir John Soane's Museum
  55, 93, **93**
Soho 66
South Bank Centre 87
Southwark Cathedral 87
Speaker's Corner **78**, 81

Tate Gallery 65, **65**
Temple 55
Thames Barrier 88, **88**
Theatre Museum 67
Tower Bridge **83**, 87–8
Tower of London 89–92,
  **89, 92**
Trafalgar Square 63
travelling around 338
  the Tube 338
Victoria & Albert
  Museum 74–5, **74, 75**
  walking tours 54–5, 62–3,
  66–7, 80–81
  Wallace Collection 94
Westminster Abbey 57–8,
  **57, 58**
Westminster Hall 62
Westminster and the
  West End 56–67
Long Melford 212
  Kentwell Hall 212
  Melford Hall 212
Long Mynd 225, 240
Longleat House 157, **157**
Longridge 375
Looe 355
Lost Gardens of Heligan 146
Lost property 341
Louth 220
Lowry, L.S. **244**, 249
Ludlow **223**, 225, 238, **238**,
  371
  Ludlow Castle 238
  St. Laurence's Church 238
Lundy Island 158
Lydford 355
Lyme Park 46
Lyme Regis 137
Lymington 351
Lynmouth 144, 355
  Exmoor National Park
  Visitor Centre 144
Lynton 144, 355–6
  Lyn and Exmoor Museum
  144

## M

Macdonald, Flora 327, 331
Macduff 318
Machynlleth 361
Mackintosh, Charles Rennie
  295, 296
Magna Carta 25–6, 99, 132
Maiden Castle 22
Maidenhead 99, 347–8
Maidstone 351
Mail boxes 338
Mainland, Orkney 332
  Maes Howe 332
  Ring of Brodgar 332
  Skara Brae 22, **325**, 332
  Standing Stones of
  Stromness 332
Mainland, Shetland 333, **334**
  Jarlshof Prehistoric Site
  333, **333**
  Mousa Broch 333
Maldon 213

Malham 259
Malmesbury 181–2
Malpas 241
Malt Whisky Trail 319
Malvern Hills 176, 180
Malvern Wells 364
Mam Tor 229, 242
Manchester 13, 33, 244, 248–9, **249**, 375
  Castlefield Urban Heritage Park 248
  Chinatown 249
  City Art Galleries 249
  Free Trade Hall 248
  G-Mex Centre 248
  Imperial War Museum North 249
  Lowry Arts Complex 249
  Museum of Science and Industry in Manchester 248–9
  Old Trafford 249
  Uppermill Textile Museum **248**
Mapledurham 195
Marble Hill House 85
Margate 125
Marlow 98, 348
Mary, Queen of Scots 58, 232, 302, 304, **304**, 314
Masham 275
  Theakston's Brewery 275
Matlock 231
Mauchline
  Burns House 293
  Gavin Hamilton's House 293
  Mauchline Church 293
  Poosie Nansie's Tavern 293
Measurements and sizes 339
Medical treatment 341
Melksham 351
Melrose 383
  Melrose Abbey 290
Melton Mowbray 371
Mên-an-Tol 147
Mersea Island 213
Mersey Beat 247
Middleton-in-Teesdale 259
Midhurst 351
Milton, John 62, 97, 109
Mingulay 331
Minsmere 222
Moffat 383
Money 339–40
Monmouth 162, 361
Montacute House 46, 157
Moore, Henry 97, 114
Moray Firth 10
Morpeth 378
Morwellham Quay 145
Mousehole 356
Much Hadham 114
Much Wenlock 371
Muck 330
Mull 330
  Duart Castle 330
Mull of Kintyre 312

Mumbles 361
Music 43–5, 283, 324

N

National Dragonfly Museum 198
National Coal Mining Museum 272
National Gallery 60–61, **60**, **61**
National Gallery of Scotland 302, **303**
National holidays 340
National Maritime Museum 88
National Mountaineering Centre 172
National Portrait Gallery 64, **64**
National Railway Museum 264
National tourist boards 341
National Trust 340
Nayland 212
The Naze 213
Neidpath Castle 288, 308
Nelson, Lord 53, 130
New Forest 138, **138**
New Lanark 296
New Milton 351–2
Newbury 351
Newcastle Emlyn 361
Newcastle upon Tyne **262**, 263, 282, 378–9
  BALTIC the Centre for Contemporary Arts 282
  Blinking Eye Bridge **262**, 282
  Tyne Bridge 282
Newmarket 207, **207**, 208
  Jockey Club 207, 208
  National Horseracing Museum 208
  National Stud 208
  Tattersalls 208
Newquay 356
Newspapers 339
Newton, Isaac 204
Newton Stewart 383
Newtown 361–2
Nidderdale 274
Norfolk 200, 216–9
Norfolk Broads **200**, 217, **217**
Norman castles 25
North Berwick 308, 383
North Downs 96
North Midlands 223–42
  hotels and restaurants 369–73
North Ronaldsay 332
North Uist 331
North York Moors 262, 276–7
North Yorkshire Moors Railway 276
Northamptonshire 198
Northeast England 10, 261–86

hotels and restaurants 376–9
  map 263
Northern Isles see Orkney and Shetland
Northumberland 263
Northumberland National Park 282
Northumbrian coast 282
Northwest England 10, 243–60
  hotels and restaurants 373–6
Northwich 371
Norwich 216, **216**, 368–9
  Castle 216
  Cathedral 28, 216
Noss Island 334
Nottingham 14, 226–7, **227**, 371
  Castle 226
  Lace Centre 226
  Museum of Costume and Textiles 226
  Tales of Robin Hood 226
Nottingham and Beeston Canal **227**

O

Oare 149
Offa's Dyke 162, 174, **174**
Okehampton 356
Old Bolingbroke 220
Old Hall Marshes bird reserve 213
Old Man of Hoy 332
Old Radnor 167
Old Sarum 133
Orford 10, **16**, 222
Orkney 325, 332
Orwell, George 41, 195, 330
Oundle 198, 364
Out Skerries 334
Outer Hebrides (Western Isles) 321, 325, 331
Oxford 177, 191–4, 364–5
  Ashmolean Museum 194
  Bodleian Library 194
  Carfax Tower 192
  colleges **191**, 192–4, **192**, **194**
  Martyrs' Memorial 194
  Museum of Oxford 192
  Radcliffe Camera 194
  Sheldonian Theatre 194
  University of Oxford Botanic Garden 192–3

P

Pabbay 331
Packing advice 336
Padstow 14, 147, 147, 356
Painswick 181, 365
Palace of Holyroodhouse **287**, 302
Pangbourne 195
Papa Stour 334
Papa Westray 332

Parking 337
Passports 336
Paxton, Joseph 34, 233
Peak Cavern 242
Peak District 224, 225, 229–31, **229**, 262
Peebles 308
Pembrokeshire Coast National Park 164–5
Pennine Way National Trail 258–9
Pennines 258–9, 260
Penrhyn Castle 168
Penrith 258, 375
Penshurst 352
Penshurst Place **118**, 119
Pentland Hills 302
Penybont 362
Penzance 356
Pepys, Samuel 38, 62, 204
Perry Green 97, 114
Perth 314–5
Pets, importing 340
Pharmacies 341
Pickering 276
Pilgrim's Way 96, 114
Pistyll Rhaeadr 174
Pitlochry 315, **315**
Places of worship 340
Plymouth 141, 145, 356–7
  Mayflower Steps 145
  National Marine Aquarium 145
  Plymouth Dome 145
  Plymouth Hoe 145, **145**
  Royal Citadel 145
Police 341
Polperro 146, 356
Pooley Bridge 375
Porlock 144
Port Appin 387
Porthmadog 168
Portmeirion 173, 173
Portree 387
Portsmouth 130
  Charles Dickens' Birthplace Museum 130
  D-Day Museum 130
  Flagship Portsmouth 130
  *Mary Rose* 130
  H.M.S. *Victory* 130, **130**
Post offices 338, 340
Potter, Beatrix 256
Potteries, The 236–7
Powis Castle **166–7**, 167
Prae Wood 111
Prior Park 156
Priston 156
Public transport 337
Pubs 16, *17*, 340
Puddletown 137

Q

Queen Elizabeth Forest Park Visitor Centre 314

R

Radio 339
Rail travel 336, 337

Ralph Cross 276
Ramsey Island 165
Ramsgate 125
Ravenglass and Eskdale
  Railway 252, **252**
Ravenstonedale 375–6
Rawtenstall 244, 250
  Weaver's Cottage 250
Reigate 348
Repton, Humphrey 32
Rhondda Heritage Park 163
Ribblehead Viaduct 258
Richard III 91
Richmond 275
Richmond Park 85
Ridgeway 135, 195
Rievaulx Abbey 277
Ripley 274
Ripley Castle 274
Ripon 274, 379
  Cathedral 274–5
River Thames 83–8
Robin Hood 226, 227
Robin Hood's Bay 276
Rochester 124, **124**
  Charles Dickens Centre
  124
Roman Army Museum 284,
  285
Romney Marsh 10, 125
Rosedale Abbey 276
Rosthwaite 376
Rothbury 283
Rousay 332
Royal Botanic Gardens at
  Kew 85–6, **86**
Royal Deeside 310, 316–7
Royal Tunbridge Wells 352
Rum 321, 330
Runnymede 99
Ruthin 174, 362
Rutland 372
Rydal Mount 256
Rye 125, **125**, 352
  Lamb House 125

**S**

Saffron Walden 200,
  209–10, **209**
St. Agnes' Island 158
St. Albans 24, 111, 348
  Cathedral 110–11, **110**
  Verulamium Museum 111
St. Andrews 304, **304–305**,
  305, 307, 320, 383
St. Bee's Abbey 251
St. David's 164, 362
  Bishop's Palace 164
  Cathedral 164
St. David's Head 165
St. Govan's Head 165
St. Ives **140**, 147, 357
  Barbara Hepworth
    Museum and Sculpture
    Garden 147
  Tate Gallery 147
St. Just-in-Roseland 147
St. Margaret's Hope 387
St. Martin's Island 158

St. Mary's Island 158
St. Michael's Mount 147
St. Peter's-at-the-Wall 213
Salisbury 131–3, 352
  Cathedral 28, 117, 131–2,
    **131**
  Mompesson House 132
  Royal Gloucesterhire,
    Berkshire, and Wiltshire
    Regiment Museum 132
Salle 218
Saltram House 46
Sanday 332
Sandringham 218, **218–9**
Sandwich 125
Scarborough 276
Scone Palace 315
Scotland 10, 287–334
Scott, Sir Walter 40, 288,
  290, 291, 298, 308, 310,
  314, 315
Scottish islanders 328–9
Scottish Lowlands 287–308
  hotels and restaurants
    379–84
  map 289
Sea routes to Britain 336
Seahouses 282
Settle–Carlisle Railway 258
Shaftesbury 352
Shakespeare, William 26,
  186–9, **188**
Shapinsay 332
  Balfour Castle 332
Shaw, George Bernard 41,
  68, 114
Sheffield 33, 372
Shepton Mallet 357
Shere 114, **114**, 348
Sherwood Forest Country
  Park 227
Shetland 13, 311, 325, 333
Shinfield 348
Shopping 340, 388–9
Shottery 189
  Anne Hathaway's Cottage
    189
Shrewsbury 239, 372
  Castle 239
  Church of St. Mary 239
  St. Chad's Church **239**
  Shropshire Regimental
    Museum 239
Sidmouth 143, 143
Silbury Hill 22, 135
*Sir Walter Scott* 314
Sissinghurst Castle Garden
  121
Skiing 320–21
Skipton 379
Skokholm Island 165
Skomer Island 165
Skye 326–7, **326–7**, **328**
  Clan Donald Centre 326
  Cuillin Hills 320, 326
  Dunvegan Castle 326
  MacCrimmon Piping
    Centre 326
  Museum of Island Life 326

Slaidburn 250
Smailholm Tower 288
Snape 222
Snowdon 172, **172**
Snowdon Mountain Railway
  172
Snowdonia National Park
  172
Solihull 365
Solway Firth 321
Somerset & Avon 141, 144,
  150–56, 157
Somerset Levels 150
South Country 10, 115–38
  hotels and restaurants
    349–53
  map 116–7
South Downs Way 127
South Midlands 175–98
  hotels and restaurants
    362–6
  map 177
South Ronaldsay 332
South Uist 331
Southwell 372
  Minster 228, **228**
Southwestern Highlands
  312–13
Southwold 222, **222**
Speedwell Cavern 242
Spey Valley **318**, 319
Speyside Way 319
Spurn Head 10
Staffa 330, **330**
  Fingal's Cave 330
Staffordshire 225
Staithes 276
Stamford 46, 221, 369
Stanton 183
Stanway 183
Staverton 357
Steep Holm 158
Stinsford 136
Stiperstones 240
Stirling 306–307, 383
  Argyll and Sutherland
    Highlanders Regimental
    Museum 307
  Argyll's Lodging 306
  Church of the Holy Rude
    306
  Mar's Wark 306
  Stirling Castle 306–307
Stockbridge 352
Stoke Bruerne 198
Stoke-by-Nayland 212, 369
Stoke-on-Trent 225, 236,
  237, 372, 373
  Etruria Industrial Museum
    237
  Royal Doulton Visitor
    Centre 237
  Spode Visitor Centre 237
  Wedgwood Visitor
    Centre 237
Stokesay Castle 240, **240**
Ston Easton 357
Stonehenge 14, 22, 117,
  134–5, **134–5**

Stourhead 157
Stow-on-the-Wold 183
Stowe 107
Stranraer 383–4
Stratford-upon-Avon 177,
  186–7, 365
  Church of the Holy
    Trinity 187
  Guild Chapel 187
  Hall's Croft 187
  Harvard House 187
  Judith Shakespeare's
    House 186–7
  King Edward VI Grammar
    School 187, **187**
  Memorial Theatre **186**, 187
  Nash's House 187
  Shakespeare's Birthplace
    186
Strath of Kildonan 324
Strathspey Steam Railway
  319
Stretham 220
The Strid 274
Stromness 332
Stronsay 332
Stroud 181
Studley Royal 274
Sudbury 212, 369
  Gainsborough House
    Museum 212
Sudbury Hall 46
Sudeley Castle 183
Suffolk 200–201, 212,
  214–5, 222
Sulhamstead 207–208, 348
Sunderland Point 250
Surrey 96, 114
Sussex 117
Sutherland 311
Sutton 352–3
Sutton Coldfield 365
Sutton Courtenay 195
Sutton Hoo 24, 41, 71, **71**,
  222
Swaledale 46, **274–5**, 275
Swan upping 14, 98
Swanage 137
Swansea 362
Sway 353
Syon House 86

**T**

Tantallon Castle 288, 308
Tarbolton 293
  Lochlea Farm 293
Tartans 317
Taunton 357
Teesdale 260
Television 339
Tenby 362
Tetbury 182, 365
Tewkesbury 178
Thame 366
Thames Path National Trail
  87
Thaxted 200, 210
  Guildhall 210
  John Webb's Windmill 210

Theater 45–6, 390
Thomas à Becket 122
Thomas, Dylan 164, **164**
Thorpe 372–3
Thorpeness 222
Thurlestone 357
Time differences 340
Tintagel 147
Tintern Abbey 162, **162**
Tipping 340–41, 343
Tiree 330
Tissington 14
Tissington Trail 230
Tobermory 387
Todmorden 244, 272
Tollesbury 213
Top Withens 259, 272
Torquay 357
Tours, organized 338
Towcester 366
Traffic accidents 341
Traquair House 291
Traveler's checks 339
Traveling to Britain 336
Treak Cliff Cavern 242
Trelissick Garden 147
Tresco 158, 158
Troon 384
Trossachs 310, 314
Trossachs Trundler 314
Truro 147
Turnberry 320, 384
Turner, J.M.W. 42, 65
Two Bridges 357

**U**
Uffington White Horse 22
Ullapool 323, 387
Unst 333
Up Helly Aa' 13, 333
Upper Teesdale 259
Upwell 220
Urquhart Castle 322

**V**
Vale of Clwyd 174
Vale of Rheidol Steam
   Railway 167
The Valleys (Wales) 10, 163
Vanbrugh, Sir John 32, 88,
   197, 210, 271
Veryan 357–8
Victoria & Albert Museum
   74–5, **74, 75**
Victoria, Queen 34, **34**, 82,
   316
Vindolanda Fort and
   Museum 284, 285

**W**
Wade's Causeway 276
Wainwright, Alfred 255,
   258
Wales 10, 159–74
   hotels and restaurants
      358–62
   map 160
Walking and climbing 320,
   338

Wallace Monument 307
Wallingford 366
Walton, Izaak 98, 129
Walton on the Naze 213
Ware 348
Warkworth Castle 282
Warminster 353
Wars of the Roses 26, 184
Warwick 366
   Castle 184–5, **184, 185**
Wasdale Head 252, 376
The Wash 220
Wastwater 252
Watership Down 130
Wayland's Smithy 195
Weardale 260
Well-dressing 14
Wellington 358
Wellow 156
Wells 151, 358
   Bishop's Palace 151
   Cathedral 151, **151**
   Vicars' Close 151
Wells Museum 151
Welney 220
Welsh Borders 174, 176
Welsh Highland Railway
   168
Wenlock Edge 225, 240
Wensleydale 46, 275
West Country 10, 139–58
   hotels and restaurants
      353–8
   map 140–41
West Kennet Long Barrow
   22, 135, 135
West Riding of Yorkshire
   272–3
West Wycombe 97, 109
   St. Lawrence's Church
      109, **109**
West Wycombe Caves 109
Wester Ross 311, 321, 323
Western Isles see Outer
   Hebrides
Westonbirt Arboretum 181
Westray 332
Weymouth 137
Whalsay 334
Wharfedale 274
Whin Sill 285
Whisky 319
Whitby 276, 379
   Captain Cook Memorial
      Museum 276
White Horse 195
White Peak 224
Whitehaven 251
Whitney-on-Wye 366
Wicken Fen 220
Wildlife 20–21, 321
Wilmcote 189
   Mary Arden's House 189,
      **189**
   Shakespeare Country
      Museum 189
Wilton House 32, 133
Wiltshire 117, 131–5
Winchcombe 183

Winchester 128–9, 353
   Cathedral 117, 128–9,
      **128, 129**
   Great Hall 129
   Pilgrim's Hall 129
   Round Table 129
   St. Cross Hospital 129
   Winchester College 129
   Wolvesey Castle 129
Windermere 376
Windsor 100–104
   Windsor Castle **96**,
      100–104, **100, 101,
      102**
   Windsor Great Park
      104
Winteringham 369
Wisbech 220
Wishaw 366
Withypool 358
Woburn 106–107
   Woburn Abbey 106,
      **106**
Wool towns 28, 212
Woolacombe 144, 358
Woolbridge Manor 137
Woolf, Virginia 41, 68, **68**,
   121
Worcester 180
   Cathedral 180, **180**
   Royal Worcester
      Porcelain Company 180
Wordsworth, William 40,
   204, 252, 254, 255, 256
Worfield 373
Wren, Sir Christopher 32,
   51, 52, 53, 54, 55, 57, 82,
   84, 88, 100, 192, 194
Wye Valley 10, 162
Wyre 332

**Y**
Yattendon 348
Yell 333
York 13, 262, 264–9, **264,
   268**, 379
   Clifford's Tower 268
   Ice House 269
   Jorvik Viking Centre 264
   Minster 28, **264**, 266–7,
      **267**
   National Railway Museum
      264
   York Castle Museum 264
   York Story 264
   Yorkshire Museum 264
Yorkshire 262, 264–77
Yorkshire Dales **258–9**,
   262, 274–5, **274–5**

# ILLUSTRATIONS CREDITS

Abbreviations for terms appearing below: (t) top; (b) bottom; (l) left; (r) right; (c) center.

Cover, (l) Jason Hawkes Aerial Collection/ Julian Cotton Photo Library. (c) Tony Stone Images (r) Powerstock. 1, Powerstock. 2/3, Tony Stone Images. 4, Bob Krist. 9, W.Voysey/AA Photo Library. 11, Brian Smith/ESP/Gamma/Frank Spooner Pictures. 12/13, Mike Goldwater/Network Photographers. 14/15, Robert Estall Photo Agency. 16, S&O Matthews/AA Photo Library. 17, Geoff Howard/Collections. 19, Sam Abell, National Geographic Photographer. 20/21, Cary Wolinsky. 22/23, Cary Wolinsky. 24, British Museum/Michael Holford. 27, Richard Turpin. 28, S.Day/AA Photo Library. 29, Thyssen Bornemisza Collection/The Bridgeman Art Library. 30/31, Private Collection/The Bridgeman Art Library. 33, Wallington Hall, Northumberland/The Bridgeman Art Library. 34, Hulton Getty. 35,Victoria & Albert Museum/e.t.archive. 36, Popperfoto. 39, RGT. 40, Hulton Getty 42, symbol 211 \f "Symbol" \s 13 David Hockney/ e.t.archive. 42/3, S&O Matthews/AA Photo Library. 44/5, Jonathan Olley/Network. Photographers. 47, W.Voysey/AA Photo Library. 50, Andrew Holt. 51, Derek Croucher/Bruce Coleman Ltd. 52, John Miller/Collections. 56, John Freeman. 57, Pictures Colour Library. 58, Simon Harris/Robert Harding Picture Library. 59, Robert Harding Picture Library. 60, Jon Hoffmann/Impact Photos. 61, The National Gallery, London/Corbis. 64, By Courtesy of the National Portrait Gallery, London. 65, Pictures Colour Library. 68, Hulton Getty. 68, Adam Woolfitt/Robert Harding Picture Library. 69, Pictures Colour Library. 70, artwork: Maltings Partnership. 71(all) The British Museum, London/Michael Holford. 72, Sir Jeremy Grayson/Bruce Coleman Ltd. 74/75 Courtesy of the V&A Museum, London. 76, Courtesy of the Science Museum, London. 77, Andrew Holt. 78(t), P.Wilson/ AA Photo Library. 78(b), T.Woodcock/ AA Photo Library. 79, e.t.archive. 81, B.Smith/AA Photo Library. 82, MKH/ Julian Cotton Photo Library. 83, Lesley Howling/Collections. 85, Pictures Colour Library. 86, Neil McAllister/Bruce Coleman Ltd. 87, Richard Turpin. 88, AA Photo Library. 89, W.Voysey/AA Photo Library. 90, Pictures Colour Library. 90/91, artwork: Maltings Partnership. 91, S&O Matthews/AA Photo Library. 92, James Bartholomew/Collections. 93, Michael Jenner. 94, M.Birkitt/AA Photo Library. 95, John Miller/The National Trust Photographic Library. 96, Roger Scruton/Collections. 98, Mark Cator/ Impact Photos. 99, Patrick Ward/Corbis.

100, Paul Almasy/symbol 211 \f "Symbol" \s 13 Corbis. 101, W.Voysey/AA Photo Library. 102, Rex Features. 102/103, artwork: Maltings Partnership. 104/105, Mark Cator/Impact Photos. 106, Woburn Abbey. 107, Private Collection/The Bridgeman Art Library. 108/109, Sir Jeremy Grayson/Bruce Coleman Ltd. 109, C.Jones/AA Photo Library. 110, Tony Page/Impact Photos. 111, Verulamium Museum, St. Albans/The Bridgeman Art Library. 112, Fotomas Index. 113, Pictures Colour Library. 114, AA Photo Library. 115, D.Forss/AA Photo Library. 117, S&O Matthews/AA Photo Library. 118, D.Forss/AA Photo Library. 119, AA Photo Library. 120, S&O Matthews/AA Photo Library. 121, Pictures Colour Library. 122, Sonia Halliday Photographs. 123, Canterbury Cathedral, Angelo Hornack/ Corbis. 124, Robert Hallmann/ Collections. 125, Pictures Colour Library. 126, David Tomlinson/Bruce Coleman Ltd. 127, T.Souter/AA Photo Library. 128/129 D.Forss/AA Photo Library. 130, W.Voysey/AA Photo Library. 131, Spectrum Colour Library. 132, S.Day/AA Photo Library. 133, Neil Campbell-Sharp/ The National Trust Photographic Library. 134, Robert Harding Picture Library. 135, Michael Jenner. 136(t), Towner Art Gallery, Eastbourne/The Bridgeman Art Gallery. 136(b), John Miller/The National Trust Photographic Library. 137, Ian West/The National Trust Photographic Library. 138, W.Voysey/AA Photo Library. 139/140, Robert Harding Picture Library. 142, AA Photo Library. 143, A.Lawson/ AA Photo Library. 144, T.Teegan/AA Photo Library. 145, S&O Matthews/AA Photo Library. 146, Derek Croucher/ Bruce Coleman Ltd. 147/148(t), R.Moss/ AA Photo Library. 148(b), Pictures Colour Library. 149, Derek Croucher/ Bruce Coleman Ltd. 150, H.Williams/AA Photo Library. 151, John Worrall/Bruce Coleman Ltd. 152, Stapleton Collection, UK/The Bridgeman Art Library. 153, M.Birkitt/AA Photo Library. 155, S&O Matthews/AA Photo Library. 156, Courtesy of The American Museum in Britain, Bath. 157, Jason Hawkes Aerial Collection/Julian Cotton Photo Library. 158, Mike Pooler/Collections. 159, C.Jones/AA Photo Library. 161, Joe Cornish/The National Trust Photographic Library. 162, H.Williams/ AA Photo Library. 163, I.Burgum/AA Photo Library. 164, National Museum of Wales, Cardiff/The Bridgeman Art Library. 165, Joe Cornish/The National Trust Photographic Library. 166, Ian Shaw/The National Trust Photographic Library. 169(tl/tr), Pat Aithie/AA Photo Library. 169(bl/br), C.Jones/AA Photo Library. 170, AA Photo Library. 172, C.Jones/AA Photo Library. 174, J.Tims/AA Photo Library. 174, C.Jones/AA Photo Library. 175, S.Day/AA Photo Library. 176, Michael St. Maur Sheil. 178, S.Day/AA Photo Library. 179, John D.Beldom/

Collections. 180, C.Jones/AA Photo Library. 181, F.Stephenson/AA Photo Library. 182(tl/tr), S.Day/AA Photo Library. 182(b), Tony Souter/AA Photo Library. 183, S.Day/AA Photo Library. 184, Michael Jenner. 185, F.Stephenson/ AA Photo Library. 186, PBK. 187, Adam Woolfitt/Robert Harding Picture Library. 188, Adam Woolfitt/Robert Harding Picture Library. 189(t), Donald Cooper/ Photostage. 189(b), Robert Harding Picture Library. 190, Pictures Colour Library. 191, Homer Sykes/Impact Photos. 192, A.Lawson/AA Photo Library. 194, Julian Cotton Photo Library. 195, V.Potter/AA Photo Library. 196, Michael Glover/Bruce Coleman Ltd. 197, A.F.Kersting. 198, David Hartley/Rex Features. 199, A.Baker/AA Photo Library. 200, John D.Beldom/Collections. 202, Adam Woolfitt/Robert Harding Picture Library. 203, M.Birkitt/AA Photo Library. 204, Robert Harding Picture Library. 206/207/208, M.Birkitt/AA Photo Library. 209, L.Whitwan/AA Photo Library. 210, S&O Matthews/AA Photo Library. 211, A.F.Kersting. 212, W.Voysey/ Viewfinder. 213, W.Voysey/AA Photo Library. 214, The National Gallery, London/e.t.archive. 215, Colin R.Chalmers/The National Trust Photographic Library. 216, Liz Stares/ Collections. 217, John D.Beldom/ Collections. 219(t), Nadia McKenzie/The National Trust Photographic Library. 219(b), Pictures Colour Library. 220, John Worrall/Bruce Coleman Ltd. 221, Michael Jenner. 222, P.Davies/AA Photo Library. 223, R,Surman/AA Photo Library. 224, C.Jones/AA Photo Library. 225, A.J.Hopkins/AA Photo Library. 226, M.Bikitt/AA Photo Library. 227, PBK. 228(t/b), R.Newton/AA Photo Library. 229, Joe Cornish/The National Trust Photographic Library. 230(t), A.J.Hopkins/AA Photo Library. 230(b), A.J.Hopkins/AA Photo Library. 231(t/l), P.Baker/AA Photo Library. 231(b), Andy Traynor/AA Photo Library. 232, M.Birkitt/AA Photo Library. 233, A.J.Hopkins/AA Photo Library. 235(t), Hawkley Studios/The National Trust Photographic Library. 235(b), Geoff Morgan/The National Trust Photographic Library. 236, Pictures Colour Library 237, Courtesy of the Trustees of the Wedgwood Museum, Barlaston, Stoke-on-Trent. 238, M.Allwood-Coppin/AA Photo Library. 239/240/241, C.Jones/AA Photo Library. 242, Brian Shuel/Collections. 243, S.Day/AA Photo Library. 244, L.S. Lowry, The Bandstand, Peel Park, Salford, York City Art Gallery/The Bridgeman Art Library. 246, S.Day/AA Photo Library. 247, Rex Features. 248, AA Photo Library. 249, C.Molyneux/AA Photo Library. 250, J.Beazley/AA Photo Library. 251/252, E.A.Bowness/AA Photo Library. 253, Joe Cornish/The National Trust Photographic Library. 254(l), John Hammond/The

CREDITS **399**

C R E D I T S

National Trust Photographic Library. 254/5, S.Day/AA Photographic Library. 255, R.Surman/AA Photo Library. 257(tl), S.Day/AA Photo Library. 257(tr), Ted Bowness/AA Photo Library. 257(c), S.Day/AA Photo Library. 257(br), C.Lees/AA Photo Library. 259, Granville Harris/Bruce Coleman Ltd. 260, G.Rowatt/AA Photo Library. 261, R.Newton/AA Photo Library. 262, Graeme Peacock. 264, R.Rainford/Robert Harding Picture Library. 265, L.Whitwam/AA Photo Library. 266/7, artwork: Maltings Partnership. 267, L.Whitwam/AA Photo Library. 268, Michael Jenner. 269, R.Newton/AA Photo Library. 270, AA Photo Library. 271, R.Newton/AA Photo Library. 273(tl), Hulton Getty. 273(tr), A.Baker/AA Photo Library. 273(c), L.Whitwam/AA Photo Library. 273(bl), P.Wilson/AA Photo Library. 275, Mark Mawson/Robert Harding Picture Library. 277(t), S.Gregory/AA Photo Library. 277(bl/br), P.Baker/AA Photo Library. 278, C.Lees/AA photo Library. 279, T.Woodcock/AA Photo Library. 281, Leslie Garland. 283, Joe Cornish/The National Trust Photographic Library. 285, J.Beazley/AA Photo Library. 286, C.Lees/ AA Photo Library. 287/289, K.Paterson/ AA Photo Library. 290, M.Alexander/AA Photo Library. 291, J.Beazley/AA Photo Library. 292, K.Paterson/AA Photo Library. 293, Malcolm Innes Gallery, London/The Bridgeman Art Library. 294, AA Photo Library. 295, Stephen Gibson Photography/AA Photo Library. 297, David Robertson/Still Moving. 298, Doug Corrance/Still Moving. 299, AA Photo Library. 300, D.Corrance/AA Photo Library. 303, AA Photo Library. 304, Mary Evans Picture Library. 305, Barry Lewis. 306(t/b), S.Day/AA Photo Library. 307(l/r), K.Paterson/AA Photo Library. 308, M.Taylor/AA Photo Library. 309, Allan G.Potts/Bruce Coleman Ltd. 312/13, symbol 211 \f "Symbol" \s 13 Pinhole Productions/Still Moving Picture Company. 315, R.Elliott/AA Photo Library. 316(l), J.Beazley/AA Photo Library. 316(c), R.Weir/AA Photo Library. 316/17, AA Photo Library. 317, M.Taylor/AA Photo Library. 318, J.Henderson/AA Photo Library. 319, Bruce Coleman Ltd. 320, Alasdair Macfarlane/Still Moving Picture Company. 321, Robert Lees/Still Moving Picture Company. 322, J.Beazley/AA Photo Library. 324, S.Day/AA Photo Library. 325, E.Ellington/AA Photo Library. 326/7, J.Henderson/AA Photo Library. 328, M.Alexander/AA Photo Library. 329(l), Mark Pepper/Still Moving Picture Company. 329(r), R.Elliott/AA Photo Library. 330, Henry McInnes/Still Moving Picture Company. 331, symbol 211 \f "Symbol" \s 13 EOLAS/Still Moving Picture Company. 332, Michael Jenner. 333, E.Ellington/AA Photo Library. 334, David Robertson/Still Moving Picture Company. 335, Bo Zaunders/CORBIS.

**Published by the National Geographic Society**

John M. Fahey, Jr., President and Chief Executive Officer
Gilbert M. Grosvenor, Chairman of the Board
Nina D. Hoffman, Executive Vice President,
President, Books and School Publishing
Kevin Mulroy, Vice President and Director, Book Division
Marianne Koszorus, Design Director
Charles Kogod, Director of Photography
Elizabeth L. Newhouse, Director of Travel Publishing
Barbara A. Noe, Senior Editor and Series Editor
Cinda Rose, Art Director
Carl Mehler, Director of Maps
Joseph F. Ochlak, Map Editor
Gary Colbert, Production Director
Richard S. Wain, Production Project Manager
Lawrence Porges, Editorial Coordinator
Kay Kobor Hankins, Caroline Hickey, Contributors

Edited and designed by AA Publishing (a trading name of Automobile Association Developments Limited, whose registered office is Norfolk House, Priestley Road, Basingstoke, Hampshire, England RG24 9NY. Registered number: 1878835).

Betty Sheldrick, *Project Manager,* David Austin, *Senior Art Editor*
Rachel Alder, *Senior Editor,* Jo Tapper, *Designer*
Simon Mumford, *Senior Cartographic Editor*
Nicky Barker-Dix, Helen Beever, *Cartographers*
Richard Firth, *Production Director*
Picture Research by Suzanne Williams
Drive maps drawn by Chris Orr Associates, Southampton, England
Cutaway illustrations drawn by Maltings Partnership, Derby, England

**Reprinted with updates 2001, 2004**

Copyright © 1999, 2001, 2004 National Geographic Society. All rights reserved. No part of this book may be reproduced or transmitted in any form or by any means, electronic or mechanical, including photocopying, without permission in writing from the National Geographic Society, 1145 17th Street N.W., Washington, D.C. 20036-4688.

**Library of Congress Cataloging-in-Publication Data**
National Geographic Traveler. Great Britain.
    p. cm.
    Includes index.
    ISBN 0-7922-7425-3 (alk. paper)
    1. Great Britain—Guidebooks.  I. National Geographic Society (U.S.)  11. Title: Great Britain.
DA650.N29  1999
914.104'859—dc21               99-11700
                              CIP

Printed and bound by Mondadori Printing, Verona, Italy. Color separations by Leo Reprographic Ltd., Hong Kong. Cover separations by L.C. Repro, Aldermaston, U.K.

Visit the Society's Web site at http://www.nationalgeographic.com

The information in this book has been carefully checked and to the best of our knowledge is accurate. However, details are subject to change, and the National Geographic Society cannot be responsible for such changes, or for errors or omissions. Assessments of sites, hotels, and restaurants are based on the authors' subjective opinions, which do not necessarily reflect the publisher's opinion. The publisher cannot be responsible for any consequences arising from the use of this book.

**Special Offer!** Order today and get one year of National Geographic Traveler, the magazine travelers trust, for only $14.95. Call 1-800-NGS-LINE and mention code TRAC3A6.

**Travel the World** with National Geographic Experts: www.nationalgeographic.com/ngexpeditions.

# NATIONAL GEOGRAPHIC
# TRAVELER

## A Century of Travel Expertise in Every Guide

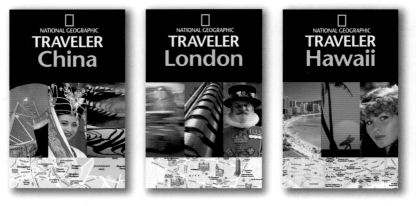

- **Amsterdam** ISBN: 0-7922-7900-X
- **Arizona** ISBN: 0-7922-7899-2
- **Australia** ISBN: 0-7922-7431-8
- **Barcelona** ISBN: 0-7922-7902-6
- **Boston & Environs** ISBN: 0-7922-7926-3
- **California** ISBN: 0-7922-7564-0
- **Canada** ISBN: 0-7922-7427-X
- **The Caribbean** ISBN: 0-7922-7434-2
- **China** ISBN: 0-7922-7921-2
- **Costa Rica** ISBN: 0-7922-7946-8
- **Cuba** ISBN: 0-7922-6931-4
- **Egypt** ISBN: 0-7922-7896-8
- **Florence & Tuscany** ISBN: 0-7922-7924-7
- **Florida** ISBN: 0-7922-7432-6
- **France** ISBN: 0-7922-7426-1
- **Germany** ISBN: 0-7922-4146-0
- **Great Britain** ISBN: 0-7922-7425-3
- **Greece** ISBN: 0-7922-7923-9
- **Hawaii** ISBN: 0-7922-7944-1
- **Hong Kong** ISBN: 0-7922-7901-8
- **India** ISBN: 0-7922-7898-4

- **Ireland** ISBN: 0-7922-4145-2
- **Italy** ISBN: 0-7922-7562-4
- **Japan** ISBN: 0-7922-7563-2
- **London** ISBN: 0-7922-7428-8
- **Los Angeles** ISBN: 0-7922-7947-6
- **Mexico** ISBN: 0-7922-7897-6
- **Miami and the Keys** ISBN: 0-7922-7433-4
- **New Orleans** ISBN: 0-7922-7948-4
- **New York** ISBN: 0-7922-7430-X
- **Paris** ISBN: 0-7922-7429-6
- **Prague & Czech Republic** ISBN: 0-7922-4147-9
- **Rome** ISBN: 0-7922-7566-7
- **San Diego** ISBN: 0-7922-6933-0
- **San Francisco** ISBN: 0-7922-7565-9
- **Spain** ISBN: 0-7922-7922-0
- **Sydney** ISBN: 0-7922-7435-0
- **Taiwan** ISBN: 0-7922-6555-6
- **Thailand** ISBN: 0-7922-7943-3
- **Venice** ISBN: 0-7922-7917-4
- **Washington, D.C.** ISBN: 0-7922-7903-4

## AVAILABLE WHEREVER BOOKS ARE SOLD